MANUAL OF
CRITICAL CARE

FRANK B. CERRA, M.D., F.A.C.S.

Professor of Surgery,
Director, Surgical Critical Care;
Director, Nutrition Support Service,
University of Minnesota,
St. Paul-Ramsey Medical Center,
Minneapolis/St. Paul, Minnesota

With 186 illustrations

The C. V. Mosby Company

ST. LOUIS · WASHINGTON, D.C. · TORONTO   1987

MOSBY

A TRADITION OF PUBLISHING EXCELLENCE

Editor: Karen Berger
Developmental editor: Terry Van Schaik
Assistant editors: Beth Campbell, Sandra L. Gilfillan
Project editor: Suzanne Seeley
Manuscript editors: Jean Babrick, Mary Drone, Claire Genovese
Book design: Diane Beasley
Cover design: Diane Beasley
Production: Kathy A. Burmann, Timothy O'Brien

Printed in the United States of America

The C. V. Mosby Company
11830 Westline Industrial Drive, St. Louis, Missouri 63146

Library of Congress Cataloging-in-Publication Data

Manual of critical care.

Includes bibliographies and index.
1. Therapeutics, Surgical—Handbooks, manuals, etc.
2. Critical care medicine—Handbooks, manuals, etc.
I. Cerra, Frank B. [DNLM: 1. Critical Care—handbooks.
2. Postoperative Care—handbooks. WX 39 P7388]
RD49.P63 1986 616′.028 86-16324
ISBN 0-8016-1010-9

C/MV/MV 9 8 7 6 5 4 3 2 11/B/154

Contributors

William Becker, M.D.

Fellow, Trauma/Critical Care,
University of Minnesota,
St. Paul-Ramsey Medical Center,
Minneapolis/St. Paul, Minnesota

Jon Berlauk, M.D.

Assistant Professor, Anesthesiology;
Associate Director, Surgical Intensive Care,
University of Minnesota,
Minneapolis, Minnesota

Daniel M. Canafax, Pharm.D.

Associate Professor in Pharmacy Practice,
University of Minnesota,
Minneapolis, Minnesota

Frank B. Cerra, M.D.

Professor of Surgery;
Director, Surgical Critical Care;
Director, Nutrition Support Service
University of Minnesota,
St. Paul-Ramsey Medical Center,
Minneapolis/St. Paul, Minnesota

Jack Crumbley, M.D.

Instructor in Surgery,
University of Minnesota,
Minneapolis, Minnesota

Tom Davin, M.D.

Assistant Professor of Medicine;
Chief of Nephrology Section,
University of Minnesota,
St. Paul-Ramsey Medical Center,
Minneapolis/St. Paul, Minnesota

Clifford Deutschman, M.D.

Fellow, Anesthesia/Critical Care,
Johns Hopkins University,
Baltimore, Maryland

David Dunn, M.D.

Assistant Professor of Surgery,
University of Minnesota,
Minneapolis, Minnesota

John Fath, M.D.

Fellow, Trauma/Critical Care,
University of Minnesota,
St. Paul-Ramsey Medical Center,
Minneapolis/St. Paul, Minnesota

Ian Gilmour, M.D.

Assistant Professor, Anesthesiology;
Associate Director, Surgical Intensive Care,
University of Minnesota,
Minneapolis, Minnesota

Henry J. Mann, Pharm.D.

Assistant Professor of Pharmacy Practice,
Univesity of Minnesota,
Minneapolis, Minnesota

John Mawk, M.D.

Assistant Professor of Neurosurgery,
University of Nebraska
Lincoln, Nebraska

John W. McBride, M.D.

Assistant Professor of Medicine and Cardiology,
University of Minnesota,
St. Paul-Ramsey Medical Center,
Minneapolis/St. Paul, Minnesota

Marvin A. McMillen, M.D.

Assistant Professor of Surgery;
Director, Surgical Critical Care,
Downstate Medical Center,
Brooklyn, New York

Terry Quigley, M.D.

Instructor in Surgery,
University of Minnesota,
Minneapolis, Minnesota

John H. Rodman, Pharm.D.

St. Jude's Hospital,
Memphis, Tennessee

Arthur D. Santos, M.D.

Fellow, Trauma/Critical Care,
University of Minnesota,
St. Paul-Ramsey Medical Center,
Minneapolis/St. Paul, Minnesota

Lynn D. Solem, M.D.

Assistant Professor of Surgery;
Director, Burn Unit,
University of Minnesota,
St. Paul-Ramsey Medical Center,
Minneapolis/St. Paul, Minnesota

Pradub Sukhum, M.D.

Assistant Professor of Medicine and Cardiology,
University of Minnesota,
St. Paul-Ramsey Medical Center,
Minneapolis/St. Paul, Minnesota

Preface

The history of the care of the critically ill and injured reflects the progress of research and the development of medical technology. Hospital areas designated for intensive nursing began with the advent of the ventilator; the emphasis was on ventilation and its management. Invasive physiologic monitoring developed as a therapeutic tool. Patient care began to fertilize research; research began to impact patient care. The focus shifted from blood pressure to cardiac output, to perfusion, and then to oxygen consumption. Now the era of organ-specific assessment and monitoring has begun. The practice has also shifted from one of monitoring to one of therapeutic intervention preoperatively, intraoperatively, and postoperatively.

That the reduction of morbidity and mortality does not reside just in the physiology has become apparent. Rather, the restoration and maintenance of oxygen transport has opened the door to the monitoring of and eventual manipulation of cell metabolism. This is the state of the art in the 1980s. As an outgrowth of this, the biochemist has now come to the bedside. The common problems in the ICU have now also attracted the interests of the cell-cell "interactionist." The mediators of the metabolic response to injury are being identified and characterized. Common pathways of antigen processing and the systemic metabolic response are being recognized. In short, cell biology and molecular biology as diagnostic and therapeutic tools have arrived in the ICU.

These advances in knowledge and technology have saved many lives, an act that before was not possible. As with all advances, new problems have become evident. Critical care is resource-intensive and expensive. Ethical and legal dilemmas as to institution, appropriateness, and withdrawal of therapy have become common. New clinical syndromes have emerged, the organ failure syndrome being an important example. For the patient who has survived the ICU, rehabilitation becomes a re-source-intensive sequela. Because the patient's metabolic response to injury involves all organ systems, each with its own reserve, multiple consultants are a frequent practice pattern. Indeed, "consultantitis" is not an uncommon problem for the patient, with each specialty focusing on "its organ" with less attention to the interorgan interactions, the frequently necessary trade-offs in organ reserves, or the patient as a whole.

Out of the process has emerged a multidisciplinary fund of knowledge and experience with new treatment regimens and reductions in morbidity and mortality.

Because the field is rapidly expanding in knowledge and application, the common knowledge base must be integrated into student, resident, and fellow training programs so that the surgical practitioner can directly apply more of the discipline as part of the care armamentarium. In this way the overall standard of practice continues to improve and benefit patients. Within this context, research and development must continue and insight must be gained into the pathologies, etiologies, and treatments of disease and also into the ethical and legal dilemmas. The many "practice" problems that exist must be resolved.

It is to assist in the dissemination of the common knowledge base that this book is written. It attempts to present in a logical and concise manner the knowledge and application of physiologic and metabolic principles that have evolved over the last 25 to 30 years. Much of this development is the direct result of advances in surgery and the quest for adequate treatments of the surgical problems of trauma and sepsis and the need to continue developing safe, effective surgical techniques.

To these latter ends, the University of Minnesota Hospitals continue to be a leader. Under the direction of its Chairman, Dr. John Najarian, the Surgical Intensive Care Units continue to be dedicated to the mission of care, teaching, and research and exist and develop in an environment of academic stimulation and excellence.

May you find this communication useful in your daily practice and study.

FRANK B. CERRA

Contents

xi

GENERAL PRINCIPLES: PHYSIOLOGY AND METABOLISM OF ICU PATIENTS

PART I

RESTORATION AND MAINTENANCE OF OXYGEN TRANSPORT

1

Overview of the problem

Frank B. Cerra

As critical care techniques improve and knowledge increases, more patients are surviving trauma and major surgery. However, it continues to be apparent that the events of the initial hours profoundly affect the patient's subsequent course. Recent studies have focused on cell metabolism, with emphasis on restoration and maintenance of oxygen transport. Groups of patients have been identified for whom clinical criteria are unreliable; for these patients an intensive, systematic algorithmic approach has improved mortality and reduced the subsequent incidence of organ failures.

BASIS OF QUANTITATIVE RESTORATION OF OXYGEN TRANSPORT

One of the major findings in research on the metabolic-physiologic response to surgery, trauma, and sepsis is that humans in these states show an adaption much different from that seen in humans in the "normal," or nonstressed, fasting state.

A. Stress state responses
 1. Activating agents induce mediator activity; mediator activity modulates systemic response.
  a. Activating agents
   (1) Dead tissue
   (2) Injured tissue
   (3) Dividing microorganisms (e.g., virus, fungus, bacteria)
   (4) Hematomas (e.g., pelvic, retroperitoneal)
   (5) Some antigen-antibody reactions
   (6) Perfusion deficits
  b. Known mediating systems
   (1) Central nervous system

(2) Macroendocrine system
(3) Microendocrine and/or cell-to-cell mediator system

c. System responses

Characteristic	Starvation	Stress
Cardiac output	$--$*	$++$*
Resistance	NC*	$--$
O_2CI	$--$	$++$
Energy expenditure	$--$	$+++$
Mediator activation	NC	$++$
R/Q	0.75	0.85
Fuel	Fat	Mixed
Proteolysis	$+$	$+++$
Gluconeogenesis	$+$	$+++$
Ureagenesis	$+$	$+++$
Protein oxidation	$+$	$+++$
Lipolysis	$++$	$+++$
Responsiveness to outside substrate	$++++$	$+$
Ketosis	$++++$	$+$
Rate of development of malnutrition	$+$	$++++$

*$-$ means decrease; $+$ means increase; NC means no change.

2. Mediator activity modulates end-organ response.
   a. Response is dynamic, with an uncomplicated case having peak response on day 3 after injury and resolving by day 7.
   b. Response's failure to abate or a response resurgence indicates the presence of a new activator event.
   c. Various stratification systems quantitate the process for clinical use. These schemes are necessary as clinical criteria, evaluating degrees of organ failure correlates poorly with the degree of existing metabolic activation.* An example of a stress stratification schema:

Stress level	Clinical type*	Urinary nitrogen loss (g/day)	Plasma lactate (mM/L)	O2CI (ml/m2)	Plasma glucose (mg/dl)	Estimated caloric need (Kcal/day)
0	Starvation	<5	0.5 ± 5	90 ± 10	100 ± 20	BEE†
1	Elective surgery	5-10	1.2 ± 0.2	130 ± 6	150 ± 25	1.3 × BEE
2	Polytrauma	10-15	1.5 ± 0.5	140 ± 6	200 ± 25	1.5 × BEE
3	Sepsis	>15	>2.5	170 ± 10	250 ± 25	2.0 × BEE

*Approximately 70% specific.
†Basal energy expenditure.

    d. Failure to achieve these responses after injury is associated with increased mortality (e.g., survival correlates with the ability to increase cardiac output at $r = 0.86$ at $P < 0.02$).

B. Flow-dependent oxygen consumption

    Flow-dependent oxygen consumption can occur as a result of general surgery, trauma, pancreatitis, sepsis, acute cardiogenic states, and the adult respiratory distress syndrome. These significant increases in oxygen consumption with increases in cardiac output have occurred in situations in which clinical criteria of perfusion were felt to be adequate. Observed metabolic alterations have resolved with the restoration of perfusion (e.g., the lactate/pyruvate ratio returning to normal).

    1. Flow dependency in pancreatitis

Observations	CI	O_2CI	Significance
18	2.5	115	$p < 0.03$
16	3.5	158	$p < 0.03$
16	4.4	175	NS
8	5.4	200	NS
2	6.7	210	NS

    2. Flow dependency in hypovolemia (Fig. 1-1)

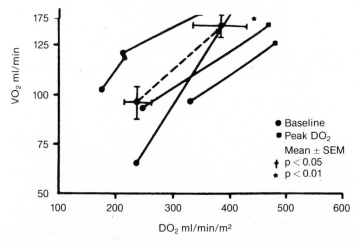

Fig. 1-1. Hypovolemic shock: effect of increase in oxygen delivery (Do_2) on consumption (Vo_2) in five patients. (From Kaufman, B., and Rachow, E.C.: Chest **85:**336, 1984.)

3. Flow dependency in sepsis (Fig. 1-2)
4. Flow dependency in adult respiratory distress syndrome (Figs. 1-3 and 1-4)
5. Venous oxygen tension is not related to oxygen consumption. This has been observed for mixed venous oxygen saturation and for the relationship between cardiac output and venous oxygen tension, saturation, or the arteriovenous oxygen content differences (Fig. 1-5).

C. Multiple systems organ failure (MSOF)
  1. The MSOF syndrome remains the cause of death in over 90% of surgical patients in the intensive care unit.
  2. One of the major contributing factors in MSOF is unrecognized hypoperfusion or a failure to adequately restore oxygen transport.

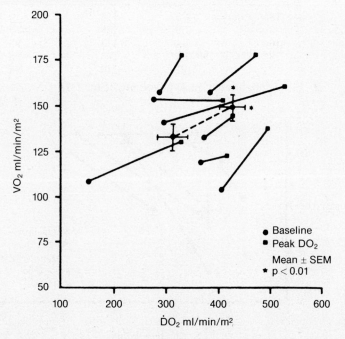

Fig. 1-2. Septic shock: effect of increases in oxygen delivery (DO_2) on oxygen consumption (VO_2) in eight patients (*CI*, Cardiac index; *SvO₂*, mixed venous blood % saturation; *PvO₂*, mixed-venous PO_2 torr.) (From Kaufman, B., and Rachow, E.C.: Chest **85**:336, 1984.)

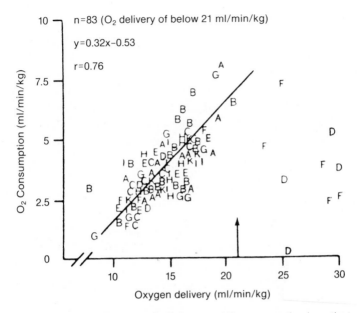

Fig. 1-3. Relationship between O_2 delivery and O_2 consumption in patients with adult respiratory distress syndrome (ARDS). (From Danek, S.J., et al.: Am. J. Respir. Dis. **122:**387, 1980.)

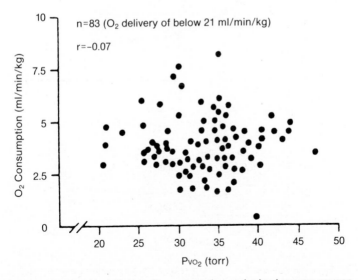

Fig. 1-4. Relationship between O_2 consumption and mixed venous oxygenation (Pv_{O_2}). (From Danek, S.J., et al.: Am. J. Respir. Dis. **122:**387, 1980.)

   3. Longitudinal studies through surgery are particularly illustrative of inadequate perfusion unrecognized by clinical criteria (Fig. 1-6).
D. High-flow states
   Pathologic states in which the physiology is one of high flow and low resistance represent states in which the higher cardiac output is largely nutrient. Data from end-stage liver disease patients undergoing surgical procedures are revealing.

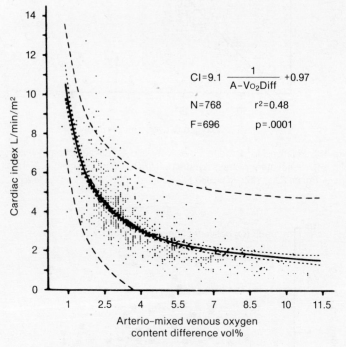

$$CI = 9.1 \frac{1}{A-Vo_2Diff} + 0.97$$

N=768 r^2=0.48

F=696   p=.0001

$CI = 7.5 - 2.9 \log A-Vo_2Diff$
N=768 r^2=0.52   F=842   p=.0001

$CI = -2.1 + 0.8 \, Svo_2$
N=768 r^2=0.32   F=359   p=.0001

$CI = -1.6 + 0.13 \, Pvo_2$
N=768 r^2=0.33   F=373   p=.0001

Fig. 1-5. Graph of cardiac index in relation to difference in oxygen content between arteries and veins. *CI,* Cardiac index; Svo_2, mixed venous blood % saturation; Pvo_2, mixed venous Po_2 mm Hg. (From Karwande, S., Siegel, J.H., and Cerra, F.B.: Surg. Forum, **31:**26, 1980.

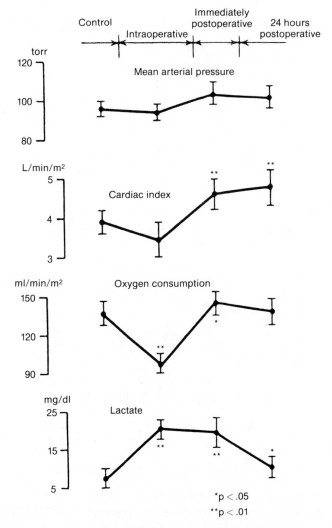

Fig. 1-6. Mean arterial pressure (MAP), cardiac index (CI), oxygen consumption (Vo_2), and arterial blood lactate concentrations obtained preoperatively (control), intraoperatively, immediately postoperatively, and next morning. *Dots,* Mean values; *vertical bars,* standard error of mean. Notice reduced Vo_2 associated with increased lactate levels. (From Waxman, K., Nolan, L., and Shoemaker, W.C.: Crit. Care Med. **10:**96, 1982. © 1982, The Williams & Wilkins Co., Baltimore.)

Group I—Flow reduced

(N = 13)	Baseline	Preanhepatic	Postanhepatic
Lac	2.6 ± 0.4	6.9 ± 0.9*	9.4 ± 0.7*
Lac/Pyr	55.0 ± 12.0	46.0 ± 6.0	55.0 ± 8.0
CI (n = 4)	8.2 ± 1.2	—	3.8 ± 0.5*

Group II—Flow restored

(N = 5)	Baseline	Preanhepatic	Postanhepatic
Lac	4.4 ± 0.9	7.8 ± 0.9*	9.9 ± 1.0*
Lac/Pyr	18.0 ± 2.0†	18.0 ± 1.0†	26.0 ± 2.0†
CI	10.8 ± 2.0	10.7 ± 0.1	10.5 ± 0.1†

LAC in millimoles/L; CI in L/min.
*$p < 0.01$ to prior column by matched pair student t.
†$p < 0.01$ to Group 1 by group student t. Values are mean ± S.E.M.

E. Low-flow stress states
   1. Patients in stress states who have an inappropriately low flow have an increased mortality risk. With proper therapy, the flow can frequently be reversed, with a concomitant improvement in the survival rate.
   2. Data from acutely cardiogenic sepsis are revealing, as seen in these physiologic indexes before and after nitroglycerine paste (NP).

Index	Pre-NP	Post-NP	P
RAP (mm Hg)	11.0 ± 3.0	5.7 ± 1.7	0.05
CI (L/min m²)	1.27 ± 0.31	2.5 ± 1.0	0.01
tm (sec)*	17.0 ± 9.7	8.8 ± 6.3	0.05
TPR (dyne-cm × 10⁻⁵)	3773.0 ± 916.0	1507.0 ± 322.0	0.01
A-VO₂ (vol%)	7.4 ± 2.1	5.0 ± 1.0	0.02
O₂ consumption (ml/m²)	91.0 ± 14.0	114.0 ± 23.0	0.02

*Cardiac mixing time, an index of contractility [5].

F. Anemia and hypermetabolism
   In hypermetabolic states, the presence of anemia becomes a significant correlate of mortality:

Hemoglobin (g/dl)	O_2 content (vol %)	Patients (no.)	Mortality (%)
7.5-9.9	9.8-12.9	58	72
10.0-12.4	13.0-16.1	80	64
12.5-15.0	16.2-19.2	31	42
15	19.2	13	23

G. Resuscitation parameters

Resuscitation from states of hypovolemia and sepsis is frequently monitored by—and judged complete by—measurements of pulmonary artery pressure and pulmonary capillary wedge pressure. In these states, a shift in ventricular compliance can occur such that restoration of adequate end-diastolic volume and cardiac output requires higher-than-usual filling pressures.

H. Oxygen transport and mortality

A reduction in mortality from trauma may strongly correlate with the increased use of invasive restoration of oxygen transport.

1. Fig. 1-7 shows the results of one study attempting to prove this correlation.

2. In another setting, prospective, randomized studies attempted to compare oxygen transport restoration by ob-

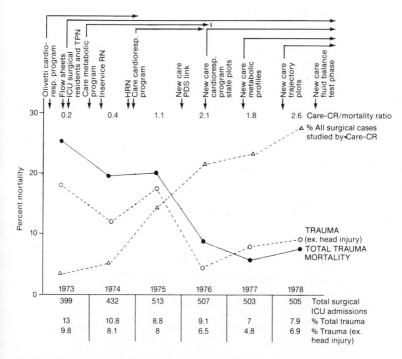

Fig. 1-7. Yearly mortality from 1973 to 1978 for trauma in intensive care units. (From Powers, S.R., and Marmal, R.: Ann. Surg. **178:**265, 1975.)

jective criteria with the usual clinical criteria of restoration (e.g., skin temperature and color, urine output, nail bed perfusion, mental activity).

  a. Objective criteria:
- (1) Cardiac index at least 50% above normal for non-stressed person
- (2) Blood volume at least 500 ml greater than normal, with a wedge pressure under 20 torr
- (3) Oxygen delivery greater than 600 ml/min
- (4) Oxygen consumption greater than 170 ml/min
- (5) Usual blood pressure
- (6) Vascular resistance index less than 250 dyne sec/cm/m^2
- (7) Nutritional support

  b. Significant reduction occurred in respiratory failure requiring ventilatory support, sepsis, renal failure, cardiac failure, and multiple organ failure.

  c. Mortality data

	Control	Protocol
Number of patients	143	80
Mortality	35%	12.5%

3. At the same institution:

  a. Pulmonary artery (PA) catheterization with the outlined optimized values appeared to result in reduced mortality.

  b. Comparing PA catheterization with optimal values to standard practice with either a pulmonary artery catheter or a central venous catheter showed the following:

	Mortality
Central venous pressure (CVP) with usual methods	29%
PA with usual methods	34%
PA with optimized values	4%

PRINCIPLES OF OXYGEN TRANSPORT

A. Criteria for oxygen delivery equal to oxygen demand (see also Chapter 4)

  1. No bedside technique currently exists for determining how much oxygen the tissues would like to consume.

2. Two techniques measure the amount consumed
   a. The product of cardiac output and the arteriovenous oxygen content difference
   b. Expired gas analysis
3. Two absolute criteria for adequate oxygenation
   a. Absence of flow-dependent oxygen consumption
   b. Metabolic indexes consistent with the absence of an oxygen deficit (e.g., a normal lactate/pyruvate ratio)

B. When oxygen delivery is not equal to oxygen demand
   An inequality of supply and demand requires implementing a planned approach to affect both parameters, the specifics depending on the clinical circumstances.
   1. Variables available to manipulate
      a. Tissue demand: temperature, pH, endocrine, drugs, fuel
      b. Normalization of content: PaO_2 that gives over 95% saturation; hemoglobin at 13 g/dl
      c. Improvement of distribution: volume, dilation; constriction
      d. Flow change: preload, contractility, afterload
   2. The endpoint remains having oxygen delivery equal to oxygen demand.
   3. Once achieved, the decisions involved maintaining equalization most efficiently.
      a. From the cardiac standpoint, doing flow work is usually less costly than doing pressure work.
      b. In some settings temporarily increasing lung water may be necessary to adequately restore perfusion.
   4. In general, the sicker the patient, the more quantitative criteria are necessary, particularly for pressure monitoring.
      a. Pressure has a relationship to volume only within the limits of the compliance of the system in which it is being measured.
      b. In such compliant systems, large changes in volume can occur with little change in pressure
      c. The pressure changes only occur
         (1) After large losses of volume, in which case flow is usually severely reduced

  (2) When the vascular capacity is nearly full
 d. Fluid challenges are necessary to maintain the blood volume in those ranges where sensitivity of pressure for volume exists.
 e. Flow is a much more accurate measurement and is much more sensitive to volume changes.
 f. Attempts are made in these settings to predict flow from mixed venous oxygen tension, saturation of from the arteriovenous oxygen content difference. The predictability of these parameters for cardiac output is quite poor and not very reliable.
C. General principles (Fig. 1-8).
 1. Oxygen consumption appropriate for the existing level of metabolic stress
 2. Arterial Po_2 that provides at least 95% saturation
 3. Hemoglobin 13 g/dl
 4. Cardiac output at a level to achieve the appropriate level of oxygen consumption at the normalized oxygen content; PCWP under 20 torr (mm Hg)

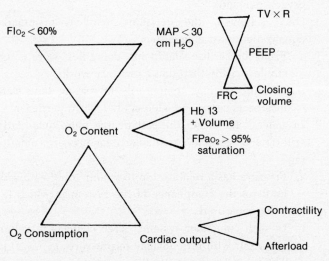

Fig. 1-8. The balancing triangles of oxygen transport. The system is interdependent, and altering one variable alters the entire relationship. The key variable for survival appears to be oxygen consumption.

     5. Resistance under 800 dyne sec/cm
     6. Fuel support
     7. Mean airway pressure under 30 to 35 cm water
     8. Inspired oxygen percentage under 60
D. Application
     1. Who and when to invade
       a. Cases for which data exist: pancreatitis; severe sepsis; septic shock; adult respiratory distress syndrome (ARDS); severe polytrauma
       b. High-risk settings: patient with athrosclerotic heart disease (ASHD) undergoing surgery with potential for hypotension and/or acute blood loss
       c. Observed response not expected
       d. Monitoring: chronic hypermetabolic states

SELECTED READINGS

Alyono, D., Ring, W.S., and Anderson, R.W.: Effects of hemorrhagic shock on diastolic properties of left ventricle, Surgery **83**:691, 1978.

Ashbaugh D.C., and Pitt, T.L.: CPAP in ARDS, J. Thorac. Cardiovasc. Surg. **57**:31, 1969.

Brunwald, E.: Regulation of circulation, N. Engl. J. Med. **290**:1124, 1974.

Cerra, F.B., and Caprioli, J.: Proline metabolism in sepsis, cirrhosis and general surgery, Ann. Surg. **190**:557, 1979.

Cerra, F.B., and Hassett, J.H.: Vasodilator therapy in clinical sepsis with low output syndrome, J. Surg. Res. **25**:180, 1978.

Cerra, F.B., and Siegel, J.H.: Correlations between metabolic and cardiopulmonary measurements in patients after trauma, general surgery, sepsis, J. Trauma **19**:621, 1979.

Cerra, F.B., and Siegel, J.H.: The hepatic failure of sepsis: cellular versus substrate, Surgery **86**:409, 1979.

Cerra, F.B., and Siegel, J.H.: Septic autocannibalism, Ann. Surg. **192**:570, 1980.

Clowes, G.H.A., and Del Guercio, L.R.M.: Circulatory response to trauma of surgical operations, Metabolism **9**:67, 1960.

Clowes, G.H.A., and Vucini, M.: Circulatory and metabolic alterations associated with survival and death in peritonitis, Ann. Surg. **163**:866, 1966.

Danek, S.J., et al.: Dependence of O_2 uptake on O_2 delivery in ARDS, Am. Rev. Resp Dis. **122**:387, 1980.

Downs, J.B., and Douglas, M.E.: Ventilatory pattern, intrapleural pressure and cardiac output, Anesth. Analg. **56**:88, 1977.

Fath, J., Estrin J., and Cerra, F.B.: Lactate metabolism during hepatic transplantation: evidence for a perfusion sensitive population. Trans Proceedings (In press).

Forrester, J.S., et al.: Medical therapy of acute myocardial information by application of hemodynamic subsets, N. Engl. J. Med. **295**:1404, 1976.

Hess, M.L., and Hastillo, A.: Spectrum of cardiovascular function during gram negative sepsis, Prog. Cardiovasc. Disease **23**:279, 1981.

Ito, K., and Ramirez-Schon, G.: Myocardial function in acute pancreatitis, Ann. Surg. **194**:85, 1981.

Kaufman, B., and Rachow, E.C.: The relationship between O_2 delivery and consumption during fluid resuscitation of hypovolemic and septic shock, Chest **85**:336, 1984.

Mohsenfar, Z., et al.: Relationship between O_2 delivery and VO_2 in *ARDS*, Int. Crit. Care Digest **3**:36, 1984.

Nishijimi, H., Weil, M.H., and Shubin, H.: Hemodynamic and metabolic studies on shock associated with gram negative bacteremia, Medicine (Baltimore), **52**:287, 1973.

Powers, S.R., and Marmal, R.: Physiologic consequences of PEEP, Ann. Surg. **178**:265, 1975.

Rachow, E.C., Falk, J.L., and Fein, A.: Fluid resuscitation in circulatory shock: comparison of cardiorespiratory effects of albumin, hetastarch and saline solutions in patients with hypovolemic and septic shock. Crit. Care Med. **10**:230, 1982.

Rhodes, G.R., and Newell, J.C.: Increased O_2C accompanying increased O_2 delivery with Marmitol in ARDS, Surgery **84**:490, 1978.

Shoemaker, W.C., and Apple, P.: Clinical trial of an algorhithm for outcome prediction in acute circulatory failure, Crit. Care Med. **10**:390, 1982.

Shoemaker, W.C., and Apple, P.L.: Use of physiological monitoring to predict outcome and to assist clinical decisions in critically ill post-operative patients, Am. J. Surg. **146**:43, 1983.

Shoemaker, W.C.: Hemodynamic and oxygen transport patterns in septic shock: physiologic mechanisms and therapeutic implications. Perspectives in sepsis and septic shock, Soc. Crit. Care Med., Fullerton, Calif., 1985.

Shoemaker, W.C., and Carey J.S.: Hemodynamic measurements in various types of clinical shock, Arch. Surg. **93**:189, 1966.

Shoemaker, W.C., and Mohr, P.A. Use of sequential physiological measurements as guides to therapy in uncomplicated septic shock, Surg. Gyn. Obstet. **131**:245, 1978.

Sibbald, W.: Myocardial function in critically ill: factors influencing left and right ventricular performance in septic and traumatized patient, Surg. Clin. N. Am. (In press).

Seigel, J.S., and Cerra, F.B.: Physiological and metabolic correlations in human sepsis, Surgery **86**:163, 1979.

Siegel, J.H., Cerra, F.B.: Effect of survival in critically ill and injured patients of an ICU teaching society organized around a physiological CARE system, J. Trauma **20**:558, 1980.

Swan, H.J.C.: Role of hemodynamic monitoring in management of the critically ill, Crit. Care Med. **3**:83, 1975.

Waxman, K., Nolan, L., and Shoemaker, W.C.: Sequential perioperative lactate determination, Crit. Care Med. **10**:96, 1982.

Weil, M.H., and Afifi, A.A.: Expanded clinical studies on lactate and pyruvate as indicators of the severity of acute circulatory failure, Circulation **41**:989, 1970.

Wilson, R.F., and Gibson, B.S.: Use of PVo_2 to calculate CO and O_2C in critically ill surgical patients, Surgery **84**:362, 1978.

2

Airway management

Jon Berlauk

Respiratory failure is not an uncommon occurrence for patients in the surgical intensive care unit (ICU). Basic airway management skills are mandatory for physicians caring for these patients. Although acute airway obstruction can occur, the more common scenario is one of slowly progressive respiratory failure requiring intubation and mechanically assisted ventilation. An approach to management of these patients follows.

INTUBATION
Who requires intubation?

A. Most common indications in the ICU
1. Inadequate alveolar ventilation
   a. CO_2 retention causing respiratory acidosis
   b. Serum pH less than 7.30 (PCO_2 will be approximately 60 torr)
2. Intractable hypoxemia
   a. PaO_2 less than 60 torr, despite an FIO_2 greater than or equal to 0.60
   b. If patient meets above conditions and is not improving with conservative measures, endotracheal intubation required

Preparation for intubation

A. All equipment needed to handle unexpected difficulties should be assembled.
1. Assembling equipment is usually not a problem during "elective" intubations when a physician has time to "prepare for the worst."
2. It can be more important during urgent conditions when

the lack of an instrument or piece of equipment can make a difficult intubation an impossible intubation.
3. Fortunately, most critical care stations have prepackaged intubation kits.
4. The physician performing the intubation is, however, responsible for checking all equipment.
B. Equipment needed for intubation
   1. Adequate suction apparatus
      a. This is the most often forgotten yet potentially the most important piece of equipment available for a safe intubation.
         (1) Saliva and accumulated mucus often fill the hypopharynx in seriously ill patients.
         (2) Trauma during intubation can cause sufficient bleeding to obscure the anatomical features of the airway.

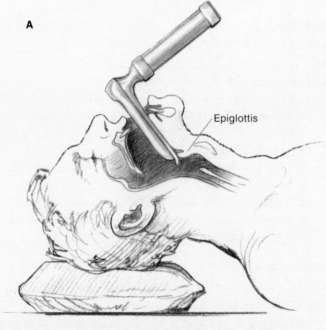

A

Epiglottis

Fig. 2-1. Proper position of laryngoscope blade during direct laryngoscopy. **A,** Distal end of the curved blade is advanced into the space between the base of the tongue and pharyngeal surface of the epiglottis (vallecula).

Continued.

(3) Finally, regurgitation caused by stimulating the gag reflex can be disasterous without adequate suction.

b. The intensivist should *personally* check the suction.

2. Laryngoscope blades and functioning laryngoscope

   a. Laryngoscope blades

      (1) The Jackson-Wisconsin blade is the prototype straight blade; the Miller blade is the most popular.

         (a) With these blades, the objective is to "pick up" the epiglottis with the tip of the blade.

         (b) The larynx is exposed (Fig. 2-1, A).

      (2) The MacIntosh blade has a broad curve.

         (a) The blade is designed for insertion into the vallecular space.

B

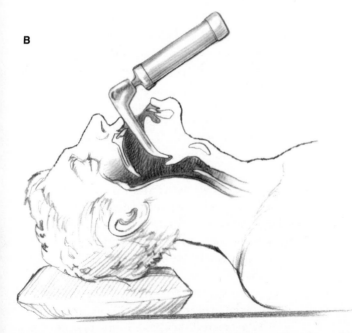

Fig. 2-1, cont'd. B, Distal end of straight blade (Jackson-Wisconsin or Miller) is advanced beneath laryngeal surface of the epiglottis. Forward and upward movement exerted along the axis of the laryngoscope blade, *arrows*, elevates the epiglottis and exposes glottic opening.

(b) Elevation of the blade will cause stretching of the hypoepiglottic ligament.

(c) The epiglottis is folded against the underside of the blade.

(d) The larynx is exposed (Fig. 2-1, *B*).

(3) All blades come in sizes appropriate for neonates to adults.

(4) At least two sizes of two different types of blades should be available.

b. Laryngoscope

Before proceeding, the intensivist should attach the laryngoscope blade to the laryngoscope handle to ensure proper functioning. Weak batteries, a loose-seated bulb, or an ill-fitting blade will interrupt an intubation at the critical moment before insertion of the endotracheal tube.

3. Endotracheal tubes

Selection of an appropriate endotracheal tube (ETT) is an important consideration for long-term intubation.

a. Under emergency conditions any ETT is appropriate; the ETT can always be replaced under more favorable conditions.

b. The tube design and material, cuff size and design, and endotracheal tube diameter to trachea diameter all determine the extent of laryngeal trauma from intubation.

c. Diameter

(1) The average adult male's trachea will easily admit an 8- to 9-mm internal diameter ETT; most women, however, require a 7-mm ETT.

(2) Because of the narrow nasal passage, a nasotracheal tube should be no larger than 7.5 mm for most adults.

d. Length

(1) Uncut endotracheal tubes are 29 cm in length.

(a) The average distance from lips to midtrachea in adults is 20 to 24 cm.

(b) Endobronchial intubation will result if a full-length tube is inserted too far.

      (c) If time allows, the ETT should be cut to 22 to 24 cm if oral intubation is planned.

      (d) A 27-29 cm tube is appropriate for nasal intubation.

  4. Magill's forceps

Designed to guide the ETT tip into the larynx, these forceps are especially useful during difficult intubations.

  5. Empty syringe

This is necessary to inflate the ETT cuff.

  6. Adhesive tape

Most endotracheal tubes are secured with tape. Often preparing the skin with tincture of benzoin before taping the tube will provide longer-lasting adhesion.

C. Drugs

  1. Local anesthetics

Under "elective" intubation conditions, using general anesthetic to perform the intubation is often inappropriate. Use of a good topical anesthetic will provide the patient comfort and better cooperation for an "awake" intubation.

    a. If available, 4% cocaine spray provides excellent analgesia and vasoconstriction.

    b. Alternatives include local anesthetic aerosols (Cetacaine, etc.) and 4% lidocaine (Xylocaine) jelly; 4% lidocaine topical anesthetic provides rapid analgesic effect for nasal or transtracheal use.

  2. Cardioresuscitation drugs

With careful preparation and adequate skill, a respiratory emergency will not develop into a cardiorespiratory arrest; however, emergency equipment should always be nearby.

Oral intubation of the unconscious patient

A. Position

  1. Fig. 2-2, *C*, shows the proper anatomical position for successful intubation.

  2. Extension and slight elevation of the head on a pillow gives the best alignment of oral, pharyngeal, and laryngeal axes.

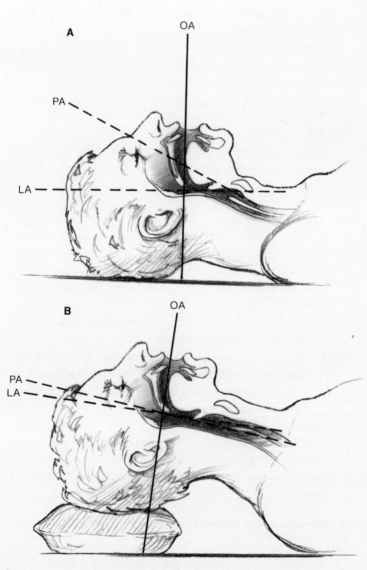

Fig. 2-2. Head position for endotracheal intubation. **A,** Successful direct laryngoscopy requires alignment of oral, pharyngeal, and laryngeal axes. **B,** Elevation of the head about 10 cm with pads under the occiput while the shoulders remain on the table aligns the laryngeal and pharyngeal axes.

Continued.

3. The mouth should be opened as widely as possible using the index and middle fingers of the *right* hand. All laryngoscopes are designed for left-hand use.

B. Procedure
1. With the blade in functioning position on the handle, the tip of the blade is inserted along the right side of the tongue.
2. When the tip of the blade passes near the base of the tongue, the entire laryngoscope is elevated at a 45-degree angle toward the feet.
   a. The practioner's left wrist should be firmly locked.
   b. The laryngoscope should *not* be used as a lever.
   c. All power necessary to elevate the mandible should come from the upper arm.
3. At this point one should be able to visualize the epiglottis easily at the tip of the blade.
   a. The patient's tongue should be entirely to the left side of the laryngoscope blade chosen.

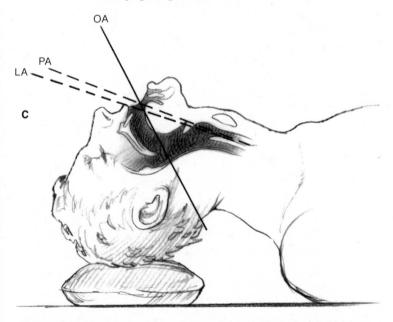

Fig. 2-2. cont'd. C, Subsequent head extension at atlanto-occipital joint creates the shortest distance and most nearly straight line from incisor teeth to the glottic opening.

   b. If the tongue overlaps the blade, reposition the blade
      to the right of the tongue.
4. Next, depending on the type of blade chosen, the epiglottis is either lifted with the blade or retracted by the
   blade (see Fig. 2-1, *A* and *B*).
   a. The vocal cords should now clearly be seen.
5. The endotracheal tube is passed through the far right
   corner of the mouth and directed toward the vocal cords.
   One should not attempt to pass the tube down the lumen
   of the laryngoscope blade; vision will be obscured, and
   the ETT can easily miss the larynx.
6. Once the ETT has been seen to pass through the cords,
   the laryngoscope is removed and the cuff is inflated.
7. The lung fields should be immediately auscultated for
   breath sounds to ensure proper ETT placement.
8. Breath sounds should be distinct and bilateral before the
   tube is securely taped.

Oral intubation of the conscious patient

This procedure is very difficult unless sufficient skill at intubation has been attained.
A. Position
   Patient compliance determines the success of this procedure, so he or she should be made as comfortable as possible.
B. Procedure
   1. The tongue, palate, and pharynx should first be anesthe-
      tized with a local anesthetic spray or jelly, which the pa-
      tient should be encouraged to gargle.
   2. With gentle manipulation and good patient cooperation,
      the laryngoscope can be introduced to the back of the
      tongue. If the area is not adequately anesthetized, the
      patient will gag and more spray should be used in this
      area.
   3. When the epiglottis is visualized, it too should be
      sprayed with local anesthetic.
   4. To provide topical anesthesia to the trachea and vocal
      cords, 2 ml of 4% topical lidocaine is drawn into a small

syringe to be injected into the larynx through the cricothy-
roid membrane.

    a. The cricothyroid notch is identified.

    b. The area is swabbed with povidone-iodine solution
(Betadine).

    c. A No. 25-gauge needle, no longer than ½ inch, is in-
serted through the membrane. By one's using a 25-
gauge, short-length needle, laryngeal trauma should
be negligible.

    d. Air bubbles should be present on withdrawal of the
syringe plunger.

    e. The lidocaine is then rapidly injected until the patient
coughs, at which time the needle is withdrawn.

  5. After these steps to provide local anesthesia, intubation
should be performed as in the unconscious patient.

    a. Since the patient is in some respiratory distress al-
ready, great care must be exercised to avoid obstructing the airway.

    b. If this happens, the patient usually objects violently
and further attempts to intubate in this manner may
be met with great resistance.

Nasal intubation of the conscious patient

A. Procedure

  1. Patient cooperation is also imperative with this procedure, so proper local anesthesia must be provided.

    a. The procedures for anesthetizing the pharynx, larynx,
and tongue should be followed, as outlined previously.

    b. In addition, the nasal passage must be adequately
anesthetized.

      (1) Each naris is checked for patency; the one that of-
fers the best airway is chosen.

      (2) The best local anesthetic to use is a 4% cocaine
solution, soaked in a pledget.

        (a) It provides superior analgesia.

        (b) It also provides vasoconstriction to help mini-
mize nosebleeds.

    (3) If local anesthetic spray is used, the chosen nasal passage must be thoroughly anesthetized.

2. A tube of the proper length is generously lubricated and passed with firm, gentle pressure perpendicular to the plane of the face.
   a. Usually mild resistance is encountered while passing the turbinates.
   b. A sudden loss of resistance is usually encountered as the tube passes into the pharynx.
3. The patient's head is placed in the "sniff position" (see Fig. 2-2).
4. The patient's mouth is closed and he or she is instructed to breathe as deeply as possible through the nose.
5. While listening at the end of the endotracheal tube, one slowly advances the tube toward the larynx.
   a. Very loud distinct breath sounds ensure proper alignment.
6. When the tip of the ETT is at the opening of the larynx, passage into the larynx is attempted only on inspiration when the cords are open.
   a. The tube should not be forced, because the vocal cords may easily be damaged.
   b. Usually, if the tube touches the larynx, the patient will stop breathing momentarily.
7. If the tube does not pass easily, it should be withdrawn a few centimeters and repeat the attempt.
   a. The tube should be advanced *only* on inspiration.
   b. Repeated failure to pass the tube indicates that the ETT is hanging up on the anterior or posterior laryngeal lip.
   c. Further elevation and flexion of the head may help align the axes.
8. If the breath sounds disappear when the ETT is advanced, two explanations exist.
   a. The tube is directed to either side of the larynx.
      (1) If the ETT is directed left or right, the tube will not advance, and a bulge can be felt to either side of the larynx externally.
      (2) The tube should be withdrawn a few centimeters,

rotated 45 to 90 degrees in the proper direction, and advanced again.

 b. The tube is displaced posteriorly in the esophagus.

  (1) If the tube enters the esophagus, the breath sounds will disappear, but the tube is easily advanced.

  (2) Further *flexion* of the head may be necessary to correct the alignment.

9. If despite all of these maneuvers the intubation is unsuccessful, direct visualization with the laryngoscope will be necessary.

 a. The ETT can be visualized in the posterior pharynx and directed toward the larynx.

 b. Often an associate can externally displace the larynx for proper alignment for intubation.

 c. If not, the Magill forceps should be used to pick up the end of the ETT and direct it into the larynx.

 d. Care must be exercised to avoid tearing the cuff with the forceps.

Precautions

A. When the physician is using an awake oral/nasal intubation technique on a patient who is in significant respiratory distress, someone should be assigned to watch the patient.

1. In attempting to place the endotracheal tube, the physician is often concentrating solely on the larynx.

2. The patient's vital signs, skin color, and ability to continue with the procedure should be monitored by a second person.

3. During difficult intubations, frequent rest periods, during which 100% oxygen is administered to the patient, are necessary to prevent more serious complications.

B. For patients with cervical spine injuries or suspected injuries, flexion or extension of the neck is contraindicated.

C. In cases of high cervical spine instability, the simple alignment of the oropharyngeal and laryngeal planes has potentially devastating complications. In such situations the nasotracheal route or cricothyrotomy may be the procedure of choice.

BRONCHOSCOPY

Flexible fiber-optic bronchoscopy is becoming an important adjunct in the airway care of critically ill patients. With prolonged intubations, bronchoscopy is used to assess the presence and progression of airway injury. It is also a good technique for assessing "edema status" in clinical risk situations: neck surgery, trauma, and laryngeal edema. In such circumstances, extubating over the bronchoscope is sometimes useful. A few considerations are necessary if bronchoscopy is to be performed safely.

A. Flexible bronchoscopy can be performed with local or general anesthesia.

1. If an ill patient who can tolerate the procedure, local anesthesia (as described for oral intubation of a conscious patient) is preferable.

2. Avoiding respiratory depressants is advantageous.

B. Seriously ill patients often will not tolerate the procedure under local anesthesia, or they already require mechanical ventilation because of respiratory failure.

1. In these patients, fiber-optic bronchoscopy must be performed through an endotracheal tube.

a. If a flexible bronchoscope is placed through a 8.0-mm ETT, the cross-sectional area unoccluded by the bronchoscope is equivalent to a 5.5-mm ETT. Attempts to adequately ventilate an adult will be difficult.

b. A 9.0-mm ETT with bronchoscope provides a cross-sectional area equivalent to a 7.0-mm ETT. For safety, this size tube should be placed whenever possible.

2. Special adapters with a rubber membrane and swivel connection have been developed to allow continuing mechanical ventilation during bronchoscopy.

a. PEEP should be continued if the patient requires this modality, but airway pressures must be monitored closely.

b. Prior to the bronchoscopy, the patient should be placed on 100% FIO_2 and continued throughout the procedure.

c. If the mechanical ventilator does not monitor airway

pressure and expiratory volume, separate monitors must be attached.

d. If the fiber-optic bronchoscope is too large for the ETT, expiratory obstruction occurs with increased end expiratory pressure and decreased expiratory volumes. Pneumothorax could result.

3. During the actual bronchoscopy, frequent arterial blood gas analyses are required.
    a. Only short periods of selective endobronchial occlusion with the bronchoscope will be tolerated without the occurrence of atelectasis, hypoxemia, and hypercapnia.
    b. Aspiration through an empty suction channel results in the same problems.
4. Since ventilation is controlled, the use of respiratory depressants is not contraindicated.
    a. Morphine sulfate in small intravenous doses provides good sedation and analgesic effect in these patients.
    b. If the patient exhibits cardiovascular instability, the morphine is seldom the cause.
    c. All monitors of ventilatory adequacy should be rechecked and bronchoscopy discontinued briefly.

AIRWAY ROUTE CHOICE AND COMPLICATIONS

A. Tracheostomy complications
    1. Loss of cough—suction dependent
    2. Contamination down to carina
    3. Erosion into innominate artery
    4. Stenosis
    5. Tracheobronchitis
    6. Tracheomalacia
    7. Site infection with or without systemic sepsis
    8. Cross-contamination of neck or subclavian central line
    9. Dislodgement
B. Endotracheal tube complications
    1. Loss of cough—suction dependent
    2. Tracheal contamination
    3. Oronasopharyngeal erosion and/or hemorrhage
    4. Sinusitis with or without systemic sepsis

     5. Glottic, supraglottic, or tracheal injury, particularly in the presence of side-to-side head motion

     6. Increased airway resistance if tube is too small relative to anatomic airway or to minute ventilation

     7. Bronchial intubation

     8. Dislodgement from "tonguing effect" in patients with intact reflexes

     9. Less effective secretion control

C. Minimizing complications

     1. Correct size of tube

     2. Meticulous local care (securing, washing, dressing)

     3. Toileting routines

     4. Limiting side-to-side head motion

     5. Judicious suctioning technique

     6. Endoscopic monitoring for prolonged intubation or tracheostomy

     7. Cognizance of tube length relative to patient anatomy

     8. Using tracheostomy when necessary

     9. Clearing hypopharyngeal "adherent" secretions before extubation

    10. Sinus roentgenograms periodically during prolonged NT intubation

Oral versus nasal endotracheal route

A. Oral

     1. Advantages

        a. Larger tubes can be used

        b. Better toileting

        c. Bronchoscopy easier

     2. Disadvantages

        a. Hyperextension/extension of head necessary for intubation

        b. More tooth or tongue and lip injuries

        c. Oral hygiene more difficult

        d. More laryngeal trauma

B. Nasal

     1. Advantages

        a. Better patient comfort

     b. Less side-to-side motion
     c. Accidental extubation less frequent
  2. Disadvantages
     a. Smaller tubes necessary
     b. Less effective toilet
     c. Nasal bleeding
     d. Sinusitis

Mechanical airway resistance

A. Factors involved
    1. Tube diameter   3. Minute ventilation
    2. Tube length   4. Turbulence
B. General considerations
    1. A 7-mm tube of standard length has about the same resistance as the normal glottis. A tube of less than 7 mm has a rapidly rising resistance; above 7 mm it has less resistance.
    2. At high minute ventilations, even a large tube can be the source of an increased flow resistance.
    3. Monitoring resistance
       a. Observe the patient with spontaneous ventilation for signs of increased respiratory work. The use of accessory respiratory muscles during inspiration (unusual) and expiration is an early clinical sign.
       b. In ventilated patients, the differential between peak pressure and plateau pressure is useful. It should be under 10 cm water. More than 10 cm water indicates increased airway resistance, one cause of which is an inappropriately small endotracheal tube or tracheostomy. Other causes include secretions, bronchospasm, and conditions that displace airspace, such as pleural effusion or pneumothorax.

Complications after extubation

A. Laryngeal edema
    1. This uncommon complication can be devastating.
    2. It can occur immediately or take several hours to develop.

3. It is occasionally infectious and has even been seen with *Serratia marcescens*.
4. Management
   a. Patient should sit up
   b. Cold mist/oxygen
   c. Racemic epinephrine nebulizations (0.2 to 0.4 mg in 2.5 ml normal saline)
   d. Steroids (Decadron, 0.3 to 0.5 mg/kg)
   e. Antibiotics if infectious cause suspected
   f. Physician must be prepared to reestablish an airway either by tube or tracheostromy
B. Chronic problems
   1. Tracheal stenosis
   2. Cord scarring, granulomas, papillomas
   3. Tracheal granulomas
   4. Loss of "high" voice
   5. Arytenoid dislocation
   6. Cord paralysis

Granulomas, arytenoid dislocation, and cord paralysis can cause *acute* upper airway obstruction after extubation. *The physician should treat extubation with the same caution as intubation and be prepared to reestablish an airway!*

ETT versus tracheostomy

A. Mortality associated with procedures
   1. Elective tracheostomy—3%
   2. Emergent tracheostomy—6% to 15%
   3. ETT—1%
B. Bacterial invasion is eight times more common with tracheostomy
C. Stenosis
   1. Occurs in 98% of patients who have had a tracheostomy performed
   2. Clinically significant in 11% of tracheostomy patients
   3. Twenty-one-day ETT—19% stenosis, none clinically significant

When to do a tracheostomy

A. After 21 to 28 days of ETT; when the clinical situation clearly indicates prolonged intubation, particularly in elderly and/or malnourished patients
B. Patients who will obviously need lifelong suction (e.g., quadraplegics, patients with postarrest encephalopathy)
C. Severe head and neck trauma
D. Upper airway burn or caustic inhalation
E. Tracheomalacia syndrome

If a fresh tracheostomy is dislodged during an ICU procedure, it is frequently prudent to *reintubate the patient orally,* and reinsert the tracheostomy tube electively in a calm, controlled fashion.

Cricothyroidotomy versus tracheostomy

Cricothyroidotomy is easier to perform in the emergent situation than tracheostomy and can be performed in a patient who has been cricothyroidotomized or tracheatomized more easily than a repeat tracheotomy. However, neither the long-term complications nor the preferability of tracheostomy compared to cricothyroidotomy has been determined.

3

Ventilation

Ian Gilmour
Marvin A. McMillen

Intensive care units developed in part because of the increased recognition of the role of pulmonary dysfunction in critical illness. Patients with a significant degree of lung disease may do quite well in their everyday lives until illness supervenes, at which point their compromised lung function becomes life threatening. Unfortunately, significant degrees of pulmonary dysfunction may be present with little evidence from the patient's history or physical examination. In either case, trauma, surgery, or other precipitating factors often unveil the dysfunction, even when there has been no specific insult to the lungs.

From a systems point of view, the components of pulmonary

PHYSIOLOGIC COMPONENTS OF PULMONARY FUNCTION

A. Chest wall: ribcage and overlying tissue, abdominal contents
B. Muscles of respiration: inspiration—diaphragm; accessory—intercostals and strap muscles; exhalation, accessory—rectus abdominus, obliques, intercostals
C. Cardiovascular system: right side of the heart; pulmonary vascular bed; left side of the heart
D. Pulmonary parenchyma; V/Q relationships—alveolar/capillary membrane; surfactant
E. Airway: upper airway—large; lower airway—small
F. Lung as an endocrine/metabolic organ
G. Reticuloendothelial function of the lung
H. Neural influences on breathing and the lung

---

function include the neurohumoral control system, the musculoskeletal system, and the airways and lung parenchyma itself. Dysfunction in any one system can lead to compromise and failure of ventilation and oxygenation.

This chapter approaches the support of pulmonary function from a systems point of view. Thus pulmonary care will be discussed in terms of physiologic components and will proceed to a consideration of support principles and techniques. Specific diseases will be discussed in Chapter 12, "Pulmonary Dysfunction."

Dysfunction of any component can lead to pulmonary compromise or failure.

A. Chest wall dysfunction
  1. Anatomic
    a. Kyphoscoliosis
    b. Obesity
    c. Instability (e.g., flail chest, surgically induced)
    d. Surgically induced instability
  2. Pathologic—acquired
    a. Rib fractures
    b. Pleural effusions, abscesses, tumors
    c. Pneumothorax
    d. Intraabdominal processes (e.g., ascites, peritonitis)
  3. Other
    a. Pain
    b. Rheumatologic abnormalities
B. Neuromuscular dysfunction
  1. Central nervous system
    a. Pharmacologic
      (1) Narcotics, barbiturates, sedatives
      (2) Anesthetics
    b. Pathologic
      (1) Trauma
      (2) Hemorrhage
      (3) Emboli
      (4) Tumor
      (5) Herniation
      (6) Infection

2. Spinal cord
   a. Trauma
   b. Tumor
   c. Infection: polio, Guillain-Barré syndrome
   d. Multiple sclerosis, amyotrophic lateral sclerosis
3. Peripheral nerve
   a. Pharmacologic
      (1) Muscle relaxants.
      (2) Bacterial toxins
      (3) Antibiotics—aminoglycosides
      (4) Paraneoplastic syndromes
   b. Trauma
   c. Myasthenia gravis
   d. Multiple systems organ failure
4. Muscular
   a. Primary muscular disease
      (1) Muscular dystrophy
      (2) Myositis
   b. Acquired dysfunction
      (1) Malnutrition   (2) Disuse atrophy
5. Diaphragm
   The diaphragm and intercostal muscles interact dynamically to decrease intrathoracic pressure and expand the lung. The diaphragm, using the abdominal content as a fulcrum, pulls the ribcage outward and upward, with the intercostal muscles performing an enabling function. Loss of both intercostal and abdominal wall muscles in quadriplegia causes severe decreases in inspiratory efficiency, even when diaphragmatic function is intact. The intercostal and strap muscles can produce inspiration in the absence of diaphragm function, particularly in the upper ribcage. However, these muscles require prolonged "training" before they can sustain this activity.

   Chronic obstructive pulmonary disease (COPD) also impairs diaphragmatic function. Because the lung hyperinflates, the diaphragm is forced down, shortening the muscle fibers and decreasing contractility. During inspiration, the ribcage is pulled down and in rather than up and out. Frequently there is contraction of inspiratory muscles during expiration, and vice versa. Because the diaphragm is as susceptible to autocannibalism as other muscles, severe multiple systems organ failure often results in diaphragm depletion. Care should be taken in these circumstances to avoid rapid weaning.

C. Cardiovascular system—pulmonary hypertension
  1. Right-side heart dysfunction (high CVP, high RVEDP, low cardiac output [CO], high, normal, or low PAP).
     The right side of the heart is thin walled and drapes around the left ventricle in a crescentlike form. Its pressure (25-40/0) and afterload (PVR) are relatively low. Although right-side infarcts are uncommon, right ventricular dysfunction commonly occurs with excess volume or increased afterload.
     a. Right ventricle infarcts
     b. Pulmonary hypertension (see following discussion)
     c. Left ventricle failure
     d. Myopathy
        (1) Right heart—carcinoid
        (2) Panmyocardial
           (a) Idiopathic
           (b) Alcohol
           (c) Viral
           (d) Atherosclerotic
           (e) Radiation
           (f) Adriamycin
           (g) Nutritional
           (h) Chagas' disease
           (i) Postpartum
           (j) Hemochromatosis
           (k) Rheumatologic
  2. Chronic pulmonary hypertension often causes right-side heart hypertrophy
     a. Increased PVR resulting from loss of pulmonary vascular bed, fibrosis, or excessive blood flow in a compromised lung
        (1) Emphysema
        (2) Primary pulmonary hypertension (young females)
        (3) Recurrent pulmonary emboli

(4) Congenital heart disease with increased pulmonary blood flow (particularly with hypoxic and acidotic vasoconstriction superimposed)
  b. Increased pulmonary venous pressure
    (1) Left ventricular hypertrophy or failure
    (2) Valve disease (mitral, aortic)
    (3) Pulmonary vein thrombosis
  c. Vasomotor
    (1) Chronic hypoxia and acidosis
  d. Combination of increased PVR and vasomotor
    (1) COPD
    (2) Cystic fibrosis
    (3) Kyphoscoliosis
    (4) Chronic restrictive disease
3. Acute pulmonary hypertension (PAP = CO × PVR)
  a. High flow per se does not cause increased PAP; PVR must also be increased.
    (1) Systemic septic response
    (2) Cirrhosis
    (3) Obesity
  b. Increased PVR
    (1) Can occur at level of arterioles, capillary, interstitium, or on the venous side
    (2) CNS dysfunction–increased ICP
    (3) Increased autonomic activity—on waking up from anesthesia, pain, overdose of epinephrine
    (4) Pulmonary embolism
    (5) Left-side heart failure or fluid overload
    (6) Pulmonary parenchymal disease—adult respiratory distress syndrome (ARDS)
  c. Reflecting changes in transthoracic pressure gradient
    (1) Positive pressure ventilation
    (2) Acute increases in airway resistance—bronchospasm, airway obstruction
  d. Acute increases in PAP are often reflected in the right side of the heart by dilation of the chambers. This can produce acute dextrorotation and encroachment of the septum on the left ventricular cavity, reducing left ventricular compliance and output.

(1) Ultrasound is useful in this situation for diagnosis. A shift of the septum into the left ventricle with a small left-sided chamber and dilation of the right-side heart chamber can frequently be seen.

(2) Equalization of pressures across the heart can occur (pseudotamponade syndrome).

(3) The restrictiveness of the pericardium is thought to be a major cause of the response.

4. Management depends on etiology: acute versus chronic

   a. Acute

      (1) Treat underlying disease

      (2) Symptomatic therapy

         (a) Control of hypoxia and acidosis

         (b) Control of bronchospasm

         (c) Control of right heart failure

         (d) Control of pulmonary vascular tone

   b. Chronic

      (1) In ICU, therapy of chronic pulmonary hypertension primarily related to treatment of cor pulmonale and respiratory symptoms

      (2) Other considerations

         (a) Avoid intubation and ventilation if possible

            i. Difficult to wean—high morbidity and mortality

            ii. Swan-Ganz catheter helpful primarily for measuring cardiac output and PVR, not for assessment of the left side of the heart

         (b) If condition is severe, elective surgery may be contraindicated

         (c) Treatment of right-side heart failure

            i. Decrease afterload

               a. Treat hypoxia, hypercarbia, acidosis

               b. May respond to pulmonary vasodilators; often complicated by systemic effects; vasodilation may also increase V/Q mismatch

               c. Some report that hydralazine is effective with fewer side effects

  ii. Decrease preload
   a. Often complicated by very low left-side heart filling pressures and low cardiac output
   b. Therapeutic alternatives include better fluid management, diuresis, and capacitance vessel dilation (NTG)
  iii. Improve inotropy
   a. Some effect simply by decreased preload
   b. Inotropes: dopamine, dobutamine

D. Pulmonary parenchyme
 1. Surfactant
  Surfactant-secreting cells (type II granular pneumocytes) are part of the alveolar epithelium. Surfactant is a combination of phospholipids (especially dipalmityl lecithin) which decrease the surface tension of water. Without surfactant the lung requires 20 to 30 torr of pressure to keep the alveoli open; with surfactant, only 3 to 5 torr of pressure are required.

  Disorders of surfactant

  a. Excess surfactant—pulmonary alveolar proteinosis
   (1) Treatment is by bronchopulmonary lavage
  b. Depletion of surfactant by hypoxia or direct cell damage
   (1) ARDS
    ARDS leads to atelectasis and increased lung water, both of which decrease compliance and cause hypoxia.
   (2) Pulmonary edema resulting from either left-side heart failure or increased hydrostatic pressure
   (3) Atalectasis, pneumonia
    The surfactant disappears rapidly from collapsed alveoli and may take several days to regenerate. This disparity is one of the justifications for high V_T ventilation.

2. Ventilation-perfusion relationships
   a. This refers to the matching of ventilation and perfusion in the lungs.
   b. Although V/Q in normal healthy adults is 0.8, within any given healthy adult, V/Q ranges from 0.6 at the base of the lung to 4 at the apex in the upright individual.
      (1) This difference reflects primarily the effect of gravity on the distribution of ventilation and perfusion.
      (2) Because most of the perfusion and the majority of the ventilation are directed to dependent lungs, gas exchange is very efficient and the A-a O_2 in a healthy young adults is less than 10 to 15 torr. A-a O_2 increases with age.

$$(Pa_{O_2} = 105 - \frac{age}{2})$$

so that normal Pa_{O_2} falls from the 95 to 100 range into the 75 to 80 range in septugenarians.
   c. Any disease process that disturbs the matching of ventilation and perfusion in the lung will cause deterioration of gas exchange.
      (1) This includes almost all pulmonary diseases and potentially all serious cardiac dysfunction.
         (a) Other factors that can do this are anemia, increased energy expenditure, vasodilating drugs, hypovolemia, and low cardiac output.
      (2) The severity of the disturbance of gas exchange is much greater for O_2 than the CO_2, primarily because of the shape of their dissociation curves.
         (a) CO_2 has a linear curve at physiologic Pa_{CO_2} (20 to 80 torr).
            i. Regional deterioration of CO_2 exchange can be offset by hyperventilation.
         (b) O_2 has a sigmoid curve.
            i. At P_{O_2} below 60 torr, small changes in Pa_{O_2} cause very large changes in Hb saturation; above P_{O_2} 60 torr, even large

changes in PaO_2 cause small changes in Hb saturation and O_2 content.

   ii. Hyperventilation will have only a minimal effect on PaO_2.

$$PaO_2 = (P_B - P_{H_2O})FIO_2 - \frac{PaCO_2}{0.8}$$

d. The relationship between V and Q may be seen as a continuum between ventilation without perfusion (dead space for V_D) and perfusion without ventilation (shunt).

  (1) Any decrease of V/Q (i.e., a relative decrease in ventilation) will affect oxygenation preferentially.

  (2) Any increase of V/Q will affect CO_2 exchange preferentially.

  (3) In any given patient with pulmonary disease, areas of high, low, and normal V/Q coexist.

e. The shunt equation $[Qs/Qt \; \frac{(CcO_2 - CaO_2)}{(CcO_2 - CVO_2)}]$ estimates the amount of low V/Q by considering the lung as a three-compartment model and assuming that any decrease in the PaO_2 is a result of shunt. Normal shunt calculated in this way is less than 5%. Increases in shunt fraction associated with pulmonary disease often respond to treatment (PEEP, diuresis, cough, large breaths).

3. Compliance

a. The relationship of a change in volume to a change in pressure or $\frac{\Delta V}{\Delta P}$.

b. Decreased compliance means that lungs or chest wall are stiff. A lung with decreased compliance requires extra work for ventilation.

  (1) Causes of decreased compliance of lung

    (a) Increased lung water

      i. Cardiogenic pulmonary edema

      ii. Noncardiogenic pulmonary edema

    (b) Fibrosis

      i. Primary

      ii. Late-stage ARDS, etc.

(c) Tumor—primary or metastatic lung cancer, especially when interstitial

(d) Pneumonia

(e) Atelectasis

(f) Pleural: effusion, pneumothorax, pleural scarring

(2) Causes of decreased compliance of chest wall: kyphoscoliosis, abdominal binder/ascites/mass, obesity, etc.

(3) At the bedside, compliance changes can be estimated from the pressure gauge in patients receiving ventilation therapy.

(a) An increase in P_{max} may result from increased airway resistance or decreased compliance of lung or chest wall.

(b) The plateau pressure (Pei) reflects primarily compliance.

   i. $P_{max} - Pei > 5$ to 7 cm H_2O indicates a significant component of airway resistance (patient or machine).

   ii. Increased Pei indicates decreased compliance.

E. Airway dysfunction

1. Small airways (obstructive lung disease)

The most commonly encountered small airway dysfunctions are reactive airway disease (bronchospasm or asthma) and chronic bronchitis (smoker's lung, COPD).

a. Usual pathologic findings

(1) Contraction of bronchial smooth muscles (asthma and COPD)

(2) Edema (asthma)

(3) Infection, mucosal damage, increased secretions (COPD)

b. Physiologic results

(1) Air trapping/prolonged expiration

(2) Secretion plugging of small airways

(3) Acute respiratory acidosis–respiratory failure

c. Frequent ICU precipitating factors (COPD)

(1) Viral or bacterial superinfection

    (2) After thoracoabdominal surgery

    (3) Systemic septic response with increased ventilation demands

  d. There may or may not be associated wheezing

    (1) "Tight chest"—acute, prolonged expiration with bronchospasm, little air motion and no wheezing

    (2) Classic wheezing—high-pitched expiratory rhonchi

  e. May be mimicked by:

    (1) Left-side ventricular failure

    (2) Noncardiac pulmonary edema

    (3) Bronchomalacia or tracheomalacia

    (4) Dynamic airway compression syndrome

  2. Large airway dysfunction

    a. Causes of large airway dysfunction

      (1) External: compression from tumor, thoracic aortic aneurysm, lymph nodes

      (2) Internal: tumor, foreign body, too-small endotracheal tube, tracheal stenosis, tracheomalacia, or bronchomalacia

      (3) Chest deformity (kyphoscoliosis)

    b. Bronchoscopy is a useful diagnostic tool.

    c. Flow-volume loops are diagnostic, but not useful in an intubated patient.

F. Metabolic/endocrine lung function

  1. Synthesizes

    a. Surfactant

    b. Prostacycline/thromboxane

  2. Activates

    a. Angiotension I to angiotension II

  3. Inactivates

    a. Serotonin

    b. Bradykinin

    c. Prostaglandins

  4. Stores

    a. Norepinephrine   b. Histamine

  5. Malignancies of the lung, especially oat cell carcinoma and bronchial adenomas, may produce a variety of small peptide hormones.

G. Pulmonary defense mechanisms and the reticuloendothelial function of the lung
  1. Upper airway
     a. Moisture
     b. Heat
     c. Anatomic barriers—nasal vibrissae, etc.
  2. Lower airway
     a. Cough—requires neural, muscular, and cord function
     b. Mucus—mucous glands or goblet cells
     c. Cilia cause cephalad flow of mucus
        (1) Ciliary function is impaired by increased FIO_2, low humidity, foreign bodies such as endotracheal tubes, cold, or infection.
        (2) It improves with terbutaline or other beta agonists.
  3. Alveolus
     a. Blood-borne
        (1) Granulocytes clear bacteria; rapid turnover
        (2) Lymphocytes
            (a) Responsible for cellular immunity
            (b) Produce IgG, IgA
     b. Fixed: macrophage
        (1) Phagocytose bacteria opsonized by IgG or IgA
        (2) Involved with antigen processing and cellular recruitment in the inflammatory response
        (3) Very sensitive to tissue O_2 tension; activated by hypoxia
     c. Secretory IgA
        (1) May inhibit microbial growth or aggluinate bacteria
        (2) Activates complement
     d. IgM
        (1) Not present in normal lung
        (2) Present in inflammation
     e. IgE
        (1) Common in bronchial mucosa and hilar nodes
        (2) Probably regulates vascular or membrane permeability
H. Chemical control of ventilation

1. Peripheral
   a. Carotid and aortic bodies respond primarily to hypoxia, secondarily to $[H^+]$
   b. Carotid body responsible for hypoxic drive
   c. Little increase in afferent output until $PaO_2 < 50$ to 60 torr; coincides with shoulder of Oxy/Hb dissociation curve
   d. Narcotics and sedatives depress output
2. Central—medullary centers (close to cerebrospinal fluid in the fourth ventricle
   a. Primarily responds to change in $[H^+]$. However, as central chemoreceptor is inside the blood brain barrier, $[H^+]$ changes cause slow reaction, $[PaCO_2]$ changes cause fast reaction.
   b. Acid-base response is subordinate to hypoxic response.

THERAPY OF PULMONARY DYSFUNCTION AND PULMONARY SUPPORT

Proper therapy of pulmonary disorders is a two-part process. The first goal is to maintain an adequate PaO_2; the second part is to discern the components of the pulmonary system that are in disarray and to correct or support them. Both parts usually proceed simultaneously and entail decisions about whether the response being observed is a normal one, whether it needs external support, and what external support is necessary. Frequently what can be done is limited by the underlying pulmonary and cardiac status or the nature of the acute episode. Mechanical ventilation then is usually necessary.

Thus there are general goals of pulmonary support, criteria for mechanical ventilation application and removal, and general goals of mechanical ventilation (Table 3-1).

General goals of pulmonary support

1. Maintain adequate PaO_2 (Hb saturation $> 90\%$)
2. Use lowest possible FIO_2 ($\leq 50\%$)
3. Prevent/control/treat atelectasis
4. Aggressive pulmonary toilet

5. Prevent/control pneumonia
6. Minimize resulting cardiovascular dysfunction
7. Control systemic pathologic conditions

A. Oxygen—the goal of oxygen therapy is adequate tissue oxygenation.

1. Use FIO_2 to achieve Hb saturation of at least 90% when Hb concentration and binding capacity are normal.
2. Increasing the FIO_2 usually elevates the PaO_2; in areas of lung with low V/Q, changing FIO_2 will have less effect. When the calculated shunt approaches 30%, changing FIO_2 will have little effect on PaO_2.
3. Without a history of chronic respiratory failure with hypercapnia ($\uparrow PaCO_2$), FIO_2 should be used as clinically appropriate. If there is a history of respiratory failure, hypoxic respiratory drive should be suspected and therapy should be started at lower oxygen concentrations.
4. High-flow delivery systems (Venturi mask) are superior

Table 3-1. Parameters for bedside monitoring

Parameters	Monitoring methods	Normal values
Ventilation	Respiratory rate (RR)	15 3/min
	Tidal volume (VT)	5-7 cc/kg
	Minute ventilation (V)	70 cc/kg
	Maximum voluntary ventilation (MVV)	60-50 L/min (varies with sex and age)
	Maximum inspiratory force (MIF)	$>(-70$ cm $H_2O)$
	Forced expiratory volume—1 sec (FEV_1)	> 70% predicted
Gas exchange	PaO_2	$PAO_2 - \dfrac{age}{2}$
	$PaCO_2$	35-45 torr
	PaO_2/FIO_2	400-500 (varies with age)
	A-a DO_2	10-20 torr (varies with age and FIO_2)
	Qs/Qt	<5%
	Cardiac output—ventilation/perfusion scan	70 ml/kg/min
Airway spasm	Clinical exam, FEV_1,	
FRC	measured at bedside by nitrogen washout, He dilution	

to low-flow systems (nasal prongs) in maintaining a constant FIO_2.

5. When a patient is in extremis, FIO_2 should be maximal. Oxygen toxicity is unimportant in this setting.

6. Actual oxygen delivery to the patient depends not only on FIO_2 but on fresh gas flow and patient demand (respiratory rate, V_T, inspiratory flow rate). The delivery system must ensure that FIO_2 approaches the desired concentration.

7. Exposure of the human lung to high FIO_2 (>50%) for longer than 12 hours may cause lung oxygen toxicity—a form of ARDS; this may be caused by free superoxide radicals; FIO_2 should be ≤0.5 whenever possible.

B. Prevention/treatment of atelectasis and secretions

1. Moist warm air

   a. Dry air inhibits tracheal mucus flow, which exacerbates tracheobronchitis

   b. Cool air increases heat loss and may increase airway resistance

2. Coughing—a cough occurs when a patient increases his or her intrathoracic pressure against a closed glottis (Valsalva maneuver) and then suddenly opens the glottis.

   a. Resultant air movement (velocities reach several hundred miles per hour) is an effective method of mobilizing mucus.

   b. Well-performed coughs from total lung capacity (TLC), when combined with large breaths and appropriate respiratory therapy, are extremely useful in mobilizing secretions.

   c. Compromised cough is one of the negative aspects of tracheal intubation.

3. Incentive spirometry (IS) versus IPPB

   a. Most acute respiratory disease is characterized by an absolute or relative fall in FRC

   b. Most effective treatment is frequent deep breaths. Unfortunately, many postoperative patients will not—and most patients with serious pulmonary dysfunction cannot—take big breaths. Under such circumstances, patients should be forced (intermittent positive pressure breathing [IPPB]) or encouraged (IS) to take big breaths.

(1) Volume-oriented IPPB seems to be useful, especially in patients who cannot or will not take a big breath (>15 cc/kg).

(2) In patients who can take big breaths, IS may supply encouragement. Incentive spirometers must be properly used to be effective; this requires almost as much nursing or respiratory therapist time as old-fashioned deep breathing and coughing.

4. Nebulizers: various types of medications may be effective with fewer side effects when delivered directly to the respiratory tract by aerosol.

   a. Although particle size is of some importance in delivery, this is offset somewhat by the fact that as particle size decreases and delivery improves, the waterload also increases.

   b. Large volumes of very small droplets (ultrasonic nebulizers) may cause increased airway resistance.

5. Mobilization

   a. Aggressive mobilization is especially beneficial in the immediate postoperative period, because pressure of the abdominal viscera against the diaphragm is decreased in the upright position, leading to a higher FRC. Larger tidal volumes and stronger cough may be obtained.

   b. For the patient with severe pulmonary dysfunction who is receiving mechanical ventilatory support, however, benefits are not as clear-cut. In such patients, the prone position can be beneficial.

      (1) For a variety of reasons, pulmonary disease tends to be worse in a dependent lung. As a result, ventilation-perfusion mismatch is increased, because the body's ability to divert pulmonary blood flow is limited.

      (2) PEEP, chest physiotherapy, suctioning, and

large-volume ventilation are largely ineffective, because they primarily affect relatively healthy, more compliant lung.

(3) In the prone position

(a) Relatively normal lung is now dependent and thus ventilation and perfusion are better matched

(b) FRC increases as abdominal contents moves away from diaphragm

(c) Gravity augments drainage of mucus rather than inhibiting it

(d) Particularly effective in patients with disease localized to dorsal lung

c. Special beds

(1) Rotating beds seem to reduce pulmonary complications in patients who are bedridden and who cannot ambulate (e.g., patients with head injury).

(2) Access problems do occur

(3) Roentgenograms are frequently of reduced quality.

6. Chest percussion (P&PD)

a. Appears to be effective when ciliary activity has been decreased, as in cystic fibrosis, bronchiectasis, and chronic bronchitis. Gravity, vibration, and percussion seem to increase clearance of mucus.

b. There are no data to support segmental selectivity.

c. Most likely to be of benefit when performed "antigravity" (i.e., in the position opposite that mainly used by the patient—for the supine patient, prone; for the mobile patient, head downward).

d. Indicated only for large sputum volumes and/or a weak cough.

7. Suctioning

Suctioning in the intubated patient is necessary. It may also be of help in the nonintubated patient with copious secretions and a poor cough (nasotracheal suctioning). However, there are several problems.

    a. Catheter usually goes to right mainstem. A coudé tip catheter can be directed into the left lung more frequently, but these catheters are more expensive.

    b. Considerable mucosal trauma occurs, which may cause ulceration with bleeding and infection, and occasionally tracheomalacia. Suctioning should be done only when necessary and with minimal effective suction pressure.

    c. Suctioning involves interruption of ventilation and has been associated with hypoxia, hypercarbia, bronchospasm, and loss of continuous distending pressure (CDP or PEEP).

        (1) Suctioning for patients on high levels of CDP should be done while maintaining the CDP.

        (2) Suctioning for patients with elevated intracranial pressure should be done only when necessary for short periods, and patients should be sedated during these periods with barbiturates to minimize the effect on intracranial pressure.

        (3) Patients with reactive airway disease should receive bronchodilators when intubated, should be suctioned as little as possible, and should be extubated as early as possible.

        (4) All patients should receive 100% oxygen immediately before, during, and immediately after suctioning.

  8. Bronchoscopy

    a. If secretions are thin and atelectasis is acute, bronchoscopy is probably no more effective than aggressive respiratory therapy.

    b. When mucus is thick and atelectasis is subacute or chronic, bronchoscopy may be helpful.

    c. Primary indication is diagnosis—suctioning, washing, brushing, biopsy.

C. Assisted ventilation

  1. Criteria for assisted ventilation

    a. $PaO_2 \leq 60$ with $FIO_2 \geq 50\%$

    b. $PaCO_2 > 50$ with pH < 7.3

    c. Tachypnea with signs of impending respiratory failure such as tachycardia, hypertension, sweating, anxiety.

2. Disease causing acute respiratory failure
   a. Parenchymal or airway
      (1) Severe pneumonitis
      (2) Adult respiratory distress syndrome (ARDS)
      (3) COPD with acute exacerbation
      (4) Pulmonary embolism
      (5) Airway obstruction (foreign body)
      (6) Severe bronchospasm
      (7) Pulmonary edema
      (8) Lung contusion
   b. Nonparenchymal
      (1) Neurologic
         (a) Acute—head injury
         (b) Chronic—ALS, Guillain-Barré, polio to maintain adequate VA
         (c) Spinal cord injury, nerve injury to maintain adequate VA
      (2) Chest wall
         (a) Pneumothorax
         (b) Hemothorax
         (c) Flail chest
      (3) Metabolic
         (a) Drug overdose
         (b) Hypermetabolism states

GENERAL GOALS OF MECHANICAL VENTILATION

1. Maintain adequate Pao_2 (Hb saturation > 90%)
2. $FIO_2 \leq 50\%$
3. Mean arterial pressure (MAP) < 30 to 35 cm water
4. Use a mode of ventilation that meets the physiologic demands of the existing clinical setting
5. Prevent muscle atrophy
6. Prevent ventilator dependency
7. Meet the general goals of pulmonary support
8. Wean as soon as possible

3. Types of ventilators

Pressure-cycled	Time-cycled	Volume-cycled	Flow-cycled
Bird Mark 7, 8	Baby Bird IMV Bird Bird Mark II Bourns BP 2000 (pressure limited)	Bennett MA-1, 2 (pressure limited) Bourns Bear 1, 2 (pressure limited) Ohio 560 CCV (pressure limited) Siemens 900 B or C (pressure limited) Emerson 3PV Engstrom 300	Bennett PR-2

a. Regulation of the inspiratory-expiratory cycle
  (1) Definition of terms
    (a) Cycling: mechanism by which inspiration is terminated (e.g., pressure, time, volume, flow)
    (b) Limiting: Alternate method of termination of the ventilatory cycle, either for reasons of safety (pressure limit) or to increase the ventilator's usefulness (volume limited)
  (2) Pressure cycled: not useful in patients with abnormally high airway resistance or abnormally low compliance, or in patients who are restless, anxious or have voluminous secretions (i.e., ICU patients)
    (a) Expired volume may be monitored with a spirometer, but this does not increase control over volume delivery
    (b) Usually inexpensive
  (3) Time-cycled: Delivered volume is a function of both flow and time. By varying these parameters one can control not only volume but also I/E ratio and mean intrathoracic pressure.
    (a) Volume determined by measuring exhaled gas
    (b) These ventilators could conceivably be at a disadvantage when resistance is very high, but they are not greatly affected by compliance within their capacity. Price varies.

(4) Volume-cycled: These machines will deliver a preset volume, regardless of pressure requirements within the limits of their capability.
  (a) Not greatly affected by resistance or compliance
  (b) Most volume-cycled ventilators may be pressure limited to try to control barotrauma
  (c) Usually expensive
(5) Flow-cycled: not currently available.
(6) Machine compliance: all ventilators have an inherent compliance volume related to compression of gases and distention of tubing.
  (a) As a result, a predictable fraction of each breath recorded by the spirometer does not actually go to the patient but is lost in the tubing.
  (b) Most ventilators have a compliance of between 2 and 4 $cc/cm/H_2O$ or about 100 cc/breath in the 70 kg adult. This is of little consequence in an adult but may be significant in an infant or small child. Therefore, adult ventilators should not be used in pediatrics.

4. Types of ventilator support (Fig. 3-1)
  a. CPAP: continuous positive airway pressure; PEEP: positive end expiratory pressure

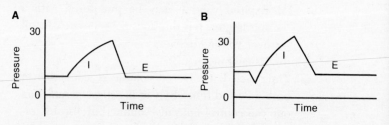

Fig. 3-1. Controlled mode ventilation with positive end-expiratory pressure (CMV with PEEP or CMV with CDP). Depicted are different modes of mechanical ventilation that illustrate the different means of interacting among the ventilator, patient, and distending pressure. **A,** Controlled-mode ventilation with positive end-expiratory pressure (CMV with PEEP). **B,** Assist-mode ventilation with PEEP or CDP. **C,** Continuous positive airway pressure (CPAP). **D,** Spontaneous ventilation with PEEP. **E,** Intermittent mandatory ventilation (IMV). **F** and **G,** IMV with CDP (it may be CPAP, **F,** or EPAP, **G**).

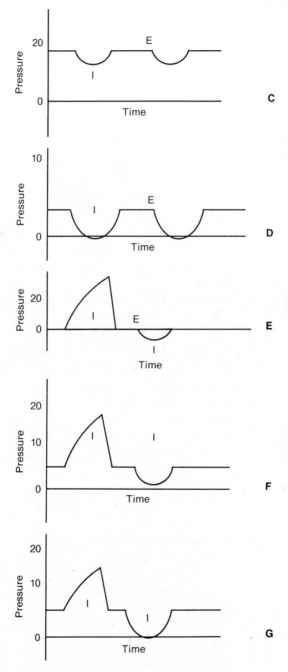

Fig. 3-1. For legend see opposite page.

(1) Two methods of exerting continuous distending pressure (CDP) by which transpulmonary pressure (PTP) is increased and functional residual capacity (FRC) rises.

(2) This may be done by mask but is more often done after intubation.

(3) Increase in FRC is usually associated with an improved V/Q.

(4) CDP will, by increasing intrathoracic pressure (ITP), lead to a decrease in venous return, which may be beneficial (CHF) or deleterious (shock).

b. IMV: intermittent mandatory ventilation

(1) Type of ventilation whereby sufficient mechanical breaths are given to maintain a 7.35 < pH < 7.45. Otherwise, the patient breathes spontaneously.

(2) The IMV support rate may be increased if the respiratory rate is greater than 30/min, the minute ventilation is greater than 10 L, or the cardiovascular system is unstable.

(3) Increased A-a DO_2 (hypoxia) usually treated separately by increasing the CDP (PEEP or CPAP), FIO_2, or other appropriate maneuvers (diuresis, etc.)

(4) Fewer cardiovascular side effects; lower MAP; increased work of breathing relative to continuous mandatory ventilation (CMV)

(5) Minute ventilation is the sum of the machine (guaranteed by the machine) and the patient breaths.

c. CMV: continuous mechanical ventilation

(1) Every breath is mechanical: *assisted* when the patient effort triggers delivery, or *controlled* when the machine delivers volume regardless of patient effort.

(2) There are no convincing data to demonstrate that assisted ventilation is superior to controlled physiologically.

(a) Psychologically, however, the inability of a

patient to get a breath when he wants it may
be devastating.

5. Ventilator controls
   a. Tidal volume and rate.
      (1) The tidal volume (V_T) for a normal resting person
      breathing spontaneously is 5 to 7 cc/kg, with
      rates of 15 ± 3/min; the same rate and volumes
      on CMV result in progressive atelectasis. To
      avoid this problem, the same V is delivered, but
      with a V_T of 10 to 15 cc/kg and rate of 8 to 10/
      min.
      (2) Estimates of appropriate V_T are based on lean
      body weight, which may be overestimated in an
      obese patient and underestimated in an ampu-
      tee.
      (3) Exceptions to above criteria
         (a) Restrictive disease, either acute (ARDS,
         pneumonia) or chronic (fibrosis, kyphosco-
         liosis); slightly smaller volumes may decrease
         the risk of barotrauma (see "Compliance, p.
         42")
         (b) In diseases like COPD with or without em-
         physema, when compliance and resistance
         are increased, larger tidal volumes and
         slower rates are beneficial, because they al-
         low maximal time for exhalation and thus
         avoid gas trapping.
      (4) Respiratory acidosis or alkalosis should generally
      be controlled by changing rate and not tidal vol-
      ume.
   b. FIO_2: the goal of therapy is a PaO_2 of 60 to 90 torr
   (assuming normal Hb and cardiac output). This will
   result in normal oxygen content (15 cc/100 cc/blood)
   when saturation is greater than 90%.
      (1) Initial FIO_2 should be higher than thought nec-
      essary with subsequent adjustments on the basis
      of blood gases.
      (2) In FIO_2 of 100% can be appropriate during CPR
      and other critical situations, or to achieve a PaO_2
      of 50 to 60 torr.

c. Sensitivity
   (1) Sensitivity is the patient effort required to trigger the pressure, flow, or volume signal, which initiates a machine-assisted breath or in the case of demand valve CPAP or IMV systems, opens the demand valve.
   (2) Sensitivity should be adjusted so that only 1 to 2 cm of H_2O change registers on the machine's pressure gauge before the ventilator responds. In many ventilators, this pressure is measured in the machine; the pressure change in the patient's thorax often greatly exceeds this. Such sensing systems greatly increase the work of breathing.
d. Flow rates: most patients are comfortable at flows of about 40 to 60 L/min. With these flows, even at rates of 20 breaths/min in the 70-kg adult, the I/E ratio will exceed 1:1, thus minimizing cardiovascular side effects. Flow rates should be increased if gas trapping is a problem or when the patient needs it (i.e., very high rate, severe dyspnea)
e. Flow pattern
   (1) Usually sine wave or square wave
   (2) In the majority of cases, flow pattern has little effect on gas exchange
   (3) Accelerating and decelerating patterns are available and may occasionally be helpful
f. Sighs
   (1) Most machines have a built-in sigh capacity. Sighs are purported to be useful in preventing atelectasis.
   (2) There is no convincing evidence that sighs ($V_T >$ 20 cc/kg) augment the effect of large V_T (10 to 15 cc/kg), and they may increase barotrauma
g. CDP: continuous distending pressure (including PEEP, EPAP and CPAP). When compliance is reduced, CDP may infrease P_{TP} sufficiently during exhalation to prevent atelectasis. Actual reversal of at-

electasis occurs during inspiration (whether with spontaneous or mechanical inspiration) when transpulmonary pressure is much larger.

6. Inspiratory pause and I/E ratio
   a. Early workers in mechanical ventilation discovered that cardiovascular side effects were prohibitive when the I/E was greater than 1:1 (i.e., inspiratory time > expiratory time)
   b. Many ventilators have built-in safety devices that prevent I/E exceeding 1:1.
   c. Studies in neonates show improved gas exchange after inverting the I/E in the treatment of IRDS and meconium aspiration.
      (1) Inspiratory time is increased either by slowing inspiratory flow or by holding full inflation. This is not widely accepted as being beneficial in adults.

7. Airway closure: as the volume of lung tissue surrounding the small airways decreases, the airways decrease in size and eventually reach their critical closing volume. Although a cause-and-effect relationship has not been established, airway closure is a rational physiologic explanation for atelectasis associated with obesity, surgery, and the perioperative period. The lung volume at which airway closure is first detected is the closing capacity (CC). In healthy adults, FRC exceeds CC until age 63 in the upright position and age 45 in the supine position.
   a. When FRC decreases, as in obese patients or those who have acute lung disease, CC may exceed FRC and small airway closure will occur during tidal ventilation. This increases the possibility of atelectasis, because even very small decreases in tidal volume or in regional time constants may prevent reopening of these airways. CDP increases FRC, which is thought to help keep small airways open and prevent airway closure. Unfortunately, the areas of the lung most likely to increase in volume with CDP are relatively normal with better compliance.

b. CDP seems to:
   (1) Distend patent airways, thereby decreasing resistance to air flow
   (2) Open collapsed airways, thus exposing more alveoli to large increases in transpulmonary pressure (PTP) provided by VT.

8. CDP effects (including PEEP, CPAP, and FPAP)
   a. Increase functional residual capacity (FRC) by increasing PTP to:
      (1) Decrease A-a DO_2
      (2) Keep small airways open and prevents atelectasis.
         (a) Increase in FRC more dramatic in compliant (relatively healthy) lung. At high levels of CDP or with large VT, this may lead to overdistention of these alveoli, with local increases in pulmonary vascular resistance and redistribution of perfusion to poorly ventilated lung.
   b. Cardiovascular side effects
      (1) Cause an increased ITP, with subsequent decreases in venous return. This is probably the most important cardiovascular side effect. Fortunately, the less compliant the lung, the less pressure is transmitted to the pleural space and the less severe the side effects.
      (2) May increase pulmonary vascular resistance and thus affect right ventricular afterload, eventually causing dilation of the right ventricle.
      (3) The effect on the left side of the heart is controversial. Some patients will increase left-side heart output, possibly as a result of improved filling pressure: an increase in FRC usually causes a decrease in pulmonary vascular resistance and a decrease in right ventricular afterload. CDP may also decrease left ventricular end diastolic volume, if as the right side of the heart fails and the right ventricular end-diastolic volume increases the interventricular septum shifts

into the left ventricle, thus increasing left ventricular afterload.

(4) May alter prostacycline/thromboxane ratio, with consequent effects on the left side of the heart and critical organ perfusion, including the lung.

(5) May decrease lung lymph flow.

9. "Best PEEP"

a. Although the goal of decreasing ventilation-perfusion abnormalities with CDP is admirable, the assumption that the whole lung is affected equally is inaccurate. Focal changes are the rule.

b. PEEP may have unwanted effects

(1) Distending normal alveoli more than abnormal, leading to barotrauma

(2) Shunting blood away from the better ventilated alveoli to the poorer ventilated ones by local increases in PVR

(3) Deleterious effects on cardiac output

c. One school of thought is that "best PEEP" is that which allows satisfactory oxygenation while avoiding overdistention of lung units and decreased cardiac output. To determine this, PEEP is increased by 2 or 3-cm increments, usually from 5 to 15 or 20 cm of H_2O. Arterial blood gases, shunt, cardiac output, PVR, and total static lung compliance are measured. "Best PEEP" is that which gives the best PO_2 at the lowest cost in terms of cardiac output and right-side heart work (reflected in PVR) and pulmonary compliance.

d. Others believe that "best PEEP" is that at which PaO_2 is highest or shunt is least, usually less than 15%. Any amount of PEEP up to 50 cm of H_2O ("super PEEP") is employed to achieve this end; cardiac output is maintained by whatever means necessary

e. There are no data that prove one "best PEEP" superior to another.

f. Super PEEP advocates, however, tend to use IMV and CPAP, whereas others usually use less PEEP and more mechanical support.

10. Weaning from PEEP
    a. Significant levels of PEEP (greater than 5 cm H_2O) should never be abruptly discontinued.
    b. Most patients who have been on PEEP for any length of time become hypervolemic as a part of the compensation for decreased venous return, and possibly increased antidiuretic hormone (ADH) secretion.
       (1) Abrupt discontinuation of PEEP may provoke increases in lung water, even if PEEP is discontinued only for short periods, such as for suctioning and monitor readings. For this reason and because stopping PEEP for monitor readings creates an artificial and unstable situation, PEEP at significant levels ($>$ 5 cm H_2O) should not be abruptly discontinued.
       (2) The effect of PEEP on transmural or "true" vascular filling pressures can be measured using an esophageal balloon to estimate pleural pressure.

$$P_{TM} = P_{vasc} - P_{PL}$$

11. VD/VT: dead space–tidal volume ratio
    a. Normal VD/VT is 0.3. This reflects anatomic dead space (nose, pharynx, trachea and bronchi) plus physiologic dead space (areas of high V/Q).
    b. Endotracheal or tracheostomy tubes decrease anatomic dead space.
       (1) This is offset during PPV because the airways distend with each positive pressure breath.
       (2) Distribution of ventilation is such that physiologic dead space is slightly higher with PPV.
    c. Most pulmonary disease is associated with mismatch of ventilation and perfusion and increases in both dead space and shunt.
    d. The ultimate cause of increased dead space is pulmonary embolism.
    e. A VD/VT of $>$ 0.6 is often associated with failure to wean from ventilatory support.
12. Special cases in ventilatory support

a. Inappropriate hyperventilation (pH > 7.45 with $PaO_2 > 60$)
   (1) Causes
      (a) Psychogenic—anxiety and pain
      (b) Reflex
          i. Pulmonary—increased lung water or other problems stimulate various lung receptors and reflex hyperventilation occurs
          ii. Central
             a. Hiccough
             b. Metabolic—liver disease, diabetic ketoacidosis (recovery phase)
             c. CNS injury
      (c) Iatrogenic
          i. Excessive V ordered
          ii. Excessive sensitivity on ventilation—self-triggering
          iii. Machine failure
          iv. Leak in system
   (2) At pH > 7.50, alkalosis may affect important enzyme functions, as well as cause arrhythmias, affect nerve conduction, and reduce cerebral blood flow.
   (3) Treatment
      (a) Treat metabolic component
      (b) Check for iatrogenic problems
      (c) Analgesia with or without sedation (not useful with reflex hyperventilation)
      (d) IMV—switch from more mechanical to more spontaneous ventilation
      (e) Increase PEEP; this may be useful in cases in which hyperventilation results from pulmonary reflexes associated with atelectasis or increased extravascular pulmonary water
      (f) Add dead space; this is only appropriate in psychogenic and pulmonary reflex stimulation and not useful for central hyperventilation.
      (g) Paralyze with muscle relaxant; this is the therapy of last resort. Usually appropriate

when hyperventilation is causing cardiovascular side effects or when $PaCO_2 < 20$ torr.

   b. One-lung ventilation

     (1) Unilateral dysfunction may occur with down lung syndrome, aspiration, trauma, unilateral pulmonary edema, lobar or lung collapse, and bronchopleural fistulae.

     (2) Double lumen tubes permit individualization of therapy.

     (3) If single lumen tubes are used, the normal lung with better compliance and resistance receives more than its share of ventilation maneuvers, while the diseased lung does not benefit.

     (4) For double lumen tubes, when two ventilators are used it is not essential that the ventilators be synchronized.

13. Weaning from ventilator

   a. Successful weaning depends on the patient's ability to perform the required respiratory work. If ventilatory work is low and patient strength is relatively high, weaning may proceed quickly. If the opposite is true, then weaning must proceed more slowly.

   b. Fast weaning (usually in postoperative patients): if NIF > 40, IC > 15 cc/kg, go to T-piece, check blood gases after 20 minutes, and extubate. Although vital capacity and negative inspiratory force

---

WEANING CRITERIA

1. Patient is improving
2. Patient is alert and responsive
3. $PaO_2/P_1O_2 > 200$
4. Resting minute ventilation < 10 L/min
5. Resting minute ventilation can be doubled
6. NIF > (-20 cm H_2O)
7. Vital capacity > 15 ml/kg body weight
8. Respiratory rate < 30 breaths/min
9. $V_D/V_T < 0.6$

(NIF) are useful, they do not correlate well with endurance. Thus a long-term ventilator patient may have excellent weaning parameters initially but fade very quickly as the diaphragm fatigues. *Do not equate weaning with extubation. Successful weaning does not mandate extubation, and patients may be intubated without requiring mechanical ventilatory support.*

c. Slow weaning: Indicated following long-term ventilatory support or when the diaphragm is adversely affected by disease or malnutrition.

   (1) Usually with IMV.

   (2) Start with IMV set at the patient's rate; decrease as tolerated. Follow with blood gases (watch for increased A-a DO_2, acidosis) and with vital signs (respiratory rate < 3, pulse and blood pressure stable).

   (3) Deterioration in any of these parameters would suggest that ventilatory support should be increased. Do not allow the patient to fatigue to the point of acidosis; the severe diaphragmatic fatigue associated with this will require 24 to 48 hours for recovery.

   (4) Alternatively, or when weaning stalls at low IMV, try spontaneous breathing on T-piece (Brigg's adapter) or CPAP. Alternate periods of spontaneous breathing with CMV. Gradually increase frequency and duration of spontaneous breathing. (See discussion on Systems, p. 67, for problems with IMV.)

d. The difficult-to-wean patient

   (1) Usually occurs in the severely compromised patients with underlying obstructive disease who has required prolonged ventilatory support.

   (2) Each time weaning reaches a critical level, ventilatory failure occurs, forcing the resumption of full mechanical support.

   (3) For weaning to be successful, either work of breathing must decrease or patient strength

must increase. To decrease the work of breathing, check the following:

(a) Resistance and compliance

  i. Resistance may be elevated by underlying obstructive disease, with augmentation by accumulated secretions in small airways and bronchospasm secondary to acute bronchitis, the presence of a foreign body (endotracheal tube) in the airway, and atelectasis.

  ii. Compliance may be decreased by excessive extravascular pulmonary water, ARDS, infiltrates, and atelectasis.

  iii. Every effort should be made to treat these, including aggressive antibiotic therapy, bronchodilation (even in the absence of a history of COPD), pulmonary toilet, and aggressive attempts to reexpand atelectatic lung.

  iv. Beta-adrenergic drugs not only bronchodilate, but they also may preserve ciliary activity and flow of mucus. Aminophylline seems to increase diaphragm contractility.

(b) Metabolic rate

  i. Oxygen consumption and CO_2 production may be so high as to overwhelm the weakened ventilatory apparatus.

  ii. Causes of high metabolic rate and excessive CO_2 production include high glucose (as opposed to protein-sparing) hyperalimentation, fever, sepsis or even excessive muscle activity. Excessive muscle tone may follow CNS injury, or high requirements for ventilatory work.

(c) Continuous distending pressure (PEEP)

  i. In the acutely dysfunctional lung, achievement of a normal or supranormal FRC with CDP may be lifesaving.

    ii. If the FRC is maintained at this level after recovery, work of breathing will be excessive. Accordingly, CDP should be decreased as pulmonary function improves, down to a level of 3 to 5 cm H_2O if possible.

(d) Blood gases

    i. Before weaning, the patient's blood gases must be as close to normal for that patient as possible. Weaning should not be attempted in the face of significant metabolic acidosis or hypoxia, because this will require respiratory compensation.

    ii. Conversely, although metabolic alkalosis will decrease ventilatory requirements, a significant decrease in V will cause atelectasis and deterioration of lung function.

(e) Tube size

    i. A small airway will increase the work of breathing. In the debilitated patient, this can be crucial.

    ii. In most adult males an ETT with an internal diameter of 8.0 mm is desirable; in adult females, a 7.0 mm ETT is acceptable.

    iii. Excessively large ETTs are associated with more severe upper airway damage.

    iv. Occasionally benefits may be achieved by switching from nasal to oral ETTS or by increasing diameter as little as 0.5 mm.

       a. Tracheostomy is frequently beneficial in this group of patients.

(f) Systems

    i. Many commercially available weaning systems, both IMV and CDP have inherent inefficiencies, which may be significant enough to cause failure to wean. This may range from sticky one-way valves to inefficient demand valves or poorly designed effort-sensing systems.

    ii. Be prepared to switch from one system to another when appropriate.

(g) Secretions

    i. Excessive secretions suggest continued infection

    ii. Obtain cultures and treat as appropriate

(h) Compliance

    i. Look for atelectasis, increased extravascular pulmonary water, effusions, etc.

    ii. Treat as appropriate

        a. Remember that PPV, pain, narcotics are associated with ADH secretion.

        b. Humidified gas during ventilation decreases insensible water loss by at least 50% in the euthermic patient;

CHECKLIST FOR TROUBLESHOOTING WHEN WEANING IS DIFFICULT

1. Is airway obstruction present that would reverse with bronchodilator therapy?
2. Is the endotracheal tube too small?
3. Are secretions a problem?
4. Is breathing depressed by drugs?
5. Is nutrition a problem?
6. Is hypercapnia resulting from metabolic alkalosis?
7. Is neuromuscular disease present?
8. Is diaphragmatic function intact?
9. Are psychological factors such as adequate sleep, calm environment, and reassurance being neglected?
10. Is the $Paco_2$ after mechanical ventilation lower than the patient's usual $Paco_2$?
11. Does the patient have hypoxic respiratory drive?
12. Would the patient benefit from a tracheostomy?

Modified from Soggin, C.H.: Weaning respiratory patients from mechanical support, J. Respir. Dis. **1**(7–8):12, 1980.

modify fluid administration accordingly.

(4) To monitor and improve the strength of respiratory muscles, check the following

    (a) Muscle function—are the diaphragm and other ventilatory muscles functioning normally? Suspect neuromuscular dysfunction when hemidiaphragm is elevated; there is repeated unilateral atelectasis; surgery or trauma in area of diaphragm, phrenic nerve, respiratory center; clinical signs of diaphragm weakness—"rocking boat" respiration.

    (b) Muscles unable to sustain necessary minute ventilation

        i. Usually because of disuse atrophy or malnutrition. May also result from other causes: drugs like aminoglysosides or residual muscle relaxants or the peripheral neuropathy of multiple system organ failure.

        ii. Respiratory exercise and nutrition can prevent or treat most of these problems.

(5) Psychologic

    (a) Difficult-to-wean patients often slip into a manipulative, passive-dependent mode.

    (b) They are very frightened by the weaning efforts and may prefer the security of the ventilator.

    (c) Most patients' fundamental fear is of dying, and the staff should interact with them in a way that demonstrates that they are considered viable, recoverable human beings.

    (d) If depression becomes a major problem, psychiatric help and counseling may have real benefit.

    (e) Ensure that the patient is not suffering pain that is inhibiting successful weaning.

14. High-frequency ventilation (HFV)

  a. HFV is a system of ventilation using small tidal volumes ($<$ 5 cc/kg) and high respiratory rates ($>$ 60 breaths/min). This may be achieved by oscillation of extremely small volumes (5 to 10 cc) at very high rates (1000 to 3000 breaths/min) or by slightly more conventional means (jet or pressure ventilation) with V_T of 1 to 5 cc/kg and rates of 60 to 150 breaths/min.

   b. Recent data reveal no significant advantage over standard methods in the treatment of ARDS. Experimental therapy of bronchopleural fistula and other unilateral disease has been promising.

D. Muscle strength: chronically ill patients who have autocannibalized their own muscle mass as an energy source develop a reversible myopathy.

   1. Once nitrogen loss has been arrested through appropriate nutrition and the acute illness stabilized, a program of active physical therapy should be begun.

   2. The patient should be responsible for a portion of his or her minute ventilation (IMV or T-piece weaning), while avoiding diaphragmatic fatigue.

   3. Daily vital capacity and NIF should be recorded.

   4. General mobilization with periods in bedside chair or commode, active extremity exercise while in bed.

   5. When the patient is ready for it, there is no better morale booster than the "bag walk," when patient, attendants, and a gaggle of trailing IV poles go for a stroll in and around the ICU.

E. Bronchospasm—contraction of airway smooth muscle leading to increased resistance. A common part of many pulmonary diseases apart from asthma and chronic bronchitis.

   1. Bronchodilators

      a. Catecholamines

         (1) Epinephrine—0.3 cc subcutaneously (0.2-1) every 4 to 6 hours

            (a) Action: beta and alpha agonist

            (b) Indications—severe acute bronchospasm, anaphylaxis

            (c) Side effects—arrhythmias, hypertension

            (d) Relative contraindications—glaucoma, atherosclerotic heart disease

  (2) Isoproterenol (Isuprel)—nonspecific B_1 and B_2
b. Synthetic beta$_2$ agonists—terbutaline, isoetharine, albuterol, metaproterenol
  (1) Administered—wet or dry aerosol, subcutaneously or p.o.
  (2) Action—relatively specific beta$_2$ activity; bronchodilators
  (3) Indications—increased airway tone
  (4) Side effects—hypotension, tachycardia
  (5) Contraindications (relative)—arrhythmias, allergy
c. Methylxanthines
  (1) Aminophylline
    (a) Action—phosphodiesterase inhibitor; increases intracellular AMP, leading to relaxation of bronchial smooth muscle
    (b) Indications—decreased diaphragm contractility, decreased respiratory drive, increased airway tone
    (c) Side effects—tachycardia (additive with beta agonists), increased gastric secretion, mild diuretic effect
    (d) Contraindications—in patients with active peptic ulcer disease, may increase secretions.
d. Steroids—not useful in treatment of acute episodes of bronchospasm; takes 6 hours to peak effect. Probably indicated during bronchospasm in anyone with previous steroid dependent asthma or in a patient with bronchospasm unresponsive or poorly responsive to other agents, as well as in anaphylaxis. May usually taper rapidly.
  (1) Action—IgE and mast cell stabilization. Although available both for systemic and local (aerosol) administration, aerosols are not appropriate in an acute episode.
e. Cromolyn sodium—20 mg inhaled q.i.d.
  (1) Action—inhibits degranulation of mast cells
  (2) Indications—extrinsic asthma; not useful in acute attacks.

   (3) Side effects—bronchospasm, cough, angioedema
  f. Parasympatholytic—ipratropium bromide, glycopyr-
   rolate, atropine
    (1) Action—decreases parasympathetic bronchial
     tone
    (2) Side effects—tachycardia, dry mucous mem-
     branes, hyperthermia
 2. Control infection
 3. Control excessive lung water
 4. Look for dynamic compression syndrome, tracheobron-
  chomalacia, or intraluminal or extraluminal masses.

SELECTED READINGS

Bartlett, R.H. (editor): Respiratory care in surgery, Surg. Clin. North Am. **60**(6):1319, 1980.

Bomalski, J.S. et al.: Inferior vena cava interruption in the management of pulmonary embolism, Chest **82**(6):767, 1982.

Brindley, G.V., et al.: Pulmonary resection in patients with impaired pulmonary function, Surg. Clin. North Am. **62**(2):199, 1982.

Collins, J.A.: The acute respiratory distress syndrome, Adv. Surg. **11**:171, 1977.

Fishman, A.P. (editor): Pulmonary diseases and disorders, New York, 1980, McGraw-Hill Book Co.

Fishman, A.P. (editor): Update: pulmonary diseases and disorders, New York, 1982, McGraw-Hill Book Co.

Glenn, W.L., Hogan, J.F., and Phelps, M.L.: Ventilatory support of the quadriplegic patient with respiratory paralysis by diaphragm pacing. Surg. Clin. North Am. **60**(5):1055, 1980.

Grace, M.P., and Greenbaum, D.M.: Effect of positive end-expiratory pressure on cardiac performance in patients with cardiac dysfunction, Crit. Care Med. **7**:143, 1979.

Greenbaum, D.M.: Positive end-expiratory pressure, constant positive airway pressure, and cardiac performance, Chest **76**:248, 1979.

Greenbaum, D.M., et al.: Continuous positive airway pressure without tracheal intubation in spontaneously breathing patients, Chest **69**:615, 1976.

Greenfield, L.J., and Jay, S.J.: Immediate management of massive pulmonary embolism, Chest **82**(6):775, 1982.

Hammond, G.L.: Acute respiratory failure, Surg. Clin. North Am. **60**(5):1133, 1980.

Kirby, R.R., et al.: High level positive end-expiratory pressure (PEEP) in acute respiratory insufficiency. Chest **67**:156, 1975.

Kirby, R.R., et al.: Cardiorespiratory effects of high positive end-expiratory pressure, Anesthesiology **43**:533,

Kirchner, J.A.: Trachesotomy and its problems, Surg. Clin. North Am. **60**(5):1093, 1980.

Lewis, F.R.: Thoracic trauma, Surg. Clin. North Am. **62**(1):97, 1982.

Lutch, J.S., and Jurray, J.F.: Continuous positive-pressure ventilation: effects on systemic oxygen transport and tissue oxygenation, Ann. Int. Med. **76:**193, 1972.

Pepine, C.J.: Coronary circulatory effects of increased intrathoracic pressure in intact dogs, Chest **72:**72, 1977.

Pontoppidan, H., Laver, M.B., and Geffin, B.: Acute respiratory failure in the surgical patient, Adv. Surg. **4:**163, 1972.

Powers, S.R., and Dutton, R.E.: Correlation of positive end-expiratory pressure with cardiovascular performance, Crit. Care Med. **3:**64, 1975.

Qvist, J., et al.: Hemodynamic responses to mechanical ventilation with PEEP, Anesthesiology **42:**45, 1975.

Robotham, J.L., et al.: A reevaluation of the hemodynamic consequences of intermittent positive pressure ventilation, Crit. Care Med. **11:**783, 1983.

Sabiston, D.C. (editor): Pulmonary embolism. In Davis, C.: Textbook of surgery, New York, 1981, W.B. Saunders Co.

Suter, P.M., Fairly, H.B., Isenberg, M.D.: Optimum end-expiratory pressure in patients with acute pulmonary failure, N. Engl. J. Med. **292:**284, 1975.

Tsarbaugh, R.F., and Lewis, F.R.: Respiratory insufficiency, Surg. Clin. North Am. **62**(1):121, 1982.

Werko, L.: The influence of positive pressure breathing on the circulation in man, Stokholm Alb Bonniers, Boktryckeri, 1947.

4

Cardiovascular responses

Frank B. Cerra

The metabolic response to injury obligates an increase in flow in response to an increase in metabolic demand. Patients in whom this process can occur, or can be allowed to occur, have a statistically increased probability of survival. In short, oxygen delivery needs to be kept equated with oxygen demand. This need necessitates two processes with current technology:

1. Getting oxygen delivery to equal demand from the point of view of "sitting at the heart" and looking toward the tissue
2. Obtaining that equality with the greatest efficiency

A. Criteria of oxygen delivery equal to oxygen demand
   1. In practice, no direct way exists to measure how much oxygen the tissue wants to consume. We can measure total body consumption by the following equation:

   $$O_2C = CO \times DVo_2, \text{ where}$$

   O_2C where is oxygen consumption L/min
   CO is cardiac output
   DVo_2 is arteriovenous oxygen content difference
   2. The criteria for achieving equality, then, are indirect:
      a. No flow-dependent oxygen consumption or its corrolary, a level of O_2 consumption appropriate to the existing level of stress
      b. Metabolic criteria indicating adequate O_2 supply (i.e., a lactate/pyruvate ratio under 20)

B. When oxygen delivery is not equal to demand, three components may be manipulated:
   1. Tissue demand

      2. Oxygen content and blood volume/distribution

      3. Cardiac output (CO)

C. Tissue demand

    1. Variables

      a. pH

      b. Temperature

      c. Drugs to change oxygen use or change the tissue/blood interface

      d. Nutrient supply, substrate manipulation, and metabolic support

      e. Correction of endocrinopathies

      f. Electrolyte/osmolar abnormalities

      g. Ion/element deficiences, for hypophosphatemia, hypomagnesemia

    2. That oxygen in tissue has other than metabolic functions is becoming increasingly apparent. Its function as an antibiotic has been demonstrated as well as its central role in regulating macrophage function of wound healing and in Kupffer cell–hepatocyte interactions.

    3. The tissue/blood interface is the critical interface. The ability to influence it selectively is limited to such maneuvers as:

      a. Maintaining blood volume

      b. Stimulating alpha- and/or beta-receptors

      c. Directing vasoconstricting or vasodilating

D. Oxygen content

    1. Variables

      a. Hemoglobin (Hb)

      b. Pao_2

      c. Oxyhemoglobin interaction

      d. Dissolved oxygen

      e. Total delivery

    2. As presented in "sick" patients, an Hb $\sim$ 13 g% seems associated with improved survival. This seems to represent a balance of viscosity and myocardial work. In high-CO states, the work necessary in maintaining O_2 delivery at an Hb of 10 g% is much greater than at an Hb of 13 g%.

3. The minimum PaO_2 is one that allows at least 95% saturation of Hb. Newer concepts of the nonmetabolic roles of oxygen may necessitate PaO_2 above this level. Data should be forthcoming. Dissolved oxygen is the product of PaO_2 and the solubility coefficient, 0.0036. In practice this latter volume is of little bedside use.

4. The relationship between O_2 and Hb results in the greatest amount of O_2 carrying. The relationship is reversible and depicted in the O_2 dissociation curve (Fig. 4-1). The P_{50} describes the oxygen tension at which 50% saturation is achieved. It is useful in assessing the position of the curve.

   a. The curve shifts to the right in a number of settings, making tissue unloading easier and lung loading harder.

     (1) Acidosis

     (2) Elevated temperature

     (3) Anemia/altitude

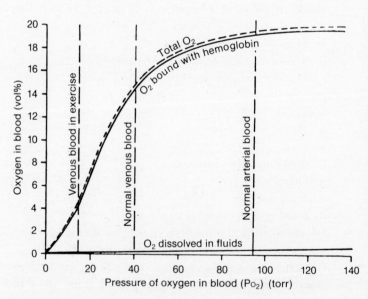

Fig. 4-1. Oxyhemoglobin dissociation curve. (From Guyton, A.C.: Physiology of the human body, ed. 6, Philadelphia, 1984, W.B. Saunders Co.)

       (4) Addison's disease

       (5) Thyrotoxicosis

       (6) Drugs, for example, methylprednisolone

   b. A shift to the left makes tissue unloading harder and lung loading easier.

       (1) Hypothermia

       (2) Alkalosis

       (3) Carbon monoxide

       (4) Old blood

       (5) Hypophosphatemia

   c. Most shifts are self-regulating. The basic triangle of oxygen transport, then, becomes that seen in Fig. 4-2.

E. Cardiac output

   1. The function of CO in this setting is to provide the flow to allow adequate delivery of the content. Thus two reasons exist for manipulating CO.

     a. To achieve O_2 delivery = O_2 demand

     b. To achieve maximum efficiency in obtaining O_2 delivery = O_2 demand

        The two manipulatable components are:

$$CO = HR \times SV$$

    where

    HR is heart rate
    SV is stroke volume.

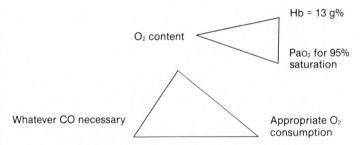

Fig. 4-2. The basic triangles of oxygen transport. The key variable is appropriate O_2 consumption. It is also important to note that all variables are interdependent.

2. Heart rate

Manipulation is situation specific.

a. HR too high

(1) Myocardial perfusion is, in part, inversely dependent on HR.

(2) Too high becomes absolute at ~140 beats per minute and relative below that in settings of apparent cardiac ischemia (pain, electrocardiogram changes) and/or risk of ischemia.

(3) Dysrhythmias are discussed in Chapter 13.

b. HR too low

(1) With the CO fixed, a reduction in HR necessitates an increase in SV. If the increased SV can be met, the decreased HR may be of little consequence.

(2) Below an absolute level of 40 to 50 beats per minute under stress conditions, a pacemaker may be necessary. Above that, HR range is a relative judgment that depends on whether the increased SV can be met without "congestive" failure.

(3) Dysrhythmias are discussed in Chapter 13.

3. Stroke volume

a. SV has three components: preload, contractility, and afterload. The basic relationship is described in the Starling curves. These are a family of responses of SV to left ventricular end-diastolic volume (LVEDV), each curve representing this relationship at a defined afterload and contractility (Fig. 4-3).

(1) With end-diastolic volume changes, LVEDV movement up and down the curve occurs.

(2) With an increase in contractility or a reduction in afterload, the response curve shifts up and the position on this curve usually shifts up and to the left.

(3) With a reduction in contractility or an increase in afterload, the response curve shifts down and the position on the curve usually shifts down and to the right.

b. With manipulations of SV, preload should be done

first. Alterations in contractility and afterload are dependent on preload.

  c. The decision of contractility versus afterload manipulation is situation specific.

    (1) Afterload reduction requires adequate contractility to achieve the desired effect; it is also less costly in terms of work.

    (2) Inotropic support requires work, particularly if an increase in HR is stimulated.

4. Predicting CO

  a. Because of the relationship between O_2C, CO, and DVO_2, DVO_2 has been used to predict CO, as have been PVO_2 and SVO_2.

  b. Data on this relationship demonstrate a very poor predictability in critical care settings.

  c. In certain settings, some utility exists (e.g., using

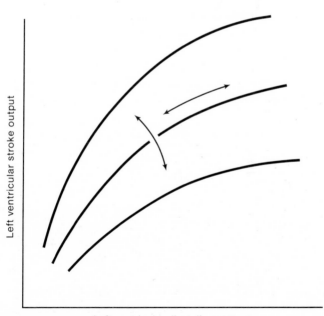

Fig. 4-3. Curve for Starling Law showing relationship between preload, contractility, and afterload.

SVO_2 to detect reductions in CO during PEEP-effect curves).

5. Compliance

In practice, we can measure HR and SV, but not LVEDV. We then infer LVEDV from pressure. This relationship of change in volume to a change in pressure is compliance.

a. Pressure measures the force per unit area on a transducing surface. As such, it tells little directly about volume. Because of compliance relationships, data from pressure can be used to imply changes in volume, within the limits of the closed system and the compliance of that system (Fig. 4-4).

(1) As volume is increased, eventually pressure increases. The relationship is linear, however, only in a narrow range, essentially the range when vessel dilitation is nearly completed.

(2) When volume is lost, vessel size reduces; pressure is maintained until large reductions in volume have occurred. Thus pressure/volume

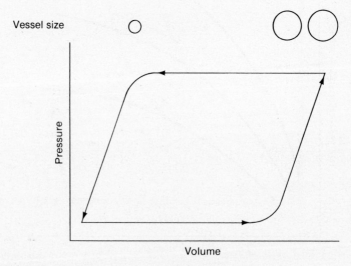

Fig. 4-4. Vessel size according to pressure and volume. Thus changes in pressure are only sensitive to changes in volume at the extremes.

changes are linear only in a relatively narrow range. In these settings, if pressure is to imply volume, the system must be kept full.

b. Fig. 4-5 depicts left ventricular compliance relationships.
   (1) At the same filling pressure a change in compliance can and does cause a change in LVEDV and SV.
   (2) Decreased compliance occurs in:
      (a) Myocardial ischemia
      (b) Shock
      (c) Pericardial effusion
      (d) Inotropic support
      (e) PEEP
   (3) Increased compliance occurs in:
      (a) Afterload reduction
      (b) Cardiomyopathy

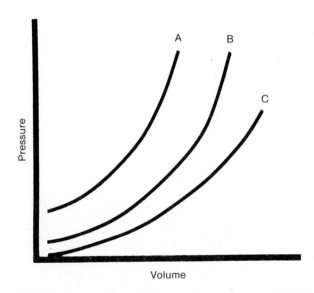

Fig. 4-5. Ventricular compliance is decreased *A*, by myocardial ischemia, shock, pericardial effusion, inotropic agents, and positive end-expiratory pressure and increased, *C*, by vasodilators, cardiomyopathy, and ischemic relief. *B*, Normal compliance.

        (c) Malnutrition

        (d) Relief of ischemia or inotropic support

   6. Relationship of compliance effects to Starling effects

      a. These relationships are depicted in Figs. 4-6 to 4-9. Because of these interactions, pressure monitoring, specifically the pulmonary capillary wedge pressure (PCWP), cannot distinguish between contractility changes and compliance changes. As an index of blood volume, then, PCWP becomes insensitive and nonspecific. It seems to measure capillary hydrostatic pressure. This can give information on the propensity to form lung water. It also becomes a barometer for

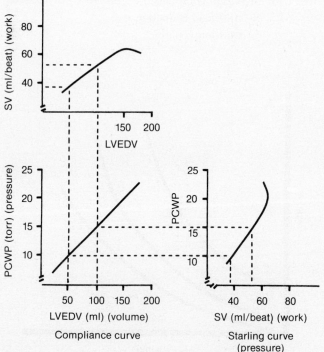

Fig. 4-6. Starling curves assuming a linear compliance curve. Note that the two Starling curves are mirror images. (Adapted from Grossman, W., et al.: *Circulation* **56:**845, 1977.)

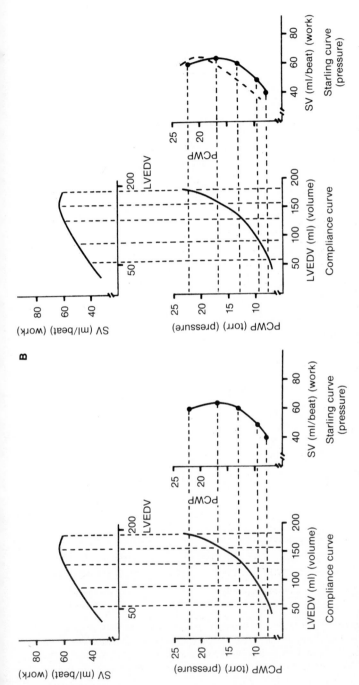

Fig. 4-7. A, Starling curves assuming a normal ventricular compliance curve. Note that the Starling curves are not mirror images. **B,** The same relationships as in **A** with the mirror image curve added (*dashed curve*). (Adapted from Grossman, W., et al.: Circulation **56**:845, 1977.)

the effectiveness of myocardial performance in distribution of fluid load. As such, it can give information about the effective blood volume (see entry *c*, opposite); that is, it acts as a guide to ventricular filling pressure.

b. By measuring CO and SV and then determining ejection fraction; LVEDV can be calculated.

$$\text{LVEDV} = \frac{\text{stroke volume index}}{\text{left ventricular ejection fraction}} \ \text{ml/n}^2$$

EF can now be estimated by beside ECHO in a reasonably reliable way.

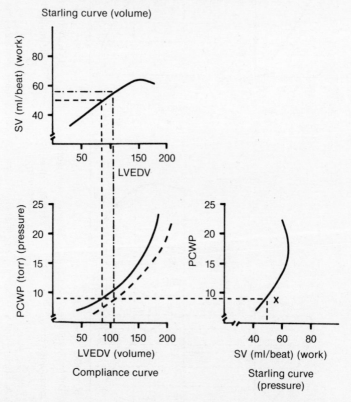

Fig. 4-8. Increase in compliance *(dashed curve)* as after treatment with a vasodilator. Note that if only pulmonary capillary wedge pressure *(PCWP)* is measured, contractility appears to have improved. (*SV* is stroke volume and *LVEDV* is left ventricular end-diastolic volume.) (Adapted from Grossman, W., et al.: Circulation **56:**845, 1977.)

c. Judgment of "adequate blood volume" requires test of fluid loading (e.g., 250 ml saline).
   (1) If PCWP stays constant and SV and CO increase:
      (a) A positive response to fluids has occurred.
      (b) A benefit is likely until CO increases so that O_2 delivery $= O_2$ demand, or filling pressure begins to rise to an undesirable level.
   (2) If PCWP markedly increases with little change in CO or SV:
      (a) A nonpositive response has occurred—whether from contractility failure or decreased compliance cannot be determined.

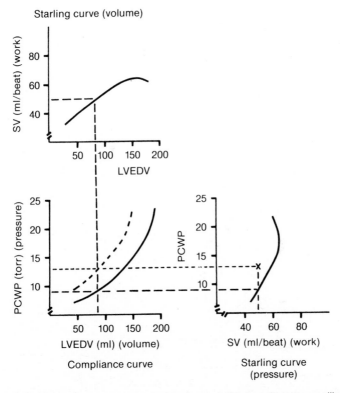

Fig. 4-9. Decreased compliance *(dashed curve).* If only pulmonary capillary wedge pressure is measured, contractility appears to have decreased. (*SV* is stroke volume and *LVEDV* is left ventricular end-diastolic volume.) (Adapted from Grossman, W., et al.: Circulation **56:**845, 1977.)

  (b) Therapy other than fluids, however, is needed (e.g., inotropic support and afterload reduction) until O_2 delivery $= O_2$ demand.

F. Cardiopulmonary interactions

 The heart and lung are inseparably connected. Consequently, changes in one affect the function of the other.

 1. Changes in cardiac function affecting pulmonary lung water have been discussed.

 2. Pulmonary artery hypertension

  a. The pulmonary resistance *origins* are in:

   (1) Arterioles

   (2) Capillaries and veins

   (3) The left side of the heart

  b. The pulmonary resistances are:

$$\text{Total} = \frac{\text{PAP} - \text{CVP}}{\text{CO}} = 1 + 2 + 3$$

$$\text{Arteriolar} = \frac{\text{PAP PWP}}{\text{CO}} = 1$$

$$\text{Pulmonary} = \text{Total} - \text{arteriolar} = 2 + 3$$

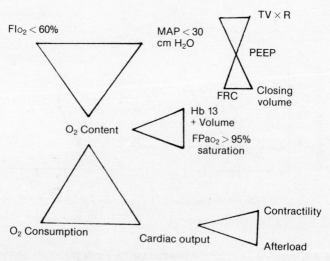

Fig. 4-10. The balancing triangles of oxygen transport. The system is interdependent, and altering one variable alters the entire relationship. The key variable for survival appears to be oxygen consumption.

Flow is usually not a cause of increased resistance. High flows, however, can significantly contribute to resistance.

c. Acute arteriolar resistance changes respond well to a number of arteriolar dilating agents.

(1) Nitroprusside

(2) Dobutamine

(3) Isoproterenol

d. Acute increases in pulmonary artery resistance are associated with right ventricular dilution, septal shift, dextrorotation of the heart, and a reduction in left ventricular output, the so called pseudotamponade syndrome, as pressures become equalized across the heart.

e. Positive pressure ventilation is discussed in Chapter 3.

G. Thus, the "triangles of life" must be balanced and kept balanced (Fig. 4-10).

SELECTED READINGS

Alderman, E.L., and Glantz, S.A.: Acute hemodynamic interventions shift the diastolic pressure-volume curve in man, Circulation **54**:662, 1976.

Alderman, E.L., and Stanton, A.G.: Acute hemodynamic interventions shift the diastolic pressure-volume curve in man, Circulation **54**:662, 1976.

Alyono, D., Ring, W.S., and Anderson, R.W.: The effects of hemorrhagic shock on the diastolic properties of the left ventricle in the conscious dog, Surgery **83**:691, 1978.

Bemis, C.E., et al.: Influence of right ventricular filling pressure on left ventricle and dimension, Circ. Res. **34**:498, 1974.

Berggren, S.: The oxygen deficit of arterial blood caused by nonventilating parts of the lung, Acta Physiol. Scand. suppl. 11:1, 1942.

Bove, A.A., and Santamore, W.P.: Ventricular interdependence, Prog. Cardiovasc. Dis. **23**:365, 1961.

Braunwald, E., and Ross, J.: Control of cardiac performance. In Berne, R.M., and Sperelakis, N.: Handbook of physiology the cardiovascular system, Baltimore, 1979 Williams & Wilkins, pp. 533-80.

Brodie BR, et al.: Effects of sodium nitroprusside on left ventricular diastolic pressure-volume relations, J. Clin. Invest. **59**:59, 1977.

Calvin, J.E., Driedger, A.A., and Sibbald, W.J.: An assessment of myocardial function in human sepsis utilizing ECG gated cardiac scintigraphy, Chest **80**:579, 1981.

Calvine, J.E., Driedger, A.A., and Sibbald, W.J.: Does the pulmonary capillary wedge pressure predict left ventricular preload in critically ill patients? Crit. Care Med. **9**:437, 1981.

Calvin, J.E., Driedger, A.A., and Sibbald, W.J.: Positive end-expiratory pressure (PEEP) does not depress left ventricular function in patients with pulmonary edema, Am. Rev. Respir. Dis. **124:**121, 1981.

Calvin, J.E., Driedger, A.A., and Sibbald, W.J.: The hemodynamic effect of rapid fluid infusion in critically ill patients, Surgery **90:**61, 1981.

Civetta, J.M., Gabel, J.C., and Laver, M.B.: Disparate ventricular function in surgical patients, Surg. Forum **22:**136, 1971.

Clowes, G.H.A., et al.: Circulating factors in the etiology of pulmonary insufficiency and right heart failure accompanying severe sepsis (peritonitis), Ann. Surg. **171:**663, 1970.

Deher, G.J., et al.: The end-systolic pP/V index: a sensitive parameter for the scintigraphic detection of left ventricular dysfunction in patients with coronary artery disease, Circulation **62**(4, Part 2):III, 1980.

Dehmer, G.J., et al.: Non-geometric determinations of right ventricular volume from equiligrium blood pool scans, Am. J. Cardiol. **49:**78, 1982.

Fleming, W.H., Bowen, J.C., and Petty, C.: The use of pulmonary compliance as a guide to respiratory therapy, Surg. Gynecol. Obstet. **134:**291, 1972.

Forrester, J.S., et al.: Filling pressure in the right and left sides of the heart in acute myocardial infarction: a reappraisal of central-venous-pressure monitoring, N. Engl. J. Med. **285:**190, 1971.

Forrester, J.S., et al.: Early increase in left ventricular compliance after myocardial infarction, J. Clin. Invest. **51:**596, 1972.

Friedman, E., Grable, E., and Fine, J.: Central venous pressure and direct serial measurements as guides in blood-volume replacement, Lancet **2:**609, 1966.

Gentzler, R.D., Briselli, M.F., Gault, J.H.: Angiographic estimation of right ventricular volume in man, Circulation **50:**324, 1974.

Glantz, S.A., and Parmley, W.W.: Factors which affect the diastolic pressure volume curve, Circ. Res. **42:**171, 1978.

Grossman, W.: Appendix: normal values. In Grossman, W., editor: Cardiac catheterization and angiography, Philadelphia, 1976, Lea & Febiger, p. 329.

Grossman, W., et al.: Contractile state of the left ventricle in man as elevated from end-systolic pressure-volume relations, Circulation **56:**845, 1977.

Guyton, A.C., Lindsey, A.W., and Gilluly, J.J.: The limits of right ventricular compensation following acute increases in pulmonary circulatory resistance, Circ. Res. **2:**326, 1954.

Guzman, P.A., et al.: Transseptal pressure gradient with leftward septal displacement during the Mueller manoeuvre in man, Br. Heart J. **46:**657, 1981.

Jardin, F., et al.: Influence of positive end-expiratory pressure on left ventricular performance, N. Engl. J. Med. **304:**387, 1981.

Korr, K.S., et al.: Hemodynamic correlates at right ventricular ejection fraction measured with gated radionuclide angiography, Am. J. Cardiol. **49:**71, 1982.

Krayenbuhl, H.P., et al.: Is the ejection fraction an index of myocardial contractility? Cardiologia **53:**1, 1968.

Lategola, M., and Rahn, H.: A self-guiding catheter for cardic and pulmonary arterial catheterization and occlusion, Proc. Soc. Exp. Biol. Med. **84:**667, 1953.

Laver, M.G., Strauss, H.W., and Pohost, G.M.: Right and left ventricular geometry: adjustments during acute respiratory failure, Crit. Care Med. **7:**509, 1979.

Lozman, J., Powers, S., and Older, J.: Correlation of pulmonary wedge and left artrial pressures, Arch. Surg. **109:**270, 1974.

Maddahi, J., Berman, D.S., and Matsuoka, D.T.: A new technique for assessing right ventricular ejection fraction using rapid multiple-gated equilibrium cardiac blood pool scintigraphy, Circulation **60:**581, 1979.

Marshall, R.C., et al.: Assessment of cardiac performance with quantitative radionuclide angiography, Circulation **56:**820, 1977.

Maughn, W.L., et al.: Instantaneous pressure-volume relationship of the canine right ventricle, Circ. Res. **44:**309, 1979.

McIntyre, K., and Sasahara, A.A.: Determinants of right ventricular function and hemodynamics after pulmonary embolism, Chest **65:**534, 1974.

Mehmel, H.C., et al.: The linearity of the end-systolic pressure-volume relationship in man and its sensitivity for assessment of ventricular function, Circulation **63:**1216, 1981.

Parker, J.O., and Case, R.B.: Normal left ventricular function, Circulation **60:**4, 1979.

Prewitt, R.M., et al.: Effect of positive end-experatory pressure on left ventricular mechanics in patients with hypoxemic respiratory failure, Anesthesiology **55:**409, 1981.

Prewitt, R.M., and Wood, L.D.H.: Effect of altered resistive load on left ventricular systolic mechanics in dogs, Anesthesiology **56:**195, 1982.

Sibbald, W.J., Calvin, J., and Driedger, A.A.: Right and left ventricular preload and diastolic ventricular compliance: implications for therapy in critically ill patients. In Shoemaker, W.C., Thompson, L.W., editors: Critical care: state of the art, vol. 3. Fullerton, California, 1982, Society of Critical Care Medicine, Ch III (f).

Sibbald, W.J., Cumingham, D.R., and Chin, D.N.: Non-cardiac pulmonary edema? Chest **84:**452, 1983.

Sibbald, W.J., Driedger, A.A., and Meyers, M.L.: Biventricular function in ARDS, Chest **84:**126, 1983.

Sibbald, W.J., et al.: Pulmonary microvascular clearance of readiotracers in human cardiac and noncardiac pulmonary edema, J. Appl. Physiol. **50:**1337, 1981.

Sibbald, W.J., et al.: Concepts of the pharmacologic and non-pharmacologic support of cardiovascular function in the critically ill surgical patient. In Hechtman, H.B., editor: Surgical Clinics of North America.

Smith, P.K., et al.: Cardiovascular effects of ventilation with positive end-expiratory pressure, Ann. Surg. **195:**121, 1982.

Starling, E.H.: The linacre lecture on the law of the heart. Delivered at St. John's College, Cambridge, in 1915. London, 1918, Longmans, Green and Co.

Stein, P.D., et al.: Performance of the failing and non-failing ventricle of patients with pulmonary hypertension, Am. J. Cardiol. **44:**1050, 1979.

Stool, E.W., et al.: Dimensional change of the left ventricle during acute pulmonary arterial hypertension in dogs, Am. J. Cardiol. **33:**868, 1974.

Sutherland, G.R., et al.: Anatomic and cardiopulmonary responses to trauma with associated blunt chest trauma, J. Trauma **21:**1, 1981.

Swan, H.J.C., et al.: Catheterization of the heart in man with the use of a flow-directed ballon-tipped catheter, N. Engl. J. Med. **283:**447, 1970.

Vlahakes, G.J., Turley, K., and Hoffman, J.I.: The pathophysiology of failure in acute right ventricular hypertension: hemodynamic and biochemical correlations, Circulation **63:**87, 1981.

5

General monitoring

David Dunn
Frank B. Cerra

Monitoring means observing to detect an aberration from some predetermined norm(s) or performing some specific task. As such, it is a process applied to a clinical setting and is therefore difficult to quantitate. The "tools" of monitoring vary from pure clinical observation to sophisticated quantitation. Thus it is possible to have only principles or guidelines for monitoring activity.

A. When to monitor
  1. This decision is a clinical judgment based on:
      a. One's knowledge of the patient's underlying disease state
      b. The stress-event that occurred
      c. The impact of the stress-event on the patient's underlying physiologic state
      d. The risk of an adverse consequence
      e. The need for a specific physiologic intervention
  2. As a patient's clinical condition deteriorates:
      a. Clinical signs and symptoms less reliably predict or assess the existing physiologic state.
      b. The need for quantitative data increases.
      c. Multiple parameters become necessary to assess the altered physiologic state and implement a treatment plan.
  3. Severity/prognostic indexes
      a. These are accurate at the extremes, but add little to a clinical assessment in those settings (e.g., a clinician's assessment of futility is as good as or better than the current assessment systems).

    b. In the intermediate region
       (1) They provide a probability rating of a favorable or unfavorable response in the population sense.
       (2) They do not frequently provide a reliable enough basis to add or withdraw therapy in many patient settings.
       (3) They are deterministic and do not allow for advances in care (i.e., they are constrained by their data base).
    c. They do allow for some standardization of data for interinstitutional communication and comparison.
    d. Continued development is necessary to allow more effective resource allocation.
  4. Within this context, invasive physiologic monitoring is indicated:
    a. In settings in which data on efficacy are present (e.g., septic shock).
    b. In settings in which there is a high risk of complications (e.g., high-risk surgery [see Chapter 30]) that can be reduced by physiologic manipulation.
    c. When the patient's clinical course is other than expected.
    d. When a direct physiologic intervention is necessary (e.g., afterload reduction in sepsis with a cardiogenic response).

B. What to monitor
  1. This is a judgment based on the clinical setting.
    a. To assess a specific organ function (e.g., fluid-distributing capacity of the heart)
    b. To assess a systemic function (e.g., adequacy of oxygen delivery)
    c. To answer a specific question (e.g., is afterload reduction necessary?)
    d. To perform a specific function (e.g., pulmonary afterload reduction)
  2. The judgment runs a spectrum between:
    a. Clinical signs/symptoms of perfusion at one end to the invasive determination of oxygen consumption and flow at the other.

  b. The "sicker" the patient becomes, the less reliable
   are the clinical signs of perfusion adequacy and the
   greater the need for multiple parameters.
 3. Limited by the technology and expertise of the personnel present.
C. Reliable monitoring
 1. Components
  a. Choice of variables
  b. Accurate measurements
  c. Interpretation of data
  d. Planned intervention
  e. Assessment of effect and need for further interven-
   tion/therapy
 2. Interaction of the patient, physician, and monitoring per-
  sonnel/system
  a. The patient (see below)
  b. The monitoring system (see opposite page)
 3. Levels of intervention in cardiovascular monitoring.
  a. Electrocardiographic monitoring

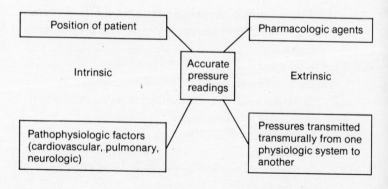

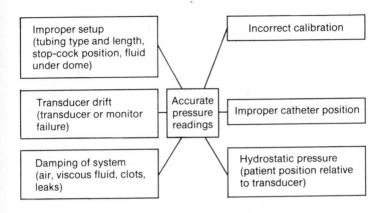

(1) Continuous monitoring of the electrocardiogram (ECG) is routine intraoperatively and in the immediate postoperative period for all patients.

(2) The following patients should have continued monitoring.

   (a) Any who have undergone a cardiovascular procedure

   (b) Any who have had another major procedure entailing large blood or intravascular volume loss or complications

   (c) Any who have a history of cardiovascular disease

   (d) Any who demonstrate any form of hemodynamic instability

(3) Automatic triggering devices are useful in the identification of arrhythmias or asystole, but they cannot supplant routine observation.

(4) Finer interpretation of changes on the ECG require a full 12-lead evaluation.

b. Blood pressure monitoring

Mean arterial blood pressure (MAP) as well as systolic and diastolic systemic pressure may be continuously monitored by an arterial pressure line connected to a pressure transducer.

(1) Typically, an attempt is made to position the catheter so that a relatively central aortic or large-artery pressure is monitored.

(2) Arterial pressure lines are useful for patients in the categories mentioned under electrocardiographic monitoring, and especially for those with hemodynamic instability in which more peripheral pressure monitoring obtained with routine sphygmomanometry may not be reliable because of peripheral vasoconstriction.

(a) Probably all patients maintained on vasoactive pharmacologic agents should be so mentioned.

(b) Patients requiring frequent arterial blood gas determinations, especially those in whom pulmonary shunt fraction determinations are required, should probably have arterial lines placed. However, the complications associated with these catheters (e.g., arterial thrombosis with ensuing ischemia) should definitely be considered and weighed against the risks of frequent percutaneous sampling.

c. Central venous pressure monitoring

The central venous pressure (CVP) is that pressure found in the great veins leading to the right side of the heart. The volume of blood in those veins, the venous tone of those veins, as well as the distensibility (compliance) of the right atrium and right ventricle influence CVP.

(1) A normal central venous pressure is between 0 and 4 torr.

(2) A, C, and V waves may often be seen on the pres-

sure tracing. (The V wave is markedly increased in tricuspid valve regurgitation.)

(a) For the right side of the normal heart, increases in CVP lead to an increase in cardiac output (CO) according to the Frank-Starling principles. This is also termed the *cardiac function curve* and is a global function parameter.

(b) Conversely, however, as CO increases, CVP decreases. This principle is physiologically defined by the systemic function curve.

(3) Causes of increased CVP include:

(a) Right ventricular failure

(b) Biventricular failure

(c) Increased intrathoracic pressure

(d) Tricuspid regurgitation

(e) Pulmonary embolism

(f) Chronic obstructive or restrictive pulmonary disease

(g) Catecholamine excess

(h) Cardiac tamponade

(i) Many authors note the increase in CVP that may occur with increased intrathoracic pressure during the use of positive-end expiratory pressure (PEEP). However, most state that monitoring may best take place without discontinuing PEEP during the measurement period, because the true physiologic status of the patient will thus be measured.

(4) The CVP is typically decreased in hypovolemia but, as noted, it may be normally low.

(5) CVP catheters are typically placed by the internal jugular, subclavian, or antecubital approach.

(a) Measurements are obtained with the patient supine and the transducer set in the same horizontal plane as the superior vena cava. Typically, this is the plane that intersects one-half the anteroposterior diameter of the chest, 4 cm inferior to the manubrium.

(b) Often these large-bore catheters are not placed for pressure monitoring, but for other reasons:

i. Venous access, when large volumes of fluid or blood must be rapidly infused

ii. Hyperalimentation and infusion of relatively hypertonic or toxic chemotherapeutic substances

iii. Patients in whom hemodynamic instability is present or suspected, unless concomitant cardiovascular disease is also present. This group of patients, which includes most patients undergoing cardiovascular procedures, diabetic patients with cardiovascular disease, and many older patients undergoing major procedures, may not be adequately monitored by CVP monitoring. These patients should have Swan-Ganz catheters placed. Younger, relatively healthy patients with normal right and left ventricular function may be monitored with the CVP.

d. Swan-Ganz catheter monitoring

As just mentioned, patients in whom no preexistent cardiovascular disease is apparent can often be managed with CVP monitoring. More complicated situations, that is, those in which such problems as concomitant hypovolemia and left-sided cardiac failure exist, require more sophisticated monitoring.

(1) The Swan-Ganz catheter may be placed by similar approaches to those mentioned for the CVP catheter.

(2) Monitoring

(a) Patients should undergo continuous ECG monitoring during insertion.

(b) Lidocaine should be available in case significant ventricular arrhythmias occur.

(c) During insertion, pressures and traces of each vessel or chamber should be measured:

Chamber or vessel	Normal pressure: mean or systolic/ diastolic
Central system veins	0 to 4
Right atrium	0 to 6
Right ventricle	20 to 30/0 to 7
Pulmonary artery	20 to 30/10 to 15
Pulmonary artery wedge pressure	6 to 13
Left atrium	4 to 8
Left ventricle	110 to 120/0 to 10
Systemic arteries	110 to 120/70 to 80

(d) A daily chest roentgenogram should be obtained to monitor for drifting of the catheter tip, which should lie in either the right or left main pulmonary artery.

(e) Ideally, positioning of this balloon flotation catheter in one of the main pulmonary arteries allows monitoring of the following parameters:

   i. Pulmonary artery systolic and diastolic pressure

   ii. Mean pulmonary artery pressure (MPAP)

   iii. Pulmonary capillary wedge pressure (PCWP)

   iv. Mixed venous O_2

   v. The cardiac output of the right side of the heart

The measurements should be done at end-expiration. The patient should not be taken off the ventilator in most settings, because pulmonary edema can occur, and the rebound in cardiac output can produce cerebral edema, particularly in the presence of high airway pressures. Intermittent tracings for documentation and charting are to be encouraged.

   vi. PWP should exceed PAP so that the catheter is not in zone III.

(f) In the normal heart, changes in CVP and PCWP closely parallel each other. The PCWP is typically related to pressure in the pulmonary veins, and thus indirectly to the left atrial pressure (LAP) and left ventricular end-diastolic pressure (LVEDP) when these are normal. At high LAP or LVEDP (>15 torr), this correlation is not as close.

(g) PCWP and MPAP also parallel each other. Typically, MPAP is 2 to 4 torr lower than the PCWP. If this correlation is established during the initial monitoring period, adequate monitoring is often possible despite loss of balloon flotation capability.

(h) Some versions of the Swan-Ganz catheter contain electrodes at various positions in the catheter that allow atrial, ventricular, or sequential atrioventricular pacing when connected to a generator pack.

(i) Multiple-lumen catheters contain an extra proximal port at 20 or 30 cm, depending on the model, which typically lies at the position of the right atrium or vena cava. This port is used for infusion during CO determinations. Those catheters which allow CO determinations have a temperature-sensitive thermistor 4 cm distal from the balloon tip. To obtain a CO measurement, a given quantity, typically 10 ml, of physiologic sterile saline at a known temperature (usually $0°$ C) is injected in the proximal port as a bolus. The thermistor probe measures the appearance and disappearance of the temperature change and sends the signal into an analog computer, which integrates the area under the curve and converts this to CO (normally 3 to 3.5 L/ min).

(j) Thermal dilution CO methods have the advantage over indicator dye dilution methods that typically use indocyanine green dye, in that the former can be repeated almost indefinitely. However, this method measures the CO of the right side of the heart. Obviously, with myocardial disease, especially that involving left-sided cardiac function, dye studies in which the dye is injected into the central system veins or right atrium and monitored in a systemic artery may be more useful, providing a measure of the left-sided CO. Both these methods are based on the Fick principle, which states that flow is proportional to the change in concentration of the indicator substance between two time points when the total amount of indicator substance added is known.

(k) When combined with systemic arterial blood pressure measurements, as well as pulmonary artery blood pressure measurements, CO is an invaluable tool in determining the basis for hypotension and shock. It should be noted that if direct pressure measurements are not available, the arteriovenous O_2 difference may give a rough estimate of CO. The venous blood must be central mixed venous blood and therefore must come from at least the low right atrium. Normal CO typically leads to 4 volumes percent arterioventricular O_2 difference, a low CO greater than 6 volumes percent difference, and high CO less than 3 volumes percent difference.

(l) Total systemic vascular resistance (TSR) can be measured by the following formula:

$$\text{TSR} = \frac{(\text{MAP} - \text{CVP}) \text{ torr } (79.8)}{\text{CO (L/min)}}$$

(m) Normal values are 1000 to 1500 dyne-sec-cm^{-5} Conversion of torr mm (Hg) to cm

H_2O can be accomplished by multiplying the value in torr by 1.36.

(n) Similarly, total pulmonary vascular resistance (TPR) can be measured in the following manner:

$$TPR = \frac{(MPAP - MPWP) \text{ mm Hg } (79.8)}{CO \text{ (L/min)}}$$

(o) Normal values are 80-200 dyne-sec-cm^{-5} The physiologically altered states that may be defined by monitoring these parameters are as follows:

	TSR	TPR	MABP	CVP	PCWP	CI
Hypovolemic shock	↑	↑	↓	↓ or nl (venous tone)	↓	↓ or nl
Cardiogenic shock						
Myocardial left	↑	↑	↓	↓ or nl	>20	<1.5
Cardiac tamponade	↑	↑	↓	↑ = PAD and PAWP	↑	↓
Neurogenic shock	↓	↓	↓	↓	↓	↑ or ↓
Septic shock						
Low CO	↑	↑ or nl	↓	↑	↓	↓
High CO	↓	↓ or ↑	↓	↓ or nl	nl	↑
Pulmonary embolism	or nl	↑	↓ or nl	↑ or nl	↓ or nl	↑ or nl

(p) The cardiac index is sometimes thought to be a more reliable indicator of cardiac function and may be obtained by using estimates of the patient's body surface area. It is thus possible to define mixed states in which components of cardiogenic and septic shock may exist (compare myocardial cardiogenic shock and high-output septic shock in terms of TSR and CO) or in which hypovolemia complicates cardiogenic or septic shock.

4. Choice of variables

The principles have been discussed and are summarized in Fig. 4-9.

D. Troubleshooting

1. Swan-Ganz catheter (Table 5-1)
2. CO monitoring (Table 5-2)

Table 5-1. Troubleshooting guide for Swan-Ganz catheter.

Problem	Possible causes	Interventions
No waveform displayed on oscilloscope	Incorrect stopcock position	Correct stopcock position
	Transducer dome loose, air in dome	Tighten transducer to dome, flush air from dome.
		Flush entire system to irrigate catheter and maintain patency.
	Poor transducer connection to plug in	Check to see that all connections are secure and properly aligned.
	Clot in catheter lumen causing total occlusion	Aspirate fluid from catheter, and irrigate with flush solution. May help to use small syringe (e.g., tuberculin syringe). IF YOU CANNOT ASPIRATE FLUID, DO NOT IRRIGATE.
	Faulty dome	Change dome
	Faulty transducer	Check function of transducer with mercury manometer system. Change transducer if faulty.
All waveforms appear damped (RAP, PAP, PWP). Reduction in the amplitude of the pulmonary artery pressure. Waveform appears more rounded, with loss of distinct characteristics.	Flush bag not fully inflated to 300 mm Hg	Check bag pressure and reinflate to 300 mm Hg.
	Presence of air in dome	Flush air from dome.

Continued.

Table 5-1. Troubleshooting guide for Swan-Ganz catheter—cont'd.

Problem	Possible causes	Interventions
Reduction in the amplitude of the pulmonary artery pressure. Waveform appears more rounded, with loss of distinct characteristics—cont'd	Presence of air bubbles in catheter lumen or intraflow system	Check system systematically for air bubbles; aspirate air if present.
	Catheter kinked (Catheter may have coiled in right atrium or during insertion; occurs more frequently with smaller catheters.)	If catheter coiling is suspected, confirm with chest x-ray film. Notify physician. With balloon deflated, physician will slowly withdraw catheter to eliminate coil and reinsert.
		Should recoiling occur, it may be helpful to instill iced saline to make catheter less pliable.
	Catheter lumen partially occluded with blood	Aspirate fluid from catheter. Irrigate with flush solution.
		Check flush system to ensure proper functioning and continuous catheter irrigation.
	Catheter occluded by wall of pulmonary artery	Have patient cough and deep breath; roll patient from side to side.
		Flush catheter slowly with small amount of solution. Solution injected with high pressure can damage vessel walls. Chest x-ray film will confirm catheter position. May need to withdraw catheter 1 to 2 cm.

Oscilloscope does not display PCWP when balloon inflated. (Pulmonary artery pressure [PAP] waveform appears normal.)	Insufficient amount of air used to inflate balloon	Deflate balloon and reinflate with proper amount of air.
	Catheter not be far enough into pulmonary artery to allow "wedging" to occur.	Present waveform will be different from earlier ones. Catheter may need to be advanced, but only if sterility has been maintained. Chest x-ray film will confirm position.
	Balloon ruptured	If balloon is ruptured, no resistance will be met during attempted inflation. DO NOT INJECT ANY MORE AIR IF BALLOON RUPTURE IS SUSPECTED; could cause air embolus. Notify physician.
		Blood may be seen at balloon inflation valve with balloon rupture.
		Overinflation or extended inflation of balloon may result in its rupture. Latex balloon absorbs blood lipoproteins, causing a loss of elasticity and increasing possibility of rupture.
		Use a syringe large enough to allow proper inflation, but small enough to prevent over-inflation of balloon Balloon inflation should never exceed 2 cc.

Continued.

Table 5-1. Troubleshooting guide for Swan-Ganz catheter—cont'd.

Problem	Possible causes	Interventions
Oscilloscope does not display PCWP when balloon inflated. (Pulmonary artery pressure [PAP] waveform appears normal.)—cont'd	Ballon ruptured—cont'd	It is recommended that PCWP be measured no more frequently than every 4 hours (unless ordered by physician.) Excessive balloon inflation increases elasticity loss, predisposing balloon to possibility of rupture.
		Syringe used for inflation should be disconnected between uses to prevent inadvertent balloon inflation. Keep inflation valve in open position at all times.
		It is recommended that catheter be used no longer than 48 hours.
Continuous PCWP waveform.	Balloon may have been kept inflated.	Deflate balloon, keep inflation valve in open position between uses, and disconnect syringe.
No characteristic PAP waveform when catheter is only partially wedged. Amplitude of PAP wave form will decrease reduction in systolic pressure. Diastolic pressure will remain unchanged.	Continuous PWP waveform is sometimes mistaken for a damped waveform.	Troubleshoot damped waveform as previously described.
	Catheter may have migrated into a distal branch of pulmonary artery and assumed a wedge position while balloon is deflated; subsequent risk of pulmonary infarction is possible.	Change position of patient. Roll patient from side to side. Have patient cough and deep breathe. Confirm position with chest x-ray film.

	Catheter migration can occur at anytime, but most frequently occurs in the first few hours after insertion. This is primarily caused by excess catheter loop in the right ventricle and increased catheter pliability from blood warming.	Withdraw catheter in 2 to 3 cm increments until good PAP waveform is obtained.
Significantly less volume of air required to produce wedge pressure.	Wedging can also occur as result of changes in patient positioning and changes in lung volume.	Inflate balloon only as necessary and record amount of air required to wedge catheter.
	Catheter tip too peripheral in pulmonary circulation	Catheter will need to be withdrawn until a wedge pressure is recorded with near maximal balloon volume.
Radical changes in PAP and PCWP readings	Inaccurate transducer calibration	Recalibrate equipment. Check transducer function with mercury manometer system.
	Transducer not at level of right atrium (phlebostatic level).	Reposition and level transducer. Mark chest at level of right atrium with felt-tip pen to ensure consistent readings.
	Air or blood in transducer dome	Flush blood or air from dome.
	Tubing not in horizontal position	Tubing falling to floor can change pressure reading. Keep tubing coiled and secured in horizontal position.

Continued.

Table 5-1. Troubleshooting guide for Swan-Ganz catheter—cont'd.

Problem	Possible causes	Interventions
Radical changes in PAP and PCWP readings—cont'd.	Reading taken with patient in different position	Consistently take readings with patient in same position. Readings are inaccurately low with patient at a 90-degree angle or with legs dangling. Accurate readings can be obtained with patient sitting up to a 45-degree angle.
	"Overwedging" of catheter	Record balloon volume required for inflation to prevent inadvertent over inflation.
		If PCWP is recorded at a low balloon volume but inflation is continuous, resultant pressure reading will be falsely high. This is thought to be caused by increased pressure of over-inflated balloon in catheter tip. As balloon is inflated, systolic pressure will continue to rise on oscilloscope.
	Changes in lung volume	Pressure readings should be averaged during several respiratory cycles.
	The normal, minimal changes of systolic and diastolic pressures during respiration will be significantly increased in	Take readings at end of expiration.

the presence of lung disease or severe heart failure or with use of mechanical ventilation.

When high pressures or large volumes are used with mechanical ventilation, PWP will be elevated during positive pressure phase, or as patient receives each mechanical breath. Additionally, the use of (CPAP) increases PWP relative to amount of continuous airway pressure applied.

Waveform of higher amplitude

Displacement of catheter tip into right ventricle. Recognized when there is no change in systolic pressure but diastolic pressure drops into range of mean RAP. Catheter can flip in and out of right ventricle into pulmonary artery. Generally, ventricular irritability will be seen when this occurs.

If ventricular irritability occurs, balloon should be inflated and advanced to pulmonary artery, provided sterility has been maintained.

Have lidocaine ready. Notify physician.

If catheter cannot be advanced, it should be withdrawn into right atrium. Care should be taken that balloon is deflated so tip can pass freely through heart valves. Balloon should be deflated whenever catheter is withdrawn, whether it be from pulmonary artery to right ventricle, or right ventricle to right atrium

Table 5-2. Troubleshooting guide for cardiac output monitoring

Source	Cause	Identification	Remedy
Nonreproducible CO measurements			
Hemodynamic	Arrhythmias (PVC, atrial fibrillation)	ECG	Do not inject during PVCs. Rarely, may need to use alternative method for obtaining CO.
Hemodynamic	Tricuspid valve regurgitation—allows for retrograde indicator flow—indicator loss	Irregular thermodilution curve shape.	Use alternative method for obtaining CO.
Hemodynamic	Mechanical ventilation can cause pronounced changes in intrathoracic pressures—cyclic changes in venous return, thus—changes in CO.	Sine wave baseline blood temperature pattern on the thermodilution curve.	Perform five or six CO measurements. Use 10 ml of iced injectate to increase signal-to-noise ratio. Obtain CO at same point in respiratory cycle (data will be skewed to reflect CO during one part of respiratory cycle).
Catheter	Catheter "whip", generally caused by hemodynamic instability, turbulent flow within heart.	Pressure waveform "fling." Irregular thermodilution curve shapes.	Obtain chest x-ray film to verify position. Reposition catheter. Use 10 ml of iced injecate. Perform five or six CO measurements.
Catheter	Catheter thermistor against wall of pulmonary artery or migration of catheter tip out to a	Wide variations in COs, interspersed with 0.00 readings and ridiculously high COs. Ir-	Reposition catheter into main branch of PA. Wedging should occur with 1 to 1.5 ml of air.

branch of PA—thermistor cannot "see" indicator.	regular or nonexistent curves. If catheter has migrated, balloon will wedge with less than 1 to 1.5 ml of air.	(Check package insert.)
Catheter	Catheter body looped in right ventricle—thermistor in ventricle, not pulmonary artery.	Irregular curve caused by inadequate mixing. Catheter's insertion depth markings indicate that an unrealistically long section of catheter is in the patient.	Obtain chest x-ray film to verify loop in right ventricle. Withdraw and readvance catheter so tip is in main branch of pulmonary artery.
User technique	Uneven injectate bath sampling (if iced syringes are used)	Ice may not be evenly distributed around injectate bath. Some syringes are allowed to cool longer than others.	Ensure that bath is evenly chilled. Allow adequate time for all syringes to cool (45 to 60 minutes).
User technique	Injections are uneven. Varied rates of injection between consecutive determinations.	Curves are not smooth and vary from one determination to another.	Inject smoothly and rapidly (less than or equal to 4 seconds).

CO lower than expected

Hemodynamic	Recirculation of indicator from a ventricular septal defect—overestimation of area is seen.	Multiple peaks on curve.	Use alternative method for obtaining CO.
Catheter	Catheter is kinked, knotted, and/or partially obstructed by thrombus at right atrium port—injectate delivered too slowly—too great a curve area.	Curve shows slow, irregularly ascending portion with "normal," more rapid curve descent. Kinking and knotting are seen on chest x-ray film.	Prevent thrombus formation with intermittent or heparinized flush. Remove knot or kink.

Continued.

Table 5-2. Troubleshooting guide for cardiac output monitoring—cont'd.

Source	Cause	Identification	Remedy
CO lower than expected—cont'd.			
User error	Injectate volume in syringe is too large.		Choose syringe size with total volume as close as possible to injectate volume.
User error	Incorrect computation constant (CC) (set too low)	Compare CC dialed into computer with CC listed for particular catheter, volume, and temperature of injectate.	Dial in correct CC. To salvage any COs already performed: $$CO\ wrong \times \frac{CC\ right}{CC\ wrong} = CO\ right$$
User technique	Injectate solution injected much too slowly	Slow, sustained ascending portion of curve with "normal" more rapid decay is observed.	Deliver injectate smoothly and rapidly (10 ml in less than 4 seconds).
CO higher than expected			
Hemodynamic	Very large heart with low stroke volume.	Very long (up to 20 seconds) lag period before onset of curve. Also, low-amplitude curve with slow return to baseline.	Use "delayed START" method.
Catheter	Catheter thermistor against wall of pulmonary artery or migration of catheter tip out into branch of artery. Both problems result in unusually high		Withdraw catheter to a main branch of pulmonary artery. Wedging should occur with 1 to 1.5 ml of air. (Check package insert.)

User technique	CO readings (10 to 60 L/min), usually interspersed with 0.00 readings. Irregular or nonexistent curves. If catheter has migrated, balloon will wedge with less than 1 to 1.5 cc of air. Injectate volume in syringe is too small.		Assure that volume injected is correct.
User technique	Incorrect CC (set too low).	Compare dialed-in CC with the appropriate CC.	Dial in correct CC to salvage any COs already performed. Use above-listed formula.
User technique	Actual injectate temperature not as cold as indicated by injectate probe in bath.	(1) Injectate is not positioned in solution prepared identically to injected solution. (2) Overhandling of syringe barrel.	(1) Follow proper procedure for injectate bath preparation. (2) Do not handle syringe barrel. Remove syringe from bath, connect it to injection port, press "START," and inject immediately.
User technique	Uneven injection technique—computer may ignore any indicator injected following pause in delivery.	Irregular curve (may have multiple peaks).	Inject smoothly and quickly.

Continued.

Table 5-2. Troubleshooting guide for cardiac output monitoring—cont'd.

Source	Cause	Identification	Remedy
CO higher than expected—cont'd.			
Hemodynamic	Low flow state (approx. 2 L/min) where the heart has low stroke volume—delayed curve onset of as much as 20 seconds following injection and initiation of "START."	9520: Curve fails to fall to 30% of peak amplitude before it resets (in 40 seconds). Curve is low amplitude and returns to baseline very slowly. 9520A: The 9520A will not begin to integrate curve without first determining certain minimum change in blood temperature in first 12 seconds—computer will reset (0.00 displayed), because it has determined that no curve is coming.	Use "delayed START" technique.
Catheter	Catheter thermistor against wall of pulmonary artery or migration of catheter tip out into a branch of artery.	Unusually high CO readings (10 to 60 L/min), interspersed with 0.00 readings. Irregular or nonexistent curves. If catheter has migrated, lumen will wedge with less than 1 to 1.5 ml of air.	Withdraw catheter to a main branch of pulmonary artery. Wedging should occur with 1 to 1.5 ml of air. (Check package insert.)
User technique	Injection made into distal lumen	9520A: Minimum area criterion must be met within 12 seconds, or computer will reset.	Inject into right atrium port.
User technique	Delayed injection		Inject immediately after initiating "START."

SUGGESTED READINGS

American College of Surgeons: Manual of surgical intensive care, Philadelphia, 1977, W.B. Saunders Co.

American College of Surgeons: Early care of the injured patient, ed. 2, Philadelphia, 1976, W.B. Saunders Co.

Anderson, R.J., et al.: Nonoliguric acute renal failure, N. Engl. J. Med. **296:**1134, 1977.

Applefeld, J.J., et al.: Assessment of the sterility of long-term cardiac catheterization using the thermodilution Swan-Ganz catheter, Chest **74:**377, 1978.

Berk, J.L.: Monitoring the patient in shock, Surg. Clin. North Am. 55:713, 1975.

Boyd, D.R.: Monitoring patients with posttraumatic pulmonary insufficiency, Surg. Clin. North Am. **52:**31, 1972.

Danielson, R.A.: Differential diagnosis and treatment of oliguria in post-traumatic and postoperative patients, Surg. Clin. North Am. **55:**697, 1975.

Espinel, C.H.: The FENa test: use in the differential diagnosis of acute renal failure, JAMA **236:**579, 1976.

Gallagher, T.J., Augenstein, J.S., and Civetta, J.M.: Monitoring of respiratory function in critical care patients, Surg. Clin. North Am. **60:**1437, 1980.

Gardner, R.M., et al.: Percutaneous indwelling radial-artery catheters for monitoring cardiovascular function, N. Engl. J. Med. **290:**1227, 1974.

Golden, M.D. (editor): Intensive care of the surgical patient, ed. 2, Chicago, 1981, Year Book Medical Publishers, Inc.

Levy, M.N.: The cardiovascular physiology of the critically ill patient, Surg. Clin. North Am. **55:**483, 1975.

Rosen, A.J.: Shock lung: fact or fancy? Surg. Clin. North Am. **55:**613, 1975.

Sise, M.J., et al.: Complications of the flow-directed pulmonary-artery catheter: a prospective analysis in 219 patients, Crit. Care Med. **9:**315, 1981.

Swan, H.J., and Ganz, W.: Use of balloon flotation catheters in critically ill patients, Surg. Clin. North Am. **55:**501, 1975.

Tooker, J., Huseby, J., and Butler, J.: The effect of Swan-Ganz catheter height on the wedge pressure–left atrial pressure relationship in edema during positive-pressure ventilation, Am. Rev. Resp. Dis. **117:**721, 1978.

Tietjen, G.W., Gump, F.E., and Kinney, J.M.: Cardiac output determinations in surgical patients, Surg. Clin. North Am. **55:**521, 1975.

Toussaint MacLaren, G.P., Burgess, J.H., and Hampson, L.G.: Central venous pressure and pulmonary wedge pressure in critical surgical illness, Arch. Surg. **109:**265, 1974.

Pardy, B.J., and Dudley, A.F.: Comparison of pulmonary artery pressures and mixed venous oxygen tension with other indices in acute haemorrhage: an experimental study, Brit. J. Surg. **64:**1, 1977.

Wilson, R.S., and Rie, M.A.: Management of mechanical ventilation, Surg. Clin. North Am. **55:**591, 1975.

PART II

RESTORATION AND MAINTENANCE OF METABOLIC FUNCTION

Metabolic response to injury

Frank B. Cerra

The systemic inflammatory response (SIR) is an integral part of the metabolic response to injury.

A. Several agents activate the systemic inflammatory response.
   1. Microorganisms
   2. Dead tissue
   3. Injured tissue
   4. Certain resolving hematomas—pelvis, retroperitoneum
   5. Antigen-antibody reactions
   6. Severe perfusion derangements
B. Physiologic, metabolic, and clinical end-organ responses then occur (Figs. 6-1 and 6-2).
C. The activator-mediator-responder relationship forms the basis of modern treatment regimens for SIR.

The systemic septic response

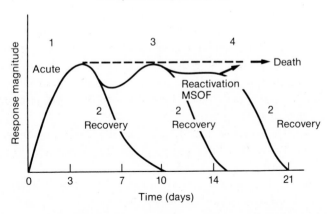

Fig. 6-1. Stages of metabolic response to injury are depicted for sepsis. Eventually, organ failure occurs, frequently ending in death.

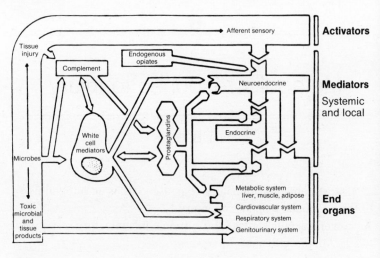

Fig. 6-2. End-organ responses represent clinical expressions after modulation by mediator systems. Activators "activate" mediators and include dead and injured tissue, perfusion deficits, and invading microorganisms.

D. *Sepsis,* a clinical term, describes the clinical manifestations of systemic inflammation by which the host responds to an invading microorganism.

END-ORGAN RESPONSE

A. Staging
   1. The time course of an end-organ responses is predictable and can be divided into stages.
   2. Because a patient can initially be seen at any stage, part of the clinical problem becomes deciding which stage the patient is in. Staging facilitates diagnosis and therapy and is useful in prognosis.
   3. The acute stage (phase 1) occurs with the onset of injury (Fig. 6-1).
      a. The response usually peaks on day 2 to 3 postinjury.
      b. The patient then enters phase 2 and continues there until recovery is complete.
      c. If the injury is severe enough, the patient enters the pathway toward death (see Fig. 6-1).
      d. Some patients have a reactivation (phase 3) of the systemic response, heralding either:

(1) A new focus of infection from which, if it is controlled, the patient will recover; *or*

(2) Onset of the multiple-system organ failure process (phase 4).

B. Clinical findings of SIR

The systemic response is a host-dependent one and therefore is *not* dependent on the type of invading organism. The diagnosis of sepsis requires the presence of at least one invading microorganism to which the host is having a systemic response. The significant discriminating variables for predicting the presence of an outcome from sepsis are metabolic. These include plasma levels of such compounds as lactate, lactate/pyruvate ratio, acetoacetate/beta-hydroxybutyrate ratio, proline, tyrosine, phenylalanine, and methionine.

No clear delineations exist between phases. Rather, transitions occur and eventually culminate in clinical settings characteristic of each phase and on which a statistical definition can then be placed (Fig. 6-1).

1. The clinical manifestations are nonspecific and reflective of the physiologic/metabolic response.

a. With a worsening response, the following tend to occur:

(1) More metabolic encephalopathy

(2) More fever and leukocytosis

(3) More tachycardia, hyperventilation, and signs and symptoms of increased sympathometic tone

(4) The eventual onset of organ failures

(5) A usually consumptive coagulopathy with significant thrombocytopenia and abnormal coagulation tests, sometimes with bleeding

(6) Spontaneous bacteremias, frequently polymicrobial

(7) Commonly gastrointestinal tract mucosal atropy and ulceration, perhaps representing the source of the bacteremias

(8) Peripheral neuropathies

b. These clinical findings are not necessarily specific of sepsis, because they are more characteristic of inflammation in general than of sepsis.

   c. The primary response seems to occur at the cell met-
      abolic level. The best way to describe the metabolic
      characteristics may be to contrast them with the ref-
      erence state of starvation.
C. The metabolic response
   1. A starvation problem is present when the organ system
      is not able to get sufficient amounts of carbohydrate, fat,
      and protein at the cellular level. Once in the cells, the
      nutrient substrate is used normally. The etiologies of the
      failure to achieve adequate input are primarily those of
      gastrointestinal tract obstruction, infection such as *Can-
      dida* stomatitis or esophagitis, and malabsorption or mal-
      digestion.
      a. Preferential fuel
         Each organ has a preferential fuel, that is, a substrate
         that it prefers to use for energy production.
         (1) *Glucose* is the primary substrate for the brain
             and red blood cells.
         (2) *Fatty acids* are preferred by the heart, liver, and
             skeletal muscle.
         (3) *Ketone bodies* (acetoacetate and beta-hydroxy-
             butyric acid) are preferred by the heart and skel-
             etal muscle and, after adaptation, by the brain.
         (4) Branched chain *amino acids* (BcAA) (leucine, iso-
             leucine, and valine) have a moderate preference
             in skeletal muscle; the nonbranched chains have
             a moderate preference in liver.
      b. Overall metabolic characteristics (Fig. 6-3)
         (1) There is reduced resting metabolic expenditure.
         (2) The neurohumeral system provides little active
             metabolic regulation.
         (3) Glucose is the predominant fuel early; fat as ke-
             tone bodies and fatty acids become the main fuel
             with time (in days).
         (4) New glucose comes from amino acids after he-
             patic glycogen is used up.
         (5) The regulation is responsive to exogenous sub-
             strate; for example, adding glucose, fat, or amino
             acids individually or in combination acts to re-

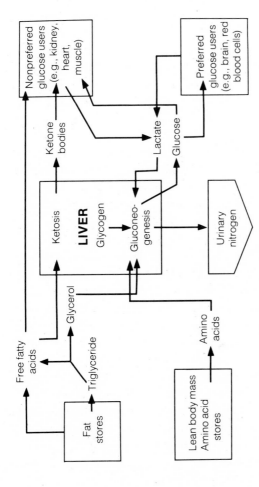

Fig. 6-3. Acute nonstress fasting metabolism. Initial flow of substrate is designed to provide glucose for obligate and nonobligate glucose users. With time, ketones and fats become main energy substrates, resulting in a reduction in daily urinary nitrogen excretion.

duce new glucose formation and the mobilization
of fat and amino acids.

c. Metabolic details (see Fig. 6-3)

(1) The system makes glucose available for all tissues.

(a) Hepatic glycogen only lasts a few hours.

(b) *Gluconeogenesis* occurs from amino acids,
and nitrogen is excreted in the urine.

(2) The relatively low insulin levels promote *lipolysis*.

(a) *Free fatty acids* become a fuel source for
nonpreferred glucose users and become
available in the liver for ketone body formation.

(b) *Ketone body* production increases, and ketones become the predominant fuel. With
time, the brain also uses it as a fuel.

(c) *Glycerol* (a sugar) serves as a gluconeogenic
substrate. With time, renal gluconeogenesis
becomes prominent.

(3) *Amino acids* are mobilized, serving as gluconeogenic fuel. The BcAA are also oxidized in the peripheral (nonhepatic) tissue.

(4) The *protein-sparing mechanisms* that develop (in
days) act to conserve protein and reduce urinary
nitrogen loss.

(5) The *respiratory quotient*, the ratio of CO_2 produced to O_2 consumed starts high (0.9 to 1.0),
indicating predominant glucose oxidation, and
falls to the 0.6 to 0.7 range, indicating predominant fat oxidation.

d. Nutrition support principles.

By supplying the necessary substrates in the right
combinations, the net rates of lypolysis, proteolysis,
and gluconeogenesis can be reduced (protein-sparing
therapy) or can be converted to the "fed" or anabolic
state. This later state of full nutritional support has
both positive nitrogen and caloric balance. If calories
are supplied in excess, fat formation (lipogenesis) oc-

curs and the respiratory quotient exceeds 1, CO_2 production increases, and fat sometimes deposits in nonfat tissue (fatty liver). *Exercise* stimulates nitrogen retention and helps to produce a positive nitrogen balance.

2. Altered metabolic states

   Altered metabolism exists when, from the reference of starvation, substrate use is altered even though substrate supply is adequate. Such states are now known to exist in settings of surgical stress, cancer, cirrhosis, sepsis, and possibly in liver failure and during pregnancy (Table 6-1).

   a. *Surgical stress* runs a spectrum of response from low (level 0) to high (level 3) (Table 6-2). The magnitude of the response depends on the stimulus (level 0 in starvation vs. level 3 during sepsis) and on host factors. Once activated, the response runs a regulated time course and abates unless a new stimulus (more surgery or a complication) ensues.

      (1) Mediator systems.

         The onset of tissue injury or infection activates the mediator systems that subsequently modulate the cellular metabolic machinery (Table 6-3 and Fig. 6-2).

Table 6-1. Origin of reduced lean body mass

	Starvation	Metabolic disorder* (trauma/sepsis)
Resting energy expenditure	−†	+ +
Respiratory quotient	Low (0.7)	High (0.85)
Mediator activation	−	+ + +
Regulatory responsiveness	+ + + +	+
Primary fuels	Fat	Mixed
Proteolysis	+	+ + +
Branched chain oxidation	+	+ + +
Hepatic protein synthesis	+	+ + +
Ureagenesis	+	+ + +
Urinary nitrogen loss	+	+ + +
Gluconeogenesis	+	+ + +
Ketone body production	+ + + +	+

*The disorders run a spectrum; a midrange value is used in this comparison.
†−, reduced; +, increased in scale (+, little to + + + +, great).

Table 6-2. The stratification of stress*

	Stress level and clinical example			
	0 (Nonstressed starvation)	1 (Elective surgery)	2 (Polytrauma)	3 (Sepsis)
Urinary nitrogen loss (g/day)	<5	5 to 10	10 to 15	>15
Plasma lactate ($\mu M/L$)	100 ± 50	1200 ± 200	1200 ± 200	2500 ± 500
Plasma glucose (mg/dl)	100 ± 20	150 ± 25	150 ± 25	250 ± 50
Oxygen consumption index (ml/M^2)	90 ± 10	130 ± 6	140 ± 6	160 ± 10
Glucagon/insulin	2 ± 0.5	2.5 ± 0.8	3.0 ± 0.7	8 ± 1.5

*Mean ± standard deviation.

Table 6-3. Metabolic effects of various mediators

Mediator	Muscle	Liver	Adipose	Lipolysis	Carbohydrate metabolism Glycogenolysis	Gluconeogenesis	Protein metabolism Proteolysis
Cortisol	Enhances proteolytic effects of other mediators	Promotes gluconeogenesis	Enhances catecholamine-mediated lipolysis	++	−	+++	+++
Catecholamine	Glycogenolysis Proteolysis	Glycogenolysis	Lipolysis	++++	++++	++	+
Glucagon	Mobilizes amino acid pools, protein degradation	Activates glycogenolysis and gluconeogenic enzymes		+++	++	+++	+
Growth hormone			Mobilizes fat	++	−		−
White cell mediators	Thermogenesis by altering their hypothalamic control Mediates proteolysis	Increase uptake of amino acids, increase synthesis of acute phase reactants				+	+++
Prostaglandins	Mediate proteolysis Modulate insulin effects on muscle	May activate/ deactivate metabolic enzymes	Mediate antilipolytic effect, lipolytic effects	++	++	++	+++

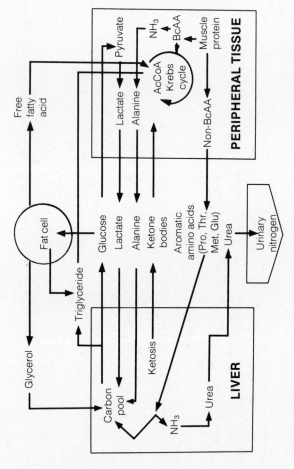

Fig. 6-4. Moderate-to-severe stress metabolism. Gluconeogenesis becomes less suppressible; there is increased oxidative use of the BcAA. There is increased use of carbohydrate, fat, and amino acids as fuel sources. If stimulus persists, result is a rampant form of acquired protein-calorie malnutrition.

(a) Activation of the *neurohumoral* (autonomic and humoral) systems promotes glycogenolysis, gluconeogenesis, proteolysis, and lipolysis.

(b) *Mediator activation* also produces or enhances these end-organ responses. Such mediators include endotoxin, leukocyte endogenous mediator, complement, prostaglandin, and peptides of various lengths.

(2) Metabolic characteristics

The mediators modulate the *metabolism* to a degree that relates to the level of stress. The more activation there is, the more end-organ response occurs. The result is a spectrum of response that changes with time. Initially there is a lag or ebb phase in which little response is demonstrated. The flow or response phase then begins, peaks 3 or 4 days after stress, and usually abates in 5 to 7 days. The precise characteristics vary with patient and stimulus, but the overall pattern is the same. If the response does not spontaneously abate, a complication is usually present that is frequently septic in nature. Thus exact metabolic characteristics seen vary with time in any given case. The process is dynamic.

(a) General characteristics of stress metabolism (see Figs. 6-4 and 6-5, Tables 6-1 and 6-2)

   i. Stress metabolism is a dynamic, changing process.

   ii. Resting energy expenditure increases.

   iii. The respiratory quotient ranges from 0.8 to 0.88, indicating the use of carbohydrate, fat, and protein as fuels.

   iv. *Amino acid* requirements are increased to meet energy demands and the increased demands of hepatic protein synthesis.

   v. Urinary nitrogen loss is increased; the degree of loss depends on the existing

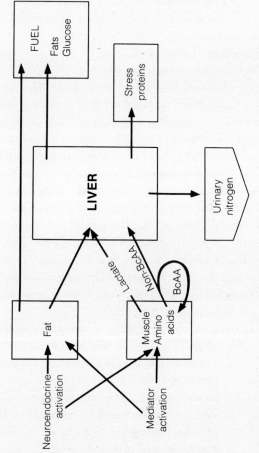

Fig. 6-5. Moderate-to-severe stress metabolism. Neuroendocrine and intrinsic mediator systems modulate metabolic machinery to mobilize fat and amino acid stores to provide a continuous supply of substrate for production of stress protein. Increased urinary nitrogen excretion is one result of process.

level of stress and the preexisting muscle mass.

vi. The suppressibility of the process relates inversely to the level of stress. The more stress there is, the less the processes of lipolysis, proteolysis, and gluconeogenesis are suppressible by the exogenous administration of glucose, fat, or amino acids.

(b) Details of stress metabolism

i. Fat and amino acids are mobilized rapidly and simultaneously. The BcAA are oxidized mainly in the periphery; the non-BcAA are used as fuel and synthetic substrate in the liver. All amino acids are used to meet the synthetic demands of acute-phase protein production. Urea production increases and urinary nitrogen excretion rises. The increased proteolysis is reflected in the increased urinary excretion of 3-methylhistidine (3-MeH).

ii. There is increased use of fatty acids and triglycerides as fuel as stress increases. In late sepsis, the ability to clear triglycerides decreases and hypertriglyceridemia and lipemia can occur. At this time the respiratory quotient may exceed 1, indicating net lipogenesis and increased CO_2 production. Other reasons for the triglyceride intolerance include reduced lipoprotein lipase activity in fat and muscle and possibly altered intracellular transport related to carnitine deficiency or malfunction.

iii. Gluconeogenesis increases and becomes harder to suppress. The mass flow of glucose to the periphery as well as its uptake by the cell either alone or in response to insulin remains normal. However, much more glucose is converted to lactate instead of being oxidized to CO_2 and water.

iv. The increased lactate production, in the absence of a problem with oxygen transport, is accompanied by an increase in pyruvate so that the lactate/pyruvate ratio remains within a reasonably normal range.

v. Ketone bodies are produced by the liver, but not to the extent seen in starvation. In addition, the β-hydroxybutyrate/acetoacetate (BOHB/AcAc) ratio rises, indicating some fall in mitochondrial redox potential.

vi. The dynamic nature of the response is reflected in the changing substrate patterns. A patient proceeds through the various levels of stress on the way to recovery or to death. Thus a patient may start at level 1, move to level 2, and then to level 3 and return to an earlier level as the response abates.

vii. In late sepsis leading to death, hepatic protein synthesis fails and a cellular energy production/utilization problem becomes apparent. It is as if there were a sequential fuel failure of glucose, then fat, and then amino acids.

3. Multiple system organ failure (MSOF) seems to represent the late metabolic sequalae of the systemic inflammatory process and carries a high mortality rate.

a. It also exists in stages (Table 6-4).

b. At a point, the metabolic changes are irreversible and death inevitably results, frequently taking 14 to 28 days.

c. Characteristics of transition to MSOF:

(1) A propensity to develop hepatic cholestasis and hepatic steatosis occurs in most patients.

(2) Frequently biliary sludging and sometimes acalculous cholecystitis occur.

(3) The plasma amino acid profile becomes very similar to that in cirrhotic hepatic failure.

(4) The liver also shows an associated decrease in amino acid clearance. Hence, the plasma levels of most amino acids rise, particularly those of phenylalanine, tyrosine, methionine, threonine, and proline.

(5) The BOHB/AcAc ratio decreases.

(6) Hepatocyte culture and Kupffer cell coculture systems demonstrate a macrophage-mediated alteration in protein synthesis.

(7) Hepatic failure is believed to be the dominant organ failure at this point and to be the major contributor to mortality.

(8) Gut malnutrition is usually present with the attendant changes in gut microflora induced by the disease process and chronic administration of antibiotics.

(9) Triglyceride intolerance occurs or worsens, frequently necessitating the elimination of triglycerides from the nutrition regimen.

Table 6-4. Criteria for early and late MSOF

Parameter	Early	Late (liver failure present)
Mentation	Light coma	Deep coma
Respiratory distress syndrome	Present	Advanced
Bilirubin	3-4 mg%	>8 mg% and rising
Creatinine	2-3 mg%	>3 mg% and rising
BUN/Cr ratio	Normal	↑ (off nutrition)
Muscle mass	±	Autocannibalism
Lactate	1.5 mmol/L	>2 mmol/L
BOHB/AcAc Ratio	Normal	Increased
Phenylalanine	<80 M/L	>80 M/L
Triglycerides (12 hr fasting)	<250 mg%	>250 mg%
O_2CI	>160 ml/M^2	<130 ml/M^2
VCO_2	<5 ml/kg	>5 ml/M^2
N-balance (on nutrition)	Equilibrium or positive	>5 g/day

(10) At this point, the transition to the clinical syndrome of MSOF has been made.
  d. Settings for transition to MSOF
    (1) Persistently uncontrolled source(s) of infection
    (2) New source(s) of infection
    (3) Persistent oxygen transport deficit
    (4) Pre-existing or developing malnutrition
    (5) Pre-existing liver disease or immunosuppression
    (6) Prolonged period of circulatory shock that precedes the sepsis or occurs with it
  e. Staging MSOF
    (1) Given the clinical findings and the observed metabolic alterations, it is possible to stage the degree of MSOF (see Table 6-4).
    (2) Likewise, one can quantitatively grade the degree of metabolic stress and clinically stratify patients so that similar kinds of patients can be studied and prognostic probabilities given (see Table 6-2).
D. Physiologic changes
  The changes in physiology reflect the changes in metabolism. The physiologic changes appear to at least reflect the direct influence of the mediator systems and the indirect influence of the increased cellular metabolic demands imposed by the systemic metabolic response. Precisely what fraction of the physiologic response is derived from these two driving forces is unclear. Which organ or organ system is a principal consumer is also unclear: liver, heart, white cell, macrophage, muscle. Fig. 6-6 summarizes the physiologic responses; Fig. 6-7 summarizes the metabolic correlates.
  1. Initial physiologic response
    a. Vascular capacity increases.
    b. The existing blood volume necessary to maintain ventricular preload and systemic perfusion increases. Generally, the resuscitation volume necessary to restore perfusion is nearly twice that of the normal blood volume.
    c. The systemic vascular resistance falls to an inappropriately low level for the existing level of cardiac out-

put. This afterload-reducing effect is characteristic of the mediated response states, particularly sepsis.

d. The decrease in vascular resistance and the increase in vascular capacity are intimately related.

e. The rapid emptying of the pulmonary blood volume with the associated acute worsening of the pulmonary shunt is an adverse effect.

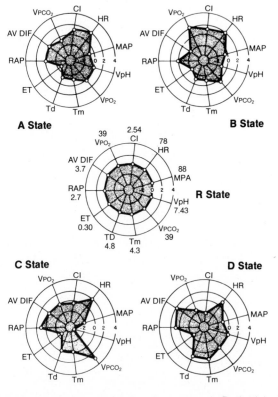

Fig. 6-6. Heavy circle in central polar plot represents R physiologic state. Mean values for each of the physiologic parameters among patients classified in R state are shown. In corners are polar plots of means of physiologic parameters in states A, B, C, and D. Each parameter has been normalized in terms of standard deviations from its mean value in R state. *CI*, cardiac index (L/min/M^2); *HR*, heart rate (beats/min); *MAP*, mean arterial pressure (torr); *VpH*, venous pH; *VPCO_2*, venous CO_2 tension (torr); *VPO_2*, venous O_2 tension (torr); *Tm*, cardiac mixing time (sec); *Td*, pulmonary dispersive time (sec); *ET*, cardiac ejection time (sec); *AV DIF*, A-VO_2 difference (vol%); and *RAP*, right atrial pressure (cm H$_2$O). (From Simmons, R.L., and Howard, R.J., eds.: Surgical infectious disease, New York, 1982, Appleton-Century-Crofts, p. 318.)

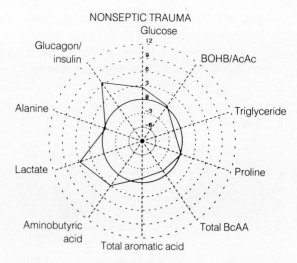

Glucose 5.5 ± 2 mM/L
BOHB/AcAc 5 ± 1
Trig. 1200 ± 150 μM/L
Proline 204 ± 43 μM/L
Total BcAA 450 ± 169 μM/L

NONSTRESSED CONTROL
mean ± SD

TAA 119 ± μM/L
ABU 3 ± 2 μM/L
Lactate 600 ± 152 μM/L
Alanine 332 ± 269 μM/L
Glg./Ins. 2 ± 0.5

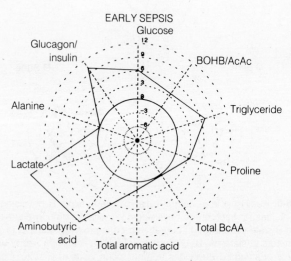

Fig. 6-7. Dark inner circle represents mean value for each variable (on radians) from fasting, nonstressed man. Each dotted circle then represents 3 or 4.5 standard deviations from that control mean. Plotted on this grid are mean values for each variable at peak metabolic response for nonseptic trauma, cirrhosis with surgery, and sepsis. The states thus become statistically defined.

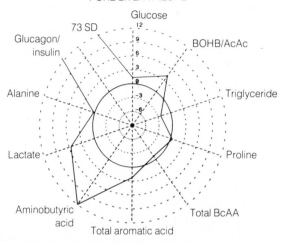

PURE LIVER FAILURE

Glucose 5.5 ± mM/L
BOHB/AcAc 5 ± 1
Trig. 1200 ± 150 μM/L
Proline 204 ± 43 μM/L
Total BcAA 450 ± 169 μM/L

NONSTRESSED CONTROL

mean ± SD

TAA 119 ± μM/L
ABU 3 ± 2 μM/L
Lactate 600 + 152 μM/L
Alanine 332 ± 269 μM/L
Glg./Ins. 2 ± 0.5

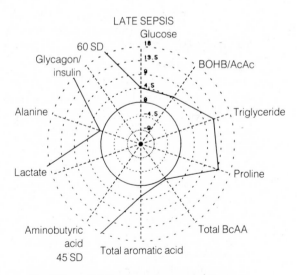

Fig. 6-7, cont'd. For legend see opposite page.

    f. Failure of the high cardiac output, low systemic vascular resistance state to develop usually indicates inadequate fluid resuscitation, preexisting myocardial dysfunction, or acquired myocardial failure.

    g. High cardiac output seems to be nutrient in nature.

        (1) O_2 consumption is usually twice that of normal.

        (2) Flow-dependent oxygen consumption is observed until the high cardiac output state is achieved.

        (3) Lactate/pyruvate ratios remain elevated until the high-flow state is achieved.

        (4) Patients who cannot mount and/or sustain this high output state have an increased mortality.

2. Intermediate physiologic response

    a. As the process continues, central venous hemoglobin desaturation fails to occur.

    b. The high cardiac output initially compensates, and the high V_{O_2} and V_{CO_2} are maintained. The arteriovenous oxygen content then becomes inappropriately narrow for the existing level of cardiac output.

    c. This phenomenon continues, and the total body oxygen consumption falls despite large volumes of oxygen delivery to the periphery.

    d. Although the precise nature of the cellular regulation occurring and/or the defects present are unclear, the primary needs appear to be oxygen and fuel substrate.

    e. Initial therapy is aimed at restoring oxygen transport.

3. Late physiologic response

    a. In the late MSOF or late sepsis phase, abnormal processes appear, including:

        (1) Increased oxygen delivery

        (2) Reduced resistance

        (3) Increasing oxygen consumption

        (4) Respiratory quotient over 1

        (5) Triglyceride intolerance

        (6) Increased lactate level with a normal lactate/pyruvate ratio

    (7) Rising plasma amino acid levels, particularly the hepatically cleared amino acids

    (8) A rising BOHB/AcAc ratio

    (9) Unrestricted ureagenesis

  b. At this point, energy availability and substrate utilization seem to become abnormal and a full deficit seems to exist.

  c. Hepatic failure seems to become the prominent feature.

THE MEDIATORS

The mediator systems involved are complex. The following all seem certain about the mediator systems:

1. That they are involved; that they control the degree and duration of the metabolic response; and that their interaction is poorly understood (see Fig. 6-5).

2. The central nervous system, autonomic outflow, white cell-macrophage microendocrine systems, and the classic macroendocrine systems are involved in the activation, maintenance, and abatement of the systemic metabolic response. Precisely how those systems interact or are regulated is unclear.

3. Other metabolic products that have regulatory capacity also seem to be present, such as octopamine, interleukin 1-a (IL1-A), products of malnutrition (e.g., carnitine deficiency), and as yet undiscovered agents.

PRINCIPLES OF METABOLIC SUPPORT

The concept of activator-mediator-responder provides a useful framework within which to discuss current treatment regimens and future treatment research.

Activator control

The first principle of activator control is to remove or control the source of the activator and to prevent the occurrence of new sources.

A. Source control

  1. Early, aggressive surgery is frequently necessary.

2. Invasive line management protocols assume a central role in the daily care regimens.
3. Because pulmonary complications are some of the most frequent, aggressive pulmonary management is essential to:
   a. Keep the functional residual capacity at an appropriate level
   b. Promote good toileting of secretions
   c. Treat infections
   d. Care for artificial airways
   e. Maintain appropriate airway patency
      (1) Early ambulation and keeping the chest upright are useful measures even in the presence of active mechanical ventilation.

B. Antibiotics
   Antibiotics are a mainstay of source control in settings in which dividing microorganisms are involved.
   1. Appropriate monitoring is necessary to assure correct doses and a minimum of complications.
   2. Because drug interactions are becoming a major problem in the modern critical care unit, daily input from a trained pharmacist is essential.
   3. There is renewed interest in the use of oxygen as an antibiotic.

Mediator control

The primary means of controlling mediator activity is controlling the source of the mediator. Antimediator pharmacologic therapy is now in various stages of testing. After considerable interest in steroids and at least one encouraging clinical trial, a prospective randomized clinical trial is now nearly completed. New trials of other antimediators or mediator regulators are beginning. Other approaches such as immune stimulation with vitamin A and the use of such antioxidants as vitamin E are still experimental.

Responder support

A. Because the primary substrate support is oxygen, the first objective is always to restore and maintain oxygen transport.

1. This seems best done by objective criteria:
   a. No-flow dependent oxygen consumption
   b. Appropriate level of existing oxygen consumption
   c. A normal lactate/pyruvate ratio. Because other means of regulating pH are usually in use the measurement of pH alone is frequently inadequate, and lactate and pyruvate levels become useful parameters.
2. Once restored, oxygen transport does not remain a primary determinant of survival, as long as delivery and demand are equal.
3. The principles involved are:
   a. To keep a PaO_2 that gives at least 95% saturation at a hemoglobin of 13 g%.
   b. Then to adjust the cardiac output until the criteria of adequacy are maintained. Because of the data on oxygen as an antibiotic, maintaining higher PaO_2 may be desirable in some settings.
4. Once oxygen transport is restored and can be maintained, the remaining principles are designed to improve efficiency, to borrow from one organ to pay another, and to minimize complications.
   a. These principles involve the following manipulations:
      (1) To keep the FIO_2 under 60%
      (2) To keep the mean airway pressure under 35 cm H_2O
      (3) To minimize myocardial work by the appropriate balance of preload, afterload reduction, and inotropic support
   b. Critical care patients with sepsis develop protein calorie malnutrition as a principal manifestation of the mediated metabolic response. In patients who were previously malnourished or remain hypermetabolic, this rapidly developing malnutrition is felt to be a major contributing factor to morbidity, mortality, and length and expense of subsequent rehabilitation.
      (1) The mediator systems change the substrate needs and fuel requirements from those of standard starvation.

      (a) Amino acid requirements increase to meet the needs of increased protein synthesis and the increased use of amino acids as oxidative fuels.

      (b) The ability to use glucose as an energy source becomes limited in sepsis.

      (c) Fat is increasingly relied on as an energy source until late in the MSOF process.

  (2) With appropriate stratification for the degree of metabolic stress, the nutritional requirements can be determined (Table 6-5).

      (a) When this type of metabolic support is used, many of the complications of nutritional support are no longer significant problems, and end-organ responses are improved.

      (b) The end-organ support, however, is not optimal, with under 50% of patients achieving nitrogen equilibrium, under 40% with adequate support of the visceral proteins, and under 15% with adequate support of indices associated with improved survival.

Table 6-5. Estimated substrate requirements

	Stress level			
	Starvation	**2 (Low)**	**3 (Early)**	**3 (Late)**
Nonprotein calorie-nitrogen ratio (kcal/g N)	150/1	100/1	100/1	80/1
Amino acids* (g/kg/day)	1	1.5	2	2.0 to 2.5
Total nonprotein calories (kcal/kg/day)	25	25	30	35
Total calories (kcal/kg/day)	28	32	40	50
Fractional requirements of total daily caloric load				
Amino acids (%)	15	20	25	30
Glucose (%)	60	50	40	70
Fat† (%)	25	30	35	—‡

*For currently available amino acid formulas; the amount will vary somewhat with the brand of amino acid supplement used.

†For commercially available intravenous fat preparations composed primarily of long-chain triglycerides.

‡Hypertriglyceridemia present.

(3) Further research undertaken on the higher levels of stress has indicated the following:

    (a) Increased efflux of most amino acids from muscle and visceral stores toward the liver.

    (b) Increased use of amino acids as direct oxidative fuels. This seemed particularly so for the branched chain amino acids in skeletal muscle.

    (c) Increased hepatic extraction of most amino acids early in the course of the response, with reduced extraction late in the course of the response, particularly for phenylalanine, methionine, tyrosine, cysteine, threonine, serine, alanine, and glutamine.

    (d) A potential hepatotoxic effect correlating with the large load of non-BcAAs being processed by the liver.

(4) In accordance with these observations, the amino acid solutions were redesigned to:

    (a) Increase the delivery of those amino acids with a demonstrated increased demand for protein synthesis and oxidation

    (b) Reduce the delivery of those amino acids with a reduced demand and/or potential toxic effect

    (c) Provide a final formula that would allow delivery with a reasonable volume of solution

(5) After 7 days of therapy, the modified amino acid group data demonstrated that, relative to standard amino acids

    (a) Nitrogen retention was improved and was proportionate to the amino acid load.

    (b) The higher plasma transferrin levels reflected improved visceral protein status.

    (c) The higher lymphocyte counts and lower anergy rates reflected improved general status.

(6) The effects observed were independent of the route of administration, because they were observed after enteral or parenteral administration of appropriate product.

WHAT'S NEW

A. Manipulating hormone milieu

Potentially, the hormone milieu can be manipulated so as to favor those factors tending to promote survival.

B. Source control by activator controls

With the advent of antibody production by bacterial cultures, the possibility of developing "magic bullets" has become a clinical reality.

1. Monoclonal antibody against the common internal core lipopolysaccharide/lipid A region was found to have high affinity and to be protective across five gram-negative organisms in a mouse model of intravenous gram-negative bacterial sepsis.

2. A very preliminary human study indicates possible efficacy.

3. Prospective randomized clinical trials are currently in progress.

C. Sources of alternate fuels

1. Alternate fat sources

   a. In vivo and in vitro models have demonstrated a potential immune-inhibitory effect of the parenteral long-chain fatty acid triglyceride emulsions.

   b. These effects are not observed with the medium-chain fatty acid triglyceride emulsions.

   c. Early clinical studies with intravenous medium-chain fat formulations are showing excellent clearance, utilization as an energy source, and absence of clinical toxicity.

2. High-energy phosphate levels are low when measured in the setting of late sepsis-MSOF.

   a. In experimental settings, failure to regenerate adenosine monophosphate (AMP) in ischemic liver injury is associated with a serum glutamic oxaloacetic transaminase leak and a reduction in amino acid clearance.

   b. In postischemic myocardium, where the regeneration of AMP is likewise a problem, the administration of ribose was associated with an increased AMP and adenosine 5′−triphosphate production and an improvement in systolic function.

c. Consequently, the use of ribose and other hexose shunt fuels such as sorbitol and xylitol are under intense investigation.

D. The gut's role in pathogenesis

The evidence is mounting that the gut may play a prominent role in the pathogenesis of the persistent hypermetabolic state.

1. In the presence of ischemic colonic ulcers, this phenomenon is easy to understand.
2. Other evidence indicates, however, that a relationship may exist in the absence of mucosal ulcers.
3. Potential effectors include:
   a. Gut malnutrition
   b. Alterations in gut microflora from nonuse
   c. Alterations in flora from certain types of feedings and/ or antibiotics.
   d. Bacterial overgrowth of the small intestine with an increased toxic load to the liver.
   e. Possible Kupffer cell activation and induced hepatocyte dysfunction.
4. For these reasons, together with fewer complications and lower cost, early, aggressive enteral nutrition with tubes distal to the pylorus are becoming the dominant mode of nutritional support in this group of patients.

SELECTED READINGS

Abrams, J., Barke, R., and Cerra, F.B.: Quantitative evaluation of clinical course in surgical ICU patients: the data conform to catastrophe theory, J. Trauma 24:1028, 1984.

Askanzai, J., et al.: Nutrition and the respiratory system, Crit. Care Med. 10:163, 1982.

Askanzai, J., et al.: Respiratory changes induced by the large glucose loads of total parenteral nutrition, JAMA 243:1444, 1980.

Attebery, H.R., Sutter, V.L., and Finegold, S.M.: Effect of a partially chemically defined diet on normal human fecal flora, Am. J. Clin. Nutr. 25:139, 1972.

Baracos, V., et al.: Stimulation of muscle protein degradation and prostaglandin E_2 release by leukocyte pyrogen: a mechanism for the increased degradation of muscle proteins during fever, N. Engl. J. Med. 308:553, 1983.

Biesel, W.R., and Wannemacher, R.W., Jr.: Gluconeogenesis, ureagenesis and ketogenesis during sepsis, JPEN 4:277, 1980.

Blackbourn, G.L., et al.: Branched chain amino acid administration and metabolism during starvation, injury and infection, Surgery **86**:307, 1979.

Cerra, F.B.: Hypermetabolism, organ failure and metabolic support surgery. (In press.)

Cerra, F.B.: Profiles in nutritional management: the trauma patient (Monograph), Chicago, 1982, Medical Directions.

Cerra, F.B., and Hassett, J.H.: Vasodilator therapy in clinical sepsis with low output syndrome, J. Surg. Res. **25**:180, 1978.

Cerra, F.B., et al.: Branched chain metabolic support: a prospective, randomized, double-blind trial, Ann. Surg. **199**:3, 1984.

Cerra, F.B., et al.: Nitrogen retention in critically ill patients is proportional to the branched chain load, Crit. Care Med. **11**:775, 1983.

Cerra, F.B., et al.: Septic autocannibalism: a failure of exogenous nutritional support, Ann. Surg. **192**:570, 1980.

Cerra, F.B., et al.: Correlations between metabolic and cardiopulmonary measurements in patients after trauma, general surgery, and sepsis, J. Trauma **19**:621, 1979.

Cerra, F.B., et al.: The hepatic failure of sepsis: cellular versus substrate, Surgery **86**:409, 1979.

Cerra, F.B., et al.: Branched chains support postoperative protein synthesis, Surgery **92**:192, 1982.

Chernow, B., Rainey, T.G., and Lake, C.R.: Endogenous and exogenous catecholamines in critical care medicine, Crit. Care Med. **10**:409, 1982.

Clowes, G.H.A., Jr., George, B., and Ryan, N.T.: Induction of accelerated proteolysis and amino acid release from skeletal muscle by a potent nonprotein factor in the plasma of septic patients. In McConn, R., editor: Role of chemical mediators in the pathophysiology of acute illness and injury, New York, 1982, Raven Press, pp. 327-341.

Clowes, G.H.A., Jr., et al.: Muscle proteolysis induced by a circulating peptide in patients with sepsis or trauma, N. Engl. J. Med. **308**:545, 1983.

Demetriou, A., et al.: Effects of vitamin A and beta carotine on intra-abdominal sepsis, Arch. Surg. **119**:161, 1984.

Dietze, G.J., et al.: Evidence for an involvement of kinins and prostaglandins in the modulation of the action of insulin induced by changes in the energy state in skeletal muscle tissue. In McConn, R., editor: Role of chemical mediators in the pathophysiology of acute illness and injury, New York, 1982, Raven Press, pp. 297-315.

Dunn, D.L., Bogard, W.C., and Cerra, F.B.: Murine monoclonal antibodies against endotoxin: comparison of type specific and cross reactive clones, Surgery; In press.

Fath, J., et al.: Alterations in amino acid clearance during ischemia predicts hepatocellular ATP changes, Surgery; In Press.

Hassett, J., et al.: Multiple systems organ failure: mechanisms and therapy, Surg. Ann. **14**:27, 1982.

Heideman, M., and Hugli, T.: Anaphylatoxin generation in multiple systems organ failure, J. Trauma **24**:1038, 1984.

Iapichino, D., et al.: The main determinants of nitrogen balance during total parenteral nutrition in critically ill injured patients, Intensive Care Med. **10**:251, 1984.

Kaufman, B., and Rachow, E.C.: Relationship between O_2 delivery and consumption during fluid resuscitation of hypovolemic and septic shock, Chart **85**:336, 1984.

Keys, A., et al.: The biology of human starvation, Minneapolis, 1950, University of Minnesota Press.

Kinney, J.M.: The effect of injury on metabolism, Br. J. Surg. **54**:435, 1967.

Knighton, D.R., et al.: Oxygen tension regulates the expression of angiogenesis factor by macrophages, Science **221**:1283, 1983.

Long, C.L., et al.: Muscle protein catabolism in the septic patient as measured by 3-methylhistidine excretion, Am. J. Clin. Nutr. **30**:1349, 1977.

Madoff, R.D., et al.: Prolonged intensive care: worth the price? Arch. Surg. **120**:698, 1985.

Moyer, E.D., et al.: Multiple system organ failure. VI. Death predictors in the trauma-septic state—the most critical determinants, J. Trauma **21**:862, 1981.

Moyer, E.D., et al.: Multiple systems organ failure. III. Contrasts in plasma amino acid profiles in septic trauma patients who subsequently survive and do not survive—Effects of intravenous amino acids, J. Trauma **21**:263, 1981.

Mullin, T.J., and Kirkpatrick, J.R.: Substrate composition and sepsis, Arch. Surg. **118**:176, 1983.

Oppenheim, J.J., et al.: Lymphokines: their role in lymphocyte responses: properties of interleukin I, Fed. Proc. **41**:257, 1982.

Rodemann, H.P., and Goldberg, A.L.: Arachidonic acid, prostaglandin E2 and F2 influence rates of protein turnover in skeletal and cardiac muscle, J. Biol. Chem. **257**:1632, 1982.

Shoemacher, W.C., and Apple, P.L.: Use of physiologic monitoring to predict outcome and to assist clinical decisions in critically ill, Am. J. Surg. **146**:43, 1983.

Siegel, J.H., and Cerra, F.B.: Physiological and metabolic correlations in human sepsis, Surgery, **86**:163, 1979.

Waxman, K., Nolan, L., and Shoemacher, W.C.: Sequential perioperative lactate determination, Crit. Care Med. **10**:96, 1982.

Weissman, C., et al.: Amino acids and respiration, Ann. Intern. Med. **98**:41, 1983.

West, M.A., et al.: Pure Kupffer cells mediate a biphasic modulation of hepatocyte protein synthesis after exposure to septic stimulae. Surgery, **98**:388, 1985.

Wiles, J., and Cerra, F.B.: The systemic septic response: does the organism matter? J. Crit. Care Med. **8**:55, 1980.

Wilkons, T.D., and Long, W.R.: Changes in the flora of the cecal mucosa of mice fed a chemically defined diet, Bacteriol. Proc. **71**:113, 1971.

Wilmore, P.W., et al.: Effect of injury and infection on visceral metabolism and circulation, Ann. Surg. **192**:491, 1980.

Wilmore, P.W., Mason, A.P., Jr., and Pruitt, B.A., Jr.,: Impaired glucose flow in burned patients with gram-negative sepsis, Surg. Gynecol. Obstet. **143**:720, 1976.

7

Acid-base balance

Jon Berlauk

ARTERIAL BLOOD GASES

While a thorough understanding of blood gas physiology is desirable, the critical care physician can resort to simple and practical guidelines to interpret arterial blood gas (ABG) data. By systematically approaching each value in the ABG report (i.e., $pH/Pco_2/HCO_3^-$), the physician can interpret the patient's acid-base status without the use of nomograms. In essence, this method keys on the Pco_2.

1. The measured pH is observed. This is ultimately the most important value. Any therapeutic maneuvers should be directed to "normalizing" pH, not Pco_2 or HCO_3^-.
2. The measured Pco_2 is used to calculate a predicted pH. This is correlated with the measured pH.
3. The HCO_3^- is used to predict normal compensation versus abnormal metabolic derangements.

Principles

A. The pH
   1. Normal values
      a. For ABG analysis, assume that $Pco_2 = 40$ torr (mm Hg) and $pH = 7.40$ are absolute normal values. Respiratory alkalosis is the only primary acid-base disorder that will be fully compensated for. If a patient's body is allowed to normally compensate for a primary acid-base disorder, he or she will never overcompensate (i.e., the pH will determine if the primary disorder is an acidotic or alkalotic disorder). However, once therapeutic interventions are instituted, the measured pH may reflect overzealous iatrogenic compensa-

tion. Unfortunately, most patients in a critical care setting are subject to numerous assaults on acid-base physiology, so ABG data must be correlated with therapy.

    b. Initially, the pH value determines whether the patient is alkalotic or acidotic.

B. The P_{CO_2}

    1. Fluctuations in P_{CO_2} result in nearly instantaneous and, more importantly, predictable changes in blood pH.

    2. The measured P_{CO_2} is treated as though the change from normal P_{CO_2} were acute, and the following rules are applied.

        a. Rule 1: An acute increase in $P_{CO_2} = 10$ torr will decrease the blood pH $= 0.05$ unit.

        b. Rule 2: An acute decrease in $P_{CO_2} = 10$ torr will increase the pH $= 0.1$ unit.

        c. Using these two equations, one can readily predict a pH, assuming changes in P_{CO_2} alone are responsible for pH changes.

           (1) If the predicted and measured pH correlate well, an acute respiratory disorder is present.

           (2) If the predicted and measured pH are 180 degrees opposite, a primary metabolic disorder exists.

           (3) If the predicted pH and measured pH do not correlate, but are both acidotic or both alkalotic, several possibilities exist.

              (a) Renal compensation has occurred.

              (b) The patient has a combined disorder (i.e., respiratory alkalosis and metabolic alkalosis). The combined disorders are immediately evident from ABG data, because the measured pH will be even more acidotic or alkalotic than the pH predicted by the P_{CO_2}.

              (c) A mixed acid-base disorder exists (i.e., respiratory acidosis with metabolic alkalosis). These disorders are often more difficult to discern; consequently the critical care physician often resigns himself or herself to a less than complete interpretation of the ABG data or relies on a nomogram.

C. Blood bicarbonate
  1. Blood bicarbonate is the principal buffer against drastic changes in pH that would occur with changes in P_{CO_2}.
  2. This buffering occurs in two steps.
      a. A rapid re-equilibration of HCO_3^-, as described by the Henderson-Hasselbalch equation, occurring in minutes
      b. Regeneration of HCO_3^- through renal mechanisms, which occurs over 24 to 36 hours
      c. The following rules apply.
          (1) Rule 3: An acute increase in P_{CO_2} = 10 torr will be buffered by an increase in $HCO_3^- \simeq 1$ mEq/L. (Upper limit: $HCO_3^- \simeq 30$ mEq/L)
          (2) Rule 4: An acute decrease in P_{CO_2} = 10 torr will be buffered by a decrease in $HCO_3^- \simeq 2.5$ mEq/L. (Lower limit: $HCO_3^- \simeq 18$ mEq/L)

ABG ANALYSIS

Rule 1: An acute increase in P_{CO_2} = 10 torr will decrease blood pH $\simeq 0.05$ unit.

Rule 2: An acute decrease in P_{CO_2} = 10 torr will increase the pH $\simeq 0.1$ unit.

Rule 3: An acute increase in P_{CO_2} = 10 torr will be buffered by an increase in $HCO_3^- \simeq 1$ mEq/L. (Upper limit: $HCO_3^- \simeq 30$ mEq/L)

Rule 4: An acute decrease in P_{CO_2} = 10 torr will be buffered by a decrease in $HCO_3^- \simeq 2.5$ mEq/L. (Lower limit: $HCO_3^- \simeq 18$ mEq/L)

Rule 5: A chronic increase in P_{CO_2} = 10 torr will be compensated by an increase in $HCO_3^- \simeq 2.5$ to 3.5 mEq/L. (Upper limit: $HCO_3^- \simeq 45$ mEq/L)

Rule 6: A chronic decrease in P_{CO_2} = 10 torr will be compensated by a decrease in $HCO_3^- \simeq 5$ mEq/L.

Rule 7: Metabolic acidosis—expected P_{CO_2} = 1.5 (HCO_3^-) + 8 ± 2; also, usually P_{CO_2} = last two digits of the pH.

Rule 8: Metabolic alkalosis—an increase in HCO_3^- = 10 will cause a rise in $P_{CO_2} \simeq 6$ torr. (Upper limit: P_{CO_2} = 55 torr)

Rule 9: A pH change = 0.1 pH unit is equivalent to 6 to 7 mEq HCO_3^- per liter of HCO_3^- distribution.

Rules 3 and 4 give an estimation of Henderson-Has-selbalch re-equilibration.

 (3) Rule 5: A chronic increase in P_{CO_2} = 10 torr will be compensated by an increase in HCO_3^- ≈ 2.5 to 3.5 mEq/L. (Upper limit: HCO_3^- ≈ 45 mEq/L)

 (4) Rule 6: A chronic decrease in P_{CO_2} = 10 torr will be compensated by a decrease in HCO_3^- ≈ 5 mEq/L. (Lower limit: HCO_3^- ≈ 12 to 15 mEq/L)

 Rules 5 and 6 give a prediction of renal compensation.

D. Summary

 1. All decreases in P_{CO_2} cause a greater magnitude of change in pH or HCO_3^- than do increases in P_{CO_2} (i.e., alkalosis > acidosis).

 2. Most changes are in fractions of 10 (i.e., 1/10, 5, 2.5, etc.).

 3. Interpretation of ABG data by the just-described method assumes that the acid-base problem is respiratory (P_{CO_2}) and that compensation occurs via a renal mechanism. If the underlying pathologic condition is metabolic in origin, compensation would obviously now occur via the respiratory system. Use of the first two rules will quickly identify an acid-base disorder as metabolic, because the measured pH will be exactly opposite that predicted (i.e., acidotic instead of alkalotic).

 4. One cannot determine if compensation is inadequate or normal using these rules. Mixed disorders would be missed.

  a. Limits of P_{CO_2} compensation for metabolic disorders follow:

   (1) Rule 7: Metabolic acidosis—expected P_{CO_2} = 1.5 (HCO_3^-) + 8 ± 2; also, usually P_{CO_2} ≅ last two digits of the pH.

   (2) Rule 8: Metabolic alkalosis—an increase in HCO_3^- = 10 will cause a rise in P_{CO_2} ≅ 6 torr. (Upper limit: P_{CO_2} = 55 torr)

E. Deciding whether therapeutic intervention is necessary
  1. The most important value in this decision is the pH.
     a. Most of the normal physiologic compensatory mechanisms will attempt to "normalize" the pH, not the Pco_2 or HCO_3^-. The physician should do the same.
  2. Simple respiratory disorders can be easily corrected if a patient is receiving mechanical ventilation.
  3. If not, serious respiratory disorders require intervention to control ventilation.
  4. Treatment of metabolic disorders, especially metabolic acidosis, is less difficult.
     a. Rule 9: A pH change $= 0.1$ pH unit is equivalent to 6 to 7 mEq HCO_3^- per liter of HCO_3^- distribution.
     b. This rule is far from exact not only because HCO_3^- distribution varies with age but also because it varies with the underlying pathologic condition causing acidosis.
     c. For these reasons, along with the fact that the bicarbonate is injected into the intravascular space, not the "bicarbonate space," the first administration of HCO_3^- is always limited to one-third to one-half of the calculated dose.
     d. While one can accurately estimate changes in HCO_3^- because of changes in Pco_2, the reverse is not true.
     e. The only method available to determine Pco_2 after an injection of HCO_3^- is to measure to ABG levels again.

METABOLIC ACID-BASE DISORDERS
Metabolic acidosis

Of the four primary acid-base disturbances, metabolic acidosis is perhaps the most interesting. Numerous clues to the etiology of the acidosis are available via the interplay of serum anions and cations (i.e., the anion gap). Coupled with clinical information, these data often make a precise diagnosis possible.
A. Physiology
  1. Acid buffer system
     A nonstressed adult will produce between 40 and 100 mEq of acid daily as byproducts of normal intermediary

metabolism. This acid is in the form of H_2SO_4, H_3PO_4, and other minor organic acids. To buffer this continual production of acid requires extracellular buffers, predominantly HCO_3^-, intracellular buffers, and the skeletal system. Eventually the kidneys must excrete the acid and resynthesize lost HCO_3^-. Overproduction of acid, loss of buffer stores, or underexcretion of acid can disrupt this delicately balanced system. Regardless of the mechanism of acidosis, medullary chemoreceptors will respond by stimulating respiration. The resulting hypocapnia will return pH toward normal, but compensation is never complete. ABG analysis should show the adequacy of respiratory compensation. The PCO_2 should equal the last two digits of the pH. Winter's formula, a more sophisticated calculation, states: Expected PCO_2 = 1.54 $[HCO_3^-]$ + 8.6 + 1.1. If the PCO_2 falls outside these limits of compensation, a mixed disorder may exist.

2. Acid load excretion

   Acid load depends on renal tubular ability to excrete H^+ and ammonia normally. H^+ secretion occurs in both proximal and distal tubular cells and depends on intracellular production of H^+, carbonic anhydrase (CA) concentration, and PCO_2. In the proximal tubule, H^+ secretion is most dependent on PCO_2. In the distal tubule, H^+ secretion is independent of PCO_2 and mainly dependent on CA concentration. In either tubular cell, CO_2 combines with H_2O under the influence of CA. H^+ is secreted into the tubular fluid in exchange for Na^+. The HCO_3^- is reabsorbed into the blood as $NaHCO_3$ (Fig. 7-1). In the proximal tubule, H^+ in the tubular fluid will recombine with tubular HCO_3^-, and either carbonic acid or CO_2 will diffuse back into the tubular cell. However, in the distal tubule, H^+ is combined with secreted buffers to be excreted. Phosphate is the primary buffer available. Transfer of H^+ into the distal tubular lumen will continue in the face of a steep H^+ gradient to a pH $\sim$ 4.3 via this mechanism. Further H^+ secretion is then dependent on ammonia (NH_3) production. Ammonia production is dependent on intracellular K^+ concentra-

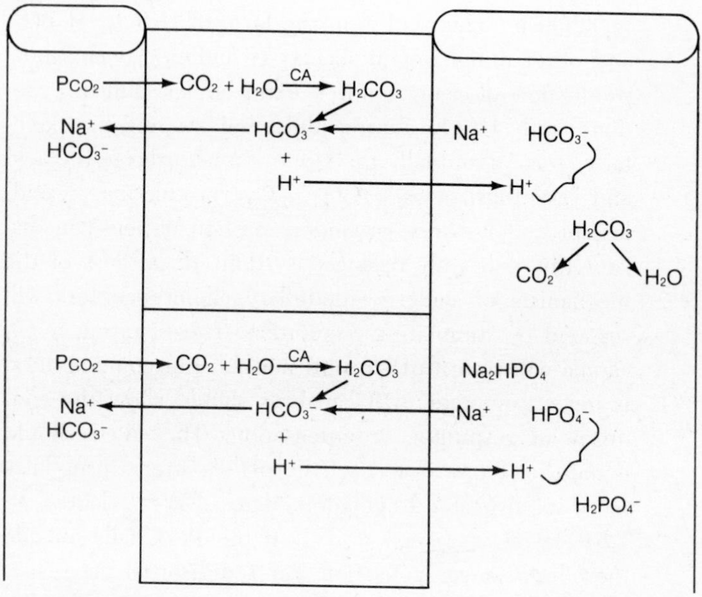

Fig. 7-1. Excretion of acid load. (*CA*, carbonic anhydrase.)

tion. Hyperkalemia inhibits ammonia formation, and hypokalemia stimulates ammonia formation as well as chloruresis. Importantly, not only is H^+ secretion necessary to excrete the acid load, this is the only available mechanism for generation of new HCO_3^-. K^+ for Na^+ exchange also occurs in the distal tubule, but new HCO_3^- is not generated and absorbed via this process.

B. Differential diagnosis

 1. The "anion gap" (AG) is a manifestation of electrolyte patterns resulting from the interplay of serum anions and cations.

   a. The AG is usually estimated using serum Na^+, Cl^-, and HCO_3^-. $AG \simeq Na^+ - (Cl^- + HCO_3^-)$.

   b. Because K^+ is usually low and fairly constant, it is ignored.

   c. The normal AG is about 12 mEq/L.

   d. One must recognize, however, that the term *anion gap* is a misnomer since it implies a normal disequilibrium between cation and anion concentration.

(1) In reality, ionic equilibrium is achieved by unmeasured anions (UA) and unmeasured cations (UC). $Na^+ + UC = (Cl^- + HCO_3^-) + UA$.

(2) The AG therefore is $UA - UC$.

e. The AG's clinical usefulness goes beyond differentiation of acidoses. An abnormal AG may suggest other disorders.

CAUSES OF INCREASED ANION GAP

A. Decreased unmeasured cation:
  1. Hypokalemia, hypocalcemia, hypomagnesemia
B. Increased unmeasured anion:
  1. Organic anions: lactate, ketone acids
  2. Inorganic anions: phosphate, sulfate
  3. Proteins: hyperalbuminemia (transient)
  4. Exogenous anions: salicylate, formate, nitrate, penicillin, etc.
  5. Incompletely identified: anion accumulating in paraldehyde, hyperosmotic hyperglycemic nonketotic coma
C. Laboratory error:
  1. Falsely increased serum sodium
  2. Falsely decreased serum chloride or bicarbonate

CAUSES OF DECREASED ANION GAP

A. Increased unmeasured cation
  1. Increased concentration of normally present cation: hyperkalemia, hypercalcemia, hypermagnesemia
  2. Retention of abnormal cation: IgG globulin, lithium, Tris buffer
B. Decreased unmeasured anion
  1. Hypoalbuminemia
C. Laboratory error:
  1. Systematic error: hyponatremia caused by viscous serum, hyperchloremia in bromide intoxication
  2. Random error: falsely decreased serum sodium, or falsely increased serum chloride or bicarbonate level

(1) Bromide intoxication

(2) Multiple myeloma

(3) Disorders of divalent cations

f. The primary use of the AG, however, remains dividing metabolic acidosis into normal vs. elevated AG (see the box below).

   (1) Whenever HCO_3^- is lost leading to metabolic acidosis, another organic anion must replace the bicarbonate to maintain equilibrium.

THE METABOLIC ACIDOSES

Normal anion gap

A. Hypokalemic acidosis
  1. Renal tubular acidosis
     a. Proximal
     b. Distal
  2. Diarrhea
  3. Posthypocapneic acidosis
  4. Carbonic anhydrase inhibitors
     a. Acetazolamide (Diamox)
     b. Mafenide (Sulfamylon)
  5. Ureteral diversions
     a. Ureterosigmoidostomy
     b. Ileal bladder
     c. Ileal ureter
B. Normokalemic/hyperkalemic acidosis
  1. Early renal failure
  2. Hypoaldosteronism
  3. Hydronephrosis
  4. HCl, NH_4Cl, ArgHCl, Lys·HCl

Elevated anion gap

A. Chronic renal failure
B. Diabetic ketoacidosis
C. Alcoholic ketosis
D. Fasting
E. Defect in gluconeogenesis
F. Aspirin intoxication
G. Paraldehyde overdose
H. Methanol poisoning
I. Ethylene glycol poisoning
J. Lactic acidosis
  1. Type A 2. Type B

---

(2) If this anion is Cl^-, it will be measured.

(3) The resultant acidosis is hyperchloremic metabolic acidosis or normal AG acidosis.

(4) All other anions are unmeasured and the AG is elevated.

(5) Normal AG acidosis can be further sub-divided into hypokalemic versus normokalemic/hyperkalemic variants.

2. Hypokalemic hyperchloremic metabolic acidosis

   a. Renal tubular acidosis

      (1) Renal tubular acidosis may be either proximal (type II) or distal (type I or classical).

      (2) Both types are characterized by bicarbonate wastage in the face of systemic acidosis.

      (3) Proximal tubular acidoses are associated with numerous phospho-gluco-amino tubular dysfunction disease states in addition to bicarbonate wastage.

         (a) An acidic urine is possible when the systemic acidosis becomes severe enough.

      (4) Distal tubular acidosis is characterized by an inability to acidify urine despite severe systemic acidosis.

      (5) In either type, the depleted HCO_3^- reserves are replaced with Cl^-.

   b. Diarrhea

      (1) Diarrhea is one of the more common causes of acidosis.

         (a) Intestinal losses of $NaHCO_3$ and $KHCO_3$ lead to extracellular fluid (ECF) hypobicarbonemia and relative hyperchloremia.

         (b) The kidneys will sense the volume loss and attempt to restore renal blood flow via Na^+ reabsorption.

         (c) The accompanying anion reabsorbed will favor the more abundant Cl^-.

         (d) The associated hypokalemia will stimulate ammoniagenesis, thus facilitating H^+ excretion.

    (e) The reparative process of new HCO_3^- generation, however, usually takes several days.

  c. Posthypocapneic acidosis

    The normal renal compensation for a chronic hypocapnia is a reduction in serum HCO_3^-. A sudden increase in P_{CO_2}, even to values near normal, would not be compensated by a commensurate rise in HCO_3^-.

  d. Carbonic anhydrase inhibitors

    Both acetazolamide (Diamox) and mafenide (Sulfamylon) inhibit carbonic anhydrase.

    (1) In the renal tubular cell this inhibition leads to loss of K^+ and HCO_3^-.

    (2) This effect of acetazolamide is used clinically to treat severe metabolic alkalosis unresponsive to conventional therapy.

  e. Ureteral diversions

    If urine is allowed prolonged contact with intestinal mucosa, the epithelium will absorb urinary Cl^- for HCO_3^-.

    (1) This is an unusual complication unless the ileal bladders are large or obstruction occurs.

    (2) It is most common following ureterosigmoidostomies.

3. Hyperkalemic/normokalemic hyperchloremic metabolic acidosis

  a. Early renal failure

    Hyperkalemia will inhibit ammonia formation, thus impairing H^+ excretion.

    (1) Renal failure is associated with expanded ECF, which will in turn depress HCO_3^- reabsorption.

    (2) Later in the course of renal failure, accumulation of organic acids leads to an elevated AG acidosis.

  b. Hypoaldosteronism

    Aldosterone stimulates both distal H^+ secretion and K^+/Na^+ exchange. A deficiency of aldosterone will lead to hyperkalemia and HCO_3^- wasting.

  c. Hydronephrosis

    Hydronephrosis as well as chronic pyelonephritis lead

to either impaired renin secretion or a refractory tubular response to aldosterone.

d. Addition of HCl, NH$_4$Cl, etc.

4. Elevated anion gap acidosis

Elevated anion gap acidosis is characterized by accumulation of an anion other than Cl$^-$. A list of the more common anions is given on p. 154.

a. Chronic renal failure (CRF)

The acidosis CRF causes is the result of a number of mechanisms resulting in decreased nephron mass, decreased H$^+$ secretion, and decreased ammonia production. Progressive damage results in accumulation of PO$_4$$^{-2}$, SO$_4$$^{-2}$, and other organic anions.

b. Diabetic ketoacidosis

c. Alcoholic ketosis

d. Fasting acidosis

(1) Obese patients are more prone to fasting acidosis.

e. Defects in gluconeogenesis

Ketosis and accumulation of acetoacetate and β-hydroxybutyrate characterize these diseases.

f. Aspirin intoxication

(1) Aspirin acts centrally to stimulate respiration while peripheral metabolism causes overproduction of acid.

(a) In adults this situation leads to a combined metabolic acidosis and respiratory alkalosis.

(b) Often children will manifest only metabolic acidosis.

(2) In addition to an elevated AG, these patients have an elevated prothrombin time.

(3) A diagnostic clue is a P$_{CO_2}$ lower than as calculated by Winter's formula.

g. Paraldehyde poisoning

h. Methanol poisoning

i. Ethylene poisoning

(1) Both methanol and ethylene glycol, found in common household products, cause severe metabolic acidosis accompanied by neurologic symptoms ranging from stupor to coma.

(2) A diagnostic clue is a measured serum osmolality 10 to 15 mOsm greater than that calculated from the Na^+, BUN, and glucose, because of the low molecular weight compounds, methanol and ethylene glycol.

$$\text{Serum osmolality} \cong 2Na^+ + \frac{BUN}{3} + \frac{Glu}{18}$$

j. Lactic acidosis
   (1) Type A
       (a) Numerous conditions of clinically apparent tissue hypoxia cause type A lactic acidosis (i.e., tissue oxygen supply does not meet tissue oxygen demand).
           i. Severe anemia
           ii. Hemorrhagic shock
           iii. Septic or cardiogenic shock
           iv. Heart failure
       (b) Normal physiologic responses to correct the inadequate cardiac output usually exacerbate poor tissue perfusion, and a vicious cycle is created.
   (2) Type B
       (a) Type B lactic acidosis results from clinically inapparent tissue hypoxia.
       (b) Numerous disorders such as diabetes mellitus, uremia, tumors, and liver failure, as well as drugs such as ethanol, biquanides, and streptozotocin interfere with normal O_2 utilization by tissues.
       (c) Possible etiologies include increased NADH/NAD ratio, inability to reoxidize reducing equivalents, or subclinical hypoxia.
C. Effects of acidosis
   The effects of acidosis are widespread. Often the physiologic response to an increased Pco_2 (respiratory acidosis) is more pronounced than a similar degree of acidosis caused by an elevated serum H^+ level, but this varies with different organ systems.

1. Vasculature

   Of greatest concern to the clinician are the effects of acidosis on the cardiovascular system.

   a. With the exception of the pulmonary vasculature, all vascular beds appear to dilate in response to acidosis (see Table 7-1).

      (1) Because acidosis does cause a release of catecholamines peripherally, direct dilation effects are attenuated or overridden.

2. Cardiac

   a. Acidosis causes direct myocardial depression.

      (1) Again, catecholamines attenuate this response until pH = 7.20.

   b. Further acidosis causes marked cardiac depression.

      (1) The mechanism of action is thought to be an alteration in the myocardial calcium cycle rather than interference with energy metabolism.

   c. Both acidosis and catecholamines cause an increase in phase 4 depolarization of the SA node leading to tachycardia.

   d. Acidosis causes pacemaker cell membrane instability that can lead to dysrhythmias.

Table 7-1. Summary of organ vascular responses to acute acidosis

		H^+	CO_2
Brain	Direct	0	− −
	Sympathetic		?
Coronary	Direct	−	−
	Sympathetic	?	?
Pulmonary	Direct	0+	0+
	Direct + hypoxia	+ +	+ +
	Sympathetic + hypoxia	+ +	+ +
Renal-splanchnic	Direct	−	− −
	Sympathetic	+	+ +
Muscle-skin	Direct	−	− −
	Sympathetic	+	+
Uterus	Direct	−?	− −
	Sympathetic	?	0

+, Vasoconstriction.
−, Vasodilation.

3. Pulmonary
   a. In the lung, pH affects both vasculature and bronchi.
      (1) CO_2 effects are more potent than H^+ effects.
      (2) However, either acidosis causes pulmonary vaso-constriction and bronchodilation.
      (3) The vasoconstrictor effect is small under normal alveolar oxygen tensions, but is greatly exaggerated by hypoxia (hypoxic pulmonary vasoconstriction).
4. Brain ECF and cerebral blood flow (CBF)
   a. The brain ECF is normally more acidic than tissue ECF.
   b. Because of the blood-brain barrier, CO_2 readily crosses into the brain while H^+ does not.
   c. Therefore, during metabolic acidosis, brain ECF will change in the same direction but not nearly to the same degree.
   d. In addition, the choroid plexus, or brain kidney, adjusts HCO_3^- in much the same way the kidney does, only more quickly.
   e. The CBF is controlled by brain ECF, not serum pH. CBF will change $\sim$ 4%/torr CO_2 change.
      (1) Because of the brain "kidney," however, changes in CBF are transient.
5. Catecholamine
   The catecholamine release caused by acidosis is partially responsible for demargination of leukocytes leading to leukocytosis.
6. Hyperkalemia
   Hyperkalemia secondary to acidosis is more apt to occur with accompanying dehydration, insulin deficiency, or CRF.
7. Hypercalcemia
   Decreased protein binding and increased mobilization of Ca^{++} from bone causes hypercalcemia.
8. Emesis
   Severe acidosis can stimulate emesis.
   a. The loss of gastric juice will ameliorate the acidosis.
D. Treatment
   1. $NaHCO_3$ therapy

a. NaHCO$_3$ therapy is the mainstay for most cases of metabolic acidosis.

b. While judicious use of NaHCO$_3$ may be lifesaving, controversy still surrounds this therapy for certain conditions.

(1) While no consensus is available as to which pH should be treated, cardiac output does begin to fall at pH = 7.20.

(2) The controversy about NaHCO$_3$ therapy revolves around treatment of diabetic ketoacidosis and most cases of type A lactic acidosis.

(a) Appropriate fluid, electrolyte, and insulin therapy alone will reverse ketoacidosis.

(b) Clinical treatment of *reversible* type A lactic acidosis results in normal metabolism of accumulated lactate to either glucose through gluconeogenesis or CO$_2$ and H$_2$O through oxidation.

(c) HCO$_3$$^-$ is a by-product of either metabolic pathway.

(d) Consequently, overaggressive HCO$_3$$^-$ therapy can lead to "overshoot alkalosis."

(e) Of concern is the inability to predict the increase in Pco$_2$ associated with NaHCO$_3$ therapy.

i. This increase in Pco$_2$ will rapidly cause a further acidification of an already acidic brain ECF.

ii. Theoretically, obtundation could occur if the brain ECF acidoses were severe enough.

(3) Another theoretic concern is the rapid shift to the left in the oxyhemoglobin curve.

(a) Acute acidosis causes a shift to the right.

(b) However, 2,3-DPG levels are diminished with chronic acidosis, essentially returning the P$_{50}$ to normal.

(c) NaHCO$_3$ therapy will correct serum pH, but "unmask" the compensation and theoretically lead to tissue hypoxia.

(4) Hypernatremia and fluid overload caused by NaHCO$_3$ therapy may be of concern in certain patients with CRF and acidosis. 1 ampule of NaHCO$_3$ contains 50 mEq Na$^+$ (1000 mEq/L).

(5) In critically ill patients, rapid shifts of intracellular calcium and potassium ions could lead to fatal arrhythmias.

    (a) Judicious use of bicarbonate is always advised.

    (b) While the "bicarbonate space" may increase as much as 200% in severe acidosis, the drug is initially injected into the intravascular space.

    (c) The effects of injecting a calculated bicarbonate deficit into this smaller space should be apparent.

Metabolic alkalosis

The hallmark of metabolic alkalosis is a sustained hyperbicarbonatemia. This can occur through loss of acid, loss of volume, exogenous bicarbonate, or imbalances in the renal-adrenal axis, usually acting through an aldosterone mechanism.

A. Physiology

Alkalinization of serum will eventually lead to alkalinization of the cerebrospinal fluid (CSF). Alkalinization of medullary chemoreceptors will depress respiration. The resulting hypercapnia will return pH toward normal, but compensation will never be complete. The PCO_2 can be expected to rise about 6 torr for each 10 mEq/L rise in HCO$_3^-$. Maximal CO$_2$ compensation is approximately 55 torr. If the measured PCO_2 falls outside these limits, a mixed disorder should be suspected.

In contrast to metabolic acidosis, in which accumulated H$^+$ is excreted entirely by tubular mechanisms, renal compensation for hyperbicarbonatemia is chiefly controlled through changes in glomerular filtration rate (GFR). Under normal conditions, bicarbonate reabsorption, like Na$^+$ reabsorption, changes directly with the GFR, resulting in little change in excreted bicarbonate. This process is probably mediated through changes in tubular size and the adequacy of H$^+$ secretion by renal tubules. Under conditions of volume depletion, the kidney will protect renal blood flow by avid Na^+ reabsorption. The accompanying anion reabsorbed will favor the more abundant HCO_3^-, leading to hyperbicarbonatemia. A vicious cycle leading to increasingly severe alkalosis would ensue were it not for the renal tubular maximum (Tm) of bicarbonate. The renal tubule maximal capacity to reabsorb HCO_3^- is approximately 27 to 29 mEq/L. A higher tubular concentration of filtered HCO_3^- is excreted. Although the respiratory compensation for alkalosis will elevate PCO_2 and the elevated PCO_2 will enhance H^+ secretion (and HCO_3^- reabsorption) in the proximal tubule (see Fig. 7-1, p. 152), this increase in HCO_3^- reabsorption is minor. Therefore, if the GFR remains constant, large amounts of HCO_3^- are excreted after the Tm for HCO_3^- is reached, preventing severe systemic alkalosis.

Additional controlling influences of HCO_3^- hemostasis exist: (1) adrenocortical hormones, (2) serum Ca^{++}, (3) serum Cl^-, and (4) the integrity of the countercurrent system in the renal medulla.

B. Differential diagnosis

The differential diagnosis of metabolic alkalosis is divided between those alkaloses which are saline responsive and those which are not (Table 7-2).

Table 7-2. Metabolic alkalosis

Saline responsive (urinary chloride level < 15 mEq/L)	Saline unresponsive (urinary chloride level > 15 mEq/L)
Diuretic therapy	Normotensive:
Cystic fibrosis	Bartter's syndrome
Gastric losses	Severe potassium depletion
Poorly absorbed anions	Refeeding alkalosis
Posthypercapneic alkalosis	Hypercalcemia/hypoparathyroidism
Villous adenoma	Hypertensive:
Exogenous alkali ingestion	Hyperaldosteronism
Massive blood transfusion	Hyperreninism
	Liddle's syndrome
	11- or 17-adrenal hydroxylase deficiency
	Licorice ingestion
	Carbenoxalone

1. If the diagnosis is not clinically evident, measurement of urinary electrolytes, particularly urine Cl^-, will aid in the diagnosis.
   a. Saline-responsive alkaloses generally have a urinary Cl^- below 15 mEq/L because of avid Cl^- retention.
   b. Saline-unresponsive alkaloses have several unique characteristics.
      (1) They exhibit tubular dysfunction caused by imbalances in the renal-adrenal axis.
      (2) Cl^- wasting is a predominant feature.
      (3) Often hypertension accompanies these alkaloses.
2. Saline responsive
   a. Contraction alkalosis
      (1) Loss of ECF leading to "contraction alkalosis" is the common denominator in the following disorders.
         (a) Diuretic therapy
         (b) Cystic fibrosis
         (c) Gastric losses
      (2) Fluid lost is rich in Cl^- and poor in HCO_3^-.
         (a) The kidneys will detect a decrease in circulating volume and avidly retain Na^+ and HCO_3^-. Diuretic therapy and cystic fibrosis usually cause only a minor alkalosis.
         (b) The stomach, however, like the kidney, is capable of net HCO_3^- synthesis if H^+ is lost through vomiting or gastric aspiration.
            i. Severe metabolic alkalosis can result from prolonged gastric losses.
            ii. HCO_3^- will be absorbed to protect RBF via proximal tubule mechanisms.
            iii. Furthermore, aldosterone release will increase both H^+ and K^+ for Na^+ exchange in the distal tubule (Fig. 7-2).
            iv. H^+ excretion results in generation of new HCO_3^-, which is reabsorbed.
            v. Hypokalemia will stimulate ammonia formation genesis, which will facilitate the H^+ excretion.

       vi. A similar aldosterone effect underlies the alkalosis of vigorous diuresis.

b. Poorly absorbed anions

Many antibiotics are poorly absorbed anions containing Na^+. Through unclear mechanisms, perhaps involving aldosterone, Na^+ is reabsorbed. This leaves the anion to be excreted with K^+ or H^+ to maintain electroneutrality.

c. Posthypercapneic alkalosis

Renal compensation for a chronic respiratory acidosis is "unmasked" when the PCO_2 is lowered to normal limits too quickly.

d. Villous adenoma

These rare colonic polyps cause a diarrhea rich in Cl^- that will lead to an alkalosis through mechanisms described under contraction alkalosis.

e. Exogenous alkalosis

f. Massive blood transfusions

Any salt of a strong acid taken in excess can overwhelm the kidneys' ability to excrete HCO_3^-.

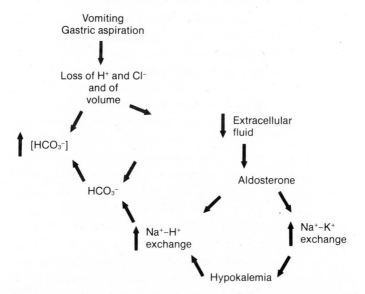

Fig. 7-2. Progression of metabolic alkalosis as a result of prolonged gastric losses.

(1) Whole blood contains large amounts of citrate as preservative.

(2) Massive transfusions can lead to severe alkalosis when the accumulated citrate is metabolized to bicarbonate.

3. Saline unresponsive

This group of disorders (Table 7-2) involves imbalances in the renal-adrenal axis and is very difficult to discuss in simplified terms. Suffice it to say that aldosterone and K^+ deletion play important roles in these mineralocorticoid alkaloses.

C. Effects of alkalosis

Too often clinicians are more concerned with a mild acidosis than with a significant alkalosis. Most of the physiologic derangements caused by alkalosis, either clinically significant or theoretic, lead to tissue hypoxia. For this reason, correction of severe alkalosis (i.e., pH > 7.55), is critical in seriously ill patients.

1. Pulmonary

a. As is true with acidosis, pulmonary bronchi and vasculature respond more dramatically to changes in P_{CO_2}, causing alkalosis than to hyperbicarbonatemia.

(1) The major effect of hypocarbia (or alkalosis) is bronchoconstriction.

(a) Presumably, this response will protect against areas of lung with high V/Q ratios.

(b) If serious pulmonary disease is present, however, this reflex could convert an area of relative shunt to an absolute shunt and increase pre-existing hypoxemia.

(c) In fact, improved oxygenation has been observed with the addition of 5% CO_2 to inspired gases in this clinical situation.

(2) In addition, both dynamic and static lung compliance decrease with hypocarbia.

(a) Whether this change is caused by decreased functional residual capacity secondary to additional areas of low V/Q or to decreased surfactant production remains unclear.

     (3) The hypoxic pulmonary vasoconstrictive reflex, which shunts blood from poorly ventilated areas of lung, is blunted with alkalosis, further aggravating hypoxemia.

2. Cardiovascular

  a. Alkalosis will cause coronary artery vasoconstriction, a response mediated via perivascular pH.

     (1) This can lead to a decrease in myocardial blood flow.

     (2) While the cardiac output may actually increase with spontaneous hyperventilation, respiratory alkalosis caused by mechanical ventilation depresses cardiac output.

     (3) This is largely caused by the effects of positive pressure ventilation.

     (4) When combined, however, with a decrease in myocardial blood flow, the depression of cardiac output may be accentuated.

     (5) Again, this could lead to tissue hypoxia.

  b. Ionic shifts in myocardial pacemaker cells are probably responsible for arrhythmias secondary to alkalosis.

     (1) These arrhythmias can occur without a history of previous heart disease.

     (2) They usually occur above pH 7.55.

     (3) They are usually more common in patients who are taking digitalis.

     (4) They are uniformly refractory to conventional antiarrhythmic therapy.

     (5) Fortunately, these arrhythmias are usually junctional or supraventricular, but they can be life-threatening.

     (6) The only effective treatment is reversal of the alkalosis.

3. O_2 consumption

Several studies have shown an increase in O_2 consumption secondary to alkalosis as high as 25% above basal levels.

   a. The mechanism appears to be an increase in phosphofructokinase enzymatic activity with an alkalotic pH.
   b. In the face of a depressed cardiac output, tissue hypoxia could result.
4. Cerebral blood flow
5. Hypokalemia
6. Hypoglycemia
   Ionic homeostasis is not only important for cardiovascular stability but also for neuromuscular function. Decreased ionized calcium leads to paresthesias and muscle spasm.
7. P_{50} shift
   A shift to the left of the P_{50} oxyhemoglobin curve causes an increased affinity for Po_2 and, again theoretically, can lead to tissue hypoxia.
D. Treatment
   1. Saline responsive
      a. Saline administration will correct hypovolemia and allow Na^+, Cl^- and HCO_3^- to enter the distal tubule in high concentration.
         (1) Here a poorly defined anion exchange mechanism retains Cl^- and excretes HCO_3^-.
         (2) The Cl^- anion is essential to the restoration of normal circulating volume.
      b. Potassium replacement
         (1) Because of severe K^+ losses, replacement of 300 to 1,000 mEq may be necessary to restore potassium balance.
            (a) Unless cardiovascular instability or emergency surgery indicates rapid replacement, it is best to avoid replacing more than 10 mEq/hour.
            (b) Rates of 40 mEq/hour or greater have been accomplished safely, but only under conditions of intensive monitoring.
      c. Acetazolamide (Diamox) therapy
         (1) Not uncommonly, critical care patients are overloaded in total body water, but alkalotic.

      (a) In these circumstances, short-term acetazol-
amide therapy is effective, provided the patient has adequate renal function.

      (b) Because both K^+ and HCO_3^- are lost via ace-
tazolamide therapy, careful attention to potassium replacement is required.

  d. Acidifying agent

In rare cases of severe alkalosis, especially if life-
threatening arrhythmias supervene, acidifying agents
may be required.

    (1) Ammonium, arginine, or lysine hydrochlorides
may be used.

      (a) These agents are metabolized, however, to
urea and HCl.

      (b) The resulting azotemia may limit their useful-
ness.

    (2) Acidification using 0.1 to 0.2 M percent HCl so-
lution is safe, provided the infusion is given via a
large cental vein and limited to 20 mEq/hour.

      (a) Frequent blood gas determinations are neces-
sary to monitor this therapy.

2. Saline unresponsive

Alkaloses that are not saline responsive defy simplistic
therapeutic intervention.

  a. Severe potassium depletion plays a prominent role in
these alkaloses, and aggressive replacement is necessary.

  b. Further therapy must be directed at the underlying
cause.

RESPIRATORY ACID-BASE DISORDERS

While metabolic acid-base disorders are produced by disturbances in organic acid production or excretion relative to bicarbonate, respiratory acid-base disorders result from alterations in
normal pulmonary CO_2 excretion.

A. Physiology

During normal intermediary metabolism, an adult will produce 15,000 to 20,000 mmol of CO_2 daily. Blood is the primary buffer for the drastic changes in pH that would nor-

mally accompany such CO_2 production. Oxyhemoglobin ($pK_a = 6.7$) is more acidic than reduced hemoglobin ($pK_a = 6.9$). This fact allows reduced hemoglobin to absorb approximately 0.7 mmol H^+ for each millimole of O_2 released without a subsequent change in pH. The hydrogen ion at the tissue level is supplied from CO_2 through the action of carbonic anhydrase.

The increased concentration of CO_2 at the tissue level facilitates the unloading of O_2 from oxyhemoglobin (Bohr effect). CO_2 diffuses into the red blood cells. In the cells, CO_2 is hydrated through the action of carbonic anhydrase. Dissociation to form H^+ and HCO_3^- follows immediately. Reduced hemoglobin buffers the H^+. The excess concentration of HCO_3^- will diffuse out of the red blood cells, and Cl^- replaces the excess to maintain electroneutrality (chloride shift). Total CO_2 is finally carried in one of four forms: (1) HCO_3^- (70%), (2) carbamino compounds (20%), (3) H_2CO_3 (<10%), and (4) a small fraction as dissolved CO_2. While both the reactions for O_2 release from oxyhemoglobin and H^+ buffering by reduced hemoglobin are thermodynamically favorable, the main driving force is the continual depletion of O_2 and the concentration gradient of CO_2.

When venous blood carrying a high total CO_2 concentration reaches the lung, the concentration gradients for O_2 and CO_2 are reversed. The reactions that occurred at the tissue level are also reversed. This time, however, reactions proceed against a thermodynamically unfavorable gradient. Here, the continual depletion of end products determines the rate and direction of reactions. Additionally, the increased concentration of O_2 facilitates the unloading of CO_2 from hemoglobin (Haldane effect).

The CO_2-carrying capacity of blood is nearly linearly related to P_{CO_2}, unlike the sigmoid relationship between oxygen-carrying capacity and P_{O_2}. Therefore, no "saturation" phenomenon for CO_2-carrying capacity is seen. The excretion of CO_2 varies directly with P_{CO_2} and alveolar ventilation. The normal lung has an enormous capacity for CO_2 excretion. Overproduction of CO_2 leading to a saturation of this excretion mechanism is unknown. Medullary chemoreceptors are exquisitely sensitive to changes in P_{CO_2} so that relatively small changes in arterial P_{CO_2} will result in dramatic changes in alveolar ventilation. This results in a sensitivity balanced system to regulate excretion to production and maintain a stable P_{CO_2}. If a person doubles his alveolar ventilation, he nearly halves his P_{CO_2} and vice versa. Any imbalance in the steady state linking excretion to production is transient. For example, an unexpected and sustained increase in alveolar ventilation not triggered by an increase in arterial CO_2 concentration will lower the alveolar CO_2 partial pressure. The lower Pa_{CO_2} will diminish the excretory gradient of CO_2 from blood to lungs; thus CO_2 release from reduced hemoglobin will become even less thermodynamically favorable. Eventually, a new steady state will be achieved but at a lower P_{CO_2}. At this point the P_{CO_2} will drop no further. The consequences of hypoventilation follow a similar logic.

B. Respiratory acidosis

Simple respiratory acidosis is characterized by an elevation of P_{CO_2}. Since renal compensation for an acute rise in P_{CO_2} requires 36 hours or more, the degree of acidemia produced by abrupt and sustained elevation in P_{CO_2} is mainly dependent on the plasma and intracellular buffers described before. Generally, a 10 torr rise in P_{CO_2} is accompanied by a 1 mEq/L rise in HCO_3^- through buffering reactions, which occur in minutes. The maximal compensation is 30 mEq/L HCO_3^-. Over a period of hours to days, the kidneys will compensate for a chronic elevation in P_{CO_2} both by reabsorbing all filtered bicarbonate and secreting H^+ in the distal tubule. H^+ combines with ammonia and is excreted, thereby generating new HCO_3^-. This excretion of H^+ and generation of HCO_3^- will compensate only to a P_{CO_2} of 60 torr. Above a P_{CO_2} of 60 torr, the urine will remain free of bicarbonate, but serum pH will rapidly fall. The impairment of H^+ excretion is probably caused by the poisonous effect of high P_{CO_2} on tubular ammonia production. Chronic compensation results in an increase in HCO_3^- of 2.5 to 3.5 mEq/L for each 10 torr rise in P_{CO_2}. The limit of compensation is approximately $[HCO_3^-] = 45$ mEq/L. This sustained reabsorption of bicarbonate must be accompanied by a chronic loss of chloride so severe hypochloremia may be present.

C. Differential diagnosis

1. The causes of respiratory acidosis could theoretically be divided into those of overproduction of CO_2 and those of underexcretion. Increased production of CO_2 to the extent of overwhelming the excretory mechanism of normal lungs is virtually unknown. Therefore, underexcretion of CO_2 either because of primary pulmonary disease or a nonpulmonary cause of hypoventilation divides the differential.

2. Various tables have divided respiratory acidosis between "central depression of ventilation" and "primary pulmonary disease." Others divide respiratory acidosis between "acute" and "chronic" causes of hypercapnia. Ultimately these classifications are less than satisfactory clinically.

3. Because the respiratory disorders all culminate in an abnormal gas exchange, the simple calculation of alveolar-arterial (A-a) gradient would better differentiate respiratory acid-base disorders.

   a. The calculation of the A-a gradient is derived from Dalton's law and is usually used to differentiate causes of hypoxemia.

$$P_{AO_2} = FIO_2 (PB - P_{H_2O}) - P_{ACO_2} \left[FIO_2 + \frac{1 - FIO_2}{R} \right]$$

   where

   P_{AO_2} is alveolar O_2 pressure
   PB is barometric pressure
   P_{H_2O} is partial pressure of H_2O
   P_{ACO_2} is alveolar CO_2 pressure

   (1) This seemingly complex equation for alveolar O_2 concentration can be reduced to

$$Pa_{O_2} = 149 - 1.2\ Pco_2$$

   if the patient is breathing room air. The only major assumption is that the respiratory quotient (R) = 0.8.

(2) If the patient is breathing inspired O_2, the equation becomes

$$Pa_{O_2} = FI_{O_2} (713) - 1.2 \ P_{CO_2}$$

since P_{H_2O} is usually 47 torr.

(3) The calculated Pa_{O_2} minus the measured Pa_{O_2} gives the A-a gradient.

(4) The normal gradient is ~10 torr because of physiologic shunt, but this gradient increases to ~20 torr with age.

(5) The causes of a widened A-a gradient (i.e., greater than 20 torr) include:

    (a) V/Q abnormality (with a myriad of causes)

    (b) Intracardiac or intrapulmonary shunt

    (c) A diffusion limitation (for O_2)

(6) All of these causes can be characterized under abnormal cardiopulmonary system.

(7) The causes of normal A-a gradient with hypercapnia include all other noncardiopulmonary reasons for hypoventilation including such diverse causes as drug overdose, neuromuscular diseases, abnormal thoracic cage, and sleep apnea.

(8) Clinically this differentiation would be useful to follow a particular ill patient.

    (a) For example: chest pain, tachypnea, hypoxemia, and an elevated P_{CO_2} is less likely to be a major pulmonary embolus if the A-a gradient did not widen from a previous calculation.

        i. One precaution must be remembered. The A-a gradient will increase with increasing FI_{O_2}, so unless an appropriate table of values is handy, interpretation of the first A-a gradient should be made on room air.

D. Effects of acidosis

The widespread effects of acidosis, both metabolic and respiratory, were listed in the metabolic acidosis section of this chapter. In many organ systems the effect of acidemia caused by elevation of P_{CO_2} is more pronounced than a similar degree of acidemia caused by accumulation of fixed acids.

E. Treatment

The therapy for respiratory acidosis is aimed at restoring alveolar ventilation and treating the underlying cause.

1. Treatment of acute and self-limited disorders may require endotracheal intubation and mechanical ventilation.

   a. If substantial renal compensation has already occurred, care should be taken to normalize the pH and not the P_{CO_2} to avoid posthypercapneic alkalosis.

   b. In the case of chronic CO_2 retention, the patient tolerates acidemia better.

      (1) Consequently, more conservative therapy is probably indicated, because these patients are notoriously difficult to wean from mechanical ventilation.

      (2) In any case, only in circumstances of severe life-threatening acidemia, when mechanical ventilatory support is not immediately available, should bicarbonate therapy be used.

F. Respiratory alkalosis

Simple respiratory alkalosis is characterized by a low P_{CO_2} induced through inappropriate hyperventilation. As in respiratory acidosis, the compensation occurs in two phases. Cellular buffering is complete in 5 to 10 minutes. Renal compensation follows later. Acute compensation for an abrupt lowering of P_{CO_2} of 10 torr is a fall in $[HCO_3^-] \cong 2.5$ mEq/L. The maximal limit of this compensation is approximately 18 mEq/L. Over a period of days, renal compensation occurs, and 5 mEq/L of HCO_3^- are lost for each sustained 10 torr drop in P_{CO_2}. With sustained hyperventilation, both plasma H^+ and CO_2 concentrations are decreased. Consequently, both factors decrease availability of renal tubule cell hydrogen ion for excretion. This will decrease proximal tubular reabsorption of bicarbonate and prevent new bicarbonate generation. Potassium (and Na^+) is lost with bicarbonate, and chloride is retained. The electrolyte pattern of hyperchloremia and hypokalemia may mimic some of the metabolic acidoses (see metabolic acidosis). The maximal limit of bicarbonate loss is 12 to 15 mEq/L. It should be noted that chronic respiratory alkalosis is the only simple acid-base disorder that can completely compensate. The reason for complete compensation is unknown.

G. Differential diagnosis

As with respiratory acidosis, numerous methods of classifying these respiratory alkalosis disorders exist.

1. Calculation of the A-a gradient will again differentiate primary disorders of the cardiopulmonary system from all other causes.

   a. This calculation can reveal serious pulmonary problems in the face of apparently adequate Po_2.

   b. On the other hand, most of the pulmonary causes of respiratory alkalosis are partially reflex in nature, because hypocapnia can occur in the absence of hypoxia.

2. Unexplained hyperventilation and respiratory alkalosis should initiate a search for peritonitis, gram negative sepsis, or aspirin intoxication.

   a. Respiratory alkalosis may be one of the earliest signs of these conditions.

H. Therapy

1. Any patient with a pH > 7.55 should have therapy directed toward treatment of the underlying disorder.

2. Symptomatic patients require more aggressive correction of their alkalemia.

   a. This may require some form of rebreathing apparatus, as simple as a paper bag or as complex as breathing 5% CO_2 via a mask or T-piece apparatus.

   b. In severe conditions when patient compliance is low or unobtainable, more extreme measures must be taken.

      (1) Acetazolamide therapy works well in metabolic alkalosis, but poorly in respiratory alkalosis because of the low tubular hydrogen ion and CO_2 concentration.

      (2) Administration of 0.1M HCl intravenously via a large central vein may be necessary.

      (3) Controlled ventilation using muscle relaxants should only be used as a last therapeutic measure.

8

Fluids and electrolytes

Jack Crumbley

Appropriately administered fluid and electrolyte therapy requires a thorough knowledge of normal body composition and the functional compartmentalization of body constituents.

CONSTITUENTS OF BODY COMPOSITION

A. Water
  1. Total body water (TBW) is the single largest constituent of the human body.
     a. Its highest concentrations occur in blood, muscle, and viscera.
     b. Lower concentrations are found in fat and connective tissues.
     c. Water content tends to decrease with age, from a high of 80% of body weight for a full-term infant to 58% in a 1-year-old child and 54% in an adult.
     d. Because of differences in body fat content, the percentage of TBW is about 10% higher in men than in women.
  2. TBW can be divided into two major compartments based on the differential concentrations of the two major cations, potassium and sodium.
     a. Potassium-rich intracellular fluid (ICF) makes up about 55% of total body water (higher in men than in women and in leaner individuals with larger muscle mass).
     b. Sodium-containing extracellular fluid (ECF) makes up 35% of TBW or 23% of body weight.
        (1) ECF can be further divided into the interstitial fluid (75% of ECF) and blood plasma (25% of ECF or 5% of body weight).

Predicted normal TBW can be calculated from the formulas for adults (see Fig. 8-1):

$$\text{Males: } \frac{\text{TBW (L)}}{\text{Body weight (kg)}} \times 100 = 79.45 - 0.24 \text{ (wt)} - 0.15 \text{ (age)}$$

$$\text{Females: } \frac{\text{TBW (L)}}{\text{Body weight (kg)}} \times 100 = 69.81 - 0.2 \text{ (wt)} - 0.12 \text{ (age)}$$

B. Electrolytes

The major electrolytes are sodium, potassium, and chloride. Total body sodium and potassium have a very tight correlation with TBW. The normal Na/K ratio is 0.85 in males and 1.0 in females, reflecting ECF and ICF volumes. The ratio rises toward 1.5 during a variety of illnesses, probably as a result of edema in trauma, sepsis, or cardiac and renal insufficiency, and/or loss of ICF volume in advanced malignancy or malnutrition.

1. Sodium

    a. Sodium is the major extracellular cation.

    b. Total body sodium amounts to 50 to 60 mEq/kg of body weight.

        (1) The exchangeable sodium is about 40 mEq/kg or 65% of total body sodium (TBNa), the remaining being very slowly exchangeable skeletal sodium.

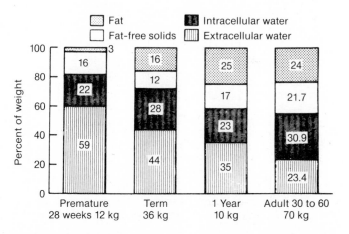

Fig. 8-1. Body composition by age. (From Randall, H.T.: Fluid, electrolyte, and acid-base balance, Surg. Clin. North Am. **56:**1019, 1976; based on data from Widdowson and Moore)

2. Potassium
   a. Potassium is the major intracellular cation.
      (1) Total body potassium is approximately 45 mEq/kg.
      (2) It can be considered fully exchangeable.
      (3) Ninety-eight percent of total body potassium is present within cells.
3. Chloride
   a. Chloride is the major extracellular anion.
      (1) Total body chloride is about 33 mEq/kg.
      (2) Ninety percent of total body chloride is extracellular.
      (3) Intracellular chloride is poorly exchangeable and is present mostly in red cells, gonads, gastric mucosa, and skin.

Fluid components

Fig. 8-2 demonstrates the approximate chemical composition of the three major fluid compartments: ICF, interstitial fluid, and plasma. Plasma and interstitial fluid differ only in plasma's higher protein content.

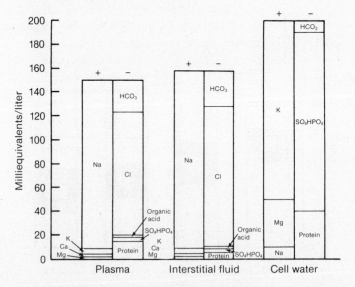

Fig. 8-2. Approximate chemical composition of body fluids. (From Randall, H.T.: Fluid, electrolyte, and acid-base balance, Surg. Clin. North Am. **56:**1019, 1976.)

Normal values

Normal serum electrolyte values vary somewhat among clinical laboratories. Reasonable values are listed in Table 8-1.

Principles governing water balance (Fig. 8-3)

A. Starling-Landis: interstitial fluid/plasma

The Starling-Landis hypothesis explains the volume equilibrium between the protein-rich plasma and interstitial fluid (Fig. 8-4).

1. Fluid flow across the capillary wall occurs as a balance between capillary hydrostatic pressure, forcing fluid out and the colloid oncotic pressure exerted by the plasma proteins tends to draw fluid in.

2. Fluid may be considered to leave at the arterial end of

Table 8-1. Normal electrolyte concentration of serum

Electrolytes	Range of normal, including laboratory-method variance	Reliability of laboratory test—95% confidence limits
Cations		
Sodium	136-145 mEq/L	± 3 mEq
Potassium	3.5-5.0 mEq/L	± 0.2 mEq
Calcium	4.5-5.5 mEq/L	± 0.1 mEq
	(9.0-11.0 mg/dl)	
Magnesium	1.5-2.5 mEq/L	± 0.04 mEq
	(1.8-3.0 mg/dl)	
Anions		
Chloride	96-106 mEq/L	± 2.0 mEq
CO_2 (content)	24-28.8 mEq/L	± 0.2 mEq
TCO_2		
Phosphorus (inorganic)	3.0-4.5 mg/dl	Considerable variance as a result of analytic problem
	(1.9 to 3.25 as $H PO_4^=$	
Sulfate (as S)	0.8-1.2 mg/dl	Method dependent
	(0.5-0.75 mEq/L as $SO_4^=$	
Lactate	0.7-1.8 mEq/L	Method dependent
	(6 to 16 mg/dl)	
Protein	6.0-7.6 gm/dl	Method dependent
	(14-18 mEq/L)	
	Depends on albumin	

From Randall, H.T.: Water, electrolytes and acid-base balance. *In* Goodhart, R.S., and Shils, M.E. (eds.): Modern Nutrition in Health and Disease, 5th ed. Philadelphia, Lea and Febiger, 1973. Used with permission.

the capillary and return at the venous end where the hydrostatic pressure is 30 torr lower.

3. With pertubations, dynamic equilibrium maintains the plasma volume.

B. Darrow-Yannet: interstitial/intercellular fluids

The Darrow-Yannet hypothesis explains volume equilibrium across the cell membrane between the interstitial and intracellular spaces.

1. In Fig. 8-5 the height of the column represents osmolarity; the width represents volume.

2. The volume flux occurs along an osmotic gradient, since the membrane is freely permeable to water.

3. Sodium is the principle regulator of extracellular fluid volume.

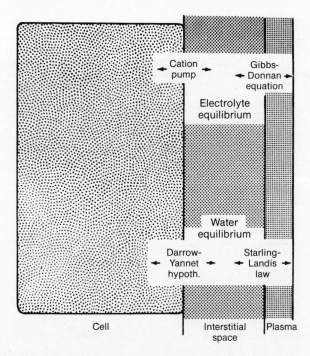

Fig. 8-3. Principles governing the electrolyte and water equilibrium between fluid compartments. (From Zimmermann, B.: Fluid and electrolyte balance in surgical patients. In Sabiston, D.C. [editor]: Davis-Christopher Textbook of surgery, Philadelphia, 1972, W.B. Saunders Co.)

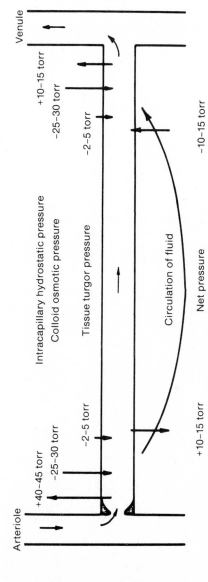

Fig. 8-4. Starling-Landis hypothesis of fluid distribution between plasma and ICF compartments. (Reproduced with permission from Pitts, R.F.: Physiology of the kidney and body fluids, 3rd edition. Copyright © 1974 by Year Book Medical Publishers, Inc., Chicago)

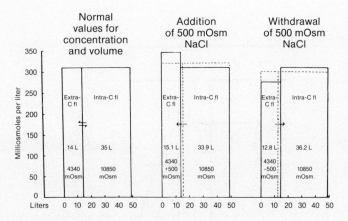

Fig. 8-5. The Darrow-Yannet diagram describes movement of water between the intracellular fluid and extracellular fluid caused by changes in extracellular sodium concentration. (From Zimmermann, B.: Fluid and electrolyte balance in surgical patients. In Sabiston, D.C. [editor]: Davis-Christopher textbook of surgery, Philadelphia, 1972, W.B. Saunders Co.)

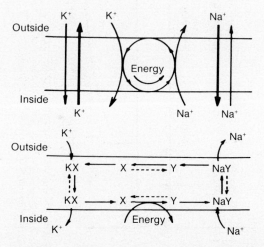

Fig. 8-6. The sodium-potassium ATP-ase pump. **A,** Passive diffusion of ions *(straight arrows); curved arrows,* active transport **B,** Hypothetical coupled carrier mechanism. (**A** reproduced with permission from Pitts, R.F.: Physiology of the kidney and body fluids, 3rd edition. Copyright © 1974 by Year Book Medical Publishers, Inc., Chicago. **B,** from Glynn, I.M.: J. Physiol., **134:**278, 1956.)

    a. From equilibrium, if the osmolarity of the ECF is increased by the addition of sodium or the loss of water, the intracellular compartment will shrink as water leaves to expand the extracellular compartment.

    b. Conversely, with addition of water to ECF or withdrawal of sodium, the free flux of water across the osmotic gradient expands the intracellular compartment.

4. The principle is of particular importance in the hyponatremia of the syndromes of inappropriate ADH (see below) and water intoxication as a cause of cerebral edema and increased intracranial pressure.

C. Ionic flux across cell membrane

The action of the sodium-potassium ATPase pump controls ionic flux across the cell membrane (Fig. 8-6).

1. This membrane-bound, energy-dependent ion exchange mechanism removes sodium from the cell while transferring potassium from the ECF to the ICF.

2. The mechanism maintains the sodium and potassium compartments.

3. It also maintains the transmembrane potential required for the excitability and conductivity of nerve and muscle.

D. Gibbs-Donnan: ionic equilibrium/capillary wall

The Gibbs-Donnan Rule (Fig. 8-7) explains the ionic equilibrium across the capillary wall.

1. Although the capillary membrane is freely permeable to water and ions, the negatively charged plasma proteins are trapped within the intravascular compartment.

STARTING CONDITION		EQUILIBRIUM CONDITION	
5 Pr$^-$ 5 Na$^+$	10 Cl$^-$ 10 Na$^+$	5 Pr$^-$ 5 Na$^+$ 4 Cl$^-$ 4 Na$^+$	6 Cl$^-$ 6 Na$^+$
1	2	1	2

Fig. 8-7. The Gibbs-Donnan equilibrium. The effect of nondiffusible protein anions on the distribution of diffusible cations and anions under closed-system conditions. (Reproduced with permission from Pitts, R.F.: Physiology of the kidney and body fluids, 3rd edition. Copyright © 1974 by Year Book Medical Publishers, Inc.)

2. If a nondiffusable ion (protein) is on one side of a membrane permeable to all other ions, the diffusable ions will distribute themselves unequally so that the following conditions are met:

   a. Total anions must equal total cations on each side of the membrane.

   b. On the side containing the protein, the concentration of the diffusable anions must be less, and the concentrations of the diffusable cations must be greater than on the side containing no protein.

   c. The osmotic pressure on the side containing protein (oncotic pressure) will be slightly greater than on the side containing no protein, and it must be balanced in some way to prevent the transfer of fluid.

   d. The products of the diffusable ions on either side of the membrane must be equal.

$$(B^+)_1 \cdot (A^-)_1 = (B^+)_2 \cdot (A^-)_2$$

In only Na^+ and Cl^- are the following present:

$$(Na^+)_1 = (Na^+)_2 \text{ and } (Cl^-)_1 = (Cl^-)_1 = (Cl^-)_2$$

The results may be different if a more diffusible anion is present.

THERAPEUTIC GOALS

The goal of fluid and electrolyte therapy of the surgical intensive care patient can be considered in three categories.

A. Maintenance of baseline requirements

   1. Adequate water, sodium, chloride, and potassium to meet normal needs of the patient whose oral intake has been curtailed

B. Compensation for observed abnormal losses

   1. Semiquantitative replacement of volume and electrolytes to offset losses from the gastrointestinal tract and wounds

   2. Accounting for sequestered fluid in third-space losses

C. Replacement of deficits

   1. Estimation of abnormal quantities of water and electrolytes

   2. Replacement or restriction of the abnormal constituents

Table 8-2. Commonly used intravenous solutions

Solutions	Glucose (g/L)	Na (mEq/L)	Cl (mEq/L)	K (mEq/L)	Ca (mEq/L)	Lactate (mEq/L)
D5W	50					
D10W	100					
D20W	200					
D50W	500					
5% D/0.9% NaCl	50	154.0	154			
5% D/0.45% NaCl	50	77.0	77			
3% NaCl		513.0	513			
Ringer's solution		147.5	156	4	4.5	
Ringer's lactate		130.0	109	4	3.0	28

Table 8-3. Commonly available parenteral additives

Solutions	Volume per ampule	mEq in ampule
7.5% Sodium bicarbonate	50	44
7.5% Potassium chloride	20	20
14.9% Potassium chloride	20	40
10.0% Calcium chloride	10	14
10.0% Calcium gluconate	10	4
25.0% Magnesium sulfate	2	4
26.8% Ammonium chloride	20	100
25% Mannitol	50	12.5 g
50.0% Glucose	50	25

THERAPEUTIC PREPARATIONS

Many preparations are clinically available for fluid and electrolyte therapy. Table 8-2 lists the composition of commonly used intravenous solutions. Table 8-3 lists commonly available parenteral additives.

MAINTENANCE THERAPY

A. Water requirements

Water requirements are based on three factors:

1. Urine output required to excrete a 24-hour solute load
2. Insensible losses from the skin and respiratory tract
3. Minus the water produced from endogenous metabolism of carbohydrates and fats

B. Solute load

1. In a fasted adult the daily solute load is about 600 mOsm.

2. Normal renal function can concentrate the urine to a specific gravity of 1.030 or 1000 to 1400 mOsm/kg urine.
3. Thus a minimal urine output of about 500 ml/day is required for solute excretion.
4. The presence of a defect in concentrating ability, or excessive catabolism related to other disease states necessitates higher urine outputs.

C. Insensible losses
   1. Insensible losses in a nonobese, afebrile patient at a comfortable temperature and humidity
      a. 500 to 800 ml/day in women
      b. 800 to 1000 ml/day in men
      c. Standardized figure of 300 to 500 ml/m^2 of surface area per day
      d. About half is respiratory and half surface evaporation

D. Endogenous water
   1. Production averages about 300 ml/day in a resting, fasted adult but can vary from 200 to 1000 ml.
   2. Production is closely related to caloric expenditure at about 10 ml produced per 100 kcal burned from body stores.

E. Net water requirement
   Addition of these elements gives us a bare minimum water requirement of about 1000 ml/day for a resting fasted adult.

Estimating average fluid requirements

A. By ideal weight for adults
   1. Active young adults (ages 16 to 30)   40 ml/kg/day
   2. Average adults (ages 25 to 55)   35 ml/kg/day
   3. Older adults (ages 55 to 65)   30 ml/kg/day
   4. Elderly (over 65)   25 ml/kg/day
B. By ideal weight for children over 5 kg through middle age
   1. First 10 kg body weight   100 ml/kg/day
   2. Second 10 kg body weight   50 ml/kg/day
   3. Weight above 20 kg   20 ml/kg/day
C. Example
   A 70-kg adult should receive $70 \times 35 = 2450$ ml by the first formula, and $(10 \times 100) + (10 \times 50) + (50 + 20) = 2500$ ml by the second.

Importance of body weight

A. Serial determination of body weight is the *most practical* indicator of hydration and water balance.
B. The recorded daily weight of patients on intravenous fluid therapy should reflect a loss of 0.3% to 0.5% of body weight per day. More rapid loss of weight gain should—in the absence of postoperative third-space losses, blood transfusions, or diuresis—suggest dehydration or overhydration, respectively.

Electrolyte requirements

For the patient deprived of normal alimentary intake for relatively short periods, only sodium, potassium, and chloride must be supplied as maintenance electrolytes.

A. Sodium
   1. Although sodium levels are greatly reduced in the urine of patients on a salt-free diet, 20 mEq/day is the minimum requirement to compensate losses by sweating and desquamation.
   2. Customarily, however, 70 mEq/day is supplied as 4 g NaCl per day.
B. Potassium
   1. A 5 to 10 mEq/day obligate potassium excretion remains in patients who have normal renal function and who are being maintained on a potassium-free solution.
   2. Thus at least 20 mEq/day must be allowed.
   3. Usually 40 to 60 mEq are given per day if renal function is adequate.
C. Chloride
   Chloride is usually supplied in quantities equal to that of sodium.

OBSERVED ABNORMAL LOSSES

In addition to maintenance fluids, abnormal losses must be measured.

A. Temperature effects
   Fever increases the body's water requirement.
   1. Fever above 38° C (100° F) requires an additional 500 ml

water per day because of the increased respiratory losses of hyperventilation.
2. Environmental temperature
The effects of increased environmental temperature depend on humidity and activity.
   a. In general, an additional 500 ml water daily should be allowed for each 2° to 3° C (5° F) above 32° C (85° F).
   b. Sweating is increased in obese patients.
   c. The salt content of sweat varies seasonally.
     (1) In the winter sweat is two-thirds isotonic.
     (2) In summer it becomes only one-third isotonic for increased evaporative cooling.

B. Gastrointestinal losses
1. The digestive system of an active person secretes 9 L of fluid daily, with the fluid composition dependent on the gut level at which the sample is taken.
   a. Approximate adult values are:
     (1) 1500 ml of saliva
     (2) 2500 ml gastric juices
     (3) 600 ml bile
     (4) more than 1000 ml pancreatic juice
     (5) 3000 ml from the jejunum
2. In the postoperative patient, large volumes are frequently drained away by or through:
   b. All but about 200 ml is reabsorbed.
   a. Nasogastric and long intestinal tubes
   b. Fistulas
   c. Cutaneous enterostomies
   d. Biliary drainage tubes
3. Tables of average values of electrolyte concentrations of various gastrointestinal secretions are useful for the measurements and replacement of short-term losses (Table 8-4).
4. The large individual variation, however, mitigates against regular sampling of large losses.

C. Urinary losses
Excessive urinary electrolyte losses may occur with a variety of disease states and medications.

1. Sodium loss
   a. Diuretic therapy
   b. During the recovery period following ATN and post-obstructive diuresis
   c. Medullary cystic disease
2. Potassium loss
   a. Diuretic therapy
   b. Corticosteroid administration
   c. Renal tubular acidosis
   d. Metabolic alkalosis
   e. Hyperaldosteronism
3. Regular laboratory measurement of urine electrolytes is the best guide to the replacement of inappropriate renal electrolyte excretion.

D. Internal fluid shifts
   Internal fluid shifts complicate the "balance-sheet" method of fluid and electrolyte therapy.
   1. Third-space loss
      a. Third-space loss is the sequestration of water, electrolytes, protein, blood, and osmotically active debris within an area of tissue injury and water from the two major active body fluid compartments.
         (1) This loss occurs to some extent in any postoperative patient.

Table 8-4. Electrolyte composition of gastrointestinal secretions: average (range)

Secretion	Na^+ (mEq/L)	K^+ (mEq/L)	Cl^- (mEq/L)	HCO_3^- (mEq/L)
Saliva	60	20	15	50
Gastric	60 (30-90)	10 (4-12)	90 (50-150)*	0
Pancreatic fistula	140 (135-155)	5 (4-6)	75 (60-110)	80 (70-90)
Bile	145 (135-155)	5 (4-6)	100 (80-110)	45 (35-50)
Midjejunum	105 (70-125)	5 (3.5-6.5)	100 (70-125)	10 (10-20)
Ileostomy	120 (90-140)	5 (4-10)	105 (60-125)	20 (15-50)
Diarrhea	(25-50)	(35-60)	(20-40)	(35-45)

*Lower in achlorhydria

 (2) It may be extreme in:
  (a) Burns
  (b) Crush injuries
  (c) Peritonitis
  (d) Pancreatitis
  (e) Long-bone fractures
  (f) Soft-tissue infections and abscesses
  (g) Pneumonitis
  (h) Edema distal to venous or lymphatic obstruction

 b. Fluid may also be sequestered within body cavities, such as the pleural space or peritoneum, and within the hollow viscera of the gastrointestinal tract with ileus or obstruction.

 c. The difficulty in replacing these third-space losses is that unless evacuated or drained in some way, they are not apparent as decreases in weight but are suggested only by hemodynamic parameters.

 d. Unlike the other losses previously discussed, these deficits are only temporary.
  (1) With the resolution of the tissue injury or other cause, large volumes can be rapidly returned to

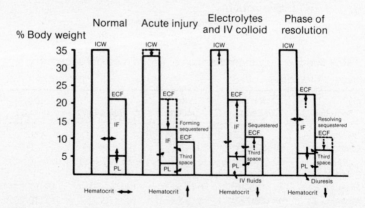

Fig. 8-8. The creation and resolution of third space losses. *ICW*, Intracellular water; *ECF*, extracellular fluid; *IF*, interstitial fluid; *PL*, blood plasma. (From Randall, H.T.: Surg. Clin. North Am. **56**:1019, 1976.)

the functional fluid compartments and mobilized into the circulation (Fig. 8-8).

(2) This change can create problems of water and electrolyte overload that physiologic or therapeutic diuresis must clear.

SALT AND WATER DISORDERS
Acute volume depletion

Acute volume depletion is almost entirely ECF loss.

A. Salt and water are lost in various proportions.
   1. If the loss is isonatremic, the ECF tonicity is unaffected.
   2. Water loss in excess of salt (e.g., sweating, severe diarrhea, or other gastrointestinal loss) produces hypernatremia. Water then enters the ECF from the ICF, and symptoms are blunted.
   3. Hypotonic replacement (water drinking or ill-designed intravenous therapy) may produce hyponatremia.

B. Diagnosis
   1. Symptoms parallel the volume lost.
      a. A deficit of 2% of body weight produces thirst and oliguria.
      b. A 4% weight loss represents a 20% ECF volume deficit and causes oliguria, tachycardia, and postural hypotension.
      c. Shock and acute tubular necrosis follow a 6% (30% ECF) body weight loss.
   2. No practical laboratory method exists for diagnosis.
      a. The serum sodium is not a guide to volume depletion but is a reflection of the tonicity of fluid lost and the volume and concentration of any replacement.
      b. The BUN is elevated out of proportion to creatinine levels.
      c. The urine specific gravity will be elevated toward 1.03.
      d. Urine sodium will be low, usually less than 10 mEq/L.

C. Treatment
   Treatment is both to replace the lost fluid and to control the source of loss.

1. Central venous pressure monitoring or the use of Swan-Ganz catheterization may be warranted in patients with limited cardiac reserve.
2. A good indicator is the continued production of high-specific-gravity, low-sodium urine. Falling specific gravity and rising sodium often herald acute tubular necrosis (ATN).
3. A reasonable replacement for isotonic loss is Ringer's lactate or normal saline alternated 2:1 with 1/6 M $NaHCO_3$. Large volumes of glucose-containing solutions should be avoided to prevent osmotic diuresis.
4. Serum potassium should be closely monitored to detect the hypokolemia that may follow the resolution of the metabolic acidosis of hypoperfusion.

Hypernatremia: disorders of renal concentration ability

Any pathologic condition that prevents the elaboration of a maximally concentrated urine will produce hypernatremia. This group of disorders results either from low levels of circulating antidiuretic hormone (ADH) or the inability of the kidney to respond to the hormonal direction.

Classification (Fig. 8-9)

A. Hypernatremia with low total body sodium
   These patients lose both salt and water, but with a greater water loss than sodium loss.
   1. Extrarenal sources of loss
      a. Profound sweating (see previously discussed temperature and baseline requirements)
      b. Gastrointestinal losses, the classic one being cholera
   2. Diagnosis
      a. Patients exhibit signs of hyponatremia.
      b. Since no renal abnormality exists, urine osmolarity will be high (> 10mEq/L).
      c. When renal losses of hypotonic fluid occur with the osmotic diuresis of glucose, mannitol, urea, or radiologic contrast material, the urine will be hypotonic or isotonic.

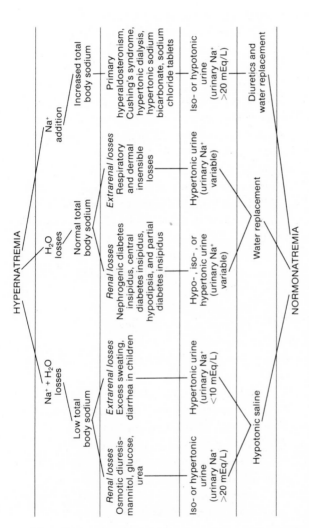

Fig. 8-9. The diagnostic and therapeutic approach to the hypernatremic patient. (From Berl, T., et al.: Kidney Int. **10**:117, 1976.)

  (1) The specific gravity may, however, be very high because of the osmotic agent.
  (2) The urine sodium will also be higher, usually more than 20 mEq/L.
B. Hypernatremia with normal total body sodium
   If water is lost without sodium, the ECF becomes hypertonic and water enters the ECF from the cells; thus overt volume contraction does not often occur and these patients may appear euvolemic.
   1. Extrarenal water loss
      a. Causes are evaporative (e.g., respiratory tracheostomy, hyperventilation) or dermal (psoriasis, high environmental temperature, fever)
      b. Diagnosis
         (1) Urine osmolarity will be very high, because the ADH-renal mechanisms are intact and urine sodium will be determined by the patient's sodium intake.
         (2) Symptoms and signs
            (a) Azotemia   (d) Disorientation
            (b) Fever   (e) Coma
            (c) Oliguria   (f) Convulsions
         (3) Hypotension is a late finding.
   2. Renal water loss
      Renal water loss is much more common.
      a. Causes
         (1) Pituitary diabetes insipidus
         (2) Nephrogenic diabetes insipidus (DI)
            (a) Hypophyseal DI (about half the cases)
            (b) Head trauma
            (c) Neoplasma (primary or breast metastasis)
            (d) Encephalitis
            (e) Sarcoidosis
            (f) Surgical hypophysectomy
         (3) Trauma produces transient or permanent DI, depending on the site of the lesion.
            (a) Nuclear destruction is permanent.
            (b) Lesions below the median eminence produce transient DI.

        (4) Nephrogenic DI
           (a) Congenital
           (b) Acquired, rarely severe (3 to 4 L water lost per day)
               i. Chronic renal disease
              ii. Hypokalemia
             iii. Hypercalcemia
             iv. Various drugs
              v. Sickle cell anemia

  b. Diagnosis
    (1) DI develops in three stages:
       (a) Initial diuretic phase of several hours to a week.
       (b) Antidiuretic phase as antidiuretic hormone (ADH) leaks from injured axons, lasting hours to days. During the period, continued water administration can produce profound hyponatremia.
       (c) A second diuretic phase
          The response to exogenous vasopressin and historic data differentiate pituitary and nephrogenic DI.
           i. Pituitary DI
              a. Usually sudden
              b. Great polyuria and polydipsia
              c. Invariable nocturia
              d. Marked preference for iad water
           ii. Nephrogenic DI
              a. Variable onset
              b. Moderate urine volumes
              c. No nocturia

C. Hypernatremia with increased total body sodium
The least common hypernatremia results from exogenous salt administration.
  1. Causes
    a. Excessive $NaHCO_3$ therapy
    b. Hypertonic saline infusion from therapeutic abortion
    c. Saltwater drowning

    d. Oral intake of sodium (e.g., salt tablets or error in baby formula mixing)
  2. Urinary sodium excretion is large

Clinical manifestations

A. The cellular dehydration associated with hypernatremia is responsible for most symptoms and signs.

  1. Restlessness   5. Coma
  2. Irritability   6. Seizures
  3. Lethargy   7. Death
  4. Hyporeflexia

B. Hypernatremia, especially acute, carries a 45% to 70% mortality, with neurologic sequelae common among survivors.

Treatment

The primary goal of therapy is the restoration of normal ECF volume and tonicity. Therapy thus depends on what has been lost.

A. Isotonic saline may be used to overcome hemodynamic instability.

B. This is followed by infusion of the appropriate crystaloid.

C. Calculation of water deficit in patients with pure water loss depends on the serum sodium levels and body weight.

$$\text{Nl vol TBW (L)} = 0.6 \text{ body weight (kg)}$$

$$\frac{\text{Nl serum } [\text{Na}^+] \times \text{TBW}}{\text{Measured serum } [\text{Na}^+]} = \text{Current TBW}$$

$$\text{Body water deficit} = \text{normal TBW} - \text{Current TBW}$$

D. Rate of correction is critical and should not exceed 2 mOsm/hr to prevent cerebral edema and seizures.

Hyponatremia: disorders of renal diluting capacity

The disorders of renal diluting capacity most frequently express themselves as hyponatremia with (1) ECF volume depletion, (2) modest ECF volume excess, or (3) edema with marked ECF volume excess. These disorders are caused by either persistent ADH release despite hyposmolarity or renal pathologic conditions, producing a decrease in glomerular filtration or in-

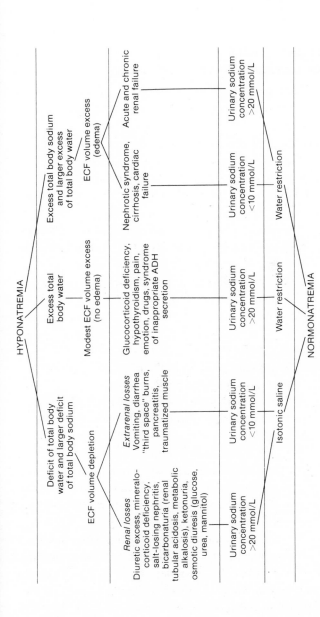

Fig. 8-10. The diagnostic and therapeutic approach to the hyponatremic patient. (From Berl, T., et al.: Kidney Int. **10**:117, 1976.)

crease in proximal tubular sodium and water reabsorption, or both, which robs the distal nephron of fluid with which to dilute the urine.

Classification (Fig. 8-10)
Hyponatremia with low total body sodium

A. Extrarenal losses
1. Gastrointestinal losses represent the major sources of extrarenal loss.
    a. With normal renal function, the hypovolemia of vomiting, nasogastric suction, and diarrhea stimulates maximal urinary sodium retention (urine $Na^+ < 10$ mEq/L, often 1 to 2 mEq/L) and high urinary osmolarity.
    b. If vomiting produces metabolic alkalosis, however, the bicarbonate load demands Na^+ as a cation for excretion.
        (1) Urinary sodium increases above 20
        (2) Urinary chloride decreases below 10
    c. Third-space losses sometimes fall into this category as well.
B. Renal losses
1. Renal losses may be of multiple origin.
    a. Diuretic therapy (Fig. 8-11)
        (1) Urinary sodium is not low (>20 mEq/L), because the kidney is the source of the loss
    b. Advanced chronic renal failure (GFR < 10 ml/min)
        (1) Prevents maximal dilution of the urine.
        (2) Raises minimum urinary sodium concentration (e.g., medullary cystic disease, polycystic disease, renal tubular acidosis, renal salt wasting with less severe impairment).
        (3) Uremia also produces hyponatremia because of its osmotic effect as the body increases extracellular fluid (water) to maintain tonicity, thus decreasing serum NA.
    c. Renal insufficiency
        Produces hyponatremia and hypovolemia associated

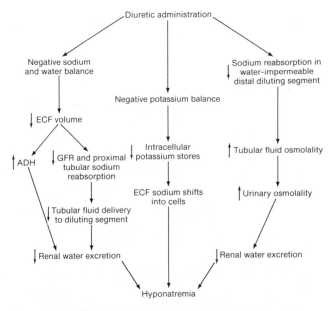

Fig. 8-11. The mechanism of diuretic-induced hyponatremia. (From Schrier, R.W.: Renal and electrolyte disorders. Boston, 1980, Little, Brown & Co.)

with hyperkalemia and urinary sodium concentrations greater than 20 mEq/L.

    d. Osmotic diuresis

        (1) Because the filtered solute carries sodium with water, urinary sodium concentration is high (>20 mEq/L) despite volume depletion.

        (2) Hyperglycemia further lowers serum Na by another mechanism.

        Water shifts from the ICF into the hyperosmolar ECF, lowering serum sodium by 1.6 mEq/L for every 100 mg percent rise in blood glucose.

Hyponatremia with normal total body sodium

When hyponatremia is associated with neither hypovolemia nor edema, an excess in TBW leads to only a modest expansion of ECF.

A. Causes
   1. ADH excess
      a. Pain
      b. Emotion
      c. Surgical injury
         (1) Expanded ECF with hyponatremia is the most common fluid and electrolyte disorder of surgical patients.
   2. The syndrome of inappropriate ADH secretion (SIADH) is the paradigm of this group of disorders.
      a. Malignant tumors, pulmonary and cerebral disorders, stress, and drugs have been implicated.
      b. The diagnostic criteria are strict:
         (1) Hyponatremia with hyposmolarity (serum $Na^+ <$ 120)
         (2) Urine less than maximally dilute (urine $Na^+ > 30$)
         (3) Normal renal, thyroid, and adrenal function
         (4) No clinical evidence of volume depletion or overload
         (5) Patient not taking diuretics
         (6) Disappearance of abnormalities following water restriction
      c. Hypothyroidism is yet another cause of this disorder and results from elevated ADH levels as well as intrarenal sodium transport deficiencies.

Hyponatremia with normal and decreased total body sodium
Clinical manifestations

The clinical manifestations of hyponatremia are caused by hyposmolarity.

A. Most are neurologic and thought to result from cerebral edema.
   1. Lethargy, apathy, disorientation, anoxia, nausea, agitation, and muscle cramps are associated with abnormal sensoria, hyporeflexia, hypothermia, and seizures.
   2. Most patients become symptomatic at Na^+ level of 120.
B. Acute hyponatremia is associated with a mortality of up to 50%, but gradually developing hyposmolarity is better tolerated.

Treatment

A. For those patients with neurologic signs of hyponatremia, prompt increase in serum osmolarity is indicated.

  1. Hypertonic saline works rapidly, but with the danger of volume overload.

  2. A more appropriate therapeutic approach is the elimination of excess water.

    a. Loop diuretics

    b. Replacement of electrolyte losses with hypertonic solutions

    c. Calculation for excess water to be removed:

Current body water (L) = 0.6 Current body weight (kg)

$$\text{ECF osmolarity} = 2\,([Na] + [K]\ mEq/L) + \frac{\text{Urea (mg percent)}}{2.8} + \frac{\text{Glucose (mg percent)}}{18}$$

Total body solute (mOsm) = Current volume TBa × Plasma osmolarity (mOsm/1)

$$\text{Normal volume body water} = \frac{\text{Total body solute (mOsm)}}{\text{Desired plasma osmol}\left(\dfrac{mOsm}{L}\right)}$$

Current volume − Normal volume = Body water excess (L)

    d. Elevation of serum sodium to 130 is sufficient.

B. Chronic stable hyponatremia requires treating the underlying disorder (hormone replacement). For SIADH the following guidelines are effective:

  1. If serum sodium is less than 125 mEq/L, water intake should be restricted to less than sensible and insensible losses until the serum sodium levels return to normal.

  2. Once the serum sodium level is normal, water intake should be restricted to sensible and insensible loses plus urine output.

  3. Demeclocycline (Declomycin, Declostatin) 300 to 600 mg twice a day may be useful in decreasing the need for water restriction in chronic cases. Lithium and phenytoin (Dilantin) may also be effective. Note that demeclocycline causes nephrotoxicity in patients with cirrhosis.

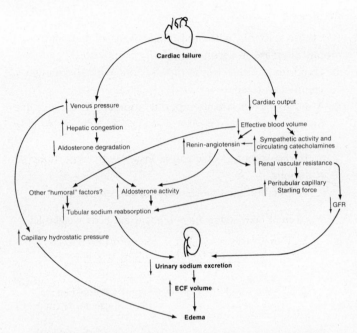

Fig. 8-12. Mechanism of the sodium retention of cardiac failure.

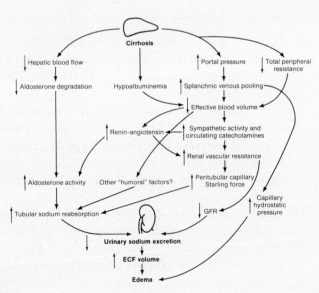

Fig. 8-13. Mechanism of the sodium retention of cirrhosis: the underfilling theory.

Hyponatremia with increased total body sodium
Edematous disorders

A. Causes
1. Congestive heart failure (Fig. 8-12)
2. Hepatic failure with cirrhosis and ascites (Fig. 8-13)
3. Nephrotic syndrome (Fig. 8-14)
4. Advanced chronic renal failure

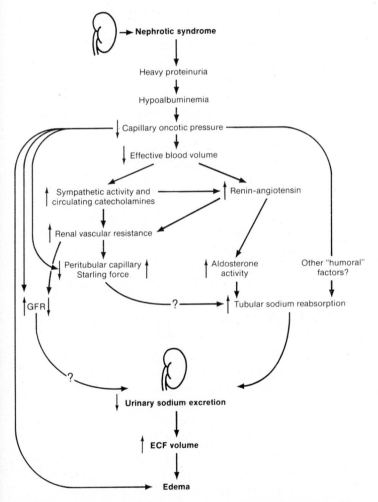

Fig. 8-14. Mechanism of the sodium retention of nephrotic syndrome. (From Schrier, R.W.: Renal and electrolyte disorders, Boston, 1980, Little, Brown & Co.)

B. Treatment
1. General principles for treating edematous disorders are as follows:
   a. Treatment of the primary disorders
      (1) Adequacy of diuretic therapy in congestive failure
      (2) Use of steroids to reduce proteinuria in nephrotic syndrome
      (3) Judicious use of albumin infusions in both nephrotic syndrome and cirrhosis to increase plasma oncotic pressure
         (a) In nephrosis, albumin is rapidly cleared and is of value only in the transient treatment of life-threatening hypotension.
         (b) Although albumin is slowly cleared in patients with cirrhosis, the expansion of blood volume may promote variceal bleeding.
   b. Salt and water intake are evaluated.
      (1) Restriction of sodium intake to 1 to 2 g/day can only *prevent* further increase in the positive sodium balance.
      (2) Hyponatremic patients should have their water intake limited to insensible losses (500 to 700 ml/day) plus measured urinary losses.
   c. The edema is mobilized.
      (1) Bed rest, particularly in the presence of cardiac failure, may produce diuresis.
      (2) Elastic stockings and LeVeen peritoneovenous shunting may also be of benefit.
   d. Indications for diuretic therapy are evaluated.
      (1) Impaired respiratory function
         (a) Pulmonary edema
         (b) Ascites elevating diaphragm with compromised ventilation
      (2) Impaired cardiovascular function of fluid overload
      (3) Excess fluid causing discomfort or physical limitations
      (4) To allow ingestion of sodium-containing (and

therefore more palatable) food, increasing caloric intake

2. General principles for treating ascites:
   a. Daily measurement of body weight with careful follow-up
   b. Stable renal and hepatic function are required for diuretic therapy.
   c. Trial of bed rest and low sodium diet before diuretic therapy (may produce diuresis in 15% of patients).
   d. Daily weight loss of 1 to 2 lb if ascites plus edema is present or 0.3 lb if there is ascites only.
   e. End-point of therapy should be maximal patient comfort with minimal diuretic-induced complications.
   f. The following regimen has been suggested:
      (1) Restrict sodium (10 to 40 mEq/day); effective alone in 5% to 15% of cases.
      (2) If no diuresis in 3 to 4 days, add spironolactone (Aldactone, 100 mg/day). Increase dose every 3 to 5 days until urinary sodium is increased; effective in 40% to 60% of cases.
      (3) If no diuresis with spironolactone 400 mg/day, add furosemide (Lasix, 20 to 80 mg/day)

SERUM MINERAL DISORDERS
Normal potassium metabolism

A. Concentration/distribution

Although physiologically potassium is the most abundant cation, several factors combine to make its serum concentration less than an ideal reflection of total body potassium.

1. The extracellular pool represents only 2% of total body stores.
   a. The normal serum (ECF) concentration is 3.5 to 5.5 mEq/L, compared to an intracellular concentration of 150 to 160 mEq/L.
   b. Since the muscle mass makes up a large portion of this intracellular pool, total body potassium varies significantly with age, sex, and body habitus.

2. Alteration in serum pH level can produce significant variations in serum potassium concentration through effects on renal excretion as well as through intercompartmental shifts (Fig. 8-15).
   a. Reduced potassium excretion occurs during the early stages of both metabolic and respiratory acidosis.
   b. Increased potassium excretion occurs during alkalosis.
   c. Changes in intracellular pH probably cause alterations in uptake from the peritubular ECF, thus changing the excretory pattern.
3. The relationship between serum and total body potassium concentrations is not linear (Fig. 8-16).
   a. As the total body potassium level increases above normal, the serum potassium level rises sharply.
   b. With developing total body potassium deficit, however, the corresponding document in serum potassium becomes smaller and smaller, tending to underestimate the magnitude of the deficit.

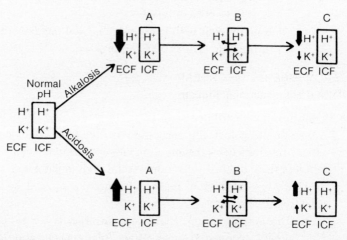

Fig. 8-15. Redistribution of ECF and ICF potassium and hydrogen ions in response to ECF pH. *I:* Alkalosis. *A,* H$^+$ concentration decreases. *B,* H$^+$ moves out of cells down its concentration gradient; K$^+$ moves in to maintain electrical neutrality. *C,* The result is the hypokalemia of alkalosis. *II:* Acidosis. *A,* H$^+$ concentration rises. *B,* H$^+$ moves into cells down its concentration gradient, K$^+$ moves out to maintain electrical neutrality. *C,* The result is the hyperkalemia of acidosis. (From Schrier, R.W.: Renal and electrolyte disorders, Boston, 1980, Little, Brown & Co.)

    4. These factors, combined with ECF, potassium's major role in the maintenance of membrane potentials and electrical excitation, require that therapy of potassium balance disorders be delicate, emergent, and precise.

B. Absorption/excretion

    1. The normal diet contains 50 to 100 mEq/day of potassium.

    2. About 10 mEq is lost daily in the stool and sweat.

    3. The kidneys excrete the majority of potassium.

       a. The following factors influence renal potassium excretion:

          (1) Aldosterone

          (2) Acid-base balance

          (3) Tubular flow rate–sodium delivery

          (4) Sodium intake

          (5) Diuretics

          (6) Intracellular potassium concentration and peritubular potassium uptake

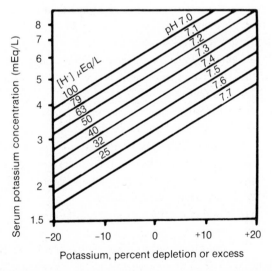

Fig. 8-16. Relationship of serum potassium concentration, total body potassium, and extracellular fluid pH. Note that the ordinate is a log scale. (From Schrier, R.W.: Renal and electrolyte disorders, Boston, 1980, Little, Brown & Co.)

b. Urinary potassium excretion may vary from a minimum of 5 mEq/L to 100 mEq/L, depending on the ingested load.

c. With renal failure, however, fecal losses can increase substantially.

d. Although the glomerulus filters potassium, a fairly constant 90% is actively reabsorbed in the proximal tubule and loop of Henle.

e. The distal tubule and collecting duct regulate urinary potassium excretion by a secretory process influenced by aldosterone, acid-base balance, and tubular fluid delivery.

Hypokalemia

A. Possible types
   1. Hypokalemia with normal total body potassium
   2. Total body deficits not reflected by hypokalemia
   3. Hypokalemia representing a total body deficit
B. Causes
   1. The most common cause of hypokalemia with normal body stores is:
      a. Respiratory alkalosis
      b. In long-distance runners and other endurance-trained athletes, hypokalemia may be evident without total body deficit.
      c. Occasionally, hypokalemia may be absent in the presence of severe total body depletion, producing alterations of cellular membrane transport of potassium. The rapid correction of the underlying abnormality may unmask florid signs of hypokalemia. This situation may occur in:
         (1) Metabolic acidosis (most common)
         (2) Uremia
         (3) Congestive heart failure with pulmonary edema
   2. Potassium deficit, demonstrated by presence of hypokalemia, usually results from:
      a. Poor potassium intake
      b. Inappropriate renal losses

   c. Poor nutrition (e.g., alcoholics, the elderly, the NPO hospital patient with inappropriate free intravenous feedings, and clay eaters, an unusual adult pica seen among blacks in the southeastern United States)

   d. Periods of rapid anabolism (e.g., recovery from anemia and preoperative hyperalimentation following the cachexia of malignancy)

   e. Excessive gastrointestinal loss
     Gastrointestinal loss is the most common cause of potassium depletion.

     (1) Upper gastrointestinal sources

       (a) Vomiting

       (b) Nasogastric suction

       (c) Fistulae

     (2) Calculation of the potassium deficit from the observed volume lost and the potassium concentration of gastric juice (10 mEq/L) will underestimate the severity of depletion, and thus potassium replacement, because the calculation does not consider the obligate kaliuria of metabolic alkalosis.

     (3) Lower gastrointestinal potassium sources

       (a) Diarrhea, or laxative abuse

       (b) A long ileal conduit ureteral diversion or ureterosigmoidostomy in patients with permanent lower urinary tract abnormalities

     (4) Endocrine diarrheagenic syndromes

       (a) Islet cell tumors of the pancreas (Zollinger-Ellison syndrome)

       (b) Carcinoid syndrome

       (c) Medullary carcinoma of the thyroid

       (d) Watery diarrhea–hypokalemia–achlorhydria syndrome (WDHA)

3. Urinary loss

   a. Renal potassium wasting (see gastrointestinal problems, above)

   b. Excessive mineralocorticoid effect

     (1) Primary (e.g., aldosteronoma—Conn's syndrome

        (2) Secondary (e.g., cirrhosis, nephrotic syndrome, congestive heart failure treated with diuretics)

    c. Juxtaglomerular cell hyperplasia (Bartter's syndrome, ACTH-secreting tumors, therapeutic administration)

    d. Glycyrrhizic acid ingestion (licorice has an aldosterone-like effect)

    e. Renal tubular acidosis

    f. Osmotic diuresis (glycosuria or mannitol administration)

    g. Diuretic therapy

C. Manifestations

  1. Perhaps most critical are the cardiac effects resulting from alterations in transmembrane potentials.

    a. The classic electrocardiographic changes of hypokalemia are flattening of the T wave, the appearance of a U wave following the T, S-T segment depression, and arrhythmias (Fig. 8-17).

      (1) The flat T wave and prominent U wave may lead to an incorrect measurement of the Q-T interval

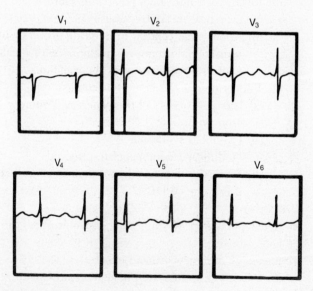

Fig. 8-17. The EKG in hypokalemia. (From Schrier, R.W.: Renal and electrolyte disorders, Boston, 1980, Little, Brown & Co.)

(which is really the Q-U interval). Such prolongation of the "Q-T" interval may erroneously suggest hypocalcemia.

    (2) Arrhythmias are predominantly atrial and ventricular prematurity.

  b. Hypokalemia can exacerbate digitalis toxicity and may result in certain arrhythmias common to this condition (e.g., paroxysmal atrial tachycardia with block).

2. Neuromuscular effects depend not on the absolute level of ECF potassium but on ECF to ICF ratio; thus the neuromuscular manifestations may be less than expected.

  a. Neuromuscular excitability decreases with hypokalemia producing:

    (1) Adynamic ileus

    (2) Paraesthesias

    (3) Weakness

    (4) Hyporeflexia

    (5) Irritability

    (6) Stupor

  b. Autonomic instability can result in orthostatic hypotension.

  c. Of uncertain cause is the polydipsia that is often present.

  d. In patients with liver disease, encephalopathy may be exacerbated.

3. Carbohydrate intolerance, expressed as an abnormal GTT that improves with potassium replacement, may result from decreased insulin secretion.

4. Because potassium is a mild vasodilator, it is probably in part responsible for the relaxation of muscular precapillary sphincters in response to exercise. The failure of this response may be responsible for the ischemic rhabdomyolysis observed in hypokalemia.

5. Hypokalemia affects the kidney in at least two ways.
The effects of hypokalemia contribute to continued potassium loss from other sources. However, examination of the urinary potassium concentration can provide clues

to the diagnosis if it is not immediately apparent Fig. 8-18.

  a. If the urinary potassium concentration is less than 20 mEq/L, the source of potassium depletion is probably gastrointestinal or is of shorter than one week's duration.

  b. Hypokalemia also comprises the ability of the kidney to maximally concentrate the urine.

    (1) The result is the "paradoxical aciduria" (pH 6.1 to 7.0) seen with hypokalemic alkalosis and occasionally with hypophosphatemia.

D. Treatment

  1. Prevention

    The best therapy for hypokalemia is prevention. Oral supplementation can avoid the depletion resulting from chronic administration of thiazide or loop diuretics and steroids and should be considered in patients receiving digitalis.

  2. Parenteral maintenance

    Parenteral maintenance therapy requires 40 mEq/day in adults. Estimating the severity of depletion is difficult (Fig. 8-16) because of fluctuation in serum potassium levels with pH.

  a. For every change of 0.1 pH unit, an estimated reciprocal change of 0.6 mEq/L occurs in the serum potassium.

  b. Furthermore, progressive depletion results in smaller and smaller decreases in serum potassium, while excesses result in a rapidly rising ECF concentration.

  c. The therapeutic rate, route, and preparation depend on the severity of the deficit and associated symptoms.

    (1) The following guidelines seem reasonable for intravenous therapy:

      (a) Adequate urine output should be established, or at least the renal status should be known, before intravenous potassium administration.

      (b) Frequent serum potassium determinations are appropriate during replacement.

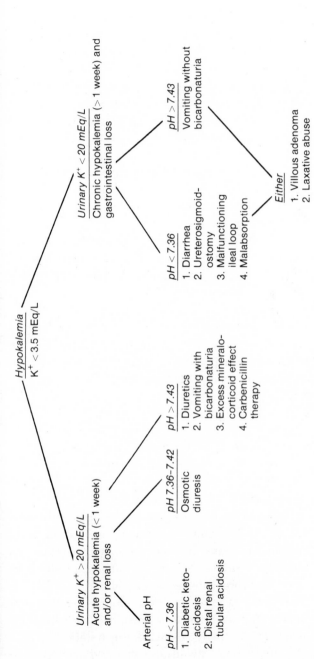

Fig. 8-18. The utilization of urinary potassium concentration and serum pH to assess the source of hypokalemia. (From Schrier, R.W.: Renal and electrolyte disorders, Boston, 1980, Little, Brown & Co.)

      (c) In asymptomatic patients with serum levels greater than 2.5 mEq/L, 10 to 20 mEq/hr for 100 to 200 mEq/day may be safely given.

      (d) For patients with rhabdomyolysis, muscle weakness, or arrhythmias, up to 40 mEq/hr (*twice* the normal total intravascular potassium) may be given, as long as the EKG is continuously monitored and the serum potassium is checked every 100 mEq.

      (e) Consideration should be given to the potassium salt used for replacement.

        i. The alkalotic patient requires potassium chloride.

        ii. For the patient with metabolic acidosis (renal tubular acidosis or diabetic ketoacidosis), potassium bicarbonate or citrate will be more effective.

  3. Oral maintenance

    For mild, asymptomatic deficits, oral therapy is preferred and a variety of preparations is available. For the hypokalemia of hyperaldosteronism, spironolactone (Aldactone) is the appropriate treatment.

Hyperkalemia

A. Maintenance

    The body's defense against hyperkalemia consists of mechanisms for the maintenance of both external and internal balance (Fig. 8-19).

  1. External balance

    a. Even in advanced renal failure (creatinine clearances as low as 5 ml/min), if urine volume is adequate, adaptive increases in renal potassium excretion can maintain external balance despite relatively large acute and chronic increases in load.

    b. Hyperkalemia provides direct adrenal stimulation of aldosterone secretion in a classic feedback loop, independent of the renin-angiotensin system.

      (1) Aldosterone stimulates the sodium-potassium ATP-ase pump in the distal nephron.

      (2) This action produces a kaliuria, facilitated by local increases in peritubular ECF potassium concentration.

  2. Internal balance

    a. Even when urinary excretion is temporarily overwhelmed, excesses in the small extracellular potassium pool can be shifted intracellularly.

      (1) Insulin plays at least a permissive role in this cellular uptake.

      (2) Evidence suggests that at extreme degrees of hyperkalemia, a feedback control loop with insulin may be operative.

      (3) The elevations in plasma glucagon levels occurring in hyperkalemia probably reflect the attempt to maintain normal glucose levels in the face of hyperinsulinemia.

    b. The hyperkalemia frequently present in untreated diabetes or hypoaldosteronism indicates the importance of these hormones in potassium homeostasis.

B. Causes

  1. Decreased renal excretion is the main cause of hyperkalemia.

  2. However, the ability of the distal nephron to clear a potassium load suggests an additional cause for hyperkalemia if the serum creatinine is under 10 mg/dl.

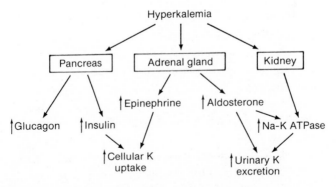

Fig. 8-19. Organ response to hyperkalemia. (From Schrier, R.W.: Renal and electrolyte disorders, Boston, 1980, Little, Brown & Co.)

3. Potassium-sparing diuretics (e.g., spironolactone, triamterene) produce severe hyperkalemia in a variety of patients, including those taking or with:
   a. Potassium supplements
   b. Mild to moderate renal insufficiency
   c. Diabetes
   d. Addison's disease (hypoadrenalcorticism), especially when salt depleted
   e. Either primary or hyporeninemic hypoaldosteronism
4. Endogenous potassium loads that can saturate physiologic defense include:
   a. Massive hemolysis
   b. Rhabdomyolysis of alcohol intoxication or crush injury
   c. Tissue destruction of major burns (compounded by hypovolemia and oliguria)
   d. Cancer radiation or chemotherapy
5. Exogenous sources include:
   a. Potato chips (also a source of excess Na intake).
   b. Dried fruits
   c. Salt substitutes
   d. Large doses of intravenous potassium penicillin
   e. Massive blood transfusion (30 mEq/L of 10-day-old whole blood)
6. Like hypokalemia, hyperkalemia may result from the redistribution of potassium in acid-base disturbances.
   a. Metabolic or respiratory acidosis may produce hyperkalemia with normal total body stores.
   b. Other sources of redistribution hyperkalemia include:
      (1) Digitalis intoxication
      (2) Arginine infusion
      (3) Intravenous glucose administration to diabetics
C. Manifestations
   1. Cardiac
      a. The sequential EKG changes (Fig. 8-20) are as follows:
         (1) Tall-peaked T waves
         (2) Widening QRS complex
         (3) Increasing P-R interval

        (4) Decreasing amplitude of both the P and R waves

        (5) Blending of S and T waves into the classic sine wave pattern of hyperkalemia

    b. Ventricular arrhythmias and asystole soon follow.

  2. Neuromuscular

    a. Sequence

        (1) Initial hyperexcitability as the decreasing resting transmembrane potential depolarizes toward threshold

        (2) Weakness and paralysis when the membrane can no longer generate an action potential

    b. These effects are limited to the peripheral nervous system and muscles. CNS manifestations of hyperkalemia are rarely seen.

D. Treatment

  1. Errors in potassium determination may lead to errors in therapy.

    a. Long tourniquet times when drawing venous samples can increase serum concentration by 2.7 mEq/L.

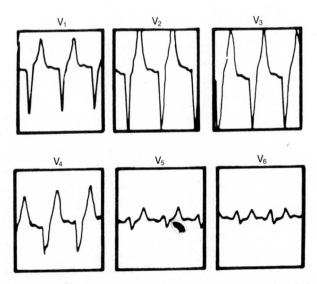

Fig. 8-20. The EKG in hyperkalemia. (From Schrier, R.W.: Renal and electrolyte disorders, Boston, 1980, Little, Brown & Co.)

b. Cellular elements of the blood can release their potassium-rich contents into the serum sample if it is not rapidly decanted.

c. Hemolysis of red cells from agitation is a common source of error.

d. Samples with platelet counts over 1 million or leukocyte counts over 70,000 should have plasma rather than serum potassium determination, because these elements may release their potassium stores during coagulation.

2. Treating hyperkalemia must also include the underlying disorder can be corrected. This alone is usually adequate therapy for serum potassium concentrations below 6.5.

3. Patients with ECG changes, neuromuscular symptoms, or serum levels over 6.5 require emergency temporizing measures.

a. Antagonize potassium effects

Intravenous calcium lowers the membrane threshold, restoring the normal voltage difference between resting and threshold levels for generation of action potentials.

(1) Calcium gluconate (5 to 10 ml of a 10% solution) may be given over 2 minutes.

(2) Administration is repeated if no effect occurs in 5 minutes.

(3) If there is still no result, calcium therapy should be abandoned.

(4) When present, the effect lasts 30 to 60 minutes.

b. Redistribute potassium from ECF

(1) Bicarbonate or glucose and insulin effectively redistribute potassium.

(2) One ampule (44 mEq) of $NaHCO_3$ may be given over 5 minutes and repeated in 15 minutes.

(a) The effect begins in 15 minutes and lasts 1 to 2 hours.

(b) $NaHCO_3$ cannot be mixed with calcium-containing fluids, because calcium carbonate forms an insoluble precipitate (intravenous limestone).

      (c) Continued administration of $NaHCO_3$ can lead to hypernatremia and volume overload in oliguric patients.

    (3) Glucose and insulin can be administered in a variety of formulas.

      (a) 500 ml of 10% glucose with 10 units of regular insulin

      (b) Five units of regular insulin with 25 g of D50W over 5 minutes reduces the infused volume

      (c) One thousand milliliters of D10W plus 90 mEq of $NaHCO_3$ given with 25 units of regular insulin subcutaneously, 300 ml in the first 30 minutes, the rest over 2 to 3 hours

      (d) Effects begin in 30 to 60 minutes and last several hours

  c. Eliminate potassium

    (1) Potassium can be removed from the body with peritoneal or hemodialysis, or more practically, with ion exchange resins.

    (2) Sodium polystyrene sulfonate (Kayexalate) removes about 1 mEq/g (7 to 12 g per heaping teaspoon). Kayexalate therapy imposes a large sodium load as 1.3 to 1.7 mEq of sodium are released for every 1.0 mEq potassium bound.

      (a) Forty grams given orally in divided doses produce a 1.0 mEq/L decrease in serum potassium in 24 hours in anephric patients. A single Kayexalate enema can reduce serum potassium by 0.5 to 1.0 mEq/L.

      (b) Oral administration is recommended and consists of 20 to 50 g in 100 to 200 ml of 20% sorbitol every 3 to 4 hours, up to five doses in 24 hours. The sorbitol produces diarrhea that prevents impaction of the resin and generates some potassium loss itself.

      (c) Rectal administration is required in patients with ileus, when a more rapid effect is de-

sired, or when the patient cannot tolerate oral administration.
  i. A Fleet enema prep is performed.
  ii. Hourly doses of 50 g of Kayexalate powder plus 50 g of sorbitol plus 200 ml of D20W are given and should be retained as long as possible.

Normal calcium and phosphorus metabolism
Calcium

A. The divalent cation calcium is essential in a variety of physiologic activities.
  1. Regulation of membrane permeability and neuromuscular excitation and conduction
  2. Smooth, skeletal, and cardiac muscle excitation—contraction coupling
  3. Bone hydroxyapatite crystal deposition
  4. Synthesis and release of acetylcholine
  5. Lactation
  6. Blood coagulation
  7. Intercellular bonding and the formation of ground substance
  8. Activation of certain enzyme systems
B. Calcium distribution
  1. Ninety-nine percent total body calcium is bound within a relatively active skeletal pool.
  2. One percent is distributed among the intracellular, interstitial, and intravascular compartments.
  3. Normal total serum calcium falls between 8.8 and 10.4 mg percent (2.20 to 2.60 mM/L) in adults, with slightly wider limits in younger age groups.
    a. About 40% is nondiffusable and bound to the albumin (85%) and globulin (15%) serum protein fractions.
    b. About 60% is diffusable.
      (1) Ten percent is complexed to bicarbonate, citrate, phosphate, and to a lesser extent lactate and sulfate.
      (2) Fifty percent is present as free ionized cation.

C. Ionized cation

The ionized calcium is of greatest direct physiologic significance.

1. Because 1 g of albumin can bind 0.7 to 0.8 mg of calcium and 1 g of globulin can bind 0.16 mg, one can make a rough estimate of the changes that occur with altered serum protein.

2. Serum pH and sodium concentrations affect protein binding.

   a. Alkalosis and hyponatremia may increase the binding of calcium to albumin, reducing the size of the ionized pool.

   b. Hence severe alkalosis can produce signs of tetany despite a normal serum calcium level.

   c. The opposite effects occur with acidosis and hypernatremia.

   d. Some estimate that for every 0.1 pH unit change, an inverse change in the ionized fraction of 0.17 mg/dl results (some authors give 0.16 mg/dl).

   e. A directly proportional change of 0.12 percent occurs in protein-bound calcium.

D. Calcium absorption

1. About 1.0 g of dietary calcium is ingested daily, of which about half is absorbed.

2. Factors that tend to increase the solubility of calcium salts enhance calcium absorption, and vice versa. For example, the insoluble calcium-fat complexes present in steatorrhea greatly increase fecal calcium loss.

3. The hormonal effects of parathyroid hormone and vitamin D on calcium absorption will be discussed below.

4. Endogenous fecal calcium loss makes up about one fourth of daily calcium excretion, with 300 to 400 mg as daily urinary loss.

Phosphorus

A. Phosphorus, the most abundant intracellular anion (100 mM/L), is physiologically important in many systems, highlighted by its roles in:

1. Nucleic acids functioning in cellular reproduction, protein synthesis, and genetics
2. Carbohydrate metabolism as hexose and creatinine phosphates
3. Energy transfers in intermediary metabolism
4. Phosphate buffers in the maintenance of stable pH balance
5. Regulation of oxygen transport via the 2, 3-DPG of red cells

B. Phosphorus distribution
   1. Eighty percent of total body phosphorus (700 g) is present outside cells in bone.
   2. About 9% of total body phosphorus is to be found in skeletal muscle.
   3. Total serum phosphorus is about 12 mg/dl, of which 8 mg percent is phospholipids and 1 mg/dl is phosphoesters.
   4. This leaves the clinically reported inorganic phosphorus of 2.0 to 5.0 mg/dl (0.65 to 1.62 mM/L), which is completely ionized and under hormonal control.

C. Excretion
   1. Approximately 10% of the daily intake is excreted into the feces.
   2. Ninety percent is excreted into the urine as titratable acid. Urinary excretion is regulated by glomerular filtration and by way of parathyroid hormone–controlled tubular reabsorption.
   3. Phosphorous excretion depends on three factors:
      a. Presence of parathyroid hormone (PTH)
      b. Serum calcium
      c. Dietary phosphate load
   4. The tubular reabsorption of phosphate (TRP) is normally 80% to 90% of the filtered load at normal phosphorus levels.
      a. It should rise above 90% when the serum phosphorus falls below 2.5 mg/dl.
      b. It will be inappropriately low (<80%) in cases of hyperparathyroidism.

Calculating calcium-phosphorus product

A. Within the limitations imposed by biologic systems, a clinically useful calcium-phosphorus product can be calculated for diagnostic purposes.
   1. For example, the value is low in rickets, but higher in growing children and quite high in patients developing metastatic calcifications.
   2. The "normal value" is 30 to 40 in adults and 40 to 55 in growing children.
   3. Caution in the use of this concept is in order, since some authors feel that its use is an oversimplification.
      a. It varies only under extreme conditions, such as the decrease in serum calcium following an acute rise in serum phosphorus.
      b. The contrasting relationships do not hold for acute changes in serum calcium.
   4. Perhaps the use of the calcium-phosphorus product should be limited to the determination of the etiologies of rickets and osteomalacia.

Hormonal control

Calcium and phosphorus balance is under the hormonal control of PTH, the D vitamins, and perhaps thyrocalcitonin. A feedback loop tightly controls serum calcium levels via the secretion of PTH. No feedback loop is present for phosphorus, resulting in wider variation in serum phosphorus values.

A. Parathyroid hormone (PTH)
   1. Cyclic adenosine monophosphate (C-AMP) mediates PTH release, depending on the serum ionized calcium level.
   2. Epinephrine and falling serum magnesium may also stimulate PTH secretion.
   3. PTH raises serum calcium levels by:
      a. Vitamin D–dependent osteocytic and osteoclastic bone resorption
      b. Net calcium resorption by the distal nephron
      c. Increasing calcium absorption from the gastrointestinal tract by its effects on vitamin D metabolism
   4. PTH also decreases the tubular reabsorption of phosphate below 80%, producing net phosphate excretion.

B. D vitamins
   1. The body obtains the fat-soluble D vitamins in two ways:
      a. From the diet (dependent on normal fat absorption) as vitamins D_2 (ergocalciferol) and D_3 (cholecalciferol)
      b. From endogenous D_3 production in the skin by the action of ultraviolet irradiation on 7-dehydrocholesterol.
   2. During enterohepatic circulation, which is entirely feedback controlled, cholecalciferol is converted into 25-OH cholecalciferol.
   3. The kidney further hydroxylates 25-OH-D to one of the following:
      a. The 100 times more potent $1,25\text{-}(OH)_2D$ under the stimulation of increased PTH or low serum phosphorus
      b. The less potent $24,25\text{-}(OH)_2D$, which inhibits PTH secretion
   4. Deficiency in the active metabolites of the D vitamins can result from several situations.
      a. Inadequate intake and/or decreased production (excess pigmentation)
      b. Reduced absorption (steatorrhea)
      c. Renal or hepatic insufficiency resulting in decreased conversion
      d. Increased hepatic catabolism and excretion (phenobarbital administration)
   5. Several mechanisms exist by which $1,25\text{-}(OH)_2$ cholecalciferol increases serum calcium and phosphorus.
      a. Increased intestinal absorption of calcium and perhaps phosphorus
      b. Enhanced calcium and phosphorus reabsorption from bone
      c. Most importantly, the increased tubular reabsorption of phosphorus and perhaps calcium
   6. The vitamin D analog dihydrotachysterol, is more potent in mobilizing calcium from bone and has been used in the treatment of hypoparathyroidism.

C. Thyrocalcitonin

Thyrocalcitonin, produced by the parafollicular cells (C cells) of the thyroid gland, has an uncertain role in normal calcium and phosphorus metabolism.

1. This peptide hormone is produced in medullary carcinoma of the thyroid.
2. Its clinical uses include:
   a. Antagonizing PTH in severe hypercalcemia
   b. Promoting bone mineralization in osteopenic metabolic bone diseases
3. Its actions result in decreased serum calcium and phosphorus concentrations, by several mechanisms:
   a. By inhibition of bone resorption, its major action
   b. Probably by increasing bone formation
   c. By increasing the renal excretion of phosphorus, calcium, sodium, and potassium
   d. By decreasing phosphorus absorption in the gut

Hypocalcemia

A. Causes

1. The most common cause of hypocalcemia is hypoalbuminemia. Because the ionized calcium is normal, no symptoms are produced and no treatment is required.
2. Vitamin D_1 deficiency can cause clinically significant hypocalcemia.
   a. The causes of vitamin D deficiency may be:
      (1) Nutritional
      (2) Malabsorptive (gastrectomy, sprue, chronic pancreatitis, cirrhosis, laxative abuse, intestinal bypass)
      (3) Metabolic (anticonvulsant drugs, renal insufficiency, hepatic dysfunction, abnormalities in PTH secretion or serum phosphate concentration)
      (4) Hypoparathyroidism is a common cause of symptomatic hypocalcemia and may be:
         (a) Postsurgical
         (b) Idiopathic

(c) A component of multiple endocrine dysfunction (e.g., DiGeorge syndrome)

(5) Caused by hypomagnesemia

(6) Certain cancers can produce hypocalcemia by:

(a) Secretion of thyrocalcitonin (e.g., medullary carcinoma of the thyroid and oat cell carcinoma of the lung

(b) The rapid deposition of calcium salts in osteoblastic metastases, as has been reported in prostate and breast cancer

(7) Hyperphosphatemia can produce hypocalcemia by a variety of mechanisms discussed below.

(8) Acute pancreatitis can cause hypocalcemia by:

(a) The formation of calcium soaps in abdominal fat

(b) The glucagon-mediated release of thyrocalcitonin

(9) Finally, a variety of substances bind calcium in the gut (sodium phytate–containing cereals, and oxalate in spinach and rhubarb) or in the blood (ethylenediaminetetraacetic acid [EDTA], citrate in massive transfusions) and can precipitate hypocalcemia crises in those with a predisposition.

B. Symptoms

1. Paraesthesias

2. Tetany

a. Carpopedal spasm

b. Chvostek's sign—facial contraction on tapping the seventh nerve in front of the ear.

c. Trousseau's sign—carpopedal spasm after 3 minutes of brachial ischemia with a blood pressure cuff.

3. Confusion

4. Seizures

5. Sometimes a prolonged Q-T interval on ECG.

C. Treatment

1. Therapy of acute symptomatic hypocalcemia should be prompt, because delay may further aggrevate tetany and lead to seizures and cardiac arrest.

2. Manifestations generally clear with the administration of 10 to 20 ml of 10% calcium gluconate (9 mg/ml of elemental calcium) given intravenously over 5 to 15 minutes.

3. Ten percent calcium chloride is also available but contains four times the calcium of the gluconate solution.

4. Further therapy can be by IV drip of calcium gluconate (600 to 800 mg Ca/L) in D5W until oral therapy can be instituted.

5. Hypocalcemia that is refractory to replacement, or in patients with alcoholism, pancreatitis, or malabsorption, should suggest hypomagnesemia (see next section) and will resolve with adequate replacement of magnesium stores.

D. Postsurgical hypocalcemia

1. Although hypocalcemia following thyroid or parathyroid surgery is generally transient and mild, one must watch carefully for its development.

2. Symptoms usually do not appear until the first or second postoperative day.

3. Possible causes include:

   a. Vascular compromise of residual parathyroid tissue

   b. Inadvertent resection of parathyroid tissue in thyroid surgery

   c. "Hungry bones" after removal of adenomatous or hyperplastic glands for primary hyperparathyroidism

4. Treatment measures depend on the severity and duration of hypocalcemia.

   a. As long as the serum calcium remains above 7.0 to 7.5, no therapy is indicated and symptoms often clear by the fourth or fifth day.

   b. Severe symptoms or a serum calcium below 7.0 requires parenteral therapy, as outlined previously.

   c. The persistent postoperative hypocalcemia of patients such as those with osteitis require additional care.

      (1) A low-phosphorus diet (restricted milk and meat)

      (2) 1.5 to 3.0 g of elemental calcium daily. Options include:

         (a) Glubionate calcium (Neo-Calglucon)—15 ml four times a day

   (b) Calcium carbonate (Titrilac)-400 mg Ca/5 ml
    or 170 mg calcium tablets
   (c) 250 or 500 mg calcium tablets
  (3) Vitamin D supplementation as cholecalciferol (vitamin D_2—1.25 mg, 50,000 unit capsules), dihydrotachysterol (Hytakerol—0.125 mg tablets) or 12,25 dihydroxycholecalciferol (Rocaltrol—0.25 and 0.5 mg capsules) may be required to enhance intestinal absorption.
 d. For postoperative patients, Hytakerol, 0.625 mg daily, tapered over 1 week to 0.125 mg daily, has been suggested.
 e. Usually therapy can be stopped within 4 weeks; rarely, however, oral calcium and vitamin D may be required for over a year.

DIFFERENTIAL DIAGNOSIS OF HYPERCALCEMIA

Hyperparathyroidism
 Primary: Adenoma, carcinoma, hyperplasia, multiple endocrine adenomatosis syndromes
 Secondary: Malabsorption, vitamin D deficiency, chronic renal failure
 Tertiary: Following renal transplantation
Neoplasm
 Malignant tumors metastatic to bone
 Tumors secreting PTH-like substance
 Tumors secreting non-PTH-like substances
Hypervitaminosis
 Vitamin A intoxication
 Vitamin D intoxication
Granulomatous disease
 Sarcoidosis
 Tuberculosis
Hyperthyroidism
Adrenocortical insufficiency
Immobilization
Milk-alkali syndrome
Thiazide diuretics
Paget's disease

E. Chronic hypocalcemia (secondary hyperparathyroidism)
   1. Control of chronic hypocalcemia (e.g., patients with renal insufficiency) depends on controlling hypercalcuria (4 mg/kg/day) while maintaining serum calcium above 8.0 mg percent.
   2. Therapeutic mainstays include:
      a. Calcium supplementation
      b. Oral phosphate restriction
      c. Phosphate-binding gels
      d. Vitamin D administration
   3. High vitamin D doses may also be required (200,000 units of vitamin D_2/day) but should be approached gradually.
   4. Thiazides can enhance the calcemic action, but furosemide aggravates hypercalcuria.

Hypercalcemia

A. Differential diagnosis
   The differential diagnosis of hypercalcemia encompasses a large number of conditions (see Table 8-5). The most common in the general population is hyperparathyroidism; however, among in-hospital patients, the second most common cause, malignancy, becomes first.
B. Classification
   1. Classically, patients with primary hyperparathyroidism can be divided into three groups:
      a. Those without overt bone disease but with kidney stones or nephocalcinoses
      b. Those with bone disease but without stones
      c. Those with neither bone disease nor stones
   2. Additionally, hypertension, pancreatitis, possibly peptic ulcer disease, cholelithiasis, soft tissue and articular calcification, and neuromuscular and psychiatric disorders have been associated with primary hyperparathyroidism.
C. Causes
   1. Malignant
      a. Breast   d. Colon
      b. Lung   e. Thyroid
      c. Kidney   f. Myeloma

Table 8-5. Differential diagnosis of hypercalcemia

	Serum			PTH	Urine		Special
	Ca^{++}	$PO_4^{=}$	Alk Phos		Ca^{++}	$PO_4^{=}$	
Primary hyperparathyroidism	↑	↓	N-↑	↑	↑	↑	Serum $Cl^-/PO_4^= > 30$
Secondary hyperparathyroidism	N-↑	↑	N-↑	↑↑	→↑	→↑	Cheave's renal failure
Vitamin D intoxication	↑	↑	→↓	↓	↑	↓	Ectopic calcification
Metastatic carcinoma	↑	N	N	↓	↑	N	Other signs of metastasis
Multiple myeloma	↑	N	N-↑	↓	N-↑	N-↓	Bence Jones protein, roentgenograms
Sarcoidosis	↑	N-↓	N	↓	↑	↑	Chest roentgenograms, hepatosplenomegaly, Kurim test
Milk-alkali syndrome	↑	N	N		N-↓	N-↓	Positive history, renal failure
Paget's disease	N-↑	N	↑	N-↓	↑	N	Roentgenograms

2. Nonmalignant
   a. Functioning parathyroid adenomas have been found in patients with malignancies of the breast, liver, kidney, pancreas, uterus, lung, and myeloma.
   b. Patients with granulomatous disease appear to have hypercalcemia based on increased vitamin D sensitivity, since they respond to glucocorticoids, which are known to inhibit calcium absorption by the intestine. Whether this increased sensitivity causes the hypercalcemia of Addison's disease is not known.
   c. The stimulation of osteoclasts by thyroid hormone produces the hypercalcemia of hyperthyroidism. The persistence of elevated serum calcium in the euthyroid patient should suggest another etiology.

D. Diagnosis
   1. Symptoms
      a. The symptoms of hypercalcemia include:
         (1) Vomiting
         (2) Diffuse abdominal pain
         (3) Constipation
         (4) Polyuria to the point of dehydration and azotemia
         (5) Marked muscular weakness and fatigue
         (6) Obtundation
         (7) Coma
      b. The severity of symptoms varies greatly and is somewhat dependent on the rate of rise of serum calcium.
   2. Laboratory findings of primary hyperparathyroidism
      a. Usual findings include:
         (1) Hypercalcemia
         (2) Normal to low normal serum phosphorus
         (3) Normal to elevated serum chloride
         (4) Tubular resorption of phosphate lower than 85%
         (5) Elevated nephrogenous urinary cyclic AMP
         (6) Elevated serum PTH
      b. In addition, a serum chloride-phosphorus ratio above 30 is not found in hypercalcemia from causes other than primary hyperparathyroidism

E. Treatment
  1. Saline diuresis
     a. The only therapy effective for the rapid lowering of serum calcium is saline diuresis.
     b. Normal saline should be alternated with 0.5 N saline at a rapid rate (250 to 500 ml/hr) to produce volume expansion.
     c. If cardiac and renal function permit, a CVP of at least 10 cm H_2O should be achieved.
     d. Diuresis can be further stimulated with furosemide (10 to 40 mg every 2 to 4 hours).
     e. Further volume should be given, appropriate to the replacement of urinary water and electrolyte losses.
     f. Dehydration must be prevented or recurrent hypercalcemia will develop.
     g. Unfortunately, saline diuresis is difficult to maintain for long periods, and adjunct modalities must be used.
  2. Glucocorticoids
     a. Glucocorticoids are effective in 24 to 48 hours in the following cases:
        (1) Vitamin D intoxication
        (2) Granulomatous disease
        (3) Myeloproliferative and non-PTH-secreting tumors
     b. They are not effective in hyperparathyroidism.
     c. Hydrocortisone (3 to 4 mg/kg of body weight/24 hr) may be followed by an oral, maintenance dosage of prednisone (10 to 40 mg/day).
  3. Salmon calcitonin
     In cases of severe hyperparathyroidism, salmon calcitonin (Calcimar) inhibits bone resorption and promotes renal excretion of calcium, sodium, and phosphorus, producing a 1 to 3 mg/dl fall in serum calcium.
     a. A 15-minute skin test is required with 1 MRC unit before therapy.
     b. The recommended starting dose is 4 MRC units/kg of body weight, injected subcutaneously or intramuscularly every 12 hours.

   c. The dose may be increased at daily intervals to a maximum of 8 MRC units/kg of body weight every 6 hours.

   d. Although calcitonin has been used in the long-term treatment of Paget's disease, the doses are much smaller, and calcitonin should be considered inappropriate for the long-term therapy of hypercalcemia.

4. Mithramycin

   a. In low doses (15 to 25 mg/kg of body weight) given intravenously, the cancer chemotherapeutic agent mithramycin produces a significant fall in serum calcium level within 12 to 24 hours, lasting 3 to 7 days.

   b. Repeated doses often lead to toxicity, thus limiting the drug's use on a long-term basis.

5. Prostaglandin inhibitors

Prostaglandin inhibitors (e.g., indomethicin, aspirin) may be useful because of humoral agents produced by certain neoplasms.

6. Phosphate

   a. Although the least effective, phosphate therapy has the advantage of being suitable for chronic as well as acute therapy.

   b. Phosphates should be used only after volume loading and diuresis has been established.

   c. They are never used in patients with hyperphosphatemia (hypervitaminosis D).

   d. Intravenous therapy is extremely hazardous and has been associated with severe soft tissue calcification (see "Hypophosphatemia"), renal cortical necrosis, and rapid pulmonary calcification.

   e. Doses of 20 to 30 mg of elemental phosphorus per kg of body weight every 12 hours have been suggested.

     (1) Oral doses of either Phosphosoda (600 mg P/5 ml, three or four times a day) or Neutra-Phos (250 mg P/capsule, 2 to 3 capsules three or four times a day) are well tolerated.

     (2) Phosphate may be given as a 100 ml Fleet retention enema twice a day.

(3) A major potential complication is metastatic calcification, including renal failure resulting from nephrocalcinosis.

(4) Calcium-blocking agents can be effective in controlling cardiac toxicity (verapamil, nifedipine, diltiazem)

Hypophosphatemia

Hypophosphatemia is an abnormally low concentration of inorganic phosphorus in serum and does not always reflect total body phosphorus depletion. Likewise, severe depletion in body phosphorus stores may exist with normal serum phosphorus.

A. Causes

The causes of hypophosphatemia are legion and have been divided into groups according to the severity of hypophosphatemia produced (see box on opposite page).

B. Consequences

The consequences of severe hypophosphatemia are also numerous:

1. Red blood cell dysfunction results from 2,3-DPG and ATP depletion, leading to limited oxygen release to tissues, erythrocyte rigidity, and hemolysis.

2. Leukocyte dysfunction, with alterations of chemotaxis and phagocytosis, results from interference with ATP synthesis and may contribute to the infectious complications of hyperalimentation and burn injury.

3. Metabolic encephalopathy is manifested by irritability, apprehension, weakness, numbness, paresthesias, dysarthria, confusion, obtundation, seizures, and coma.

4. Rhabdomyolysis has occurred in alcoholic hypophosphatemics.

5. Metabolic acidosis results from decreased excretion of titratable acid in the urine as well as depression of ammonia production by the renal tubular cell.

6. Congestive cardiomyopathy may occur and appears to be completely reversible with appropriate treatment.

7. Potential long-term sequellae of hypophosphatemia include hepatocellular and renal dysfunction, ketoacidosis, and peripheral neuropathy.

CONDITIONS ASSOCIATED WITH MODERATE HYPOPHOSPHATEMIA (1.0 to 2.5)

A. Intracellular shifts
1. Respiratory alkalosis
a. Gram-negative bacteremia
b. Hepatic coma
c. Primary hyperventilation
d. Thyrotoxicosis
e. Salicylate poisoning
2. Metabolic alkalosis
3. Administration of:
a. Sugars—glucose, fructose, lactate, glyceral
b. Hormones—insulin, gastrin, epinephrine, glucagon, corticosteroids
4. Recovery from hypothermia
B. Deficiency of phosphorus absorption
1. Starvation/malabsorption
2. Vitamin D deficiency
3. Antacid administration
4. Chronic alcoholism
C. Increased phosphorus excretion
1. Hyperparathyroidism
2. Diuretic therapy
3. Renal tubular defects
4. Volume expansion
5. Hypomagnesemia
6. Hyperaldosteronism
D. Uncertain
1. Acute gout
2. Hypokalemia
3. Carcinoma

CONDITIONS ASSOCIATED WITH SEVERE HYPOPHOSPHATEMIA (<1.0)

A. Pharmacologic binding of phosphate in the gut by antacids
B. Thermal injury, diuretic and recovery phase
C. Hyperalimentation
D. Nutritional recovery syndromes
E. Severe respiratory alkalosis
F. Diabetic ketoacidosis—treatment phase
G. Alcohol withdrawal

C. Treatment

The therapy of hypophosphatemia is hazardous, and some of the effects listed above may be only slowly or poorly reversible. Therefore, emphasis must be on prevention rather than correction of this disorder. Unlike some other electrolyte disturbances, hypophosphatemia is not such an emergency that phosphate must be given before a diagnosis can be rendered. As stated earlier, hypophosphatemia can exist without phosphate depletion, and often correcting the underlying cause will obviate the need for supplemental phosphate. Deficits may be corrected by the intravenous route or the oral route, although complications are more likely by the former. Intramuscular phosphorus administration is contraindicated.

1. Intravenous administration
   a. Complications of intravenous phosphate administration include:
      (1) Hyperphosphatemia, which may lead to hypotension
      (2) Metastatic deposition of calcium phosphate
      (3) Hypocalcemia
         (a) Soft tissue calcifications are likely if the calcium-phosphorus product rises above 60.
         (b) They may occur with alarming speed.
         (c) Possible sites include the lung, eye, kidney, and coronary arteries.
         (d) Acidosis decreases and alkalosis potentiates the risk of this complication.
      (4) The administration of large amounts of potassium phosphate may lead to hyperkalemia.
      (5) Dehydration from osmotic diuresis
      (6) Hypernatremia
   b. Contraindications to the administration of phosphate include:
      (1) Hypercalcemia
      (2) Hyperphosphatemia
      (3) Oliguria or renal failure
      (4) Hypoparathyroidism
      (5) Evidence of tissue necrosis

   c. Raising the serum phosphorus much above 1.0 mg percent is not necessary by the intravenous route.

   d. Calcium and phosphorus preparations *cannot* be given simultaneously through the same IV line.

   e. Several regimens have been suggested:

     (1) An initial dose of 2.5 to 5.0 mg/kg of body weight intravenously over 6 to 8 hours, additional doses according to response. Diabetic ketoacidosis may initially require 500 mM daily to correct large deficits.

     (2) For alcoholics, 50 to 75 mM intravenously for 24 hours will maintain serum phosphorus at 2.0 to 3.0 mg/dl.

   f. Maximum dosage should be considered 7.5 mg/kg of body weight/6 to 8 hr.

   g. Serum phosphorus must be monitored closely.

Oral supplements

A. Skim milk is well tolerated and contains about 1 g (33 mM) of inorganic phosphorus per quart. Milk is especially well suited for the cachectic patient.

B. Alternatively for moderate hypophosphatemia:

   1. Neutra-Phos (7 mEq K, 7 mEq Na, 250 mg P/capsule)

   2. Although these doses would produce diarrhea in most patients, diarrhea is much less likely in phosphate-depleted patients.

Hypokalemia and hypomagnesemia

A. Severe hypophosphatemia with phosphate depletion is frequently complicated by hypokalemia and hypomagnesemia.

B. Ampules of potassium phospate, 10 ml ($KH_2PO_4 \cdot K_2HPO_4^-$ 4 mEq K, 93 mg or 2 mM P/ml), can be added to intravenous fluids to correct hypokalemia as well as hypophosphatemia.

C. A similar sodium preparation is also available.

Hyperphosphatemia

A. Causes

   1. Hyperphosphatemia is most commonly associated with

renal insufficiency, occurring chronically when the glomerular filtration rate falls below 30.
2. It frequently occurs in acute renal failure.
3. Other associations include:
   a. Hypoparathyroidism
   b. Increased catabolism
   c. Neoplastic diseases treated with cytotoxic agents, usually leukemias and lymphomas (contrast with the hypophosphatemia present in rapidly growing untreated malignancy)
4. Administration of vitamin D
5. As a complication of phosphate administration in treatment of hypophosphatemia

B. Consequences
1. Hyperphosphatemia frequently produces hypocalcemia, an observation that led to the treatment of hypercalcemia with phosphates.
2. It is responsible for the secondary and tertiary hyperparathyroidism of chronic renal failure.
3. The other major complication of hyperphosphatemia is metastatic calcification (discussed earlier).

C. Treatment
1. Hyperphosphatemia is best treated by dietary phosphate restriction (reduced milk and meat) and the use of phosphate-binding gels (Basaljel, Amphojel, Alternajel, and Dialume).
2. In chronic renal failure, the serum phosphate should ideally be kept at 4 to 5 mg/dl.

Normal magnesium balance

Magnesium, the body's fourth most common cation, is important in the activation of several enzyme systems, and is involved in cellular metabolism and in the electrical activity of nerve and muscle. Calcium and magnesium have complex interdependent relationships.

A. Distribution
1. Of the 25 g total body magnesium, only a small amount is present in the extracellular fluid.

2. Sixty percent of the total body magnesium is present in bone at a calcium to magnesium ratio of 50:1.
3. This ratio does not, however, reflect the fact that 30% of bone magnesium is fully exchangeable.
4. Muscle contains another 20% of body stores.
   a. Magnesium is second only to potassium as the intracellular cation of highest concentration.
5. Serum magnesium concentration is closely maintained at levels between 1.40 and 1.90 mEq/L (0.7 to 0.95 mM/L).
   a. In contrast to calcium, only 20% is protein bound.
   b. Thus variations in serum protein concentration have less effect on serum magnesium levels.

B. Absorption and excretion
   1. Average dietary magnesium content is about 300 mg (25 mEq) daily.
   2. Absorption varies, with intake at around 50% ± 25%.
   3. Calcium and magnesium absorption appears somewhat interdependent, although the relationship is far from clear.
   4. Urinary magnesium excretion varies over a 50-fold range, from a low of 10 to 12 mg (1 mEq) per day.
      a. Glomerular filtration and tubular reabsorption with a measurable Tm appears to be the mechanism of regulation, although urinary magnesium excretion varies with that of other cations.
      b. Sodium or calcium loading increases magnesium excretion, along with increased excretion of the excess cation, implying a common carrier protein for reabsorption.

Hypomagnesemia

A. Causes
   May occur as a result of defective gastrointestinal absorption of magnesium or with renal magnesium wasting.
   1. Magnesium depletion is most severe in patients with a high fecal fat content.

      a. Idiopathic steatorrhea
      b. Diseases of the distal ileum
      c. Short bowel syndrome
      d. Partial gastric resections
      e. Biliary fistulae
  2. Kwashiorkor-type protein malnutrition
  3. Alcoholism
  4. Concurrent hypophosphatemia and alcohol-stimulated increased urinary excretion.
  5. Chronic diuretic therapy, especially mercurials
  6. Mercurials
  7. Bartter's syndrome
  8. Hyperaldosteronism
  9. Hypercalcuria
 10. Syndrome of inappropriate ADH (SIADH)
 11. In diabetic ketoacidosis, rehydration and insulin therapy lead rapidly to hypomagnesemia and occasionally to frank tetany. Perhaps magnesium replacement should be regularly included in the therapy of diabetic ketoacidosis.
 12. Excessive vitamin D administration
 13. Possibly with amphotericin B toxicity
 14. Possibly in hypoparathyroidism following parathyroidectomy

B. Consequences
  1. Manifestations
      a. Lethargy   d. Nausea
      b. Generalized weakness e. Apathy
      c. Anorexia   f. Personality changes
  2. In the absence of hypocalcemia or alkalosis, the following may occur:
      a. Muscle fasciculations
      b. Tremors
      c. Positive Chvostek's and Trousseau's signs (see "Hypocalcemia")
      d. Generalized tetany (a bad prognostic sign)
  3. Although magnesium depletion produces hypocalcemia, the external calcium balance remains neutral or posi-

tive, implying a derangement in the internal control mechanism for calcium.

4. Magnesium depletion is also associated with hypokalemia, which may exacerbate symptoms, with the development of hypokalemic alkalosis.

   a. The low PTH levels, hypocalcemia and its direct effects, and hypokalemia will resolve with replacement of magnesium alone.

   b. Furthermore, the hypocalcemia and hypokalemia of magnesium depletion will remain resistant to replacement therapy with these cations until magnesium stores are repleted.

   c. Therefore, hypocalcemia refractory to replacement therapy should suggest underlying hypomagnesemia.

C. Treatment

   1. Oral route

   2. Parenteral route

      a. The intravenous route should be reserved for patients with seizures or tetany and avoided in children because of the danger of hypotension (intravenous magnesium has a direct vascular smooth muscle relaxing effect).

      b. Although in the absence of renal insufficiency overtreatment is unlikely, caution seems warranted:

         (1) Check deep-tendon reflexes before each intravenous dose.

         (2) Delay further therapy in the absence of reflexes.

      c. With compromised renal function, cautious administration and close monitoring of serum magnesium levels are in order.

   3. A reasonable treatment program for adults with normal renal functions* is outlined here:

      a. Intramuscular route: (50% $MgSO_4$)

         Day 1: 4 ml (16.3 mEq/mg) every 2 hours × 3, then every 4 hours × 4

         Day 2: 2 ml (8.1 mEq/mg) every 4 hours × 6

         Day 3-5: 2 ml (8.1 mEq/mg) every 6 hours

---

*From Flink, E.B.: Therapy of magnesium deficiency, Ann. N.Y. Acad. Sci. **162**:901, 1969.

  b. Intravenous route: (50% $MgSO_4$)

  Day 1: 12 ml (49 mEq/mg) in 1000 ml solution containing glucose over 4 hours, followed by 10 ml (40 mEq/mg)/1000 ml fluid over 10 hours × 2 L

  Days 2 to 5: 12 ml (49 mEq/mg) daily, distributed uniformly in the day's intravenous fluids

  c. Oral therapy: (MgO)

  Most patients can tolerate 250 to 500 mg (12.5 to 25 mEq mg) four times daily without developing diarrhea. This produces 20 to 25 mEq of absorbed magnesium daily for patients with primary magnesium malabsorption and renal magnesium wasting.

  d. Alternative partenterial methods: (10% $MgSO_4$)

  Useful for patients with frank tetany is 1 to 2 g/mg (10 to 20 ml, 8.1 to 16.3 mEq/mg) intravenously over 15 minutes. If clinical response is favorable, further dosage as above, intramuscularly. If no response, repeat as long as deep tendon reflexes are present.

Hypermagnesemia

A. Causes
  1. Hypothermia
  2. Renal insufficiency
  3. Adrenocortical insufficiency
  4. Use of magnesium-containing antacids (Mylanta, Maalox) or laxatives (milk of magnesia, $MgSO_4$) by patients with chronic renal insufficiency

B. Consequences

  The manifestations of acute magnesium intoxication result from central and peripheral neuromuscular and cardiac depression and a direct effect on vascular smooth muscle.

  1. Above 4 mEq/L, the following events occur:
    a. Depression of deep tendon reflexes
    b. Nausea
    c. Vomiting
    d. Hypotension
  2. Above 7 mEq/L
    a. Muscular weakness
    b. Areflexia

3. At 8 to 10 mEq/L
   a. Flaccid quadriplegia and respiratory paralysis
4. Above 12 to 15 mEq/L
   a. Coma
   b. Cardiac depression with prolonged Q-T intervals, A-V block
   c. Cardiac arrest

C. Treatment
   Therapy should be directed at antagonizing magnesium's effects and reducing serum levels by eliminating the source of excess magnesium.
   1. Renal function present
      a. Furosemide diuresis with 0.5 N NaCl volume replacement.
      b. Calcium gluconate (15 mg calcium/kg over a 4-hour period) administration
   2. Renal insufficiency
      a. Peritoneal dialysis or hemodialysis with a magnesium-free dialysate can reduce the serum magnesium level effectively in 4 to 6 hours.
   3. Respiratory depression or cardiac abnormalities present: As little as 5 to 10 mEq calcium gluconate can reduce effects.
   4. Calcium administration should be the first step in treating symptomatic hypermagnesemia.

SELECTED READINGS

Brenner, B.M., and Rector, F.C., Jr., (editors): The kidney, ed. 2, Philadelphia, 1981, W.B. Saunders Co.

Emmett, M., and Narins, R.G.: Clinical use of the anion gap, Medicine **56**:36, 1977.

Maxwell, M.H., and Kleeman, C.R., (editor): Clinical disorders of fluid and electrolyte metabolism, ed. 3, New York, 1980, McGraw-Hill Book Co.

Narins, R.G., and Emmett M.: Simple and mixed acid-base disorders: a practical approach, Medicine **59**:161, 1980.

Schrier, R.W.: Renal and electrolyte disorders, ed. 2, Boston, 1980, Little, Brown & Co.

9

Coagulation

Marvin A. McMillen

The first portion of this chapter addresses itself to the problem of the patient with either an abnormal prothrombin time (PT), partial thromboplastin time (PTT), or thromboplastin time (TT) or the patient whose blood continues to ooze from wound surfaces and puncture sites several days postoperatively. In this group, coagulopathy from lack, inhibition, or breakdown of clotting factors or platelet absence or dysfunction may be responsible. The second portion of this chapter deals with patients who have thrombotic tendencies and outlines diagnostic management principles.

BRIGHT RED BLEEDING

The most common cause of bright red bleeding from surgical wounds and drain sites in the immediate postoperative period is the overlooked or insecurely ligated vessel. Primary consideration should be devoted to the advisability of reexploration. The absence of clotting factors should be diagnosed, and the factors replaced concomitantly. As a general rule, blood loss from chest wounds in excess of 250 ml/hr is an indication for reexploration, and blood loss from intraabdominal wounds in excess of 100 ml/hr requires surgical reevaluation. Blood loss that is increasing almost always necessitates reexploration. However, the acceptable postoperative blood loss varies with the procedure, and when large raw surfaces have been left after long and difficult procedures, the likelihood of finding single-vessel bleeders as the responsible source is less likely. Vigorous replacement with fresh frozen plasma and platelets (if necessary) should suffice in this case. On the other hand, a persistent loss of 25 to 50 ml/hr after a routine sigmoid colectomy may imply a missed mesenteric venous bleeder and thereby require reexploration despite a relatively low volume loss. For the purposes of calculating losses in wound dressings, a 4-inch × 4-inch gauze pad holds approximately 10 ml of blood, and an "ABD" pad holds approximately 30 ml.

PHYSIOLOGY OF CLOT FORMATION

Clot formation represents a dynamic interplay of multiple hemic elements. Vessel walls, tissue thromboplastins, platelets, clotting factors, and fibrinolysins all interact in an integrated fashion that represents the first step in the healing process. Intravascular activation of clotting factors does not normally occur. In this section we will examine clotting in terms of its component parts, and in subsequent sections on pathophysiology and treatment we shall review the role of each part in the sum of the whole.

A. The blood vessel's role in hemostasis

    1. Mechanical—vasoconstriction

        a. Although mechanical forces alone are thought inadequate to effect hemostasis, the simultaneous release of serotonin may play an important role in platelet adherence and agglutination.

        b. Capillaries and venules, however, lack vasamedial smooth muscle, and thus "spasm" plays a minor role in hemostasis from these vessels.

    2. Tissue factors

        a. Platelet adherence and aggregating factor.

            (1) Platelets do not adhere to normal vessel intima.

            (2) They do readily adhere to collagen, vessel basement membrane, and microfibrils.

            (3) Adenosine diphosphate (ADP) released from damaged cells also elicits platelet aggregations.

        b. Tissue factor III reacts rapidly with factor VII to initiate the extrinsic clotting mechanism, leading to rapid thrombus formation.

        c. Collagen may also activate factor XII and thereby also trigger the intrinsic clotting mechanism (Fig. 9-1).

B. The intrinsic clotting mechanism (measured by the PTT)
  1. The cascade mechanism represents a series of enzymatic steps wherein each enzyme catalyzes the one following it in the sequence.
  2. Each enzyme can transform more than one substrate molecule.
    a. Thus factor XII levels are measured in micrograms.
    b. Fibrinogen (factor I) is measured in milligrams.

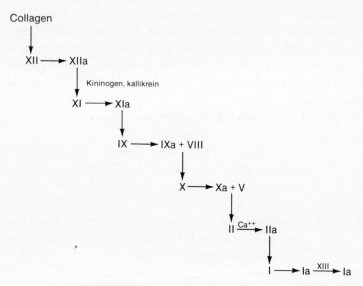

Fig. 9-1. Intrinsic clotting mechanism.

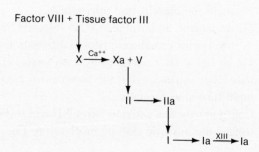

Fig. 9-2. Extrinsic clotting mechanism.

3. Factor production
    a. Factors I, II, V, VII, IX, X produced by hepatic parenchymal cells, reduced in liver disease
    b. Factors II, VII, IX, X production dependent upon vitamin K
    c. Factor VIII produced perhaps by reticuloendothelial system
    d. Factors XI and XIII produced by an unknown source
C. The extrinsic clotting mechanism (measured by the PT) (Fig. 9-2)
    1. The exact role that the extrinsic mechanism plays in invivo clotting is not well defined. Tissue thromboplastin released at the site of injury probably accelerates the clotting reaction by increasing the amount of activated thrombin.
D. Fibrinolysis (Fig. 9-3)

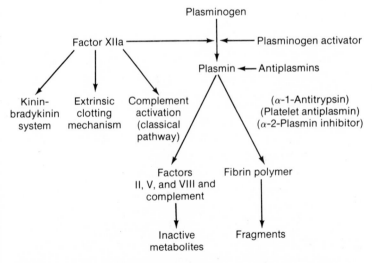

Fig. 9-3. Fibrinolysis. The intima of blood vessels contains large amounts of plasminogen activator that initiates fibrinolysis. This may be the mechanism by which patients with intravascular clotting clear peripheral thrombi. The clinical importance of the plasminogen activator is suggested by the demonstration of low vessel fibrinolysin activity in patients with recurrent peripheral venous thrombosis. The new vascularity of neoplastic processes does not contain plasminogen activator and may represent a nidus for the coagulopathy encountered in neoplasia.

1. Factor XII triggers the clotting cascade, the kinin system, complement activation, and the fibrinolysins.
2. Other plasminogen activators also trigger the fibrinolytic system and enhance clot lysis.

E. Platelets
1. Platelets play an essential role in clot formation by:
   a. Adhering to areas of injury
   b. Agglutinating to each other to form a plug
   c. Releasing phospholipid factor III to initiate the intrinsic system
   d. Passively providing clotting factors adherent to their surface
2. Platelets also play a role in clot retraction.
3. Platelet surface plasmin initiates fibrinolysis.

PATHOPHYSIOLOGY OF THROMBUS FORMATION AND LYSIS
Platelet dysfunction

A. Manifestation
1. Petechial rash
2. Mucosal ooze
3. Slow ooze from raw surfaces
4. Leak from line sites

B. Assessment
1. The Rumpel-Leed test: Blood pressure cuff inflated to 40 mm Hg and left in place for 5 minutes.
   a. Normal: Three to five petechia develop in 5 minutes, although individuals with increased capillary fragility may develop 10 to 20 petechiae.
   b. Abnormal: In platelet coagulopathy, a shower of petechia occurs.
2. Peripheral smear: A platelet estimate of 5 to 8 hpf roughly correlates with a count of 250,000.
3. Bone marrow examination: The presence of 1 megakaryocyte per 10 hpf correlates with normal platelet production.
4. Standardized bleeding time (Ivy): laboratory/technician specific.

C. Causes of platelet dysfunction
1. Central (bone marrow) decreased production

a. Microenvironment
  (1) Congenital
    (a) Wiskott-Aldrich syndrome with low IgA, eczema, and thrombocytopenia
    (b) Maternal thiazides
    (c) Fanconi's pancytopenia
    (d) Thrombocytopenia, absent radius (TAR) syndrome
    (e) Cytomegalovirus (CMV) and rubella
  (2) Acquired
    (a) Drugs—especially methotrexate
    (b) Alcohol
b. Stem cell—megakaryocyte
  (1) Radiation
  (2) Cystosine arabinoside, cyclophosamide (Cytoxan), busulfan, methotrexate, and 6-mercaptopurine.
c. Thrombopoeitin–differentiation arrest—usually congenital
  (1) B_{12} deficiency   (2) Iron deficiency
d. Infiltrative diseases
  (1) Carcinoma, leukemia, lymphoma, neuroblastoma
  (2) Myelofibrosis
  (3) Gaucher's disease
  (4) Osteopetrosis
  (5) Miliary tuberculosis
2. Peripheral increased destruction
  a. Mechanical
    (1) Burns or hypothermia
    (2) Giant cavernous hemangioma (Kasbach-Merritt syndrome)
    (3) Splenomegaly (e.g., Felty's syndrome in rheumatoid arthritis)
    (4) Portal hypertension
    (5) Transplant rejections; microangiopathic anemia-like mechanism
  b. Immunologic
    (1) Idiopathic thrombocytopenic purpura (ITP)
    (2) Autoimmune diseases—lupus, rheumatoid arthritis

    (3) Drug-related autoimmune diseases—procainamide hydrochloride (Pronestyl)

    (4) Quinine, quinidine—antibody against drug stuck to platelet's surface, not platelets

  c. Drug related

    (1) Thiazides

    (2) Sulfonamides

    (3) Heparin

    (4) Gold salts

    (5) Antilymphocyte globulin

  d. Infections

    (1) Bacterial sepsis—two thirds of patients with gram-negative sepsis have platelet counts > 150,000, one third have platelet counts > 50,000

    (2) Rickettsial—Rocky Mountain spotted fever, typhus, typhoid, and diphtheria

    (3) Granulomatous diseases—tuberculosis, histoplasmosis, and brucellosis

    (4) Parasites—malaria and trypanosomiasis

    (5) Viruses—CMV, infectious mononucleosis, and mumps

3. Dysfunction

  a. Congenital

    (1) Membrane: paroxysmal nocturnal hemoglobinurea (PNH)—abnormal activation and C_4 receptors on red cells and platelets result in autolysis; may also be related to episodes of thrombosis and hepatic vein thrombosis (Budd-Chiari syndrome) seen in PNH

    (2) Adhesion defects: Bernard-Soulier—giant platelets, defective adhesion

    (3) Agglutination defects: thrombasthenia—decreased aggregation (markedly impaired clot retraction)

    (4) Defective release reaction

  b. Acquired

    (1) Uremia: probably from excess guanidinosuccinate

    (2) Liver disease

    (3) Myeloproliferative disorders

      (a) Essential thrombocythemia

      (b) Polycythemia vera

      (c) Myeloid metaplasia

      (d) Chronic myelogenous leukemia

      (e) Myeloma and Waldenstrom's macroglobulinemia

    (4) Drugs

      (a) Aspirin

      (b) Dextran

      (c) Carbenicillin

      (d) Quinidine and quinine (gin and tonic drinker's thrombocytopenia)

      (e) Heparin

      (f) Nonsteroidal anti-inflammatory agents

      (g) Nitroprusside

      (h) Cephalosporin antibiotics

D. Platelet destruction syndromes

  1. Idiopathic thrombocytopenic purpura (ITP): ITP is a disease of unknown cause in which platelets are destroyed by an IgG antiplatelet antibody, usually to a platelet-specific antigen.

    a. Diagnosis

      (1) Clinical signs

        (a) Petechiae

        (b) Epistaxis

        (c) The mucosal-type bleeding encountered in platelet dysfunction

        (d) Rarely splenomegaly

      (2) Tests results

        (a) Peripheral smears: rare platelets/hpf

        (b) Bone marrow aspirate: megakaryocytes present in normal or increased numbers

        (c) Bleeding time: prolonged

        (d) Rumple-Leed test: positive

        (e) PT and PTT: normal

        (f) Clot retraction: decreased

        (g) Sera: will agglutinate normal patient's platelets

        (h) Radioimmunoassay: platelets coated with IgG.

This latter phenomenon is the basis for the antiplatelet antibody assay.

b. Acute ITP
   (1) Occurs in pediatric patients most frequently between ages 2 and 6
   (2) Has no predilection
   (3) Commoner in the cold months
   (4) Febrile viral illness usually precedes it
   (5) Course is self-limited
   (6) Steroids are of questionable efficacy

c. Chronic ITP
   (1) Characteristics
      (a) A disease of adults
      (b) Has threefold female predominance
      (c) Onset is insidious
      (d) Course characterized by exacerbations and relapses
      (e) Mortality is 7% to 10% and death is usually from intracranial bleeding when peripheral counts are below 10,000
   (2) Medical management of chronic ITP
      (a) Platelet count: 30,000 to 100,000
         i. Acceptable for outpatient management
         ii. Need extra platelets in event of surgery
      (b) Platelet count: 20,000 to 50,000
         i. Manifestations
            a. Epistaxis   *d.* Oral bleeding
            b. Petechiae   *e.* Menorrhagia
            c. Purpura
         ii. Steroids needed
            a. Acute dose: prednisone 1 mg/kg/day.
            b. Appropriate tapering after 2 weeks of stabilization.
            c. If 1 mg/kg/day is insufficient, another 10% will respond to 2 mg/kg/day.
            d. This program will achieve remission in 70% of patients.
      (c) Platelet count: <10,000
         i. Illness is life threatening

      ii. Need platelet superconcentrates (1 to 2/ day) (and bolus intravenous steroids— methylprednisolone sodium succinate (Solu-Medrol), 2 gm intravenously every 6 hr, or hydrocortisone sodium succinate Solu-Cortef, 100 mg every 6 hr)

  (3) Surgical management in chronic ITP

    (a) Indications

      i. Recurrent episodes

      ii. Recurring minor or more than two severe bleeds

      iii. High steroid requirements

      iv. Steroid intolerance

    (b) Preoperative preparation should include:

      i. Adequate steroid supplementation for both stress and platelet preservation

      ii. Platelet superpack immediately prior to surgery may be useful

      iii. A second superpack hanging during surgery

    (c) Although most patients will have a prompt increase in platelet counts postoperatively, further platelets should be available.

    (d) Operative mortality rate is less than 1%.

    (e) In patients who relapse, a postoperative liver-spleen scan should be obtained in search of an accessory spleen (found in 10% of the population) that may have been missed at the time of operation.

  (4) In patients refractory to both steroids and splenectomy, cyclophosamide (Cytoxan), azathioprine (Imuran), or vincristine may have therapeutic benefit.

2. Thrombotic thrombocytopenic purpura (TTP): TTP is a syndrome of microangiopathic hemolytic anemia associated with fluctuating neurologic abnormalities. This is a highly malignant syndrome with a 65% mortality within 90 days of presentation.

    a. Causes

      (1) A primary lesion of small vessels may be the triggering event.

      (2) However, primary coagulopathic, autoimmune, or infectious etiologies have also been suggested.

    b. Diagnosis

      (1) Clinical presentation: Neurologic abnormalities, anemia, throbocytonia, renal failure, mild jaundice.

        (a) Vary from mild to fulminant

        (b) Plethora of presenting symptoms reflects ischemic injury to the central nervous system, lungs, heart, viscera, or kidneys

        (c) Fever is present in 90% of the patients

        (d) Splenomegaly is present in 30%

      (2) Test results

        (a) Peripheral smears: damaged red cells (burr cells), red cell fragments, and marked reticulocytosis (immature red blood cells)

        (b) Bilirubin: raised in 90% of patients

        (c) Proteinuria and microscopic/gross hematuria are present in most patients

    C. Treatment

      (1) The primary therapy is plasmapheresis.

      (2) Platelet-inhibiting drugs are occasionally useful.

  3. Posttransfusion purpura (PTP): An exceedingly rare cause of thrombocytopenia, PTP occurs 5 to 8 days after transfusion therapy. Thrombocytopenia is profound and the risk of an intracranial hemorrhage is high. All reported cases have been in parous women, and a specific platelet antigen (Pl^{Al}) has been implicated as the target of a serum antibody.

    a. Treatment

      (1) Transfused platelets are ineffective.

      (2) Exchange transfusion or plasmapheresis has been recommended.

      (3) Steroids may be of benefit.

      (4) The disorder is usually self-limited, and resolution occurs within 10 to 48 days.

FACTOR DEFICIENCY

A. Inadequate production
  1. Factor VIII deficiency (hemophilia A) represents about 85% of clinical hemophilia.
      a. Patients with severe hemophilia
        (1) Have less than 1% factor VIII
        (2) May present in infancy with intracranial bleeding or bleeding after circumcision
        (3) Develop ecchymoses readily (but seldom petechiae)
        (4) Are plagued by intraarticular hemorrhage and hemarthroses, usually of the weight-bearing joints, which are painful and ultimately crippling
        (5) Trauma need not accompany hemorrhage. Hemorrhage into rectus sheath may mimic acute abdominal pain or appendicitis. Spontaneous hemorrhage into the fascial plane of the neck may produce acute pharyngeal obstruction.
      b. Patients with moderate hemophilia
        (1) Have from 1% to 5% factor VIII
        (2) Have an attenuated form of the disease with occasional hemarthroses
      c. Patients with mild hemophilia
        (1) Have 5% to 30% factor VIII
        (2) May be asymptomatic until dental extraction or surgery

Table 9-1. Coagulation test findings in hereditary factor deficiencies

Disorder	Abnormal	Normal
Hemophilia (factor VIII); Christmas disease (factor IX); factors XI, XII (Hageman); von Willebrand's	APTT	PT
Factor VII	PT	APTT
Factors II (prothrombin), V, X; dysfibrinogenemias; deficiency of or inhibitor to one or more coagulation factors, DIC, vitamin K deficiency, broad-spectrum antibiotics, malabsorption, liver disease	APTT, PT	
Factor XIII (fibrin F stabilizing factor), von Willebrand's, dysfibrinogenemias, Osler-Weber-Rendu, Ehlers-Danlos, vasculitis		PT, APTT

d. Therapy

Therapy is directed at obtaining a factor VIII level of 30% of normal.

(1) Factor VIII concentrate

(a) One unit factor VIII concentrate equals amount of factor VIII in 1 ml of blood.

(b) A patient with severe hemophilia, then, will require one unit of concentrate per kg of body weight per 2% increase in clotting or 15 units of concentrate per kg of body weight for 30% to 60% raised as an acute dose. Since the half-life of factor VIII is 12 hours, replacement of half this amount is necessary every 12 hours until the bleeding ceases or until the tenth postoperative day.

(c) Lyophilized antihemophilic factor has a significant (though small) risk of hepatitis. It may, however, be the preferred method for patients who are already known to be hepatitis B anti-

Table 9-2. Protocol for replacement of coagulation factors

Factor	Percent of normal required Minor surgery	Major surgery	Material	Dose per Kg	Repeat (hr)
I (fibrinogen)	20	40	Cryoprecipitate	0.3 bag	48
II (prothrombin)	40	40	Plasma	20 ml	24
V	10	15	Plasma	10 ml	12
VII	10	20	Plasma	10 ml	6
VIII	40	80	Concentrate*	40 units	6†
IX	40	80	Concentrate‡	80 units	6§
X	15	20	Plasma	10 ml	24
XI	?	?30	Plasma	20 ml	48
XII	?	?	None	None	
XIII	5	5	Cryoprecipitate	0.1 bag	48
			or plasma	5 ml	48
VWF	50	?	Cryoprecipitate	0.6 bag	8

*Or cryoprecipitate.
†Or better given 5 units kg hr.
‡Or plasma.
§Dose—40 units kg or preferably 5 units kg hr.
From Watson-Williams EJ: Medical evaluation of the preoperative patient, Med. Clin. North Am. **63:**1183, 1979.

gen positive. There is also concern that the HTLV-III virus may contaminate this preparation, but screening of potential commercial donors for HTLV-III antigenemia may soon ameliorate this problem.
- (2) Cryoprecipitate
    - (a) Dosage
        - i. One bag (80 to 100 units)/2 kg
        - ii. One-half the amount repeated every 12 hours
- (3) Fresh-frozen plasma (FFP), though readily available, requires large volumes for replacement. However, in an emergency situation, its use may be life-saving.
- (4) Factor VIII inhibitor
    - (a) Approximately 10% of patients with severe hemophilia will develop factor VIII inhibitor, an antibody which quickly inactivates transfused factor VIII.
    - (b) Levels of inhibitor may range from moderate to severe and may even require plasmapheresis to maintain adequate factor VIII levels.
    - (c) Steroids in large doses (prednisone, 60 mg/day) orally may be tried, but evidence to document their efficacy is slight.
2. Factor IX deficiency (Christmas factor)
   Factor IX deficiency accounts for about 15% of cases of clinical hemophilia. It is clinically indistinguishable from factor VIII deficiency and also presents in severe, moderate, and mild forms.
   - a. Therapy
       - (1) Options available
           - (a) Cryoprecipitate
           - (b) FFP
           - (c) Konyne (see Chapter 28)
       - (2) Dosage
           - (a) For surgery: acute 40 to 60 units/kg
           - (b) For hemarthrosis: 20 units/kg
           - (c) For maintenance: 10 to 20 units/kg/day, 5 units/kg

(3) Konyne and hepatitis

The temptation to use Konyne to reverse the effects of dicoumarol (Coumadin) or replace the vitamin K–dependent factors should be resisted because of the incidence of hepatitis. Aquamephyton (10 mg intravenously) is effective within 8 to 12 hours, and the patient may be supported with FFP until then.

3. Von Willebrand's disease

Von Willebrand's disease manifests as an autosomal dominant disorder of factor VIII carrier protein and platelet dysfunction. A combination of low factor VIII levels and abnormal platelet agglutination is observed clinically.

a. Clinical manifestation
   (1) Tends to become more severe with age.
   (2) Epistaxis, ecchymoses, and menorrhagia are common.
   (3) Severe hemorrhage at time of surgery is not common, but can occur.
   (4) Postpartum hemorrhage is uncommon, probably because of large amount of tissue thromboplastin (factor VII) in placenta.
   (5) Hemarthrosis is rare.

b. Laboratory findings
   (1) Elevated PTT
   (2) Normal PT
   (3) Prolonged modified bleeding time
   (4) Platelet counts normal
   (5) Platelet agglutination in response to ADP decreased
   (6) Hemophiliac plasma corrects abnormal PTT in Von Willebrand's patient

c. Treatment
   (1) Cryoprecipitate, which contains both factor VIII and factor VIII carrier protein
   (2) Though uncommon, Von Willebrand's disease should always be considered in either the male or female patient who hemorrhages excessively in surgery.

4. Factor XI deficiency
   a. Clinical manifestation
      (1) Quite mild
      (2) Ecchymoses
      (3) Epistaxis
      (4) Menorrhagia
      (5) Postdental or postoperative hemorrhage
      (6) Hemarthroses uncommon
   b. Laboratory findings
      (1) PTT markedly elevated
   c. Treatment
      Because the quantitative amount of factor XI is small and the half-life quite long (40 to 84 hours), most patients will correct with only small amounts of plasma.
5. Factor XII deficiency
   Factor XII deficiency (Hageman factor) is not commonly associated with clinical or surgical bleeding. Coagulation proceeds normally and no replacement is required. The disorder is not uncommon and accounts for the markedly abnormal PTT sometimes found in preoperative coagulation studies in asymptomatic patients.
6. Deficiencies or abnormalities of fibrinogen (factor I)
   Congenital deficiencies or abnormalities of fibrinogen are quite uncommon but usually present in childhood in the offspring of consanguinous parents. Familial occurrences of dysfunctional fibrinogen have been reported, but the majority of patients will have a benign course, without replacement therapy. The incidence of wound dehiscence is, however, reported to be higher in these patients, reemphasizing the importance of clot formation as the first step in healing and suggesting that appropriate technical considerations such as retention sutures be applied.
7. Other factors
   Autosomal recessive deficiencies of clotting—factor II, V, VII, and X, though rare and of variable penetrance, should be considered in the face of unexplained postoperative oozing or menorrhagia in the patient without other discernible cause.

8. Factor XIII deficiency

Factor XIII converts fibrin monomer to a more stable matrix of fibrin polymer by catalyzing the formation of peptide bonds between chains.

a. Clinical manifestations of factor XIII deficiency
   (1) Oozing from the cord at birth
   (2) Ecchymoses
   (3) Hematomas and oozing from minor abrasions
   (4) Hemarthrosis uncommon
   (5) Higher incidence of intracranial hemorrhages than in other hereditary bleeding disorders
   (6) Recurrent spontaneous abortions
b. Laboratory findings
   (1) PT: normal
   (2) PTT: normal
   (3) Clots: soluble in 5-M urea.
c. Treatment

   Because of the extremely long half-life of the factor (>150 hours), effective hemostasis will occur with as little as 2 to 3 ml of FFP/kg every 2 to 4 weeks. Cryoprecipitate also contains factor XIII.

9. Coagulation disorders in the patient with hepatic disease

Factors I, II, V, VII, IX, and X, produced in the liver, are markedly decreased in patients with end-stage cirrhosis. These same factors probably also decrease in the terminal hepatic failure of the multiple-organ system failure syndrome. In chronic liver disease accompanied by portal hypertension, splenomegaly may occur, and the concomitant sequestration of platelets may aggravate the bleeding problem. Platelet production is decreased as part of the marrow pancytopenia of nutritional deprivation, and platelet destruction is increased.

a. Treatment
   (1) Platelet counts in excess of 100,000 are adequate, 50,000 to 100,000 equivocal, and beneath 50,000 definitely in need of replacement
   (2) FFP, remembering that it will provide a volume load that the patient may have difficulty handling
   (3) Nutritional support

SURGERY AND CARE OF THE CRITICALLY ILL PATIENT ON ORAL DICUMAROL ANTICOAGULANTS

A. Uses of dicumarol (Coumadin)
1. Thrombotic cerebrovascular accidents
2. Ulcerating carotid plaques
3. Postmyocardial infarct
4. Deep venous thrombosis and pulmonary embolus prevention
5. After cardiac valve replacement

B. Dosage
1. Usual oral loading dose: 10 to 20 mg daily for 3 days followed by 2.5 to 7.5 mg every other day or daily
2. Monthly protimes are used to adjust the dose to give 1½ to 2 times the normal prothrombin time (11 to 13 sec)
3. Affected by
   a. Intestinal absorption
   b. Degree of albumin binding (competition with other drugs)
   c. Body stores of vitamin K
   d. Hepatic metabolism

C. Effects of dicumarol (Coumadin) maintenance
1. Decreases levels of factors II, VII, IX, X and the VIII and V antagonist protein C
2. The oral or intravenous administration of 50 mg Aquamephyton orally or intravenously reverses the effects in the patient with a normal liver. The oral route takes 10 to 12 hours; the intravenous route takes 4 to 6 hours.
3. The incidence of "rebound" thrombosis is very low.
4. In the emergency setting, FFP will restore normal clotting quite rapidly.

INCREASED FACTOR DESTRUCTION

A. Diffuse intravascular coagulation (DIC)
Many critically ill, trauma, and septic patients develop the syndrome of diffuse intravascular coagulation.
1. Predisposing conditions
   a. Infections
      (1) Bacterial
         (a) Endotoxinemic—*E. coli*

      (b) Polysaccharide-encapsulated organisms—*E. coli*, Klebsiella, pneumococci, *H. influenza*, some protei, meningococcus

      (c) Hemolysins—*C. perfringens*

  (2) Viral—CMV, herpes

  (3) Mycotic—Histoplasma, Asperigillus

  (4) Protozoal—malarial

b. Inflammatory

  (1) Vasculitis—polyarteritis, lupus

  (2) Hemolysis

      (a) Paroxysmal nocturnal hemoglobinuria

      (b) Transfusion reaction

  (3) Snakebite—complement activation and defibrination

c. Neoplastic—especially mucin-secreting adenocarcinomas

  (1) Prostate, pancreas, lung, stomach, colon, breast

  (2) Leukemias

d. Toxic/metabolic

  (1) Drugs

  (2) Snakebite

  (3) Liver disease—cirrhosis/acute yellow atrophy

e. Traumatic

  (1) Crush injury

  (2) Fat embolism and adult respiratory distress syndrome (ARDS)

  (3) Massive central nervous system injury—phospholipid release

  (4) Burns

  (5) Hypotension, shock, and acidosis

f. Mechanical

  (1) After open heart surgery (common but seldom of major clinical impact)

  (2) Giant hemangioma (Kasbach-Merrit syndrome)

g. Obstetric

  (1) Abruptio placenta

  (2) Septic abortion and chorioamnonitis

  (3) Amniotic fluid embolus

  (4) Retained dead fetus

       (5) Hydatidiform mole

       (6) Hypertonic saline abortion

       (7) Toxemia

       (8) Septic pelvic thrombophlebitis

   h. Miscellaneous

2. Diagnosis

   a. Clinical presentation

       (1) Generalized ooze from venipuncture, line sites, and even several-day-old wounds.

   b. Laboratory findings

       (1) PT elevated

       (2) PTT elevated

       (3) Long thrombin time

       (4) Low platelet count

       (5) Low quantitative fibrinogen

       (6) Red cells on a peripheral smear show marked fragmenting

       (7) Fibrin-split products elevated

       (8) PO_2 decreasing

       (9) Pulmonary compliance increasing

     (10) Chest x-ray may show interstitial pattern consistent with ARDS. Any internal organ may be ischemically compromised but a rising blood urea nitrogen and creatinine require prompt attention with volume and diuretics.

3. Treatment

   a. Treatment should be directed at discovery and therapy of the underlying cause. In the critically ill patient, DIC is often not the cause of the patient's death, but a harbinger of it. Surgery should be performed if necessary to resolve infection.

   b. Heparin, though seemingly of theoretic value, has seldom been effective in clinical use and is probably indicated only when ischemic symptoms of a vital internal organ present or when limb-threatening thrombosis occurs.

   c. Steroids

       (1) Large doses of steroids may accelerate DIC and are not indicated in the treatment of it.

(2) The benefits of steroids in treating the underlying disease should not be sacrificed, however, because of a theoretic or unproved risk of coagulopathy.

   d. Factor replacement

     (1) Cryoprecipitate offers some volume advantages over FFP, but either will do in an emergency.

     (2) A platelet count <50,000 can result in clinical bleeding and should be corrected with platelet administration. In the presence of bleeding, platelets counts of at least 100,000 should be maintained whenever possible.

B. Excessive fibrinolysis—patients with clinical bleeding whose blood forms a stable clot at 37° C which lyses in 10 to 20 minutes should be considered to possibly have disordered fibrinolysis.

  a. Congenital

     (1) Kindreds have been reported with abnormal plasminogen activity and excessive thrombus formation.

     (2) However, congenital absence of plasminogen activity itself is probably incompatible with life.

  b. Acquired

     (1) Primary

       (a) Excessive amounts of plasminogen activator release. For example:

         i. Urokinase from metastatic prostate carcinoma or endogenous plasminogen activator released after shock

         ii. Anoxia

         iii. Sepsis

         iv. Surgery or cardiopulmonary bypass

       (b) Impaired plasminogen activator breakdown in liver disease

         i. Particularly aggravated after portocaval shunting

         ii. May be the initial stimulator to a DIC

       (c) Acquired fibrinolysins, especially in terminal leukemia. Other proteases capable of degrading fibrinogen appear and may become clinically significant

(2) Secondary

   (a) Excessive fibrinolysis is a component of most diffuse intravascular coagulopathy.

   (b) Diagnosis

      i. No reliable laboratory examination exists.

      ii. The presence of persistent oozing in a postoperative patient in the right clinical setting may suggest its presence and justify the empiric use of therapy if the situation appears sufficiently desperate.

   (c) Treatment

      i. Epsilon aminocaproic acid (EACA; Amicar)

         a. Initial dose: 5 g orally or by slowly intravenously

         b. If bleeding continues, 1 g/hr for 8 hours or longer

         c. No more than 30 g per 24 hours

DISORDERS OF HYPERCOAGULABILITY AND THROMBOSIS
Deep venous thrombosis

A. Clinical manifestation

  1. Calf pain and unilateral edema is associated with 50% of patients who subsequently develop pulmonary embolus.

  2. Slight tenderness of the deep femoral vein or no discomfort at all may be the only symptoms.

  3. Unchanged or worsening symptoms after anticoagulation suggest a torn soleus muscle masquerading as a positive Homan's sign.

B. Radiologic studies

  1. Doppler ultrasound—loss of venous augmentation over femoral vein with calf compression

  2. Venogram

C. Treatment

  1. A chest roentgenograms and blood gas studies should be obtained as a baseline, even in the young patient who has no history suggestive of pulmonary embolus.

2. Lung perfusion/ventilation scan should be obtained in any questionable case.
3. Full heparinization
   a. 10 to 15 mg/kg as a bolus
   b. Continuous hourly infusion of 5 to 10 mg/kg to obtain an activated PTT of 1½ to 2 times the control or a thrombin time of 1½ to 2 times normal
4. Thrombolytic therapy
   a. Advantages
      (1) Directly lyses deep venous thrombi.
      (2) May reduce hemodynamic disturbances and restore circulation to normal.
      (3) May prevent damage to deep veins and valves and subsequent chronic venous insufficiency.
      (4) May decrease the likelihood of permanent pulmonary hypertension.
      (5) Has not been associated with converting deep venous thrombosis (DVT) to pulmonary emboli. (The National Institutes of Health has recently recommended careful study of thrombolytic agents in the treatment of DVT and pulmonary emboli.)
   b. Contraindications
      (1) Active internal bleeding
      (2) Recent cardiovascular accident or other intracranial bleeding.
   c. Surgical intensive care unit (SICU)–acquired DVT
      The incidence of SICU-acquired DVT or pulmonary embolus is rare. Routine prophylactic anticoagulation is not routinely performed. Each case is individualized and a decision for prophylaxis made (e.g., prior history, physical examination, hypercoagulable, not ambulated).
      In general, if prophylaxis is to be useful, it needs to be started before the onset of prolonged bedrest. Bleeding is very common in SICU patients and mitigates against the use of heparin. In such settings, vena caval umbrellas are used when the risk/benefit ratio is deemed acceptable.

d. Thrombosis from line placement

Upper extremity thrombosis from line placement is common and usually of little clinical significance. Very symptomatic and/or progressive cases may require anticoagulation.

e. Fibrinolytic agents used in deep venous thrombosis and pulmonary embolism

(1) Urokinase

(a) Loading dose: 2,000 CTA units/pound or 4,400 CTA units/kg over 10 min

(b) Maintenance dose: 2,000 CTA units/hr for 12 to 24 hr

(2) Streptokinase

(a) Loading dose: 250,000 CTA units over 20 to 30 min

(b) Maintenance dose: 100,000 units/hr for 24 hr

ANTITHROMBIN III DEFICIENCY

Antithrombin III, or heparin cofactor, controls the mechanism of thrombus formation by inhibiting factors II, V, IX, X, and XII. Antithrombin III is an acute phase reactant, produced by the liver. Low-dose heparin (5,000 units subcutaneously every 8 hours) probably functions to prevent deep venous thrombosis and subsequent pulmonary emboli by potentiating antithrombin III. Therapeutic heparinization results in decreased levels of antithrombin III after 4 or 5 days, manifested by a hypercoagulable state if heparin is suddenly withdrawn.

A. Congenital

1. Presentation

a. Recurrent DVT

b. Pulmonary emboli

c. Family history of sudden death

2. Treatment

a. Resistant to conventional doses of heparin, PT, and PTT unaffected.

b. Fresh-frozen plasma (10 to 15 ml/kg/day) required to render the patient susceptible to heparinization.

c. Prophylaxis with dicumarol (Coumadin) should be lifelong.

B. Acquired
  1. Presentation: Often an inordinate heparin requirement to achieve effective anticoagulation
  2. Etiologies
     a. Liver disease: The inability to produce antithrombin III may result in patients with liver disease and elevated PT/PTT being paradoxically difficult to anticoagulate. Giving FFP, which contains antithrombin III may make them suddenly overly anticoagulated and result in severe bleeding.
        (1) Cirrhosis
        (2) Hepatitis
        (3) Terminal hepatic failure of sepsis
     b. Diabetes mellitus   d. Drugs
     c. Vascular disease

THROMBOGENESIS SECONDARY TO PLATELET PATHOLOGY

A. Paroxysmal nocturnal hemoglobinuria
   In this disorder, red cell and platelet membranes bear an abnormal receptor for the C_4 component of complement. Red cells undergo chronic (and sometimes decompensated) hemolysis and the complement-mediated membrane defects result in osmotic instability, the basis for the Ham's sugar-water test. Platelet adhesion and agglutination are normal.
   1. Results
      a. Chronic low-grade thrombosis
      b. Tendency toward central venous thrombosis of the renal veins, hepatic veins (Budd-Chiari syndrome) and the inferior vena cava
   2. Laboratory studies
      a. Ham's sugar-water test
B. Thrombocytosis
   1. Primary (malignant disease of megalokaryocytes)
      a. Causes
         (1) Essential thrombocytosis
         (2) Polycythemia vera
         (3) Chronic granulocytic leukemia
         (4) Idiopathic myelofibrosis
      b. Platelet counts >1 million and as high as 14 million

   c. Bleeding common with primary thrombocytosis, less common with secondary

   d. Treatment

     (1) Busulfan or other antimetabolites

  2. Secondary—less morbid and lower mortality

   a. Causes

     (1) Infections

       (a) Recovery from acute infection

       (b) Gonorrheal arthritis, tuberculosis

     (2) Inflammatory

       (a) Rheumatoid arthritis

       (b) Periarteritis nodosa

       (c) Wegener's granulomatosis

       (d) Sarcoidosis

       (e) Acute rheumatic fever

       (f) Ulcerative colitis

       (g) Regional enteritis

       (h) Cirrhosis

     (3) Neoplastic

       (a) Carcinoma

       (b) Hodgkin's disease and other lymphomas

     (4) Drugs

       (a) Vincristine   (b) Epinephrine

     (5) Iron-deficiency anemia

     (6) After splenectomy

     (7) Other

       (a) Osteoporosis

         i. Rebound after B_{12}

         ii. After chemotherapy

       (b) Platelet counts >400,000 associated with clinical thrombosis

   b. Presentation: Bleeding uncommon

   c. Treatment: If thrombotic, may need aspirin, heparin, or plasmapheresis

HYPERVISCOSITY SYNDROMES

1. Patients with polycythemia vera, multiple myeloma, and Waldenstrom's macroglobulinemia have both increased blood viscosity resulting in small vessel stasis and increased platelet adherence.

a. Treatment
  (1) Chemotherapy directed at the cause of the disorder is the primary therapy.
  (2) Plasmapheresis and anticoagulants may be effective in acute thrombosis.

PROTEIN C DEFICIENCY

Protein C is a vitamin K–dependent antagonist of factors VIII and V. A deficiency of this blood protein is familial and is associated with a hypercoagulable state. Patients may present with major vein thrombosis that may be peripheral or central (portal, renal, caval). Anticoagulants are indicated.

SUGGESTED READINGS

Bell, W.R., et al: Thrombocytopenia occurring during the administration of heparin, Ann. Intern. Med. **85**:155, 1976.

Clinics in hematology: Thrombosis, Philadelphia, 1981, W.B. Saunders Co.

Colman, R.W., et al. (editors): Hemostasis and thrombosis, Philadelphia, 1982, J.B. Lippincott.

Evans, B.E.: Dental treatment of hemophiliacs: Evaluation of dental program (1975-1976) at the Mount Sinai Hospital International Hemophilia Training Center, Mt. Sinai J. Med. **44**:409, 1977.

Hampson, W.G.J., et al.: Failure of low-dose heparin to prevent deep vein thrombosis after hip-replacement arthroplasty, Lancet **2**:795, 1974.

Harris, W.H., et al.: Aspirin prophylaxis of venous thromboembolism after total hip-replacement, N. Engl. J. Med. **297**:1246, 1977.

Hirsh, J., et al.: A practical approach to the diagnosis, prevention, and treatment of venous thromboembolism, New York, 1981, Grune & Stratton.

International multicenter trial: prevention of fatal postoperative pulmonary embolism by low doses of heparin, Lancet **2**:45, 1975.

Leyvrax, P.F., et al.: Adjusted versus fixed-dose subcutaneous heparin in the prevention of deep-vein thrombosis after total hip replacement, N. Engl. J. Med. **309**:954, 1983.

New perspectives in aspirin therapy, Am. J. Med. Suppl. June 14, 1983.

Nunn, J.F., and Freeman, J.: Problems of oxygenation and oxygen transport during hemorrhage, Anesthesia **19**:206, 1964.

Sikorski, J.M., Hampson, W.G., and Staddon, G.E.: The natural history of aetiology of deep vein thrombosis after total hip replacement, J. Bone Joint Surg. **B63**:171, 1981.

Thomas, D.J., et al.: Effect of hematocrit on cerebral blood flow in man, Lancet **2**:941, 1977.

Thompson, A.R.: Manual of hemostasis and thrombosis, 1983, F.A. Davis.

Wasserman, L.R., and Gilbert, H.S.: Surgical bleeding in polycythemia vera, Ann. N.Y. Acad. Sci. **115**:112, 1964.

Wessler, S., and Gitel, S.N.: Warfarin: from bedside to bench, N. Engl. J. Med. **311**:645, 1984.

10

Metabolic support

Frank B. Cerra

Malnutrition, once developed, affects all organ systems except the central nervous system. The effects include a loss in mass, function, and "reserve" capacity to respond to a severe and/or sustained-stress stimulus. Under these latter circumstances, significant malnutrition becomes a contributing factor to morbidity, length of stay, and probably rehabilitation time to functional recovery. Table 10-1 summarizes the spectrum of structural and functional changes associated with the malnutrition process.

Applying the principles of classic starvation nutrition to the stress of surgery, trauma, and sepsis has shown two general effects: (1) poor end-organ support in a high percentage of patients as evaluated by nitrogen retention, visceral proteins and indexes of metabolic well-being (anergy, lymphocyte count); and (2) the appearance of new complications, such as increased levels of carbon dioxide production, prolonged ventilation times, hepatic steatosis and cholestasis, and multiple organ dysfunction.

In these stress settings, then, principles different from those of classic starvation states are operative. This information has led to the development of principles of stress nutrition that seem to result in better support with fewer complications. This chapter is a summary of these support principles as currently conceived and practiced in adult patients.

Portions of this chapter have been taken from Cerra, F.B.: Pocket manual of surgical nutrition, St. Louis, 1984, The C.V. Mosby Co.

Table 10-1. Demonstrable end-organ alterations in malnutrition

Organ	Anatomic	Physiologic
Heart	Four-chamber dilation Atrophic degeneration with necrosis and fibrosis Myofibrillar disruption	Q-T prolongation, low voltage, bradycardia; decreased cardiac output, stroke volume, and contractility. Preload intolerance. Diminished responsiveness to drugs.
Lung	Emphysematous changes Pulmonary infarcts Reduced bacterial clearance Muscle atrophy	Pneumonia Decreases in functional residual capacity, vital capacity, and maximum breathing capacity Depressed hypoxic/hypercarbic drives
Hematologic	Stem cell failure Depressed erythropoietin synthesis	Anemia
Kidney	Epithelial swelling Atrophy Mild cortical calcification	Reduced glomerular filtration rate and inability to handle sodium loads Polyuria Metabolic acidosis
Gut	Disproportionate mass loss Hypoplastic and atrophic changes Decrease in total mucosal height	Depressed enzymatic activity Shortened transit time Impaired motility Propensity for bacterial growth Maldigestion and malabsorption
Liver	Mass loss Periportal fat accumulation	Decreased visceral protein synthesis Eventual hepatic insufficiency
White blood cell	Decreased polymorphonuclear chemotaxis Decreased lymphocyte count with reduced T-helper and increased T-suppressor and killer Decreased blastogenesis to phytohemagglutinin and mixed lymphocyte culture	Anergy Decreased granuloma formation Impaired response to chemotherapy Increased infection rate

DATA BASE

Standard starvation

A. The prototype of standard starvation serves as a reference to compare the stress metabolism of surgery, trauma, and sepsis (Table 10-2).

    1. In starvation nutrient input is lacking.

    2. Nutrient utilization is normal at the cell level.

    3. Little or no activation of metabolic mediators occurs.

    4. System is responsive to outside influence. For example, glucose administration will reduce or stop the formation of new glucose from fat stores.

    5. The basal energy requirements necessary to sustain life progressively fall.

B. Fuel supplies are progressively depleted.

    1. For both obligate and nonobligate users, glucose is the first fuel to be made available (Fig. 10-1).

    2. Hepatic glycogen stores are rapidly depleted.

    3. Muscle glycogen is not available for systemic use.

    4. Fat cannot be effectively converted to glucose.

    5. As a result the carbon for hepatic gluconeogenesis comes from amino acids, and the nitrogen is excreted as urea.

    6. Since the primary fuel is glucose, the initial respiratory

Table 10-2. Starvation versus metabolic stress

	Starvation	Metabolic disorder* Trauma/sepsis
Resting energy expenditure	↓	↑ ↑ ↑
Respiratory quotient	Low (0.7)	High (0.85)
Mediator activation	−	+ + +
Regulatory responsiveness	+ + + +	+
Primary fuels	Fat	Mixed
Proteolysis	+	+ + +
Branched chain oxidation	+	+ + +
Hepatic protein synthesis	+	+ + +
Ureagenesis	+	+ + +
Urinary nitrogen loss	+	+ + +
Gluconeogenesis	+	+ + +
Ketone body production	+ + + +	+
Rapidity of development of malnutrition	+	+ + +

*The disorders run a spectrum; a midrange value is used in this comparison.

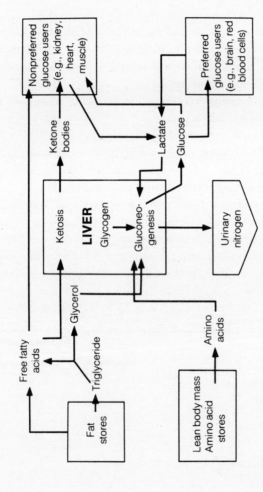

Fig. 10-1. Flow diagram of acute nonstress fasting metabolism. The initial fuel is glucose. With time, a progressive shift to fat and a recycling of glucose as lactate and alanine produces an internal protein sparing action.

quotient (R/Q) (ml CO_2 produced per ml O_2 consumed) is high.

7. With time, adaptive process begin to occur that spare amino acids by substituting other sources of carbon for glucose production and by providing alternative fuel sources.

   a. Glucose becomes less efficiently oxidized and is recycled as lactate.

   b. Fatty acids become an oxidative fuel source and promote hepatic ketone body formation, providing another fuel source.

   c. Glycerol, a sugar that forms the skeleton for triglycerides, becomes available as an alternative gluconeogenic substrate. As a result, the amount of nitrogen excreted in the urine decreases.

   d. Gluconeogenesis begins to predominate as a renal function.

   e. Consequently, some obligate glucose users, such as the brain, develop the capacity to derive major amounts of energy from ketones.

8. In this setting, 10% to 15% of the reduced energy expenditure seems to come from amino acid oxidation. The other 90% can come from glucose, almost all from fat, or from some combination of glucose and fat.

9. When 1 g/kg/day of amino acids is given with 25 to 30 nonprotein kcal/kg/day, together with the necessary amounts of salts, vitamins, and minerals, maintenance and repletion of nutritional status occurs. The latter is enhanced with an exercise program.

METABOLIC STRESS

The occurrence of surgery, trauma, or sepsis activates a new process (Table 10-3).

A. Injured tissue, dead tissue, dividing organisms, severe perfusion deficits, and some resolving hematomas activate mediator systems.

B. These systems regulate end-organ function and the clinical, physiologic, and metabolic manifestations of the response to stress (Fig. 10-2).

Table 10-3. Categories of metabolic stress

Variables for routine measurement

Stress level	Clinical example	Urinary nitrogen loss/day (g)	Plasma lactate level* (μg/L)	Plasma glucose level† (mM/L)	Insulin resistance	O₂CI (ml/min/m²)	Urinary 3-methyl-histidine excretion (μg/24 hr)
0	Starvation	<5	10 ± 5	5.5 ± 2	—	90 ± 10	<100
1	Elective general	5-10	1200 ± 200	9.5 ± 1.4	—	130 ± 6	130 ± 20
2	Polytrauma	10-15	1200 ± 200	9.5 ± 1.4	±	140 ± 6	200 ± 20
3	Sepsis	>15	3000 ± 500	16.0 ± 1.6	+	160 ± 10	450 ± 50

Variables for research use (plasma amino acid levels)

	Leucine (μg/L)	Proline (μg/L)	Phenylalanine (μg/L)	Methionine (μg/L)	Glucagon (pg/ml)	Glucagon/insulin
0	120 ± 10	200 ± 20	60 ± 15	10 ± 5	<20	2.0 ± 0.5
1	74 ± 12	213 ± 40	74 ± 8	15 ± 5	50 ± 9	2.5 ± 0.8
2	74 ± 12	213 ± 40	74 ± 8	15 ± 5	120 ± 40	3.0 ± 0.7
3	180 ± 30	300 ± 50	124 ± 17	105 ± 25	500 ± 50	8.0 ± 1.5

*In the absence of diabetes mellitus, pancreatitis, and steroid therapy.
†With a lactate/pyruvate ratio of 15:1 to 20:1.

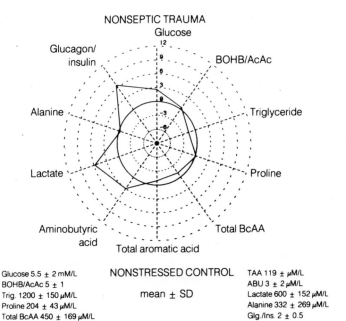

NONSTRESSED CONTROL

mean ± SD

Glucose 5.5 ± 2 mM/L
BOHB/AcAc 5 ± 1
Trig. 1200 ± 150 μM/L
Proline 204 ± 43 μM/L
Total BcAA 450 ± 169 μM/L

TAA 119 ± μM/L
ABU 3 ± 2 μM/L
Lactate 600 ± 152 μM/L
Alanine 332 ± 269 μM/L
Glg./Ins. 2 ± 0.5

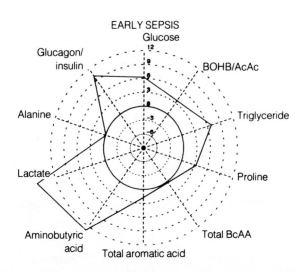

Fig. 10-2. The metabolic responses to stress are contrasted with those of standard starvation. In each depiction, the dark inner circle is the mean values for each variable for overnight resting, fasting man. Each dotted circle then represents 3 or 4.5 standard deviations from that mean. *BOHB* = Hydroxybutyrate; *Trig* = Triglyceride; *ABU* = Aminobutyric acid; *Ins* = Insulin; *AcAc* = Acetoacetate; *BcAA* = Branch chain amino acids; *Glu* = Glucagon.

Continued.

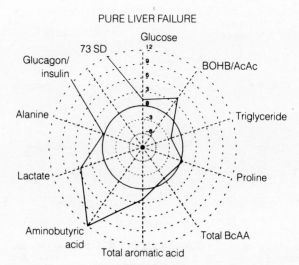

PURE LIVER FAILURE

Glucose 5.5 ± mM/L
BOHB/AcAc 5 ± 1
Trig. 1200 ± 150 μM/L
Proline 204 ± 43 μM/L
Total BcAA 450 ± 169 μM/L

NONSTRESSED CONTROL
mean ± SD

TAA 119 ± μM/L
ABU 3 ± 2 μM/L
Lactate 600 + 152 μM/L
Alanine 332 ± 269 μM/L
Glg./Ins. 2 ± 0.5

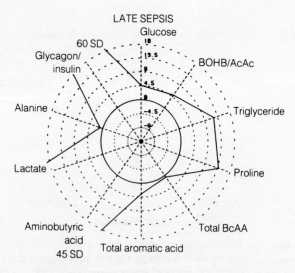

LATE SEPSIS

Fig. 10-2, cont'd. For legend see page 277.

1. This dynamic process is initiated with a lag or ebb phase during which little metabolic activity occurs.
2. The flow phase follows during which metabolic activity increases and peaks, usually on day 3 to 4 after injury.
3. The processes then abate over another 3 to 4 days unless a complication ensues.
   a. With a complication, the process reactivates and reaches a new peak.
   b. The degree of activation, and thus the peak response, depends on how much mediator is activated.
   c. The duration of the response depends on how long the mediators are activated.
   d. Thus, a large soft tissue injury that becomes infected may result in a very hypermetabolic state that persists for many days or weeks.

C. The amount of resting energy expenditure rises depending on the type of severity or the stress. (Table 10-3).
   1. The R/Q reflects the oxidation of a mixed fuel: fat, carbohydrate, and amino acids.
   2. The mediators seem to control and modulate the fuel mix.
   3. At high levels of stress, 30% to 35% of the increased energy expenditure seems to come from the oxidation of amino acids, 30% to 40% from glucose, and 30% to 40% from fat.
   4. With mediator modulation present, the system becomes less responsive to exogenous influence.
      a. Thus administered glucose has a progressively less inhibiting effect on lipolysis, proteolysis, and gluconeogenesis.
   5. Glucose and total calories in excess of the existing demands promote lipogenesis with excess carbon dioxide production and hepatic dysfunction.
      a. Hepatic steatosis is common in this setting.

D. Proteolysis increases with amino acid flux attempting to meet the demands of energy production and protein synthesis.
   1. Ureagenesis is increased.
   2. More nitrogen is present in the urine.

3. Gluconeogenesis is increased.

4. The glucose space is expanded.

5. Peripheral glucose uptake is normal, but much of the glucose becomes recycled as lactate and alanine.

   a. Thus increased plasma glucose and lactate values are a normal part of the response.

6. With appropriate attention to perfusion, the lactate/pyruvate ratio remains normal (>20).

7. Insulin does not seem to increase the oxidative use of glucose but does seem to potentiate hepatic steatosis.

E. Ketosis is relatively depressed in that hepatic ketone production is much less than it would be for a comparable duration of starvation.

1. The peripheral tissue appears able to use ketones.

2. The mediators seem to be modulating hepatic production of ketones downward.

3. Giving ketones does not seem to alter the processes significantly.

F. Malnutrition tends to develop rapidly under these conditions, taking days instead of the weeks needed in simple starvation.

1. Sometimes factoring out the effects of bed rest (disuse) on some of the parameters is difficult. Thus the need for interpretation in the clinical setting is great.

2. Isolated closed-head injuries provide a good example. Several reports have appeared with the observation of persistent excretion of large amounts of urinary nitrogen for days to weeks. However, more detailed studies that looked at a number of other parameters and coordinated them with the clinical setting indicate that the response abates in 5 to 7 days unless a complication ensues. The early nitrogen excretion appears to reflect the stress response, whereas the persistent nitrogen excretion seems to reflect bed rest and disuse in this largely young and muscular group of patients. In situations of bed rest and disuse, the nitrogen is mobilized after 4 to 5 days, about the same time the stress response would be abating after isolated closed-head injury.

G. In some instances the process reactivates, and the state of persistent hypermetabolism with or without the development of the organ failure syndromes ensues.

1. Patients who are at high risk for this problem need early, aggressive nutritional support, respective of their prior nutritional status.
2. Risk factors are known to include:
   a. Persistent/recurrent sepsis
   b. Severe perfusion shock or septic shock
   c. Surgical procedures with a high risk of technical complications
   d. Major polytrauma

PRINCIPLES OF NUTRITIONAL SUPPORT
Goals

The goals of nutrition support therapy derive from the processes of the metabolic response to injury.

A. To support organ structure and function
B. To do no harm
C. To treat malnutrition when and where present and when necessary
D. To prevent the occurrence of malnutrition in those settings in which a reasonable risk exists that it can become a significant contributor to morbidity and mortality

Timing

Nutritional support is a part of the therapeutic armamentarium for managing patients safely and effectively after surgery or trauma and during and after sepsis. The clinical judgment to treat is based on knowledge, experience, and the clinical setting. As with many therapies, definitive data that apply to a given patient in a given setting are frequently not available. Therefore, rational clinical judgment must prevail.

A. The timing of initiation of the support remains subject to debate.

1. Oxygen transport must be restored and maintained before the initiation of nutrition therapy.
2. In previously well-nourished patients in low-risk nutritional settings, waiting a few days to initiate nutritional

support and to judge recovery potential seems reasonable. Data on risk, however, are not currently available.

3. However, with a severely malnourished patient in a high-risk nutritional setting, therapy should be started as soon as possible after stabilizing oxygen transport.

4. When it becomes apparent that nutrient intake will not occur in a reasonable period of time (5 to 6 days), that nutritional stores are not reasonable, and that the acute life-threatening hemorrhage problems are controlled, support should probably be started.

5. At the other end of the judgment spectrum is a previously well-nourished patient who has received a blunt trauma injury requiring a splenectomy and who will be eating in 2 to 4 days. This patient requires only hydration and volume.

Nutritional requirements

A. Methods of calculation

There are two components of the nutritional formula that need to be calculated: the total calories and the fractional percentage of those calories that are to be supplied from carbohydrates, fat, and protein. Two methods are currently in use: the basal energy expenditure (BEE) and the resting energy expenditure (REE). Both methods provide only *approximations*, and *metabolic monitoring* must be done to ensure the appropriate response with a minimum of complications.

1. Basal energy expenditure (BEE)

a. The total caloric load is calculated for the basal state from the Harris-Benedict equations.

Male: $\text{BEE} = 66 + (13.7 \times \text{Wt}) + (5 \times \text{Ht}) - (6.8 \times \text{A})$

Female: $\text{BEE} = 655 + (9.6 \times \text{Wt}) + (1.7 \times \text{Ht}) - (4.7 \times \text{A})$

$$\text{Wt} = \text{Weight (kg)}$$
$$\text{Ht} = \text{Height (cm)}$$
$$\text{A} = \text{Age (years)}$$

(1) Some controversy exists over whether to use actual, usual, or ideal body weight. In general, ac-

tual body weight will maintain the status quo; usual or ideal body weight will allow repletion in the setting of starvation.

b. The BEE calculated is an estimate of the energy requirements at rest. For states other than basal, the BEE is multiplied by a "correction factor."

Low stress	1.3 × BEE
Moderate stress	1.5 × BEE
Severe stress	2.0 × BEE
Cancer	1.6 × BEE

c. The calculated total calories are then proportioned between carbohydrate, fat, and protein according to what the particular patient is thought to need (Tables 10-4 and 10-5). Standard starvation provides an example.

Table 10-4. Metabolic needs relative to stress level

	Stress level			
	Starvation	**2 (Low)**	**3 (High early)**	**3 (High late)**
Protein synthesis				
Total body (net)	↓*	↓	↓	↓
Hepatic	→	↑	↑ ↑	↓
Proteolysis	→	→ ↑ ↑	↑	
Estimated caloric need				
	BEE	1.3 × BEE	1.5 × BEE	2.0 × BEE
Fractional requirements of total daily caloric load				
Glucose (%)	60	↓†	↓†	↓†
Fat (%)	25	↑	↑	↓‡
Amino acids (%)	15	↑	↑ ↑	↑ ↑ ↑
Metabolic regulation				
	Normal	Present but at a higher threshold	Less responsive	Failed

* ↑, Increased; ↓, decreased; →, little or no change.
†Relative to starvation.
‡With currently available formulas.

(1) Amino acids = 1 g/kg/day × 4 cal/kg = amino acid calories

(2) Nonprotein calories = total calories − amino acid calories

(3) Nonprotein calories are supplied as 40% fat and 60% glucose

d. The patient is then monitored at 7- to 10-day intervals for a nutritional end-organ response and formula adjustments made as necessary.

2. Resting energy expenditure (REE)

a. The REE method calculates the existing level of caloric expenditure and fractional substrate use (percent carbohydrate, fat, and amino acids) at the time the analysis is done. To do this, it uses the O_2 consumption, the CO_2 production, and the urinary nitrogen excretion. Therefore it estimates what fuels are actually being oxidized and in what proportions at the time the assay is performed.

b. Prerequisites

(1) Technology to accurately measure O_2 consumption (Vo_2) in the clinical setting experienced.

Table 10-5. Estimated substrate requirements

	Stress level			
	Starvation	**2 (Low)**	**3 (Early)**	**3 (Late)**
Nonprotein calorie-nitrogen ratio (kcal/g N)	150/1	100/1	100/1	80/1
Amino acids* (g/kg/day)	1	1.5	2	2.0 to 2.5
Total nonprotein calories (kcal/kg/day)	25	25	30	35
Total calories (kcal/kg/day)	28	32	40	50
Fractional requirements of total daily caloric load				
Amino acids (%)	15	20	25	30
Glucose (%)	60	50	40	70
Fat† (%)	25	30	35	—‡

*For currently available amino acid formulas; the amount will vary somewhat with the brand of amino acid supplement used.
†For commercially available intravenous fat preparations composed primarily of long-chain triglycerides.
‡Hypertriglyceridemia present.

(2) Technology to accurately measure CO_2 production (VCO_2) in the clinical setting experienced.

(3) Urinary nitrogen determination (g/day).

(4) A guideline to judge stress level or degree of malnutrition. The system does not determine the degree of depletion of the lean body mass and thus the presence of severity of malnutrition.

3. Estimate of REE without urinary nitrogen (UN)

$$\text{REE (Kcal/day)} = (3.8 \times VO_2 + 1.2 \times VCO_2) \times 1.4$$

4. Estimate of REE and fuel mix when UN is available

a. Component calculation when fat fraction is positive (after calculation)

(1) g/day

Carbohydrate $= 4.1 \times \dot{V}CO_2$ (L/day) $- 2.9 \times \dot{V}_2$ (L/day) $- 2.5$ UN

Fat $= 1.7 \times VO_2$ (L/day) $- 1.7 \times VCO_2$ (L/day) $- 1.9$ UN

Protein $= 6.25 \times$ UN

(2) Kcal

Carbohydrate $= 4.2 \times$ g/day $= \text{kcal}_1$
Fat $\quad\quad\quad = 9.5 \times$ g/day $= \text{kcal}_2$
Protein $\quad\quad = 4.3 \times$ g/day $= \text{kcal}_3$
Total kcal/day $= \text{kcal}_1 + \text{kcal}_2 + \text{kcal}_3$

b. Component calculation when fat fraction is negative (after calculation), indicating negative fat use or fat synthesis

(1) g/day

Carbohydrate oxidized $= 14 \times VO_2$ (L/day) $- 0.19 \times VCO_2$ (L/day) $- 6.9 \times$ UN

Fat synthesized $= 1.7 \times VCO_2$ (g/day) $- 1.7 VO_2$ (g/day) $+ 1.9 \times$ UN

Carbohydrate converted $= 2.5 \times$ Fat synthesized

Protein $= 6.25 \times$ UN

(2) Kcal

Carbohydrate $= 4.2 \times$ g oxidized $= \text{kcal}_1$

Fat synthesized $=$ carbohydrate converted $= 1.1 \times$ g fat synthesized $= \text{kcal}_2$

Protein $= 4.3 \times$ g/day $= \text{kcal}_3$

Total kcal/day $= \text{kcal}_1 + \text{kcal}_2 + \text{kcal}_3$

5. Effect of quantitation

The quantitation produced only provides a reasonable base from which to start therapy. The patient must then be monitored for nutritional end-organ effect.

6. BEE versus REE

There are no current data to suggest that the REE method is any better or worse than the BEE method. For the discussions in this manual, the BEE method is used.

B. Fat, vitamins and trace elements, and electrolytes

1. Fat emulsions

a. Of the total daily calories, 4% to 8% need to be endogenous fatty acids (EFAs) to prevent EFA deficiency. This is referred to as using fat as a vitamin.

b. The other use of fat is as a calorie source. Most studies indicate that 30% to 40% of the total calories as fat seems to be most optimal.

c. Fat-free TPN for 2 weeks is frequently adequate to induce clinical EFA deficiency. Minimal fat requirements can be met with two to three 500 ml bottles of 10% fat per week for the average-size adult patient.

d. Intralipid and Travamulsin contain a soybean oil base and are 65% EFAs, containing 56% linoleic acid and 8% linolenic acid; Liposyn is safflower oil and is 77% EFA, containing linoleic acid.

2. Vitamins and trace elements

a. Precise requirements under acute or chronic stress conditions are unstudied. Currently recommended maintenance doses are listed in Table 10-6.

b. In the presence of renal failure, trace elements should be used judiciously, as they are renally excreted and poorly dialysed. A guideline is to give a maintenance dose 1 to 2 times per week.

c. In the presence of abnormal losses, increased quantities must be given; for example, active Crohn's disease may need up to 15 to 20 mg/day of zinc.

d. It is important that all the vitamins be given to avoid deficiency states. MVI-12, MVC 9 + 3, and multivitamin additive supply the maintenance vitamins as long as vitamin K is added.

3. Electrolytes

Adequate amounts of sodium chloride and intracellular electrolytes must be given. Normal plasma and total body levels of potassium, phosphorus, and magnesium need to be maintained for appropriate nutritional responses to occur. One of the major causes of a poor response or glucose intolerance is inadequate potassium.

Table 10-6. Recommended daily allowance (RDA) for vitamins and trace elements

| | Enteral RDA | Intravenous RDA | In addition to RDA | |
			During pregnancy	During lactation
Vitamin A (IU)	4000-5000	3300	+200	+400
D (IU)	400	200	+200	+200
E (IU)	12-15	10		
C (mg)	45	100	+20	+40
Folacin (µg)	400	400	+400	+100
Niacin (mg)	12-20	40	+2	+5
Riboflavin (mg)	1.1-1.8	3.6	+0.3	+0.5
Thiamine (mg)	1.0-1.5	3.0	+0.4	+0.5
Pyridoxine (mg)	1.6-2.0	4.0	+0.6	+0.5
Cyanocobalamine (µg)	3	5	+1.0	+1.0
Pantothenic acid (mg)	5-10	15		
Biotin (µg)	150-300	60		
K	70-140 µg	5 mg		
Calcium (mg)	1000		400	400
Magnesium (mg)	350		150	150
Iron (mg)	15	1		
Zinc (mg)	15		5	10
Iodide (µg)	150		25	50
Copper (mg)	2-3			
Manganese (mg)	2.5-5.0			
Chromium (mg)	0.05-0.2			
Selenium (µg)	0.05-0.2			
Molybdenum (µg)	0.15-0.5			
Phosphorus	1000		400	400

Routes of administration
Considerations

A. Duration and severity of existing malnutrition
   1. The visceral protein compartment serves as a primary amino acid reservoir and is a primary target during starvation or altered metabolism.
   2. Consequently, if gut malnutrition is severe enough, sufficient maldigestion and malabsorption will be present so as to preclude adequate gut function. This will usually become evident by hypoalbuminemia or diarrhea and a failure of a response during a feeding trial. Occasionally a biopsy is necessary.
B. Gastrointestinal tract function
   1. In the postoperative period following most elective surgical procedures, the major areas of atony and ileus are the stomach and the colon. The small bowel usually works and has been demonstrated to function during immediate postoperative feedings.
   2. If small bowel ileus is present at the end of a surgical procedure, it will usually continue postoperatively and immediate feeding usually will not work well.
   3. In severely stressed and septic states, the adequacy of the gastrointestinal tract for nutritional support has also been demonstrated.
   4. There must also be adequate absorptive surface. Consequently, situations of short bowel and some situations of fistula formation will preclude the gastrointestinal route as the sole means of nutritional support.
   5. The feeding tube should be in a position in the gastrointestinal tract to commence feedings safely and effectively, that is, distal to the pylorus during the period of gastric atony.
   6. There is evidence accumulating that gastric feeding is as effective or more effective than antacids and H_2 receptor blockers in preventing and treating stress ulcers. Candida overgrowth and invasion of esophageal or gastric mucosa seem to be much less of a problem.

C. Routes of administration
1. When identical solution and formula compositions are used, identical efficacy in nutritional support is found.
2. The enteral or parenteral formulas available may influence the route chosen. This is particularly so when special formulas are necessary in states of altered metabolism.
3. When it is imperative to know the exact amount that reaches the cell, or when the care plan necessitates the rapid onset of full support, the intravenous route is probably the route of choice.
D. Facilities and personnel
1. The necessary facilities and protocols for line care, preparation, infusion, and monitoring need to be present to minimize complications.
2. The necessary facilities and protocols for tube care, preparation, infusion, and monitoring need to be present to minimize tube and tube feeding complications.
E. Cost containment
Even with the new enteral metabolic support formulas being developed and used, enteral nutrition is still significantly cheaper.

Enteral nutrition

A. Indications
1. Oral consumption is inadequate or contraindicated.
2. Feeding tube is in an appropriate position.
   a. Adequate gastric motility is present.
   b. The tube is distal to the pylorus.
3. An appropriate enteral formula is available.
B. Absolute or relative contraindications
1. Vomiting and aspiration, unless access is distal to the ligament of Treitz and no reflux is demonstrable
2. Intestinal obstruction
3. Small bowel ileus
4. Enteroenteral or enterocutaneous fistulas
   a. Usually with high output
   b. Ascertainment of presence of adequate absorptive surface

5. Diarrhea that is uncontrollable or shouldn't be controlled and presents problems of hygiene, fluid electrolyte imbalance, or adequacy of nutritional support, such as drug-induced diarrhea or concomitant lactulose therapy
6. Upper gastrointestinal bleeding such as varices

C. Advantages relative to intravenous route
   1. Enteral nutrition avoids all the risks of central or peripheral vein cannulation.
   2. Neither solution nor tubing needs to be sterilized.
   3. It is relatively inexpensive.
   4. The intestinal mucosa is stimulated.
   5. There is frequently a reduced insulin requirement or insulin may be eliminated from the regimen.

D. Disadvantages relative to intravenous route
   1. Sometimes absorption levels are uncertain. Checking stool parameters is much more difficult and expensive. By the time this problem becomes apparent, many days may have passed. This can be a problem in some clinical settings.
   2. Aspiration can be minimized by adjusting formulas, rates of administration, and sites of administration.
   3. Gastrointestinal symptoms such as cramps, diarrhea, and bloating occur more frequently.
      a. Gastrointestinal symptoms are frequent with high fat formulas and high administration rates.
      b. Twenty-five percent of patients will experience diarrhea, necessitating discontinuance.
   4. Formulas may not be available to meet special needs. This is a rapidly disappearing problem as more metabolic-support enteral products become available.

E. Routes of administration
   1. Oral route
      a. Palatability and taste fatigue become real problems.
      b. Close monitoring may be necessary, as with calorie and protein counts.
   2. Tube feedings
      a. Accepted positions are nasogastric, nasoduodenal, and nasojejunal and by esophagostomy, gastrostomy, and jejunostomy.

(1) The newer weighted tubes will pass the pylorus by themselves in the presence of gastric motility 25% of the time.

(2) Frequently, positioning with an endoscope or under fluoroscopy is very useful.

(3) Percutaneous gastrostomy techniques with tube positioning in the stomach or duodenum are becoming increasingly useful and reliable.

   b. The newer tubes specifically designed for tube feedings are recommended. They are softer and better tolerated; they markedly reduce the risk of tracheoesophageal fistulas in patients with indwelling tracheostomies or endotracheal tubes and the degree of gastroesophageal reflux, and seem they to be much less prone to cause mucosal ulcers from contact. Many types are now available. Examples are listed in Table 10-7.

Parenteral nutrition

A. Indications

Whenever nutritional support is needed and the gut route is not available, is inadequate, or is contraindicated.

B. Absolute or relative contraindications

1. Gastrointestinal tract is functioning and is appropriate to the clinical setting.

2. Active infection or sepsis is present, at least until the source of infection is controlled and antibiotic coverage has begun.

3. Inadequate venous access, such as thrombosed or absent central veins or lack of a line to dedicate to TPN. (The triple-lumen central venous catheters usually overcome this.)

4. Unreliable patient or clinical setting.

C. Advantages relative to enteral route

1. Certainly that the amount administered gets to the cell

2. Shorter prime intervals

3. Avoidance of the problems of gut feeding such as aspiration, diarrhea, and bloating

4. Provision of total nutritional support when the gut does not work

Table 10-7. Enteral feeding tubes

Tube	Material	Length	French size	Weight	Lubricant	Stylet
Duo-Tube (Argyle/Sherwood)	Outer: polyvinyl chloride Inner: silicone	40 inches	5,6,8	Mercury Silicone	None	No
Dobhoff (Biosearch)	Polyurethane	43 inches	8	Mercury Optional	Hydromer	Optional
Entriflex (Biosearch)	Polyurethane	36 inches, 43 inches	8	Mercury	Hydromer	Optional
Keofeed (IVAC)	Silicone	43 inches	5,7.3 9,6	Mercury	None	Yes
Vitafeed (American McGaw)	Silicone	15 inches, 42 inches	5,6,8 10,14	Mercury	None	Yes
Vivonex Tungsten Tip (Norwich-Eaton)	Silicone	43 inches	8	Tungsten	None	No

D. Disadvantages relative to enteral route
   1. Necessity of sterility in preparation and administration
   2. Necessity of more specialized training and care such as administration, line care, compatibilities
   3. Greater risk of septic complications
   4. More expensive
   5. Greater risk of metabolic complications
   6. Result in gut atrophy if stimulation cannot or is not maintained

Enteral nutrition
Digestion and absorption of nutrients (Fig. 10-3)

A. Carbohydrates
   1. Major dietary sources
      a. Starches
      b. Polysaccharides
      c. Disaccharides
   2. Digestive enzymes
      a. Amylase is found in saliva and is also secreted by the pancreas.

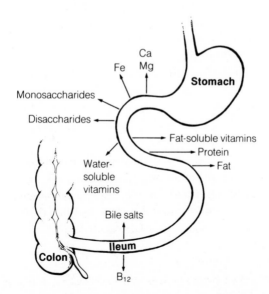

Fig. 10-3. Site of absorption of common nutrients. (From Cerra, F.B.: Pocket Manual of Surgical Nutrition, St. Louis, 1984, The C.V. Mosby Co.)

    b. Disaccharidases (maltase, sucrase, and lactase) are the brush border enzymes.

  3. Digestion and absorption

    a. Some hydrolysis occurs in the mouth, but most hydrolysis takes place in the small intestine.

    b. The component monosaccharides are subsequently absorbed into the circulation by the mucosal cells of the small intestine.

B. Lipids

  1. Major dietary sources

    a. Triglycerides

    b. Glycerophosphatides

    c. Cholesterol esters

    d. Cholesterol

  2. Digestive enzymes

    a. Esterases and pancreatic lipase are secreted ino the duodenum by the pancreas.

  3. Digestion and absorption

    a. Digestion continues in the duodenum through the hydrolysis of ester bonds by esterases. The fat is emulsified into mecelles by bile. Pancreatic lipase acts on the micelles and hydrolyzes the triglycerides into fatty acids, diglycerides, monoglycerides, and glycerol, which are then absorbed by the microvilli of the small intestine. Further hydrolysis occurs in the intestinal mucosal cells and resynthesis into new triglyceride molecules. These are released from the intestinal mucosa into the lymph, which finally empties into venous blood.

    b. Triglycerides that follow the lymphatic route are predominantly the long-chain fatty acids. Medium-chain fatty acids (10 carbons or less), because of their greater water solubility, are absorbed directly into the portal blood as free fatty acids.

C. Proteins

  1. Major dietary sources

    a. Intact proteins from meats, starches, and vegetables

    b. Albumin

    c. Casein

2. Digestive enzymes
   a. Pepsin is secreted by the stomach.
   b. A variety of pancreatic proteases are secreted by the pancreas into the duodenum.
   c. Peptidases are found within the intestinal mucosal cells.
3. Digestion and absorption
   a. Digestion begins in the stomach with pepsin hydrolysis of proteins into smaller peptides (that is, proteoses, peptones, polypeptides, and dipeptides).
   b. In the duodenum the peptides are acted on by pancreatic proteases and are further hydrolyzed by the enzymes within the intestinal mucosal cells.
   c. The final hydrolytic products that enter the bloodstream are free amino acids.

Types of formulas

A. Complete versus incomplete diets
   1. A complete diet contains all six necessary components
      a. Carbohydrate   d. Vitamins
      b. Protein   e. Minerals
      c. Fat   f. Trace elements
   2. An incomplete diet lacks one or more of the six necessary components and needs supplementation (for example, Citrotein, Hepatic Aid, Vivonex standard and high nitrogen diets, and Precision LR).
B. Lactose-free formulas

Definition	Caseinate and soy isolate–based products; lactose free, low in residue.
Composition	Largely intact protein, oligosaccharides, and long-chain fats with a limited number containing some medium-chain triglycerides (MCT).
Indications	In general, require a functional gastrointestinal tract; may be used as both supplemental or total nutrition via tube or oral consumption.
Advantages	Lactose free; most are moderately palatable and relatively inexpensive to use; free-flowing consistency allows use of small-bore feeding tubes.
Disadvantages	Quality of protein is not as high as that in milk-based or blenderized formulas.

Products	Kcal/ml	Osmolality (mOsm/kg H₂O)	Percent kcal as long-chain fat	Protein (gm)/ 2000 kcal	Amount needed to meet RDA (ml)
Isocal*	1	300	30	65	1920
Ensure*	1	450	31.5	74	1887
Sustacal HC*	1.5	650	34	81	1200
Ensure Plus*	1.5	600	32	73	2000
Sustacal*	1	625	21	120	1080
Osmolite*	1	300	16	74	1887
Magnacal*	2	590	36	70	1000
Portagen*†	1	354	5	70	960
Isocal HCN*	2	740	39	75	1500
Travasorb*	1	488	31.5	74	1900
Osmolite HN	1.0	310	17.4	83	1320
Ensure HN	1.0	470	33.6	79	1321
Ensure Plus HN	1.5	650	47.2	79	947
Nutri Aid	1.1	300	31.5	74	2000

*"Complete" formula, containing all six necessary nutrients
(carbohydrates, protein, fat, vitamins, minerals, and trace elements).
†Contains greater than 2% of kcals as long-chain fat, but may need EFA
supplementation.

C. Chemically defined formulas

Definition	Nutrients are supplied in partially "predigested" simple forms with mineral residue and free of lactose.
Composition	Protein composition varies from intact high-biological-value protein to peptide and amino acid mixtures, carbohydrate is supplied as oligosaccharides and disaccharides. In general, a minimum of fat is provided, mostly as long-chain fats.
Indications	Designed for patients with limited gastrointestinal function and/or metabolic abnormalities; may be used as total or supplemental nutrition via tube or oral consumption.
Advantages	Requires mineral digestion and absorption for use of nutrients (almost totally absorbed in duodenum and proximal jejunum), lactose free; low in viscosity; easily administered via small-bore feeding tube.
Disadvantages	High osmolality may cause gastrointestinal distress and metabolic derangements (that is, diarrhea or dehydration); significantly more expensive than diets composed of intact nutrients; relatively unpalatable in pure form.

Products	Kcal/ml	Osmolality (mOsm/kg H_2O)	Percent kcal as long-chain fat	Protein (gm)/ 2000 kcal	Amount needed to meet RDA (ml)
Precision HN*	1	557	1.1	88	2850
Precision Iso-tonic†	1	300	28	58	1560
Precision LR*	1	525-545	1.3	52	1710
Citrotein*	0.66	500	2	121	NA
Isotein HN†	1.2	300	19	114	1800
Travasorb MCT†‡	1-2	312-590	6	98	1000-2000
Travasorb Std†‡	1	560	5	60	2000
Travasorb HN†‡	1	560	5	90	2000
Vital HN†‡	1	460	4	84	1500
Criticare HN†‡	1	650	2.8	72	2000

*"Incomplete" formula, missing one or more of the six necessary nutrients.
†"Complete" formula, containing all six necessary nutrients (carbohydrates, protein, fat, vitamins, minerals, and trace elements).
‡Contains greater than 2% of kcal as long-chain fat, but may need EFA supplementation.

D. Specialty formulas
  1. Organ failure

Definition	A product designed for specific organ failure (that is, liver failure, renal failure).
Composition	Free amino acids, oligosaccharides, short- and long-chain fats; lactose free
Indications	Designed for patients with specific organ failure; requires some degree of digestion and absorption; may be administered via tube or orally consumed.
Advantages	Theoretically, nitrogen balance may be maintained and/or achieved without exacerbating the specific organ failure.
Disadvantages	May have to be supplemented with vitamins, minerals, or trace elements; high osmolality may cause gastrointestinal distress and metabolic derangements; relatively unpalatable; very expensive.

Products	Kcal/ml	Osmolality (mOsm/kg H_2O)	Percent kcal as long-chain fat	Protein (gm)/ 2000 kcal	Amount needed to meet RDA (ml)
Hepatic-Aid*	1.6	900	20	54	NA
Amin-Aid*	1.9	900	31	20	NA
Travasorb-Hepatic*†	1.1	690	3.5	53	NA
Travasorb-Renal*†	1.35	590	3.5	34	NA

*"Incomplete" formula, missing one or more of the six necessary nutrients.
†Contains greater than 2% of kcal as long-chain fat, but may need EFA supplementation.

2. Stress

A number of formulas are now available or are being developed for use following surgical procedures and during the stress response of polytrauma and sepsis. In general, these formulas are the same as those already discussed but with a lower calorie/nitrogen ratio, or they have been reformulated particularly with respect to amino acids.

a. Low calorie/nitrogen formulas

Formula	Kcal/ml	NPC/N*	Percent carbo-hydrate	Percent fat	Percent protein	Osmolality (mOsm/kg H_2O)
Sustacal	1.0	79:1	55	21	24	625
Isotein HN	1.2	89:1	52	25	23	300
Travasorb MCT	1 to 2	102:1	50	30	20	312 to 590
Vital HN	1.0	125:1	74	9.3	16.7	460
Precision HN	1.05	125:1	82	1.1	16.7	557
Travasorb HN	1.0	126:1	70	12	18	560
Trauma Cal	1.5	88:1	38	40	22	550

b. Reformulated formulas

The formulas are reformulated by increasing the proportion of BcAA and altering the proportion of other amino acids

Formula	Kcal/ml	NPC/N*	Percent carbo-hydrate	Percent fat	Percent protein/ percent BcAA	Osmolality (mOsm/kg H_2O)
Traum-Aid HBC	1.0	102:1	66.4	11	22.4/50	675
Stresstein	1.2	97:1	56.7	20	23.3/44	910
Vivonex TEN	1.0	149:1	82.2	2	15.3/33	630

*NPC/N, Nonprotein kcal/g nitrogen.

E. New modules

New modular systems are being marketed that allow complete flexibility in formula composition so that a truly tailored formula can be made. In addition, these systems are prepackaged, easily hydrated, and not labor intensive in their preparation or use.

Sources
Carbohydrate

Nutrisource carbo-hydrate	Glucose polymers	3.2 kcal/ml

Protein

Nutrisource protein	Lactalbumin, egg albumin	1 oz = 23 g protein
Nutrisource amino acids	L-amino acids (standard and modified)	1 oz = 29 g protein

Fat

Nutrisource lipid	Safflower oil, MCT	2.3 kcal/ml, 55% EFA

Vitamins, minerals, and trace elements

Nutrisource vitamins	10 g packet provides 100% RDA for essential vitamins
Nutrisource minerals for protein formulas	24 gm packet in combination with 59 g Nutrisource protein provides 100% RDA of essential minerals and trace elements
Nutrisource minerals for protein formulas (electrolyte restricted)	Same as above but essentially Na^+, K^+, and Cl^- free
Nutrisource minerals for amino acids	24 g packet provides 100% RDA of essential minerals and trace elements
Nutrisource minerals for amino acids (electrolyte restricted)	Same as above but essentially Na^+, K^+, and Cl^- free

Parenteral nutrition
Solutions available

A. Intravenous fat emulsions
1. These emulsions are of long-chain fatty acid triglycerides. Linoleic acid and its metabolic derivative, ararachidonic acid, are essential nutrients in humans. Linoleic acid cannot be made from other fats in humans and therefore must be supplied. Most agree that linolenic acid is probably essential in newborns, infants, and children and possibly in adults after long-term total parenteral nutrition. During total parenteral nutrition, EFA needs to be given, as the glucose seems to inhibit mobilization of endogenous stores. This is using "fat as a vitamin."
2. The other use of current intravenous fats is as a source of calories. Once given, the fat particles (0.4 to 2.0 μ) are coated with a hydrophilic layer of apoprotein and phospholipid. Some is reprocessed in the liver to very low–density lipoprotein. Clearance is rapid and is usually complete in 8 to 10 hours after administration of an infusion of 500 ml of 10% fat given at 50 ml/hr. When stored, the fat seems to appear primarily in cardiac and skeletal muscle. Clearance by cardiac and skeletal muscle, liver, spleen, and kidneys occurs for use as a caloric source. The chylomicrons are hydrolysed by lipoprotein lipase, and the free fatty acids and glycerol are absorbed. Re-esterification then occurs. When the need for fat calories arises, hydrolysis again occurs and the long-chain fatty acids are transported into the mitochondria for beta oxidation and adenosine 5'-triphosphate (ATP) production. This transport is energy dependent and requires carnitine. Carnitine is a quarternary ammonium substance produced by the liver that facilitates long-chain fatty acid transport across the mitochondrial membrane as acylcoenzyme A esters.
   a. Lipoprotein lipase is a hormonally sensitive enzyme. It is stimulated by insulin and thyroid hormone and is inhibited by epinephrine and glucagon. Heparin also activates lipoprotein lipase.
3. The intravenous fats are cleared in a two-phase process.

Until peripheral clearance mechanisms are saturated, the fat is removed at a rate proportional to dose. Once clearance is saturated, the removal rate becomes constant. Exactly when this saturation occurs is very difficult to predict, particularly under stress conditions. When it oc-

---

UNIVERSITY OF MINNESOTA HOSPITALS & CLINICS
PHYSICIAN'S ORDERS (STANDING ORDERS)

ORIGINATED BY (PHYSICIAN)	ORIGINATED	REVIEWED
Frank B. Cerra	2/82	

PATIENT IDENTIFICATION PLATE

TITLE:

ADULT ENTERAL FEEDING: Page 1 of 1

ADMINISTRATION AND MONITORING

Formula desired: _____.

Aspirate residuals q 4h. Call H.O. with _____ cc return.

Flush feeding tube with _____ cc of _____ q 4h, after feeding and meds.

Hang fresh feeding q 8h.

Check tube placement q shift or before intermittent feeding.

Change feeding bag and tubing q 24h.

Elevate HOB 30-45°.

Daily weights; I&O.

Diabetic urines q 6h.

Calorie/protein counts (notify dietitian)

Administration of Feedings (choose one)

( ) Continuous Administration

1. Initiate at _____ str. at 50 cc/hr
2. Increase volume (rate q 12h by 25 cc/hr to _____ cc/hr, as tolerated.
3. When desired volume reached THEN increase strength (1/4 to 1/2 to 3/4 to full strength) q 12hr to _____ strength, as tolerated.

( ) Intermittent Administration

1. Initiate at _____ str/ at 100 cc/fdg. followed by _____ cc H$_2$O q _____ h, _____ times a day.
2. On Day 2, increase to _____ cc/fdg. (not to exceed 400cc/fdg.), as tolerated.
3. On Day 3, increase to full strength, as tolerated.

( ) Routine Monitoring

1. GNE q d x 3, then Monday and Thursday.
2. MAD, Mg, P Day 1 and then q Monday.
3. PT, albumin, retinol binding protein Day 1 and q Monday.

Special Lab Screening (as indicated)

( ) Nitrogen Balance Study - 24 hour urine collection on ice - 12M to 12M for urea nitrogen, to Chemistry.

( ) Skin Testing - mumps, candida and PPD intermediate strength.

PSO2-608

SIGNATURE OF PHYSICIAN	DATE
M.D.	

21931, JUN 81   ORIGINAL - MEDICAL RECORD   COPY - PHARMACY

PHYSICIANS ORDERS

Fig. 10-4. University of Minnesota Hospitals and Clinics physician's orders: adult enteral feeding—administration and monitoring. (From Cerra, F.B.: Pocket Manual of Surgical Nutrition, St. Louis, 1984, The C.V. Mosby Co.)

curs, lipemia and inappropriately elevated plasma triglyceride levels occur. The fat can then layer out in the plasma, form globules in the liver and spleen, be cleared as a particle by macrophages, and possibly contribute to "blockade" and pulmonary failure or insufficiency.

a. It is therefore necessary to monitor the rate of intravenous fat clearance periodically, particularly under stress conditions. One regimen is to provide 500 ml of 10% fat at 50 ml/hr and check for lipemia or elevated triglycerides 10 hours after the infusion. If lipemia is present or the triglyceride level exceeds 250 mg/100 ml, clearance is abnormal and the intravenous fat should be given at a reduced rate or should be stopped and "used as a vitamin."

b. If intravenous fat is not used as a part of a TPN regimen, the biochemical changes of long-chain fatty acid deficiency appear in about 7 days with clinical findings at 4 weeks. To prevent this, 500 ml of 10% fat needs to be given at least twice weekly. Treatment of clinical deficiency seems to require daily therapy for 7 to 10 days.

c. The question of what to do in cases of familial hyperlipidemia is unanswered. Deficiency states need to be treated. Fat clearance may still be normal or adequate, although perhaps with reduced dosage or administration rate. Use of fat as calories in this setting is judgmental and needs to be individualized.

4. Composition
   a. Fatty acid

Type	Safflower oil (%)	Cottonseed oil (%)	Soybean oil (%)
Linoleic	77	53	54
Linolenic	—	—	7.8
Oleic	13	17	26
Palmitic	7	25	9
Arachidonic	—	—	—
Stearic	2.5	2.8	2.9

b. Emulsions

| | Content/500 ml | | |
Type	Intralipid	Liposyn	Travamulsion
Soybean oil	50 gm	—	50 gm
Safflower oil	—	50 gm	—
Cottonseed oil	—	—	—
Egg yolk phospholipid	6 gm	6 gm	6 gm
Soybean phospholipid	—	—	—
Glycerol	11.3 gm	12.5 gm	12 gm
Sorbitol	—	—	—
Xylitol	—	—	—

5. Intravenous fat alone has significant protein-sparing qualities. These can be advantageously used by combining fat with glucose as a calorie source. Most practitioners agree that 20% to 40% of calorie intake should be as fat. Currently, it is not recommended to exceed 60% of the calorie intake as fat and to not exceed 2.5 g/kg/day in adults and 4 g/kg/day in infants and children, assuming clearance capacity is normal.

   a. In general, the emulsions are nearly iso-osmolar with serum and can therefore be given by peripheral vein.

   b. Common practice is not to mix emulsions with other nutrient solutions but to administer them through a separate angioaccess or with a Y-connector near the portal of entry. This practice will probably change in the near future, however, as the capacity to mix with other nutritional solutions is now available.

6. New fats. Intravenous forms of medium- and short-chain fats have been reformulated and are entering the testing stage. They may be available in the 1980's.

B. Standard amino acid solutions

The composition of some standard amino acid solutions are listed in Table 10-8. In clinical practice, one formula seems to be as efficacious as the other.

C. Modified amino acid solutions

It is very important to use each of these solutions only for what it was designed. For example, hepatamine should be used for hepatic encephalopathy in a setting of chronic liver disease or for nutritional support in end-stage fibrotic liver disease where standard amino acid formulas have failed. Stress formulas are used for stress conditions or surgery, sepsis, and trauma where nutritional support is needed. Even here the formulas vary, and thought needs to be given to choice and timing. It is probably not correct to use a formula high in aromatic amino acids during the phase of sepsis at which aromatic amino acids are elevated. The stress formulas currently available include Branch amine and Freamine HBC.

1. The historical background emerged from in vitro and in vivo animal experimentation and human investigations.
   a. Oxidation of the BcAA leucine, isoleucine, and valine is increased under conditions of surgery, trauma, and sepsis.

Table 10-8. Amino acid content of some amino acid solutions for parenteral nutrition

	Travasol (8.5%) (Travenol) (g/100 ml)	Freamine III (8.5%) (McGaw) (g/100 ml)	Aminosyn (8.5%) (Abbott) (g/100 ml)
Essential amino acids			
L-Isoleucine	0.406	0.590	0.620
L-Leucine	0.526	0.770	0.810
L-Lysine	0.492	0.620	0.624
L-Methionine	0.492	0.450	0.340
L-Phenylalanine	0.526	0.480	0.380
L-Threonine	0.356	0.340	0.460
L-Tryptophan	0.152	0.130	0.150
L-Valine	0.390	0.560	0.680
Nonessential amino acids			
L-Alanine	1.760	0.600	1.100
L-Arginine	0.880	0.810	0.850
L-Histidine	0.372	0.240	0.260
L-Proline	0.356	0.950	0.750
L-Serine	—	0.500	0.370
L-Tryosine	0.034	—	0.044
Glycine	1.760	1.90	1.100
L-Cysteine	—	<0.020	—
Total nitrogen (g/L)	14.3	13.0	13.4
BcAA (% w/v)	15.6	23.3	24.2

b. One major site of increased oxidation is skeletal muscle.

c. Liver extracts BcAA in accord with its need for protein synthesis.

d. BcAA in the experimental setting, particularly leucine, can have a metabolic regulatory function, part of which is a promotion of protein synthesis. BcAA may also act to reduce proteolysis under stress conditions.

e. When BcAA are given to nonstressed humans, the plasma levels rise rapidly.

2. Double-blind, randomized, prospective studies under conditions of surgery, polytrauma, sepsis, and multiple-systems organ failure using an isocaloric, isonitrogenous model have demonstrated advantages to BcAA-modified protein solutions in a setting of balanced nutritional support.

a. Improved nitrogen retention.

b. Positive nitrogen balance as early as one day following injury when they are given in sufficient quantities.

c. Improved support of hepatic protein synthesis at least as measured by plasma transferrin.

d. Improved total body protein synthesis as measured by nitrogen retention and 3-methylhistidine excretion.

e. Improved white blood cell function as evaluated by absolute lymphocyte count and anergy testing.

f. Improved hepatic protein synthesis.

3. Under conditions of surgical, trauma, or septic stress, the data indicate additional considerations for the BcAA-modified protein solutions.

a. BcAA should be given in the context of a balanced amino acid mix.

b. At least 0.8 g/kg/day BcAA is needed to observe the nitrogen retention effect.

c. BcAA should be given in a setting of balanced calories and calories in appropriate amounts, such as 40% fat and 60% glucose or glucose calories alone.

d. The presence of significant stress is required to observe the nitrogen retention effect (Fig. 10-5), such as

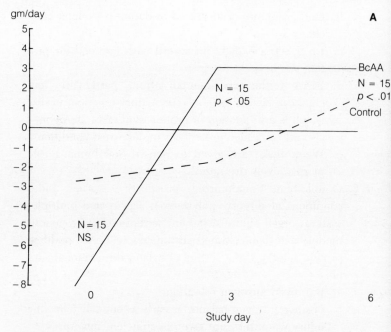

Fig. 10-5. A, In double blind, randomized, prospective studies with isonitrogenous, isocaloric input, nitrogen balance became positive during stress response in those patients receiving modified amino acids. It is impossible to achieve this effect 1 day after injury. **B,** Dark inner circle represents mean value for each variable from day of injury for both control and branch chain amino acids (BcAA). Each dotted circle represents 3 standard deviations from that mean. Plotted are the plasma levels on the sixth day of the study for control and BcAA. The BcAA levels rose on the sixth day as the stress response abated. **C,** BcAA total parenteral nutrition (TPN) versus standard TPN. Effect of nutritional support on nitrogen balance during stress response is depicted. When altered requirements of stress state are supplied, better and more rapid nitrogen retention is achieved. (**A** from Cerra, F.B., et al.: Branched chains support postoperative protein synthesis, Surgery **92:**192, 1982; **B** and **C** from Cerra, F.B.: Pocket manual of surgical nutrition, St. Louis, 1984, The. C.V. Mosby Co.)

Continued.

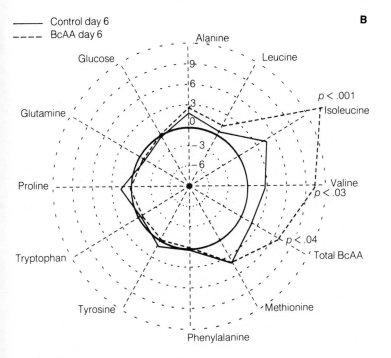

——— Control day 6
- - - - BcAA day 6

Alanine

Glucose

Leucine

Glutamine

$p < .001$ Isoleucine

Proline

Valine
$p < .03$

$p < .04$

Tryptophan

Total BcAA

Tyrosine

Methionine

Phenylalanine

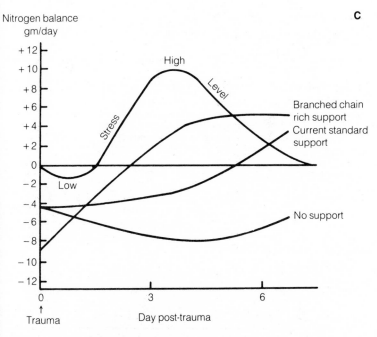

Nitrogen balance
gm/day

C

+ 12

+ 10

High

+ 8

Level

+ 6

Branched chain
rich support

+ 4

Current standard
support

+ 2

Stress

0

- 2

Low

- 4

- 6

No support

- 8

- 10

- 12

0   3   6

↑
Trauma   Day post-trauma

Fig. 10-5. For legend see opposite page.

baseline nitrogen excretion of over 8 g/day in the absence of any nutritional support.

e. BcAA should not be used in the absence of significant stress and should be stopped and standard amino acids used when the stress response has adequately abated.

f. The dosing guidelines seem to be similar to those outlined under stress. Monitoring of stress level is necessary to decide when to start BcAA, how much to give, and when to stop them. There are no data as yet to support one formula as more beneficial than another.

Solution combinations

A. Solutions for stress states that provide a 100:1 calorie to nitrogen ratio are listed in Table 10-9.

B. Solutions for standard TPN that provide 150:1 calorie to nitrogen ratio are listed in Table 10-10.

C. Current guidelines indicate that the modified amino acid formulas should be used in the same dose as the standard amino acid formulas, except that they should only be used for the indication for which they were formulated; for ex-

Table 10-9. Standard formulas for parenteral nutrition (100:1) (to provide 100 nonprotein kcal/gm nitrogen)

Formulas	Regimen A: no fat	Regimen B: moderate fat	Regimen C: low fat
TPN solution			
Dextrose	20%	10%	15%
Amino acids	4.25%	4.25%	4.25%
Lipid	None	200 ml of 20% fat emulsion/ L TPN	200 ml of 10% fat emulsion/L TPN
Composition of intake (% of total intake)			
Carbohydrate	80%	41%	58%
Protein	20%	19%	20%
Fat	0%	40%	22%
Nonprotein kcal:g N	95:1	103:1	99:1

ample, for acute sepsis in which a 4.25% amino acid solution is desired, the 4.25% modified amino acids would be used at a dose commensurate with the level of stress.

Other additives

A. The usual electrolyte requirements are listed in Table 10-11.
B. Individual electrolyte salt additives are available as listed below. The choice of salt depends on the status of acid base

Table 10-10. Standard formulas for parenteral nutrition (150:1) (to provide 150 nonprotein kcal/g nitrogen)

Formula	Regimen D: no fat	Regimen E: moderate fat	Regimen F: low fat
TPN solution			
Dextrose	30%	20%	25%
Amino acids	4.25%	4.25%	4.25%
Lipid	none	200 ml of 20% fat emulsion/ L TPN	225 ml of 10% fat emulsion/L TPN
Composition of intake (% of total fat)			
Carbohydrate	86%	58%	71%
Protein	14%	13%	13%
Fat	0%	29%	16%
Nonprotein kcal:g N	143:1	151:1	153:1

Table 10-11. Adult electrolyte requirements for parenteral nutrition

	Usual electrolyte requirement/24 hours	Standard concentration/L TPN
Sodium (mEq)	60-100	35
Potassium (mEq)	60-100	30
Magnesium (mEq)	10-20	5
Calcium (mEq)	10-15	5
Phosphorus (mmole)	20-45	15
Chloride (mEq)	*	†
Acetate (mEq)	*	†

*Varies with acid-base status.
†Varies with amino acid product used.

balance, abnormal losses requiring replacement, renal and cardiac function, and disease-specific needs.

1. Sodium—chloride, acetate, lactate, phosphate
2. Potassium—chloride, acetate, phosphate
3. Magnesium—sulfate
4. Calcium—gluceptate, gluconate, chloride
5. Phosphorus—sodium potassium

C. Vitamin requirements in the basal state can be met with 10 ml MVI-12 per day added to the TPN solution. Vitamin K requirements can be met by adding 5 mg/day to the TPN solution. The precise requirements during stress or disease states are unknown.

D. A number of trace element formulas are currently commercially available. They will usually provide the basal state needs of zinc, copper, chromium, and manganese when added to the TPN solution. The precise requirements under stress and in disease states are largely unknown. As with vitamins, it seems prudent to give at least the basal requirements every day unless there are reasons not to, such as in renal failure.

1. Some disease state needs are known, as in the increased need for zinc in diarrheal states and in burns.
2. Trace elements are largely cleared by the kidney. In renal failure, the dose needs to be reduced. In general, trace elements are poorly dialyzed. A prudent regimen seems to be to reduce administration to twice weekly unless there are abnormal needs or signs of toxicity or deficiency.
3. Newer trace elements such as selenium and molybdenum are quite expensive and probably are needed only on a daily basis in the presence of a deficiency state or after a long period of time on TPN.

Administration techniques

A. Route
1. Peripheral vein parenteral nutrition. Administration of 5% to 10% dextrose plus amino acids supplemented by intravenous fat emulsion to provide 2000 kcal/day.
2. Central vein parenteral nutrition. Administration of

greater than 10% dextrose plus amino acids to provide 2000 to 4000 kcal/day; fat also may be included.

3. Considerations
   a. Goal of nutritional therapy
      (1) Total vs. supplemental parenteral nutrition
      (2) Nutritional requirements
   b. Viability of peripheral veins
   c. Length of therapy
   d. Fluid tolerance
   e. Risks of central line.

B. Techniques
   1. Central TPN

Initiation	Begin slowly (e.g., 40 ml/hr); increase rate over 48 hours to maximum desired rate.
Discontinuation	Gradually taper over 24 hours or rapidly taper by decreasing rate to 40 ml/hr for 2 to 4 hours and then discontinue.
Exception	Intermittent TPN may be infused 10 to 18 hours/day with initiation and discontinuation over 1 to 2 hours.

   2. Peripheral TPN

Initiation	May begin at maximum desired rate
Discontinuation	May discontinue without tapering

   3. Cyclic TPN
      A technique for intermittent administration used in home TPN, for patient convenience, or for treatment of the complications of fatty liver or end-organ response failure. The TPN is given over 10 to 16 hours, the rate is turned down, and the TPN is then discontinued. An example regimen follows:
      TPN 80 ml/hr for 1 hr
      TPN 150 ml/hr for 14 hr
      TPN 40 ml/hr for 2 hr
      TPN off for 7 hr
      This technique requires increased fluid tolerance over a shorter period of time and is difficult in the presence of diabetes mellitus or other states of glucose intolerance.

4. Fat emulsions (peripheral or central)

Initiation	Test dose: administer at 1 ml/min × 30 minutes; if there are no adverse reactions, advance to desired rate (not to exceed 125 ml/hr for 10% fat emulsion and 60 ml/hr for 20% fat emulsion).
Discontinuation	May discontinue without tapering.

Complications and their management
Failure to achieve desired effects

Failure to achieve desired effects is one of the most commonly encountered problems. It is frequently unrecognized unless appropriate monitoring is done. In such settings, expensive therapy is applied and unnecessary complications occur. Monitoring is relatively cheap and is effective in efficiently providing useful therapy with a minimum of problems. Even when monitored, however, failure to achieve the nutritional effects does occur.

A. Causes in starvation states
   1. Inappropriate calorie load
   2. Inappropriate amino acid load
   3. EFA, vitamin, or trace element deficiency
   4. Low total body potassium, magnesium, and phosphorus
   5. Malabsorption/maldigestion
   6. Need for cyclic TPN
   7. Presence of a complication or an unrecognized metabolic disorder

There is a small group of patients who do not seem to respond to continuous nutrient administration. Cyclic regimens will usually correct the problem. The precise reason is unknown but is believed to be related to the presence of a starvation interval.

B. Causes in metabolic states
   1. Inappropriate calorie/nitrogen ratio
   2. Inappropriate calorie mix of glucose and fat
   3. Not enough or too much amino acid or an inappropriate formula
   4. Essential fatty acid, trace elements, or vitamin deficiency
   5. Presence of a complication
   6. Presence of a metabolic problem not amenable to metabolic therapy

7. Malabsorption/maldigestion

8. Low total body potassium, magnesium, and phosphorus

In these settings, assessment of metabolic status will usually indicate which cause is present and the course of action necessary.

Parenteral complications

The best treatment for any complication is prevention. An awareness of the potential problems and the factors that potentiate them will facilitate their prevention.

A. Substrate intolerance

Table 10-12 outlines the common metabolic complications and their management. The hepatic dysfunction that occurs is common and generally is reversible.

1. Hepatic dysfunction

   a. Predisposing disease states

      (1) Good supporting data with TPN in the presence of prematurity or low birth weight; presence of cirrhosis or sepsis.

      (2) Marginal supporting data in malignancy, in stress states, and in settings of prior malnutrition.

   b. Solution composition. An excess or deficiency of carbohydrate, fat, or amino acids can contribute:

      (1) Long-chain fatty acid deficiency.

      (2) Excess intravenous fat in neonates, infants, and adults (greater than 2 to 2.5 gm/kg/day in adults).

      (3) Glucose calories in excess of demand.

      (4) Excessive amino acid loads in infants.

      (5) Specific amino acids such as tryptophan were once implicated as were the preservatives.

      (6) The lack of unspecified amino acids has been suggested.

   c. Liver histology

      (1) Child. Extramedullary hematopoiesis, cholestasis, periportal inflammation. Fibrosis has been observed but the data supporting the theory that it results from TPN are quite circumstantial and unproved.

      (2) Adult

      (a) Steatosis, both in periportal hepatocytes and Kupfer cells, cholestasis, periportal inflammation.

      (b) A time course observed in adults:

2 to 10 days TPN	Steatosis
10 to 20 days TPN	Cholestasis and ↑ alkaline phosphate
20 to 30 days TPN	↑ Alkaline phosphate and bilirubin; cholestasis and duct proliferation, steatosis
More than 30 days TPN	Periportal inflammation

Table 10-12. Substrate intolerance

Problem	Predisposing factors	Management
Hyperglycemia	Stress, corticosteroids, pancreatitis, diabetes mellitus, peritoneal dialysis	↓ Dextrose intake (decrease rate of infusion or ↓ dextrose concentration) and substitute fat calories; insulin infusion
Hypoglycemia (rare)	Abrupt withdrawal of dextrose, insulin overdose	↑ Dextrose intake; ↓ exogenous insulin intake
Excess CO_2 production	Excess dextrose intake	↓ Dextrose intake, balance calories as fat and dextrose
Hyperlipidemia (↑ cholesterol, ↑ triglycerides)	Stress, familial hyperlipidemia	↓ Fat intake or discontinue if indicated
Serum amino acid imbalance	Stress, hepatic failure, hepatitis	Modify amino acid intake if indicated or ↓ amino acid intake
Abnormal liver function tests (↑ AST, ↑ alkaline phosphatase, ↑ billirubin)	Stress, infection, cancer, excess carbohydrate intake, excess total calorie intake, EFA deficiency, trace element deficiency	↓ Dextrose intake (substitute as fat); ↓ total calorie intake; provide essential fatty acids and trace elements; look for sledge in biliary tree
Coma	Hyperosmolar, nonketotic; hepatic failure; sepsis	Fluids, salt, insulin; find and treat sepsis; change amino acid load or formula; find/treat other cause of hepatic failure

d. Enzyme patterns occur with equal likelihood in infants, children, and adults. They do not correlate with the history. The patterns involve changes in the canalicular function enzymes (CFE)—alkaline phosphatase, GGT, 5^1NT, bilirubin—and/or the hepatocellular enzymes (HPC)—AST and serum glutamic pyruvic transaminase (SGPT)

(1) Canalicular function patterns

    (a) Hepatocellular enzymes remain normal.

    (b) CFE rise soon after the onset of TPN, peak at ~14 days, and return to normal in 4 to 10 weeks.

    (c) The pattern is usually seen within 21 days of starting TPN.

    (d) Alkaline phosphatase can rise 2 to 3 times normal; the GGT up to 15 times normal; the bilirubin up to 10 times normal.

    (e) The alkaline phosphatase peak preceeds the bilirubin peak.

(2) Hepatocellular-canalicular patterns

    (a) HPC and CFE rise after the onset of TPN, peak in 1 to 3 weeks, and return to normal within 4 weeks after stopping therapy.

        i. AST and alkaline phosphatase peak on the nineteenth day, bilifubin on the twenty-second day.

        ii. CFE rise soon after TPN is started; then HPC enzymes rise, peaking about 4 weeks after the CFE (which peak 3 to 6 weeks). The pattern is usually seen within 49 days of starting TPN.

d. Therapy

(1) Treat any predisposing conditions as well as possible; liver biopsy if needed. Frequently, TPN receives the "blame" for abnormal liver function tests when another problem is presnt but is undiagnosed, is not suspected, or is not looked for.

(2) Adjust calorie mix and amino acid load.

(3) Start cyclic TPN.

(4) Switch to tube feeds.

(5) Assure adequate vitamin and trace-element replacement; check for vitamin toxicities.

(6) As a last resort and if the clinical setting is justifiable, stop the nutritional support and see if improvement occurs.

(7) Check for biliary sledge. If present, improvement can sometimes be achieved with metronidazole or cholecystokinin.

(8) Work up other causes—pancreatitis, sepsis, calculus, or acalculus cholecystitis.

B. Fluid, electrolyte, and acid-base problems

The commonly observed problems are outlined in Table 10-13.

C. Complications of infections

Identifying catheter sepsis in the acutely stressed patient who has multiple potential sources of fever may be difficult. Catheter sepsis is defined as a septic episode in which no other site of infection is obvious, the fever resolves on catheter removal, and cultures of the catheter tip and peripheral blood grow the same organism. The general steps to be taken in a patient receiving parenteral nutrition who develops an elevated temperature are:

1. Discontinue the TPN solution, change tubing, administer D5 half-normal saline at the same rate through the same catheter.

2. Culture blood (from central venous pressure and peripherally), sputum, urine, as well as other appropriate sites for bacteria and fungi.

3. Monitor vital signs.

4. If the source of infection is found, treat appropriately and reinstitute parenteral nutrition infusion.

5. If no source is found, continue D5½ normal saline infusion for 12 hours. If temperature then returns to normal, reinstitute parenteral nutrition infusion.

6. If temperature remains elevated, remove catheter and administer fluids peripherally.

7. If the clinical situation warrants it, remove the central line immediately.

8. When the patient has been afebrile 48 hours, parenteral nutrition may be restarted through a new central line.

The incidence of catheter sepsis can be minimized through proper care of the catheter insertion site and by limiting the use of the central line to administration of only the parenteral nutrition solution. Catheter sepsis usually resolves spontaneously, because once the catheter has been removed, the bacteremia or

Table 10-13. Fluid, electrolyte, and acid-base abnormalities

Problem	Predisposing factors	Management
Hypovolemia	Gastrointestinal fluid losses, osmotic diuresis	↑ Fluid intake
Hypervolemia	Renal failure, excess fluid intake, cardiac failure	↓ Fluid intake, diuretics
Hyponatremia	Gastrointestinal losses, fluid overload, diuretics	↑ Or ↓ sodium depending on cause; change diuretics
Hypernatremia	Dehydration; ↑ Na	↑ Fluid intake
Hypokalemia	Gastrointestinal losses, diuretics, anabolism	↑ Potassium intake; ↓ Na
Hyperkalemia	Renal failure	↓ Potassium intake
Hypophosphatemia	Phosphate-binding antacids, anabolism, phosphate-free dialysate	Discontinue phosphate-binders, ↑ Phosphorous intake
Hyperphosphatemia	Renal failure, formulas that come with phosphate	↓ Phosphorous intake; change formula
Hypomagnesemia	Diarrhea, malabsorption, anabolism	↑ Magnesium intake
Hypermagnesemia	Renal failure	↓ Magnesium intake
Hypocalcemia	Hypoalbuminemia, chronic renal failure	↑ Calcium intake (with CRF only)
Hypercalcemia	(Rare)	↓ Calcium intake
Metabolic acidosis	Diarrhea, high output gastrointestinal fistulae, renal failure; excess amino acid intake; drugs	↑ Acetate in TPN, ↓ Chloride in TPN; ↓ amino acid intake; stop drugs
Metabolic alkalosis	Gastric losses	↑ Chloride in TPN, ↓ acetate in TPN

fungemia will usually clear in 2 or 3 days. Exceptions occur and might include critically ill and/or immunocompromised patients or those who continue to need central lines and antibiotics.

D. Nutritional complications

1. Most of the nutritional complications associated with parenteral nutrition develop after many weeks to months of an inappropriate intake of a particular nutrient. However, in the acutely stressed patient who has a preexisting condition of malnutrition, nutritional deficiencies may develop earlier in the course of parenteral nutrition if the regimen is lacking in any nutrient. It is therefore important to include EFAs, vitamins, and trace elements in at least maintenance doses in all patients receiving parenteral nutrition. If specific deficiencies are identified, replacement doses should be given.

2. Nutrient toxicities may also develop but are usually the result of chronic accumulation particularly of fat-soluble vitamins or trace elements. These toxicities result from either excessive intake or reduced elimination. Trace element intake should be reduced in patients with renal failure to prevent potentially toxic accumulation as a result of decreased renal excretion.

E. Complications of intravenous fat

1. The intravenous administration of fat is characterized by its safety in the clinical setting as long as clearance is normal.

2. It should not be given to patients with abnormal clearance unless there is some mitigating circumstance. Such states of abnormal clearance may be congenital or may occur during sepsis of pancreatitis. If lipid clearance is normal during pancreatitis, it seems to be safe to use. There seems to be no data connecting intravenous fat as a causative agent for pancreatitis.

3. Acute effects

   a. Displacement of bilirubin from albumin
   b. Thrombocytopenia (usually not less than $80,000/mm^3$)
   c. Thrombophlebitis
   d. Fever, urticaria, dyspnea, diplopia, and blurred vision can occur as can headache, abdominal cramps,

nausea, vomiting, and diarrhea. Switching the brand of fat will frequently eliminate these problems.

4. Chronic administration
   a. No increased arthrogenesis has been observed with chronic use in home TPN.
   b. Kupfer cell deposition has been observed and is of unknown clinical significance.
   c. Eosinophilia in greater than 5%.
   d. Reversal of steatosis caused by excess glucose administration.

5. When the recommended dosage is exceeded, the recommended administration rate is exceeded or clearance is abnormal and fat is still given:
   a. Creaming occurs in the plasma and a setting analagous to fat emboli seems to occur.
   b. Fat loading of the macrophage system has been observed in neonates and infants.
   c. Transient abnormalities of pulmonary function have been observed (for example, reductions in diffusion capacity).

6. In vitro data have been reported to show decreased white cell function. The clinical confirmation and significance of these observations are currently unknown and under investigation.

7. There are currently little or no clinical data indicating better clearance of intravenous fat with the addition of low doses of heparin.

F. Incompatibilities
The field of drug compatibilities is complex and confusing. As administration systems and solutions change, so do the medications that can be safely mixed with them. It is strongly recommended that the administering physician communicate closely with the pharmacy department to obtain up-to-date compatibility information.

With the new admixture–administration systems giving glucose, fat, amino acids, and additives in the same package, a frequent update on drug compatibility will be necessary.

Enteral complications

Although the complication rate is usually less, significant problems can and do arise. Appropriate monitoring will minimize these problems and usually facilitate efficient, cost-effective therapy with a good nutritional response.

A. Table 10-14 lists some mechanical complications of enteral nutrition.
B. Table 10-15 lists some of the gastrointestinal complications of enteral nutrition.
C. Table 10-16 lists some of the metabolic complications associated with enteral feedings.
   1. Peritoneal dialysis
      The additional problems of glucose absorption from the peritoneum and protein loss through the peritoneum are present in patients receiving this technique who also need nutritional support.
      a. Glucose absorption
         The data indicate variability. A reasonable and useful formula is:

$$\text{g glucose absorbed/L} = 11.3\ X - 10.9$$
of dialysate instilled

$$X = \text{average glucose concentration (g/100) for all dialysate instilled/24 hour period}$$

Adjustments for this absorption may be necessry or advisable in patients receiving nutritional support, particularly in the presence of glucose tolerance and diabetes mellitus.

   b. Protein is lost with each exchange of peritoneal dialysate. The amount is variable, particularly in the presence of peritonitis. A reasonable and useful estimate is:

0.5 g/L dialysate with normal peritoneum
1.0 g/L dialysate with peritonitis

Adjustment in amino acid load or replacement with albumin may be necessary on an individual patient basis, for example, for a critically ill, hemodynamically unstable diabetic patient with advanced malnutrition and in need of peritoneal dialysis.

Table 10-14. Mechanical complications associated with enteral nutrition therapy

Complication	Possible causes	Prevention/therapy
Pharyngeal irritation Esophageal/mucosal erosion Otitis media	Large-bore vinyl or rubber feeding tubes for prolonged periods of time	Small-bore polyurethane or silicone feeding tube
Obstruction of the feeding tube lumen	Particulate matter from crushed medications administered through the tube; incompletely dissolved formula secondary to poor mixing technique	Thorough crushing of medications and mixing of enteral formula; flushing of feeding tube after medication administration and whenever feedings are interrupted; use of an infusion pump to maintain a constant flow rate, streptokinase to open a tube plugged with formula (100 units)
Gastroesophageal reflux with pulmonary aspiration of gastric contents/aspiration pneumonia; gastric retention	Altered gastric motility; patient's head of bed not elevated adequately; altered gag reflex; gastric feeding; rapid duodenal or jejunal feeding	Elevation of the patient's head of bed greater than or equal to 30 degrees at all times; continuous infusion administration technique; feeding tube positioned distal to the ligament of Treitz
Tube displacement	Coughing, vomiting	Replace tube and confirm placement by roentgenogram

Table 10-15. Gastrointestinal complications associated with enteral nutrition therapy

Complication	Possible causes	Prevention/therapy
Cramping, distension, bloating, flatulance, borborygmi, nausea/vomiting, hypermotility	Inappropriate formula administration (e.g., rapid increase in rate/volume, rapid increase in concentration, or both); lactose intolerance; antibiotic therapy; cold formula; too much fat	Initiate and advance formula rate and concentration gradually; reduce rate and concentration temporarily; continuous infusion administration technique; bring formula to room temperature before use; change to lactose-free formula; lactinex prescription; ↓ fat
Diarrhea	Inappropriate formula administration	Initiate and advance formula rate and concentration gradually; reduce rate and concentration temporarily; continuous infusion administration technique
	Starvation/hypoalbuminemia	Use elemental diet initially until nutritional status improves; give course of TPN before tube feedings
	Antibiotic therapy	Lactinex granules (1 packet via tube, 3 times/day for 1 day); vancomycin therapy; stop antibiotics
	Pellagra (diarrhea, dermatitis, dimentia)	Add 100 mg nicotinamide/L enteral solution
	Compromised pancreatic function/malabsorption/short bowel syndrome/radiation enteritis/severe Crohn's disease	Bolus doses of pancreatic enzymes via feeding tube several times a day; elemental diet; refeeding bile
	Lactose intolerance	Lactose-free formula
	Contaminated formula and/or equipment	Change solutions and clean all equipment
		Antidiarrheal therapy is frequently effective. It is important to use a regularly administered dose for the best effect (e.g., LoMotil liquid 1 to 2 tsp every 6 to 8 hours. Kaotin-Pectin will absorb liquid and "firm up" the stool but do little to actually reduce the electrolyte and water loss)

Table 10-16. Metabolic complications associated with enteral feedings

Complication	Possible causes	Prevention/therapy
Glucose interolerance/hyperosmolar, hyperglycemic, nonketotic dehydration/coma	Stress (traumatic or septic) with a temporary insulin resistance; diabetes mellitus; tube feed syndrome with diarrhea or excess renal losses	Insulin administration; use of formula with 30% to 50% of calories as fat; increase free water
Hyponatremia	Dilutional states; gastrointestinal losses	Diuretic therapy; sodium replacement; control of losses
Hypernatremia	Free water loss secondary to diabetes insipidus; dehydration; bowel losses	Appropriate hydration
Hypokalemia	Dilutional states Diuretic therapy Large-dose insulin therapy Increased losses (e.g., gastrointestinal drainage, diarrhea)	Diuretic therapy; potassium supplementation; control of losses
Hyperkalemia	Metabolic acidosis secondary to renal insufficiency; diarrhea or excessive ostomy losses	Use of enteral formula with low levels of potassium; fluid replacement
Hypophosphatemia	Large-dose insulin therapy; antacids; diarrhea	Phosphate supplementation; ↓ antacids or change
Hyperphosphatemia	Renal insufficiency	Use of enteral formula with low levels of phosphate
Hypozincemia	Increased losses (e.g., gastrointestinal drainage, burns, diarrhea)	Zinc supplementation
EFA deficiency	Use of enteral formula with low fat content over a prolonged period of time	Provide a minimum of 4% of the caloric intake as EFAs (linoleic)
Excess CO_2 production/respiratory insufficiency	Use of enteral formula with a high simple sugar content	Provide an enteral formula with balanced protein, fat content; increase percent of kcals provided as fat

SUGGESTED READINGS

Askanzai, J., et al.: Nutrition and the respiratory system, Crit. Care Med. **10**:163, 1982.

Askanzai, J., et al.: Respiratory changes induced by the large glucose loads of total parenteral nutrition, JAMA **243**:1444, 1980.

Baracos, V., et al.: Stimulation of muscle protein degradation and prostaglandin E_2 release by leukocyte pyrogen: A mechanism for the increased degradation of muscle proteins during fever, N. Engl. J. Med. **308**:553, 1983.

Biesel, W.R., and Wannemacher, R.W., Jr.: Gluconeogenesis, ureagenesis and ketogenesis during sepsis, JPEN **4**:277, 1980.

Blackburn GL, et al.: Branched chain amino acid administration and metabolism during starvation, injury, and infection, Surgery **86**:307, 1979.

Cerra, F.B.: Pocket manual of surgical nutrition, St. Louis, 1984, the C.V. Mosby Co.

Cerra, F.B., et al.: Branched chain metabolic support: a prospective, randomized, double-blind trial, Ann. Surg. **199**(3):3, 1984.

Cerra, F.B., et al.: Branched chains support postoperative protein synthesis, Surgery **92**(2):192, 1982.

Cerra, F.B., et al.: Correlations between metabolic and cardiopulmonary measurements in patients after trauma, general surgery, and sepsis, J. Trauma **19**:621, 1979.

Cerra, F.B., et al.: Enteral feeding in sepsis: a prospective, randomized, double-blind trial, Presented: CSA, Montreal, 1985, Surgery (In press.)

Cerra, F.B., et al.: The hepatic failure of sepsis: cellular versus substrate, Surgery **86**(3):409, 1979.

Cerra, F.B., et al.: Nitrogen retention in critically ill paients is proportional to the branched chain load, Crit. Care Med. **11**:775, 1983.

Cerra, F.B., et al.: Septic autocannibalism: a failure of exogenous nutritional support, Ann. Surg. **192**:570, 1980.

Chernow, B., Rainey, T.G., and Lake, C.R.: Endogenous and exogenous catecholamines in critical care medicine. Crit. Care Med. **10**:409, 1982.

Clowes, G.H.A., Jr., George, B.C., Villee, C.A., Jr., et al.: Muscle proteolysis induced by a circulating peptide in patients with sepsis or trauma, N. Engl. J. Med. **308**(10):545, 1983.

Deutschman, C.S., et al.: Refeeding syndrome: transient elevation of serum liver enzymes following resumption of gut feedings in patients receiving total parenteral nutrition, Surg. Forum XXXV, October 21-26, 1984, pp. 79-82.

Fath, J., et al.: Alterations in amino acid clearance during ischemia predicts hepalocellular ATP changes. Presented: Society of University Surgeons, Boston, February, 1985. (In press.)

Hassett, J., et al.: Multiple systems organ failure: mechanisms and therapy, Surg. Annu. **14**:27, 1982.

Heideman, M., and Hugli, T.: Anaphylatoxin generation in multiple systems organ failure, J. Trauma **24**:1038, 1984.

Iapichino, D., et al.: The main determinants of nitrogen balance during total parenteral nutrition in critically ill injured patients, Intensive Care Med. **10**:251, 1984.

Keys, A., et al.: The biology of human starvation. Minneapolis, 1950, University of Minnesota Press.

Kinney, J.M.: The effect of injury on metabolism, Br. J. Surg. **54**:435, 1967.

Knighton, D.R., et al.: Oxygen tension regulates the expression of angiogenesis factor by macrophages, Science **221**:1283, 1983.

Long, C.L., et al.: Muscle protein catabolism in the septic patient as measured by 3-methylhistidine excretion, Am. J. Clin. Nutr. **30**:1349, 1977.

Madoff, R.D., et al.: Prolonged intensive care: worth the price? Presented: Western Surgical Association, November 11-14, 1984. Arch. Surg. (In press.)

Mullin, T.J., and Kirkpatrick, J.R.: Substrate composition and sepsis. Arch. Surg. **118**:176, 1983.

Oppenheim, J.J., et al.: Lymphokines: their role in lymphocyte responses; properties of interleukin I, Fed. Proc. **41**(2):257, 1982.

Rodemann, H.P., and Goldberg, A.L.: Arachidonic acid, prostaglandin E2 and F2 influence rates of protein turnover in skeletal and cardiac muscle, J. Biol. Chem. **257**(4):1632, 1982.

Siegel, J.H., and Cerra, F.B.: Physiological and metabolic correlations in human sepsis, Surgery **86**:163, 1979.

Weissman, C., et al.: Amino acids and respiraton, Ann. Intern. Med. **98**:41, 1983.

Wilmore, P.W., et al.: Effect of injury and infection on visceral metabolism and circulation, Ann. Surg. **192**:491, 1980.

Wilmore, P.W., Mason, A.P., Jr., and Pruitt, B.A., Jr.: Impaired glucose flow in burned patients with gram-negative sepsis, Surg. Gynecol. Obstet. **143**:720, 1976.

11

Metabolic monitoring

Frank B. Cerra

The dynamic nature of the metabolic processes necessitates active monitoring protocols to assess the level of metabolic stress and to determine whether or not the desired nutritional effects are being achieved (see Fig. 9-4). The most useful parameters are: expired gas analysis (R/Q, V_{O}, V_{CO_2}), nitrogen excretion, glucose intolerance (in the absence of diabetes and pancreatitis), lactate and lactate/pyruvate ratio, and the clinical setting.

A. Evaluation of lean body mass
  1. The creatinine-height index combines chemical and anthropometric data.
    a. Creatinine-height index is designed to measure skeletal muscle mass. Creatinine is the end-product of creatine metabolism. Creatinine is found mainly in skeletal muscle and is excreted in the urine. Thus the amount of creatinine excreted is thought to directly correlate with muscle mass.
    b. A 24-hour urine collection is obtained and compared as a percentage of that for a "normal" patient of the same height and sex.
    c. Considerations in interpretation.
      (1) Ideal norms are used.
      (2) Normal renal function is necessary.
      (3) Age variation and stress changes are not accounted for.
      (4) Creatinine-height index does not correlate well with measured changes in body composition.

Portions of this chapter taken from Cerra, F.B.: Pocket manual of surgical nutrition, St. Louis, 1984, The C.V. Mosby Co.

2. Nitrogen balance.
   a. Nitrogen balance is calculated as nitrogen intake minus nitrogen excretion from all sources. Stool losses do not usually exceed 1 to 2 g/day in the absence of gastrointestinal disease: skin losses range from 0.1 to 0.4 g/m^2/day. In the absence of abnormal losses, skin and stool nitrogen should not exceed 2 g/day. Urinary nitrogen has several components: urea, uric acid, ammonia, amino acids, and creatinine. Approximately 90% of the urinary nitrogen is excreted as urea (UUN), except in chronic starvation or severe stress and sepsis when it may fall to as low as 65% to 70%. In those settings, total urinary nitrogen (TUN) gives a more accurate reflection of losses. Therefore nitrogen excretion can be calculated in the absence of abnormal skin or stool losses as follows:

   Nitrogen excretion = TUN + 2 g

   (Skin and stool)

   or

   Nitrogen excretion = UUN + 20% UUN + 2 g

   *(For nonurea   (Skin and
   components)   stool)*

   b. Nitrogen intake is calculated from the protein intake. For diets, approximately 16% of the protein intake will be nitrogen. For standard amino acid formulas there is usually 1 g nitrogen for each 6.25 g protein. The precise conversion coefficient differs for each amino acid formula and is usually on the label or in the package insert or can be calculated from the amino acid composition.
   c. The UUN method tends to overestimate the nitrogen loss. The test is inexpensive, easy to do, and available in nearly all hospitals.
   d. Considerations in interpretation.
      (1) Nitrogen balance measurement requires accurate sample collection.
      (2) It is limited in nitrogen-retention diseases such as renal or hepatic failure. More elaborate formulas

become necessary with a further reduction in accuracy and a prerequisite for a steady-state condition, for example, in renal failure:

Change in *body* urea nitrogen (BUN)(g/day) =

$(SUN_f - SUN_i) \times 0.6 \times BW_i +$

    (g/L/day)   *(L/kg)*

$(BW_f - BW_i) \times SUN_f \times 1.0$

    (kg/day)   *(g/L)*   *(L/kg)*

SUN = serum urea nitrogen
f = final
i = initial
BW = body weight (kg)

and

Total urea nitrogen appearance =

   (g/day)

UUN + *Body* urea nitrogen

  (g/day)   *(g/day)*

(3) Nitrogen balance measurement is limited in the presence of abnormal skin or stool losses as in enteropathies and malabsorption syndromes. Direct measurements of stool losses in these settings can improve accuracy.

B. Plasma chemistries evaluating hepatic protein synthesis. Hepatic proteins are generally inexpensive and easy to determine. They must be interpreted in the clinical context, as there are many factors in addition to nutrition that affect them such as abnormal gut or urine losses or hydration status. However, in appropriate clinical settings they are reasonably reliable nutritional indices, as is summarized in Table 11-1. In those patients in whom low visceral proteins are caused by malnutrition, nutritional therapy will usually induce a response and favorably affect surgical morbidity and mortality.

1. Albumin

  a. Albumin has a large body pool (4 to 5 g/kg) and a long half-life (20 days). It is therefore relatively insensitive to acute changes (in days) and responds slowly to therapy.

Table 11-1. Parameters of nutritional assessment

| Test | Degree of malnutrition | | | Na_e/K_e correlation | Reflects |
	Mild	Moderate	Severe		
Ideal body weight (%)	80-90	70-80	<70	—	Total body change
Usual body weight (%)	85-95	75-85	<75	—	Total body change
Creatinine height index	—	60% to 80%	<60%	0.37	Lean body mass change
Skinfold thickness (%)*	35-40	25-35	<25	0.79	Fat mass status
Midarm circumference (%)*	35-40	25-35	<25	0.68	Lean body mass change
Albumin (gm/100 ml)	2.8-3.5	2.1-2.7	<2.1	0.67	Visceral protein status
Transferrin (mg/100 ml)	150-200	100-150	<100	—	Visceral protein status
Absolute lymphocyte count (thousands of cells/mm³)	1.2-2.0	0.8-1.2	<0.8	—	Visceral protein status and immunocompetence

*Measured against a percentile table of norms.

b. It is reduced in nephrosis; in enteropathies; in hepatic failure, with a loss of 75% to 90% of hepatic cells as in hepatitis; in dialysis, particularly peritoneal dialysis (up to 30 g/dialysis); in uremia; in third-space losses into burns and areas of sepsis; in states of hypoadrenalism or hypothyroidism; and in conditions of volume expansion.

c. Albumin is increased in dehydration and in settings of increased cortisol output or excesses of anabolic hormones, growth hormone, insulin, and estrogens.

2. Transferrin

a. Transferrin has a smaller body pool and a shorter half-life (8 to 10 days) and is therefore of greater sensitivity.

b. In settings of minimal malnutrition, transferrin concentration can be estimated from the iron-binding capacity. However, in moderate to severe states, the correlation with iron-binding capacity is not good, and direct measurements should be done.

c. As with the other visceral proteins, the concentration will vary with hydration, rates of synthesis and catabolism, and compartment exchange. The same hormone influences are also present. It is also reduced in nephrosis and in burns from urine and wound losses, respectively.

d. Serum iron stores also affect it. In iron deficiency, transferrin is elevated; in overload, it is depressed.

3. Thyroxin-binding prealbumin (TBPA)

a. Thyroxin-binding prealbumin has a small body pool and a short half-life (2 to 3 days). It transports thyroid hormone and is a carrier protein for retinol-binding protein.

b. Its synthesis is both calorie and protein dependent.

c. The same factors as previously mentioned all seem to influence thyroxin-binding prealbumin. In addition, low levels are seen in hyperthyroidism, cystic fibrosis, chronic illness, and acute stress.

4. Retinol-binding protein (RBP)

a. Retinol-binding protein has a small body pool and a

very short half-life (12 hours) and therefore is very sensitive to synthesis and utilization changes.

b. It is specific for vitamin A transport and is linked with thyroxin-binding prealbumin in a constant molar ratio.

c. It is filtered and reabsorbed by the kidney; levels rise in renal disease.

d. It also has a reduced level in liver disease, chronic illness, cystic fibrosis, vitamin A deficiency, and hyperthyroidism. It is increased by excess vitamin A administration.

C. Immunocompetence

The currently used tests are at best screening procedures for immune function. They are inexpensive and easy to do but have multifactoral components. In addition, because they are multifactorial in result, the more sophisticated tests of immune function are difficult to use at the bedside and there are few current data on their nutritional effects. The data derived from any of the tests must be interpreted in the clinical setting. Despite their problems, some of the tests are useful risk predictors and in some patient groups are affected by nutrition with a subsequent effect on risk.

1. Anergy

a. The recall skin test antigens commonly used are: mumps, second-strength purified protein derivative of tuberculin (PPD), Candida, streptokinase-streptodornase (SKSD), and trichophytin. At least three antigens need to be used in a battery. A positive response is 5 mm induration at 48 to 72 hours after planting.

b. The response is multifactoral in origin and affecting factors include steroids, radiation, chemotherapy, diseases such as sarcoidosis and collagen-vascular diseases, sepsis without malnutrition, surgery alone, malnutrition, and malignancy.

c. If anergy is present and is nutritionally reversed, prognosis is significantly improved. A trial of nutritional therapy may be necessary if the cause of anergy cannot be determined by history, physical examination, or other laboratory tests.

2. Absolute lymphocyte count
   a. Absolute lymphocyte count is probably more reliable than skin testing.
   b. It is inexpensive, fast, and the easiest of the lymphocyte tests to do.
   c. Levels less than $1200/mm^3$ can reflect a moderate level of malnutrition (Table 11-1).
   d. Many other factors affect the absolute lymphocyte count, and thus it can be interpreted only in the clinical context. Such factors include sepsis, steroids, and neoplasia.
   e. The correlation between absolute lymphocyte count and other tests of white cell function are not clearly defined at this time.

3. Whether immune function is nutritionally influenced in settings other than standard starvation is controversial at present

D. Determination of existing stress level
   Because of the dynamic nature of the response to injury and the altered nutritional needs during that time, it is necessary to know a patient's current status in the response spectrum. Landmark characteristics have been identified.

1. For routine clinical use, the most useful characteristics are urinary nitrogen excretion, the blood glucose level and its response to insulin, plasma lactate, and the oxygen consumption index.
   a. The clinical setting is only a moderate predictor of the degree of hypermetabolism. Likewise, most severity scores or prognostic indices do not predict the presence and degree of hypermetabolism well.

2. A detailed statistical comparison of prototype stress response states is found in Fig. 10-1, p. 274.
   a. The dark inner circle represents the mean values for each variable for a nonstressed man who has fasted overnight. Each dotted circle represents 3 (nonseptic trauma, early sepsis) or 4.5 (late sepsis) standard deviations above or below the mean.

      b. On that framework are plotted the peak stress-response mean values for each variable during nonseptic trauma, early sepsis, and late sepsis.

      c. The spectrum and changing characteristics of the response become readily apparent.

E. Other assessment techniques

  1. Amino acid profiles

      a. As described above, different metabolic states have characteristic plasma metabolic profiles. Some of these are summarized in Table 11-2 and Fig. 11-1.

      b. These profiles are frequently useful diagnostically in the clinical setting, such as for diagnosing the hepatic metabolic status, as part of a coma work-up, for prognosis in intensive care unit patients, and in assessing metabolic status as a prelude to designing nutritional support regimens during the stress phase.

      c. On the basis of these profiles and more sophisticated analytical tools, a better understanding of the metabolic response to stress has occurred and newer metabolic support solutions have been designed and tested in the clinical settings.

        (1) The modified amino acid solutions are now commercially available.

        (2) Alternate fat fuels are in clinical testing. These techniques seem to promote the survival of more of those patients who would have otherwise died from malnutrition.

  2. Expired gas analysis

      a. Indirect calorimetry measures O_2 consumption and CO_2 production. The ratio

$$\frac{V_{CO_2}(ml)}{V_{O_2}(ml)}$$

    is the respiratory quotient.

        (1) The ratio reflects the existing mix of fuel oxidation. In starvation with ketosis, the respiratory quotient is $0:70$. With pure glucose oxidation, it is ~ 1.0, and with mixed carbohydrate, fat, and amino acid oxidation it is ~ 0.85. When net lipo-

Table 11-2. The categorical classification of stress

	Stress level and clinical example			
	0 (Nonstress starvation)	**1** (Elective general surgery)	**2** (Polytrauma)	**3** (Sepsis)
Total urinary nitrogen (g/day)	5	5 to 10	10 to 15	>15
Glucose* (mg/dl)	100 ± 20	150 ± 25	150 ± 25	250 ± 50
O_2 Consumption index (ml/m²)	90 ± 10	130 ± 6	140 ± 6	160 ± 10
Lactate (µM/L)	100 ± 5	1200 ± 200	1200 ± 200	2500 ± 500
Insulin resistance	No	No	Yes/no	Yes
Leucine (µM/L)	120 ± 10	74 ± 12	74 ± 12	180 ± 30
Proline (µM/L)	200 ± 20	213 ± 40	213 ± 40	300 ± 50
Phenylalanine (µM/L)	60 ± 15	74 ± 8	74 ± 8	124 ± 17
Methionine (µM/L)	10 ± 5	15 ± 5	15 ± 5	105 ± 25
Glucagon (pg/ml)	20	50 ± 9	120 ± 40	500 ± 50
Glucagon to insulin ratio	2 ± 0.5	2.5 ± 0.8	3.0 ± 0.7	8 ± 1.5
Untreated respiratory quotient	0.7	0.85	0.85	0.85 early, 1.0 late

*In the absence of diabetes, pancreatitis, or steroid therapy.
†With a normal lactate to pyruvate ratio of between 15:1 and 20:1.

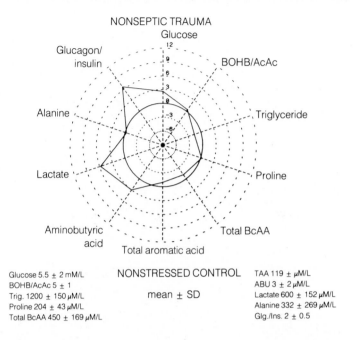

NONSEPTIC TRAUMA

Glucose 5.5 ± 2 mM/L
BOHB/AcAc 5 ± 1
Trig. 1200 ± 150 μM/L
Proline 204 ± 43 μM/L
Total BcAA 450 ± 169 μM/L

NONSTRESSED CONTROL

mean ± SD

TAA 119 ± μM/L
ABU 3 ± 2 μM/L
Lactate 600 ± 152 μM/L
Alanine 332 ± 269 μM/L
Glg./Ins. 2 ± 0.5

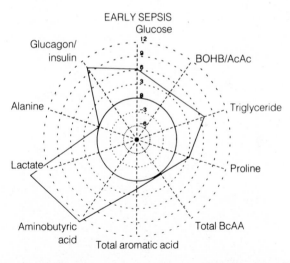

Fig. 11-1. Dark inner circle represents the overnight mean value for each variable (on radians) from a nonstressed man who has lasted overnight. Each dotted circle then represents 3 or 4.5 standard deviations above or below that control mean. Plotted on this grid are mean values for each variable at peak stress response for nonseptic trauma, early sepsis, and late sepsis. Spectrum and changing characteristics of the response become readily apparent. (From Cerra, F.B.: Pocket manual of surgical nutrition, St. Louis, 1984, The C.V. Mosby Co.)

Continued.

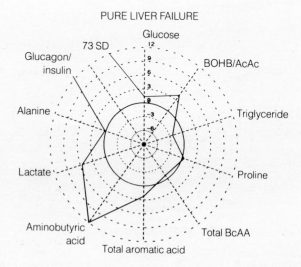

PURE LIVER FAILURE

Glucose 5.5 ± mM/L
BOHB/AcAc 5 ± 1
Trig. 1200 ± 150 μM/L
Proline 204 ± 43 μM/L
Total BcAA 450 ± 169 μM/L

NONSTRESSED CONTROL

mean ± SD

TAA 119 ± μM/L
ABU 3 ± 2 μM/L
Lactate 600 + 152 μM/L
Alanine 332 ± 269 μM/L
Glg./Ins. 2 ± 0.5

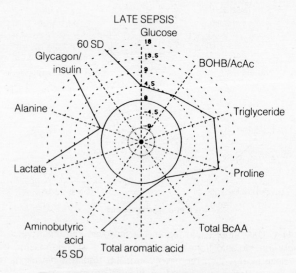

LATE SEPSIS

Fig. 11-1, cont'd. For legend see page 335.

genesis is occurring, the respiratory quotient exceeds 1.

   b. Thus, indirect calorimetry measurement is useful for several assessments.

     (1) Noninvasive oxygen consumption

     (2) Assessing the current fuel mix being oxidized

     (3) Assessing when net lipogenesis is occurring

       (a) In settings of excessive glucose administration

       (b) In settings of altered metabolism, as in late sepsis

     (4) Assessment of caloric expenditure

3. Current limitations in the technology

   a. Existing commerical technologies seem to work well in the nonintubated, nontracheostomy patient who is on room air, is not being ventilated, and is not under much stress.

   b. These commercial techniques are also reasonably reliable in intubated/tracheostomy patients who are being ventilated or who can be directly connected to the analyzer system. $FIO_2 \leq 50\%$ is usually required.

   c. Technician dependence in achieving steady-state data is very high. Documentation of level of activity, constancy of FIO_2 (V), tidal volume (TV), minute ventilation (MV) is necessary.

4. Increasing usefulness of expired gas analysis

   a. In replacing invasive blood gas and O_2 consumption determination

   b. In determining cardiac output

   c. In use with tissue monitors to assess the restoration of O_2 transport

SUGGESTED READINGS

Apelgren, K.N., Rombeau, J.L., and Twomey, P.L.: Comparison of nutritional indices and outcomes in critically ill patients, JPEN **10**:305-307, 1982.

Caldwell, M.D., and Kennedy-Caldwell, C.: Normal nutritional requirements, Surg. Clin. North Am. June, 1981.

Cerda, J.J., and Baumgartner, T.G.: Trace element requirements during total parenteral nutrition, vol. 4, July, 1982, Aspen Update.

Covelli, H.D., et al.: Respiratory failure precipitated by high carbohydrate loads, Ann. Intern. Med. **95**:579-581, 1981.

Fischer, J.E.: Nutritional assessment before surgery, Am. J. Clin. Nutr. 35:1128-1131, 1982.

Grant, J.P., Custer, P.B., and Thurlow, J.: Current techniques of nutritional assessment, Surg. Clin. North Am. June, 1981.

Heymsfield, S.B., et al.: Biochemical composition of muscle in normal and semi-starved human subjects: relevance to anthropometric measurements, Am. J. Clin. Nutr. 36:131-142, 1982.

Long, C.L., et al.: Metabolic response to injury and illness: estimation of energy and protein needs from indirect calorimetry and nitrogen balance, JPEN 3:452-456, 1979.

Long, C.L., et al.: Urinary excretion of 3-methylhistidine: an assessment of muscle protein catabolism in adult normal subjects and during malnutrition, sepsis,and skeletal trauma, Metabolism 30:765-775, 1981.

Martin, D.J.: Topical lotion for essential fatty acids, Nutr. Supp. Serv. 1:40, 1981.

Mullin, T.J., and Kirkpatrick, J.R.: The effect of nutritional support on immune competency in patients suffering from trauma, sepsis, or malignant disease, surgery 90:610-615, 1981.

Shizgal, H.M.: Body composition. In Fischer, J.E., editor: Surgical nutrition, Little, Brown & Co., 1983.

Stein, T.P.: Fat requirements for parenteral nutrition, Nutr. Supp. Serv. 1:19-22, 1981.

Trace elements in human nutrition, Dairy Council Digest 53:January-February 1982.

Wilmore, D.W.: The metabolic management of the critically ill, New York, 1977, Plenum Medical Book Co.

SECTION TWO

ORGAN DYSFUNCTION

12

Pulmonary dysfunction

Marvin A. McMillen
Ian Gilmour

A. Pulmonary embolism

Since Virchow first explored the pathophysiology of pulmonary embolism in 1846 and heparin became a means of treating hypercoagulability in the 1930's, the clinical importance of this condition has received increasing attention. The significance of pulmonary embolism in the critically ill, immobile, traumatized patient cannot be overestimated. An intensive care unit–acquired pulmonary embolism, however, is an unusual event

1. Predisposing factors
   a. Stasis
   b. Vessel injury
   c. Hypercoagulability

2. Sources of pulmonary emboli
   a. Iliac-pelvic veins—40%
   b. Femoral veins—50%
   c. Calf veins—<10%
   d. Can also embolize from upper body veins
   e. Thromboses may begin in calf veins, propagate proximally, and break off in femoral veins

3. Pathophysiology of fatal pulmonary emboli
   a. Obstruction of more than 50% of pulmonary outflow tract. Similar reduction of pulmonary vascular bed by surgical resection is not fatal; therefore obstruction alone is not the lethal factor.
   b. Acute pulmonary hypertension-vasoconstriction
   c. Acute right heart pressure overload, failure, and/or infarction

d. Reflex bronchoconstriction from platelet release of histamine and serotonin (heparin is an excellent anti-serotonin agent)

e. Thromboxane, prostaglandins, and other vasoactive substances
   (1) Inhibit hypoxic vasoconstriction
   (2) Change V/Q

f. Acute ventilation/perfusion abnormalities
   If patient survives initial insult, recanalization of vessels and return of function occur within 2 to 3 weeks.

4. Signs and symptoms—Most common are nonspecific
   a. Dyspnea, tachpnea, and or hyperpnea
   b. Tachycardia
   c. Fever
   d. Chest pain—pleuritic (or anginal). Occasionally a pleural rub, wheezing
   e. S_3, fixed splitting of S_2, right ventricular tap or heave, or other signs of right heart failure
   f. Acute hypoxemia
   g. Acute increase in pulmonary artery pressure (PAP) and/or decrease in mean arterial pressure (MAP)

5. Diagnosis
   a. Clinical presentation—suspicion alone in selected cases may be enough to initiate therapy.
   b. Initial—eliminate other diagnoses. Estimate severity.
      (1) Chest roentgenogram—volume loss, hyperlucency, effusion, infarction. Rarely diagnostic.
      (2) Electrocardiogram—S-T, QRS change in 70%; specific finding ($S_I Q_{III}$) rare
      (3) Complete blood count—rule out sepsis
   c. Evaluate cardiovascular effects
      (1) With normal cardiovascular system, PAP seldom > 40 torr
      (2) May precipitate acute right heart failure with >40% occlusion or with underlying heart disease
      (3) Systemic hypotension in about 25%; usually associated with right-side heart failure

    d. Evaluate pulmonary involvement
       (1) V/Q scans; normal perfusion scan rules out pulmonary embolism
       (2) Pulmonary angiography
    e. Evaluate deep vein thrombophlebitis
       (1) Venous Doppler ultrasound—good only above knee
       (2) Impedance plethysmography—less acurate below knee
       (3) Venogram

6. Management of pulmonary emboli
    a. Ventilatory support—as indicated from increased FIO_2, blood gases
    b. Heparinization—bolus, 20 to 30 units/kg to block degranulation of platelets by thrombin
       (1) Maintenance—10 to 15 units/kg/hr
       (2) Follow partial thromboplastin time (PTT), (1.5 to 2.5 times normal); clotting times (CT) 2 to 3 times normal
       (3) Monitor platelet count to avoid thrombocytopenia
       (4) Continue during initiation of Coumadin therapy
    c. Coumadization
       (1) The clot is usually undergoing lysis by day 10
       (2) Begin warfarin (Coumadin) on day 7 to 10
       (3) If 70 kg, 10 mg orally for 3 days then 5 mg daily; if 50–70 kg, 10 mg daily for 2 days, then 2.5 to 5 mg orally daily
       (4) The goal is a prothrombin time of $1\frac{1}{2}$ to 2 times normal
    d. Thrombolytic therapy—streptokinase, urokinase, usually in massive embolism with unstable hemodynamics
       (1) Heparin is discontinued and medication is not given until PTT is less than two times normal.
       (2) The medication is continued for 24 hours, then heparin is restarted.

(3) Relative contraindications include surgery, biopsy, or trauma within 10 days, recent cardiopulmonary resuscitation (CPR), recent serious gastrointestinal bleeding, severe hypertension, known hemostatic disorders.

(4) Venipuncture should be avoided while patient is receiving streptokinase. If venipuncture is necessary, pressure is applied afterward for 30 min.

e. Transvenous embolectomy

(1) After diagnosis and heparinization, the clot is localized angiographically and retrieved with transvenous catheter embolectomy forceps. Retrieval may require multiple passes. Heparin and warfarin treatment is as previously discussed.

f. Embolectomy (open)

(1) A median sternotomy with cardiopulmonary bypass from below or through the chest is performed.

(2) The pulmonary artery is opened and clot removed.

(3) Mortality > 60%

7. Management of recurring pulmonary emboli or when heparin in contraindicated

a. Contraindications to heparin

(1) Absolute: Recent cardiovascular accident (CVA) or recent neurosurgery, ocular surgery, or spinal surgery

(2) Relative: Recent major surgery, major trauma, intracranial neoplasm, recent gastrointestinal bleeding, guiac-positive stools, hemostatic defects, hypertension—> 200 systolic or > 110 diastolic, hematuria, heparin-induced thrombocytopenia

b. Surgical approach

(1) Caval interruption by ligation or placement of clip

(a) High morbidity and mortality

(b) Seldom used

    (2) Transvenous—cutdown or percutaneous intro-
ducer system

      (a) Clip is placed in inferior vena cava (IVC) be-
low renal veins

      (b) Greenfield filter, Mobin-Uddin umbrella,
Hunter balloon

    (3) Complications include edema, thrombosis, re-
embolization, death

B. Pneumonia

  1. Bacterial

    a. Pathogenesis is usually aspiration of organisms from
the upper respiratory tract. Excessive secretions,
poor cough, impaired nutrition, and inadequate host
defenses may all facilitate bacterial colonization,
growth, and infection. Bacterial encapsulation may
enhance pathogenicity. Gram negative colonization of
the upper respiratory and gastrointestinal tract can
occur rapidly in the intensive care unit. The gastrointestinal tract is probably the source of the gram-negative organisms. Resistant organisms result from
broad-spectrum antibiotic coverage.

    b. Right lower lobe pneumonia

      (1) Pneumococcus, 60%; *S. aureus*, 20%. Also influ-
enza A, *Streptococcus* species, and *Klebsiella
pneumoniae*. Often follow viral upper respiratory
tract illness.

      (2) Staphylococcal pneumonia is more commonly
seen after influenza A and can be particularly lethal even in healthy young adults.

    c. *Klebsiella* pneumonia

      (1) This pneumonia is more common in alchoholic
patients.

      (2) Its upper lobe location reflects the drainage of
the aspirant in the recumbent inebriate.

    d. Hypostatic (lower lobe) pneumonia

      (1) Many surgical patients with poor pulmonary toi-
let, poor cough effort, and abdominal pain may
develop first a lower atelectasis (usually left) that
then progresses to a frank pneumonia.

    (2) Prolonged nasogastric intubation may facilitate chronic aspiration.

    (3) Pathogens are as likely to be gram negative as gram positive; mixed flora including anaerobes are common.

    (4) Broad-spectrum antibiosis pending specific culture and sensitivities are recommended, but the most effective therapy is prevention with vigorous pulmonary support.

e. *Legionella* pneumonia

    (1) Severe pneumonitis that is initially lobar then bilateral and diffuse may be Legionella.

    (2) High-grade sepsis occurs and carries a 20% mortality.

    (3) High index of suspicion when pneumonia fails to respond to beta-lactamose stable (Blactan) or aminoglycoside antibiotics.

    (4) Diagnosis can be made on culture, immunofluorescence, or antibody titers.

    (5) The treatment is erythromycin intravenously, 1000 mg every 6 hours for 24 hours, then 500 mg every 6 hours for 14 days. Immunosuppressed patient may require 21 days.

    (6) If there is no response, then rifampin, 600 mg p.o. q.d. for 9 to 12 days.

f. Pneumonia in the immunosuppressed or agranulocytic patient

    (1) Neutrophils and inflammatory cells required for consolidation.

    (2) In agranulocytic or even severely dehydrated patients, tachpnea, cyanosis, hypoxia, and a widened A-a DO_2 may be the only hallmarks of an overwhelming pneumonia.

    (3) Sputa may be scanty, yet Gram stain shows a plethora of organisms.

    (4) Therapy should be broad spectrum and perhaps accompanied by white cell transfusions.

(5) Unusual organisms, i.e., anaerobes, fungi, cytomegalovirus, mycoplasma, and mycobacteria
should be ruled out.

2. Viral or mycoplasmal
a. Thought to follow viremia, usually patchy and central
in distribution.
b. Physical and chest roentgenogram findings are often
minimal with major impairment of gas exchange; often in immunocompromised or elderly patients; often
associated with decreased white count. Resolution is
frequently lengthy.
c. Superinfection should be closely watched for and aggressively treated.
d. Nonresolving pneumonias in critically ill patients
should never be ignored.
(1) Nonspecific mixed flora may mask another
pathogen. Fungal cultures for Candida, histoplasmosis, and aspergillosis should be sent and
Ziehl-Neilson stains and cultures for mycobacteria prepared.
(2) In settings in which disease is progressive, diagnosis is uncertain, and immune compromise is
present, consideration should be given to early
use of open lung biopsy.

C. Adult respiratory distress syndrome
1. Adult respiratory distress syndrome (ARDS) characterized by tachypnea, increased A-a Do_2, decreased compliance, generalized interstitial infiltrates in a setting of
known predisposition for the disease.
2. Disorders associated with ARDS
a. Sepsis (bacterial, viral or fungal)
b. Trauma, burns
c. Aspiration
d. Postresuscitation, shock, and other low flow states
e. O_2 toxicity
f. Pancreatitis
g. Noxious inhalation
h. Drug overdose

    i. Blood products

    j. Head injury

3. Possible mediators

    a. Neurogenic increase in pulmonary venous pressure

    b. Leukoagglutination and release of proteolytic enzymes

    c. Direct damage by toxic substances (burns, noxious fumes)

    d. Oxygen-free radicals

    e. Complement

    f. Endotoxin-triggers release of culpable substances.

    g. End products of ararchidonic and metabolism (prostaglandins, thromboxane, etc.)

    h. Fibrin split products

    i. Microemboli (fat or platelets or red blood cells)

    j. End result is increased pulmonary capillary membrane permeability, with increased interstitial fluid from the capillary leak. There may also be damage to the alveolar epithelium.

4. Pathophysiology

    a. Early interstitial and late alveolar edema

    b. Loss of surfactant

    c. Atelectasis/congestion

    d. Focal alveolar lining damage

    e. Cellular infiltration

    f. Fibrosis

5. Management

    a. Oxygen

        (1) Excess O_2 per se is a cause of ARDS. Attempt to maintain Hb saturation $> 90\%$ ($Pao_2 > 60$) with minimum FIO_2.

    b. Continuous distending pressure (PEEP, CPAP, etc.)

        (1) Theoretically keeps alveoli open and maintains functional residual capacity (FRC), thus decreasing V/Q abnormality. Levels necessary are controversial (See section on CDP p. 58) Combine with FIO_2 to keep $Pao_2 > 60$, $FIO_2 \leq 50\%$; increase PEEP before increasing $FIO_2 > 50\%$.

(2) Higher levels of PEEP affect the heart by decreasing venous return or pulmonary vascular resistance (PVR).

c. Positive pressure ventilation (PPV) to keep the level of respiratory work at an acceptable level

d. Maintain colloid oncotic pressure and intravascular volume
   (1) Suggestion that a COP > 18 decreases extravasation and interstitial water
   (2) Decrease total body water with fluid restriction and diuresis as appropriate; maintain blood volume and perfusion.

e. Restore and maintain systemic O_2 transport; (i.e., maintain cardiac output at an appropriate level), keep hemoglobin at 12 g%; maximize flow-dependent O_2 consumption.

f. Remove or control the cause of ARDS (see above)

g. Nutrition support

h. Drug therapy
   (1) Steroids—no benefit
   (2) Mediator antagonists—still experimental
   (3) Prostaglandins—still experimental

i. Good pulmonary care as outlined in Chapter 3

D. Aspiration
1. Acute insult—gastric contents inhaled into tracheobronchial tree trigger bronchospasm and may cause physical airway obstruction with potential for development of ARDS. May be direct damage to both the lining of airways and capillary endothelium. The end result is a diffuse intense hemorrhagic pneumonitis and ARDS.
   a. Etiology not simply hydrochloric acid (HCl); experimental HCl aspiration is a self-limited disease whereas aspiration of gastric contents often produces prolonged severe illness. Severe sequalae may result even when pH of gastric content > 2.5, probably because of airway obstruction with particulate matter and development of pneumonia and because of initiation of ARDS mechanism.
2. Pneumonia—may progress to lung abscess.

a. Causes
  (1) Anaerobic organisms are the usual causal agents.
    (a) *Bacteroides* species
    (b) *Fusobacterium nucleatum*
    (c) Peptostreptococcus
    (d) Microaerophilic streptococcus
  (2) Aerobes—less common
    (a) *Staphylococcus aureus*
    (b) *Diplococcus pneumoniae*
    (c) Enterics and Pseudomonas
b. Management
  (1) Control airway by intubation to prevent further aspiration and allow specific treatment
  (2) Aggressive suction and lavage; send aspirate for pH, culture, etc.
  (3) Ventilation with PEEP, aggressive pulmonary toilet, mechanical assist, O_2 as needed
  (4) Bronchoscopy for particulate matter
  (5) Role of antibiotics and steroids controversial
c. Aspiration of particulate antacid can also produce very severe pulmonary dysfunction
E. Obstructive lung disease
  1. Bronchoconstrictive or bronchospastic disorders
  Bronchoconstriction is most commonly encountered in reactive airway disease or asthma and in chronic bronchitis (smoker's lung). Patients diagnosed as being asthmatic primarily have reversible obstruction, although asthma and bronchitis can coexist. Asthma may be further subdived into intrinsic (pediatric, atopic) or extrinsic (acquired).
    a. Pathophysiology of asthma
      (1) Bronchial smooth muscle—contraction and eventual hypertrophy
      (2) Vasodilation—edema
      (3) Increased mucous secretion with plugging
      (4) Eosinophilia
    b. Diagnosis
      (1) A presumptive diagnosis that obstructive lung disease is present can be made on clinical

grounds. A laboratory diagnosis of reactive airway disease is made on the basis of pulmonary function tests (PFTs), demonstrating a 25% improvement in flow and/or volume with bronchodilators.

(2) Patients often have increased FRC and residual volume and decreased expiratory reserve volume (ERV) because of gas trapping. In late stages of chronic obstructive pulmonary disease (COPD) and during acute asthma attacks, vital capacity (VC) may be decreased.

(3) Gas exchange is usually compromised in COPD. It may be normal between attacks of asthma.

(4) Most asthma attacks often follow a predisposing event, such as allergen exposure or viral upper respiratory infection.

c. Mediators of atopic response in asthma

Histamine	Mast cells
Leukotrienec	Mast cells and neutrophils
Eosinophilic chemotactic factor of anaphylaxis	Mast cells, basophils
Neutrophil chemotactic factor	Mast cells, basophils
Platelet activity factor	Mast cells, basophils
Prostaglandin	Mast cells, basophils, platelets

d. Other settings in which bronchospasm occurs include

(1) Foreign body aspiration or introduction (e.g., endotracheal tube [ETT])

(2) Drug-induced—beta-blocking agents, histamine release (morphine sulfate)

(3) Exercise

(4) Cold

(5) Infection

e. Signs and symptoms

(1) Dyspnea, tachypnea, obvious use of accessory muscles of exhalation; audible wheezing either externally or by stethoscope, prolonged exhalation, signs of autonomic activity. In late stages

obvious decrease in VT with gasping respirations, cyanosis, and respiratory failure

(2) Dynamic airway compression syndrome

(a) Usually prior bronchitis (COPD).

(b) Occurs during expiration in presence of either patient agitation or high minute ventilation. Initially difficult to differentiate from bronchospasm.

(c) Tends to disappear abruptly when patient is sedated or paralyzed.

(d) Transthoracic pressure gradient during forced expiration collapses larger airways.

(e) When diagnosis is confirmed, extubate during heavy sedation.

  i. Variant occurs after prolonged mechanical ventilation and tends to manifest during weaning particularly when high minute ventilation (V) is necessary.

2. Chronic obstructive pulmonary disease

Although the stereotypes of the "pink puffer" or "blue bloater" are effective teaching tools, most patients fall somewhere along a spectrum from pure bronchitis (obstructive) to pure emphysema.

a. Types

(1) Bronchitis—chronic airway irritation/infection with voluminous sputum, bronchospasm, and edema leading to permanent scarring with edema; destruction of normal defense mechanisms.

(2) Emphysema—obliteration of normal alveolar anatomy with coalecence to form large air spaces. Almost always associated with severe obstructive disease.

(3) Bronchiolitis—rare in adults

(a) Toxic gas exposure—Cl, NH_3, SO_2, $O_3{}^-$, NO_2, phosgene

(b) Infectious—viral

(c) Airway edema with wheezing on expiration; may progress to pneumonitis/ARDS picture

b. Diagnosis

	Primarily bronchitic	Primarily emphysematous
Clinical		
Dyspnea at rest	Maybe	Usually
Dyspnea on exertion	Yes	Yes
Hyperinflation	Usually	Yes
Productive cough	Yes	Maybe

	Bronchitis	Emphysema
Physical findings		
Uses accessory muscles of inspiration	Maybe	Yes
Uses accessory muscles of expiration	Yes	Often
Cyanosis	Maybe	Often
Clubbing	Maybe	Often
Wheezing	Often	Maybe
Laboratory values		
Increased hemoglobin	Maybe	Usually
Chest roentgenogram	Nonspecific	Bullae
PFTs	VC $\rightleftharpoons$	$\downarrow$
	RV $\uparrow$	$\uparrow \uparrow$
	FEV$_1$ $\downarrow$	$\downarrow$

c. Treatment
   (1) Avoid excessive sedation, narcotics; Consider regional block for analgesia
   (2) Aggressive mobilization, chest physiotherapy
   (3) Aggressive bronchodilator therapy
   (4) Mucolytics—questionable efficacy
   (5) Antibiotics—as indicated; often advisable in bronchitis
   (6) Avoid fluid overload, anemia
   (7) Monitor blood gases, respiratory rate, blood pressure, heart rate
   (8) Avoid intubation/ventilation if possible; see Chapter 3 for ventilation parameters; use PEEP judiciously

      (9) In operating room: choose incision to minimize pain, respiratory embarrassment; avoid unnecessary surgery; extubate as soon as possible to allow effective cough

      (10) Early ambulation

F. Smoke inhalation
  1. General
     a. 10% to 25% of hospitalized burn patients
     b. Injury due to the toxic products carried in smoke—a suspension of gas and particles
        (1) Location and severity of injury depend on: type of chemicals, concentration of chemicals, solubility, length of exposure.
        (2) Highly soluble chemicals tend to dissolve in upper airway; NH_3, HCl, SO_2.
        (3) Insoluable tend to localize in lower airways: aldehydes, phosgene, oxides.
     c. Hypoxemia results from: V/Q abnormality, airway obstruction, decreased cardiac output, carbon monoxide.
  2. Increased risk settings
     a. Steam
     b. Plastics
     c. Loss of consciousness
     d. Enclosed space
     e. Associated burns of face and/or upper airway
  3. Symptoms and signs: May take 12 to 48 hours to develop
     a. Dizziness, headache, seizures, coma, confusion
     b. Dyspnea, cough, stridor, tachypnea, soot in sputum
     c. Arrhythmia
     d. Nausea and vomiting
  4. Tests
     a. ABG
     b. Carboxyhemaglobin
     c. Chest roentgenogram
     d. ECG
     e. Spirometry

5. Therapy
    a. Intubation criteria
       (1) Stridor
       (2) Burns of palate, tongue, pharynx
       (3) Respiratory failure
    b. Bronchoscopy may be used to assess extent and severity of injury or need for intubation
    c. Oxygen
    d. Therapy for carbon monoxide if needed
    e. Toilet, bronchodilators
    f. No prophylacic steroids or antibiotics
G. Carbon monoxide (CO) intoxication
    1. CO binds to hemoglobin forming carboxyhemoglobin. Hemoglobin has 210 times greater affinity for CO than for O_2. Carboxyhemoglobin also releases O_2 only at much lower tissue O_2 levels.
    2. Normal CO levels
       a. Nonsmokers, 1%
       b. Smokers, 6%
       c. Garage workers, 3% to 15%
    3. CO Hb levels and symptoms
       Symptoms are accelerated by altitude or anemia, or factors that left-shift the O_2 dissociation curve.
       a. 0% to 10%—usually none
       b. 10% to 20%—dyspnea on exertion, headache, throbbing temples
       c. 20% to 30%—irritability, dizziness, confusion, visual disturbances; all from cerebral edema
       d. 40% to 60% syncope, chest pain, seizures, apnea, coma
    4. Management
       a. High flow (>40 L/min); high concentrations (dose to 100%) O_2 until CO < 8% to 15%

FIO_2	CO half-life
20%	210 min
100%	30-40 min
2atm	10-25 min
95% O_2 + 5% CO_2	20 min

b. Supportive measures—cardiac, respiratory, etc.
c. Hyperbaric chamber consideration
   (1) CO > 40%
   (2) CO > 25% with Hb < 10 g% or with angina, ECG changes, seizures, pregnancy, history of cardiac disease
d. Sequelae depend on severity and duration of insult; may include myocardial infarction, liver necrosis, basal ganglion dysfunction, etc.
e. Monitor
   (1) PaO_2 does not correlate with CO Hb level or with O_2 content. Therefore monitor either O_2 content or CO Hb level.
   (2) Blood gases to rule out respiratory depression, metabolic acidosis
   (3) ECG
   (4) Chest roentgenogram
   (5) Clinical parameters

SELECTED READINGS

Alberts, W.M. et al.: The outlook for survivors of ARDS, Chest **84**:272, 1984.

Alderson, P.O., et al.: The Role of 133Xe ventilation studies in the scintigraphic detection of pulmonary embolism, Radiology **120**:633, 1976.

Bell, W.R., and Simon, T.L.: A comparative analysis of pulmonary perfusion scans with pulmonary angiograms, Am. Heart J. **92**:700, 1976.

Bell, W.R., and Simon T.L.: Current status of pulmonary thromboembolic disease: pathophysiology, diagnosis, prevention and treatment, Am. Heart J. **102**:239, 1982.

Bell, W.R., et. al: The clinical features of submassive and massive pulmonary embolism, Ann. Intern. Med. **62**: 355, 1977.

Bellamy P.E., and Oye, R.K.: ARDS: hospital charges and outcome according to underlying disease, Crit. Care Med. **12**:622, 1984.

Biello, D.R., et al.: Interpretation of inderterminate lung scintigrams, Radiology **133**:189, 1979.

Biello, D.R., et al.: Ventilation-Perfusion studies in suspected pulmonary embolism, Am. J. Radiol. **133**:1033, 1979.

Bone, R.C.: Diagnosis of causes for acute respiratory distress by pressure-volume curves, Chest **70**:740, 1976.

Bone, R.C.: Treatment of adult respiratory distress syndrome with diuretics, dialysis, and positive end-expiratory pressure, Crit. Care Med. **6**:135, 1978.

Bone, R.C.: Treatment of severe hypoxemia due to the ARDS, Arch. Intern. Med. **140**:85, 1980.

Bone, R.C. (editor): ARDS, Clin. Chest Med. **3**:1982.

Braun S.D., et al.: Ventilation-perfusion scanning and pulmonary angiography. AJR **143**:977, 1984.

Canham E.M., et al.: Mepacrine but not methylprednisolone decreases acute edematous lung injury after injection of phorbol myristate ecetate in rabbits, Am. Rev. Respir. Dis. **127**:594, 1983.

Cheely, R., et al.: The role of noninvasive tests versus pulmonary angiography in the diagnosis of pulmonary embolism, Am. J. Med. **70**:17, 1981.

Crapo, R.O.: Smoke inhalation injuries, JAMA **246**:1694, 1981.

Danek, S.J., et al.: The dependence of oxygen uptake on oxygen delivery in the adult respiratory distress syndrome, Am. Rev. Respir. Dis. **122**:387, 1980.

Eaton, R.J., et al.: Cardiovascular evaluation of patients treated with PEEP, Arch. Intern. Med. **143**:1958, 1983.

Elliott, C.G., et al.: Pulmonary function and exercise gas exchange in survivors of adult respiratory distress syndrome, Am. Rev. Respir. Dis. **123**:492, 1981.

Fein, A.M., et al.: The risk factors, incidence, and prognosis of ARDS following septicemia, Chest **83**:40, 1983.

Flick, M.R., and Murray, J.F.: High-dose corticosteroid therapy in the ARDS, JAMA **251**:1054, 1984.

Genovisi, M.G.: Effects of smoke inhalation, Chest **77**:335, 1980.

Hallman, M., et al.: Evidence of lung surfactant abnormality in respiratory failure, J. Clin. Invest. **79**:673, 1982.

Holzapfel, L., et al.: Static pressure-volume curves and effect of positive end-expiratory pressure on gas exchange in ARDS, Crit. Care Med. **11**:571, 1983.

Hull, R.D., et al.: Impedance plethysmography using the occlusive cuff technique in the diagnosis of venous thrombosis, Circulation **53**:696, 1976.

Hull, R.D., et al.: Pulmonary angiography, ventilation lung scanning, and venography for clinically suspected pulmonary embolism with abnormal perfusion lung scan, Ann. Intern. Med. **98**:891, 1983.

Hull, R.D., et al.: A randomized trial of diagnostic strategies for symptomatic deep vein thrombosis, Thromb. Haemost. **50**:160a, 1983.

Hyers, T.M., editor: Pulmonary embolism and hypertension, Clin. Chest Med. **5**:1984.

Jardin, F., et al.: Influence of PEEP on left ventricular performance, N. Engl. J. Med. **304**:387, 1981.

Johnsrude, I.S.: Pulmonary embolism, Curr. Probl. Diagn. Radiol. **2**:5, 1982.

Kaplan, R.L., Sahn, S.A., and Petty, T.: Incidence and outcome of the respiratory distress syndrome in gram-negative sepsis, Arch. Intern. Med. **139**:867, 1979.

Kipper, M.S., et al.: Longterm follow-up of patients with suspected pulmonary embolism and normal lung scan, Chest **82**:411, 1982.

McNeil, B.J.: A diagnostic strategy using ventilation-perfusion studies in patients suspected for pulmonary embolism, J. Nucl. Med. **17**:613, 1976.

Mills, S.S.R., et al.: The incidence, etiologies, and avoidance of complications of pulmonary angiography in a large series, Radiology **136**:295, 1980.

Mohsenifar, Z., et al: Relationship between O_2 delivery and O_2 consumption in the adult respiratory distress syndrome, Chest **84**:267, 1984.

Moser, K.M.: Pulmonary embolism, Am. Rev. Respir. Dis. **115**:829, 1977.

Neuhaus, A., et al.: Pulmonary embolism in respiratory failure, Chest **73**:460, 1978.

Novelline, R.A., et al.: The clinical course of patients with suspected pulmonary embolism and a negative pulmonary arteriogram, Radiology **126**:561, 1978.

Progressive pulmonary insufficiency and other pulmonary complications of thermal injury, J. Trauma **15**:366, 1975.

Rakow, E.C., Fein, A., and Seigel, J.: The relationship of the colloid osmotic-pulmonary artery wedge pressure gradient to pulmonary edema and mortality in critically ill patients, Chest **82**:433, 1982.

Robin, E.D.: Overdiagnosis and overtreatment of pulmonary embolism: The emperor may have no clothes, Ann. Intern. Med. **87**:775, 1977.

Secker-Walker, R.H.: On purple emperors, pulmonary embolism and venous thrombosis, Ann. Intern. Med. **98**:1006, 1983.

Sevitt, S.: Venous thrombosis and pulmonary embolism, Am. J. Med. **33**:703, 1962.

Shimada, Y., et al.: Evaluation of the progress and prognosis of ARDS, Chest **76**:180, 1979.

Sibbald, W.J., et al.: Alveolo-capillary permeability in hyman septic ARDS, Chest **79**:133, 1981.

Watts, W.J., and Weg, J.G.: Thromboembolic disease in critically ill patients, Clin. Challenge Cardiopul. Med. **4**:1, 1983.

Weil, M.H., et al.: Relationship between colloid osmotic pressure and pulmonary artery wedge pressure in patients with acute cardiorespiratory failure, Am. J. Med. **64**:643, 1978.

13

Dysrhythmias

John W. McBride

Disorders of rhythm are a common occurrence in surgical intensive care unit (SICU) patients. Since occasionally they are life threatening and require immediate therapy, a basic knowledge of rhythm disorders is essential to the management of these patients. The goals of this chapter will be as follows:

A. To present an organized approach to the interpretation of rhythm strips and electrocardiograms (ECGs)
B. To briefly discuss the dysrhythmia moving from the:
   1. Sinoatrial (SA) node and atrium; then to the
   2. Atrioventricular (AV) node or junctional tissue; then to the
   3. Ventricle
C. To include diagnostic possibilities and approach to therapy

INTERPRETATION OF RHYTHM STRIPS AND ELECTROCARDIOGRAMS

Proper identification and management of dysrhythmias requires a methodologic approach. The most effective method requires starting at the SA node and working down through the AV node, bundle branches and their subdivisions, and finally, to the ventricle.

SA node activity

Because there is no direct evidence of SA node function, one must look to tissue that responds to the SA node. When the SA node depolarizes, the impulse escapes into the atrium and causes the atrium to depolarize.

A. P wave
   The P wave on the electrocardiogram (ECG) represents atrial muscle depolarization.

1. The normal vector of atrial muscle depolarization is directed anteriorly, inferiorly, and to the left, with a frontal plane axis of 45 degrees ± 30 degrees.
   a. In a given lead, then, P waves will have a constant P configuration with a constant interval between P waves and a normal or usual axis.
   b. The P wave on a 12-lead ECG will be:
      (1) Upright in leads I, II, III, AV$_F$
      (2) Inverted in AV$_R$
      (3) Either upright or inverted in AV$_L$
   c. The usual monitor leads, II or V$_2$, will show upright P waves, upright or biphasic in V$_1$.
2. To contrast
   a. P waves are generally fairly small and the most angular.
   b. T waves are larger and somewhat angular.
   c. U waves are the most rounded deflections.
3. This information can be useful in identifying P waves superimposed on other portions of the complex and in differentiating P, T, and U waves (Fig. 13-1).

B. Atrial dysrhythmias
   Conduction through the AV node to the ventricle usually, but not invariably, follows. Alteration in conduction below the atrium is a function of AV node disease and will be discussed later.
   1. *Normal sinus rhythm* is normally directed atrial activity with constant P configuration at rates of 60 to 100 beats

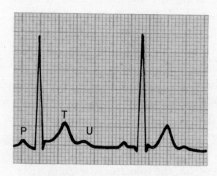

Fig.13-1. Morphology of P, T, U.

per minute (beats/min), regardless of whether or not conduction below the atrium (AV node or ventricle) occurs (Fig. 13-2, *A*).

2. *Sinus tachycardia* is atrial activity at rates greater than 100 beats/min (Fig. 13-2, *B*).

    a. Sinus tachycardia is seen in congestive heart failure, febrile states, excitement or anxiety, physical exercise, hyperthyroidism, or response to catecholamine discharge.

    b. Treatment is usually directed at the underlying physiologic state.

3. *Sinus bradycardia* is normal atrial activity at rates less than 60 beats/min (Fig. 13-2, *C*).

    a. Sinus bradycardia may appear in various circumstances.

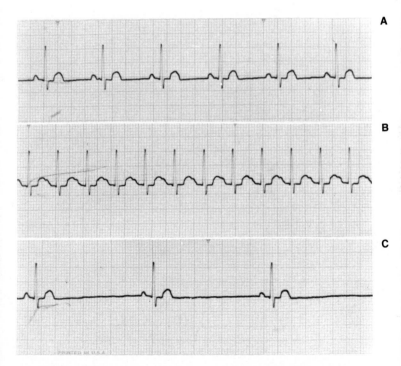

Fig. 13-2. A, Sinus rhythm. **B,** Sinus tachycardia. **C,** Sinus bradycardia.

(1) Young or elderly people, often in association with sinus arrythmia (see below)

(2) Hypothermia

(3) Hypothyroidism

(4) Well-conditioned athlete

(5) Sick sinus (node) syndrome (see below)

4. Sinus arrhythmia (Fig. 13-3) is often associated with sinus bradycardia and is seen in the same setting. The P configuration is constant, but the P-P interval varies, usually with respiration.

5. Atrial premature complexes (APCs) occur as the name implies, early or prematurely (Fig. 13-4).

a. They come from the atrium or internodal pathways and depolarize the atrium in a configuration different from the usual pattern.

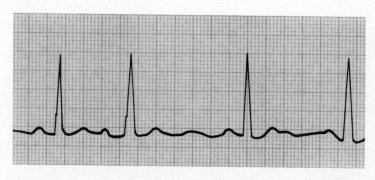

Fig. 13-3. Sinus arrhythmia.

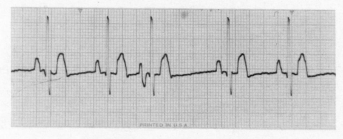

Fig. 13-4. Atrial premature complex.

    b. APCs may enter the SA node, depolarize it, and reset the SA pacemaker. An *imperfect compensatory pause* results.

    c. In unusual circumstances, APCs may not reset the pacemaker. A *perfect compensatory pause* results.

6. *Supraventricular tachydysrhythmias* arise from the AV node or above.

    a. *Sinus tachycardia* is a form of atrial tachydysrhythmia, described previously (see Fig. 13-2).

    b. *Atrial tachycardia* is a series or run of three or more atrial premature complexes (Fig. 13-5). Other forms include distinct categories such as *paroxysmal atrial tachycardia* or *AV nodal reentry tachycardia* or the *essential form of atrial tachycardia* (Fig. 13-6). It occurs because of a dissociation in depolarization pathways through the AV node (Fig. 13-7).

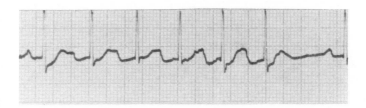

Fig. 13-5. Atrial tachycardia.

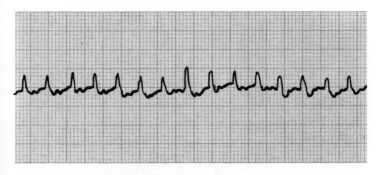

Fig. 13-6. AV nodal reentry tachycardia.

(1) The impulse travels down a single pathway until it reaches tissue containing a difference in ability to maintain conduction forward *(antegrade, orthograde)*.

(2) The wave of depolarization is conducted rapidly down one pathway through the AV node, depolarizing the ventricle (Fig. 13-7, *A*).

(3) It may conduct more slowly down the other limb (Fig. 13-7, *B*) and reach the lower end of the combined pathway after the faster pathway has not only completely undergone depolarization, but has also repolarized.

(4) The impulse fractionates (Fig. 13-7, *B*) and continues down through the lower conduction system to depolarize the ventricle and also continues *retrograde* into the repolarized opposite limb, the faster pathway.

(5) Since the slower pathway repolarizes more quickly than the fast pathway does, the slower pathway has repolarized by the time the impulse traverses the fast pathway in retrograde fashion.

(6) The impulse again traverses the slower pathway antegrade. (Fig. 13-7, *D*).

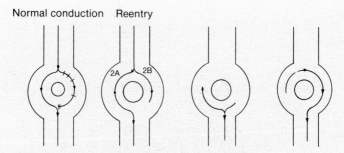

Fig. 13-7. Reentry mechanism.

(7) This continuous circular conduction allows the ventricle to be discharged at a more rapid rate.

(8) This *microreentry pathway* is in the AV node; hence the name "AV nodal reentry tachycardia." The rhythm strip shows a narrow QRS tachycardia at approximately 120 to 250 beats/min, usually at 180 beats/min (Fig. 13-6). P waves are not evident.

(9) These rhythms are often seen in the absence of underlying recognizable heart disease.

(10) Effective treatment consists of breaking up the critical timing between the fast and slow pathways that allow the dysrhythmia to be sustained.

    (a) *Carotid sinus massage* may be effective. Avoid such a maneuver in patients with carotid artery disease when possible. If such maneuver is urgently needed to control the rhythm, auscultate the vessels. Ideally, electrocardiographic monitoring should be used for carotid massage. Practically, it can be done by palpating the radial, brachial, axillary, or femoral pulse if electrocardiographic monitoring is not available and hypotension or symptoms dictate urgent therapy.

    (b) Once the carotid artery is located, it can be gently but firmly compressed in a rotatory motion to partly include flow.

    (c) Pressure is reduced in the carotid sinus, which reflexly increases vagal discharge.

    (d) When the pulse suddenly returns to normal, massage should be promptly terminated.

    (e) Theoretically, left carotid sinus massage may be more effective than massaging the right, since the SA node and the right carotid artery share more similar nerve supplies and, similarly, the left carotid artery and AV node share similar nerve supplies.

(f) The *Valsalva maneuver* or the combination of Valsalva maneuver plus left (or right if left is unsuccessful) carotid massage may also be effective.

(g) Positioning the patient in Trendelenberg with or without the above maneuver may also be effective.

(h) If the above fail to terminate the dysrhythmia, verapamil, 5 to 10 mg intravenously over 1 to 2 minutes, is the drug therapy of choice. If the dysrhythmia suddenly terminates after injection of a portion of the dose, the injection should be stopped.

(i) If 10 mg verapamil alone is unsuccessful, carotid massage or Valsalva plus carotid massage may be added.

(j) If none of the above maneuvers is successful, *cardioversion* should be carried out. The energy required is usually low, from 5 to 25 joules, with or without intravenous diazepam for its amnestic activity. Occasionally the ventricular rate may exceed the internal electrical circuitry of the cardioverter so that the cardioverter cannot detect an R wave. In this instance, the synchronizer switch should be turned off and the patient defibrillated. Ventricular defibrillation may result; in that case, subsequent defibrillation will be required.

c. Nonessential form of atrial tachycardia*

The underlying ECG is usually abnormal and often shows frequent atrial premature complexes.

(1) These may occur in runs of atrial tachycardia at rates of 120 to 150 beats/min, usually at rates of approximately 130 beats/min.

---

*This is an older term and is seldom used. But, because it is slower and connotes underlying disease, it may still be clinically useful.

(2) This form generally suggests underlying cardiac or pulmonary disease.

(3) Treatment is directed at the underlying disease and may include correction of electrolytes or arterial gases. The use of bronchodilators and the treatment of pneumonia when present may be effective.

d. Atrial tachycardia with block (Fig. 13-8)

  (1) Characteristics

    (a) P waves of a constant configuration with a rate greater than 100 beats/min, often as high as 150 to 170 beats/min occur.

    (b) Atrial activity at this rate bombards the AV node with varying degrees of penetration (*decremental conduction*).

    (c) Not every P wave is followed by a QRS.

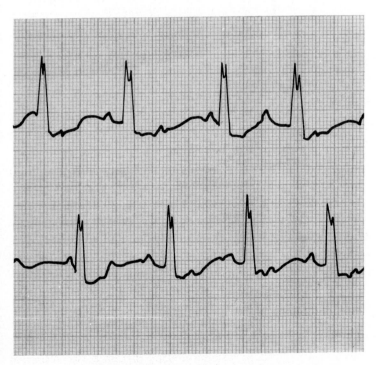

Fig. 13-8. Atrial tachycardia with block.

    (d) Often the P waves that result in QRS complexes have varying P-R intervals.

    (e) Therefore the ventricular response is irregular and rapid.

  (2) Causes

    (a) This dysrhythmia is frequently caused by digitalis toxicity. Occasionally, atrial tachycardia with block is seen in the absence of digitalis. The P-R and the R-R intervals are usually regular in these cases.

  (3) Treatment

    (a) Treatment consists of withholding digitalis and giving potassium chloride for hypokalemia if hypokalemia is present.

    (b) Magnesium sulfate has also been used.

    (c) Beta-inhibitors such as propranolol may reduce the atrial rate or AV conduction.

e. Multiform atrial tachycardia (MAT) or chaotic atrial rhythm (Fig. 13-9), are purely descriptive terms for the rhythm.

  (1) Characteristics

    (a) A given lead has at least three different P configurations with varying P-P intervals, and a rate greater than 100 beats/min.

    (b) A QRS follows each P wave, often with a varying P-R interval.

  (2) Probable setting—any situation that leads to atrial fibrillation

    (a) Pulmonary disease

      i. Chronic obstructive pulmonary disease

      ii. Pulmonary embolus

      iii. Pneumonitis

    (b) Acute left ventricular failure (e.g., acute myocardial infarction)

    (c) Mitral valve disease (especially mitral stenosis)

    (d) Thyrotoxicosis

    (e) As an intermediate rhythm between normal

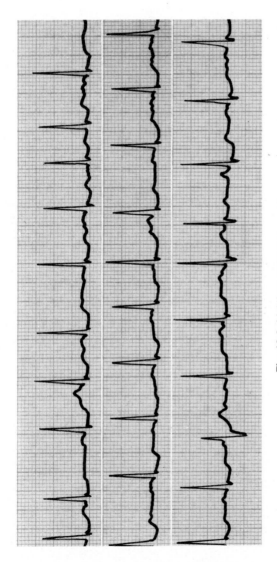

Fig. 13-9. Multiform atrial tachycardia.

sinus rhythm and atrial fibrillation, from either one to the other.

(3) Treatment

(a) Treatment includes correction of the underlying disease, (e.g., hypoxia, pneumonitis, fluid and/or electrolyte abnormalities).

(b) Occasionally one may have to use digitalis, calcium antagonists (especially verapamil), or beta inhibitors, especially shorter-acting agents such as propranolol, to control heart rate.

7. Wandering atrial rhythm (Fig. 13-10)

a. Characteristics

(1) The original term refers to a minimum of three consecutive sinus complexes, followed by an organized, progressive change in the P configuration, usually with a decreasing P-R interval as the impulse wanders to the AV node.

(2) The P wave becomes inverted and occurs either in front of or behind the QRS complex.

(3) It can also occur within the QRS, but cannot then be seen.

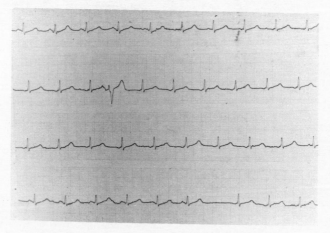

Fig. 13-10. Wandering atrial pacemaker (to AV node).

(4) The inverted "AV nodal" P wave continues for a minimum of three complexes, then wanders back to the SA node.

(5) This rhythm, unlike MAT, is rare.

(6) The dysrhythmia usually causes no symptoms.

b. Probable settings

  (1) Abnormal physiologic states

    (a) Chronic obstructive pulmonary disease

    (b) Acute exacerbations of pulmonary disease

    (c) Cirrhosis

    (d) Hepatic disease

    (e) Electrolyte disturbance

c. Treatment

  (1) Treatment is directed at the underlying disorder.

8. Atrial flutter (Fig. 13-11)

a. Characteristics

  (1) Atrial activity is organized but occurs at 220 to 350 beats/min, most often at 300 beats/min.

  (2) Atrial activity has a sawtooth appearance, especially in standard leads II, III, and AV_F, with the sawteeth pointing down.

  (3) Not every flutter wave (FF) conducts through the AV node.

  (4) A regular narrow QRS at a rate of 150 beats/min should suggest atrial flutter with 2:1 conduction (two FF complexes for each QRS complex).

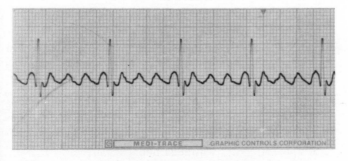

Fig. 13-11. Atrial flutter with 4:1 block.

    b. Probable setting

        (1) Absence of medications such as:

            (a) Digitalis

            (b) Quinidine

            (c) Procainamide

            (d) Disopyramide

            (e) Beta-inhibitors or calcium antagonists (that may slow atrial conduction)

                i. Pulmonary disease

                ii. Acute ischemic heart disease

                iii. Mitral stenosis

    c. Treatment

        (1) Carotid sinus massage (see AV nodal reentry tachycardia) may decrease AV conduction and thereby allow evidence of atrial activity to be more clearly defined.

        (2) The above medications may slow AV conduction with a slower, more controlled atrial rate.

        (3) Conversion may successfully be carried out, often at low energy such as 10 to 25 or 50 joules.

            (a) Patients are usually rendered sleepy and amnestic by intravenous boluses of diazepam until speech is slurred and/or counting backwards is impaired.

            (b) Either anterior-posterior paddles or two anterior paddles are applied with a firm pressure of 20 to 25 pounds.

            (c) Synchronized cardioversion is carried out.

            (d) Occasionally the rhythm will be converted to atrial fibrillation that can be converted to sinus rhythm by one of two means.

                i. Repeat cardioversion is performed usually at higher energy such as 50 to 100 or 200 joules.

                ii. If nothing other than medication is given to control ventricular responses, the rhythm may spontaneously convert within 24 hours.

9. Atrial fibrillation

No organized atrial activity is seen (Fig. 13-12). Clinical setting is identical to atrial flutter.

a. Characteristics

(1) The baseline is *undulating*.

(2) Atrial activity (ff) bombards the AV node at 350 to 600 times per minute.

(3) The AV node responds by blocking most of this activity, so QRS complexes occur at a much slower rate and at irregular intervals.

(4) Suggested terms for the ventricular response include:

(a) Atrial fibrillation with a rapid ventricular response (>100 beats/min)

(b) Atrial fibrillation with a controlled ventricular response (60 to 100 beats/min)

(c) Atrial fibrillation with a slow ventricular response (<60 beats/min)

(5) Atrial fibrillation is often categorized as *coarse* or *fine*.

(a) Atrial fibrillation can *only* by called *coarse* if the amplitude of the undulations is large in the presence of a 1 mV calibration signal.

(b) *Fine* atrial fibrillation *requires* low-amplitude undulation in the presence of a 1 mV calibration signal.

(c) In the absence of the calibration signal, the

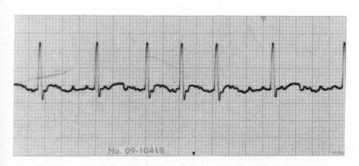

Fig. 13-12. Atrial fibrillation with rapid ventricular response.

magnitude of the undulations may relate to the position of the gain control knob on the monitor.

(d) Atrial fibrillation coarsens if an intervention causes large undulations to occur without a change in gain control.

(e) The same coarse/fine terminology is true of ventricular fibrillation.

b. Treatment

Treatment is aimed at controlling the ventricular response or at restoring the rhythm to sinus.

(1) Ventricular rate control may be achieved by oral or intravenous digitalis.

(a) Digoxin is stored in lean body mass; thus lower doses may be required in smaller patients or small-boned obese patients.

(b) Digoxin, 0.5 to 0.75 mg, may be given initially.

(c) The patient should be reevaluated in 30 minutes to 2 or 3 hours.

(d) If the rate is still excessive, a second, perhaps smaller, dose of 0.25 to 0.5 mg may be given, with reassessment in another 2 to 6 hours.

(e) Doses should be ordered and given individually after patient assessment.

(f) When the rate is controlled, a single daily maintenance dose may be substituted for subsequent parenteral doses.

(g) Digitalis may be pushed to excess during attempted rate control and may cause toxicity; ventricular ectopy, ventricular tachycardia, first- or second-degree AV block.

(h) Gastrointestinal toxicity with nausea/vomiting and central nervous system toxicity such as fatigue, confusion, or yellow vision may occur.

(2) Ventricular rate control may also be attained by using oral or parenteral beta-inhibitors.

(a) Propranolol may be used, 0.5 to 1.0 mg intravenously every 5 minutes, to rate control or to a maximum 0.1 to 0.2 mg/kg.

(b) Alternatively, propranolol or other beta-inhibitors in equivalent doses could be given orally as 10 to 20 mg.

(c) Peak plasma levels occur in approximately 1½ to 2 hours.

(d) If rate control is not achieved at that time, larger doses can be given.

(e) Propranolol, metoprolol, pindolol, and timolol are stored in fat; thus larger doses will be required in obese people.

(f) If beta-inhibitors are contraindicated, calcium antagonists may be used.

    i. Verapamil has the greatest negative chronotropic effect and is orally available in 80- and 120-mg tablets given at 6- to 8-hour intervals.

    ii. Verapamil also has the greatest overall negative inotropic effect and therefore must be used cautiously, if at all, in patients with heart failure.

    iii. Verapamil can also be used in individual intravenous doses not to exceed 10 mg in one bolus to achieve rate control, or by constant intravenous infusion beginning at 0.005 mg/kg/min.

(3) Restoration of sinus rhythm can be achieved medically or by cardioversion.

(a) If the duration of known atrial fibrillation is <5 days, immediate cardioversion may be used (see "Atrial flutter", p. 371). The energy necessary is generally higher, from 50 to 200 joules.

(b) If the duration of atrial fibrillation is 5 days or longer, treatment may be initiated with anticoagulants, first with heparin and subsequently with coumadin for 2 to 3 weeks before cardioversion. It should be continued for at least 1 week after cardioversion to prevent thromboembolism.

(c) Pharmacologic agents also considered include quinidine, procainamide, and disopyramide.

　i. These agents slow atrial conduction; thus the rate of AV node bombardment is reduced. Paradoxically, this may allow an increase in the number of impulses conducted through the AV node and therefore a faster ventricular response.

　ii. Conduction through the AV node should be slowed by digitalis, beta-inhibitors, or calcium antagonists before medical conversion with the agents named above.

　iii. As many as five doses of 200 mg of quinidine may be given every 2 hours until conversion or diarrhea.

　　a. If conversion does not occur, the dose may be increased the following day to 300 mg every 2 hours for 5 days.

　　b. The QRS and Q-T duration should be monitored. An increase of 25% above baseline is reason to proceed cautiously. An increase by 50% above baseline is an indication to withhold the drug and monitor carefully until the QRS and/or Q-T is back to within 25% above baseline. Failure to do this may result in drug-induced ventricular tachycardia, ventricular fibrillation, or torsade des pointes. Management of these rhythms includes withholding the drug, administering bicarbonate or infusing a continuous epinephrine or isoproterenol by adding 2 mg to 500 ml D/W and infusing at 2 to 5 mg/min, by providing temporary pacing, or a combination of the above.

(d) An *outpatient method* of chemical conversion during oral anticoagulation includes controlling the ventricular rate with digoxin.

    i. Five to 7 days before electrical conversion, 200 mg of quinidine are orally given every 6 hours. Beware of the interaction between digitalis and quinidine that might increase the digitalis plasma concentration by one and one-half to two times.

    ii. Up to 30% of those who can be successfully converted may do so before electrical conversion.

    iii. If electrical conversion is necessary, the patient may obtain a plasma digoxin concentration as an outpatient one day, with the dose of digoxin withheld the next day, and be admitted for elective cardioversion.

10. The sick sinus (node) syndrome
    a. Disorders
      (1) *Marked sinus bradycardia* in the absence of drugs that cause the reduced rate.
      (2) Drug-resistant sinus bradycardia
        Atropine-, epinephrine-, isoproterenol-resistant
      (3) Second-degree SA block or sinus exit block
        The SA node fires, the atrium responds continuously until the SA node fires but the impulse does not escape into the atrial muscle to cause depolarization, so no P wave occurs. However, a perfect atrial compensatory pause may follow,

with subsequent SA node firing and atrial response (Fig. 13-13)

(4) Third-degree SA block with no evidence of atrial activity

A lower escape mechanism, either AV nodal (junctional) or His-Purkinje (ventricular), must take over or the patient is asystolic.

(5) Abnormally long pause following an atrial premature complex

No lower escape complex (Fig. 13-13)

(6) Prolonged sinus node recover time during atrial pacing

>1500 msec; not drug-induced

(7) Atrial fibrillation with slow ventricular response in the absence of drugs that slow AV conduction

Ordinarily, this is evidence of AV nodal dysfunction rather than SA nodal dysfunction. The two are often found together, however, and historically this has been considered a manifestation of sick sinus syndrome.

(8) Cardioversion of atrial fibrillation resulting in SA or atrial standstill for the same reason as (7) above

  (a) Bradycardia-tachycardia syndrome

  Patients with this syndrome have periods of bradycardia interrupted by periods of tachycardia. Syncope can occur with a change in rhythm, but usually occurs when the "tachy" variety changes to the "brady" variety. This is the only variety that may carry an increased risk of embolic strokes, so anticoagulation therapy has been suggested.

  (b) Characteristics

    i. Patients with the sick sinus syndrome may have nonspecific symptoms of fatigue, palpitations, syncope, weakness, dizziness.

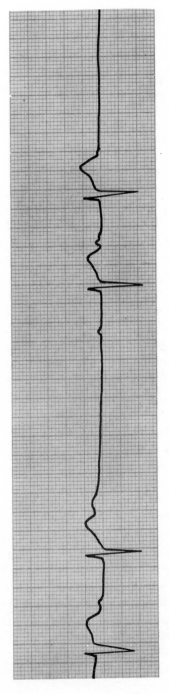

Fig. 13-13. Second-degree SA block or sinus exit block (advanced form). Second-degree AV block, Mobitz I or Wenckebach

(c) Treatment

    i. Pacing has not been shown to correct these symptoms.

    ii. No therapy is helpful unless the symptoms can be demonstrated to occur with the dysrhythmia. Correction of the latter may then affect the former.

· · ·

To this point, the dysrhythmias discussed involved SA node function or atrial muscle depolarization. AV node function is usually intact (except in the specific instances of slow atrial fibrillation in the sick sinus syndrome). Therefore normal AV conduction and conduction below the AV node are expected.

C. AV nodal or junctional dysrhythmias

The following conduction disturbances will involve the AV node or bundle branch systems. Normal SA and atrial function is to be expected unless combined conduction disturbances occur. When these occur, atrial conduction disturbances are identified first and AV nodal conduction second. The *complete correct* interpretation requires both.

1. AV nodal or junctional premature complexes (NPC) (Fig. 13-14) result in *premature* antegrade depolarization of the ventricle from an AV nodal focus.

    a. Characteristics

      (1) The complexes may or may not result in a retrograde depolarization of the atrium.

      (2) If depolarization results, however, the P axis will be posterior, superior, and to the right, directed toward the right shoulder (AV$_R$) with P inversion I, II, III, and AV$_F$.

      (3) Whether the inverted P wave precedes or follows the QRS will depend on whether the conduction is most delayed on the ventricular or atrial side of the AV nodal pacemaker focus.

      (4) If conduction occurs to the atria and ventricle simultaneously or does not occur to the atria, no P wave will be seen.

2. Nodal or junctional escape complexes (Fig. 13-15)

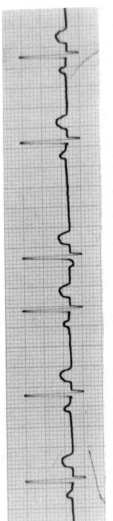

Fig. 13-14. Nodal or junctional premature complex

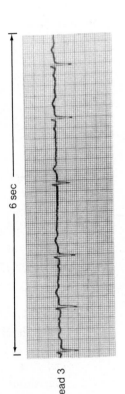

Lead 3

Fig. 13-15. Nodal or junctional escape complex.

a. Characteristics

These are similar to NPCs except that they occur *late* after the expected normal complex should have occurred, but did not.

b. Treatment

Neither this nor NPC requires treatment, although a search for underlying physiologic disposition (e.g., hypoxemia, ischemia, electrolyte disturbance) should be undertaken.

3. In the absence of SA nodal activity, an *AV nodal* or *junctional escape rhythm* at 40 to 60 beats/min (the usual spontaneous rate of the AV node) is expected.

4. *AV nodal or junctional tachycardia* is an AV nodal rhythm in excess of 100 beats/min, usually caused by a physiologic abnormality (Fig. 13-16).

a. Treatment

No specific treatment is required, but a search for the underlying abnormality should be conducted.

b. Cause

(1) Physiologic abnormality

5. Accelerated AV node rhythm (60 to 100 beats/min) "Accelerated" is an accepted term for rates greater than usual for a given pacemaker outside the SA node, but less than 100.

a. Causes

(1) Following diagnosis, a search for the underlying cause should be made.

(2) One possible cause is digitalis toxicity, especially when one sees *atrial fibrillation with regularization of the ventricular rate,* which is atrial fibrillation with an accelerated junctional (AV nodal) pacemaker (Fig. 13-17).

b. Treatment

(1) Digitalis is discontinued.

(2) Any potassium deficit is repleted.

(3) Use of magnesium sulfate or beta-inhibitors is considered.

(4) Underlying cause is treated.

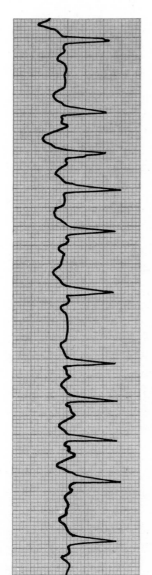

Fig. 13-16. Nodal or junctional tachycardia.

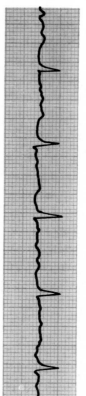

Fig. 13-17. Atrial fibrillation with an accelerated nodal (junctional) rhythm.

6. *AV nodal reentry tachycardia*

See paroxysmal atrial tachycardia, above (Fig. 13-6)

7. AV nodal block

a. First-degree AV block (Fig. 13-18)

(1) Characteristics

(a) SA node function and the atrial response should be normal, so that constant configuration P waves with normal P axis and rate 60 to 100 beats/min are usually present.

(b) Conduction is delayed through the interatrial pathways or AV node so that the P-R interval is prolonged beyond 0.18 to 0.22 seconds, depending on the atrial rate. A QRS complex, however, follows each P wave.

b. Second-degree AV block

Considering four types is useful.

(1) Mobitz I or Wenckebach (Fig. 13-19)

(a) Characteristics

i. SA node function and atrial response are normal.

ii. The impulses show progressive delay through the AV node so that the P-R interval increases.

iii. Since the P-R interval increases, the R-P interval must shorten as does the R-R interval. Finally, a P wave occurs

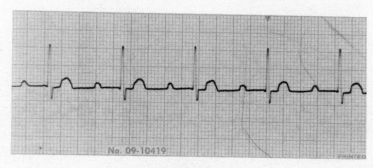

Fig. 13-18. AV block.

without the following QRS (QRS is dropped).

iv. QRS complexes must follow at least two consecutive P waves, in order to detect the increase in P-R interval.

v. The conduction delay is between the atrial depolarization complex (P wave) and the His bundle. Usually, this interval is 85 to 165, m̄ 120 msec, but may be increased by 40 to 80 msec.

vi. The QRS is usually narrow unless associated-conduction defects such as bundle branch blocks are present.

vii. The initial P-R interval is usually long.

viii. Conduction often varies (e.g., 3:2 or 4:3 atrial/ventricular) responses.

(b) Settings

i. Inferior myocardial infarctions

ii. Digitalis excess

iii. Primary conduction system disease

(c) Treatment

i. Observation is indicated in the first two settings.

ii. Discontinuing digitalis is also indicated in the second setting.

iii. Pacing may rarely be indicated in symptomatic primary conduction disease.

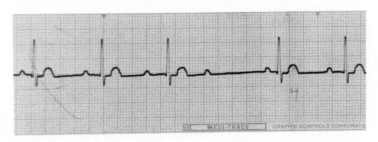

Fig. 13-19. Second-degree AV block, Mobitz I or Wenckebach.

(2) Mobitz II (Fig. 13-20)
  (a) Characteristics
    i. SA and atrial function are normal.
    ii. The defect is between the His bundle and the ventricle, usually 35 to 55 msec.
    iii. Since an increase here of only 10 to 20 msec will result in an abnormally long His-to-ventricle conduction, the P-R interval will be only slightly affected.
    iv. Therefore the P-R interval is usually not prolonged and is usually constant before the "dropped" QRS.
    v. QRS complexes are usually wide, ≥ 0.12 sec.
  (b) Setting
    i. Anterior infarctions
    ii. Primary conduction disturbances (e.g., those resulting from fibrosis)

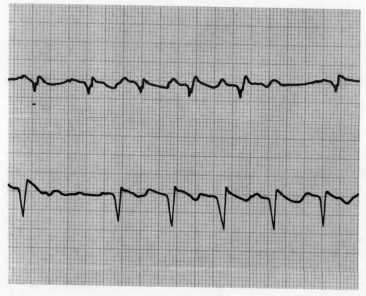

Fig. 13-20. Second-degree AV block, Mobitz II.

(c) Treatment

Since Mobitz II is usually seen as a forerunner of more advanced conduction abnormalities, temporary or permanent pacing is frequently indicated.

(3) Second-degree AV block with 2:1 conduction (Fig. 13-21)

This is a separate type only if the rhythm strip is too short or the context in which the conduction disturbances is seen is not known. Such conduction interspaced with Wenckebach is as likely to be Wenckebach as is that seen in the inferior infarction. When 2:1 conduction is interspersed with Mobitz II or in anterior infarction, it is likely to be Mobitz II. When 2:1 conduction is isolated, one cannot be certain whether it is Mobitz I or Mobitz II, since one

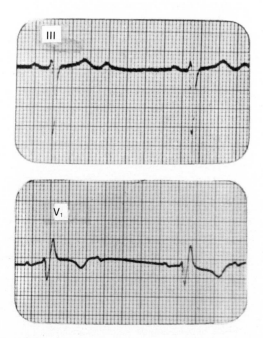

Fig. 13-21. Second-degree AV block with 2:1 conduction.

cannot tell whether the P-R interval is lengthening before the missing QRS.

(4) An advanced form of AV block exists when two or more P waves appear without following QRS complexes (Fig. 13-22). Some authorities would label this Mobitz II. However, it occasionally appears with characteristics similar to Mobitz I, hence, it is called a specific type here.

   (a) Setting

      i. Myocardial ischemia or infarction

      ii. Primary conduction disturbances

   (b) Treatment

      These patients should have electrical pacing.

c. Third-degree AV block (Fig. 13-23)

   (1) Characteristics

     (a) Sinus and atrial functions are normal.

     (b) The problem is at the AV node or below.

     (c) Older terminology differentiated *AV block* from *AV dissociation*. The former is usually caused by an anatomic abnormality affecting the AV node. The SA node fires at 60 to 100 beats/min, but because of the AV node disease, no AV conduction occurs. A lower pacemaker takes over: either the AV node or junction with a narrow QRS at a rate of 40 to 60 beats/min, or lower in the His-Pur-

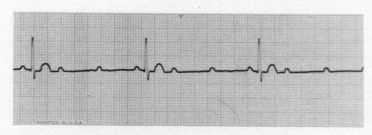

Fig. 13-22. Second-degree AV block, advanced form.

kinje system with a wide QRS (≥ 0.12 sec) at < 40 beats/min. It is important in describing third-degree AV block to state the location of the pacemaker that depolarizes the ventricles (e.g., *third-degree block with an AV nodal [junctional] pacemaker, or third-degree AV block with a ventricular [His-Purkinje] pacemaker*).

(2) Treatment

    (a) Temporary or permanent pacing is the most effective, safest form of therapy.

    (b) Temporarily, an epinephrine or isoproterenol infusion may be used to improve AV conduction or to increase the rate of the lower pacemaker.

    (c) Either infusion is made by adding 2 or 3 mg to 500 ml of 5% dextrose in water or normal saline. With 3 mg in 500 ml, 10 µgtts/min equals 1 µg/min. The usual infusion rate is 1 to 5 µg/min (10 to 50 mgtts/min).

(3) AV dissociation with an accelerated AV node or junctional pacemaker

Occurrence of a physiologic abnormality that accelerates the AV node

    (a) Characteristics

        i. The SA node continues to control the atrium at 60 to 100 beats/min, usually at the lower end.

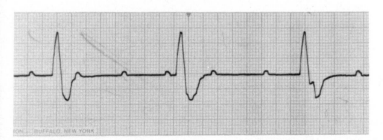

Fig. 13-23. Sinus rhythm, third-degree AV block with idioventricular rhythm.

        ii. The AV node, however, is accelerated
            to discharge faster than the atrial rate.
    (b) Physiologic abnormalities
        i. Fluid and electrolyte changes
        ii. Hypoxia
        iii. Drug effects
    (c) Cause
        i. Atrial fibrillation with an accelerated
          junctional pacemaker caused by digi-
          talis toxicity (Fig. 13-16)
        ii. Other physiologic abnormality

BUNDLE BRANCH CONDUCTION DEFECTS

Consider the right ventricle as an anterior ventricle, the left
as posterior, and two thirds to three fourths of the septum as
functionally part of the left ventricle. Fig. 13-24, depicting the
heart in cross section, portrays the relative muscle mass of the
two ventricles. The impulse travels from the SA node to the AV
node, to the right and left bundle branch systems. The impulse
then depolarizes the septum from each bundle. Since the septum is functionally mostly left ventricle, the vector for its de-

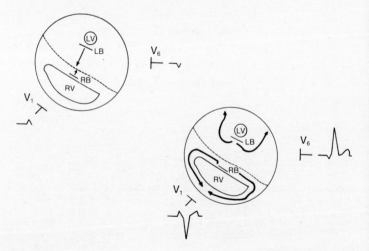

Fig. 13-24. Depolarization vectors. ECG shown represents the sum of various
depolarization vectors.

polarization is directed anteriorly and to the right, resulting in a "septal r" in V_1 and a "septal q" in V_{5-6}. The vector for the next major part of ventricular depolarization is directed toward the left because of the large left ventricular mass, causing S in V_1 and R in V_6.

A. Right bundle branch block (Figs. 13-21 and 13-25)
  1. Characteristics
     a. The initial and middle parts of ventricular depolarization are normal in duration and direction, if not in magnitude.
     b. However, as the impulse goes through the right ventricular muscle, it is delayed. Terminal conduction delay results.
     c. This terminal conduction delay is directed anteriorly, superiorly, and to the right.
     d. Hence, terminal slurred S waves are seen in I, AV_L, V_6, and terminal slurred R' in AV_R and V_1.

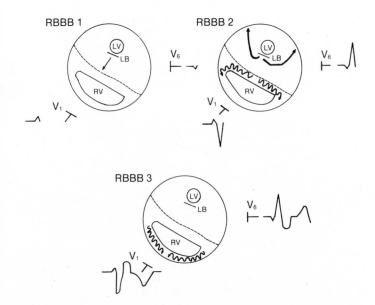

Fig. 13-25. Effect of right bundle branch block on depolarization vector. Because of the block, net vector is altered, as seen on ECG.

B. Left bundle branch block (Figs. 13-26 and 13-27)
   1. Characteristics
      a. The septum is depolarized from right to left, causing a Q in V_1 and r in V_{5-6}.
      b. The larger muscle mass of the left ventricle causes the second part of ventricular depolarization also to be directed to the left and posteriorly.
C. The left bundle has two divisions, the anterior-superior division and a posterior-inferior division.
   1. The easiest leads to examine to determine axis are leads I and II. (See Table 13-1 and Fig. 13-28).

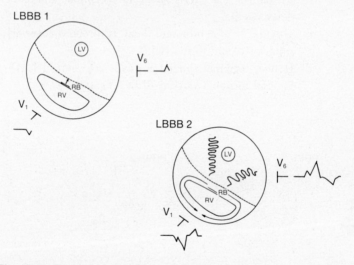

Fig. 13-26. Effect of left bundle branch block on depolarization vector. Because of the block, net vector is altered, as seen on ECG.

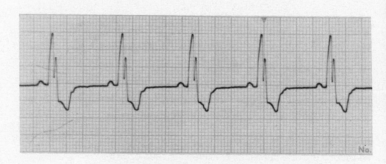

Fig. 13-27. Left bundle branch block.

Table 13-1. Axis deviation and its interpretation

Lead		Axis (degrees)	Interpretation
I	Positive	−30 to +90	Normal
II	Positive		
I	Positive	−30 to −90	Left axis deviation
II	Negative		Left anterior hemiblock
			Left anterior fascicular block: does not widen QRS more than 0.013 seconds
I	Negative	+90 to +150	Right axis deviation
II	Positive		Compatible with a left posterior hemiblock, left posterior fascicular block: does not widen QRS more than 0.017 seconds

NORMAL AXIS

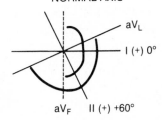

If I is (+) and II is (+), axis is –30° to +90°

LEFT ANTERIOR FASCICULAR BLOCK

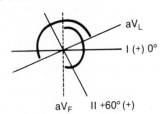

If I is (+) and II is (–), axis is –30° to –90°

RIGHT AXIS DEVIATION

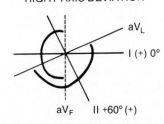

If I is (–) and II is (+), axis is +90° to +150°

Fig. 13-28. Cardiac electrical axes. Axis is most easily determined in leads I and II. The effect of bundle branch block is shown here.

2. A block in the former causes the axis to shift to the left in the frontal plane, usually equal to or greater than 45 degrees (Fig. 13-28).

   a. If lead I is positive, the vector must be between +90 and −90 degrees. If lead II is positive, the axis must be between −30 and +90 degrees normal (Fig. 13-28).

   b. If I is positive and II is negative, the axis must be between −30 to −90, left axis deviation or left anterior fascicular block (Fig. 13-28).

   c. A left posterior hemiblock (Fig. 13-27) is harder to diagnose without previous tracings, since right axis deviation can occur in patients with chronic lung diseases as well as in young people and may be a normal variant.

      (1) It does not usually widen the QRS more than 0.017 sec.

      (2) The importance of the hemiblocks is that they may be seen in pulmonary and other problems, and they may also be forerunners of a more advanced heart block in anterior infarctions or underlying primary conduction disease.

PREEXCITATION SYNDROMES

A. Lown-Ganong-Levine (LGL) syndrome

   1. Characteristics (Fig. 13-29)

      a. This syndrome has normal sinus activity, P configuration, and P-P interval.

      b. The P-R intervals, however, are short, which may represent accelerated AV conduction ("greasy AV node").

      c. The QRS duration is normal.

      d. The syndrome includes paroxysms of supraventricular tachycardia (SVT), probably resulting from nodal reentry tachycardia.

      e. A normal ECG, as shown in Fig. 13-29 with short P-R intervals (<0.12 sec) in the absence of SVT should not be labeled LGL.

B. Wolff-Parkinson-White (WPW) syndrome

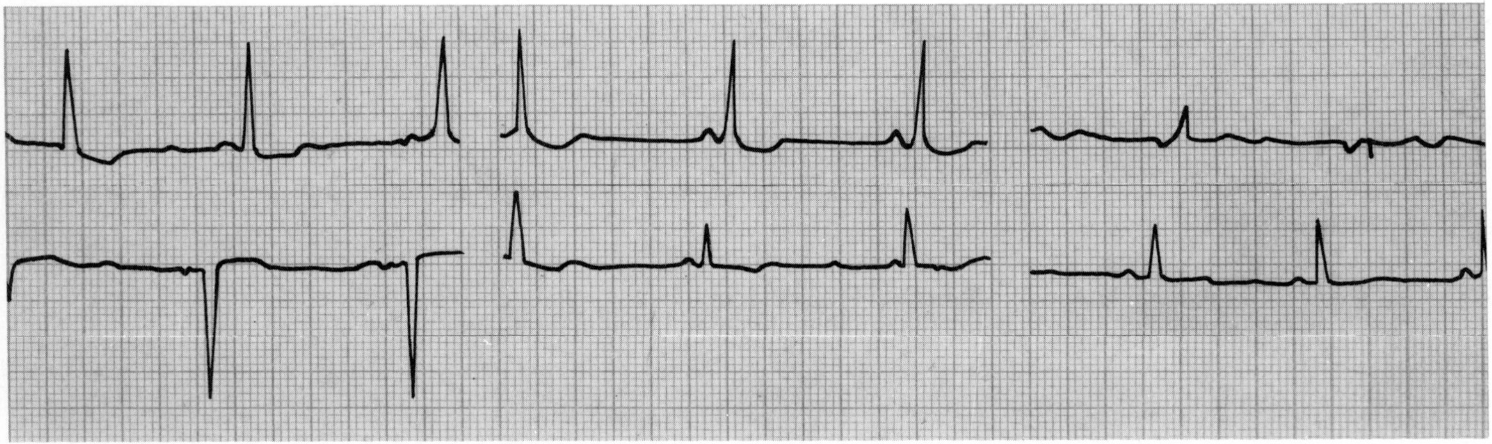

Fig. 13-29. Preexcitation syndromes are commonly seen arrythmias in the ICU. Depicted is the LGL variety (**A**). This needs to be contrasted with a normal ECG (**B**).

Continued.

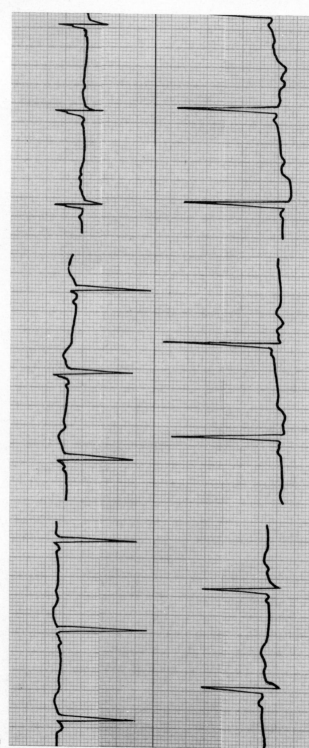

Fig. 13-29, cont'd. Preexcitation syndromes are commonly seen arrythmias in the ICU. Depicted is the LGL variety (**A**). This needs to be contrasted with a normal ECG (**B**).

B

1. Characteristics (Fig. 13-30)
    a. This group of syndromes is characterized by normal P configuration and normal P-P interval.
    b. A short P-R interval is followed, however, by an initial conduction delay (delta waves) and wide QRS complexes.
    c. The overall Q-T interval is usually normal.
    d. The atrium depolarizes in the usual fashion, but the ventricle "preexcites" either through accessory pathways between the atrium and ventricle (Kent fibers), or by bypassing portions of the AV node to enter ventricular muscle (Mahaim fibers).
    e. Runs of SVT are caused by macroreentry mechanisms. These are usually antegrade through the AV node and retrograde through the accessory pathways (narrow QRS).
    f. The most dangerous dysrhythmia is atrial fibrillation, in which the ventricle is not protected by the AV node.
        (1) Conduction to the ventricle may occur at 350 to 600 times per minute.
        (2) Immediate cardioversion or defibrillation is necessary.
2. Treatment
    a. Agents used to prevent SVT and WPW include quinidine and beta-inhibitors.

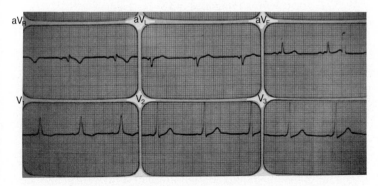

Fig. 13-30. Preexcitation syndrome, Wolff-Parkinson-White.

   b. Digitalis and calcium antagonists have been used, but they are potentially dangerous.

   c. Long-term therapy should be decided in consultation with a cardiologist or a knowledgeable internist to avoid worsening the dysrhythmia.

VENTRICULAR DYSRHYTHMIAS

   SA, atrial, and AV node functions are usually normal.

A. Premature ventricular complexes (PVCs)

   1. Characteristics

      a. The impulse arises below the AV node, usually in the His-Purkinje system.

      b. The complex is wide and bizarre.

      c. *Uniform PVCs* are multiple PVCs of the same configuration (Fig. 13-31).

      d. *Multiform PVCs* are two or three different configurations occurring in a single lead. These are more dangerous than uniform PVCs (Fig. 13-32).

      e. An *interpolated PVC* occurs between two normal complexes without interrupting the P-P interval and without causing a QRS to be "dropped" (Fig. 13-31).

   2. Treatment

      a. Treatment may include lidocaine bolus and infusion, parenteral bretylium or procainamide, especially if detected in acute myocardial infarction.

      b. Oral agents such as quinidine, procainamide, or disopyramide may be used. Occasionally beta-inhibitors or calcium antagonists may be used.

      c. If underlying heart disease is absent, PVCs do not require treatment.

B. Ventricular escape complex (Fig. 13-23)

   A late ventricular complex may occur when normal complex fails to occur when expected. Such a complex is termed a *ventricular escape complex*. The search should be aimed at determining why normal conduction from above did not occur.

C. Ventricular bigeminy (Fig. 13-33)

   Ventricular bigeminy is the alternating of ventricular premature complexes with normal complexes. A fixed interval

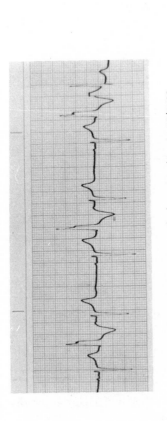

Fig. 13-31. Interpolated ventricular premature complexes.

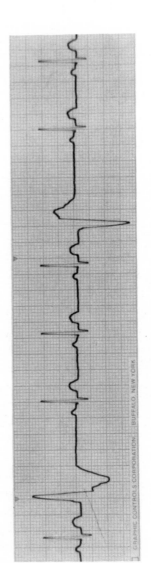

Fig. 13-32. Multiform ventricular premature complexes.

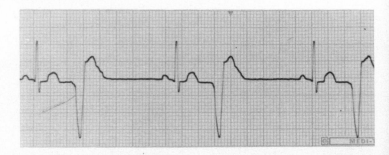

Fig. 13-33. Ventricular bigeminy.

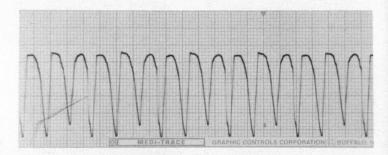

Fig. 13-34. Ventricular tachycardia.

between the normal complex and the PVC (constant coupling interval) suggests a reentry mechanism. A sequence of three or more PVCs indicates that *ventricular tachycardia* has occurred.

1. Treatment
   a. A search for ischemia or other underlying heart disease should be conducted.
   b. Treatment should be lidocaine bolus and infusion, parenteral bretylium or procainamide, or other oral antidysrhythmic agents.
   c. A key in the differentiation of ectopy from supraventricular complexes with aberrancy is the identification of P waves preceding QRS complexes by intervals compatible with normal conduction.

D. Tachydysrhythmias

Tachydysrhythmias are referred to as *wide QRS tachycardias* (Fig. 13-34) when determining whether they represent ventricular tachycardia or SVT with aberration is difficult. The following guidelines help to differentiate these tachycardias. No criterion is infallible in differentiating ventricular from SVT.

Whether QRS complexes are *monophasic, diphasic,* or *triphasic* relates to the number of times they cross the baseline. Complexes may be *monophasic* or *diphasic* in some leads and *triphasic* in other leads, so that it is most useful to look at a full 12-lead ECG. A diphasic complex may represent aberrancy if, for instance, the initial R wave of a right bundle branch block is absent because of an anterior septal myocardial infarction. Only a QR will be seen. Often, ectopy will result in a complex that crosses the baseline one less time than the normal complex if examined in multiple leads, whereas aberrancy will result in complexes that cross the baseline one more time than the usual complexes. (Fig. 13-36).

Fusion complexes are those that fuse normal conduction through the AV node with an ectopic focus lower down and thus create a wide bizarre complex.

Undue prematurity refers to those complexes that come so early in the cardiac cycle that they cannot be conducted through the AV node.

Previous anomalous complexes refer to previous ECGs in which a QRS complex was seen and could be readily identified. In a subsequent ECG in the same lead, a complex of the same configuration that can be identified is probably ectopic, whereas a previously obvious aberrant complex is probably aberrant in the later ECG.

V_{1-6} *reversal* refers to the horizontal plane in which the useful progression from V_{1-6} actually reverses. This occurs for V_6 to V_1.

A *frontal plane axis* directed toward AVR suggests that the impulses come from around the AV node or below.

Ashman's phenomenon suggests that the complex ending a short cycle preceded by a longer cycle is likely to be supraventricular with aberrancy. Unfortunately, ventricular bigeminy would fulfill Ashman's criteria so that a better term is *cycle sequencing* (Fig. 13-35).

In *cycle sequencing* one looks at the sequence of cycles. If the R-R intervals are getting farther apart, the heart is slowing. Conduction is slowing and the mechanism for aberrancy is established. A complex that ends that short cycle is likely to be supraventricular with aberrancy. If, on the other hand, the heart is speeding up so that the R-R intervals are getting shorter, conduction is improving. An abnormal complex that ends those decreasing cycles is most likely to be ventricular.

DIFFERENTIATING ECTOPY FROM ABERRANCY

	Ectopy	Aberrancy
P Waves	None preceding QRS	Precede QRS by reasonable interval
Initial QRS vector	Abnormal	Normal
Middle QRS vector	Abnormal	Normal in direction
Terminal QRS vector	Abnormal	Terminal slurring—right branch bundle block pattern
	Monophasic or diphasic	Usually triphasic—r smaller than R^1 in V_1
Coupling interval	Fixed—"Rule of bigeminy"	Usually variable
	Cycle sequencing	Ashman phenomenon—cycle sequencing
	Fusion complexes	
	Undue prematurity	
	Previous anomalous complexes ≥ 0.16 sec	Previous aberrant complexes ≤ 0.12 sec
QRS duration		
Frontal plane axis	Toward right shoulder	
	V_{1-6} reversal	

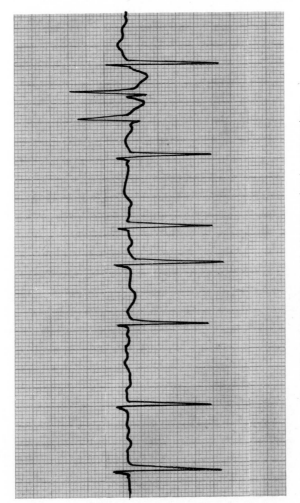

Fig. 13-35. Atrial fibrillation with aberrancy (cycle sequencing).

E. Ventricular fibrillation

The absence of organized ventricular activity and the presence of an undulating activity characterize ventricular fibrillation (Fig. 13-36).

1. Treatment

   a. Treatment consists of cardiopulmonary resuscitation, intravenous lidocaine or bretylium, and/or defibrillation.

   b. The airway may be managed by oral airway, pocket mask or bag-valve-mask, esophageal airway, or endotracheal intubation and oxygenation.

   c. Medications to be considered after the initial measures include epinephrine, 0.5 to 1.0 mg (5 to 10 ml of 1:10,000), at 5-minute intervals, see JAMA Standards, 1985–1986.

   d. Other useful agents in special circumstances include atropine, 0.5 to 1.0 mg, intravenously every 5 minutes to a maximum of 2.0 or 3.0 mg.

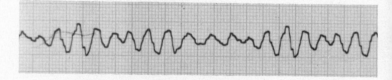

Fig. 13-36. Ventricular fibrillation.

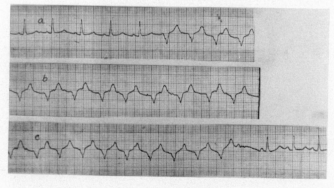

Fig. 13-37. Accelerated isochronic (isorhythmic) ventricular rhythm.

F. Accelerated isochronic (isorhythmic) ventricular rhythm in acute myocardial infarction (Fig. 13-37)
  1. Characteristics
     a. This may occur in acute myocardial infarction, either anteriorly or interiorly.
     b. The patient's sinus rhythm may be interspersed with brief runs, usually less than 30 complexes of an idioventricular rhythm that may begin with either a premature or an escape complex.
     c. Characteristically, the ventricular rhythm occurs at approximately the same rate as the sinus rate.
     d. If the ventricular rate occurs at 60 to 100 beats/min (faster than the usual idioventricular rate, but slower than a tachycardia, i.e., <100 beats/min), a useful term is *accelerated isorhythmic ventricular rhythm.*
     e. If the sinus rate and the idioventricular rhythm occurs at a rate greater than 100 beats/min, a useful term is *isorhythmic ventricular tachycardia.*
  2. Treatment
     a. These rhythms do not usually precede ventricular fibrillation and usually do not require active therapy.
     b. Observation is necessary.
     c. Occasionally the dissociation between atria and ventricles results in the loss of the atrial contribution to ventricular filling, with a subsequent reduction in cardiac output. In this case, atrioventricular sequential pacing or suppression of the isorhythmic rhythm may be necessary.
G. Torsade des pointes (Fig. 13-38)

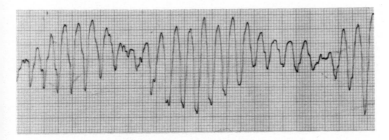

Fig. 13-38. Torsade des pointes.

1. Cause
   a. Torsade des pointes is usually caused by drug therapy, such as with quinidine or procainamide.
2. Characteristics
   a. Usually a marked widening of the Q-T interval precedes it.
   b. This rhythm starts with a PVC and degenerates into ventricular tachycardia that shows characteristic rotation around a point.
3. Treatment
   a. Treatment includes infusing isoproterenol or epinephrine and/or temporary pacing at the same time one stops the offending agent.

14

Acute myocardial infarction

Arthur D. Santos
Frank B. Cerra

Although a myocardial infarction (MI) acquired in the surgical intensive care unit (SICU) is unusual, MIs do occur in surgical patients, with the peak incidence at 3 to 5 days postoperatively. For these reasons, a working knowledge of ischemic myocardial injury is necessary for surgeons. In uncertain diagnostic conditions and in the presence of acute MI, care plans should be developed by or in consultation with medicine and/or cardiology staff.

A. Diagnosis
 1. Criteria
   a. Clinical signs, symptoms, and history
   b. Enzyme analysis
   c. Electrocardiogram (ECG)
 2. Clinical presentation
   a. Precipitating event
   b. Pain—examples are:
    (1) New
    (2) Change in old pattern
    (3) Unrelieved by rest or nitroglycerine
    (4) Retrosternal or parasternal
    (5) Radiation: jaw, neck, back, arms
    (6) "Indigestion"
   c. Sympathomimetic signs
   d. Arrhythmia
 3. Enzyme analysis
   a. There is a direct relationship between CPK-MB generation and:
    (1) Pulmonary artery end diastolic pressure

        (2) The clinical findings of pump failure

        (3) The size of the infarction

    b. CPK-MB

        (1) Starts to rise at ~6 hours; peaks at 6 to 18 hours; is back to normal in 48 to 72 hours

  4. ECG

    a. High incidence of ventricular fibrillation and other dysrhythmias in the first hour

    b. Pathologic Q waves; patterns of Q waves present

        (1) May require several days to appear

        (2) May not appear (e.g., subendocardial)

        (3) More typical patterns:

Cardiac location	ECG changes seen	ECG leads changes seen
Inferior	Negative Q and T Positive, high ST	II–III–AVF
Anterior	Negative Q and T Small R wave Positive ST	V_1–V_2
Anterolateral	Loss R wave Inverted T waves Small R wave	V_2–V_6 V_1
Anteroseptal	Deep QS	V_1–V_3
Lateral	Negative Q High ST	AVL I V_3–V_6
Posterior	Tall, dominant R waves	V_1–V_2
Apical	Loss R wave Inferior changes	V_5–V_6

  5. Differential diagnosis

    a. Pulmonary embolism

    b. Pericarditis, pericardial effusion, and/or tamponade

    c. Hypovolemic and/or septic shock

    d. Acute mitral regurgitation

    e. Acute VSD/muscle rupture

    f. Esophageal spasm or rupture

B. General hemodynamic patterns

  1. a. Normotensive

    b. Hyperdynamic

    c. Hypotensive

        (1) Hypovolemic

        (2) Contractility loss

    d. Hypertensive

    e. Pump failure

    f. Cardiogenic shock

2. ECHO—May be useful in assessing wall motion, aneurysm, VSD, pericardial effusions and/or ejection fraction

3. Clinical subsets

    a.

Subsets	Cardiac index $(L/min/m^2)$	PCWP $(torr)$	Mortality $(\%)$
I. No lung congestion or systemic hypertension	2.7 ± 0.5	12 ± 7	2
II. Lung congestion	2.3 ± 0.4	23 ± 5	10
III. Systemic hypoperfusion	1.9 ± 0.4	12 ± 5	25
IV. Both lung congestion and systemic hypoperfusion	1.6 ± 0.6	27 ± 8	55

    b.

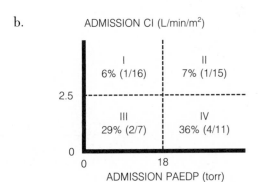

C. Therapeutic principles

  1. Cardiac factors in O_2 supply and demand

    a. O_2 demand

      (1) Frequency of pressure development

      (2) Rate of pressure development

      (3) Ventricular volume/mass

    b. O_2 supply

      (1) Diastolic time

      (2) Perfusion pressure

      (3) Collateral resistance

      (4) Wall tension

    c. Manipulatable factors
      (1) Heart rate
      (2) Preload
      (3) Afterload (impedance)
      (4) Contractibility

2. Reduce O_2 demand therapies
    a. Control anxiety
    b. Bed rest
    c. Control pain
    d. Unloading therapy
    e. Control heart rate (e.g., <110)

3. Improve oxygen supply therapies
    a. Oxygen
    b. Correct anemia
    c. Correct hypovolemia
    d. Systemic unloading
    e. Diuresis
    f. Balloon pumping
    g. Clot dissolution
    h. Angioplasty
    i. Surgery

4. By subset

Subset	*PCWP*	*CI**	*Rx to consider*
Normal	≤12	2.7-3.5	None
Hyperdynamic	≤12	>3.0	Beta-blocker
Hypotension (second degree to hypovolemia)	≤9	<2.7	Fluid
Failure (mild)	18-22	<2.5	Diuretics
Failure (severe)	>22	<1.8	Vasodilators + diuretics
Cardiogenic shock	>18	<1.8	Inotropes/intraaortic balloon pump

*$L/min/m^2$

5. Pain control
   a. Morphine sulfate
   b. Streptokinase
   c. Nitrates/nitroglycerine
   d. Beta-blocking agents
   e. Calcium channel—blocking agents
   f. IABP
6. Afterload reduction with vasodilation
   a. Indications
      (1) To relieve ischemia
      (2) To improve pump function and ventricular emptying
   b. Vasodilators
      (1) Relax epicardial arteries
      (2) Reduce wall tension
      (3) Reduce work
      (4) Can increase ischemia if aortic perfusion pressure and/or distal coronary perfusion pressure are reduced too far
   c. Nitroglycerine/nitrates
      (1) Effects

Pathophysiologic changes observed in CHF	Effect of intravenous nitrate therapy	Effect of nitroprusside
↑ SVR	↓ SVR	↓ SVR
↑ LVEDVol	↓ LVEDV	↓ LVEDV
↑ LVEDP	↓ LVEDP	↓ LVEDP
↑ PRELOAD	↓ PRELOAD	↓ PRELOAD
↑ AFTERLOAD	↔AFTERLOAD	↓ AFTERLOAD
↓ CI	↔CI or sl ↓	↑ CI
↑ PCWP	↓ PCWP	↓ PCWP
↓ SV	↑ SV*	↑ SV
↑ LVFP	↓ LVFP	↓ LVFP
Pulmonary edema	↓ Pulmonary edema	Pulmonary edema ↓
↑ PVP	↓ PVP	↓ PVP
↑ HR	N/C or sl ↑	N/C↔HR or sl ↑
BP	↓	↓
Mean PAP	↓	↓

*Depending on presence or absence of liver failure

(2) Nitroglycerine
(a) Dosage and administration

Application	Dosage and administration
A. Ischemic heart disease	
1. Unstable angina	a. 10 to 15 µg/min continuous infusion increased 5 to 10 µg/min every 3 to 5 minutes until angina relieved, headache occurs, or mean arterial pressure drops > 20 torr; titrate infusion rate against arterial blood pressure in hypertensive patients
	b. 50 to 100 µg bolus for acute ischemia followed by continuous infusion
2. Acute MI	
a. For infarct size reduction	a. 10 to 15 µg/min continuous infusion increased 5 to 10 µg/min. every 3 to 5 minutes until angina is relieved, headache occurs, or mean arterial pressure drops > torr.
b. For left ventricular failure	Follow pulmonary capillary wedge, systemic pressures, cardiac output
	Determine optimal position on cardiac function curve
B. Congestive heart failure	a. 50 to 200 µg bolus if acute ischemia coexists (experimental) or same as 2a
C. Surgical applications	
1. Hypertension during and after CABG	a. As in 1b, titrate against blood pressure with arterial line
2. Deliberate hypotension	Infusion rates may be higher, up to 500 µg/min

(b) Side effects
    i. Reversible and dose-dependent
    ii. Hypotension
    iii. Bradycardia
    iv. Headache
    v. Hypoxemia
    vi. ↑ Intracranial pressure

       vii. Nausea, vomiting

      viii. "Coronary steal"

   (c) End points

       i. Pain relief/worsening

      ii. BP $\leq$ 100 torr or $>$ 10% decrease

     iii. HR $>$ 10 BPM rise

     iv. ST segment improves/worsens

      v. PAO_2 drop of 10 torr

  (3) Nitroprusside

   (a) Start 0.5 µg/kg/min; upper limit 8 to 10 µg/kg/min

   (b) Mix in D5W and keep out of contact with light

   (c) Metabolized to thiocyanate

       i. Level 10< mg/dl probably safe

      ii. Toxicity: delerium, blurred vision, tinnitus

   (d) Also forms cyanide

       i. Initial presentation is acidosis

      ii. It generally becomes a problem at doses over 5 to 6 µg/kg/min

     iii. Treatment is thiosulfate

   (e) Other side effects and end points the same as for nitroglycerine

   (f) Also of great use in hypertensive crisis and management of hypertension in the postoperative period

D. Beta-blocking agents

  1. Comparison to other agents (Table 14-1)

  2. Mechanisms

    a. Decrease heart rate

    b. Decrease blood pressure

    c. Impair platelet aggregation induced by catecholamines, collagen

    d. Right shift oxyhemoglobin curve

  3. Useful in:

    a. Control of heart rate

    b. Relief of angina

    c. Control of arrhythmias

    d. Perhaps in reducing infarct size

Table 14-1. Relative cardiac effects of various drugs

	Nitrates	β-Blockers	Calcium blockers		
			Nifedipine	Verapamil	Diltiazem
Heart rate	Reflex ↑	↓ ↓	↕ or Reflex ↑	↓	↓
Heart size	↓				
Contractility	Reflex ↑	± ↑ / ↓	± → / ↓' Reflex ↑' or	± ↓ / ↓' Reflex ↑' or	↕ / ↓' Reflex ↑' or
Coronary artery tone	↓	↔ ↑ (acute)*	↔	↔	↔
Peripheral tone	↓ ↓	↑	↓ ↓	↓ ↓ / ↓ ↓	↓ ↓ ↓
Heart block	↔	↑	↔	↓	↓

*Peripheral resistance falls back toward baseline with long-term beta-blocker administration.

   e. Probable effect in reducing late mortality/reinfarction
       rate and mortality
   4. Dosages
       a. Propranolol (intravenous)
           (1) 0.5 to 1.0 mg bolus for rate control or therapy of
                arrhythmias
           (2) Repeat as needed or until complication (e.g.,
                bradycardia, contractibility failure, broncho-
                spasm)
           (3) In MI, 0.1 to 0.2 mg/kg in three divided doses 5
                minutes apart have been used for loading, fol-
                lowed by conversion to PO (40 mg)
       b. Propranolol (oral)
           (1) Dose to desired effects of complications
           (2) In MI, up to 180 to 240 mg/day have been used
E. Calcium channel–blocking agents
    1. No apparent advantage of one or another in acute MI
        therapy
    2. Have the theoretical advantages of:
        a. Decreasing myocardial work
        b. Increasing coronary blood flow and cerebral blood
            flow
        c. Reducing afterload
        d. Reducing platelet factor 3 and therefore platelet ag-
            gregation
        e. Reducing contractility
    3. Comparison
        a. See "Comparison to other agents"
        b. See Tables 14-2 and 14-3

Table 14-2. Relative cardiac effects of calcium channel blocking
agents

Characteristic	Verapamil	Nifedipine	Diltiazem
SA node automaticity	↓ ↓	None	↓
AV node conduction	↓ ↓ ↓	Little	↓ ↓
Myocardial contractility	↓ ↓	↓	↓
Peripheral vascular re- sistance	↓ ↓	↓ ↓ ↓	↓
Heart rate	↑ ↓	↑	Little
Cardiac output	↓ ↑	↑	Little

Table 14-3. Clinical pharmacology of Ca^{++} antagonists

	Dosage	Absorption	Onset of action	Plasma (t½)	Metabolism and elimination	Comments
Nifedipine	3-10 µg/kg IV 10-20 mg/6-8 hr, SL or PO	>90% SL and PO	<1 min IV <3 min SL <20 min PO	4 hr	90% bound to plasma protein—metabolized to an acid or lactone drug and metabolites excreted 80% in urine	No known adverse drug interaction; may be used together with beta-blocker Side effects: Hypotension Dizziness Flushing Nausea
Verapamil	75-150 µg/kg IV 80-160 mg/8 hr PO	>90% PO	<2 min IV <30 min PO	5 hr	90% bound to plasma protein—extensively metabolized (de-methylated) in liver; 85% first pass hepatic elimination after PO administration	Addition of beta-blocker may cause AV block Side effects: Hypotension Dizziness AV block
Diltiazem	75-150 µg/kg IV 60-90 mg/8 hr PO	>90% PO	<30 min PO	4 hr	Little bound to plasma protein—extensively deacetylated; drug and metabolites excreted 80% in urine	Addition of beta-blocker may cause AV block Side effects: Hypotension Dizziness Flushing Bradycardia

SUGGESTED READINGS

Aronow, W.S.: Clinical use of nitrates: Nitrates in congestive heart failure. Mod. Concepts Cardiovasc. Dis. **48**:37, 1979.

Baaske, D.M., Yacobi, A., and Amann, A.H.: Intravenous nitroglycerin; a review. Am. Pharmacol. **NS22**(2):36, 1982.

Chiarello, M., et al.: Comparison between the effects of nitroprusside and nitroglycerin on ischemic injury during acute myocardial infarction. Circulation **54**:766, 1976.

Epstein, S.E., et al.: Protection of ischemic myocardium by nitroglycerin: experimental and clinical results. Circulation **53** (supp. I), 191, 1976.

Fisher, J., et al.: Chapter 9. Cardiogenic shock: Pathophysiology and therapy. In Yu, P.N. and Goodwin, J.F. (editors): Progress in Cardiology, ed. 11, Philadelphia, 1982. Lea & Febiger.

Flaherty, J.T., et al.: Comparison of the intravenous nitroglycerin and sodium nitroprusside for treatment of acute hypertension developing after coronary artery bypass sugery. Circulation **65**:1072, 1982.

Ganz, W., et al.: Intracoronary thrombolysis in evolving myocardial infarction. Am. Heart J. **101**:4, 1981.

Hill, N.S., et al.: Intravenous nitroglycerin: a review of pharmacology, indications, therapeutic effects and complications. Chest **79**:69, 1981.

Markis, J.E., et al.: Myocardial salvage after intracoronary thrombolysis with streptokinase in acute myocardial infarction. N. Engl. J. Med. **305**:777, 1981.

May, G.S., et al.: Secondary prevention after myocardial infarction: A review of short-term acute phase trials. Prog. Cardiovasc. Dis. **25**: 335, 1983.

Opie, L.H.: Myocardial infarct size: Part I. Basic considerations. Am. Heart J. **100**:355, 1980.

Opie, L.H.: Myocardial infarct size. Part II. Comparison of anti-infarct effects of beta-blockade, glucose-insulin-potassium, nitrates and hyaluronidase. Am. Heart J. **100**:531, 1980.

Rackley, C.E., et al.: Modern approach to myocardial infarction: determination of prognosis and therapy. Am. Heart J. **101**:75, 1981.

Reduto, L.A., et al.: Coronary artery reperfusion in acute myocardial infarction: beneficial effects of intracoronary streptokinase on left ventricular salvage and performance. Am. Heart J. **102**:1168, 1981.

Rentrop, K.P., et al.: Acute myocardial infarction: intracoronary application of nitroglycerin and streptokinase. Clin. Cardiol. **2**:354, 1979.

Rentrop, P., et al.: Selective intracoronary thrombolysis in acute myocardial infarction and unstable angina pectoris. Circulation **307**, 1981.

Ribner, H.S., et al.: Acute hemodynamic responses to vasodilator therapy in congestive heart failure. Prog. Cardiovas. Dis. **25**:1, 1982.

Rutsch, W., et al.: Percutaneous transluminal coronary recanalization: procedure, results, and acute complications. Am. Heart J. **102**:1178, 1981.

Ryder, R. et al.: β-blockers—decrease myocardial demand and inhibit effects of catecholamines. Decrease ventricular arrhythmias and infarct size. N. Engl. J. Med. **308**:614, 1983.

15

Pacemakers

Pradub Sukhum

INDICATIONS

Opinions differ among physicians and institutions about when and how temporary cardiac pacing in surgical intensive care units (SICUs) is considered and utilized. In general, however, the indications for temporary cardiac pacing fall into these categories: therapeutic, prophylactic, hemodynamic improvement, diagnostic, and tachyarrhythmia management.

A. Therapeutic pacing

1. Therapeutic pacing is used in patients with symptomatic bradycardia who cannot be managed reliably and effectively by either medical or clinical measures. For example, an elderly man who has episodes of Adams-Stokes attacks with a third-degree atrioventricular (AV) block will need temporary pacing while he is waiting for a permanent pacemaker implantation.

2. Temporary cardiac pacing may also be required in cases in which severe and intractable bradycardia has been precipitated by drugs such as digitalis, beta-inhibitors, or other antiarrhythmic agents.

3. Symptomatic sinus node dysfunction (significant and inappropriate sinus bradycardia, sinus arrest, or sinoatrial exit block), which includes the bradycardia-tachycardia syndrome, may appear differently among individuals or sometimes even in the same individual. When these arrhythmias occur continuously or repeatedly, pacing is indicated.

B. Prophylactic pacing

1. Sinus node dysfunction with infrequent and unpredictable significant episodes of sinus pause (sinus arrest or si-

noatrial exit block) is an indication for prophylactic pacing category.

2. A long-standing controversy exists about the necessity for pacing in an acute myocardial infarction.

   a. It is generally agreed that pacing is needed in the third-degree AV block patient who is hemodynamically and/or electrically unstable.

   b. For various types of bundle branch blocks complicating acute myocardial infarction (more often the anterior wall), the decision of whether or not to use prophylactic pacing should be based on such factors as:

      (1) The percentage of these patients who may develop third-degree AV block and its consequences

      (2) The physician's experience in handling such cases

      (3) The possibility of potential complications from pacing

   c. Table 15-1 lists an approach to temporary pacing in cases involving acute myocardial infarction.

Table 15-1. Temporary pacing in acute myocardial infarction

	Degree	Location/type of block	Pace
Acute inferior myocardial infarction	Second	AV node/Wenckebach	No
		His bundle/Mobitz II (rare)	Yes
	Third	Usually AV node	No* Yes†
Acute anterior myocardial infarction		Right bundle branch block	No
		Bifasicular block	Yes
		(Right bundle branch block plus left anterior or left posterior fascicular block)	No
		Left bundle branch block	
	Second	Mobitz II	Yes
	Third	Usually complete bundle branch block or trifasicular block	Yes

*Existence of an adequate escape pacemaker and hemodynamic stability.
†Existence of an inadequate escape pacemaker and/or hemodynamic instability.

3. Temporary prophylactic pacing may also be used in patients who are at high risk of developing significant bradycardia when they are undergoing procedures or surgery (e.g., cardiac catheterization, cardiac angiography, or surgery under general anesthesia in patients with some degree of AV block or intraventricular block). However, the chance that patients undergoing noncardiac surgery under general anesthesia will develop complete AV block from preexisting bifascicular block is very remote.

C. Pacing for hemodynamic improvement

1. In certain patients, such as who have undergone cardiac surgery with an inadequate heart rate, hemodynamic status may be improved by pacing.

2. The more physiologic types of pacing, such as atrial demand (AAI) or A-V sequential ventricular inhibit (DVI), may further augment stroke volume by preserving A-V synchrony.

3. When this technique is used, cardiac output and the patient's status should be monitored appropriately.

D. Diagnostic application

1. A simultaneous recording of the atrial intracardiac electrogram (ICE) (for P wave identification) and the surface electrocardiogram (ECG) for QRS identification can be very helpful in the diagnosis of some arrhythmias.

2. A skillful operator and more elaborate equipment will be required for more sophisticated diagnostic studies. Most of these studies are done in the special electrophysiologic laboratory on an elective basis.

E. Tachyarrhythmia management

1. Although significant developments have been made in the pacing management of certain tachyarrhythmias, the technique has not been as widely used for tachyarrhythmias as it has been for bradycardia.

a. The conventional drug approach for preventing and terminating the tachycardias, together with direct current–cardioversion, continues to dominate the field.

   b. The latest work on rapid or burst pacing and catheter cardioversion/defibrillation will eventually lead to important changes in this area.

2. Those tachyarrhythmias that can be effectively terminated by the pacing technique are:
   a. Atrial flutter (Waldo type I)
   b. Supraventricular tachycardia (SVT) of the AV nodal reentrant type
   c. SVT associated with accessory pathway type

3. Although offering considerable promise, ventricular tachycardia interruption by the burst stimuli method can also induce ventricular fibrillation or acceleration of the ventricular tachycardia rate.

4. Pacing techniques are not effective in the conversion of atrial fibrillation.

5. Proper pacing for management of tachycardias requires:
   a. A knowledgeable and experienced team
   b. Fluoroscopic equipment
   c. Special types of pacing and recording equipment

6. ICUs interested in using this technique should make sure they are adequately prepared to use this procedure safely and properly; otherwise, they should continue to rely on pharmacologic or direct current—cardioversion/defibrillation treatment.
   a. Table 15-2 shows a state-of-the-art comparison for three methods of tachycardia therapy.

7. The various pacing techniques used for treatment of tachycardia are:
   a. Prevention
      (1) Rate support pacing
      (2) Overdrive suppression pacing
   b. Rate control without tachycardia termination
      (1) Continuous rapid pacing
      (2) Paired and coupled pacing
   c. Termination
      (1) Slow competitive or underdrive pacing
      (2) Dual-demand and dual-chamber pacing
      (3) Autoscan pacing

Table 15-2. Comparison of the three methods of tachycardia therapy

	Requirement	Effectiveness	Prevention of recurrent tachycardia	Treatment of coexisting bradycardia	Repeated application	Diagnosis capability	Patient discomfort during treatment	Side effects and complications
Pacing	Knowledgeable experienced team	+ + − − + + +, In certain arrhythmias	+, But not reliable	+ + + +	Advantage over direct current—cardioversion	+ + + − − + + + +	−, Except during insertion	See complications and pacemaker system malfunctions section
Pharmacologic	Readily available	+ + − − + + +	+ + +	−, May induce bradycardia or deteriorate it		+, When used as therapeutic trial	+, From side effects of drugs	Multiple side effects of drugs, possible cardiovascular depressant Antiarrhythmic drugs can induce arrhythmias
Direct current—cardioversion or defibrillation	Readily available	+ + + +	−,	−, May induce bradycardia following cardioversion		−,	+ + + +. Should not be done on fully conscious patient	Skin burning, possible myocardial damage Cardioversion can induce arrhythmias

(4) Orthorhythmic pacing
(5) Overdrive pacing, entrainment, decremental ramp technique
(6) Burst pacing

EQUIPMENT AND TECHNIQUE

The technique selected will vary with the situation, purpose, experience, and resources available. For instance, despite its potential danger, one of the quickest methods to initiate cardiac pacing is the percutaneous technique. In less urgent cases, and when no fluoroscopy is available, pacing may be done by inserting a balloon tip-catheter utilizing intracardiac electrographic guidance. Fluoroscopic guidance should be employed when stabilization and good capture assurance is important.

A. Transcutaneous technique
  1. Advantage
    a. The rapidity by which the electrical stimulation of the heart can be established
  2. Disadvantages
    a. It is unreliable.
    b. There is painful and violent extracardiac (i.e., chest wall) muscle contraction as a result of the high electrical current.
    c. It is difficult to monitor the ECG.
    d. These inherent problems have caused this technique to fall into almost total disuse in the past decade.
  3. The recent interest in emergency medicine and cardiopulmonary resuscitation has led to the introduction of new and improved equipment and may revive this technique.
    a. Electrodes have been modified by replacing the smaller metal plate with a larger adhesive pad for better skin attachment and increased surface area. Electrode placement can be an anteroposterior type (Fig. 15-1).
    b. The stimulus characteristic, duration, and amplitude, have been updated for better cardiac capture; at the same time, less painful extracardiac stimuli are created.

    c. Although this equipment is commercially available, it is still being evaluated for its effectiveness.

B. Transthoracic technique

    Some institutions occasionally use the transthoracic technique, another emergency cardiac pacing technique. Currently the transthoracic cardiac pacing set comes in a sterile, disposable package. It is available from two manufacturers, each using a slightly different approach, as listed in Table 15-3.

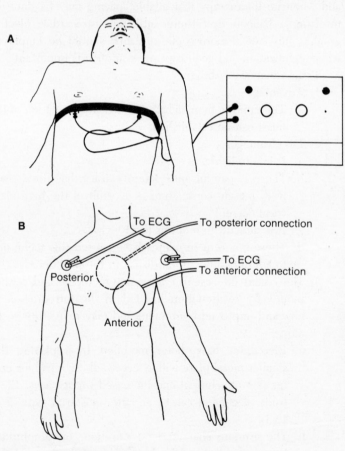

Fig. 15-1. Transcutaneous technique of temporary cardiac pacing. **A,** Early equipment and electrode application. **B,** Current equipment and electrode placement (see p. 423).

1. Technique
   a. Although the transthoracic needle can be inserted through the left parasternal area (about the fourth intercostal space), the subxyphoid approach is preferred.
      (1) The latter approach has less chance to damage blood vessels (e.g., intercostal, internal mammary, or coronary arteries).
      (2) The right ventricular internal dimension from subxyphoid approach is larger.
      (3) If the procedure is done during or in anticipation of cardiac resuscitation, the subxyphoid approach allows more room to carry out the procedure.
   b. To enter the right ventricular (RV) cavity, the needle should be inserted at the left border of the subxyphoid notch.
   c. The needle angle to the anterior abdominal wall is about 30 to 40 degrees and should point approximately straight up toward the suprasternal notch or slightly toward either shoulder (Fig. 15-2). This direction may be different from that of the pericardiocentesis technique in which the needle is directed toward the right shoulder to avoid the RV cavity or any cardiac chambers.
   d. With the Elecath transthoracic set, blood aspiration

Table 15-3. Comparison of the available transthoracic pacing sets

	Elecath*	LSCI†
Type	Unipolar (extracardiac anode)	Bipolar (allow conversion to unipolar but may have short circuit problem)
Transthoracic needle size	18-gauge	21-gauge
Blood aspiration or drug administration (checking intracavitary position)	Yes	No

*Pace-Jector, Electro-catheter Corp.
†USCI transthoracic temporary pacing electrode kit.

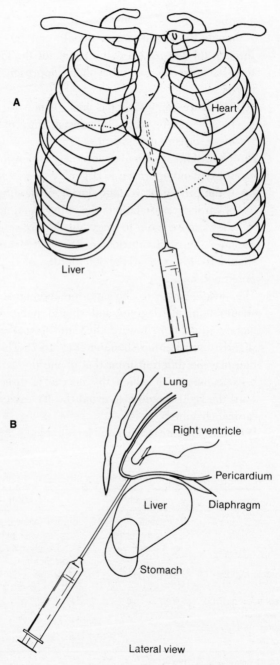

Fig. 15-2. Illustration of the subxyphoid temporary transthoracic cardiac pacing technique (see p. 425). **A,** Anterior view. **B,** Lateral view.

will help ensure that the cardiac chamber has been entered (presumably the RV cavity).

e. To advance the pacing stylet into the RV cavity, the locking hub is loosened and the stylet is advanced to the mark on the wire.

f. Extra care is necessary in withdrawing the needle so that the position of the stylet is not disturbed.

g. The stylet can now be connected to the external pulse generator via the special connector provided.

h. The electrical stimulation can be initiated at about 10 mA (or higher) in the asyncronous mode at an appropriate rate.

i. Further adjustments may be made according to the specific requirements and conditions during the procedure.

j. The stylet position may need to be adjusted slightly for better cardiac capture and/or improved stimulation threshold.

2. ICU staff members wishing to use this procedure should be thoroughly familiar with the detailed technique and equipment to avoid any life-threatening time delays during cardiopulmonary resuscitation.

3. This technique is an emergency short-term approach. It *must* be replaced as soon as possible with the transvenous endocardial technique which offers more stability, greater reliability, and less serious complications.

4. Problems

   a. In general, this approach has a low success and/or survival rate.

      (1) The major reason for this is that the technique is almost always used as the last ditch effort to revive a patient who has failed to respond to routine cardiac resuscitation.

      (2) The cardiac tissue, by then, is too far hypoxic to respond to electrical stimuli or may present as electromechanical dissociation.

   b. When inexperienced personnel do the procedure, cardiopulmonary resuscitation may have to be interrupted for long periods of time. This factor tends to

discourage the use of this technique in the early stages of the cardiac resuscitation procedure.
  c. The transthoracic technique can also induce significant complications, such as liver or stomach puncture, pneumothorax, and cardiac wall laceration.
  d. Uncontrolled patient movement and significant respiratory motion can increase the risks of these complications.
  e. This technique should *never* replace the transvenous appoach on a noncritical emergence case.
C. Esophageal technique
  With a good technique and proper equipment, short-term atrial pacing from a catheter placed in the esophagus can be achieved in a high percentage of cases. Patient discomfort does not allow for longer periods of atrial pacing by this mode.
  1. Benefits
    a. Helps to obtain an esophageal electrogram for the diagnosis of arrhythmias
    b. Provides short-term atrial pacing for tachycardia (e.g., it can induce or terminate certain forms of SVT treatment).
  2. Necessary equipment
    Multichannel ECG monitor or recorder for simultaneous recording of surface ECG and esophageal electrogram is required. For a more critical diagnostic electrogram, a faster recorder or strip chart speed (>25 mm/sec) and a different frequency bandpass filter may be required.
  3. For pacing, the distance of the electrodes (anode-cathode) should be about 3 cm apart, and the pulse generator should have a pulse duration of up to 10 msec.
  4. Currently esophageal pacing of the ventricle is usually ineffective and unreliable.
D. Temporary epicardial technique
  Temporary epicardial wire attachment during cardiac surgery has become more and more popular in recent years. Some institutions are using it routinely.
  1. To fully accomplish more physiologic pacing and to aid in arrhythmia diagnosis, both atrial and ventricular wires

are needed in a bipolar configuration, although conversion to a unipolar system may sometimes be necessary.

2. Except for the catheter, the equipment and technique for arrhythmia diagnosis and pacing are the same as those used in other methods, such as the transvenous approach.

E. Transcutaneous endocardial technique

The transvenous technique is regarded as the standard, and is the most reliable mode of temporary pacing in critical care units, except for patients who have undergone cardiac surgery and who already have a temporary epicardial wire attached.

1. Endocardial pacing catheters

The endocardial pacing catheters range in size from 4 to 7 French. They are made with different wire type and are constructed of various kinds of materials (Table 15-4).

a. Basically, the stiffer types should be inserted under fluoroscopic guidance.

(1) These catheters may become slightly less rigid while they are within the patient's body.

(2) Once the catheter's tip is in good position in the RV apex, these firmer catheters tend to stay in place better than the softer types.

(3) Because of the stiffness, however, cardiac perforation is possible.

b. The other type of catheter is constructed of a softer material so it can be passed down the bloodstream into the RV cavity without the need for skillful manipulation under fluoroscopy.

(1) The position of the catheter tip can be monitored by an ICE.

(2) The "semifloating" catheter is usually only a 4 French size and is quite soft. The use of this catheter is declining in favor of the balloon-tip flow-directed pacing catheter.

(3) Without fluoroscopic visualization, the position of this balloon-tip catheter within the RV cavity cannot be accurately determined.

(4) Stabilizing the catheter depends on wedging of

Table 15-4. Comparison of the temporary transvenous pacing catheters and techniques

Catheter	Size	Stiffness	Site of entry*	Designed to be used with	Catheter stability
Regular	5 Fr or 6 Fr	Stiff	All	Fluoroscopy	Better
Ballon-tip	4 Fr or 5 Fr	Soft	All†	ICE	Less
J-curve balloon-tip‡	5 Fr	Soft	Femoral vein	ICE	Less
Multipurpose balloon-tip hemodynamic and pacing catheter	7 Fr	Soft	Not from femoral vein Prefer from right side	Pressure & ICE	Less

*Brachial, subclavian, internal jugular, femoral.
†Less successful from brachial and femoral vein.
‡Swan-Ganz Flow-Directed J-Tip (Femoral) Pacing Catheter, Edwards Laboratories.

the catheter under the trabeculae of the RV apex and the route of the catheter's entry in relationship to the patient's movement following the catheter placement.

(5) Although associated with only minor local complications, the arm vein is among the less desirable routes to use because the patient's arm motion frequently dislodges the catheter or possibly may cause a perforation of the heart. Tables 15-4 and 15-5 summarize and compare these catheters and techniques.

2. Precautions

a. Regardless of the type of catheter selected or the route of entry chosen, good aseptic technique should always be followed.

b. Because of potential major complications such as pneumonthorax or arterial puncture with bleeding occuring, it is crucially important to be thoroughly familiar with subclavian vein and internal jugular vein cannulation.

Table 15-5. Temporary tranvenous pacing and route of entry comparison

Route of entry	Access	Complications	Patient's mobility	Catheter position stability
Subclavian	Percutaneous	Pneumothorax Thorax Arterial puncture Nerve damage	Not limited	Good
Internal jugular	Percutaneous	Same as above	Less limited	Good (except with extensive neck motion)
Femoral vein	Percutaneous	Thrombosis and emboli Arterial puncture Hematoma	Limited leg motion	Good
Brachian vein	Surgical cut down or percutaneous	Phlebitis Cardiac perforation	Limited arm motion	Not good

3. Fluoroscopic guidance
   a. Upper vein entry (internal jugular, subclavian, and brachial veins)
      (1) Approach
         (a) Once the catheter tip is in the right atrium (RA), and if the catheter tip is sufficiently curved and pointed toward the tricuspid valve (TV), the catheter may be advanced across the valve into the RV cavity (Fig. 15-3, *A*).
            It may further advance into the RV outflow tract or the RV apex. More often, however, the catheter tip is not curved enough and catches on the RA lower medial wall while it is being advanced to cross the TV (Fig. 15-3, *B*). It may also enter the coronary sinus or inferior vena cava (IVC).
         (b) A better technique is the loop formation in the RA. The catheter curve tip is rotated in the RA and advanced until it catches the RA lateral wall (Fig. 15-3, *C*). Advancement of the catheter from this position will result in a loop formation with the catheter tip migrating superiorly (Fig. 15-3, *D*).
         (c) Once the loop is big enough (the catheter tip is in the upper RA lateral wall), the catheter is rotated so the catheter tip points medially toward the TV (Fig. 15-3, *E*).
         (d) The catheter may cross the TV this time, or it may be necessary to withdraw and/or rotate to get the catheter tip flipped across the upper edge of the TV into the RV (Fig. 15-3, *F*).
         (e) The catheter then quickly advances into the RV outflow tract and across the pulmonary valve into the pulmonary artery.
         (f) The catheter tip in the RV outflow tract may cause ventricular arrhythmias. This is the same technique of right heart catheterization that has been successfully performed for the past decades. It is also one of the techniques

used to avoid an accidental coronary sinus entry.

(g) Following this, the catheter is gradually withdrawn back into the RV. It may sometimes be necessary to shake the catheter to help drop the catheter tip into the middle RV floor (Fig. 15-3, G).

(h) Finally, the catheter is advanced into the RV apex (hopefully wedged under the trabeculae)

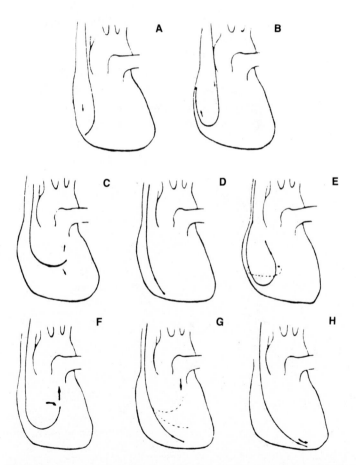

Fig. 15-3. Diagram of the temporary transvenous catheter insertion technique under fluoroscopic guidance from the "upper vein" entry (see p. 432).

under both fluoroscopic guidance (Fig. 15-3, *H*) and ICE guidance (Figs. 15-4 to 15-7). The ICE helps assess the relationship of the electrode tip with the endocarium-myocardium, and thereby indicates better threshold and stabilization, and reduces the chances of perforation.

(2) Problems

In practice, some difficulty may occur in accomlishing certain of these steps.

(a) The experienced operator will know how and when some stops should be repeated and modified.

(b) The manipulation of the catheter inside the cardiovascular system can sometimes cause arrhythmias and possible perforation. An inexperienced operator should not attempt any new and potentially dangerous techniques.

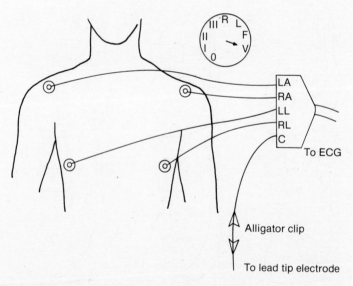

Fig. 15-4. Diagram of the technique to obtain the unipolar intracardiac electrogram. Note that the recording is done with the lead selector at the chest lead position.

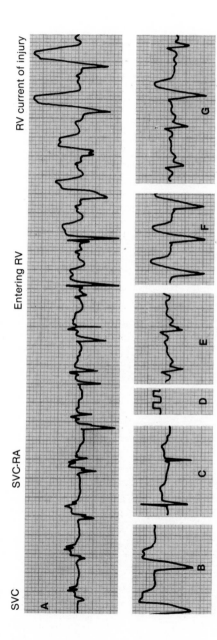

Fig. 15-5. **A,** A unipolar intracardiac electrogram (*ICE*) rhythm strip recorded from the distal (tip) electrode while the catheter is being advanced from a position in the superior vena cava (*SVC*) through the right atrium (*RA*) across the tricuspid valve (*TV*) and into the right ventricle (*RV*). The ST elevation (RV current of injury) appears when the distal electrode makes contact (or makes some impact) with the RV endocardium. **B,** A unipolar ICE from the distal electrode demonstrates the RV current of injury, indicating the distal electrode is in contact with the RV endocardium. **C,** Measurement of the *bipolar* intracardiac spontaneous QRS amplitude can roughly be made from this bipolar ICE. This is one method of checking the sensing threshold. The tracing is obtained by connecting the ECG monitoring equipment arm leads to the distal and proximal terminals of the pacing catheter with the lead selector in Lead I position. **D,** A calibration signal of 1 mV for measurement of the ICE voltage. **E,** The surface ECG (Lead II) tracing of this patient who is in normal sinus rhythm and left bundle branch block. **F,** A surface ECG tracing during stimulation threshold checking. **G,** A surface ECG tracing during sensing threshold checking.

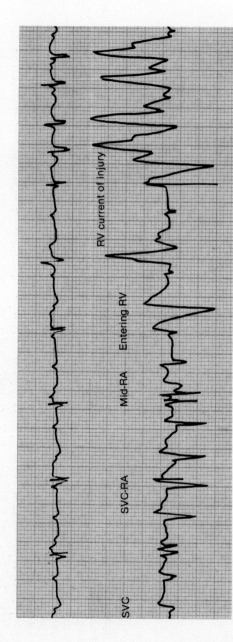

Fig. 15-6. Simultaneous recording of a surface ECG (tracing *A*) and the unipolar ICE from the distal electrode (tracing *B*) in a patient with complete heart block. These simultaneous tracings assist in better identification of the P wave and QRS complexes on the ICE, while the catheter is passing from the position in the SVC through the RA into the RV. Notice the significant change in P wave (reducing) and QRS complex (increasing) amplitude as soon as the catheter tip crosses the TV in Figs. 15-5, 15-6, and 15-7. (See abbreviations in Fig. 15-5.)

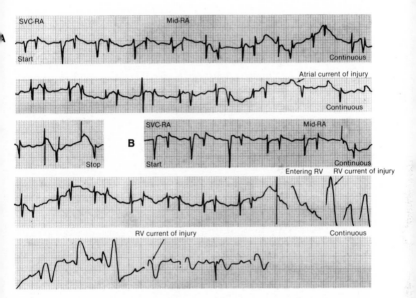

Fig. 15-7. A, A continuous unipolar ICE tracing from the distal (tip) electrode while the catheter is passing slowly from the SVC-RA junction into the RA. The atrial current of injury indicates the tip electrode touching or catching the RA wall. Further advancement of the catheter from this position may not achieve entry into the RV. **B,** The catheter is withdrawn back to SVC-RA junction and is readvanced again with a slight catheter rotation. This time the catheter enters the RV without catching the RA wall (see abbreviations in Fig. 15-5).

b. Femoral vein entry
   (1) Approach
      (a) For this approach, the use of a catheter with some curve to its tip is preferred.
      (b) A loop may be formed in the RA medially or laterally.
      (c) Then with some rotation and adjustment (advancing or withdrawing) of the catheter, the catheter will pass across the TV and can be advanced toward the RV apex.
      (d) Occasionally, while advancing the catheter, a loop can be formed within the IVC by catching the catheter tip with one of the IVC tributary veins.
      (e) ICE to establish catheter position can also be monitored as previously mentioned.
4. Electrogram guidance technique
   a. Equipment
      (1) The equipment required in this technique can be as simple as regular ECG equipment that runs either by battery or alternating current (AC) power with the patient electrically isolated. Most of the current equipment is of the latter type, which requires periodic checks for current leakage.
      (2) A better choice is ECG monitoring equipment with a monitor scope, a chest lead recording system, and a capability of simultaneously displaying and/or recording more than one lead.
      (3) When the balloon-tip flow-directed catheter is used, one must take great care to line up the curve tip so that when inserted into the RA, it will point medially towards the TV. This will facilitate the catheter crossing the TV.
   b. Entry point
      The upper veins in order of ease of RV entry are: right internal jugular, left subclavian, right subclavian, and left internal jugular. Whether the upper veins or femoral vein is the route of entry for a special J-curve balloon-tip catheter, the balloon should be in-

flated right after the catheter tip has passed through the sheath used in the percutaneous technique. This technique will help prevent the catheter tip from advancing into undesirable tributary veins. Fig. 15-4 illustrates the ECG hookup for unipolar intracardiac electrogram monitoring. If more than one lead can be simultaneously monitored, lead II is preferred for the surface ECG.

(1) Upper vein entry

    (a) The antecubital vein entry is not recommended because of a low rate of successful insertion and poor stabilization.

    (b) The unipolar ICE recorded from the catheter distal (tip) electrode is shown in Figs. 15-5 to 15-7.

    (c) With a length marker on the catheter, the operator can estimate the position of the catheter while it is being advanced. The catheter position should correlate with the ICE. For example, if the length marker reads 60 cm from skin entry of the right internal jugular approach and the ICE has not displayed the RV pattern, the catheter may not have entered the RA, it may have passed the RA into the IVC, or it may have formed a loop within the RA.

    (d) The important ICE landmarks are:

        i. The SVC-RA junction

        ii. The moment that the catheter crosses the TV

        iii. The final position within the RV cavity

    (e) With the catheter in mid-high SVC, the ICE shows both inverted P wave and a QRS complex. The pattern looks like the aVR tracing of the 12-lead surface ECG.

    (f) At the SVC-RA junction, there is a characteristic deeply inverted P wave and usually a smaller QRS complex (Figs. 15-5 to 15-7).

    (g) Within the RA, the P wave becomes biphasic

or even upright as the catheter advances from a superior to an inferior position. The P wave amplitude gradually decreases and the GRS amplitude gradually increases.

(h) As soon as the catheter crosses the TV, the QRS amplitude suddenly increases significantly, and it becomes necessary to reset the gain control to a lower scale. The P wave is now quite small, and, in fact, the ICE looks similar to the VI pattern of the 12-lead surface ECG with a very high voltage QRS.

(i) Before the balloon is deflated, the catheter should be advanced a few more centimeters beyond the TV so that it will stay within the RV.

(j) When the catheter is advanced and the tip electrode touches the endocardium, the ST segment will elevate (current of injury).

(k) Provided thresholds are acceptable, this position or one in which the catheter is advanced slightly further is recommended as the final placement.

(2) Femoral vein entry

(a) This approach requires a specially made J-curve balloon-tip flow-directed pacing catheter.

(b) The curved tip *must* be lined up medially and the balloon inflation timed.

(c) The catheter marker for helping estimate the catheter position should be used along with the unipolar ICE recorded from the distal (tip) electrode.

(d) When the catheter is in the IVC, the ICE looks like the interior leads of the 12-lead surface ECG.

(e) Occasionally, when the catheter tip is in the RA and being advanced further, the catheter tip may not cross the TV, but will be pushed up to the high RA or SVC position. This can be identified on the ICE. The catheter should be withdrawn gradually, because this manipulation may make it possible for the tip to cross the TV.

(f) Occasionally, the catheter may need a slight rotation to help facilitate entry into the RV cavity.

(g) The balloon should be deflated with the catheter tip about 3 cm beyond the TV.

(h) Under ICE guidance, the catheter is further advanced while one watches for current of injury to develop.

5. Threshold measurement

The external ends of the pacing catheter are attached to the external pulse generator directly or via the extension cord. The distal (tip) electrode is always connected to the cathode (negative) pole of the pulse generator. Care should be taken to ensure proper and tight contact of all the connectors. When the pacemaker is used with an inhibit mode, both stimulation and sensing thresholds need to be checked for proper overall functioning.

The thresholds, particularly the stimulation threshold, should be checked once a day (or more if necessary) during use to see if the catheter electrode tip is moving out of good position or other complications are resulting in a rising threshold.

a. Sensing threshold measurement

The sensing threshold may be checked first if pacing is not required immediately or if the patient's spontaneous ventricular rate is high (i.e., arbitrarily more than 100 beats/min).

(1) With the pacemaker turned off, the rate control is set at lower than the patient's ventricular rate.

(2) Then the current control is set at about 3 mA (or high enough to demonstrate a pacing artifact "spike" on the ECG monitor).

(3) The sensing control is set at the furthest clockwise position. This is about 1 mV.

(4) The pacemaker is then turned on. The flashing

light or needle deflection sensing indicator shows the pacemaker is sensing properly all the time.

(5) The alternative method is to watch the ECG monitor for the pacing artifact "spike" that occurs from improper sensing.

    (a) If the pacemaker sensing function is working, gradually rotate the control counterclockwise, and at the same time observe any one of the sensing indicators until it loses sensing.

    (b) The position just before it fails to sense is considered to be the sensing threshold.

    (c) This is equivalent to the patient's spontaneous QRS amplitude in mV as detected by the pulse generator.

(6) Unipolar and bipolar QRS voltage can also be measured from the ICE, or the voltage can be read directly from the pacing system analyzer.

    (a) A number higher than 4 mV is considered to be good.

    (b) A slightly lower figure may be accepted in a difficult case; but when the figure is too low, the pacing catheter should be repositioned.

(7) The sensing may then be reduced to one third, or at the most clockwise position, provided that oversensing of other signals (e.g., T wave or P wave) does not occur.

b. Stimulation threshold measurement

(1) With the pacemaker in OFF position, the output is set at about 3 mA.

(2) The rate is set at 15% to 20% higher than the patient's spontaneous rate.

(3) With the pacemaker turned ON, the ECG monitor is observed to see if the pacemaker has taken over and has captured the ventricle completely without missing inappropriately.

(4) The current control is then gradually rotated counterclockwise (to a smaller current) until the pacemaker misses capturing the ventricles.

(5) The last current position before it loses capturing is considered to be the stimulation threshold.

    (a) A stimulation threshold of 1 mA or lower is conventionally considered adequate.

    (b) A high current such as 2 or 3 mA requires catheter repositioning.

(6) The final current may be set as three times higher, or conventionally at 3 mA.

(7) During the stimulation threshold, difficulty or confusion may occur in patients who have premature complexes, sinus capture, or atrial fibrillation with rapid irregular response.

6. External pulse generator

The simple external pulse generator for temporary ventricular or ventricular inhibit (VVI) pacing is available from several manufacturers.

a. The same pulse generator can be used for AAI.

b. It can be used with transthoracic, transvenous and temporary epicardial techniques.

c. Their basic function and control dials are similar.

    (1) There are ON/OFF, current, rate, and sensitivity controls.

        (a) The ON/OFF control is usually hidden and/or requires two separate hand operations to prevent accidental turn ON and most important of all turn OFF.

        (b) The current control usually ranges from 0 to about 20 mA.

        (c) The rate control is usually from 30 to 180 BPM.

        (d) The sensitivity control is somewhat confusing. At the most counterclockwise position, it is usually labeled "Async" (asynchronous), which means that the pacemaker will function in the asynchronous or fixed rate mode. Clockwise rotation from the Async position reveals numbers that may start with 20 and decrease down to 1 at the most clockwise position. These numbers are approximations of the patient's spontaneous QRS voltage. If the pacemaker is sensing properly at the setting of 5, but fails at 6, it can be stated that the sensing threshold is about 5 mV or that the patient's spontaneous QRS voltage as detected by the pulse generator through the pacing catheter is about 5 mV.

7. Special-purpose external pacemaking
   a. Currently available units
      (1) High-rate atrial pacing
      (2) Tachycardia induction and termination devices
      (3) AV DVI pacing
   b. Potentially available units
      (1) External atrial synchronous ventricular inhibit
      (2) Fully automatic
   c. On some models, usually in the older units, the external end of the catheter connects to the models sideways.
      (1) This connection can cause a catheter break because of acute bending at the connecting site.
      (2) Other types may develop a loose connection or obstruction if the tightening knob is rotated in the opposite direction.
      (3) These problems can become frustrating and dangerous in an emergency or pacemaker-dependent case.
   d. Most of the latest models have vertical connectors that require no rotation and thus have avoided some of the problems mentioned.
   e. The battery should be changed periodically and the date of the battery change should be labeled on the pulse generator or written in the log book.
      (1) For more detail, the approximate hours of use may be kept so that the battery changing time can be varied for safety.

(2) Extra batteries must be kept on hand for immediate use at all times.

COMPLICATIONS

Regardless of the technique, temporary cardiac pacing is by no means without hazard. Some of the complications and their magnitude have already been mentioned earlier as the various techniques were described.

A. External electrical complications

Alternating current electric-powered appliances and equipment used for the patient can induce electric shock (microshock and macroshock) to the patient and patient-specific organ systems.

1. Facilitating
   a. Electrical leakage from equipment
   b. Improper equipment grounding
   c. Low electric-resistant pathways
   d. Electrical grounding of the patient
2. Prevention
   a. The alternating current electrically run products and electric outlets should be of the patient isolation type.
   b. They should be periodically checked for electrical leakage.
   c. Wet skin has a much lower electrical-resistant pathway than dry skin.
   d. The pacing catheter provides the lowest resistance and the most direct electrical pathway between the heart and the outside environment.
   e. The pulse generator, particularly the connector and the catheter terminals, should be covered with an insulating material, such as a surgical glove. However, the nontransparent glove makes visualization of the pulse generator control dial and the ability to check the connector more difficult.

B. Complications occurring during catheter insertion
   1. Arterial puncture or cannulation
      a. During the percutaneous technique, accidental arterial puncture, particularly unrecognized arterial cannulation with a larger size dilator-sheath, can occur and can induce bleeding and hematoma. This complication may be more serious in patients with coagulation defects.
   2. Pneumothorax
      a. Pneumothorax is perhaps the most publicized complication of subclavian vein puncture, and to a lesser degree, internal jugular vein puncture.
      b. Knowledge and experience in subclavian and internal jugular vein puncture is crucially important to keep these complications as minimal as possible.
   3. Cardiac perforation
      a. Cardiac perforation can occur when the stiff electrode catheter is used.
      b. Fortunately, cardiac tamponade does not always follow.
      c. These patients should be observed and monitored carefully once the complication is suspected.
   4. Arrhythmias
      a. Arrhythmias may develop when the catheter irritates either the RA or the RV wall.
      b. More serious ventricular arrhythmias are common during the pacing catheter insertion in acute myocardial infarction or in other ventricular tachyarrhythmic–prone patients.
   5. Nerve trunk and lymphatic vessel drainage
   6. Catheter knotting
C. Complications occurring during the pacing period

1. Thrombophlebitis, thrombosis, and emboli
   a. Thrombophlebitis is not rare when the peripheral veins are used.
   b. With the use of the percutaneous technique, the true incidence of thrombophlebitis, thrombosis, and emboli associated with the larger and more central veins may not be easily detected clinically.
2. Local infection and systemic sepsis
   a. The incidence of local infection and systemic sepsis can be minimized by using proper aseptic technique during catheter insertion and during the maintenance of the catheter entry site. This technique should be no different from hyperalimentation or hemodynamic catheter care.
3. Psychological and emotional
   a. The phrases, "Your heart stops beating," or "Your heart is beating too slow," are frightening to any individual who hears them.
   b. Imagining that they will be dependent on an electronic gadget to keep them alive is another big uncertainty these patients have to face.
   c. Not surprisingly, the psychological and emotional impact on patients who are being treated with a pacemaker is significant.
   d. Patient education and reassurance, together with persistent demonstration of the pacemaker's reliability, are important keys to minimizing this problem.

PACEMAKER SYSTEM MALFUNCTIONING/TROUBLESHOOTING

Table 15-6 lists the common pacemaker system malfunctions, diagnostic approaches, and correction actions. These malfunctions may occur continuously or intermittently.

Table 15-6. Pacemaker system malfunctions

Problems	Causes	Remarks	Diagnostic approaches	Corrective actions
Pacing artifacts (spikes) are not visualized	Pulse generator unintentionally turned off	Check first	Check ON/OFF switch	Turn pulse generator on
	Output (mA) setting at a low level		Check output (mA) setting	Set output (mA) at appropriate level
	Pacing artifacts do not show well in certain ECG monitoring leads, particularly the bipolar system and the non-fade monitoring scope or computer printout		Check ECG lead	Select ECG lead for better pacing artifact display
	Battery depletion		Check battery voltage (available in the newer models, but not always reliable)	Change battery if it has low voltage or when in doubt
			If pacing indicator is flashing, check all connectors, particularly rotation type	Correct direction of rotation and tighten all connectors
	Open and/or short circuit. Most common cause is a loose connection, and occasionally a broken catheter or the extension cord wire	Check first	Check for catheter or wire fracture; some may not be readily noticeable (ICE) and chest x-ray (CXR) can be helpful.	When in doubt, change connector
				Convert to unipolar system, if one of the catheter connector terminals is broken

	Cause		Diagnosis	Action
	Oversensing; either cardiac signal such as P or T wave or extracardiac signals such as electrical or electromagnetic interference around or on patient, and false signal from partial loose connection or wire fracture		Check sensing threshold and ICE; check for electrical and electromagnetic interference.	Adjust sensing Eliminate or improve electrical or electromagnetic interference sources
Inconsistent or no capture	ECG artifacts are simulating pacing artifacts		Usually occurs randomly Can be continuous and relatively rate-stable (e.g., IV drip system induced artifacts)	Eliminate ECG artifact
	Sensing failure resulting in pacing in refractory period		Diagnose sensing failure first	Correct sensing failure
	Battery depletion		Check battery voltage (available in newer models, but not always liable)	Change battery if it has low voltage or when in doubt.
	Output (mA) set too low		Check stimulation threshold	See output (mA) appropriately
	Stimulation threshold rise mostly due to catheter tip electrode movement or dislodgement (usually accompanies sensing malfunction)	Probably most common cause	Check stimulation threshold CXR may not show significant catheter position change.	If the threshold is too high (e.g., more than 5 mA), reposition the catheter.

Continued.

Table 15-6 Pacemaker system malfunctions—cont'd.

Problems	Causes	Remarks	Diagnostic approaches	Corrective actions
	Catheter perforation may cause pacing and sensing malfunction		CXR, ICE, development of pericardial friction rub may assist in diagnosis	Withdraw catheter into the RV cavity under fluoroscopic and ICE guidance
	Pulse generator malfunction			When in doubt, change unit
Improper sensing	Oversensing (see above).			Use asynchronous (flexed) mode, if there is no danger of precipitating ventricular arrhythmia.
	ECG artifacts are simulating pacing artifacts (see above).			
	Low sensing threshold (low voltage of the ICE spontaneous QRS complex).		Check the sensing threshold	Convert to unipolar system
	Can occur with adequate stimulation threshold			Reposition catheter
	Usually results from catheter tip electrode movement or dislodgement.			
	Pulse generator malfunction			Change unit when in doubt

SUGGESTED READINGS

Fisher, J.D.: Role of electrophysiologic testing in the diagnosis and treatment of patients with known and suspected bradycardias and tachycardias. Prog. Cardiovasc. Dis. 24:25, 1981.

Gallagher, J.J., et al.: Esophageal pacing: a diagnostic and therapeutic tool. Circulation 65:336, 1982.

Hindman, M.C., et al.: The clinical significance of bundle branch block complicating acute myocardial infraction. 2. Indication for temporary and permanent pacemaker insertion. Circulation 58:689, 1978.

Roberts, J.R., and Greenberg, M.I.: Emergency transthoracic pacemaker. Ann. Emerg. Med. 10:600, 1981.

Waldo, A.L., et al.: Temporary cardiac packing: applications and techniques in the treatment of cardiac arrhythmias. Prog. Cardiovasc. Dis. 23:451, 1981.

Zoll, P.M.: Resuscitation of the heart in ventricular standstill by external electric stimulation. N. Eng. J. Med. 247:768, 1952.

16

Cardiopulmonary resuscitation

Frank B. Cerra

The outcome in cardiopulmonary resuscitation (CPR) is related, in part, to the interval between the loss of and the subsequent reestablishment of effective perfusion. Presented here is an outline of CPR technique as recommended for adults by the American Heart Association. A more detailed discussion of individual components is presented in other chapters.

In the intensive care unit (ICU) setting, CPR may be necessary for a variety of people and situations, ranging from an intubated patient on ventilation therapy who is connected to multiple intravenous lines to a visitor in proximity to the ICU who has a cardiac arrest. An approach that can be tailored to this spectrum is presented here.

A. Initial assessment
   1. Verify unconsciousness
   2. Call for help
   3. Position
      a. Extended supine position
      b. If spinal injury suspected, use logroll technique
B. Establishment of airway
   1. No cervical spine injury
      a. Head tilt and neck lift
      b. Head tilt and chin lift
   2. Suspected/actual cervical spine injury
      a. Maintain neck in stabilized, neutral position
      b. Chin lift
      c. Nasal/oral airway may be useful
C. Ventilation
   1. Check for spontaneous breathing
   2. Ventilate

    a. Mouth-to-mouth

       (1) Pinch nose shut

    b. Mouth to nasal

    c. Bag and mask

    d. Esophageal airway

    e. intubation and bag

    f. Cricothyroidotomy and bag

       (1) Needle and jet ventilation

3. Four quick, full breaths in rapid succession to reinflate lungs

4. Obstruction—no endotracheal tube or tracheostomy

    a. Detection

       (1) Unable to ventilate

       (2) Excessive effort to ventilate

       (3) No airflow on passive expiration

       (4) Chest does not rise on ventilation

       (5) No breath sounds on ascultation

    b. Management

       (1) Reposition head

       (2) Back blows—four in succession with heel of hand

       (3) Abdominal thrust, except in late pregnancy or obesity

       (4) Finger sweep

       (5) Laryngoscopy

       (6) Cricothyroidotomy

D. Circulation

  1. Assessment

    a. Presence or absence of carotid pulse

    b. Do not listen for heartbeat

  2. Closed chest compression (see the box on p. 454)

    a. Position patient:

       (1) Supine

       (2) fixed, hard, flat surface

    b. Correct hand placement:

      Heel two fingerbreaths above xiphisternal notch

    c. Compression and timing of ventilation

  3. Open chest

    a. Subject of renewed interest

| Number of rescuers | Ventilation | | Cardiac compression | | | | CVR* |
	Rate	Switch roles	Compressor	Rate	Depth	Switch roles	
Adult/ large child	1	2	After two breaths	Two hands	80/min	1.5-2 in (4-5 cm)	After 15 strokes	15:2
	2	12/min (after every five compressions)	None	Two hands	60/min	1.5-2 in (4-5 cm)	None	5:1

*CVR, compression/ventilation ratio.

    b. Settings of ineffective closed chest techniques
        (1) Fresh median stenotomy
        (2) Chest too stiff, large, or deformed
        (3) Settings where chest already open
E. Arrhythmias
    The complete discussion is presented in the chapter on dysrrhythmias. For brevity, therapy of four common ventricular dysrrhythmias encountered in CPR is outlined. Table 16-1 contains adult dosages of CPR drugs.

Table 16-1. Adult CPR drugs/dosages

Drug	Dosage/route	Comments
Packaged in prefilled syringes containing ampule each		
Sodium bicarbonate	Initial intravenous bolus of 1 mEq/kg, then 0.5 mEq/kg every 10-15 minutes	Do not put in intravenous line with catecholamines or calcium Stop when pH is ≥7.2
Epineprine	0.5-1 mg bolus	Effective intratracheally
Lidocaine	Initial bolus of 1 mg/kg then 2-4 mg/min by continuous infusion	Effective intratracheally
Atropine	0.5-1 mg (5-10 ml) intravenously	Not more than 2 mg total dose
Calcium chloride	0.5 g (½ ampule) intravenously over 1-2 min	Do not put in intravenous line with bicarbonate solutions
Packaged in single-use glass vial		
Procainamide	Give 1000 mg loading dose in 100 mg increments every 5 min, then 1-4 mg/min by continuous intravenous infusion	
Isoproterenol	Add 1 vial (1 mg) to 500 ml of 5% dextrose in water (2 μg/ml). Give as intravenous infusion at a rate of 2-20 μg/min.	Now used primarily for chronotropic effect on heart, until pacemaker can be inserted
Dopamine	Add 1 vial (200 mg) to 500 ml of 5% dextrose in water (400 μg/ml). Give as intravenous infusion at a rate of 2-20 μg/kg/min.	Drug of choice for cardiac inotropic effects

Continued.

Table 16-1. Adult CPR drugs/dosages—cont'd.

Packaged in single-use glass vial—cont'd

Bretylium tosylate	Ventricular fibrillation: 5-10 mg/kg (0.1-0.2 mg/kg) by bolus intravenous injection	Antiarrhythmic agent with minimal negative inotropic effects
	Repeat every 10-15 min until arrhythmia is halted or a total dose of 30 mg/kg is reached	Enhances ability to convert ventricular fibrillation
	Ventricular tachycardia: Dilute 500 mg (10ml) to 50 ml and give 5-10 mg/kg intravenously over 8-10 min, then 1-2 mg/min by continuous infusion.	
Norepinephrine (levarterenol)	Add 2 vials to 1000 ml of 5% dextrose in water (15 μg/ml)	Vasoconstrictor with poor inotropic effect; visceral ischemia common.
	Give as intravenous infusion at an initial rate of 2-10 μg/min	Use only if dopamine or isoproterenol is not available
	Increase as needed	

1. Ventricular asystole
   a. Epinephrine
   b. Atropine
   c. Calcium
   d. Repeat epinephrine and calcium
   e. Isoproterenol
   f. Defibrillation
   g. Pacemaker
   h. Intracardiac epinephrine
2. Ventricular fibrillation
   a. Defibrillation
      (1) Warn everyone so no one is touching patient/bed
      (2) Paddles: aortic and apex position
      (3) 200 to 300 joules DC current, repeat at 400 joules if needed
      (4) Evaluate
      (5) Second attempt, if needed

    b. Refractory to defibrillation
       (1) Correct acidosis and hypoxemia
       (2) Epinephrine and defibrillation
       (3) Other drugs
          (a) Lidocaine
          (b) Bretylium tosylate
          (c) Procainamide
  3. Ventricular tachycardia
    a. Synchronized cardioversion
    b. Lidocaine
    c. Correct acidosis/hypoxemia
    d. Bretylium tosylate
    e. Procainamide
    f. Overdrive transvenous pacemaker
  4. Electromechanical dissociation (profound cardiogenic shock) ECG with relatively normal ventricular complexes with no palpable pulse
    a. Correct acidosis and hypoxemia
    b. Epinephrine, isoproterenol, calcium
    c. Fluid bolus (e.g., 500 ml over 20 min); check for bleeding
    d. Tension pneumothorax-needle thoracostomy
    e. Cardiac tamponade
    f. Consider open chest massage
F. Complications of CPR
  1. Gastric distension
    a. Role to side and compress epigastrium
    b. Nasogastric tube
  2. Pneumothorax
  3. Skeletal trauma
  4. Myocardial contusion/tamponade
  5. Lung contusion
  6. Liver laceration

SELECTED READING

McIntyre, K.M., and Lewis, A.T., eds.: Textbook of advanced cardiac life support, Dallas, American Heart Association.

17

Renal dysfunction

Tom Davin

Acute renal failure, a general term, means that the kidneys cannot clear the blood of waste. It does not imply a specific cause. In general, acute renal failure can be divided into three broad categories: prerenal failure, postrenal failure, and renal failure caused by intrinsic damage to the kidneys. This chapter will review causes, diagnosis, management, and prognosis of these conditions as they relate to the intensive care unit (ICU).

PRERENAL FAILURE

Prerenal failure (prerenal azotemia) occurs when a kidney does not receive sufficient perfusion to maintain an adequate glomerular filtration rate (GFR). Prerenal failure sets the stage for renal parenchymal injury. It is part of a continuum of renal injury that ranges from readily reversible prerenal azotemia through varying degrees of acute tubular necrosis to cortical necrosis.

A. Causes
1. Dehydration/hypovolemia
   a. Vomiting
   b. Ostomy loss
   c. Diarrhea
   d. Nasogastric tube losses
   e. Diuretic use
   f. Fever
   g. Rashes/burns
   h. Surgical: exploration during abdominal surgery
   i. Third-space losses: pancreatitis, ascites, bowel obstruction, ileus
   j. Blood loss

2. Reduced perfusion
   a. Low cardiac output states
   b. Vascular obstruction
      (1) Renal vein thrombosis
      (2) Arterial: stenosis, thrombosis, dissection, embolus
3. Abnormal regulation
   a. Sepsis
   b. Systemic inflammatory states
   c. Cirrhosis
   d. Nephrotic syndrome
   e. Drugs that interfere with renal autoregulation, e.g., prostaglandin synthesis inhibitors in states of decreased renal perfusion and angiotensin-converting enzyme inhibitors in the setting of bilateral renal artery stenosis.
   f. Aggressive antihypertensive or afterload reduction, especially in patients with hypertension.

B. Diagnosis
   1. History
      a. General medical patient
         (1) Vomiting or diarrhea
         (2) Diuretic intake
         (3) Severe congestive heart failure
         (4) History of peripheral vascular disease claudication amputations that suggests arterial disease
         (5) History of liver disease
         (6) Use of drugs that may affect renal perfusion in certain settings, e.g., afterload-reducing agents, angiotensin-converting enzyme inhibitors, prostaglandin synthesis inhibitors.
      b. Postoperative patient (in addition to above)
         (1) Inappropriate weight loss. A patient not receiving parenteral nutrition should lose 0.2 to 0.3 kg/day.
         (2) Unreplaced or inadequately replaced body secretions
   2. Physical examination
      a. Decreased skin turgor assessed in areas least affected by dramatic weight loss (e.g., over sternum or forehead)

  b. Dry mucous membranes, except in mouth-breathing patient
  c. Orthostatic blood pressure changes
    (1) Often studies are difficult to perform.
    (2) Changes may be drug-induced.
    (3) Underlying disease (e.g., diabetes) may cause changes.
  d. Signs of congestive heart failure or low-output state
  e. Abdominal distension and/or ileus or signs of bowel obstruction
  f. Cardiac arrhythmias
  g. Abdominal bruits, decreased peripheral pulses, decreased hair growth on distal legs which suggest generalized arthrosclerosis
3. Laboratory studies
  a. Urinalysis
    (1) Hyaline casts
    (2) Fine granular casts
    (3) No hematuria
    (4) No significant proteinuria
  b. Urinary electrolytes
    (1) Low fractional secretion of sodium (<1) suggestive but not diagnostic. The fractional excretion of sodium may be falsely high with diuretic use or salt-losing nephropathy.
  c. Elevated blood urea nitrogen (BUN)/creatinine ratio
    (1) This generally indicates prerenal origin.
    (2) In settings where the creatinine does not reflect the GFR, this ratio can be misleading (e.g., advanced protein or protein and calorie malnutrition when the creatinine is disproportionately low).
    (3) Advanced prerenal settings can and do cause elevations of the creatinine when the GFR reduction is great enough (e.g., severe dehydration).
4. Hemodynamic testing
  a. Testing helps to differentiate prerenal and renal parenchymal injury, particularly in postoperative patients with pulmonary disease who are on a ventilator with or without positive end-expiratory pressure (PEEP).

    b. Hemodynamic parameters are assessed with pulmonary artery wedge and cardiac output measurements.

    c. In certain circumstances, despite optimal filling pressures and excellent cardiac output, perfusion of visceral organs may be compromised (e.g., states of abnormal regulation).

  5. Radiologic studies

    a. Renal ultrasound is very useful in differentiating prerenal and renal parenchymal damage from postrenal damage. The test is 98% sensitive in detecting hydronephrosis, with a 74% specificity.

    b. Radionuclide imaging can be useful in determining renal perfusion. In patients in whom the arterial blood supply to one or both kidneys is in question, this study provides a noninvasive means of assessing perfusion.

C. Management

  1. The site of renal failure is determined to be prerenal.

  2. The patient's hemodynamic status is optimized.

    a. See "Renal parenchyma."

  3. Fluid and electrolyte imbalance is corrected.

  4. Dialysis is performed if needed. See "Renal parenchyma."

  5. Nutritional support is provided. See "Renal parenchyma."

D. Prognosis

  See "Renal parenchyma."

POSTRENAL FAILURE

Postrenal failure or obstruction occurs when both ureters (in a patient with two kidneys) are blocked.

A. Causes

  1. Prostatic disease

  2. Stones

  3. Pelvic or retroperitoneal malignancy (cervix, colon, ovary, lymphoma)

  4. Trauma with clots obstructing ureters or urethra or retroperitoneal bleeding

  5. Surgical error (e.g., ligation of ureters)

6. Bladder tumor
7. Periureteral fibrosis
8. Papillary necrosis (especially in diabetes, sickle cell disease)
9. Urethral stricture or tumor

B. Diagnosis
1. History
   a. General medical patient
      (1) Kidney stones
      (2) Single kidney
      (3) Pelvic malignancy or lymphoma
      (4) Urinary hesistancy or frequency in older men
      (5) Hematuria
      (6) Flank pain
   b. Postoperative patient (in addition to above)
      (1) Wide fluctuations in urine output
      (2) Complete anuria
2. Physical examination
   a. Large prostate
   b. Pelvic mass
   c. Large bladder
3. Laboratory studies
   a. Urinary electrolytes
      (1) Low fractional excretion of sodium (<1) signifies early obstruction.
      (2) High fractional excretion of sodium (>3) signifies late obstruction.
4. Radiologic studies
   a. The abdominal plain film can detect radiopaque kidney stones.
   b. Renal ultrasound is very useful in ruling out obstruction because it lacks risk and is very sensitive (see p. 461).
   c. Intravenous pyelography is used less frequently since the arrival of ultrasonography and radionuclide imaging and because of the known toxicity of radiocontrast agents. But it still can be of great use, as are retrograde studies, in defining the precise nature and location of obstructive process.

    d. Rarely obstruction is present without dilation or ultrasound because of an infiltrative process or in very early obstruction. In both these instances retrograde pyelography would be necessary to make the diagnosis.

C. Management
1. The patient's fluid status is carefully assessed. Deficit replacement is initiated if patient is dehydrated; fluids are withheld if patient is overloaded.
2. The cause of renal failure is determined to be postrenal.
3. Obstruction is relieved by appropriate means dictated by circumstances.
4. Ongoing fluid and electrolyte losses are carefully replaced unless the patient is fluid-overloaded.
5. Dialysis is performed. See "Renal parenchyma."
6. Nutritional support is provided. See "Renal parenchyma."

D. Prognosis
See "Renal parenchyma."

RENAL PARENCHYMA

Intrinsic or parenchymal renal disease is the widest and most varied category of acute renal failure.

A. Causes
Causes are similar in medical and postoperative settings, although certain diagnoses are much less likely postoperatively. The most common causes of postoperative parenchymal renal disease are starred. Varying degrees of ATN and cortical necrosis can be considered to be more severe manifestations of decreased renal perfusion (see section on renal failure); however, in these conditions endogenous and exogenous nephrotoxins are present as well.

  *1. ATN
A syndrome in which there is temporary loss of kidney function. This loss is not immediately responsive to correction of renal hypoperfusion.
  *2. Allergic interstitial nephritis
An allergic reaction to a drug resulting in renal interstitial inflammation

3. Metabolic derangements
   Hypercalcemia and hyperuricemia
4. Glomerulonephritis and systemic vasculitis
   Usually associated with systemic disease mediated by immune complex deposition in vessel walls. May also occur in response to drugs.
5. Cholesterol emboli
   A syndrome resulting from the release of small fat emboli into the circulation, usually after angiography.
6. Cortical necrosis
   A syndrome in which parts or all of the renal cortex becomes necrotic. This syndrome occurs in settings of severe ischemia, usually associated with a complication of pregnancy or DIC.

B. Diagnosis
   1. History
      a. General medical patient
         (1) Underlying disease associated with glomerulonephritis or vasculitis (e.g., systemic lupus erythematosus, Wegener's granulomatosis, polyarteritis nodosa, Goodpasture's syndrome, recent upper respiratory infection)
         (2) Recent tissue injury known to be associated with renal damage (ATN)
            (a) Hemolysis
            (b) Crush injury with rhabdomyolysis
            (c) Seizures with rhabdomyolysis
            (d) Coma or overdose resulting in prolonged period of immobility associated with rhabdomyolysis
         (3) Recent use of ATN-inducing nephrotoxic drugs (e.g., aminoglycosides, cyclosporin A, cisplatin, some fluorinated anesthetic agents, amphotericin B, tetracyclines)
         (4) Contrast studies in susceptible individuals
            (a) Diabetics with renal insufficiency
            (b) Patients with preexisting renal disease of any cause

      (c) Susceptible patients receiving repeated contrast studies at short intervals

      (d) Dehydrated patients

      (e) Patients with multiple myeloma

  (5) Recent angiography in patients with arthrosclerosis (cholesterol emboli)

      (a) The effect of these cholesterol or fat emboli on renal function can be delayed for several weeks.

  (6) Recent use of drugs known to be associated with interstitial nephritis (e.g., penicillins, cephalosporins, cimetidine, nonsteroidals, and many more)

  (7) Recent episode of hypotension

  (8) Exposure to organic solvents (glycols, hydrocarbons)

  (9) Heavy metal exposure

  (10) Recent episode of decreased renal perfusion even without overt hypotension

  (11) Recent use of drugs known to decrease renal perfusion under certain circumstances (e.g., captopril, nonsteroidal antiinflammatory drugs)

  (12) ATN is especially likely when there are both ischemic and nephrotoxic insults

b. Postoperative patient

The historical antecedents of parenchymal renal failure are the same as those in the medical patient. However, in most cases of postoperative renal failure, a single cause is not demonstrable. Typical contributing factors are:

  (1) Hypotension

  (2) Sepsis

  (3) Tissue necrosis

  (4) Use of nephrotoxic antibiotics

  (5) Recent trauma or surgery that might have led to an anastomotic leak or abscess formation with or without factors (1) through (4) above

2. Physical examination
   a. ATN
      (1) Oliguria
      (2) Presence of ischemic or necrotic tissue
      (3) Very rarely, anuria in severe ATN or cortical necrosis
   b. Allergic interstitial nephritis
      (1) Skin rash
   c. Cholesterol emboli
      (1) Abdominal bruits
      (2) Peripheral emboli
   d. Rhabdomyolysis
      (1) Muscle swelling or tenderness
      (2) Ischemic limb
   e. Glomerulonephritis or systemic vasculitis
      (1) Skin rash
      (2) Arthritis
      (3) Pleural or pericardial rub
3. Laboratory studies
   a. Urinalysis
      (1) ATN—distinctive urinalysis
         (a) Dirty brown, pigmented, coarse granular casts
         (b) Renal tubular cells and renal tubular cell casts
      (2) Allergic interstitial nephritis
         (a) White cell casts
         (b) White cells
         (c) Proteinuria (usually not in the nephrotic range)
         (d) Occasional hematuria
         (e) Rarely, red blood cell casts
      (3) Acute glomerulonephritis
         (a) Red cell casts
         (b) Hematuria
         (c) High-grade proteinuria
   b. Urinary electrolytes
      (1) High fractional secretion of sodium (>3) is suggestive but not diagnostic of ATN.

        (2) Low fractional excretion of sodium (<1) suggests prerenal azotemia.

        (3) Low FENA also occurs in glomerulonephritis during early obstruction, in contrast-induced nephropathy, and in some cases of less severe ATN with concomitant sodium-retaining state (e.g., liver failure, sepsis, dehydration).

    c. Wright's stain for eosinophils

        (1) Presence in urine suggests allergic interstitial nephritis.

        (2) Presence in serum suggests allergic interstitial nephritis or cholesterol emboli.

    d. Urine dipstick

        (1) Positive for hemoglobin in the absence of red cells suggests rhabdomyolysis.

    e. Serologic testing

        (1) Serologic testing is suggested in cases where systemic vasculitis or immune-mediated glomerulonephritis is suspected, depending on circumstances. Serum complement, antinuclear antibody, and Australia antigen may all be useful in making the diagnosis.

  4. Hemodynamic testing (renal parenchyma)

    a. See "Prerenal failure."

  5. Radiologic testing

    a. For renal ultrasound, see "Prerenal failure."

    b. Radiologic study to look for is intraabdominal catastrophy (e.g., abcess, anastomotic leak). CT scan, indium scan, gastrointestinal (GI) contrast studies can all be of use.

C. Management

  1. The cause of renal failure is determined to be renal parenchyma.

  2. The patient's hemodynamic status is optimized.

    a. Even in patients clinically suspected of having ATN, the filling pressures should be brought up to an optimal range on the basis of clinical findings and hemodynamic monitoring. This can usually be accomplished within a matter of hours. Even if hemodynamic parameters seem adequate a trial of fluid is often warranted.

b. If improvement is not dramatic after optimization of hemodynamic status, mannitol or furosemide can be tried to improve renal function.

(1) Both mannitol and furosemide may dilate renal arterioles and increase solute clearance.

(2) Either or both of these drugs might help changes in renal blood flow distribution and tubular obstruction.

(3) Many nephrologists believe that mannitol or furosemide given shortly after the onset of acute renal failure or prior to the insult in patients perceived to be at high risk may change the course of the illness.

(4) If the patient does not respond to an optimization of hemodynamic status, 12.5 to 25 g of mannitol is given intravenously. If the patient responds, a 20% mannitol drip can be started.

(5) If no response occurs to the initial dose of mannitol, it should be stopped to avoid fluid overload.

(6) If no response to mannitol occurs, furosemide can be given in increasing doses up to a dose of 300 to 400 mg.

(7) If still no response occurs, metolazone (Zaroxolyn) can be given (5 to 10 mg orally)

(8) If a response to furosemide occurs, a furosemide or furosemide/mannitol drip can be used (e.g., 250 ml of D5W, 200 mg of furosemide, and 12.5 g of mannitol).

(9) However, if continuous very high doses of mannitol or furosemide are required to maintain urine output, persistent administration of either of these drugs is probably not warranted.

(10) Fig. 17-1 presents a summary of this approach.

(11) If the patient is fluid overloaded, furosemide should be used in preference to mannitol because the mannitol can worsen the fluid overload.

(12) Even though renal function may not improve with mannitol or furosemide, increasing urine output may be advantageous in the fluid and nutritional management of ICU patients.

3. Fluid and electrolyte management
   a. Salt and water overload
      (1) Total body salt and water overload are common in acute renal failure.
      (2) In a patient who is already salt- and water-overloaded when the diagnosis of acute renal failure (ARF) is made, the appropriate conservative treatment is salt and water restriction and diuretic use.
      (3) Hyponatremia, which often accompanies salt and water overload in acute renal failure, is a dilutional hyponatremia caused by more water than sodium.

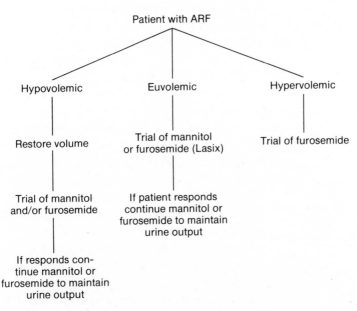

Fig. 17-1. Management strategies in ARF.

b. Volume depletion
  (1) In patients who are volume depleted when diagnosed, normal saline or appropriate volume expander should be given until the volume status is judged normal.
c. Normovolemia
  (1) In the normovolemic patient, fluid and electrolyte salt and water requirement should be based on the patient's obligatory salt and water losses, which can be quite variable.
  (2) In acute renal failure without oliguria, salt and water requirements may be quite large.
  (3) In oliguric acute renal failure, severely restricting the patient's intake of both salt and water may be necessary.
  (4) The general rule is that the patient judged normovolemic with total body salt and water stores judged as normal should receive ongoing loss plus insensible loss.
  (5) Measuring the concentration of sodium in body fluid secretion is often helpful, since appropriate replacement fluid can then be chosen.
d. Hyperkalemia and acidosis
  (1) The normal kidneys excrete approximately 1 mEq/kg of acid per day.
    (a) In acute renal failure, this function of the kidneys is severely compromised. Thus patients with acute renal failure generally develop a metabolic acidosis.
  (2) Acidosis can be treated with sodium bicarbonate in patients who are not salt and water overloaded.
  (3) The kidneys are also the primary regulators of potassium balance.
    (a) In oliguric acute renal failure, hyperkalemia is often a problem, the extent of which usually depends on the degree of oliguria, the rate of potassium administration, and the rate of the body's potassium production.

(4) Severely catabolic patients, patients with severe acidosis, and patients who are absorbing blood from the gastrointestinal tract or other body spaces may develop high levels of potassium.

(5) In acute renal failure, potassium intake must almost always be restricted.

(6) Frequent monitoring of the serum potassium level and acid-base status is essential.

(7) Mild hyperkalemia can be treated by correcting metabolic acidosis with sodium bicarbonate and administering sodium polystyrene sulfonate (Kayexalate), a cation exchange resin.

   (a) The dose of Kayexalate is usually 1 g/kg.

   (b) Because Kayexalate is an ion exchange resin, reduction in potassium is associated with positive sodium balance.

   (c) Because Kayexalate tends to be constipating, it is usually given with sorbitol.

   (d) A common dose of Kayexalate is 50 g Kayexalate with 100 or 200 ml of 20% sorbitol given orally or 50 g of Kayexalate and 200 ml of 20% sorbitol given rectally as a retention enema.

(8) In moderate hyperkalemia, when it is necessary to bring the potassium concentration down more rapidly, the above measures are also recommended.

   (a) In addition, the infusion of glucose and insulin will cause cellular uptake of potassium. Close monitoring of blood sugar is necessary.

   (b) Numerous protocols for the administration of glucose and insulin have been devised (e.g., 250 ml of 20% glucose with 10 to 15 units of regular insulin).

   (c) If a central line is being used, the glucose can be administered as a 50% solution, thus reducing the fluid volume.

(9) In severe hyperkalemia with electrocardiogram (ECG) changes, in addition to other measures, calcium gluconate or calcium chloride should be infused under ECG monitoring.

(10) When the above measures are required in the setting of acute renal failure, dialysis is usually indicated.

4. Dialysis is instituted when indicated.

   a. Indications for dialysis

The five basic indications for dialysis in acute renal failure are hyperkalemia, acidosis, congestive failure, uremia, and fluid overload. Most people start dialysis in acute renal failure when the serum creatinine reaches 8 to 10 and BUN reaches approximately 100. Once begun, dialysis is continued on a regular basis until renal function spontaneously improves. Dialyzing from crisis to crisis or waiting until the patient absolutely needs dialysis is unwise. Early and frequent dialysis probably decreases the mortality of acute renal failure.

(1) Hyperkalemia usually occurs in patients who are oliguric and/or have considerable cell breakdown. The latter occurs in:

(a) Patients with leukemia and lymphoma who are treated with chemotherapy

(b) Catabolic patients

(c) Patients who are bleeding and reabsorbing a large amount of blood from the GI tract or other body spaces

   i. Hyperkalemia is the most urgent indication for dialysis because of its effect on cardiac conduction.

   ii. In the settings of renal failure dialysis is usually indicated for a potassium of greater than 6. Rapidity of rise of potassium is a critical factor in deciding to dialyze. A rapidly rising serum potassium in a patient with acute renal failure is an urgent indication for dialysis (see "Rapidity of change").

(2) Acidosis

Acidosis per se is a rare indication for acute dialysis. However, when acidosis is associated with fluid overload, it can be a particularly difficult problem. Correction of the condition with sodium bicarbonate is difficult because of the sodium load.

(3) Combined hyperkalemia, acidosis, and congestive heart failure usually necessitate acute dialysis.

(a) For example, most physicians would initiate dialysis in an oliguric patient with a serum creatinine of 7, a potassium of 5.5, moderate acidosis, and a mild congestive heart failure, though all of these could perhaps be managed conservatively.

(4) Rapidity of change

The rapidity of change of one or more of the above factors also influences the need for dialysis, as noted above.

(a) For example, an oliguric patient whose serum potassium rises rapidly from 4 to 6 in 4 hours should be dialyzed even though the serum potassium is not extremely high.

(b) In this case, the rapidity of increase in serum potassium and the presence of renal failure make it likely that conservative medical management will not suffice in controlling the serum potassium.

(5) Uremic pericarditis

A fairly rare indication for dialysis in acute patients is the onset of uremic pericarditis.

(a) When this complication occurs in a patient with acute renal failure, it is an indication for dialysis and will usually respond to dialysis treatment.

b. Duration and frequency

The needs of the patient dictate the duration and frequency of hemodialysis treatments.

(1) Very catabolic patients or patients with large intravenous fluid requirements should be dialyzed more frequently.

(2) Some require daily hemodialysis.

(3) Limiting fluid deficits on each dialysis to 1 to 2 kg is advisable. However, considerably more may be removed if necessary.

c. Determining the type of dialysis

(1) *Peritoneal dialysis* uses large surface area of intraperitoneal organs as exchange membrane.

(a) Treatment

   i. Administer 2 L of peritoneal dialysis solution (similar to Ringer's lactate) 1.5% up to 4.25% glucose with high or low K^+ concentration ranging from 0 to 4 mEq/L plus 1000 units of heparin per bottle

   ii. Dwell time, duration, and volume of exchange vary with need.

(b) If Tenckhoff catheter and closed system of dialysis delivery are used, the peritoneal dialysis can be continued for long periods. Consultation with a nephrologist is desirable.

(c) Advantages

   i. Ability to remove large volumes of fluid with greater hemodynamic stability

   ii. Less equipment and personnel

   iii. No problem with vascular access, but peritoneal catheter placement needed

   iv. Catheter placement should be done by an experienced surgeon or nephrologist.

d. Disadvantages

(1) Removes solutes less well than hemodialysis (can be a disadvantage in catabolic states such as sepsis)

(2) Risk of peritonitis (reduced with Tenckhoff catheter and sterile delivery system)

      (3) Risk of spreading existing peritonitis

      (4) Hyperglycemia, bleeding, pain, diaphragmatic compression, protein loss, hypernatremia

2. Hemodialysis

Hemodialysis uses twin-coil cuprophan, hollow fiber cellulose or cuprophan, or sheet plate cuprophan kidney with roller pump. Duration of run, blood pump speed, type of membrane, and membrane surface area determine solute clearance. Ultrafiltration pressure, type of membrane, and surface area determine water loss.

  a. Advantages

      (1) Rapid clearance of solutes

  b. Disadvantages

      (1) Hypotension (treated with plasmanate saline or pressors)

      (2) Muscle cramps (treated with mannitol or hypertonic saline)

      (3) Seizures from disequilibrium (D/C run and treat with diazepam, administration of hypertonic saline)

      (4) Arrhythmias

      (5) Use of high sodium (140 mEq/L) and bicarbonate instead of acetate bath may lessen the frequency of these problems.

3. Circumstances often dictate the kind of dialysis to use.

  a. Again, the very sick catabolic patient with rapidly rising BUN, creatinine, and potassium, together with rapidly developing acidosis, is usually best dialyzed by frequent hemodialysis, because this method is the most efficient.

  b. Postoperative patients who cannot be hemodialyzed because of unstable hemodynamic status may be peritoneally dialyzed quite effectively.

      (1) The physician should always consider this option in these patients.

      (2) The cardiovascularly unstable patient whose peritoneal cavity has not been violated is an especially good candidate.

      (3) However, even the patient who has had abdominal surgery can receive peritoneal dialysis postoperatively if circumstances dictate.

  c. Recently, continuous arteriovenous hemofiltration has also been used in critically ill patients with unstable cardiovascular system.

4. Nutritional support

One of the main clinical consequences of acute renal failure is anorexia and nausea. Even if patients are not so critically ill that they cannot eat, they are often sufficiently anorectic that eating is impaired. Nutritional support is usually necessary because the average duration (see below) of acute renal failure is 2 to 3 weeks, the major complication of acute renal failure is infection, and most of these patients are recovering from major illnesses.

  a. Nutritional support should be instituted early in postoperative acute renal failure because theoretical benefits are multiple.

    (1) The protein and calorie malnutrition that would otherwise develop in the 2 to 3 week period may be avoided.

    (2) Healing and recovery from infections may be enhanced.

    (3) Management of potassium and phosphorus levels, a common problem in acute renal failure, is made easier. This benefit occurs because of the utilization of both potassium and phosphorus in maintenance of cellular mass.

  b. Parenteral nutrition is administered in acute renal failure in much the same way as in other postoperative patients with a few exceptions.

    (1) The usual percentages of glucose and amino acids are used in most cases of acute renal failure.

    (2) Both nonessential and essential amino acids are used.

    (3) In patients in whom fluid restriction is particu-

larly important, a higher concentration of glucose and amino acids is used to provide less volume.

(4) The extracellular fluid needs of the patient dictate the concentration of sodium and chloride in the fluid; i.e., if the patient's ongoing losses are primarily one-third normal saline, the hyperalimentation solution should be approximately one-third normal saline. Of course, serum sodium concentration should be followed and the electrolyte content of the fluid adjusted accordingly.

(5) Acetate should usually be added to hyperalimentation solution in patients with acute renal failure because of the acidosis associated with acute renal failure.

(6) Calcium should be added in the usual amounts in patients in whom the calcium phosphorus product is not excessive.

(7) Phosphorus and potassium should be deleted initially but added incrementally as the patient becomes anabolic. This is usually necessary to avoid clinically significant hypokalemia and hypophosphatemia.

c. Water-soluble vitamins are dialyzed off and should be added per the usual hyperalimentation prescription.

d. The needs for trace elements in patients with acute renal failure are not defined.

e. The effects of hyperalimentation on BUN rise is variable. Tolerating high levels of BUN in patients on hyperalimentation is advisable in hopes that the ill effects associated with this are offset by the improved nutritional status of the patients.

f. In patients with acute renal failure as in other patients requiring nutritional support, the enteral route should be used whenever possible. This use obviates the hazards of parenteral nutrition.

      (1) Choosing a particular type of enteral feeding involves two important considerations:

        (a) The potassium content of the formula.

        (b) In patients in whom fluid allowances are low, the number of calories per milliliter.

  6. Careful search for underlying cause of acute renal failure is undertaken.

    a. Nephrotoxic drugs are eliminated if possible.

    b. Septicemia is treated.

    c. Careful search is made for surgically correctable sources of infection (see "Prognosis").

  7. Careful attention is paid to potential infectious complications of treatment (see "Prognosis").

PROGNOSIS IN PATIENTS WITH ACUTE RENAL FAILURE

The diagnosis of acute renal failure in a postoperative patient has been associated with a very high mortality (as high as 80%). This continues to be the case despite advances in the techniques of dialysis as well as general improvement in intensive care techniques.

A. The reasons for the failure of improvements in this area over the past 20 years are not completely understood.

  1. The failure may be related to an increased willingness to take on very severely ill patients.

  2. Occurrence of acute renal failure in the postoperative period usually indicates the presence of a complication of major proportions in addition to the acute renal failure.

B. The experience at the University of Minnesota shows that those who die in acute renal failure tend to do so quickly.

  1. Median time to death after the first dialysis in a series of patients dialyzed for acute renal failure was 5 days.

  2. Patients who recovered renal function did so in a median time of 12 days after the first dialysis.

  3. By 1 month after initiation of dialysis for acute renal failure, 92% of patients in that series had either died or recovered renal function.

C. Most patients who survive acute renal failure recover their renal function.

  1. A very small number are left on chronic dialysis.

2. Many are left with renal impairment of some kind, including moderate decreases in creatinine clearance and renal-concentrating defects.

3. Most patients, however, seem to recover with insigificant renal impairment.

D. Infectious complications are the most common cause of death in acute renal failure. Although all critically ill patients who have a host of invasive procedures are subject to a variety of nosocomial infections, patients with acute renal failure should be watched especially carefully for signs of catheter-associated sepsis, pneumonia, wound infections, and other infections.

1. All unnecessary lines should be removed. A Foley catheter, for example, should be removed early in oliguric renal failure once monitoring the responses to various early treatment modalities is no longer necessary.

E. In the postoperative patient, an aggressive approach to potentially surgically correctable complications causing the acute renal failure is warranted. An anastomotic leak or intraabdominal abscess can cause renal failure with or without signs of systemic infection. In acute postoperative renal failure, intraabdominal infection should be considered.

F. As previously noted, early and frequent dialysis and nutritional support are additional measures that may reduce the high morbidity and mortality associated with postoperative acute renal failure.

SELECTED READINGS

Appel, G.B., and Neu H.C.: Nephrotoxicity of antimicrobial agents, N. Engl. J. Med. **296**:663, 772, 784, 1977.

Bennett, W.M., et al.: Guidelines for drug therapy in renal failure, Ann. Intern. Med. **86**:754, 1977.

Brenner, B.M., and Stein, J.H. (editors): Contemporary issues in nephrology, vol 6, Acute renal failure, New York, 1980, Churchill Livingstone.

Brenner, B.M., and Rector, F.C., (editors): The kidney, Philadelphia, 1986, W.B. Saunders Co.

Kjellstrand, C., et al.: Acute renal failure. In Drukker, W., Parson, F.M., Maher, J.F., (editors): Acute renal failure, The Hague, The Netherlands, 1982, Martinus Nijhoff.

Rasmussen, H.H., and Ibels: Acute renal failure: multivariable analysis of risk factors, AM. J. Med. **73**:211-218, 1982.

Schrier, R.W., Acute renal failure: Pathogenesis, diagnosis, and management, Hosp Pract., pp. 93-112, 1981.

18

Hepatic dysfunction

Frank B. Cerra

A primary attribute of the liver in the intensive care unit is its functional reserve. The underlying pathology is important primarily because it affects the functional reserve and is treatable so as to allow an increase in the functional reserve to a level that allows survival. The involvement of the liver may be primary or secondary.

A. Assessment of functional reserve

   1. Child-Stone classification

Criteria	Class A	B	C
Bilirubin (mg percent)	<2.0	2.0-3.0	>3.0
Albumin (g percent)	>3.5	3.0-3.5	<3.0
Ascites	None	Easy to control	Poor control
Encephalopathy	None	Mild	Severe
Nutrition status	Excellent	Good	Poor
Drug clearance	Normal	Some limit	Severe limit
Surgical risk	Normal	Some increase	High
Regenerative capacity	Normal	Some	Little

   2. Pugh point system: <6, good; 7-9, moderate; >10, poor

Criteria	Points		
	1	2	3
Encephalopathy grade	None	1,2	3,4
Ascites	None	Some	A lot
Bilirubin (mg percent)	1-2	2-3	>3
Albumin (g percent)	3.5	2.8-3.5	<2.8
Prothrombin time (seconds prolonged)	1-4	4-6	>6

3. Wirthlin classification
   a. 5-point system—1 each for: bilirubin >2 mg percent; albumin <3 g percent; prothrombin time over 16 sec; presence of encephalopathy; presence of history of varices
   b. Mortality risk:

   $$\% \text{ Mortality risk} = 23 \times \text{Points} + 13$$

4. The criteria that hold up in most clinical settings are ascites, elevated bilirubin, and encephalopathy. Quantitation with mortality is not precise.
   a. For these reasons, new tests are being developed. One of the most promising is amino acid clearance.
      (1) It correlates well with mortality risk in liver transplantation, in patients with cirrhosis who are undergoing surgical procedures, and in multiple-systems organ failure (MSOF).
      (2) Precise methodologies and confirmatory data will be forthcoming.

5. Limitations
   a. These classifications tend to be disease specific and primarily apply to cirrhosis.
   b. The best single preoperative predictor of mortality is the bilirubin.
   c. The enzyme liver function tests are poor predictors of hepatic function reserve.

6. In alcoholic hepatitis, the predictors of mortality are:
   a. Encephalopathy
   b. Ascites
   c. Jaundice (bilirubin >13 mg percent)
   d. Fever
   e. Classic Mallory bodies or biopsy

B. Viral hepatitis
   Agents include: A, B, non A–non B, EB_1, cytomegalovirus (CMV), and herpes.

Type	Incubation	Body fluid	Spread	Serology	Carrier	Chronic
A	2-6 wk	Stool	Fecal/oral	Acute: IgM anti-HA		
				Chronic: IgG anti-HA	Neg	Neg
B	6-24 wk	Blood Saliva Semen	Close contact	Acute: HB$_s$Ag anti-HB$_C$ Chronic: anti-HB$_s$Ag	10%	2%-3%
Non A– non B	6-24 wk	Blood	Close contact	Neg	Yes	2%-20%

C. Ischemic hepatitis
  1. Occurs after an episode of hypoxia or reduced hepatic perfusion with restoration of oxygenated blood flow
  2. May represent a reperfusion injury in a setting of subcellular ischemic injury
  3. May mimic infectious hepatitis: fever, anoxeria, malaise, jaundice, tender hepatomegaly
      a. Marked elevation serum glutamic oxaloacetic transaminase (SGOT) with little change in alkaline phosphatase
      b. SGOT leak seems to correlate with low adenosine triphosphate (ATP) levels and reduced capacity to regenerate adenosine monophophate (AMP)
  4. Frequently followed by a period of cholestasis
D. Cholestasis
  1. Elevated bilirubin, alkaline phosphatase, GGT, and bile acids
  2. Extrahepatic ductal
      a. Choledocholithiasis
      b. Pancreatic cancer
      c. Cholangiocarcinoma
      d. Ampulla of Vater carcinoma, tumors of the portal, hepatitis
      e. Common duct obstruction other than stones (bile duct stricture, papillary stenosis, pancreatic pseudocysts, sclerosis, cholangitis)

      f. Bowel rest

      g. Bowel rest with total parenteral nutrition (TPN)

  3. Intrahepatic ductal

      a. Focal abscess, carcinoma, cysts, parasites

      b. Intrahepatic biliary atresia

      c. Suppurative and nonsuppurative cholangitis

         (1) Bacterial

         (2) Immunologic (primary biliary cirrhosis, inflammatory bowel disease)

  4. Intrahepatic nonductal

      a. Virus

      b. Alcohol

      c. Drugs

      d. Sepsis/MSOF

      e. TPN

      f. Recurrent jaundice of pregnancy

      g. Postoperative cholestasis

      h. Ischemia

E. Cirrhosis

  1. Known etiologic agents or factors

      a. Alcohol

      b. Primary biliary cirrhosis

      c. Hemochromatosis

      d. Sarcoidosis

      e. Chlorpromazine

      f. Shistosomiasis

      g. Chronic active hepatitis

         (1) Viral

         (2) Autoimmune

         (3) Drug-induced

         (4) Wilson's disease

         (5) $Alpha_1$-antitrypsin deficiency

         (6) Postnecrotic

         (7) Cardiac

  2. Coagulopathy

      a. Present 85% of the time

      b. Results from:

         (1) Failure of factor production

         (2) Increased factor use

      (3) Production of abnormal factors

      (4) Platelet dysfunction

  3. Classification: as discussed

F. Portal hypertension

  1. Although cirrhosis is the most common cause, a differential must also be considered

    a. Pancreatitis

    b. Splenic vein occlusion

    c. Portal vein occlusion

      (1) Ideopathic

      (2) Pylephlebitis

      (3) Postvariceal sclerosis

      (4) Hypercoagulopathies

    d. Cirrhosis

    e. Budd-Chiari syndrome

    f. Cardiac

      (1) Pericarditis

      (2) Myocardopathies

      (3) Valve disease

    g. Atrioventricular (AV) fistula

      (1) Postneedle biopsy

      (2) Postinfectious/inflammatory

      (3) Posttraumatic

  2. Presentation

    a. Bleeding

      (1) Ulcer—duodenal, stress

      (2) Variceal

        (a) Esophageal   (d) Small bowel

        (b) Gastric   (e) Colon

        (c) Duodenal   (f) Hemorrhoids

    b. Ascites

    c. Renal failure

    d. Signs and symptoms of liver failure

    e. Altered abdominal venous drainage pattern; signs of caval obstruction in lower extremities

    f. Coagulopathy

    g. Splenomegaly

  3. Diagnosis

    a. Endoscopic demonstration of varices; congenital varices rare

    b. Elevated portal pressure measurement
      (1) Hepatic wedge measurement
      (2) Percutaneous portal pressure measurement
      (3) Splenoportography
    c. Direct surgical observation/measurement
    d. Contrast study
      (1) Splenoportography (historical)
      (2) Splenic anteriogram with venous phase study
      (3) Percutaneous portal venogram
      (4) Contrast gastrointestinal study

4. Treatment
    a. Indications
      (1) Documented bleeding episode(s)
      (2) Rarely, coagulopathy
    b. Active bleeding
      (1) Sclerosis
      (2) Balloon tamponade; follow package instructions carefully
      (3) Vasopressin
        (a) Peripheral administration
          i. 0.1-0.6 U/min
          ii. More complications
          iii. Higher doses required
          iv. Skin slough can occur
        (b) Selective splenic artery injection
          i. Lower dose
          ii. 0.1 to 0.4 U/min
          iii. Fewer complications, if selective; can reduce hepatic blood flow if not selective
    c. Complications of vasopressin
      (1) Water retention; pulmonary edema
      (2) Moderate to severe bradycardia
      (3) Arrhythmias
      (4) Myocardial ischemia
      (5) Hypertension
    d. Minimizing complications of vasopressin
      (1) Selective administration

       (2) Nitrate vasodilators

          (a) Do not seem to override the visceral reduction in blood flow.

          (b) Nitropaste; nitroglycerine drip

       (3) Strict intake and output, weights, and liberal use of diuretics

       (4) Microdose of isoproterenol; 0.25 to 0.75 μg/min in average-sized adult

5. Surgery

   a. Splenic vein thrombosis; splenectomy

   b. Decompression to systemic circuit

       (1) Angiographic demonstration of anatomy should be done.

       (2) Shunt surgery

          (a) All types seem to get encephalopathy eventually.

          (b) All types seem to control bleeding.

          (c) Childs A and B; only very selected C.

          (d) Results probably better if done several weeks after bleeding stopped and good medical and nutritional control obtained.

          (e) Full monitoring usually necessary.

          (f) Longevity probably improved.

          (g) Cost per occurrence high; when viewed against recurrent bleeding admissions, probably less.

   c. Decompression of tense ascites

   d. Percutaneous transhepatic embolization can be done when all else fails and surgery is not the next choice.

6. Medical vs. surgical considerations

   a. Surgical decompression does control bleeding.

       (1) Encephalopathy may result.

       (2) Long-term survival seems improved in the combined American data.

          (a) $P < 0.05$ at 3, 4, and 5 years

          (b) 30% versus 50% at 5 years

       (3) The type of shunt appears to make little difference in survival and incidence of encephalopathy and therefore becomes a matter of technical preference.

b. Medical therapy usually costs time and transfusion. This can and does result in reduced hepatic blood flow, a prime precipitating factor in hepatic decompensation.

    (1) At some point (e.g., 10 to 15 units acutely), a decision about surgery must be made.

c. Beta blocker therapy for acute control seems to offer no advantages.

d. Sclerotherapy can stop bleeding and be a useful adjunct in acute control.

    (1) The rebleeding rate is high.

    (2) It may offer a useful alternative in Childs C-type patients or those with low amino acid clearance.

    (3) Close communication between endoscopic and surgical services is usually in the best interest of the patient in these settings.

G. Ascites of liver disease

  1. Although cirrhosis is the most common cause, a differential must be considered

    a. Portal hypertension differential as discussed

    b. Pancreatic

    c. Primary peritonitis

    d. Infectious peritonitis

    e. Tumor, primary or secondary

    f. Bleeding

    g. Chyle

    h. Uremia

  2. Diagnosis

    a. Confirm by tap or sonography

    b. Diagnostic tap, under vision or sonography if needed; correct coagulopathy first

      (1) Gram stain

      (2) Culture

      (3) Cytology

      (4) White count and morphology

      (5) Amylase

      (6) Albumin, urea, creatinine, pH, and lactic acid dehydrogenase (LDH).

3. Complications
    a. Hypovolemia
    b. Renal failure
    c. Respiratory dysfunction
        (1) Mechanical, diaphragm compression.
        (2) May have associated plural effusions.
        (3) Taps are usually temperizing, but can improve ventilatory function.
    d. Portal hypertension
        (1) With variceal bleeding, tapping tense ascites can reduce portal pressure.
    e. Infection
    f. Malnutrition
    g. Hernias
4. Management
    a. Paracentesis
        (1) Temporary
        (2) Removal of too much (variable) can precipitate liver failure and renal failure
    b. Medical management
        (1) Bed rest
        (2) Salt restriction (1 to 2 g sodium)
        (3) Diuresis, especially if urine electrolytes show Na <10 mEq/L and K >50 mEq/L
            (a) Spironolactonic; adjust dose to correct urine electrolytes.
            (b) Occasionally, patients will respond to doses of 400 to 800 mg/day.
            (c) Avoid loop diuretics if at all possible until one is prepared to monitor and maintain blood volume.
            (d) Liver/renal failure can occur precipitously, particularly if hypovolemia occurs.
            (e) Supplemental volume expanders are sometimes helpful.
        (4) Good nutrition; takes 3 to 6 weeks for any effect
5. Surgical
    a. Peritoneovenous shunt

(1) Indications
  (a) Failure of medical therapy
  (b) Renal insufficiency of the underperfused type:
    i. Hypovolemia
    ii. Oliguria
    iii. Low urine Na (<10 to 15 mg/L)
b. Complications
  (1) Failure of shunt
    (a) Usually mechanical
    (b) Rarely, poor myocardial function; inspiratory exercises can improve this
  (2) Pulmonary edema can be minimized by emptying ascites prior to opening shunt
  (3) Infection; remove shunt
  (4) Postshunt coagulopathy
    (a) Seems to result from plasminogen in ascitic fluid
    (b) Minimized by draining ascites before opening shunt
    (c) Treat with coagulation factors and epsilon-aminocaproic acid
    (d) If severe, occlude shunt. Current recommendation is to then wait for fibrinogen to rise. When normal, irrigate peritoneal cavity with saline and reopen shunt.
c. Rarely, side-to-side portocaval shunt is indicated for ascites control. There seems to be no role for this indication in an SICU patient.

H. Renal failure
  1. As a manifestation of hypovolemia, renal failure is preventable and treatable if recognized and therapy is started.
    a. Signs and symptoms
      (1) Oliguria
      (2) Low renal plasma flow
      (3) Low urine sodium <10 to 15 mg/L
      (4) Hypovolemia
    b. Therapy requires volume
      (1) Central monitoring usually is necessary during the acute phase.

(2) See "Peritoneovenous shunt." Earlier, more aggressive use may be indicated in the presence of ascites.

2. As a manifestation of nonhypovolemic liver failure, ATN with liver failure, or as part of MSOF, renal failure usually heralds a fatal outcome (>95%).

   a. The decision to dialyse needs to be carefully discussed.

I. Hepatic encephalopathy

1. A clinical syndrome of altered consciousness reflecting the systemic effects of hepatocellular dysfunction (Fig. 18-1).

   a. 20%-40% mortality in cirrhosis; 90%-100% mortality with the liver failure of late MSOF.

   b. Staging of encephalopathy

Grade	Characteristic
0	No encephalopathy
1	Psychomotor abnormalities, agitation, fluctuant confusion
2	Impending stupor
3	Stupor
4	Coma, unresponsive to pain

2. Etiology (usually multifactorial)

   a. Perfusion disorders

      (1) Reduced blood flow

         (a) Hypovolemia, paracentesis, aggressive diuresis

         (b) Thrombosis, reduced cardiac output

      (2) Reduced oxygen delivery

         (a) Hypoxemia, anemia

   b. Overload of toxic substances

      (1) Drugs—tranquilizers, sedatives, alcohol

      (2) Ammonia-producing compounds

      (3) Excess protein administration or ingestion

      (4) Stress response of surgery, trauma, sepsis

   c. Metabolic imbalances

      (1) Electrolyte—Na, K

      (2) Acid-base

      (3) Progression of disease

3. Difficult to separate chemical abnormalities of hepatocellular dysfunction from their systemic effects
   a. Energy expenditure usually 1.5 times resting
   b. Hyperdynamic
   c. Reduced amino acid clearance, particularly for aromatic amino acids, methionine, threonine

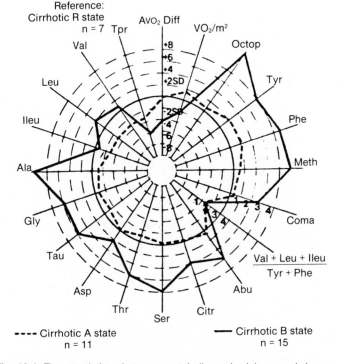

Fig. 18-1. The correlations between metabolism, physiology, and degree of encephalopathy are quite close, as seen in this diagram. The solid inner circle represents the mean value for each variable from nonstressed, nonencephalopathic cirrhotic patients. Each dotted line is 2 standard deviations from that mean. Plotted are the mean values from a large group of cirrhotic patients with early (A-state) and late (B-state) encephalopathy. *Octop* = Octopamine; *Asp* = Aspartate; *Tyr* = Tyrosine; *Tau* = Taurine; Phe = Phenylalanine; *Gly* = Glycine; Meth = Methionine; Ala = Alanine; *Abu* = aminobutyric acid; *Ileu* = Isoleucine; *Citr* = Citrulline; *Leu* = Leucine; *Ser* = Serine; *Val* = Valine; *Thr* = Threonine; *Tpr* = Systemic vascular resistance, AVo_2 = Arteriovenous oxygen content difference; VO_2/m^2 = oxygen consumption index. (From Siegel, J.H., et al.: Arch. Surg. **117**:225, Feb. 1982. Copyright 1982, American Medical Association.)

  d. Toxic compounds

   (1) Ammonia—levels correlate poorly with encephalopathy

   (2) Fatty acids, mercaptins, PgE abnormalities; precise roles are uncertain

 4. Diagnosis (Fig. 18-2)

  a. Clinical setting

  b. Spinal fluid glutamine (laboratory-specific values)

  c. Amino acid profile

  d. Amino acid clearance may be of increasing clinical utility and significance.

 5. Management

  a. General principles

   (1) Remove the cause(s)

   (2) Improve the level of hepatocellular function

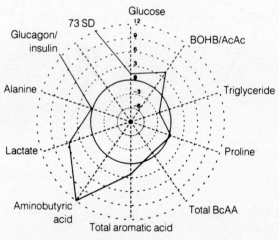

PURE LIVER FAILURE

Glucose 5.5 ± mM/L	NONSTRESSED CONTROL	TAA 119 µM/L
BOHB/AcAc 5 ± 1		ABU 3 ± 2 µM/L
Trig. 1200 ± 150 µM/L	mean ± SD	Lactate 600 + 152 µM/L
Proline 204 ± 43 µM/L		Alanine 332 ± 269 µM/L
Total BcAA 450 ± 169 µM/L		Glg./Ins. 2 ± 0.5

Fig. 18-2. The metabolic profile of pure liver failure. The organization is the same as in Fig. 18-1, except that the central reference circle is that of an overnight, nonstressed, noncirrhotic, fasting patient.

  b. Restore/maintain O_2 transport, electrolyte, acid-base status
  c. Control gut flora
     (1) Neomycin: 1.0 g into gastrointestinal tract every hour for 4 doses and then every 4 to 6 hours
     (2) Lactulose 30 ml every 3 to 4 hr to diarrhea and then reduce
  d. Metabolic support
     (1) Adequate calories
        (a) $1.5 \times$ BEE   (b) 40% of nonprotein calories
     (2) Adequate vitamins, minerals, and trace elements, particularly magnesium and zinc.
     (3) Adequate amino acids for nutritional support
        (a) 1 to 2 mg/kg/day
        (b) Use standard amino acid formula if it is tolerated without encephalopathy
        (c) Use a modified amino acid formula in the presence of encephalopathy (Fig 18-3)

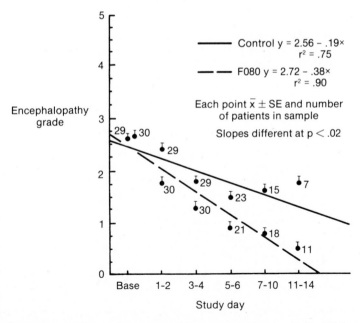

Fig. 18-3. Response of encephalopathy to treatment. (From Cerra, F.B., et al.: JPEN **9:**288, 1985, © 1985, American Society of Parenteral and Enteral Nutrition.)

SUGGESTED READINGS

Atterbury, L.E., Maddrey, W.C., and Conn H.O.: Neomycin-sorbitol and lactulose in the treatment of acute portal-systemic encephalopathy: a controlled, double blind clinical trial, Am. J. Dig. Dis. **23**:398, 1978.

Blitzer, B.L.: Fulminant hepatic failure: a rare but often lethal coma syndrome, Postgrad. Med. **68**:153, 1980.

Cerra, F.B., McMillen, M., and Angelico, R.: Cirrhosis, encephalopathy, and improved results with metabolic support, Surgery **94**:612, 1983.

Cerra, F.B., et al.: The hepatic failure of sepsis: cellular vs. substrate, Surgery **86**:409, 1979.

Clark, A.W., et al.: Prospective controlled trial of injection sclerotherapy in patients with cirrhosis and recent variceal hemorrhage, Lancet **2**:552, 1980.

Conn, H.O., and Lindenmuth, W.W.: Prophylactic portacaval anastomosis in cirrhotic patients with esophageal varices, N. Engl. J. Med. **272**:1255, 1965.

Conn, H.O., et al.: Distal splenorenal shunt vs. portal-systemic shunt: current status of a controlled trial, Hepatology **1**:151, 1981.

Elkington, S.G., Floch, M.H., and Conn, H.O.: Lactulose in the treatment of chronic portal-systemic encephalopathy. A double-blinded clinical trial, N. Engl. J. Med. **281**:408, 1969.

Fischer, J.E., et al.: Comparison of distal and proximal splenorenal shunts: a randomized prospective trial, Ann. Surg. **194**:531, 1981.

Fath, J.J., et al.: Etiology and clearance of plasma amino acids in acute hepatic failure: anhepatic man as a model, Surg. Forum **34**:32, 1983.

Goodale, R.L., et al.: Early survival after sclerotherapy for bleeding esophageal varices, Surg. Gynecol. Obstet. **155**:523, 1982.

Job, V., Coon, W.W., and Sloan, M.: Altered clearance of free amino acids from plasma of patients with cirrhosis of the liver, J. Surg. Res. **7**:41, 1967.

Langer, B., et al.: A prospective randomized trial of the selective distal splenorenal shunt, Surg. Gynecol. Obstet. **150**:45, 1980.

LeVeen, H.H., et al.: Ascites: its correction by peritoneovenous shunting, Curr. Probl. Surg. **16**:1, 1979.

Lewis, J.W., Chung, R.S., and Allison, J.G.: Injection sclerotherapy for control of acute variceal hemorrhage, Am. J. Surg. **142**:592, 1981.

Loda, M., et al.: Encephalopathy, oxygen consumption, visceral amino acid clearance and mortality in cirrhotic surgical patients. In press.

MacDougall, B.R.D., et al.: Increased long-term survival in variceal haemorrhage using injection sclerotherapy, Lancet **2**:124, 1982.

Moore, K.L., et al.: Peritoneal fibrinolysis: evidence for the efficiency of the tissue-type plasminogen activator, J. Lab. Clin. Med. **101**:921, 1983.

Munro, H.N., Fenstrum, J.D., and Wurtman, R.J.: Insulin, plasma amino acid imbalances and hepatic coma, Lancet **26**:968, 1975.

Mutchnick, M.G., Lerner, E., and Conn, H.O.: Portal-systemic encephalopathy and portacaval anastomosis: a prospective, controlled investigation, Gastroenterology **66**:1005, 1974.

Nespoli, A., et al.: Pathogenesis of hepatic encephalopathy and hyperdynamic syndrome in cirrhosis: role of false neurotransmitters, Arch. Surg. **116**:1129, 1981.

Orloff, M.J., et al.: Long-term results of emergency portacaval shunt for bleeding esophageal varices in unselected patients with alcoholic cirrhosis, Ann. Surg. **192**:325, 1980.

Raschke, E., and Paquet, K.T.: Management of hemorrhage from esophageal varices using the esophagoscopic sclerosing method, Ann. Surg. **177**:99, 1973.

Reichle, F.A., Fahmy, W.F., and Golsorkhi, M.: Prospective comparative clinical trials with distal splenorenal and mesocaval shunts, Am. J. Surg. **137**:13, 1979.

Resnick, R.H., et al.: A controlled study of the therapeutic portacaval shunt, Gastroenterology **67**:843, 1974.

Siegel, J.H., et al.: Death after portal decompressive surgery, Arch. Surg. **116**:1330, 1981.

Siegel, J.H., et al.: Pathologic synergy in cardiovascular and respiratory compensation with cirrhosis and sepsis, Arch. Surg. **117**:225, 1982.

Terblanche, J., et al.: Failure of repeated injection sclerotherapy to improve long-term survival after oesophageal variceal bleeding, Lancet **2**:1328, 1983.

Terblanche, J., et al.: Acute bleeding varies; a five-year prospective evaluation of tamponade and sclerotherapy, Ann. Surg. **194**:521, 1981.

Wapnick, S., et al.: Fibrogen, cross-linked fibrin, and their proteolysis products in ascitic fluid in hepatic cirrhosis, Surg. Forum **33**:181, 1982.

Yassin, Y.M., and Sherif, S.M.: Randomized control trial of injection sclerotherapy for oesophageal varices: an interim reort, Br. J. Surg. **70**:20, 1983.

Zieve, L.: Hepatic encephalopathy: summary of present knowledge with elaboration on recent developments, *in* Popper, H., and Schaffner, F., (editors): Progress in liver disease, vol. 6, New York, 1979, Grune & Stratton, Inc., pp. 327-341.

19

Central Nervous System

John Mawk

Successful outcome in contemporary neurosurgery has become as dependent on preoperative physiologic enhancement and postoperative monitoring as it is on good surgical technique. This chapter outlines broad principles of current neurosurgical intensive care and suggests practical regimens for applying these principles within the context of the general care principles outlined.

CEREBRAL PERFUSION

Perfusion of the brain with well-oxygenated blood containing adequate amounts of glucose is the cardinal goal in all patient care situations. The volume of the cranial contents is a fixed constant in adults and older children because of the inexpansibility of the skull; consequently, thinking of perfusion pressures is necessary.

A. Cerebral perfusion pressure (CPP) is most closely related to the intracranial pressure (ICP) and mean blood pressure (BP), according to the equation:

$$CPP = BP - ICP$$

1. At all times thinking of patient management in terms of these three pressures is necessary.
   a. Within the CPP limits, flow is dependent on cardiac output.
2. Assuming normal intracranial pressure is 10 torr (recall that normal pressure at lumbar puncture is this same value) and that the blood pressure is 120/75 (mean = 90), then:

$$CPP = 90 \text{ torr} - 10 \text{ torr}$$
$$CPP = 80 \text{ torr}$$

3. CPP between 65 to 80 torr: acceptable
4. CPP between 65 and 50: borderline brain perfusion
5. CPP below 50 torr: frank cerebral ischemia

B. Several factors influence the CPP
1. Blood pressure
   a. Raising mean arterial pressure will augment CPP only if BP is low.
   b. Because the cerebral vessels have the capacity to constrict in the presence of arterial hypertension (a phase of autoregulation that can be explained by the Bayliss effect), raising the BP to high levels becomes self-defeating.
   c. When it is desirable to increase CPP by raising BP, colloid solutions such as plasma protein fraction or salt-poor albumin should be used to expand blood volume, rather than crystalloid solutions.
      (1) Simple electrolyte solutions with low oncotic pressure may leak into damaged brain parenchyma, raise the intracranial pressure, and in turn lower CPP.
      (2) If raising CPP in this manner is necessary, monitoring of central cardiac pressures is mandatory.
      (3) In older patients or those with cardiovascular disease, Swan-Ganz catheter placement is necessary so that pulmonary artery wedge pressures (PAWP) can be judiciously elevated and cardiac output and oxygen consumption maintained at reasonable levels.
      (4) Use of dopamine may be considered if the central cardiac pressure or PAWP is already normal or high.
      (5) Neosynephrine is acceptable as an alternative drug, because the cerebral vessels are believed to be devoid of alpha-receptors.
2. Intracranial pressure
   The usual means of augmenting CPP is the lowering of ICP by the following progressive series of increasingly difficult and dangerous interventions. It is imperative

that the easiest and most reversible treatments be used before more intricate measures are undertaken.

a. Head-up positioning
   (1) Simple elevation of the head of the bed to 30 to 45 degrees has dramatic beneficial effect on increased intracranial pressure by facilitating venous return to the heart.
   (2) The head should not be allowed to turn to either side, since turning may kink the jugular veins and actually impair venous return.
   (3) The head is best held in this erect position by a small sandbag placed on either side of the head, resting loosely on the patient's shoulders.

b. Hyperventilation
   (1) The cerebral vessels are extremely sensitive to arterial carbon dioxide concentration ($Paco_2$). Small elevations of $Paco_2$ cause marked cerebral vasodilation.
   (2) Intubation and hyperventilation to a $Paco_2$ of 28 to 30 torr causes optimal cerebral vasoconstriction to occur.
      (a) These two maneuvers will control elevated ICP in a substantive proportion of neurosurgical patients.
      (b) Hypocapneic cerebral vasoconstriction may, however, lower ICP at the expense of decreasing effective perfusion in the microvasculature. Flow measurements are helpful in this decision, if they are available.

c. Mannitol
   (1) Mannitol, an inert dehydrating agent, is frequently misused.
      (a) Administering dehydrating agents is predicated on their ability to diminish brain edema through their oncotic effect.
      (b) Mannitol also has the transient salutary effect of increasing plasma volume. Urea and glycerol are also occasionally used for the same purpose.

(2) Dosage of mannitol is controversial.

    (a) In dire neurosurgical emergencies (e.g., evolving herniation syndromes), a dose of 1 g/kg of body weight should be given as a rapid intravenous bolus.

    (b) In less urgent situations, 0.25 g/kg given by infusion over 60 to 90 minutes each 4 to 6 hours produces satisfactory control of ICP in most situations.

(3) Several precautions should be taken.

    (a) A Foley catheter must always be in place before mannitol administration.

    (b) Serum osmolarity should be monitored at least every 6 hours during mannitol administration.

        i. The brisk diuresis occasioned by mannitol administration requires careful hourly input and output determination and compensatory fluid administration.

        ii. The serum osmolarity should not be allowed to rise above 315 to 320 mOsm.

    (c) Frequent electrolyte determination is also necessary.

    (d) Central cardiac pressures and PAWP measurement is essential as well as cardiac output and oxygen consumption so as to maintain reasonable blood volume status and tissue perfusion.

d. Barbiturates are somewhat effective for controlling intracranial pressure. The technique of drug administration is extremely dangerous, however, and should be carried out only in a sophisticated intensive care unit setting with all the appropriate monitoring equipment available.

(1) Barbiturates act principally by cerebral vasoconstriction.

(2) Whether barbiturates decrease cerebral metabolism sufficiently to have any noticeable effect on ICP is controversial.

(3) The decision to advance to barbiturate therapy mandates:
   (a) Swan-Ganz line placement (even in children!)
   (b) Continuous electroencephalogram (EEG) monitoring
   (c) Cooperation from the clinical laboratories so that serum barbiturate levels can be determined at any time

(4) Cardiac output should be determined before induction of barbiturate coma; in high doses, barbiturates cause myocardial depression.

(5) Sodium pentobarbital is the preferred drug, although other drugs (e.g., thiopental) may be acceptable alternatives for induction of therapeutic barbiturate coma.
   (a) A dose of 20 mg sodium pentobarbital/kg of body weight is administered by infusion over 1 hour.
   (b) An hourly maintenance dose of 1 to 1.5 mg/kg follows.
   (c) The lowest dose consistent with reducing ICP should be used. The serum barbiturate level should not, however, be allowed to rise above 30 to 40 mg/L.
   (d) A barbiturate level should be drawn at the end of the first hour and at the end of the fourth hour of treatment.
   (e) Continuous EEG monitoring is also used to assess the level of barbiturate coma. In general, a burst-suppression pattern with a periodicity of 15 to 20 seconds is desirable.

(6) Abrupt termination of barbiturate therapy will sometimes induce seizures. Barbiturates are therefore generally tapered over 3 to 4 days once intracranial pressure control has been achieved.

e. Surgical decompression of edematous brain is the most heroic means of controlling intractable intracranial hypertension.

(1) Extremely large bone flaps either laterally or frontally (the latter termed a Kjellberg procedure) are removed.

(2) This type of surgical decompression differs however, from craniotomy aimed at hematoma evacuation or lobectomy.

C. Pressure-volume curve

1. At low intracranial pressures, a given volume increment (ΔV) will produce only a small pressure rise (Δp_1).

2. The same volume increment at higher baseline ICP produces a much larger pressure change (Δp_2).

3. That is, the "tighter" or less compliant are the intracranial contents, the larger the pressure increment for given volume increment. For example, even slight arteriolar hypercapneic dilation may produce profound intracranial hypertension if the baseline ICP is modestly elevated.

4. The five sequential steps given above the ICP control all relate to leftward movement on the curve.

   a. Sinistrad movement on the P-V curve is beneficial to the patient.

   b. Rightward movement is almost always harmful.

INTRACRANIAL PRESSURE MONITORING TECHNIQUE

Three basic techniques for ICP monitoring are in use in the United States. All these devices are typically implanted in a standard frontal location approximately 2 to 3 cm from midline and 2 cm in front of the coronal suture, usually on the right side (Fig. 19-1).

A. Epidural monitoring is highly reliable and is rapidly becoming the preferred technique.

1. Approach

   a. Burr hole required for placement of the transducer

   b. Both fiberoptic and calibrated air pressure–balance sensors are commercially available.

   c. These are generally brought out through a separate stab wound in the scalp, several centimeters from the burr hole incision.

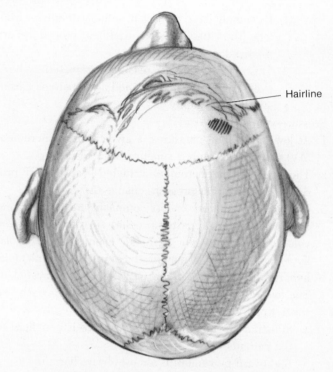

Fig. 19-1. Position of placement for ICP monitoring.

2. Advantages
    a. Freedom from the risk of meningitis
    b. Durability and reliability of the system
    c. The sensor being always at the same level as the head
3. Disadvantage
    a. Necessity of taking the patient to the operating room, since a formal burr hole is required for placement of the inducer
B. Direct measurement of cerebrospinal fluid (CSF) pressure can be accomplished by placing a catheter into the ventricle or by a subarachnoid bolt.
    1. Ventricular catheter
        a. Approach
            (1) The ventricular catheter can be placed on the ward through a twist-drill hole and brought out via separate stab wound (tunneled ventriculostomy).

    b. Disadvantages
      (1) The risk of meningitis
      (2) The inability to record pressure accurately if brain swelling collapses the ventricular cavity
    c. Advantages
      (1) The ability to treat intracranial hypertension by venting small volumes of CSF from the ventricles

2. Subarachnoid bolt
    a. Approach
      (1) A twist-drill hole is created.
      (2) The bolt is screwed into the skull.
      (3) It is necessary to penetrate the dura, having a fluid column in continuity with the convexity subarachnoid space.
        (a) A sensor can be attached at the hub of the bolt (ideal).
        (b) A fluid column can be led to a standard pressure transducer at the patient's side.
    b. Advantages
      (1) Easiest of the three systems to insert
    c. Disadvantages
      (1) Risk of meningitis
      (2) Tendency of the orifice of the bolt to become occluded with swollen brain tissue
      (3) Entry of air bubbles into the system, which interrupt the fluid column and give artifactual pressure readings

FLUID AND ELECTROLYTE CONSIDERATION IN NEUROSURGERY

Because of fear of brain edema, neurosurgical patients traditionally receive less crystalloid solution than other postoperative patients.

A. Dosage
    1. The patient who weighs 70 kg typically receives fluid administration at a rate of 75 ml/hour (1800 ml/day).
    2. Five percent dextrose in half-normal saline with 20 or 30 mEg of potassium added to each liter is an ideal intravenous solution for most purposes.

B. Monitoring
   1. Monitoring serum electrolytes at least daily is highly advisable as long as the patient's consciousness is impaired.
   2. After the patient regains consciousness, serum sodium and potassium should be checked at least twice weekly until the patient is neurologically normal or until a stable state has been reached.
C. Problems
   1. The syndrome of inappropriate antidiuretic hormone (SIADH) secretion is a frequent concommitant of head injury and even of elective brain surgery.
      a. Hyponatremia lowers the seizure threshold, so in no case should serum sodium be allowed to drop below 130 mEq/L.
      b. SIADH is best managed by fluid restriction.
      c. If hyponatremia is severe, 3% sodium chloride may be given to correct electrolyte balance more rapidly.
      d. Hypertonic saline should be given cautiously in older patients with diminished cardiac reserve.
   2. Diabetes insipidus (DI) occurs following an insult to the hypothalamus or in the situation of pituitary surgery. Removal of certain third ventricle tumors, such as craniopharyngioma, is predictably followed by DI.
      a. The first difficulty with treatment of DI lies in the correct diagnosis of the syndrome, which must be differentiated from simple postoperative diuresis.
         (1) Mild diabetes insipidus (or "relative" DI) is characterized by the production of moderately large volumes of urine (200 to 300 ml/hr) with low specific gravity.
         (2) Florid DI is characterized by the output of large volumes (300 to 400+ ml/hr) of urine with a specific gravity of 1.001 or 1.000. Urine electrolytes measurement produces confusion in florid diabetes insipidus.
      b. Many different stratagems exist for the management

of DI, but the system proposed below is both easy and safe:

(1) Questionable DI
   (a) Follow for several hours. Is this postoperative diuresis? Replace 50% of urine output.
   (b) Follow serum and urine osmolarity and electrolytes every 4 hr.
(2) Relative DI
   (a) Replace urine output 50% for several hours.
   (b) If diuresis does not stop, give 2 units aqueous pitressin intramuscularly and decrease intravenous fluid accordingly.
   (c) Follow serum electrolytes and osmolarity every 2 hr.
(3) Florid DI
   (a) Give 5 units pitressin in oil intramuscularly.* Decrease fluids to keep open.
   (b) Follow serum electrolytes and osmolarity every 2 hr.

SEIZURES

Seizures occur in a great variety of neurosurgical situations. The value of prophylactic phenytoin administration to neurosurgical patients is currently being debated. The problem which more commonly confronts the house officer is the management of seizures in patients who are not receiving phenytoin prophylactically.

A. Effects
   Seizures are extremely harmful in the neurosurgical patient.
   1. Skeletal muscle contractions which accompany seizures increase the central venous pressure, decrease the venous return to the heart, and can cause very marked elevations in the ICP very rapidly.

---

*Pitressin in oil is available only in 5 unit vials. The vial must be shaken for 5 minutes while held in warm running water to assure suspension of the agent. It is imperative that the entire ampule be given in order to ensure administration of at least some drug. Accordingly, one cannot order "2 units of pitressin in oil."

2. In addition, the respiratory changes that accompany seizures often produce intracranial hypertension.

B. Management of generalized seizures

The following regimen is recommended for control of generalized seizures.

1. Diazepam remains the agent of choice for prompt cessation of seizures.

   a. The agent should be given intravenously in 1 or 2 mg increments every 30 seconds to 1 minute, with very cautious attention to the patient's respiratory status.

   b. Depression of respiration determines the total amount of diazepam that may be safely administered.

   c. Ordinarily, giving more than 10 mg diazepam is not necessary. In no instance should the patient receive more than 15 to 20 mg of this drug intravenously.

   d. As soon as the ictal event has terminated, treatment for further seizures should be instituted, as stated below.

2. Phenytoin is the drug of choice for prevention of further seizures.

   a. Loading is accomplished by the administration of 18 mg phenytoin/kg body weight, given intravenously at a rate not to exceed 40 to 50 mg/min.

   b. Continuous cardiac monitoring should be carried out during this loading phase.

   c. Maintenance doses of phenytoin are 5.5 to 6.0 mg/kg/day, usually given in divided doses either orally or via nasogastric tube.

   d. Maintenance doses may also be given intravenously, with the same precautions as stated previously.

   e. To assure a therapeutic level, a phenytoin level should be obtained immediately following loading and daily thereafter for the first several days. Therapeutic levels of phenytoin fall in the range of 15 to 20 mg/ml.

   f. A number of patients develop either allergic or hypersensitivity reactions to phenytoin. In particular, Stevens-Johnson syndrome has been observed with phenytoin administration, usually within the first 2 weeks.

    g. The complete blood count should be checked several times during the first several weeks of phenytoin administration.

3. Phenobarbital, although an excellent anticonvulsant, depresses the sensorium. In the neurosurgical patient, this constitutes a major source of confusion in postoperative evaluation. In some cases, however, loading the patient with phenobarbital is also necessary to stop seizures.

    a. This is easily accomplished by intravenous administration of 6 to 8 mg phenobarbital/kg body weight, given as an intravenous infusion over 1 hour.

    b. Maintenance doses of phenobarbital fall in the range of 4 to 5 mg/kg/day, usually given orally or via nasogastric tube or intramuscularly in divided doses.

    c. Therapeutic barbiturate levels fall between 20 to 30 μg/ml.

C. Management of refractory seizures

1. Seizures that remain refractory to diazepam, phenytoin, and phenobarbital loading may require neurological consultation for management.

2. Every effort should be made to determine the underlying cause of the seizure, be it surgical (e.g., subdural hematoma) or medical (e.g., derangement of the major or minor electrolytes).

3. A head injury may mask alcohol withdrawal. Anyone suspected of having a seizure due to alcohol withdrawal must be protected from Wernicke's polioencephalopathy by the administration of thiamine, 100 mg intramuscularly 3 times/day.

RECOGNITION OF HERNIATION SYNDROMES

Transtentorial herniation occurs when force vectors displace the temporal lobe over the free margin of the tentorium. This produces the serious effect of pressure on the brain stem. In addition, pressure on or distortion of the ipsilateral occulomotor nerve produces pupillary changes. It is absolutely imperative that herniation syndromes be recognized prior to the development of occulomotor paresis, since this represents a late manifestation of transtentorial herniation.

A. Clinical manifestations
   1. Early
      a. Early manifestations of impending herniation, such as confusion or agitation, changes in the vital signs, or lethargy are easily confused with derangements of fluid and electrolytes, oxygenation, alcohol intoxication, etc.
      b. It is critical that thorough investigation (including computerized tomographic scanning) be carried out in any patient in whom transtentorial herniation is entertained as a possible diagnosis.
   2. Late
      a. Late manifestations of transtentorial herniation include:
         (1) Paresis of the extraoccular muscles on the side of the lesion producing herniation
         (2) A sluggish or frankly dilated pupil
         (3) A contralateral alteration in motor behavior, either a paresis of the side or stereotypic posturing of that side
      b. Although early recognition is much preferred, many patients are still salvageable at a functional level at this point
B. Management
   1. As soon as transtentorial herniation is diagnosed, the first three steps of intracranial pressure control should be instituted simultaneously and urgently.
   2. Urgent neurosurgical consultation is imperative.
   3. The patient should be fully prepared for immediate surgery and an operating room secured.

SECTION THREE

SYSTEMIC DYSFUNCTION

20

Postoperative complications

Clifford Deutschman
Frank B. Cerra

Expanding technology has helped make the practice of surgery more scientific. Nevertheless, the treatment of surgical
disease is a human endeavor and can go wrong. A number of
factors may contribute to an increase in surgical complications,
among them the widening age range of the patient population
and the ability for patients with preexiting disease to tolerate
anesthesia and surgery without prohibitive risk. Even the "per-
fect" operation, however, has an inherent failure rate, and the
conscientious practitioner is aware of this. The key to minimizing untoward outcome is anticipation of what can go wrong,
when it can go wrong, and how to prevent it from going wrong,
and, if prevention is impossible, early detection and appropriate
intervention. Understanding the physiology behind the human
response to the stress of surgical/anesthetic trauma serves to facilitate the evaluation of deviations from the normal recovery
trajectory. This, in turn, will permit early recognition and rational treatment of complications.

THE STRESS RESPONSE

When faced with a number of potentially life-threatening situations, the human organism has a characteristic response.
Changes over time in a number of metabolic and physiologic
parameters that define this pattern represent points on a continuum called the stress response. Neuro-endocrine-humoral outflow seems to modulate the stress response that has classically
been divided into three phases: ebb phase, flow catabolism, and
flow anabolism. Tissue damage releases or causes the synthesis
of "activators" which serve to activate a second level of re-

sponses collectively referred to as "mediators." These in turn
mediate a clinically detectable end-organ response. When the
response deviates from the norm or fails to resolve, a complication is usually present. Examination of the physiology of each
individual phase allows for recognition of deviations and anticipation of those complications which can cause them. To truly
anticipate requires metabolic monitoring; this permits the earliest detection of complications and facilitates treatment.

The most common deviations from the norm are the prolongation of a given phase or, if the insult is severe, a shift back
along the response trajectory to an earlier phase. An understanding of complications can be arrived at by examining each
phase.

COMPLICATIONS OF EBB PHASE

A. Ebb phase physiology
   1. While the actual "signal" that initiates the response re-
      mains unknown, ebb phase begins immediately after the
      onset of stress.
   2. One may view the phase as the organism's recognition of
      stress and its attempt to assure that vital organs are ade-
      quately supplied.
      a. In man, adequate supply means the maintenance of
         sufficient delivery of oxygen and metabolic substrate
         to heart and brain.
      b. In turn, the delivery implies adequate blood flow to
         these tissues.
   3. The time course of ebb phase depends on the severity of
      the injury.
      a. Minimal blood loss or tissue damage of only moderate
         severity will result in rapid shift into the high-level
         metabolism of the flow-catabolic phase.
      b. Even in severe injury and significant blood loss, res-
         toration of blood volume can occur via reequilibration
         of body fluid compartments or from exogenous fluid
         administration.
      c. A signal that heart and brain are "safe" seems to pro-
         duce a gradual decrease in peripheral tone and the
         onset of the flow phase.

B. Pathogenesis and pathophysiology of prolongation of ebb phase

The ebb phase seems to become prolonged when the body does not receive the neurohumoroendocrine "signal" that blood flow, O_2 delivery, and substrate mobilization are adequate to protect the heart and brain. Clinically, the presentation is one of shock. Current concepts of shock focus on an inappropriate balance of substrate supply to demand on the cellular level, with the primary effector being either physiologic or metabolic. Examples of primary physiologic effectors (see box below) have in common a failure of oxygen

---

PRIMARY PHYSIOLOGIC EFFECTORS OF PROLONGED EBB PHASE

Inadequate blood volume
  Blood volume loss—hemorrhage
  Blood component loss
    Plasma—ascites, pleural effusion, burn, third space
    Salt and water—interstitial edema, intestinal losses renal disease, fever
    Plasma/salt and water—inflammation, interstitial space collections, effusion
Volume space mismatch
  Neurogenic states
  Adrenal insufficiency
  Anesthesia, drugs
Pump failure
  Extrinsic conditions
    Inadequate preload
    Inappropriate afterload
    Mechanical—pulmonary emboli, pericardial effusion, inflammation, tamponade
  Intrinsic disease
    Preexisting—myopathy, scar tissue, valve disorder drugs, acid-base disorder, magnesium excess, phosphate deficiency, selenium deficiency, potassium and calcium disorders
    Acquired—myocarditis, valve disorder, acute infarct, drugs, calcium and potassium disorders, magnesium excess, phosphate deficiency, acidosis, selenium deficit, molybdenum deficiency
  Dysrhythmias

and substrate delivery: blood volume loss or mismatch, intrinsic or extrinsic pump failure, primary pulmonary insufficiency, or inadequate oxygen carrying capacity. Ultimately, the oxygen deficit produces an alteration in metabolism at the cellular level. Primary metabolic effectors, best represented by sepsis but also including dead and/or injured tissue and some hematomas, produce the opposite effect. In this group, unbalanced metabolism at the cellular level affecting substrate utilization leads to a compensatory alteration in physiology. Metabolic-effector shock is more often the cause of a shift from flow phase back to ebb phase and will be considered in that context later.

1. Volume insufficient to fill the vasculature-relative hypovolemia

   Inappropriate blood volume is the most common cause of prolonged ebb phase in the intraoperative and immediate postoperative period. It may also be a reason for a shift back to ebb phase metabolism later in the recovery trajectory.

   a. Up to 10% of blood volume may be lost without a change being noted in cardiac output or blood pressure.

   b. Greater losses yield a drop in cardiac output, with a loss of 20% causing a decrease in blood pressure.

   c. A significant volume deficit activates a number of physiologic mechanisms designed to conserve fluid and restore blood volume.

      (1) Baroreceptors in the right atrium, aortic arch, carotid sinus, and elsewhere along the vascular tree decrease the frequency of vagal and glossopharyngeal signals to the vasoinhibitory center of the medulla oblongata.

      (2) This in turn stimulates relays to the hypothalamus, causing an elevation in sympathetic tone with increased resistance in skin, renal, and visceral arteriolar beds, decreased venous capacitance, increased inotropy and chronotropy, and a reduction in the vagal chronotropic brake.

(3) Chemoreceptors in the carotid body and aortic arch cause stimulation of the medullary vasoconstrictor center, further increasing sympathetic discharge.

(4) Decreased blood flow to the central nervous system (CNS) causes stimulation of both the supraoptic and paraventricular nuclei of the hypothalamus and the vasoconstrictor center directly.

   (a) Hypothalamic output stimulates adrenal medullary catecholamine release and also causes antidiuretic hormone (ADH) release.

   (b) ADH effects the renal collecting duct and reduces water excretion to minimal levels.

(5) Accompanying the profound increase in peripheral tone are a reduction in postarteriolar flow, decreased renal blood flow, and concomitant drop in glomerular filtration rate (GFR). Renin secretion is increased, which activates the angiotensin/aldosterone system and leads to further vasoconstriction as well as salt and water conservation.

(6) In ongoing fluid loss, the compensatory mechanisms noted above lead to a reduction in intracapillary hydrostatic pressure.

   (a) Such a drop permits the movement of interstitial fluid into the intravascular space.

   (b) This movement causes hemodilution, decreased capillary sludging, and an expansion of the intravascular fluid compartment.

(7) These feedback mechanisms attempt to restore the fluid deficit and permit the transition from ebb to flow phase. They do so, however, at the expense of peripheral flow, lactic acidosis, and high afterload.

(8) Adequate restoration of volume will shut off the response (negative feedback). Ongoing loss or inadequate restoration in conjunction with high sympathetic tone may lead, however, to persistent hypoperfusion such that the response be-

comes self-perpetuating (positive feedback) and maladaptive.

(9) Common causes of prolonged ebb phase in general surgery and trauma include:

(a) Ongoing hemorrhage

(b) Fluid sequestration into nonfunctional compartment (the so-called "third space") due to bowel obstruction, retroperitoneal trauma, and dissection

(c) Massive soft tissue injury, which will not normally be mobilized until the flow phase has been initiated

(10) Settings for relative hypovolemia

(a) Elderly patients

(b) Patients with hypertension or heart disease

(c) Preexisting volume deficit due to chronic diuretic or vasodilator use

(d) A state of beta-blockade that may block sympathetic response mechanisms

(e) Electrolyte deficiencies, acid-base disorders (e.g., hypocalcemia or acidosis)

(f) Anesthetics causing decreased vascular tone

2. Pump failure

Inadequate left ventricular output in the absence of hypovolemia and obstruction implies an inability to generate the contractile force needed to fill the vascular tree.

a. Onset may be either acute or chronic and can be the basis for failure of substrate delivery.

b. The compensatory mechanisms triggered by insufficient volume are activated.

(1) If the underlying problem is, however, intrinsic myocardial disease particularly acute, this response can be maladaptive.

(a) Increased cardiac output means increased oxygen requirements and may potentiate a myocardial infarction or dysrhythmia.

(b) Fluid retention and increased pulmonary flow and systemic resistance may precipitate congestive failure and pulmonary edema.

      (c) The increased peripheral resistance, which may serve to maintain a blood pressure, also increases afterload and can lead to a serious mismatch of oxygen supply and demand.

    (2) Cardiogenic states secondary to extrinsic disease, i.e., pericardial tamponade, can benefit from these compensatory mechanisms.

    (3) Failure to correct the primary problem, however, will lead to positive feedback.

3. Oxygenation failure

Circulatory collapse causes a failure of substrate delivery. Likewise, failure of oxygen delivery to or uptake by circulation (i.e., hypoxemia) can produce a physiologic effector response with its consequences of altered metabolism and physiology. Blood oxygen content in turn depends on ventilation, gas exchange, and gas transport, with hypoxemia both reflecting and producing changes in all three.

  a. Failure of O_2 delivery produces its most profound alterations on the oxygen delivery system via the mechanisms noted in the preceding two sections.

  b. Increase in respiratory rate and tidal volume occurs.

  c. Less direct homeostatic control is exerted over gas exchange. However, stimulation of chemoreceptor fibers in the vagus and "spill over" from both the chemosensitive area and the inspiratory center into the vasomotor center directly stimulate sympathetic discharge.

    (1) Increased peripheral tone, positive inotropy and chronotropy, and postcapillary pulmonary venous constriction produce pulmonary blood flow redistribution. This can improve gas exchange.

    (2) Local hypoxia in the lung stimulates local vasoconstriction, also improving or rebalancing the volume quotient (V/Q).

    (3) Local factors affecting the gas transport are: pH, P_{CO_2}, temperature, and metabolic demand.

  d. Abnormalities producing hypoxemia and/or reduced oxygen delivery in the clinical setting generally arise from three distinct kinds of causes, although others exist in theory.

   (1) Hypoventilation is manifest by relative carbon dioxide retention (meaning an absolute rise in CO_2 or maintenance of normal CO_2).

   (2) Shunt and dead space constitute extremes of the second abnormality, inappropriate matching of ventilation to perfusion.

   (3) Sufficient receptor (hemoglobin, red cells) for oxygen transfer may be lacking.

 e. Anatomically, the gas-exchange system can be thought of as having four components.

   (1) The thoracic cage (thoracic, cervical and abdominal inspiratory muscles and diaphragm) functions as a bellows to create the pressure gradient needed to induce flow from environment to alveoli.

   (2) The trachea and major bronchi constitute a conduit for gas delivery.

   (3) The lung parenchyma, consisting of small airways, alveoli, interstitium and pulmonary microcirculation, permits gas exchange.

   (4) The oxygen-carrying elements of the blood provide the medium whereby O_2 may be transported to the tissues.

   (5) Prolongation of ebb phase can occur as a result of dysfunction in any or all of these components and is most easily discussed on an anatomic basis. Shifts from flow phase back to ebb phase can also be a result of hypoxemia, but will be dealt with in the context of the flow phase complications.

 f. Bellows failure
 Bellows dysfunction can produce both hypoventilation and V/Q mismatch.

   (1) True hypoventilation results only when uniform depression of respiratory excursion yields an inadequate transairway pressure gradient.

   (2) Clinically, this most often occurs in the setting

of drug intoxication, inappropriate mechanical ventilation, or infratentorial central nervous system lesions.

(3) In the awake patient, underventilation can also be a consequence of inadequate pain control, yielding shallow breathing.

    (a) Hypoxia, hyperpnea, and hypocapnea result.

    (b) Thoracotomy incisions are apt to be at the root of this syndrome, but upper abdominal, extensive laparotomy, or flank incisions involving large dissections can also be causative.

    (c) Microatelectasis occurs, whose principle manifestation seems to be fever.

    (d) If severe enough, microatelectasis occurs, usually in the lower lobes with the left side being most common.

    (e) The comatose or intoxicated patient who is underventilated will not display the anxiety or air hunger that characterize respiratory insufficiency in the awake patient, but he will exhibit reflex hyperpnea and sympathetic discharge unless the level of central depression is exceedingly great.

(4) If the cause of bellows failure is a finite CNS lesion, this increase in respiratory rate will be accompanied by a respiratory pattern that may serve to identify that region of the brain stem diencephalon involved (see the box on p. 520).

(5) For supratentorial disease to alter respiration, either herniation or a global suppression of cortical function is usually necessary. Usually this occurs with drug overdose (either abuse or iatrogenic).

(6) Only rarely does physical disruption of the thoracic cage cause hypoventilation. In general, such trauma is felt to lead to V/Q mismatch on the basis of a decrease in lung volume or restriction.

(7) Flail chest or kyphoscoliosis results in immobility of a portion of the chest wall with a decrease

---

NEUROPATHOLOGIC CORRELATES OF BREATHING ANOMALIES

Hypothalamic/forebrain damage
  Cheyne-Stokes respiration
Hypothalamic/midbrain
  Central reflex hyperpnea
Basis pontis
  Pseudobulbar paralysis of voluntary breathing
Pontine tegmentum
  Apneustic breathing
  Cluster breathing
Medulla oblongata
  Ataxic breathing
  Slow regular breathing
  Loss of automatic breathing with voluntary control (sleep apnea)
  Gasping

---

in local parenchymal excursion on inspiration and failure to develop a significant transairway pressure gradient. This results in shunt.

   (a) Further, trauma-producing flail also causes a significant underlying contusion with V/Q mismatch.

   (b) Most authors feel that the contusion is the cause of hypoxemia; as such, this is more correctly a dysfunction of parenchyma.

   (8) Diaphragmatic rupture, hemothorx, or tension pneumothorax are bellows diseases which can cause restriction on the basis of actual intrathoracic physical mass.

   (9) See the box on p. 521, top, for additional causes.

g. Conduit disruption

Although the chest wall diaphragmatic bellows generate the driving force for ambient gas delivery and gas exchange, movement also depends on the actual pressure gradient developed. This in turn is a function of patency and caliber of the conducting airways—larynx, trachea, and major bronchi.

CAUSES OF BELLOWS FAILURE

Pain
Global CNS depression
   Drug intoxication—anesthetics, narcotics, barbiturates, phenothiazines, benzoidiazapines, sleep medications
Extensive flail chest
Extensive surgery on the thoracic spine
Kyphoscoliosis
Neuromuscular disease—poliomyelitis, Guillain-Barré syndrome, myasthenia gravis, other myopathies
Nutritional depletion
Intrathoracic masses—hemothorax, pneumothorax, diaphragmatic rupture
Extensive pleural scarring

CAUSES OF CONDUIT OBSTRUCTION

Complete obstruction
   Fractured larynx
   Severe laryngeal edema or spasm
   Disrupted trachea
   Mucous plug in endotracheal tube
   Aspirated foreign body
Partial obstruction or narrowing
   Laryngospasm
   Bronchospasm
      Preexisting chronic obstructive pulmonary disease or reactive airway disease
      Fluid overload/pulmonary edema blockade
      Narrow endotracheal tube
      Extensive respirator tubing
      Constant positive airway pressure

---

(1) Narrowing or disruption of the conduit can lead to a highly significant alteration of flow.
(2) In the clinical setting, this effect may be observed in either complete or partial airway obstruction (see the box above).

(a) Obstruction is particularly important in expiration, which is normally a passive process involving elastic recoil of the pulmonary parenchyma and relaxation of the bellows.

(b) With obstruction, a dramatic increase in the work of breathing occurs as the patient struggles to inspire against increased resistance and then has to actively expire.

(c) Ultimately, this can result in air trapping in the distal airways with an increase in the functional residual capacity associated with exhaustion and substrate depletion.

(d) Both hypoxemia and carbon dioxide retention can result.

(3) Prolongation of the ebb phase will accompany acute obstructive processes that significantly impair exchange. Possible settings include:

(a) Trauma

(b) Intrathoracic surgery

(c) Laryngospasm following intubation or extubation.

(d) External compression from hematoma

(e) Foreign body aspiration

(f) Mucous plug

(g) Intra-airway bleeding

(h) Bronchospasm

    i. Most often occurring in the setting of preexisting reactive airway disease

    ii. Beta-blockade

    iii. Can also occur in the patient without previous pulmonary disease who has developed increased interstitial and alveolar fluid

(i) The endotracheal tube itself may be too narrow or become plugged with secretions; long ventilator tubing adds length to the conduit, thus increasing resistance

h. Failure of the pulmonary parenchyma

Actual oxygen exchange at the alveolar level depends on a number of factors having the final common pathway of gas diffusion through the respiratory membrane to the capillary blood. This process requires normal alveolar, interstitial, and vascular anatomy and a concentration gradient for gas exchange and appropriate distribution of blood flow.

(1) Ventilation-perfusion mismatch is the most common cause of dysfunction.

    (a) Sputum, blood, or edema fluid may fill alveoli.

    (b) Mediators or direct damage may cause vasoactive changes and a loss of surfactant and/or depression of its production. The result will be alveolar collapse and reactive edema. These increase the physical barrier to diffusion by thickening the interstitial space and locally redistributing blood flow.

(2) Processes that affect the entire lung may also result in decreased pulmonary compliance, reduced total lung volume, and increased work of breathing. This increases O_2 demand and further decreases output from the bronchiolar stretch receptors, thus potentiating sympathetic discharge.

(3) Blockage of arteriolar-capillary perfusion, as in pulmonary embolus or high-pressure edema yielding capillary collapse, may also potentiate V/Q mismatch.

(4) A contribution to the failure of O_2 to cross the alveolar-arterial interface can result from cardiogenic effects or low blood volume with decreased or stagnant blood flow. These yield an increase in physiologic dead space.

(5) Common to acute parenchymal processes that prolong ebb phase are loss of alveolar integrity, filling of the alveolar space with material that interfers with diffusion, and thickening or disruption of the interstitium.

(a) Clinically, a spectrum of disease from simple atelectasis to acute pulmonary insufficiency may be observed.

(6) Processes that affect the entire lung may also result in decreased pulmonary compliance, reduced total lung volume, and increased work of breathing. This increases O_2 demand and further decreases output from the bronchiolar stretch receptors, thus potentiating sympathetic discharge.

(7) Blockage of arteriolar-capillary perfusion, as in pulmonary embolus or high-pressure edema yielding capillary collapse, may also potentiate V/Q mismatch.

(8) A contribution to the failure of O_2 to cross the alveolar-arterial interface can result from cardiogenic effects or low blood volume with decreased or stagnant blood flow. These yield an increase in physiologic dead space.

i. Failure due to decreased oxygen carrying capacity
   Control of blood oxygen-carrying capacity is essentially a local phenomenom depending on the conditions at the site of exchange (i.e., lung or tissue).

   (1) Anemia
   (2) Altered red cell function
      (a) Acidosis
      (b) Alkalosis
      (c) Hypophosphatemia

C. Consequences of prolonged ebb phase
   1. If the loss of volume, cardiac failure, or hypoxemia is rapidly corrected, feedback mechanisms sense the return of oxygen delivery and alter the response, facilitating a shift into flow-phase metabolism.
   2. Failure to correct the underlying problem, however, leads to progressive cellular decompensation and eventually death.
   3. Cellular decompensation is reflected on the organ system level, particularly in the oxygen-deprived kidney, liver, and reticuloendothelial system. These organs and sys-

tems normally function to maintain homeostasis, clear cellular toxins, or debris and provide useful substrate.

D. Diagnosis of prolongation of ebb phase

Prolongation of the ebb phase implies the continuation of a very specific metabolic state, with ongoing decreased basal energy expenditure, elevated sympathetic output, mobilization of glycogen stores, and release of free fatty acids. Although clinical findings and history are often sufficient to make the diagnosis of profound shock, frequently these measures are inadequate to reveal deficient delivery of the cellular tissue level or to ascertain the cause and, thus, the direction of treatment. More intensive investigation may be needed, especially when doubt exists as to the cause or magnitude.

1. Relative hypovolemia
   a. Ongoing hemorrhage, fluid loss, or deficient replacement can lead to inadequate tissue perfusion.
      (1) On occasion, hemorrhage can be appreciated clinically (e.g., the postoperative patient whose abdomen becomes progressively more distended or the postthoracotomy patient with high sanguinous chest tube output).
      (2) More sensitive is serial hemoglobin determination. A drop inconsistent with intraoperative loss or hemodilution from exogenous fluid administration can be an indication for reexploration.
      (3) Continued third-space fluid loss can be anticipated based on knowledge of the underlying disease and the operative procedure.
      (4) Insensible losses to the atmosphere can be considerably underestimated in the thoracotomy patient or the patient with a prolonged intraperitoneal procedure.
      (5) Resuscitation diagnostic criteria can be divided into four levels.
         (a) Level I—clinical
            i. Tachycardia
            ii. Hypotension, particularly orthostatic
            iii. Low urine output

          iv. Loss of skin turgor, warmth, and color and mottled extremities

      (b) Level II—laboratory tests

          i. Wide AVO_2 difference

          ii. Contraction alkalosis

          iii. High Na^+, Cl^-, blood urea nitrogen (BUN), albumin

          iv. Pressure variation in time with ventilator cycle.

          v. High osmolality of serum and urine

          vi. Fluction of blood pressure (BP) with ventilator

      (c) Level III—invasive

          i. Cardiac output decreased

          ii. Peripheral resistance increased

          iii. Oxygen consumption index reduced

      (d) Level IV—research

          i. Low intramuscular oxygen tension

          ii. Low capillary oxygen tension

2. Cardiac failure

  a. In the patient with cardiac decompensation on either an acute or chronic basis, clinical criteria can be misleading.

    (1) Chronic beta-blockade, for example, will preclude some of the effects of high sympathetic tone, masking tachycardia but not vasoconstriction.

    (2) Most importantly, patients with cardiogenic states have little cardiac reserve.

      (a) A low output state can, therefore, result in hypotension, decreased urine output, cold extremities, and weak pulses.

      (b) As a result, differentiating hypovolemia from pure cardiac disease is often difficult.

      (c) Level II and usually level III criteria are often necessary to make this differentiation.

3. Respiratory insufficiency

Diagnosis of respiratory distress involves both clinical judgment and interpretation of laboratory data.

a. Clinical data are based on obtaining a useful history and performing an adequate physical examination.

   (1) Presence of tachypnea, air hunger and diaphoresis and use of accessory respiratory muscles are excellent bedside indicators of respiratory distress.

   (2) Drug intoxication or other disorders causing global suppression of the CNS can be diagnosed by the presence of a depressed level of consciousness and history abuse by review of medication sheets.

   (3) Observation of inspiratory pattern can help localize CNS lesions causing hypoventilation or a segment of flail.

   (4) The patient in obvious respiratory distress without evidence of air movement by auscultation or by placing a hand over the mouth or airway may have a mucous plug, laryngeal edema, fractured larynx, or tracheal disruption.

   (5) Decreased breath sounds confined to one side may indicate bronchial fracture, airway occlusion, or pneumothorax.

   (6) Subcutaneous emphysema may be associated with laryngeal and conduit fracture or pleural disruption.

   (7) Vigorous suction and coughing may displace a mucous plug or foreign body, thus providing both diagnosis and therapy.

   (8) Aspirated foreign bodies often occlude on expiration only, with a distinct honk audible on auscultation. Chest roentgenogram can confirm the presence of pneumothorax or foreign body.

   (9) Bronchospasm will be apparent when wheezing is heard.

   (10) Laryngospasm is a clinical diagnosis based on respiratory distress and the presence of cervical retractions, most often following extubation.

b. Generally pinpointing respiratory causes of prolonged ebb phase is easily done with the use of the above simple measures. More complicated testing and more intricate data become necessary to interpret pulmonary disease later in the course of the stress response. The diagnosis of inadequate perfusion should be made by means of the resuscitation criteria outlined above.

(1) Blood gases will indicate the presence of hypoxemia and the presence of underventilation in the CNS-depressed patient.

(2) The pH can indicate acidosis, suggestive of failure of oxygen delivery and anaerobic metabolism.

(3) An initial hypocarbia may rapidly give way to CO_2 retention as respiratory effort fails due to exhaustion. Thus, obtaining serial gases can be important.

(4) Screening chest roentgenograms are most useful in the evaluation of pneumothorax or hemothorax, pneumomediastinum, foreign body aspiration, diaphragmatic disruption, and rib fractures.

(5) Serial films will often be needed to evaluate aspiration pneumonitis and atelectasis, as well as the progressive lucency and volume increase that accompanies air trapping.

(6) Evaluating the extent of shunt in a quantitative manner involves actual cumbersome determination of arteriolar-alveolar oxygen gradient. More often, a decrease or lack of change in PaO_2, despite increased inspired oxygen content, is sufficient to estimate the presence of ventilation perfusion mismatch.

4. Oxygen transport
   Oxygen-carrying capacity is diagnosed by routine laboratory tests and clinical means.
   a. Hemolysis produces jaundice and a rise in serum bilirubin, and, if due to drug reactions, may cause a positive Coombs test.

    b. Blood gases reveal alkalosis.

    c. A low serum phosphate level may indicate 2,3-DPG depletion.

  5. Simple conditions that masquerade as shock

    At times, a postoperative patient who has undergone a relatively simple and uncomplicated procedure develops signs of shock, with evidence of increased sympathetic discharge.

    a. Suspecting a pulmonary embolus in such a case is always reasonable and prudent.

    b. Two other often unappreciated causes of high sympathetic tone are gastric dilation and urinary retention.

      (1) Both can cause extreme discomfort as well as a drop in blood pressure, tachycardia, and diaphoresis.

      (2) Both conditions, obviously, are easily relieved.

E. Treatment of prolonged ebb phase

  1. The key to treatment is diagnosis.

  2. Important points in treatment include:

    a. A high index of suspicion accompanied by knowledge of common causes of abnormalities

    b. Resuscitation by criteria with the early use of cardiac output data in conditions that are uncertain (especially in the patient who has known or suspected cardiac disease)

    c. Early reoperation in the event of uncontrolled hemorrhage

    d. Frequent clinical evaluation of respiratory efficacy and pattern

    e. Careful use and interpretation of laboratory and roentgenographic data

  3. The use of inotropic support is often beneficial.

  4. Early use of mechanical ventilation is appropriate in many cases.

  5. Appropriate dosing of pain medications is an art form learned only through experience.

COMPLICATIONS OF THE FLOW-CATABOLISM PHASE
Physiology in the flow-catabolism phase

Following successful resuscitation, ebb phase and its associated depression of metabolic rate give way to a period of heightened energy utilization. In this phase, the organism attempts to repair damaged tissue and restore the capability for normal function. Characteristics include an elevation of basal metabolism, accelerated nitrogen loss, and increased body temperature, all reflecting breakdown and use of endogenous resources; thus, the term flow catabolism is an appropriate description.

A. Flow restoration and the accompanying gradual reduction in alpha adrenergic tone results in reperfusion of both injured tissue and organ systems previously deprived of flow.

1. Resultant clearance of debris, metabolic by-products, and tissue mediators cause an alteration in neuro-humoral-endocrine modulation as a series of local products activate the second phase of the stress response.

2. Compliment, white cell mediators, the clotting cascade, endogenous opiates, and arachidonic acid metabolites are "turned on," perhaps coordinated by the macrophage system.

3. Accompanying this process is the "wash-out" phenomenon, releasing fibrin degradation products, platelet aggregates, microemboli, and other cellular debris.

4. These, in turn, mediate a systemic response designed to deliver substrate for repair to injured and/or ischemic tissue.

5. Peripheral vasodilation continues.

6. Cardiac output increases as a result of mediators themselves and a reduction in afterload.

7. Metabolism is altered to facilitate production of glucose and long- and short-chain carbon glycolytic intermediaries.

8. Lipolysis, glycogenolysis, hepatic gluconeogenesis, and cannibalization of skeletal muscle serve to provide both energy precursors and the amino acids needed for the synthesis of structural and enzymatic proteins.

B. Clinical changes become evident.

1. Serum glucose is elevated.
2. Circulating levels of triglycerides and free fatty acids are increased.
3. Serum levels of amino acids fall. The total amount of plasma amino acid, however, is increased, reflecting the increased utilization as an energy and metabolic substrate.
4. Urinary excretion of nitrogen increases markedly, a negative nitrogen balance ensues, and a drop occurs in the hepatic synthesis of non–acute-phase proteins.
5. An increase in oxygen consumption and carbon dioxide production reflects the overall rise in metabolic rate.

C. The response moves into the next phase (flow anabolism) when a signal is received that restoration of the blood-tissue interface has occurred.
   1. This signal will permit a return of normal cellular function as needed for repair.
   2. Involved in the transmission of this "message" is a "turning off" of the activation process and clearance of mediators.
   3. This generally occurs between the third and fifth postinjury or postoperative day.

D. By itself, this response is adaptive and permits the appropriate mobilization of endogenous resources needed to recover from minor trauma or uncomplicated surgery. Prolonged hypermetabolism, however, as brought about by postoperative complications occurring in this phase, will eventually deplete metabolic stores and foster a state of organ failure and acquired protein-calorie malnutrition. Complications of the flow-catabolic phase take one of two forms.
   1. Primary processes that prolong the time course of the phase
   2. Secondary processes that arise as a result of a permissive effect caused at least in part by resource depletion
      a. Some of these secondary processes in turn result in further prolongation of the phase.
   3. Either primary or secondary processes may become severe enough to result in a shift back to ebb phase.

Primary prolongation of the catabolic phase

In general, the primary causes of prolonged catabolism result from the continuation of mediator release beyond the normal 72-hour period. This can be the result of a number of processes, many of which have common ground with the causes of shock. Partial oxygen delivery deprivation or oxygen utilization impairment results in relative tissue ischemia. In addition, several other processes can result in substantial lengthening of the ebb phase without the presence of oxygen debt, e.g., tissue injury, necrotic tissue, hematoma, infection.

A. Primary physiologic effectors
   1. Fluid deficit
      a. Partial restoration of flow may be sufficient to permit the transition from ebb to flow phase but still result in significant tissue ischemia and mediator activation.
         (1) In general, this problem represents a less intense occurrence of those causes noted in the ebb phase with the added provision that third-space losses become progressively more important.
         (2) Massive tissue injury, retroperitoneal dissection, peritonitis, and bowel resection resulting in ileus lead to capillary disruption and "leak" of fluid into the interstitial compartment.
         (3) Generally, a normal catabolic phase (72 hours) is necessary for microvascular integrity to return.
            (a) Third-space losses will persist until this time and must be replaced.
            (b) Also important is replacement of insensible fluid losses (i.e., to the atmosphere in the ventilated or postthoracotomy patient) and large-scale gastrointestinal (GI) losses, as seen in fistulae, nasogastric suction, or diarrhea.
      b. Hemorrhage itself does not produce prolonged catabolism; rather, the subsequent tissue ischemia resulting from inadequate perfusion seems to be the culprit.
   2. Decreased cardiac output
      a. Cardiac output adequate to maintain blood pressure is not necessarily sufficient to perfuse ischemic tissue.

    b. An acute rise in cardiac performance is necessary to meet the demands of the flow phase.

  3. Oxygen debt

    Relative hypoxia at the tissue level can yield a reduction in peripheral tone and create a mismatch of volume and vascular space.

B. Primary metabolic effectors

  Most important of the processes that primarily prolong the catabolic phase are the primary metabolic disorders. While this group includes several less common entities, such as thyrotoxicosis or ketoacidosis, in general the surgical patient will develop a primary systemic metabolic response as part of an infection. Because the host tissue generates the response, it is independent of the invading organism.

  1. Controversy exists as to the initiating event; whatever this primary event, the result is a persistent hypermetabolism.

  2. Mediator release and persistent catabolism also appear to result from substances produced when a massive soft tissue injury or a large hematoma resolve. These processes can profoundly delay the onset of the anabolic phase.

Consequences of prolongation of flow catabolism

A. Primary end-organ response

  The activator-mediator-response pattern that the advent of the flow catabolic phase of the stress response elicits will be clinically recognizable by the end-organ responses: perfusion mismatch and pulmonary compliance, bowel and biliary function, mental status and renal perfusion. Thus, the patient develops adult respiratory distress syndrome (ARDS), ileus, bile stasis, encephalopathy, and renal insufficiency (see box on p. 534).

  1. Acute pulmonary insufficiency

    a. In the classic description, ARDS represents the pulmonary response to either an initial severe low-flow state, the persistent failure of substrate delivery or utilization, the presence of tissue injury or death, or the presence of infection.

    b. Primary pneumonias or lobar atelectasis can also pre-

**PRIMARY END-ORGAN RESPONSE TO
PROLONGATION OF THE CATABOLIC PHASE**

End-organ response	Pathological condition
V/Q mismatch or decreased compliance	ARDS or acute pulmonary insufficiency as from pneumonia
Bowel stasis	Ileus
Biliary stasis	Cholestatic jaundice, cholecystitis
Altered mental status	Encephalopathy
Renal insufficiency	Acute tubular necrosis polyuric or oliguric

---

cipitate the response. Bronchospasm and poor secretion toileting are also frequent underlying problems.

2. Ileus

a. A number of endogenous mediator substances have been implicated in the altered GI function of the catabolic state: opiates, gut hormones.

b. Exogenous substances are also factors.

(1) Narcotics exert a potent inhibitory effect on GI function.

(2) Anesthetic agents and other analgesics may have similar effects.

(3) Operative and nonoperative trauma to bowel can decrease motility for remarkably prolonged periods.

c. The substrates mobilized by the stress response are potentially important factors.

(1) Free fatty acids and certain amino acids are known inhibitors of GI motility.

(2) A role for these in poststress ileus seems likely.

3. Hepatic dysfunction and cholestatic jaundice

The hepatic response in the stressed state represents that of a primary metabolic regulator of the demand for increased substrate. An overall elevation in hepatic synthetic activity accompanies almost all acute stress states.

This is reflected in an increase in total hepatic blood flow, enzyme induction, and extraction of peripherally produced precursors for entry into gluconeogenic pathways.

a. Cholestasis is a common problem in persistent hypermetabolism and is most likely multifactorial origin.

b. The response of the liver to those entities known to prolong the flow phase has been studied in both humans and in animal models.

(1) Common to all causes of prolonged catabolism is a relative hypovolemia or an impairment of oxygen transport.

(2) This results in a drop in hepatic perfusion or impaired cellular oxygen utilization and perhaps hepatic macrophage sensitization.

(3) In hypovolemia or acute cardiogenic states, an increase in alpha-adrenergic tone will result in increased portal venous tone, as well as increased oxygen extraction across the hepatic bed.

(4) The decreased flow, however, can lead to stasis, ischemia, and hypoxia.

(a) Injury to both Kupffer and parenchymal cells has been demonstrated after as little as 60 minutes of decreased flow or oxygen delivery.

(b) Pathologically, this decrease is accompanied by enlargement of the hepatic sinusoids filled with red cell aggregates and other cellular debris.

c. Unchecked, this process can result in the multiple-systems organ failure syndrome, particularly in the presence of subsequent infection, hematoma, and soft tissue injury.

4. Acute renal failure (ARF)

A frequent complicaton of prolonged catabolism is acute renal insufficiency (defined as a GFR of between 20 and 50 ml/min/1.73^{m}) or overt renal failure (GFR < 20 ml/min/1.73m^2).

5. Encephalopathy

     a. Little attention has been focused on the mental status changes noted in prolongation of the catabolic phase.

        (1) Clinically, the picture is highly variable, ranging from diminished arousability to personality changes.

        (2) Coma may occur.

B. Sensory end-organ response

As a result of dysfunction in individual organ systems brought about by primary prolongation of the catabolic phase, a number of secondary disorders can arise. In a sense, the disorders of lung, bowel, biliary system, and kidney as well as the enhanced mediated metabolism of the prolonged catabolic phase exert a permissive effect. Thus, secondary disorders may be thought of as opportunistic. An alteration in both metabolic rate and substrate utilization results. This overall effect will be discussed in conjunction with the multiple-systems organ failure syndrome, but one of the consequences of prolonged hypercatabolism is a failure of host-mediated antimicrobial activity. This leads to a high incidence of secondary infection. In turn, these new septic episodes further prolong the flow phase.

1. Secondary pulmonary infection

     a. In most cases, the diagnosis of secondary pneumonia is first entertained with the appearance of an interstitial-subsegmental infiltrate on a chest roentgenogram that previously had demonstrated only changes consistent with ARDS. Gram-negative organisms are the rule.

     b. Pathogenesis and pathophysiology reflect the re-distribution of ventilation with associated loss of functional residual capacity (FRC) and atelectasis on both a micro- and macroscopic level.

     c. A key factor in the pathogenesis of shunt, atelectasis, and loss of FRC in the maintenance of the supine position.

     d. Pulmonary abcesses are unusual, but do occur.

2. Hematoma abscess

Secondary seeding of a large hematoma is not an uncommon occurrence.

    a. Any patient with even a transient bacteremia is at risk, as the resolving hematoma represents an ideal culture medium, with high levels of nutrients and minimal blood supply.

    b. Common organisms include those from the upper and lower GI tract and skin flora. The latter can be introduced by the placement of intravenous lines or venipuncture.

    c. Fungi and anaerobes may have a role.

3. Wound infection

   Many wound infections represent contamination at the time of surgery. However, in the immunodepressed patient, blood-borne organisms can secondarily seed a wound. This is particularly true in the surgical wound in which a fluid collection develops, either due to inadequate drainage, poor hemostasis, or lymphatic damage.

4. Sinusitis

   In the individual maintained on ventilatory support with a nasotracheal tube or a long-term nasogastric suction, the indwelling tube can block drainage of the paranasal sinuses. Purulent paranasal sinusitis can result.

5. Urinary tract infection (UTI)

   UTI represents a common form of postoperative infectious complication.

    a. Systemic sepsis and shock can occur.

      (1) The culprit most often cited is the indwelling catheter.

      (2) In male patients, long-term use of such catheters can lead to the development of prostatitis.

    b. Proper catheter care with a closed-collection system can minimize the problem.

    c. Many "bedridden" ventilated intensive care unit patients can effectively void.

6. Gastrointestinal stress ulceration

   Stress ulcers are acute erosions of the GI mucosa superficial to the muscularis mucosae. On occasion, deeper penetration is noted, with development of a chronic inflammatory reaction or perforation.

7. Postoperative cholecystitis

    a. Cholecystitis developing in the postoperative patient represents a very different disease than that noted in the population at large.

        (1) A predominance of men is about 2:1, in contrast to ordinary cholecystitis, which is heavily weighted toward women.

        (2) Older patients seem to be at increased risk, although this is variable.

    b. Among the risk factors are gut rest, ileus, and hyperalimentation, which presumably alter the stimuli to gallbladder contraction and emptying. This is in keeping with findings reporting a high incidence of gallbladder disease in patients receiving total parenteral nutrition (TPN).

    c. Various etiologies have been proposed.

        (1) Vascular etiologies may explain the incidence of this abnormality after profound shock or sepsis.

        (2) Prolonged positive pressure ventilation also correlates with cholecystitis.

        (3) Multiple transfusions seem to be associated with the disease process, presumably as the result of a high pigment load imposed by hemolysis.

        (4) Some studies on patients receiving prolonged parenteral hyperalimentation have attributed a high incidence of biliary "sludge" to intestinal anerobic bacterial overgrowth with the production of lithocholic acid. Which cases of biliary sludge progress to acute cholecystitis remains unknown.

8. Pancreatitis

The exocrine pancreas shows a characteristic response to inadequate flow in both the hypovolemic and septic settings.

    a. Autophagic vacuoles appear and may result in the catabolism of acinar cells.

        (1) If this process is checked, these vacuoles appear as characteristic inclusion structures referred to as residual bodies.

        (2) Failure to reverse the cause of relative hypoperfusion at an early stage will result in cellular self-destruction.

      (3) Digestive enzymes are secondarily released into the substance of the pancreas, further destroying tissue.

      (4) This destruction appears as postoperative or post-traumatic pancreatitis.

    b. Characteristic elevations of serum amylase and other pancreatic enzymes are noted and help confirm the diagnosis.

9. Septic phlebitis and endocarditis

    Another source of infectious complications involves the use of multiple sites for intravenous lines and the increasing reliance upon more invasive means of monitoring.

    a. In the patient who has an indwelling intravenous line for a prolonged period of time or who has had multiple venipunctures for line placement, the possibility of sepsis either subcutaneously or within the vein itself must be considered.

    b. As an extension of this process, the introduction of infectious agents into the venous system can lead to endocarditis.

C. The multiple-systems organ failure syndrome

The multiple-systems organ failure (MSOF) syndrome often represents the final common pathway for severe surgical-traumatic-septic complications. Excluding cancer, it is the most frequent cause of death in the intensive care unit and accounts for over 90% of surgical mortality.

1. MSOF can best be considered as the end result of prolonged hypermetabolism of any origin.

    a. While one-third of the patients who develop the syndrome have clear-cut sepsis and another third some form of bacteremia, the remaining group never have positive cultures.

    b. Despite this, the course of the disease is by all evidence equivalent in the three groups.

    c. Common to all, however, is a period of profound failure of substrate delivery or utilization.

2. The clinical changes that characterize MSOF are nonspecific and reflective of the underlying disorders of metabolism and physiology.

    a. As the response worsens, one may be confronted with varying degrees of encephalopathy, elevations of temperature and white count, tachycardia, hyperventilation, and the eventual onset of organ failure.

    b. Spontaneous bacteremias are frequent and often polymicrobial.

    c. Stress ulceration is common.

    d. Peripheral neuropathies are increasingly described.

    e. Varying degrees of pulmonary, respiratory, hepatic, and ultimately cardiac failure are noted.

    f. The terminal event is often cardiovascular collapse precipitated by a refractory coagulopathy.

3. MSOF syndrome represents, on the clinical level, almost any combination of primary or secondary disorders of prolonged flow catabolism.

4. On the cellular and biochemical levels, the syndrome probably represents the final common pathway to those conditions that prolong this phase.

    a. A progressive failure of substrate utilization is reflected in glucose intolerance unresponsive to increasing insulin administration, failure of triglyceride clearance, elevation of the lactate-pyruvate ratio associated with decreased peripheral extraction of oxygen, and ultimately hepatic inability to utilize amino acids as gluconeogenic precursors.

    b. Death usually follows this late-occurring phenomenon.

5. Progressive substrate depletion also has a role.

    a. Acquired malnutrition, a consequence of prolonged catabolism, almost invariably contributes to the development of the MSOF syndrome.

    b. Furthermore, malnutrition is of great importance in failure of wound healing, a complication of flow anabolism.

Diagnosis of prolongation of the flow-catabolism phase

Prolonged catabolism is exhibited by a characteristic picture of altered metabolism and/or physiology. As the organism senses the failure of oxygen or substrate delivery, it initiates mechanisms that alter metabolism in the hope of increasing substrate availability. This mechanism can be detected by metabolic monitoring.

A. Simple hypovolemia represents a primary physiologic effect and will be reflected in increased vascular resistance, elevated arteriovenous oxygen extraction, excess lactic acid production, and either acidosis or a contraction alkalosis. Cardiac failure will provide a similar picture. Hypovolemia and cardiac failure can be distinguished on the basis of actual cardiac output measurements as well as the response to therapeutic manipulation.

1. Thus, the hypovolemic patient will respond to a fluid challenge (increased preload) with an increase in cardiac output and stroke volume, a drop in peripheral resistance, AVO_2 difference and lactate production, and a normalization of pH.

2. A failing heart may be able to respond to increased preload with increased inotrophy, but often the response will be insufficient to correct the biochemical abnormalities.

3. The principles of O_2 transport restoration and maintenance are presented in Part I of this manual.

B. The metabolic changes are characteristic.

1. Metabolic changes include insulin-resistant hyperglycemia, triglyceride intolerance, and a primary failure of oxygen extraction reflected in a narrowed AVO_2 difference and a high lactate production.

2. The physiologic picture of high cardiac output and low vascular resistance seems to represent a response to the metabolic defect.

3. A discussion of these metabolic alterations is presented in Part I of this manual.

Treatment of prolongation of the flow-catabolism phase

Treatment involves adequate support while a search is made for the cause of prolongation. The support principles are presented in Part I of this manual.

COMPLICATIONS OF THE FLOW-ANABOLIC PHASE
Physiology of flow anabolism

The final phase of the recovery from stress involves a net production of metabolic precursors, both to finalize the repair process and affect repletion of those endogenous substances utilized during the hypermetabolic phase.

A. A discernible shift in metabolism occurs.
B. Depending on the nature of the individual stress process, exogenous support, and the presence or absence of sepsis, a shift in fuel balance may occur.
  1. This is reflected in a change in the respiratory quotient back toward the resting level of about 0.8.
  2. Hepatic nitrogen flux shifts from net inflow to net outflow, with most of the production being directed toward muscle.
C. Breakdown of visceral protein decreases, as does muscle catabolism. These decreases are reflected in a drop in 3-methyl histidine excretion in the urine and a decrease in serum BUN.
D. Hepatic gluconeogenesis decreases.
E. Glycogen reserves are restored.
F. Lipolysis drops and actual fat deposition can occur.
G. Support needed by organ systems falls.
H. The bulk of metabolic activity is directed toward repair of injured tissue.

Complications of flow anabolism

A. Disorders of this phase take two forms.
  1. The first is a catastrophic event.
    a. One of the following can occur:
      (1) Myocardial infarction
      (2) Pulmonary embolus
      (3) Rupture of a previously walled-off abscess
      (4) Development of a new form of systemic sepsis
    b. These are most often noted in the predisposed patient, including the elderly, the bedridden, or those with preexisting heart disease, cirrhosis, diabetes, or malnutrition.
  2. The second form of disorder involves a failure of sub-

strate availability and is reflected in poor wound healing and prolonged rehabilitation and convalescence.

    a. The predisposed patient is at greater risk.

    b. Malnutrition is a prominent feature.

    c. Exercise is an important component of therapy.

B. Determinants of adequate healing appear to involve several basic categories of effectors.

  1. Perhaps most important is the provision of adequate substrate.

    a. Since a wound is initially devoid of blood supply due to the severing of vasculature by the initial insult, substrate delivery becomes dependent upon the extent of injury and the magnitude of revascularization.

    b. Recent work has revealed the existence of a platelet-produced angiogenesis factor which, as part of the local activation sequence, induces the formation of capillaries in wounded tissue.

    c. The rate of repair depends on oxygen supply and substrate availability.

  2. Also intrinsic to the healing process, along with initial clotting and vasospasm to prevent blood loss, is thrombolysis and scavaging of debris by phagocytic white cells.

    a. This process, along with angiogenesis, will peak at about 5 days after injury in the surgical wound.

    b. This peak corresponds to the onset of the anabolic period.

  3. Local tissue environment is a factor.

    a. Due to inadequate blood supply, wounded tissue rapidly becomes hypoxic, hypercarbic, and acidotic.

    b. Cells involved in both the clearance of debris and particularly in collagen synthesis and other aspects of repair are unable to function optimally in this environment.

    c. Thus, once again, the process of physical healing coincides with the reversal of these detrimental factors, usually occurring at 5 days after injury.

    d. Epithelialization is oxygen dependent and requires reestablishment of blood supply to occur.

  4. Although the above factors relate to the delivery of sub-

strate, oxygen supply appears to be of particular importance.

    a. Function of white cells and fibroblasts, as well as reversal of acidosis and hydroxylation of lysine and proline (a key element of collagen synthesis and cross-linking) are directly O_2 dependent.

    b. Oxygen availability is also of prime importance in handling microorganisms.

        (1) While opsonization and internalization of bacteria as well as primary lysosomal degranulization can occur under anaerobic conditions, a second and highly important set of bacteriocidal mechanisms requires oxygen consumption. This involves the production of superoxides and peroxides to react with white cell myeloperoxidase and a halide to form a highly lethal hypohalide to attack invading organisms.

  5. Other substrate precursors play a role in wound healing.

    a. Glucose and fat provide fuel.

    b. Amino acids constitute both structural and enzymatic precursors.

    c. Hepatic diversion of these substances ends with the catabolic phase.

    d. Micronutrients also play a role in tissue repair and wound healing.

C. In the event of a wound complication, the following approach is rational.

  1. Diagnosis

    a. Systemic sepsis will occur with a shift back into an earlier phase of metabolism.

    b. Local wound infection will be present with redness, tenderness, and some systemic signs. Drainage may be noted.

    c. Otherwise, failure of wound healing is usually due to lack of specific nutrient, generalized malnutrition, predisposing disease, or a wound so extensive that delivery of substrate cannot be accomplished.

  2. Prevention

  Prophylaxis should involve attempts to maximize oxygen

delivery and supply macro- and micronutrients in effective quantities.

3. Treatment
    a. Treatment of a failed wound includes debridement,
       drainage, and close attention to previously mentioned
       factors.
    b. A search for recognized diabetes, cirrhosis, or mal-
       nutrition and white cell dysfunction may be in order.

D. Rehabilitation and convalescence are important components
   of this phase, particularly after a prolonged intensive care
   unit (ICU) course.

1. These should be started in the ICU.
2. These components account for at least as much and probably more expense than the ICU course.
3. Adequate nutrition is a major component.
4. Psychiatric difficulties are common.
5. Some patients never recover.
    a. This may reflect a continuation of the organ failure
       syndrome.
    b. Of those patients in the ICU over 7 days who survive
       (>60%), approximately 50% will still be functioning
       at one year.

SELECTED READINGS
The stress response

Bessey, P.Q., and Wilmore D.W.: Energy metabolism after injury. In Proceedings White Silver Springs Symposium, vol. 2, July, 1982, Mead, Johnson &
Co., p. 9.

Cerra, F.B.: Profiles in nutrition management: the trauma patient, Chicago,
1982, Medical Directions Inc.

Cerra, F.B., Siegel, J.H., and Border J.R.: Correlations between metabolic and
cardiopulmonary measurements in patients after trauma, general surgery and
sepsis, J. Trauma **19**:621, 1979.

Cuthberson, D.: The metabolic response to injury and its nutritional implications: Retrospect and prospect, JPEN **3**:108, 1979.

Fath, J.J., Meguid, M.M., and Cerra, F.B.: The hormonal and metabolic response to surgery and stress. In Lewis, R. (editor): Practice of surgery, In
press.

Lefer, A.M.: Vascular mediators in ischemia and shock, In Cowley, R.A., and
Trump, B.F. (editors): Pathophysiology of shock, anoxia and ischemia, Baltimore, 1983, Williams & Wilkins, p. 165.

Popp, M.B., and Brennen, M.F.: Metabolic response to trauma and infection.
In Fischer, J.E.: Surgical nutrition, Boston, 1983, Little, Brown & Co., p.
479.

Complications of ebb phase

Andersson, B.: Regulation of body fluids, Ann. Rev. Physiol. **39**:185, 1977.

Arturson, G., and de Verdier, C.H.: Respiratory function of the blood, In Burke, J.F. (editor): Surgical physiology, Philadelphia, 1983, W.B. Saunders Co., p. 451.

Baue, A.E.: Metabolic abnormalities of shock, Surg. Clin. North Am. **56**:1059, 1976.

Baxter, C.R.: Metabolic consequences of shock. In Proceedings White Silver Springs Symposium. vol. 1, 1982, Mead, Johnson & Co., p. 7.

Boutros, A.R., et al.: Comparison of hemodynamic, pulmonary and renal effects of use of three types of fluids after major surgical proceedures on the abdominal aorta, Crit. Care Med. **7**:9, 1979.

Calvin, J.E., Driedger, A.A., and Sibbald, W.J.: Does the wedge pressure predict left ventricular preload in critically ill patients? Crit. Care Med. **9**:437, 1981.

Carrico, C.J., and Judson, L.D.: Physiology of the mechanics of breathing. In Burke, J.F. (editor): Surgical physiology, Philadelphia, 1983, W.B. Saunders Co., p. 400.

Cerra, F.B.: Metabolic monitoring: the key to the microcirculation. In Shoemaker, W.C., and Thompson, W.L. (editors): Critical care: state of the art, vol. 3, Fullerton, Calif., 1982, Soc. Crit. Care Med.

Cerra, F.B.: Shock. In Burke, J.F. (editor): Surgical physiology, Philadelphia, 1983, W.B. Saunders Co., p. 497.

Christensson, P., et al.: Early and late results of controlled ventilation in flail chest, Chest **75**:465, 1979.

Deutschman, C.S., and Cerra, F.B.: Fluids, electrolytes, and homeostasis. In Monaco, A., et al. (editors): Textbook of surgery, Philadelphia, 1981, W.B. Saunders Co.

Guyton, A.C.: Textbook of medical physiology, ed. 6, Philadelphia, 1981, W.B. Saunders Co., pp. 289, 309, 332, 476, 491, 516, 531.

Hammon, J.W., and Sabiston, D.C.: The pulmonary circulation. In Burke, J.F. (editor): Surgical physiology, Philadelphia, 1983, W.B. Saunders Co., p. 420.

Hauser, C.J., et al.: Oxygen transport responses to colloid and crystalloid in critically ill surgical patients, Surg. Gynecol. Obstet. **150**:811, 1980.

Jones, R.H., and Sabiston, D.C.: Pulmonary embolism, Surg. Clin. North Am. **56**:891, 1976.

Lee, H.A.: Protein metabolism during anesthesia, Clin. Anesth. **1**:551, 1983.

MacLeen, L.D.: Shock: Causes and management of circulatory collapse. In Sabiston, D.C. (editor): Textbook of surgery, Philadelphia, 1981, W.B. Saunders Co., p. 58.

Mela, L.M., Miller, L.D., and Nicholas, G.: Influence of cellular acidosis and altered cation concentrations in shock-induced mitochondrial damage, Surgery **72**:103, 1972.

Meyers, J.R., et al.: Changes in functional residual capacity of the lung after operation, Arch. Surg. **110**:576, 1975.

Plum, F., and Posner, J.B.: The diagnosis of stupor and coma, Philadelphia, 1980, F.A. Davis Co., p. 34.

Shackford, S.R., et al.: The management of flail chest. A comparison of ventilatory and non-ventilatory management, Am. J. Surg. **132**:759, 1976.

Shoemaker, W.C.: Pattern of pulmonary hemodynamic and functional changes in shock, Crit. Care Med. **2**:200, 1974.

Shoemaker, W.C., et al.: Comparison of the relative effectiveness of colloid and crystalloid in emergency resuscitation, Am. J. Surg. **142**:73, 1981.

Complications of flow catabolism

Askanazi, J., et al.: Nutrition and the respiratory system, Crit. Care Med. **10**:163, 1982.

Baracos, V., et al.: Stimulation of muscle protein degradation and prostaglandin E_2 release by leukocyte pyrogen: A mechanism for the increased degradation of muscle protein during fever, N. Engl. J. Med. **308**:553, 1983.

Bessey, P.Q., and Wilmore, D.W.: Energy metabolism after injury. Proceedings White Silver Springs Symposium, 1982, Mead Johnson & Co., p. 9.

Cerra F.B., et al.: Branched chain metabolic support: a prospective randomized double-blind trial, Ann. Surg. **199**:283, 1984.

Cerra, F.B., Siegel, J.H., and Border, J.R.: Correlations between metabolic and cardiopulmonary measurements in patients after trauma, general surgery and sepsis, J. Trauma **19**:621, 1979.

Clowes, G.H.A., Jr., et al.: Muscle proteolysis induced by a circulating peptide in patients with sepsis or trauma, N. Engl. J. Med. **308**:545, 1983.

Clowes, G.H.A., Jr., et al.: Effects of parenteral alimentation on amino acid metabolism in septic patients, Surgery **88**:531, 1980.

Deutschman, C.S., et al.: Paranasal sinusitis associated with nasotracheal intubation, Crit. Care Med. In press.

Dorsey, J.S., et al.: Myocardial depression in patients on chronic calcium channel blockers given narcotic anesthesia. In press.

Hauser, C.J., et al.: Oxygen transport responses to colloid and crystalloid in critically ill surgical patients, Surg. Gynecol. Obstet. **150**:811, 1980.

Kaufman, B., and Rachow, E.C.: Relationship between O_2 delivery and consumption during fluid resuscitation of hypovolemic and septic shock, Chart **85**:336, 1984.

Law, D.K., Dudrick, S.J., and Abdou, N.I.: Immunocompetence of patients with protein-calorie malnutrition. The effects of nutritional repletion, Ann. Intern. Med. **79**:545, 1973.

Long, C.L.: Non-septic stress metabolism. In Fischer, J.E. (editor): Nutritional management of metabolic stress, Chicago, 1983, Medical Directions Inc., p. 5.

Manny, J., et al.: Myocardial performance curves as a guide to volume therapy, Surg. Gynecol. Obstet. **149**:863, 1979.

Mullen, J.L., et al.: Reduction of operative mortality and morbidity by combined preoperative and postoperative nutritional support, Ann. Surg. **192**:604, 1980.

Newsome, H.H., Jr.: The neuroendocrine system. In Burke, J.F. (editor): Surgical physiology, Philadelphia, 1983, W.B. Saunders Co., p. 208.

Rodemann, H.P., and Goldberg A.L.: Arachadonic acid, prostaglandin E2 and F2 influence the rates of protein turnover in skeletal and cardiac muscle, J. Biol. Chem. **257**:1632, 1982.

Schaper, W. (editors): The pathophysiology of myocardial perfusion, New York, 1979, Elsevier/North Holland.

Shoemaker, W.C., and Apple, P.L.: Use of physiologic monitoring to predict outcome and to assist clinical decisions in the critically ill, Am. J. Surg. **146**:43, 1983.

Sibbald, W.J., et al: Concepts in pharmacologic and nonpharmacologic support of cardiovascular function in critically ill surgical patients, Surg. Clin. North Am. **63**:455, 1983.

Solomkin, J.S., and Simmons, R.L.: Cellular and subcellular mediators of acute inflammation, Surg. Clin. North Am. **62**:225, 1983.

Waxman, K., Nolan, L., and Shoemaker, W.C.: Sequential perioperative lactate determinations, Crit. Care Med. **10**:96, 1982.

Sepsis

Burke, J.F.: The physiology of preventing infection: Preventive antibiotics. In Burke, J.F. (editor): Surgical physiology, Philadelphia, 1983, W.B. Saunders Co., p. 270.

Cerra, F.B., and Hassett, J.H.: Vasodilator therapy in clinical sepsis with low output syndrome, J. Surg. Res. **25**:180, 1978.

Cerra, F.B., et al.: The hepatic failure of sepsis: cellular vs. substrate, Surgery **86**:409, 1979.

Cerra, F.B., et al.: Septic autocannibalism: a failure of exogenous metabolic support, Ann. Surg. **192**:570, 1980.

Deutschman, C.S., et al.: Pure viral sepsis: further evidence for a host-dependent, organism independent response. In press.

Hess, M.C., Hastillo, A., and Greenfield, L.J.: Spectrum of cardiovascular function during gram negative sepsis. Prog. Cardiovasc. Dis. **23**:279, 1981.

Siegel, J.H., et al.: Human response to sepsis. a physiologic manifestation of disordered metabolic control, In Crowley, R.A., and Trump, B.F. (editors): Pathophysiology of shock, anorexia, and isedemia, Baltimore, 1983, Williams & Wilkins, p. 235.

Wiles, J., and Cerra, F.B.: The systemic septic response: does the organism matter? Crit. Care Med. **8**:55, 1980.

Pulmonary complications

Anderson, R.R., et al.: Documentation of pulmonary capillary permeability in human adult respiratory distress syndrome secondary to sepsis, Am. Rev. Respir. Dis. **119**:869, 1979.

Ayres, S.M.: Treatment of adult respiratory distress syndrome. In Cowley, R.A., and Trump, B.F. (editors) p. 387.

Bone, R.G.: Treatment of ARDS with diuretics, dialysis and positive end-expiratory pressure, Crit. Care Med. **6**:136, 1978.

Brigham, K.L.: Pulmonary edema: cardiac and non-cardiac, Am. J. Surg. **138**:361, 1979.

Demling, R.H., and Flynn, J.T.: Humoral factors and lung injury during shock, trauma and sepsis, In Crowley, R.A., and Trump, B.F. (editors): Pathophysiology of shock, anorexia, and ischemia, Baltimore, 1983, Williams & Wilkins, p. 395.

Demling, R.H., and Nerlich, M.: Acute respiratory failure, Surg. Clin. North Am. **63**:337, 1983.

Demling, R.H., Niehaus, G., and Will, J.A.: Pulmonary microvascular response to hemorrhagic shock, resuscitation and recovery, J. Appl. Physiol. **46**:498, 1979.

Fisher, P., Miller, J.E., and Glauser, F.L.: Endotoxin-induced increased alveolar capillary membrane permeability, Crit. Care Med. **4**:387, 1977.

Herrin, J.T.: The kidney. In Burke, J.F. (editor): Surgical physiology, Philadelphia, 1983, W.B. Saunders Co., p. 187.

Kirby, R.R., et al.: High level PEEP in acute respiratory insufficiency, Chest **67**:156, 1975.

Klein, J.J., et al.: Pulmonary function after recovery from adult respiratory distress syndrome, Chest **69**:350, 1976.

Modell, J.H., and Boysen, P.G.: Pulmonary aspiration of stomach contents. In Shoemaker, W.C., Thompson, W.L., and Holbrook, P.R. (editors): Textbook of Critical Care, Philadelphia, 1984, W.B. Saunders Co., p. 272.

Moore, F.D., et al.: Post-traumatic pulmonary insufficiency, Philadelphia, 1969, W.B. Saunders Co.

Parratt, J.R., and Sturgess, R.M.: The possible roles of histamine, 5-HT and prostaglandin F_{2a} as mediators of the acute pulmonary effects of endotoxin, Br. J. Pharmacol. **60**:209, 1977.

Riede, U.N., et al.: Pathobiology of the alveolar wall in human shock lung. In Cowley, R.A., and Trump, B.F. (editors): Pathophysiology of shock, anoxia, and ischemia, Baltimore, 1983, Williams & Wilkins, p. 358.

Saldeen, T.: Clotting, microembolism and inhibition of fibrinolysis in adult respiratory distress, Surg. Clin. North Am. **63**:285, 1983.

Selkurt, E.E.: Role of kidney and lung in the handling of prostaglandin E in hemorrhagic shock, Adv. Shock Res. **1**:159, 1979.

Shoemaker, W.C., and Hauser, C.J.: Critique of crystalloid vs. colloid therapy in shock and shock lung, Crit. Care Med. **7**:117, 1979.

Sibbald, W.J., and Driedger, A.A.: Pulmonary alveolarcapillary permeability in human septic respiratory distress syndrome, In Cowley, R.A., and Trump, B.F., editors: Pathophysiology of shock, anoxia, and ischemia, Baltimore, 1983, Williams & Wilkins, p. 372.

Vracko, R.: Significance of basal lamina for regeneration of injured lung, Virchows Arch. **335**:264, 1972.

Winter, P.M., and Miller, J.N.: Oxygen toxicity. In Shoemaker, E.C., Thompson, W.L., and Holbrook, P.R. (editors): Textbook of critical care, Philadelphia, 1984, W.B. Saunders Co., p. 218.

Renal complications

Anderson, R.J., et al.: Nonoliguric acute renal failure. N. Engl. J. Med. **296**:1134, 1977.

Barnes, J.L., and McDowell, E.M.: Pathology and pathophysiology of acute renal failure—a review. In Cowley, R.A., and Trump, B.F. (editors): Pathophysiology of shock, anoxia, and ischemia, Baltimore, 1983, Williams & Wilkins, p. 324.

Berndt, W.O.: Effects of acute anoxia on renal transport processes, J. Toxicol. Environ. Health **2**:1, 1976.

Cantarovich, F., et al.: High-dose furosamide in established acute renal failure, Br. J. Med. **4**:449, 1973.

Conger, J.D., and Robinette, J.B.: Pathogenetic events in ischemic acute renal failure (ARF), Kidney Int. **10**:555, 1976.

Gehr, M., et al.: Treatment of acute renal failure, In Cowley, R.A., and Trump, B.F., (editors): Pathophysiology of shock, anoxia, and ischemia, Baltimore, 1983, Williams & Wilkins, p. 341.

Hilberman M.: Renal protection. In Shoemaker, W.C., Thompson, W.L., and Holbrook, P.R. (editors): Textbook of Critical Care, Philadelphia, 1984, W.B. Saunders Co., p. 597.

Like, R.G., and Kennedy, A.C.: Prevention and early management of acute renal failure, Clin. Nephrol. **13**:73, 1980.

Tilney, N.L., and Lazarus, J.M.: Acute renal failure in surgical patients, Surg. Clin. North Am. **63**:357, 1983.

Hepatic and biliary complications

Champion, H.R., et al.: A clinicopathologic study of hepatic dysfunction following shock, Surg. Gynecol. Obstet. **142**:657, 1976.

Cowley, R.A., et al.: Pathology and pathophysiology of the liver. In Crowley, R.A., Trump, B.F. (editors): Pathophysiology of shock, anoxia, and ischemia, Baltimore, 1983, Williams & Wilkins, p. 285.

DenBesten, L.: The incidence and mechanism of gallstone formation during parenteral nutrition. In Najarian, J.S., and Delaney, J.P. (editors): Advances in hepatic, biliary and pancreatic surgery. In press.

Gately, J.F., and Thomas, E.J.: Acute cholecystitis occurring as a complication of other diseases, Arch. Surg. **118**:1137, 1983.

Howard, R.J., and Delaney, J.P.: Postoperative cholecystitis, Am. J. Dig. Dis. **17**:213, 1972.

Humphrey, C.S., and Fischer, J.E.: Endocrine control of the alimentary tract. In Burke, J.F. (editor): Surgical physiology, Philadelphia, 1983, W.B. Saunders Co., p. 373.

Long, T.N., Heimbach, D.M., and Carrico, C.J.: Acalculous cholecystitis in critically ill patients, Am. J. Surg. **136**:31, 1978.

West, M.A., et al.: Pure Kupffer cells mediate a biphasic modulation of hepatocycte protein synthesis after exposure to septic stimulae, Surgery. In press.

Pancreatic complications

Herlihy, B.L., and Lefer, D.M.: Alterations in pancreatic acinar cell organelles during circulatory shock, Circ. Shock **2**:143, 1975.

Jones, R.T., et al.: Studies of the ischemic pancreas in shock, Adv. Shock Res. **1**:197, 1979.

Jones, R.T., and Linhardt, G.: Pathology and pathophysiology of the exocrine pancreas in shock. In Cowley, R.A., and Trump, B.F. (editors): Pathophysiology of shock, anoxia, and ischemia, Baltimore, 1983, Williams & Wilkins, p. 309.

Warshaw, A.L., and O'Hara, P.J.: Susceptibility of the pancreas to ischemic injury in shock, Ann. Surg. **188**:197, 1978.

Gastrointestinal complications

Dworkin, H.J.: Gastrointestinal hemorrhage In Shoemaker, W.C., Thompson, W.L., and Holbrook P.R. (editors), Textbook of Critical Care, Philadelphia, 1984, W.B. Saunders Co., p. 591.

Humphrey, C.S., and Fischer, J.E.: Endocrine control of the alimentary tract. In Burke, J.F. (editor): Surgical physiology, Philadelphia, 1983, W.B. Saunders Co., p. 373.

Mittermeyer, C., and Riede, U.N.: Human pathology of the gastrointestinal tract in shock, ischemia and hypoxemia. In Crowley, R.A., and Trump, B.F. (editors): Pathophysiology of shock, anoxia, and ischemia, Baltimore, 1983, Williams & Wilkins, p. 301.

Multiple systems organ failure

Border, J.R., Chenier, R., and McMenamy, R.H.: Multiple systems organ failure: Muscle fuel deficit with visceral protein malnutrition, Surg. Clin North Am. **56**:1147, 1976.

Cerra, F.B., et al.: Multiple sysems organ failure. In Cowley, R.A., and Trump B.R. (editors): Pathophysiology of shock, anoxia, and ischemia, Baltimore, 1983, Williams & Wilkins, p. 254.

Eiseman, B., Beart, R., and Norton C.: Multiple organ failure, Surg. Gynecol. Obstet. **144**:323, 1977.

Complications of the anabolic phase

Hunt, T.K.: Physiology of wound healing. In Burke, J.F. (editor): Surgical physiology, Philadelphia, 1983, W.B. Saunders Co., p. 1.

Knighton, D.R., et al.: Oxygen tension regulates the expression of angiogenesis factor by macrophages, Science **221**:1283, 1983.

21

Immunologic and reticuloendothelial function in surgical and critically ill patients

Marvin A. McMillen

This chapter provides a brief outline of current cellular and humoral immune mechanisms that may be active or altered in critically ill patients. Drug dosages and other therapies are seldom provided here, since much of this information is at best theoretic and therapy is in its formative stages. Disorders in which immune dysfunction occurs are also noted. Although these conditions may be rare, their recognition and therapy may help to salvage the occasional unfortunate patient from overwhelming and decompensated sepsis.

CELLULAR MEDIATORS OF INFLAMMATION, INFECTION, AND IMMUNITY

Current research indicates that the most radical alterations in immunologic function in sepsis occur within the monocyte-macrophage and granulocyte compartment. Lymphocyte dysfunction, whether of cell-mediated T cell or humoral B cell origin, may prove important in the prevention of infection and control of viral, fungal, and certain bacterial infections; but the bulk of the response to overwhelming established bacterial sepsis is by circulating granulocytes and fixed macrophages of the reticuloendothelial system. Considerable attention is paid to these cellular functions in this chapter, and only a brief overview of lymphocyte function is provided.

Monocytes and macrophages

The mononuclear cellular population noted on peripheral smears contains both monocytoid and lymphocytoid populations.

A. Monocyte characteristics
   1. Closely related to granulocytes
   2. Derived from similar bone marrow precursors
   3. Share many of the growth factor requirements of granulocyte growth
   4. Circulating monocytes probably migrate to the periphery and become fixed macrophages
   5. Probably far more "educated" than granulocytes
B. Immunologic functions:
   1. Phagocytosis
   2. Mediate the inflammatory response
   3. Interact with other cells
      a. Process and present antigen for cytotoxic T cell development
      b. Act as helpers in antibody production
      c. Produce colony-stimulating factors, fibroblast growth factor, chemotactic factors, lymphocyte-activating factor (interleukin 1), plasminogen activator, and lactoferrin
      d. Possible secretion of inhibitory substances
C. Response to irritants
   1. Chemical and infectious irritants greatly increase the motility and phagocytic ability of macrophages.
   2. These "activated" motile cells bear plasminogen activator on their surface.
   3. The macrophage cleaves fibrin polymer to form fibrin split products, for which macrophages have another set of receptors.
   4. Complement and collagen by-products are also chemotactic for macrophages. These cells represent the first-line defense to any surgical, traumatic, or infectious insult.
   5. Once on the scene, these macrophages are primarily responsible for the recruitment of other phagocytic and inflammatory cells.

Granulocytes

A. Characteristics
   1. Granulocytes are highly differentiated, essentially end-

MACROPHAGE SECRETORY PRODUCTS

A. Growth factors
  1. Interleukin I—lymphocyte activating factor
    a. Primes precytotoxic cells
    b. Stimulates interleukin 2 secretion by T helpers
    c. Triggers endothelial release of prostacyclin
  2. Colony-stimulating factor—essential for granulocyte maturation
  3. Burst-forming activity—stimulates preerythrocyte maturation
  4. Fibroblast growth factor
B. Enzymes
  1. Lysozyme—bacteriocidal
  2. Neutral proteases (plasminogen activator, elastase, collagenase)
  3. Acid hydrolases—bacteriocidal
C. Inflammatory factors
  1. Complement components
    a. C_1, C_4, C_2, C_3, C_5, factors B, D, properdin, C_3b inactivator, and B1H
    b. Important role in lysis of bacteria and cells
    c. Some components have inflammatory effects as well
  2. Endogenous pyrogen (probably identical with interleukin 1)
    a. Causes fever by affecting hypothalamus
    b. Stimulates hepatic protein synthesis
    c. Stimulates catabolism of muscle actinomyosin
  3. Neutrophil chemotactic factor—recruits granulocytes
D. Binding proteins
  1. Transferrin
  2. Transcobalamin II
  3. Fibronectin
E. Lipids
  1. Prostaglandin E_2
  2. Thromboxane
  3. Platelet-activating factors
F. Oxygen metabolites (see granulocytes)
G. Alpha interferon
  1. May protect normal cells
  2. Induces antiviral protein (AVP) formation
  3. Stimulates "natural killer" cells

stage cells without the capacity to proliferate or reproduce themselves.

2. Neutrophils, basophils, and eosinophils have essentially four functions.
   a. Motility and chemotaxis
   b. Phagocytosis of bacteria and debris
   c. Enzyme release and mediation of inflammation
   d. Bacteriocidal effects mediated by oxygen intermediates

3. Location and life span
   a. Although granulocytes are measured in peripheral blood, the predominant intravascular defense mechanism is the fixed macrophages within the spleen and hepatic reticuloendothelial system.
   b. Granulocytes primarily function in the periphery and remain in the bloodstream only 4 to 8 hours.
   c. Their tissue survival depends on the presence or absence of infection but is probably no more than 3 to 4 days.

B. Defects of granulocyte chemotaxis
   1. In vitro mechanisms of granulocyte motility
      a. Random migration
      b. Stimulated random migration (chemokinesis)
      c. Directed migration (chemotaxis)
   2. Assays
      a. Motility: measure in vitro migration in agar
      b. Chemotaxis: measure the differences in normal motility versus that in the direction of C5a (a potent chemotactic factor)
   3. Causes
      a. Table 21-1 lists the possible causes of defective chemotaxis.
      b. C5a and degranulated neutrophil proteases are probably the most important chemoattractants.
      c. The mechanism by which granulocytes orient themselves and migrate in the direction of a gradient is currently unknown but does require energy and the products of oxidative metabolism.

Table 21-1. Causes of abnormal granulocyte chemotaxis

Intrinsic	
Defective adherence	Diabetes
	Steroids
	Salicylates
	Alcohol
Defective migration	Lazy leukocytes
	Thermal injury
	Kartagener's syndrome
Defective chemotaxis	Hyper-IgE syndrome
	Hypogammaglobulinemia
	Postmarrow transplant
	Down's syndrome
	Lupus
Other	Wiskott-Aldrich syndrome
	Rheumatoid arthritis
	Hypophosphatemia
Extrinsic	
Chemoattractants	C1r, C2, C4 ⎫
	C3 ⎬ Deficiencies
	C5 ⎭
	Immunoglobulin deficiencies
	Kinin and fibrinolysin deficiencies
	Lupus and diabetes mellitus
Chemotactic lymphokines	Mucocutaneous candidosis
	Wiskott-Aldrich syndrome
Transfer factor	Sezary syndrome
Excessive inactivators	Hodgkin's disease
	Hansen's disease
	Cirrhosis
	Sarcoidosis
Deficient inactivator	Alpha$_1$ antitrypsin deficiency
Inhibitors	Uremia
	Glomerulonephritis

C. Phagocytosis

    1. The classic defect of phagocytosis is chronic granulonatous disease. In this condition, granulocytes can ingest but not lyse microorganisms because of an absence of myeloperoxidase, an essential enzyme in the generation of bacteriocidal hypochlorous acid.

    2. Phagocytosis itself is probably not impaired in sepsis and

critical illness, but rather degranulation of lysozymes within the phagocytic vesicle is incomplete or inadequate.

D. Enzyme release and inflammation

Neutrophil lysozymal enzymes are functionally important within the phagocytic vacuole or, when the particle is too large to be ingested, outside the cell.

1. Neutrophils bear receptors for the opsonins C3b and the Fc portion of immunoglobulin.

   a. When activated, neutrophils are primed to either phagocytose or release mediators.

2. The enzyme release from specific granules is triggered by another set of neutrophil receptors for C5a and formyl-methionyl-leucyl-phenylalanine (FMLP), which is structurally similar to bacterial chemotaxins.

   a. Once outside the neutrophil, the destructive effects of these enzymes are moderated by circulating antiproteases such as alpha-1-antitrypsin and alpha-2-macroglobulin.

      (1) The severe and early emphysema and cirrhosis noted in patients homozygous for alpha-1-antitrypsin-deficiency documents the importance of these antiproteases in limiting the destructive effect of inflammatory mediators.

3. Granulocytes also secrete lactoferrin, which both binds iron and turns off colony-stimulating factor.

   a. Iron enhances bacterial growth.

   b. The iron sequestration of chronic infection may represent a homeostatic alteration to inhibit bacterial growth.

4. Eosinophils are a subgroup of granulocytes.

   a. They can inhibit the reactions triggered by IgE—mast cell activation.

   b. They also interact with immunoglobulin-coated schistosomes and other parasitic larva and lyse them via a mechanism involving cellular major basic protein (MBP).

E. Role of oxygen metabolites produced by granulocytes (Table 21-2).

Table 21-2. Oxygen metabolites produced by neutrophils

O_2^-	Superoxide anion
HO_2	Perhydroxyl radical
H_2O_2	Hydrogen peroxide
$\cdot OH$	Hydroxyl radical
$^1O_2$	Singlet oxygen
Δ^1O_2	Delta singlet oxygen
Σ^1O_2	Sigma singlet oxygen

1. Essentially, these mechanisms involve short-lived, high-energy oxygen intermediates produced:
   a. By increasing the energy of the electron (the singlet oxygens)
   b. By reducing O_2 (adding an electron) to superoxide anion and its products

F. These activities give off light that can be measured in a beta counter and are the basis for chemiluminescence studies.

G. The hydrogen peroxide produced by these reactions combines with intracellular myeloperoxidase and halide (Cl^- or I^-).
   1. The weak acids (OCl^- and I^-) produced are bacteriocidal within the granulocyte's phagosome.
   2. This mechanism is severely impaired in uncontrolled sepsis.

H. Once produced, the effects of oxygen metabolites are short lived, as ceruloplasmin and other free radical scavengers reduce their toxicity.

I. Another neutrophil mechanism utilizes molecular oxygen to alter unsaturated fatty acids such as tetraenoic arachidonate into biologically active compounds such as stable prostaglandins, thromboxanes, leukotrienes, and endoperoxidases.

Lymphocytes

A. Thymus-dependent T cells (thymic epithelium induces these cells to express a glycoprotein recognized by monoclonal antibody OKT3)
   1. Helper population (mostly OKT4 positive)
      a. Helper factors for antibody production (probably interleukin-2).

    b. Helper factor for cytotoxic cell development (interleukin-2).

    c. Lymphokines that attract and hold macrophages, granulocytes, and other lymphocytes.

2. Cytotoxic population (mostly OKT8 positive, although OKT4 positive are cytotoxic to a lesser extent)

    a. Bind and lyse virally infected cells

    b. Bind and lyse cells differing at the major histocompatability locus

3. Suppressor cells (There is a long-standing debate whether suppressor cells are a population distinct from cytotoxic cells or whether senescent cytotoxic cells demonstrate suppression of proliferation by binding Il-2 but neither proliferating nor producing more Il-2. Monoclonal antibodies to suppressor cells demonstrate a T_3-associated structure that allows one to now distinguish cytotoxic cells from suppressors, but their ontogeny is still unknown.)

    a. Inhibit proliferation of lymphocytes in vitro

4. Natural killer cells—lymphocytoid cells spontaneously cytotoxic to cultured tumor targets to which they have no prior exposure

5. Antibody-dependent cytotoxic cells

    a. T-cell population with antibody receptor for Fc.

    b. Because cytotoxic for any target coated with this antibody

6. Humoral mediators of T-cell function

    a. Il-1 Lymphocyte activity factor, endogenous pyrogen

       (1) Glycoprotein secreted by activated macrophages

       (2) Chemotactic

       (3) Stimulates precytotoxic T-lymphocytes to express a cell surface receptor for Il-2

       (4) Stimulates T-helper cells to secrete Il-2

       (5) Multiple metabolic effects (e.g., thermogenesis, proteolysis)

    b. Il-2 T cell growth factor

       (1) Produced by activated T-helper cells

       (2) Stimulates precytotoxic T cells to proliferate and mature

c. Production of both interleukin-1 and interleukin-2 is severely impaired in critically ill patients with sepsis or cancer.

7. Assays of T-lymphocyte function

a. T-lymphocyte count
Cells stain with OKT3 antibody, which is then detected by a second, fluorescing antibody. Assay can be performed with a fluorescence microscope or a fluorescent-antibody cell separator.

b. Helper/suppressor ratios—performed as in "a, above"
Helpers fluoresce with OKT4; cytotoxic/suppressor population fluoresces with OKT8. Ratio is normally 3:1; reverses to 1:2 to 1:4 in AIDS and many other serious illnesses and in burn patients.

c. Skin test antigens
While mumps and streptokinase are classically said to reflect antibody-mediated immunity and candida and tuberculosis reflect cell-mediated immunity, all four tests are dependent on antigen identification and processing by macrophages, macrophage secretory products, T-helper production of lymphokines and interleukin, the expression of receptors, and the migratory response of nonspecific lymphocytes, granulocytes, and macrophage inflammatory cells. While skin tests clearly delineate a population at risk of increased infection and surgical complications, their value in devising therapeutic strategy or determining resolution of malnutrition or sepsis is questionable.

d. Proliferative assays
Human peripheral blood lymphocytes will proliferate in tissue culture if their receptors are stimulated by antigens, in the mixed leukocyte response, or by complex carbohydrates called *lectins*. The inability of lymphocytes to respond and the presence of factors in serum to inhibit this response are part of the multiple systems organ failure seen in burns, sepsis, and AIDS.

e. Cytotoxic assays
Human peripheral blood lymphocyte stimulated for 3

days with radiated cells from an allogenic donor can lyse chromium-labeled donor cells in a 4-hour assay. The effector cells of this cell mediated lympholysis are the end products of the MLR (below). A second population of peripheral blood cells, natural killer cells, are spontaneously cytotoxic for target cells to which they have no prior exposure. A third population of cells bears an Fc receptor for antibody and can lyse cell populations bearing the antigen against which the antibody is directed.

B. Non-thymus-dependent (bursa-equivalent) cells
   1. Primarily develop into antibody-producing plasma cells
   2. Antibody production
      a. Initial steps are similar to the initial steps in production of cytolytic effectors
      b. End result is the proliferation of a specific antibody producing clone of plasma cells
   3. Antibody structure (Fig. 21-1)

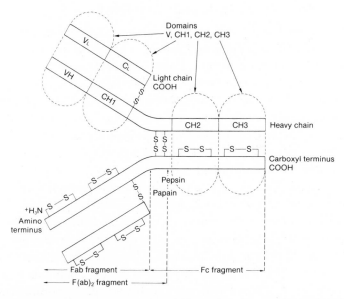

Fig. 21-1. Antibody anatomy. *V,* variable region; *C,* constant region, *H,* heavy chain component; *L,* light chain component; *S–S,* disulfide bond. From Alexander, J.W., and Good, R.A.: Fundamentals of clinical immunology, Philadelphia, 1976, W.B. Saunders Co., p. 69.

    a. Two light chains, two heavy chains, joined by disulfide bonds

    b. Both chains have constant and variable regions:

       (1) Variable region—light chain and heavy chain; site of antigen binding

       (2) Constant region—heavy chain; site of complement binding and activation

    c. Subclasses

       (1) IgA, IgM, IgG, IgE, depending on hinge

       (2) All antibody from the same class has the same constant region

       (3) All antibody made by a single clone will have the same variable region

    d. Action

       (1) By itself, antibody is not cytolytic

       (2) Complement mediates the cell damage

       (3) Both macrophages and a subclass of T-lymphocytes bind Fc portion

ACQUIRED IMMUNODEFICIENCY SYNDROME

Acquired immunodeficiency syndrome (AIDS) is thought to be transmitted by human T-lymphotropic virus type III, an RNA virus of the retrovirus group. This cytopathic virus has a trophism for the T_4 help-inducer subset of lymphocytes. Viral infection alone may be insufficient to cause the syndrome, and a long latent period of several years from time of infection seems common. A "second signal," perhaps another virus or another infection, may be necessary to develop the full-blown clinical syndrome. Affected patients will have "reversed" T_4/T_8 ratios from $3:1$ to $1:2$ or $1:4$. Immunologically, the helper factors (including interleukin-2) necessary for cytotoxic lymphocyte and B-lymphocyte maturation are absent, and affected lymphocytes cannot produce interferon. Recruitment of nonspecific inflammatory cells is also impaired. Although seropositivity for the virus identifies an individual at risk for developing the syndrome, it is not necessarily associated with the irrevocable appearance of clinical disease.

Presenting symptoms in AIDS

A. Sixty percent with opportunistic infection; 30% with Kaposi's sarcoma
B. Generalized
   1. Weight loss
   2. Inanition
   3. Generalized lymphadenopathy
   4. Fever
C. Neurologic
   1. CNS—lymphoma
   2. Cryptococcosis
   3. Candida meningitis
   4. Herpetic encephalitis
   5. Toxoplasmosis
D. Oral
   Thrush *(Candida albicans)*
E. Cutaneous—Kaposi's sarcoma
F. Pneumonia
   1. Pneumocystis carinii
   2. Cytomegalovirus (often neutropenic)
   3. Herpes simplex
   4. *Candida albicans*
   5. *Legionella pneumophilia*
   6. Histoplasmosis (disseminated)
G. Gastroenteritic
   1. Kaposi's bleeding
   2. *Salmonella typhimurium* gastroenteritis
   3. Isopsoriasis and other unusual pathogens
H. Non-Hodgkin's lymphomas and polyclonal β-cell gammopathy

COMPLEMENT

Most of the actual cytolysis accomplished by antibody is via the classic pathway of complement. Membrane perforation and the subsequent osmotic lysis of cells is mediated by the C_{6789} complex. The process is internally regulated by several inhibitors and the transitory nature of the active sites of the molecules.

A. Complement components and syndromes
1. C1 esterase inhibitor is absent in patients with *hereditary angioneurotic edema.*
    a. Setting
        These patients have chronic activation of C2 and C4 (and subsequent low levels thereof) that may be exacerbated in times of stress or infection.
    b. Possible manifestations
        (1) They may present with life-threatening, epinephrine-resistant upper airway obstruction necessitating tracheostomy
        (2) Recurrent bouts of abdominal pain
        (3) Negative laparotomy
        (4) Thrombotic tendencies because C1 esterase inhibitor also has antiplasmin effects
    c. Management
        (1) Lifetime maintenance with the drug cyproheptadine (Periactin) may decrease the number and severity of the attacks.
        (2) The androgenic steroids (and the impeded androgen danazol, which is less masculinizing) function to increase the levels of C1 esterase inhibition.
2. C2
    C2 deficiency occurs in 1/10,000 patients.
    a. Possible manifestations
        Because peripheral blood monocytes are incapable of producing C2, about 50% of patients with C2 deficiency have systemic lupus or related rheumatologic illnesses.
    b. Because C2 increases the solubility of immune complexes, its absence may result in chronic deposition of these complexes in skin, kidney, and other organs.
3. C3
    a. C3 is an important component because its cleavage product, C3a, is chemotactic and promotes granulocyte aggregation (leukoagglutination). These aggregates may play an important role in the generation of the shock-lung syndrome and the cascade of mediators that causes sepsis.

b. C3 can be activated by viral particles, bacteria, IgA and antigen-antibody complexes, and other mechanisms to trigger the alternate pathway of complement activation. This reaction is facilitated by factors B, D, and properdin, and inhibited by C3b inhibitor and factor B inhibitor. The means by which viral "clearing" occurs may be caused by "sheltering" of active C3b from its inhibitors by viral or bacterial proteins.

c. Deficiency of C3 is extremely rare but is associated with recurrent severe susceptibility to infection with pyogenic organisms. Bacteriocidal activity, chemotaxis, and opsonization are absent in the patient's sera.

d. Patients with C3b inactivator deficiency have intermittent urticaria and markedly increased susceptibility to bacterial infection.

4. C5, C6, C7, and C8

Patients deficient in C5, C6, C7, or C8 are also susceptible to infection.

HISTOCOMPATIBILITY ANTIGENS

A. Major histocompatibility antigens (class I-HLA-A, B, C, and class II-Dr) are the most prominent structures against which cytolytic T-lymphocytes and antibody are directed.

1. The class I antigens somewhat resemble immunoglobulins with a heavy chain and a beta-2 microglobulin light chain. The resemblance to immunoglobulins should not be overstretched: whereas the light chains of immunoglobulin show tremendous variation, the beta-2 microglobulins of the MHC all remain the same. (beta-2 microglobulinemia has been suggested as an early detector of transplant rejection secondary to cleavage from target cells by killer lymphocytes.) The actual cellular function of the major histocompatibility complex remains obscure, although some authors have suggested it may function as either viral receptors or play some other role in the cellular response to virus. The class II (Dr) antigen structure may function to present antigen and is itself antigenic.

B. "Minor" histocompatibility antigens, which probably abound on the cell surface, are also capable of eliciting antibody formation and cytotoxic T-lymphocyte generation.
   1. These antigens are probably responsible for the difference in renal allograft survival of 80% 5-year survival for HLA-identical sibling-donor kidneys versus 50% 5-year survival for recipients of HLA-identical cadaver kidneys.
   2. These antigens may also trigger the sometimes lethal graft-versus-host disease encountered in sibling recipients of HLA-identical bone marrow.
C. Tissue typing
   1. Serologically defined (SD) typing
      a. SD typing uses a microcytotoxic method to determine whether circulating leukocytes carry histocompatibility antigens lysed by antisera with known specificity.
      b. After 4-hour incubation, lysed cells will stain with trypan blue.
      c. Antisera of the same specificity as the individual being tested will yield a negative test result, and lysis will not occur.
      d. Antisera, unfortunately, may contain antibody to several specificities, and specificities on structurally similar histocompability antigens may cross-react.
      e. Antigens for which any question exist are so designated by the postscript "w" for "workshop."
   2. Lymphocyte defined (LD) typing
      a. LD tissue typing involves the 5-day culture of recipient leukocytes with irradiated donor cells (mixed leukocyte response or MLR).
      b. The proliferative respone is measured by the thymidine uptake on the fifth day of coculture.
      c. Ideally, LD typing involves stimulating a patient's leukocytes with his or her own irradiated cells as a control, the potential donor, and a pool of more than 20 other donors to establish a maximum response value.
      d. Homozygous typing cells (HTC), which bear only a single allele at a given LD locus, have been used to define 14 LD subtypes. This test remains clinically

disadvantageous because of the 5-day culture requirement.

e. The primed lymphocyte typing (PLT) test uses the more rapid anamnestic response seen in MLR restimulated with the same antigen.

(1) Recipient cells are stimulated by a large donor pool.

(2) Between days 10 and 14, cells are restimulated with potential donor cells.

(3) They are then observed for proliferation on days 2 and 3.

(4) Although still in its infancy, this typing method may offer a rapid means of fine level discrimination when further developed.

3. HLA crossmatch

The presence of preformed cytotoxic antibody in recipient-against-donor histocompatability antigens ensures "hyperacute rejection" mediated by complement and coagulation activation.

a. Current immunosuppression with steroids, azathioprine, antilymphocyte globulin, and cyclosporin A has no effect on hyperacute rejection.

b. However, the institution of the "final cross-match" has nearly eliminated this phenomena.

(1) Immediately before transplant, a microcytotoxicity assay is performed with recipient sera and donor cells.

(2) Any cytolysis indicates preformed antibody.

c. Although the incidence of hyperacute rejection had declined drastically with this procedure, the institution of intentional blood transfusion before transplant has increased the anecdotal reports of this phenomenon.

4. The association between HLA and disease

Certain disease states occur far more frequently with different HLA types (Table 21-3). This disease susceptibility may be a function of an immune response (Ir) gene located somewhere near the HLA locus on the seventeenth chromosome rather than of the HLA antigen itself.

Table 21-3. HLA antigens associated with specific diseases

Antigen	Condition
HLA-B27	Ankylosing spondylitis
	Reiter's syndrome
	Psoriatic arthritis
HLA-A10, B18, Dw2	C2 deficiency
HLA-A2, B40, Cw3	C4 deficiency
HLA-B7, Dw2	Multiple sclerosis
HLA-A3	Hemochromatosis
HLA-B8, Dw3	Celiac disease
HLA-B8, Dw3	Dermatitis herpetiforis
HLA-B8	Myasthenia gravis
HLA-B8	Chronic active hepatitis in children
HLA-Drw4	Active chronic hepatitis in adults
HLA-B13, Bw17	Psoriasis

SUGGESTED READINGS

Butterworth, A.E., and David, J.R.: Eosinophil function, N. Engl. J. Med. **304:**154-156, 1981.

Gallin, J.I., et al.: Disorders of phagocyte chemotaxis, Ann. Intern. Med. **92:**520, 1980.

Nathan, C.F., Murray, H.W., and Cohn, A.Z.: The macrophage as an effector cell, N. Engl. J. Med. **303:**622, 1980.

Klebanoff, S.J.: Oxygen metabolism and the toxic properties of phagocytes, Ann. Intern. Med. **93:**480, 1980.

Rosenthal, A.S.: Regulation of the immune response-role of the macrophage, N. Engl. J. Med. **303:**1153, 1981.

Acuto, O., and Reinherz, E.L.: The human T cell receptor, structure, and function, N. Engl. J. Med. **312:**1100, 1985.

Friedman, R.M., and Vogel, S.N.: Interferons, with special emphasis on the immune system, Adv. Immunol. **34:**97, 1983.

Burakoff, S.J., et al.: A molecular analysis of the cytolytic T lymphocyte response, Adv. Immunol. **36:**45, 1984.

22

Surgical infections

Frank B. Cerra

Infection remains a common cause of morbidity and mortality in the SICU. The clinical circumstances for infection are frequently confusing, because fever, leukocytosis, "toxicity," and hyperdynamic and hypermetabolic states can be caused by factors other than invading microorganisms (e.g., dead or injured tissue, resolving hematoma). The diagnosis of infection requires the demonstration of invading microorganisms. Most microbial agents seem to arise from the patient's own flora. The decision to use antimicrobial agents, however, may only require recognition of a clinical setting consistent with infection, without a clear documentation of site of origin and/or invasion.

A. Site considerations
   1. Blood
      a. Bacteremia is usually associated with an identifiable source.
      b. The source frequently requires a mechanical treatment (surgery or drainage procedure) in addition to antibiotics.
      c. The monitoring lines must always be considered as a potential source.
         (1) Peripheral and "from-the-line" cultures may be useful.
         (2) If the skin site is normal, changing the line over the guidewire is a useful and acceptable technique.
         (3) The portal of entry may also be the connectors and adapters or the solution.
         (4) If there is any question, removal of the line and site change are necessary.

(5) Catheter tips need to be cultured.

(6) *Staphylococcus epidermidis* and *Acinetobacter* sp. are not uncommon pathogens in this setting. Their occurrence is frequently a reflection of the patient's condition and not a reflection of a "break in technique."

(7) Meticulous attention to techniques in skin care, test performance, and intravenous therapy will keep the line infection rate at a minimum.

2. Abdomen

   a. A surgical or drainage procedure is usually required in addition to antibiotics.

   b. The *source* is a key factor in determining the potential pathogens.

     (1) Biliary tract: *Escherichia coli, Klebsiella, Streptococcus faecalis,* clostridia.

     (2) Colon: Gram-positive anaerobes and *Bacteroides fragilis;* enterobacteria

     (3) Small bowel

       (a) Generally devoid of much flora down to terminal ileum

       (b) Coliforms become colonized:

         i. With ileus

         ii. With obstruction

         iii. Probably with disuse

     (4) *Candida* is commonly found in the gut flora

   c. Duration of antimicrobial therapy

     (1) Criteria for response

       (a) Improvement in the clinical status of the patient

         i. Less "toxicity"

         ii. Improved mentation

         iii. Improved physiology

         iv. Lessening of the metabolic signs of sepsis

       (b) Loss of hyperpyrexia

       (c) Falling white blood cell (WBC) count

         i. Useful in predicting further infection; if the WBC count is elevated, the likelihood is increased. However, the subsequent infections tend to be nosocomial.

(2) Guidelines for cessation of antimicrobial therapy

    (a) Serious infections rarely need less than 5 days of therapy.

    (b) The average course is 9 days, with most under 12 days of therapy.

    (c) If there is no response in 3 to 4 days, reevaluation must be done.

    (d) Immunosuppressed patients may need longer courses of therapy.

    (e) The site of origin of infection may require a longer course of therapy.

        i. Hepatic abscesses—4 to 8 weeks or longer may be required.

        ii. Infected pancreatic phlegmon may require long courses of therapy.

(3) Soft tissue

    (a) The major problem is in differentiating those patients who require surgical therapy and those who do not.

        i. Factors useful in differentiating

            a. Clinical setting (e.g., trauma, perforated colon)

            b. Tempo of the disease

            c. Associated systemic toxicity

            d. Associated gas in the area; for example, retroperitoneal perforation of a colonic diverticulum that has associated rapid development of flank pain, edema, and erythema with rapid advancement, crepitus development, and septic shock has a high likelihood of being more than a simple cellulitis (Table 22-1).

(4) Procedures of help

    (a) Needle aspiration with Gram stain and culture

Table 22-1. Necrotizing surgical infections

Characteristic	Clostridial cellulitis	Clostridial myonecrosis	Synergistic necrotizing cellulitis	Necrotizing fasciitis
Setting	Trauma	Trauma, contaminated cases	Diabetes, peripheral vascular disease, perineum	Diabetes, peripheral vascular disease, trauma, contaminated cases
Onset	3-5 days	Hours-days	Days	Hours-days
Tempo	Moderate	Rapid	Rapid	Rapid
Temperature (F)	101-102	101-105	100-102	102-105
Systemic toxicity	Low	High hemolysis	High hemolysis	High hemolysis
Skin-wound appearance	±Crepitus blebs, ±necrosis, red-brown fluid, edema, extreme wound pain	Crepitus, necrosis, tan color, "bronze erysipelas," sickly sweet odor	Crepitus, blebs, necrosis, dishwater fluid edema	Red-purple color, blebs, edema, hypoesthesia
Bacteriology	Clostridia, mixed Gram+ and Gram−	Clostridia, mixed Gram+ and Gram−	Streptococcus, Bacteroides, coliforms (aerobe-anaerobe)	Bacteroides, Peptococcus, coliforms (aerobe-anaerobe)
Depth involved	Subcutaneous tissue	Muscle to skin	Skin through muscle	Skin through muscle

From Kaiser, R., and Cerra, F.B.: J. Trauma **21**:349, 1981, © 1981 The Williams & Wilkins Co., Baltimore.

(b) Local incision with:
    i. Biopsy, Gram stain and culture
    ii. Search for necrotic tissue

(5) The presence of tissue necrosis generally indicates the need for surgical debridement, in addition to antibiotic therapy.

    (a) Hyperbaric oxygen therapy may be a useful adjunct after resuscitation, debridement, and antibiotic therapy in clostridial infections, especially myonecrosis syndrome.

    (b) The major factors in survival (Table 22-2) are:
        i. Time from presentation to surgery
        ii. Appropriate surgery

    (c) The flora may range from gram positive, to anaerobic, to mixed aerobic/anaerobic, to aerobic gram negative.

    (d) The presence of an underlying source must always be considered (e.g., intraabdominal)

3. Lung

  a. A major problem is in differentiating colonization from infection.

    (1) Sputum cultures are not very reliable. Aspirates from endotracheal or tracheostomy tubes or from the transtracheal route are as reliable as possible, short of tissue biopsy.

Table 22-2. Survival

Group	N	Survived	Died	Mortality (%)
I	12	11	1	(8.3)
II	4	1	3	(75)
III	4	0	4	(100)
Overall	20	12	8	(40)

From Kaiser, R., and Cerra, F.B.: J. Trauma **21**:349, 1981, © 1981 The Williams & Wilkins Co., Baltimore.
Group I—Early recognition, antibiotics, and appropriate surgery.
Group II—Antibiotics and expectant therapy with delayed surgery.
Group III—Antibiotics and inadequate surgery.
Appropriate surgery—Incision and then excision of all necrotic tissue, regardless of extent; control of source.
Inadequate surgery—Incision and drainage without excision of all necrotic tissue.

    (2) Bronchoscopy cultures per se do not seem to add much sensitivity or specificity. The use of the covered brush may be of value.

        (a) Selective sampling of an infiltrate or cavity or a diagnostic aspirate, or washing with the covered brushes, can provide useful information.

        (b) The presence of white blood cells (WBCs) in the aspirate may or may not be useful. The presence of an endotracheal tube or tracheostomy can precipitate their presence.

    (3) Useful criteria for differentiating colonization and infection

        (a) New infiltrate or changing infiltrate, especially in one lung field

        (b) Systemic infection signs present with new infiltrate or changing infiltrate

        (c) Change in sputum color or amount with new infiltrate or changing infiltrate

        (d) Change in physiology (e.g., more shunt)

    (4) Lung biopsy

        (a) Diagnosis and therapy is changed in a significant percentage of cases.

        (b) Outcome mortality does not seem changed. This may reflect use of biopsy too late in the course of the disease to affect outcome.

b. Generally, the infections are hospital acquired, gram negative, and may have an anaerobic component.

    (1) Empiric therapy may be necessary until culture data are available.

    (2) If cultures do not show pathogens:

        (a) Virus/fungus may be present.

        (b) Antibacterial agents may do harm.

            i. Selection of more virulent or resistent strains

            ii. Potentiation of viral or fungal infection

        (c) Biopsy may be useful.

        (d) Repeat selective sampling may be useful.

        (e) Infiltrative tumors need to be considered.

c. Prophylactic intratracheal instillation of antibiotics seems to result in more virulent, subsequent infections.

d. In treating pulmonary infections with aminoglycosides, intratracheal instillation may have some use.

e. Nonresponding infiltrate
   (1) Factors
       (a) Wrong antimicrobial
       (b) Wrong dose
       (c) Superinfection
       (d) Poor drug delivery
       (e) Another disease
           i. ARDS
           ii. Tumor
           iii. Emboli
           iv. Ventricular dysfunction
           v. Constrictive pericarditis
           vi. Empyema
           vii. Multiple abscesses
   (2) Useful maneuvers
       (a) Reculture more selectively
       (b) Do serum cidal assays
       (c) Restore perfusion
       (d) Get tissue
       (e) CT scan of chest

4. Sinus
   a. Sinusitis
      (1) Should be considered in the presence of any nasal tube
      (2) Is initially seen as infection of unknown source or as nasal pus.
      (3) Maxillary sinus is most common site.
      (4) Significant percentage have sepsis; also pneumonia with same organisms as from sinus.
      (5) Diagnosis
          (a) Sinus roentgenogram and/or CT scan
          (b) Clinical setting as above
          (c) Direct aspiration
      (6) Treatment

(a) Remove the tube
(b) Antibiotics
(c) Drainage, particularly in immunosuppressed patients (e.g., transplant patients)
(d) Decongestants seem of questionable value.

B. The problem patient
1. The unknown infectious source
   a. Sources to consider
      (1) Meningitis
      (2) Otitis
      (3) Endocarditis/pericarditis
      (4) Osteomyelitis
      (5) Cholecystitis, particularly acalculous
      (6) Prostatitis
      (7) Phlebitis—central; pelvic
      (8) Interloop/retroperitoneal abscess
      (9) Pylephlebitis
      (10) Liver/spleen/lung abscess
   b. Work-up can include:
      (1) Reculture; include spinal tap (after CT scan of head) and multiple blood cultures (when patient is off antibiotics is best)
      (2) Stop antibiotics and reculture (if possible)
      (3) CT scan/sonogram
      (4) Indium-labelled WBCs and/or gallium scan
      (5) Needle aspiration of suspicious areas
      (6) Abdominal paracentesis; may include lavage
      (7) Laparotomy
2. Patient who is not responding to therapy for infection
   a. General considerations
      (1) Wrong diagnosis
      (2) Wrong therapy
      (3) Incorrect dosing
      (4) Perfusion not restored
      (5) New disease present
         (a) New infection
         (b) New organ failure
         (c) Malnutrition
      (6) Underlying organ reserve inadequate from primary disease

       (7) Multiple system organ failure syndrome

   b. Approach

       (1) Start fresh; new care team if necessary

       (2) Complete history, physical examination, and review of the record

       (3) Search for treatable disease

       (4) Care conference—open discussion frequently stimulates new ideas and approaches

       (5) Hopefully, new plan

   c. Fungus sepsis should be considered, especially *Candida*.

       (1) Mycostatin prophylaxis may be useful (e.g., 2×10^6 units orally every 8 hours or down NG tube)

       (2) Surveillance cultures should be done.

          (a) When three sites yield positive test results, a short course of amphoptericin B may be indicated (4 to 5 mg/kg, total dose).

          (b) With infection, a full course is indicated (15 to 20 mg/kg, total dose).

             i. Tissue and/or blood cultures or endophthalmitis are useful in establishing that infection is present.

             ii. Peritonitis should be considered in a situation or prior abdominal pathology that has had "adequate" therapy, especially when open bowel was present.

               a. Peritonal tap may be useful.

C. Patient with acquired immunodeficiency syndrome (AIDS)

  1. Presentations

   a. Prodromal: Fever, wasting, rectal bleeding

   b. Lymphadenopathy: May have spleenomegaly and/or skin eruptions

   c. Acute infection

   d. Kaposi's sarcoma

   e. Autoimmune syndrome: Anemia, thrombocytopenia and autoimmune antibodies

  2. Immunologic abnormalities

   a. Dysregulation of T- and B-lymphocytes

   b. OK-T4 (helper cells) decreased; OK-T5 and T8 (suppressor cells) are increased

      c. Decreased mitogen stimulation of T cells

      d. B cell antibody production may be dysregulated

      e. Anergy

      f. Decreased monocyte/macrophage chemotaxis

      g. Diminished cytotoxicity

  3. Appears to be a virally transmitted disease

      a. Agent thought to be HTLV III

      b. Can be transmitted by blood, saliva, sexual activity

      c. Virus has been found in tissues and body fluids including brain, semen, and saliva

  4. Infections handled by T cell mechanisms are seen with increased frequency.

      a. Malignancies thought to be of possible viral etiology:

          (1) Kaposi's sarcoma

          (2) Immunoblastic adenopathy

          (3) Undifferentiated lymphoma

          (4) Burkitt's lymphoma

          (5) Squamous cell carcinoma (cervix)

      b. Opportunistic infections

          (1) Virus: Herpes simplex, cytomegalovirus, Epstein-Barr, adenovirus, papova-virus.

          (2) Bacteria: Mycobacterium; *Legionella*

          (3) Fungus: *Candida*, cryptococcus, *Nocardia*.

          (4) Protozoa: *Pneumocystis*, toxomoplasma.

      c. Commonest opportunistic infection is *Pneumocystis carinii*

          (1) Ninety percent of cases diagnosed on bronchoscopy

          (2) Drug therapy of choice is trimethoprim-sulfamethoxazole

             (a) Alternate—pentamidine isethionate (Pentam)

  5. Currently no effective therapeutic treatment is available for the virus itself.

  6. Appropriate contact isolation precautions should be taken.

D. Antibacterial therapy

  1. Initial: Three general groups occur.

      a. Probable gram-positive infection

      (1) Intravenous catheter, cellulitis
      (2) Agents of value
         (a) First-generation cephalosporin
         (b) Penicillinase-resistant penicillin
         (c) If *S. epidemidis* is considered, vancomycin is the agent of choice.

  b. Probable gram-negative rod
      (1) Urinary tract, abdominal abscess
      (2) Agents of value
         (a) Aminoglycoside and a cephalosporin or broad-spectrum penicillin
         (b) If *Pseudomonas* is suspected, tobramycin or amikacin may be the preferred aminoglycosides.
         (c) In intraabdominal infections, *B. fragilis* coverage should be given: clindamycin or metronidazole are effective.
         (d) Routine enterococcus coverage is probably not justified by the risk/benefit ratio. In settings where enterococcal infection is suspected, coverage should be provided.

  c. Suspected infection
      (1) First- or second-generation cephalosporin with an aminoglycoside
      (2) Clindamycin with an aminoglycoside

  d. The data-base to support single-agent third-generation cephalosporins is growing, particularly in settings where *Pseudomonas* and/or *B. fragilis* are not the primary pathogens under consideration, and reasonable host resistence is present.
      (1) Cefoperazone, cefotaxime, Primaxin

  e. When definitive cultures are available, the antibacterial agents should be reviewed and the best coverage provided that gives the lowest risk of toxicity.

2. Factors in agent selection
  a. Suspected or actual pathogens
  b. Therapeutic margin
  c. Pharmacokinetics
  d. Status of host resistance

   e. Degree of organ failure present
   f. Local bacterial resistance patterns
   g. Availability on hospital formulary
   h. Cost
3. Agents and general considerations
   a. Aminoglycosides: gentamicin, tabramicin, amikcin, netilmicin
      (1) Active against most aerobic and facultative gram-negative rods; moderate activity against gram-positive cocci, *no* anaerobic activity
         (a) Especially good for *Pseudomonas, Serratia* and *Acinobacter* spp.
      (2) Relatively narrow therapeutic margin:
         (a) Blood level monitoring is mandatory in the SICU
         (b) Toxicity
             i. Renal dysfunction
                a. Rare on initial dosing
                b. Idiosyncratic type is uncommon
                c. Usual form is dose dependent
                d. Does not seem potentiated with use in established renal failure
            ii. Seventh nerve injury
           iii. Risk factors (see Table 22-3)
   b. Cephalosporins
      (1) Large safety margin and high therapeutic margin
      (2) First generation

Table 22-3. Risk factors in aminoglycoside toxicity

Characteristic	Nephrotoxicity	Ototoxicity
Age	+	+
Sustained high trough concentration	+	+
Elevated peak concentration	+	+
Cumulative dose	+	+
Concurrent toxic drugs	+	+
Dehydration	+	+
Dialysis	+	
Prior aminoglycoside exposure	+	+
Duration of treatment	+	+

(a) Cephalothin

(b) Excellent for staphylococci and streptococci and "easy" gram-negative rods

(c) Tend not to do well in SICU-acquired infections

(3) Second generation

(a) Expanded activity against gram-negative rods; not good for the difficult ones: *Pseudomonas, Serratia, Enterobacter, Acinetobacter* spp.

(b) Little anaerobic activity

    i. Exception is cefoxitin, which has good activity against *B. fragilis*

    ii. Those with little anaerobic activity include cefamandole, cefuroxime, cefonicid

(4) Third generation

(a) Cefotaxime, cefoperazone, moxalactam, ceftriaxone

(b) More gram-negative activity; rival aminoglycosides

(c) *Pseudomonas* still a problem, as are the difficult anaerobes

(d) Cefoperazone has almost exclusive biliary excretion

(e) Coagulopathy with bleeding can be a problem, particularly with moxalactam.

c. Penicillins

(1) Penicillin G is still the most active against streptococci.

(2) Staphylococci are still usually sensitive to methicillin, nafcillin, oxacillin

(3) The expanded penicillins

(a) Carbenicillin, ticarcillin, piperacillin, mezlocillin

(b) Rarely used alone

(c) Usually used in combination with an aminoglycoside

d. Antianaerobic agents

(1) Clindamycin, metronidazole, and chloramphenicol

(2) Clindamycin is also active against staphylococci and streptococci

(3) Metronidazole has no other antibacterial activity; it is active against *Trichomonas* and *Giardia* spp. and *Entamoeba histolytica.*

(4) Antianaerobic agents have little or no activity against aerobic or facultative gram-negative rods. Chloramphenicol has modest activity against "easy" gram-negative rods.

Table 22-4. Dosages of commonly used antibiotics

Antimicrobial	Daily adult dosage (Intravenous unless otherwise specified)	Usual dosage Interval
Aminoglycosides		
Amikacin	15 mg/kg (IV)	Every 8-12 hr
Gentamicin or tobramicin	3-5 mg/kg (IV)	Every 8 hr
Cephalosporins		
Cephalothin	4-12 g	Every 4-6 hr
Cefazolin	1.5-6 g	Every 8 hr
Cefoxitin	4-12 g	Every 4-6 hr
Cefuroxime	1.5-9 g	Every 8 hr
Cefotaxime	4-12 g	Every 4-6 hr
Macrolides; lincomycins		
Clindamycin	1-3 g	Every 8 hr
Erythromycin	1-4 g	Every 6 hr
Penicillins		
Aqueous penicillin G	2.4-24 million units (IV)	Every 4-6 hr
Ampicillin	4-12 g	Every 4-6 hr
Nafcillin, methicillin, oxacillin	4-12 g	Every 4-6 hr
Ticarcillin	12-30 g	Every 4-6 hr
Piperacillin, mezlocillin	12-24 g	Every 4-6 hr
Miscellaneous		
Chloramphenicol	4 g	Every 6 hr
Sulfamethoxazole (Trimethoprim)	8-20 mg/kg of the trimethoprim component	Every 6-12 hr
Vancomycin	25 mg/kg	Every 8-12 hr

Normal hepatic and renal function is assumed.

e. Drug dosing
   (1) An overall summary of commonly used drugs is presented in Table 22-4.
   (2) The presence of organ failures can change drug metabolism, distribution, and elimination and can thus affect dosing.
      (a) Each drug has its own characteristics.
      (b) Consultation with pharmacy personnel or a clinical pharmacy practitioner is very useful, and in some cases mandatory, to achieve proper drug dosing and maximum effect in organ failure syndromes.
      (c) Drug interactions and polypharmacy syndromes are major potential problems in SICU patients and can result in harm.
   (3) See Tables 22-5 and 22-6.

Table 22-5. Therapeutic serum concentrations (μg/ml)

	Gentamicin	Tobramicin	Amikacin
Peak			
Serious infection	6-8	6-8	20-25
Life threatening	8-10	8-10	25-30
Trough			
Serious infection	0.5-1.5	0.5-1.5	1-4
Life threatening	1-2	1-2	4-8

Table 22-6. Aminoglycoside dosages: 1-hour infusion (mg/kg)

	Gentamicin/tobramicin	Amikacin
Initial		
Dehydrated	0.75-1.5	5-7.5
Normal fluid status	1-2	7.5
Expanded ECF	1.5-2.5	7.5-10
Daily maintenance		
Normal renal function	1-1.5	15
Abnormal renal function	Adjust by renal function and serum peak/trough levels	

SELECTED READINGS

Anderson, E.T., Young, L.S., and Hewitt, W.L.: Antimicrobial synergism in the therapy of gram-negative rod bacteremia, Chemotherapy **24**:45, 1978.

Bell R.C., et al.: Multiple organ system failure and infection in adult respiratory distress syndrome, Ann. Intern. Med. **99**:293, 1983.

Eliopoulos, G.M., and Moellering, R.C.: Azlocillin, mezlocillin, and piperacillin: new broad spectrum penicillins, Ann. Intern. Med. **97**:755, 1982.

Fauci, A.S., et al.: The acquired immunodeficiency syndrome: an update, Ann. Intern. Med. **102**:800, 1985.

Hess, M.L., Hastillo, A., and Greenfield, L.F.: Spectrum of cardiovascular function during gram-negative sepsis, Prog. Cardiovasc. Dis. **23**:279, 1981.

Kaiser, R., and Cerra, F.B.: Progressive necrotizing surgical infections: a unified approach, J. Trauma **21**:349, 1981.

Klastersky, J., and Thys, J.P.: Endotracheal administration of aminoglycosides. In Whelton, A., and Neu, H.C. (editors): The aminoglycosides, New York, 1982, Marcel Dekker, Inc.

Lennard, E.S., et al.: Implications of leukocytosis and fever at conclusion of antibiotic therapy for intraabdominal sepsis, Arch. Surg. **117**:200, 1982.

Lynch, J.M., et al.: Gram-negative bacteremias: analysis of factors for clinical assessment of gentamicin resistance, Arch. Intern. Med. **141**:582, 1981.

Moore, R.D., Smith C.R., and Lietman P.S.: Risk factors for the development of auditory toxicity in patients receiving aminoglycosides, J. Infect. Dis. **149**:23, 1984.

Moore, R.D., Smith, C.R., and Lietman P.S.: The association of aminoglycoside plasma levels with mortality in patients with gram-negative bacteremia, J. Infect. Dis. **149**:443, 1984.

Moore, R.D., et al.: Risk factors for nephrotoxicity in patients treated with aminoglycosides, Ann. Intern. Med. **100**:352, 1984.

Neu, H.C.: The new beta-lactamase stable cephalosporins, Ann. Intern. Med. **97**:408, 1982.

O'Reilly, M.J., et al.: Sepsis from sinusitis in nasotracheally intubated patients, Am. J. Surg. **147**:601, 1984.

Sculier, J.P., and Klastersky, J.: Significance of serum bactericidal activity in gram-negative bacillary bacteremia in patients with and without granulocytopenia, Am. J. Med. **76**:429, 1984.

Sinanan, M., Maier, R.V., and Carrico, C.J.: Laparatomy for intraabdominal sepsis in patients in an intensive care unit, Arch. Surg. **119**:652, 1984.

23

Thermal injuries

Lynn D. Solem

BURNS—INITIAL CARE

A. Assessment considerations
   1. Airway adequacy
   2. Blood pressure and pulse
      a. Usually minimally disturbed
      b. Hypotension frequently indicative of associated trauma
   3. Level of consciousness
      a. Should be normal immediately after burn injury
      b. Decreased level may indicate
         (1) Carbon monoxide poisoning
            (a) Carboxyhemoglobin level > 40% will cause loss of consciousness
            (b) Increase is usually associated with injury occurring in a closed space
         (2) Drug abuse or alcohol abuse is frequently associated with burn injuries
         (3) Head injuries are relatively rare
   4. Need for endotracheal intubation to stent the trachea as neck edema develops
B. Management
   1. Intravenous line
      a. Necessity
         (1) *Adult* with burn over 15% of body
         (2) *Child* with burn over 10% of body
      b. Location
         (1) Can be started immediately through unburned tissue if available

(2) Can be started immediately through burned tissue because tissue has been "sterilized"

2. Immediate wound care
   a. Remove patient's clothing
   b. Wrap patient in clean sheet
   c. Delay applying antibiotic cream or ointment until wounds are properly cleaned

3. History
   a. Previous illness or surgery may indicate problems that might complicate care
      (1) Cardiovascular disease
      (2) Lung disease
      (3) Ulcer disease
      (4) Drug or alcohol abuse

4. Physical examination
   a. Routine—particular attention to the following:
      (1) External auditory canal and eardrum
         (a) Possible tympanic membrane perforation in explosion
         (b) Bleeding from fall-induced basilar skull fracture
      (2) Eyes
         (a) Corneal abrasion
         (b) Retinopathy
         (c) Perforation from explosion
      (3) Nares
         (a) Singeing   (b) Carbonaceous material
      (4) Neck
         (a) Tenderness
         (b) Crepitation
         (c) Thyroid enlargement
      (5) Abdomen
         (a) Tenderness
         (b) Examination very unreliable with overlying burn
   b. Other considerations
      (1) Peritoneal lavage if question of other major trauma exists
      (2) Digital rectal examination

(3) Evaluation of all skin
(4) Brief neurologic examination
    (a) Cranial nerve
    (b) Deep tendon reflexes
    (c) Babinski's reflexes

5. Fluid resuscitation
  a. Necessary
    (1) Burns > 15% to 20% of total body surface in *adults*
    (2) Burns > 10% to 15% of total body surface in *children*
  b. Available and equally advantageous formulas include:
    (1) Brooke
    (2) Evans
    (3) Parkland
  c. Sample regimen for Parkland formula
    (1) Provides 3 to 4 ml/kg/% burn in first 24 hours
    (2) Half given in first 8 hours
    (3) Following 24 hours includes D5W at a maintenance rate, plus:
    (4) A 3% to 5% colloid solution, 0.2 to 0.5 ml/kg/% burn, usually given in first 8 hours of day 2
  d. Determining adequacy
    (1) Demonstrated by blood pressure > 100 and
    (2) Urine output > 30 ml/hr in an adult and 1 ml/kg/hr in a child
    (3) Invasive monitoring

6. Medications
  a. Tetanus prophylaxis
    (1) All burns require tetanus prophylaxis
    (2) If victim has not had a booster in last 5 years, booster should be repeated
  b. Tetanus immunoglobulin (Hyper-Tet) recommended if:
    (1) Victim has not had booster in over 5 years
    (2) Wound is heavily contaminated
    (3) Previous immunization is uncertain
  c. Penicillin prophylaxis against streptococcus
    (1) Given for 3 to 5 days
    (2) Low-dose prophylaxis as in rheumatic fever

7. Escharotomies
   a. Fluid resuscitation causes massive edema, leading to venous stasis, which results in increased edema.
   b. Progressive edema formation may necessitate escharotomies.
   c. Need must be determined during initial burn care and in the first 24 hours after injury.
   d. Recommended approach
      (1) Immediately upon admission, escharotomies should be performed in obvious full-thickness circumferentially injured areas.
      (2) Areas of questionable depth of burn should be assessed with Doppler measurements and escharotomies performed as needed.

CLASSIFICATION OF BURNS

A. Cause
   1. Thermal (includes flame and scald burns)
   2. Electrical (contact and flash)
   3. Chemical
   4. Radiation (extremely rare)
B. Size
   1. Rule of nines
      a. Quick and easily remembered
      b. Relatively inaccurate in children
      c. The rule in adults:

Anatomic area	Surface area (%)
Head	9
Arm	9 each
Leg	18 each
Chest and abdomen	18 posterior
Perineum	1

C. Depth
   1. First degree (e.g., sunburn)
      a. Involves epidermis only
      b. Has no blistering
      c. Heals uneventfully in 3 to 7 days
      d. Requires no care other than avoidance of reinjury

2. Second degree
   a. Superficial (superficial second degree; superficial dermal)
      (1) Blistered
      (2) Heals spontaneously within 3 weeks
      (3) Has minimal scarring
      (4) Usually limited to pigment changes
      (5) Involves only the epidermis and superficial dermis
   b. Deep (deep second; deep dermal)
      (1) Requires more than 3 weeks to heal, usually 5 to 6 weeks
      (2) Causes very severe scarring
      (3) Involves the epidermis and most of the dermis, sparing only the base of the hair follicles and glands
3. Third degree
   a. Destroys all of the skin elements, including the epidermis and dermis
   b. May extend into subcutaneous fat, muscle, and bone
   c. Heals from the margins centripetally, and so requires skin grafting for coverage if diameter exceeds 3 to 4 cm
D. If indicated, transport patient to a center with facilities and personnel to provide burn care.

HYPOTHERMIA

A. Differential diagnosis of hypothermia
   1. Diabetic coma and acidosis
   2. Addison's disease, myxedema, hypopituitarism
   3. Uremia, pancreatitis, cachexia
   4. Shock states
   5. Central nervous system lesions
      a. Cerebrovascular accident
      b. Trauma
      c. Abscess
      d. Wernicke's encephalopathy
   6. Spinal cord injuries
   7. Toxic ingestion

a.	Alcohol	f.	General anesthetics
b.	Narcotics	g.	Tetracycline
c.	Chloral hydrate	h.	Tricyclic antidepressants
d.	Barbiturates	i.	Rauwolfia derivatives
e.	Phenothiazines	j.	Carbon monoxide inhalation

B. Mechanism of heat loss in hypothermia
   1. Radiation—transfer of heat to a cooler environment not in direct contact with the body
   2. Conduction—contact transfer of heat to cooler objects
   3. Convection—heat transfer by air movement
   4. Evaporation—loss is quite variable, depending on temperature, air movement, and humidity
C. Major stages of hypothermia
   1. Mild hypothermia (35° to 32.2° C, 95° to 90° F)—usually benign; moderate shivering may occur
   2. Moderate hypothermia (32.2° to 25.6° C, 90° to 78° F)—shivering stops; muscular rigidity develops; delirium, stupor, and coma may be present
   3. Severe hypothermia (lower than 25.6° C, 78° F)—death may ensue if prolonged
D. Physiologic changes
   1. Heart
      a. Initial increased output and tachycardia
      b. With lower temperature, myocardial depression
         (1) Bradycardia with markedly prolonged systole
         (2) Hypotension
      c. ECG changes—prolonged PR, QRS, QT intervals
         (1) Sinus bradycardia
         (2) Atrial flutter
         (3) Atrial fibrillation
         (4) Increased ventricular irritability with idioventricular rhythm and ventricular fibrillation (T < 30° C)
         (5) Asystole (T < 15° C)
   2. Lungs
      a. Hyperventilation
      b. As temperature falls, hypoventilation develops
      c. Bronchorrhea
      d. Thromboemboli
      e. Moderate to severe ARDS, particularly after rewarming

3. Central nervous system
   a. Clumsiness
   b. Slowed response to stimuli
   c. Ataxia
   d. Dysarthria
   e. Delirium
   f. Stupor
   g. Coma
4. Kidneys
   a. Initially cold-induced diuresis
   b. Later decreased renal perfusion and glomerular filtration rate
5. Hematologic
   a. Increased blood viscosity
   b. Thromboemboli
   c. Decreased blood volume
   d. Leukopenia
   e. Thrombocytopenia
6. Metabolic
   a. Anaerobic metabolism
   b. Metabolic acidosis
   c. Decreased basal metabolic rate
   d. Depressed drug clearance
7. Gastrointestinal tract
   a. Acute parotiditis (rare)
   b. Decreased motility and dilation
   c. Increased serum amylase
   d. Acute, sometimes fulminant, pancreatitis, particularly after rewarming
E. Management of hypothermia
   1. General supportive measures
      Hospitalization and intensive care unit management is required for all but the very mildly hypothermic patient.
   2. Laboratory
      a. Routine screening studies
         (1) Platelet counts
         (2) Prothrombin time
         (3) Fibrinogen levels
         (4) Plasma glucose, amylase
         (5) Renal function studies
      b. ABGs must be corrected for body temperature, since they are measured at a standard 37° C (98.6° F).
         (1) Effect of body temperatures on blood gases
            (a) ABGs are measured at 37° C

    (b) For each 1° C below 37° C:

        pH ↑ 0.015 units

        P_{CO_2} ↓ 4.4%

        P_{O_2} ↓ 7.2%

3. Fluid management
   a. Volume depletion is common.
   b. Fluids should be warmed by passing them through a blood warmer maintained at 98.6° to 103° F.
   c. Central monitoring can be used. Pulmonary artery catheters can precipitate arrhythmias and are best left out until after rewarming

4. Medications
   a. Most drugs are inactive and/or poorly metabolized when the core temperature is less than 32.2° C (90° F).
   b. With rewarming, overmedication can result.

5. Metabolic
   a. Correct acidosis, fluids, and electrolytes as rewarming occurs.
   b. Give glucose solutions

6. Cardiac
   a. Continuous electrocardiographic monitoring
   b. Arrhythmia management as needed
   c. The hypothermic heart is relatively unresponsive to atropine, electric pacing and, countershock. Rapid rewarming can be useful, and may be the only modality to which the arrhythmias respond.

7. Pulmonary
   a. Oxygenation by mask or endotracheal tube is frequently required.
   b. Frequent suctioning may be needed to handle increased bronchial secretions.
   c. Because pneumonia is the most common sequela of hypothermia, particular attention should be paid to its development.
   d. Fulminant ARDS can occur.

Rewarming

A. In conjunction with general resuscitative measures, a mechanism for rewarming should be instituted. Rewarming should be accomplished as rapidly as possible. A summary of rewarming techniques follows:
   1. Passive rewarming (mild hypothermia)
      a. Removal from environmental exposure and of wet clothing
      b. Dry insulating material (e.g., blankets)
   2. Active external rewarming (mild to moderate hypothermia)
      a. Immersion in heated water
      b. Heated intravenous solutions (37° C, 98.6° F)
      c. Electric blanket (37° C, 98.6° F)
   3. Active core rewarming (moderate to severe)
      a. Intragastric balloon
      b. Hemodialysis
      c. Peritoneal dialysis
      d. Extracorporeal blood warming
      e. Inhalation rewarming
B. Active rewarming may precipitate marked vasodilations, hypovolemic shock, and ventricular fibrillation.
   1. Active external rewarming has a higher mortality than do passive techniques.
   2. Active core rewarming is recommended for profound, prolonged hypothermia; where pulmonary or cardiac complications exist; or for patients with cardiac arrest.
C. Rewarming injuries
   1. Acidosis
   2. Myoglobinuria
   3. ARDS
   4. Pancreatitis
   5. Ischemic intestine
   6. Arrhythmias
   7. MSOF

24

Endocrine emergencies

Terry Quigley

Crises that occur in the surgical intensive care unit are unlikely to be a direct consequence of an endocrine organ malfunction. The signs and symptoms of endocrine organ dysfunction can be nonspecific; they frequently involve the central nervous system with attendant altered states of consciousness. A high degree of suspicion is necessary. Severe endocrine dysfunction can be lethal. These life-threatening disorders can, however, for the most part be successfully treated—if recognized. Specific disease states, with a focus on recognition, treatment, and precautions, will be discussed in this chapter.

HYPERTHYROID CRISIS (THYROID STORM)

Thyroid storm is an acute severe manifestation of thyrotoxicosis. The symptoms and signs are an exaggeration of those present in Grave's disease and represent not only a direct effect of thyroxine, but also its effect on the sympathetic nervous system secondary to catecholamine release. Thyroid storm can progress rapidly to death if not recognized and treated promptly.

A. Recognition
   1. Setting
      A variety of stresses and other disease states can precipitate thyroid storm in susceptible patients (i.e., patients with poorly controlled or unrecognized hyperthyroidism).
      a. Infection (sepsis)
         The signs and symptoms of thyroid storm can easily be confused with those of sepsis and recognition, therefore, can be more difficult.

    b. Thyroid surgery

    c. Emotional stress

    d. Hypoglycemia

    e. Diabetic ketoacidosis

    f. ICU stress

2. Clinical findings

    a. Central nervous system

        (1) Irritability

        (2) Restlessness

        (3) Confusion and stupor progressing to coma

    b. Cardiopulmonary

        (1) Tachycardia

        (2) ± Hypertension

        (3) Fever (101° to 106° F)

        (4) Overt signs and symptoms of heart failure

        (5) Tachypnea

    c. Gastrointestinal

        (1) Nausea

        (2) Vomiting

        (3) Abdominal pain

        (4) Potentially profuse diarrhea with profound fluid losses leading to dehydration, hypotension, and shock

    d. Miscellaneous

        (1) Profuse sweating may be present

        (2) Signs of persistent hypermetabolism

3. Laboratory findings

    a. Immediate laboratory tests are not helpful in making diagnoses. T_3 and T_4 levels will not differ from those in the thyrotoxic state. Treatment must not await laboratory results.

    b. Serum chemistry will be helpful in monitoring fluid replacement.

    c. Blood cultures check the possibility of sepsis.

    d. General search for septic source is warranted.

4. Roentgenograms and special studies are not helpful except as part of septic work-up.

5. Diagnosis must rest on a high index of suspicion and clinical findings in susceptible patients.

B. Treatment
1. Overall objective
   a. Eliminating end-organ toxicity
      (1) A search for identification and elimination of pre-cipitating factor is essential
   b. Blocking synthesis, impeding release, and blocking end-organ effects of thyroxine
   c. Sustaining the patient through the "storm" by general supportive measures
2. Immediate measures
   a. Propranolol (Inderal), 1 mg intravenously, followed by up to 10 mg intravenously over 3 to 4 hours (1 mg every 15 to 30 minutes) (If patient is capable of ali-mentation, 20 to 40 mg propranolol can be given or-ally every 6 hours.)
   b. Propylthiouracid, 1000 mg orally, immediately fol-lowed by 200 mg orally every 6 hours (alternatively—methimazole [Tapazole], 20 mg orally followed by 5 mg orally every 8 hours)
   c. Potassium iodide, 1 g intravenously or orally every 8 hours
   d. Systemic support
      (1) Intravenous salt solutions to maintain hydration
      (2) Supplemental oxygen to accommodate increased metabolic needs
      (3) Cooling measures as indicated
   e. Corticosteroids have been reported to ameliorate some of the symptoms associated with thyroid storm; methylprednisolone sodium succinate (Solu-Medrol), 1000 mg intravenously every 8 to 12 hours for 2 to 3 doses may be helpful
3. Sustaining treatment
   a. Continuing fluid therapy as outlined above as well as those measures aimed at blocking thyroxine synthesis and release
4. Associated conditions that occur with thyroid storm are secondary to the increased metabolic demands and can include:
   a. Angina

  b. Myocardial infarction
  c. Stroke
  d. Psychopathology
 5. Follow-up should be aimed at controlling thyrotoxicosis
     and the specific precipitating event
C. Precautions
  Thyroid storm, a very serious, life-threatening problem, demands immediate, organized, controlled action.
  1. The general support of the patient is as important as the
     specific treatment measures.
  2. Beware of thyroid storm in any patient with a previous
     history of thyrotoxicosis.
  3. Avoid stressful procedures (rapid cooling can be stress-
     ful).

HYPOTHYROID CRISIS (MYXEDEMA COMA)

  Myxedema and myxedema coma result from low or negligible levels of circulating thyroxine. The exact pathophysiology is
unclear. Usually numerous associated findings confuse the picture (hypoglycemia, adrenal insufficiency, respiratory insufficiency).
A. Recognition
  1. Setting
     Myxedema occurs as a consequence of hypothyroidism
     (most commonly in elderly women).
     a. A precipitating event is common and likely.
       (1) Sepsis
       (2) Trauma
       (3) Operation
     b. In frankly comatose patients, the diagnosis may be
        difficult, and a high index of suspicion is necessary.
  2. Clinical findings
     The signs and symptoms of hypothyroidism are almost
     invariably present:
     a. Central nervous system
       (1) Lethargy
       (2) Somnolence
       (3) Stupor progressing to frank coma
     b. Cardiopulmonary

      (1) Hypothermia (primary or secondary)

      (2) Congestive heart failure

      (3) Respiratory failure

      (4) Bradycardia with low-voltage electrocardiogram (ECG) and other dysrhythmias

  c. Gastrointestinal

      (1) Nonspecific—adynamic ileus common

      (2) Constipation

  d. Muscular

      (1) Weakness

      (2) Malaise with decreased reflexes

  e. Miscellaneous

      (1) Dry, sallow skin

      (2) General thinning hair

      (3) Edema (orbital and dependent)

3. Laboratory

  a. Immediate

      (1) Low serum sodium

      (2) Hypoglycemia

      (3) Hypoxemia

  b. Delayed

      (1) Thyroid function tests

      (2) Calcium

      (3) Blood urea nitrogen (BUN), creatinine

      (4) Thyroid-stimulating hormone (TSH) will differentiate between primary and secondary hypothyroidism

4. Roentgenograms and special studies

  a. A chest roentgenogram will show typical findings of congestive heart failure and should be part of a sepsis work-up. (A pleural effusion may also be evident.)

  b. An ECG and continued cardiac monitoring is essential.

5. Diagnosis

  a. The diagnosis must await the results of thyroid function tests.

  b. Treatment must begin, however, and the presumptive diagnosis of myxedema coma must be made on clinical grounds. A high index of suspicion is necessary.

B. Treatment
   1. Overall objective
      a. Correcting metabolic and electrolyte disturbance
      b. Identifying and eliminating precipitating event(s)
   2. Immediate treatment: general support of the patient
      a. Judicously correct electrolyte abnormalities (hyponatremia) in the event of relative volume overload.
      b. If one is relatively secure in the diagnosis of myxedema coma, levothyroxine should be administered intravenously.
         (1) 200 to 400 μg by intravenous infusion over 1 to 2 hours, followed by 50 μg/day intravenously until oral maintenance
         (2) Intense monitoring of the patient is a must to prevent toxicity
   3. Supportive therapy: primarily aimed at the general support of the patient
      a. Avoid stressful procedures.
      b. Do not actively rewarm the patient; slow passive rewarming is safest.
      c. Corticosteroids are important and guard against adrenal insufficiency during the acute treatment period. Hydrocortisone, 100 mg intramuscularly or intravenously every 8 hours for several days with a tapered withdrawal generally suffices.
C. Precautions
   1. Aggressive thyroid replacement can be as lethal as no replacement. Careful monitoring needs to be done.
   2. Most of these patients are elderly and represent a therapeutic challenge.

HYPERCALCEMIC CRISIS

Hypercalcemic crisis is a state of extreme hypercalcemia causing life-threatening symptoms, including dysrhythmias and coma. Serum calcium generally exceeds 15 mg/dl.
A. Recognition
   1. Setting
      a. Osseous metastasis, especially from breast carcinoma
      b. Hyperparathyroidism

    c. Multiple myeloma

    d. Rarely, various other causes: mild alkali syndrome, hyperthyroidism, immobilization

  2. Clinical findings

    a. Central nervous system

      (1) Drowsiness punctuated by aggitation, psychosis and bizarre behavior

      (2) Frank coma

    b. Cardiovascular-pulmonary

      (1) Dysrhythmias

      (2) Shortening of the Q-T interval on ECG

    c. Gastrointestinal

      (1) Nausea and vomiting

      (2) Vague abdominal pain

    d. Musculoskeletal

      (1) Muscular weakness

    e. Miscellaneous

      (1) Patients generally dehydrated and azotemic

      (2) Often, an associated carcinomatous cachexia contributes to the overall picture

  3. Laboratory

    a. Immediate studies to guide initial therapy

      (1) Serum calcium

      (2) Phosphorus

      (3) Electrolytes (Na^+, K^+, Cl^-, HCO_3)

      (4) Creatinine and BUN

    b. Delayed

      Close monitoring of serum calcium and electrolytes because of the nature of the therapy and the potential for large electrolyte shifts

  4. Roentgenograms and special studies are not generally helpful

  5. Diagnosis

    a. Serum measurement of calcium confirms the diagnosis.

    b. A level of 14 to 15 mg/dl is generally necessary to cause symptoms of the magnitude described above.

B. Treatment

  1. The overall objective

    a. Lowering the serum calcium levels and reversing the CNS and GI manifestations of the disease

    b. Hydration

2. Immediate treatment after determination of renal function: to hydrate the patient with a balanced salt solution

    a. Normal saline alternating with half-normal saline (up to 6 L in the first 24 hours) will decrease the serum calcium in most patients.

    b. Fluid therapy can be monitored with CVP catheter.

    c. Furosemide, 10 to 40 mg intravenously every 2 to 4 hours will promote a calcium diuresis and prevent fluid overload. Significantly lowering serum calcium takes 24 to 72 hours.

3. Sustaining therapy

    a. Continued hydration

    b. Corticosteroids if the hypercalcemic crisis is secondary to malignancy; typical dosage schedule: hydrocortisone, 300 mg intravenously every 8 to 12 hours, tapering to a maintenance dose of 25 to 50 mg of hydrocortisone equivalent daily

    c. Extremely urgent hypercalcemia

        (1) Calcitonin salmon (Calcimar) 50 to 100 MRC units intravenously every 12 to 24 hours may decrease serum calcium levels very quickly.

            (a) A test dose of 1 MRC unit should be administered subcutaneously to check for drug sensitivity.

            (b) Calcitonin will be helpful only in cases of hypercalcemia secondary to increased parathyroid hormone (PTH) production.

        (2) Mithramycin, 10 to 20 mg/kg intravenously can be administered in acute crisis.

            (a) A significant decrease in serum calcium should be evident in 24 hours.

            (b) Twice-weekly repeat doses will maintain the hypocalcemic effect.

        (3) Phosphate administration: Rarely is it indicated, and the potential severe side effects can occur from ectopic calcium deposition.

   4. Associated conditions including those expected in the milieu of metastatic carcinoma
   5. Long-term follow-up
      a. Monitor serum calcium
      b. Treat underlying disorder
C. Precautions
   1. One must determine the cause of the hypercalcemia (osseous metastasis, hyperparathyroidism, vitamin D intoxication) before instituting treatment as outlined above.
   2. If hyperparathyroidism is the etiology, operation should be considered only after 2 to 4 days of therapy.
      a. Serum calcium should be less than 12 mg/dl.
      b. Operation should be curative.
   3. Twelve to twenty-four hours are required before significant reductions in serum calcium will be seen.

HYPOCALCEMIC CRISIS

Serum calcium levels low enough to be symptomatic (generally less than 7.0 mg/dl)
A. Recognition
   1. Setting
      a. Usually as a consequence of parathyroid malfunction or absence (surgical removal)
      b. May also occur in renal failure
   2. Clinical findings
      a. Central nervous system
         (1) Excitability
         (2) Hyperreflexia
         (3) May lead to seizures and coma
      b. Cardiovascular-pulmonary
         (1) Dysrhythmias with prolonged Q-T interval on ECG
         (2) With severe crisis, laryngeal stridor and spasm possible
      c. Musculoskeletal
         (1) Hyperreflexia
         (2) Tingling of fingers and toes and around mouth
   3. Laboratory

      a. Serum calcium is low (<7.0 mg/dl), but treatment should begin immediately if diagnosis suspected.

      b. Serial calcium determinations should guide therapy.

  4. Roentgenograms and special studies: None.

  5. Diagnosis

      a. Serum calcium below normal levels

      b. Presence of the appropriate signs and symptoms

B. Treatment

  1. Overall objective

      a. Increase serum calcium

      b. Generally support the patient

  2. Immediate therapy

      a. Intravenous calcium (calcium gluconate 10%), 5 ml

      b. Dose repeated as necessary to alleviate symptoms

      c. Respiratory support should be instituted if necessary

  3. Sustained therapy

      a. Vitamin D (50,000 units daily)

      b. Oral calcium (calcium carbonate, 500 to 1000 mg orally 4 times/day)

      c. 1,25-dihydroxycholecalciferol, 0.25 mg/day, may be used but must be carefully monitored initially

  4. Associated conditions almost entirely confined to those one would expect to see in a patient after neck surgery

  5. Follow-up to: regular serum calcium check

C. Precautions

If a patient is initially seen with appropriate clinical findings after a neck operation (thyroid or parathyroid), one should not wait for a serum calcium determination to begin treatment. Small doses of intravenous calcium will not affect normocalcemic patients.

HYPOCORTISOLISM (ADDISONIAN CRISIS, ACUTE ADRENAL INSUFFICIENCY)

This is an acute deficiency of cortisol and aldosterone that may rapidly progress to circulatory collapse and death.

A. Recognition

  1. Setting

      a. An acute adrenal crisis most commonly occurs during stress (trauma, sepsis, surgery).

    b. It frequently is the result of inadequate steroid replacement in patients who have been steroid dependent and in whom the adrenal glands are suppressed.

    c. One should be particularly suspicious in patients with typical signs and symptoms in the perioperative period when exogenous steroids have been administered in the previous 2 to 3 months.

2. Clinical findings

    a. Central nervous system

      (1) Lethargy

      (2) Psychosis with confusion

      (3) Frank coma

    b. Cardiopulmonary

      (1) Prominent and life-threatening hypotension and circulatory collapse

      (2) Tachycardia

    c. Gastrointestinal

      (1) Prominent nausea and vomiting

      (2) Of special consideration is the abdominal pain that may accompany acute adrenal insufficiency; this may, in fact, mimic an acute abdominal catastrophy

      (3) Abdominal distention and diarrhea

    d. Musculoskeletal

      (1) Weakness and malaise

    e. Miscellaneous

      (1) Fever of variable magnitude

      (2) Hypothermia

3. Laboratory

    a. Immediate

      (1) Serum electrolytes and BUN are usually normal in an acute crisis secondary to inadequate replacement under stress.

      (2) If the patient has chronic adrenal insufficiency without replacement and the present circumstance is unmasking the underlying disease, hyponatremia, hypoglycemia, acidosis, and azotemia may be prominent.

    (3) Serum cortisol levels should be obtained.

    (4) A peripheral eosinophil count greater than 3%, especially after surgery, should raise one's index of suspicion.

  b. During treatment

    (1) Serum electrolytes, glucose, blood pH, and BUN monitoring is necessary.

4. Roentgenographic and special studies

Serum and urine cortisol will confirm the diagnosis but need not be the deciding factors in determining therapeutic strategy in the acute setting.

5. Diagnosis

  a. Made on clinical and laboratory results with a high index of suspicion

  b. Treatment should not wait confirmatory studies

B. Treatment

1. Overall objective

  a. Reverse the circulatory collapse

  b. Generally support the patient's vital signs during the crisis

2. Immediate therapy

  a. Intravenous fluids (normal saline [NS]) should be given.

  b. Intravenous steroids should also be administered immediately (hydrocortisone, 200 mg intravenously immediately, and then 100 mg intravenously every 6 hours until the episode has subsided).

  c. Administering mineralocorticoids is usually unnecessary since the synthetic pathway will provide adequate levels via the hydrocortisone.

3. Sustaining therapy

  a. Chronic administration of corticosteroids should be instituted.

  b. Hypokalemia may develop during the resuscitative period and should be expected.

  c. Studies to determine the etiology of the acute adrenal insufficiency can be obtained after the patient becomes stable.

    4. Associated conditions
      a. Sepsis
      b. Trauma
      c. Disseminated intravascular coagulation with adrenal hemorrhage
      d. Meningococcemia
      e. Exogenous steroid administration is most frequent and important
    5. Follow-up
      A work-up to determine etiology
C. Precautions
    1. If this disease is suspected, treatment should begin immediately.
    2. The acute administration of steroids could be life saving, and the side effects are minimal, if any, to a one-dose bolus of steroids.
    3. One must identify and treat the precipitating event (i.e., sepsis).

SYNDROME OF INAPPROPRIATE SECRETION OF ADH (SIADH)

This is characterized by the excess or continued secretion of antidiuretic hormone (ADH) from the posterior pituitary or from a malignant tumor as a paraneoplastic syndrome. Approximately 75% of the reported cases of this syndrome result from carcinoma of the lung.

A. Recognition
    1. Setting
      a. Most common: malignant lung tumor (small cell, squamous cell)
      b. Central nervous system trauma
      c. Intracranial tumors
      d. Neurologic surgery
      e. Rarely, the stress of nonneurologic surgery
    2. Clinical findings
      a. CNS
        (1) Signs of water intoxication if the syndrome is severe
          (a) Lethargy   (c) Seizures
          (b) Confusion

      (2) Frank coma

      (3) Prominent early nausea and vomiting

    b. Cardiovascular

      (1) Congestive heart failure in susceptible patients may distract from the diagnosis.

    c. GI

      (1) Prominent early nausea and vomiting

    d. Musculoskeletal

      (1) Weakness

      (2) Lethargy

  3. Laboratory

    a. Immediate laboratory

      (1) Decreased serum sodium (less than 125 mEq/L—often more severe)

      (2) Decreased serum osmolality

      (3) Elevated urine sodium with a maximally dilute urine

      (4) The low serum sodium and inappropriately elevated urine sodium should arouse considerable suspicion (Beware serum and urine electrolyte values in patients on diuretics.)

    b. During treatment

      (1) Carefully monitored serum electrolytes

  4. Roentgenograms and special studies

    a. Establish, if possible, that the patient has normal renal function.

  5. Diagnosis

    a. Established in patients with hyponatremia and increased urine sodium who correct with water restriction

B. Treatment

  1. Overall objective

    a. Minimize the effect of ADH secretion, hyponatremia, and excess total body water.

    b. Prevent seizures and coma.

  2. Immediate therapy

    a. Upon suspecting the diagnosis of SIADH, fluid (water) restriction is mandatory.

    b. If the patient has severe symptoms and urgent correction of hyponatremia is necessary, an osmotic diuresis with mannitol or urea may be instituted.

c. Hypertonic saline (2% or 3%) may be infused intravenously, but one must be cautious of overcorrection (remember that the total body fluid volume is increased).

d. Serum electrolytes should dictate therapy.

3. Sustaining therapy

a. Maintained by relative restriction

b. Demeclocycline (Declomycin), 300 mg twice daily, has been shown to be effective in patients in whom water restriction is either not possible or disadvantageous.

4. Associated conditions

Those discussed above under recognition

C. Precautions

1. Later in the course of the disease, the urine osmolality may be greater than maximally dilute, secondary to the solute diuresis and to ADH suppression by the hypoosmolar body fluids.

2. Beware of overcorrection of serum sodium with its attendant risks.

3. A variety of drugs have been reported in conjunction with SIADH. This entity, in various degrees of severity, may be more common than generally appreciated.

DIABETES INSIPIDUS

Diabetes insipidus is a polyuria secondary to an ADH deficiency resulting in renal water excretion with an inability to concentrate the urine. Urine volume can range from 2 to 16 L/day, and the onset of the disease tends to be acute (often operation or often head trauma).

A. Recognition

1. Setting

a. Most commonly seen in patients after cranial (pituitary) procedures and in patients who have sustained significant head trauma

(1) The latter presents most acutely and less predictably

b. 30% to 50% idiopathic

2. Clinical findings
   a. CNS
      (1) In patients without preexisting CNS abnormalities, thirst is perhaps the primary clinical feature.
      (2) So-called hypertonic encephalopathy may develop in patients who are denied access to water.
      (3) Somnolence progresses to stupor and coma very quickly.
   b. Cardiovascular
      (1) Dehydration resulting in hypovolemic hypotension can occur if fluid replacement is inadequate or delayed.
      (2) Note: In conscious patients who can voice their thirst and can be kept hydrated, a remarkable lack of associated symptoms exists.
3. Laboratory studies
   a. Immediate
      (1) Studies should help distinguish diabetes insipidus from a solute diuresis (diabetes mellitus, hyperosmolar nonketosis) or nephrogenic diabetes insipidus or other renal concentrating dysfunction.
      (2) Simultaneous serum and urine electrolytes and osmolality will show the relative concentrating ability of the kidney and dictate water and electrolytes replacement.
   b. Delayed
      (1) Continued monitoring of serum electrolytes is helpful in the management of replacement fluids.
4. Roentgenographic and special studies
   a. Withholding water to see if a concentrated urine can be produced is a simple and effective way to make the diagnosis.
      (1) Two-hour measures of urine and plasma osmolality can be made during fluid restriction.
      (2) Patients with pituitary diabetes insipidus will not have urine osmolality greater than serum osmolality with water restriction.
      (3) A provocative test with the subcutaneous administration of vasopression (5 units) should demon-

strate an increase (about 50%) in urine-concentrat-
ing ability.
5. Diagnosis
Diagnosis is established by tests as outlined above in
polyuric patients without the ability to concentrate their
urine.
B. Treatment
1. Overall objective
a. Maintain hydration
b. Reserve the hyperosmotic encephalopathy, if present
2. Immediate treatment
a. Intravenous fluid replacement with hypotonic balanced salt solutions, 0.25% NS or D5 0.25 NS.
b. Sufficient fluid should be administered to decrease
the serum sodium concentration (Na^+) by approximately 1 mEq/L every 1 to 2 hours. This should prevent cerebral edema and seizures.
3. Sustaining therapy
a. Therapy should be adequate to maintain fluid and
electrolyte balance.
b. Also, hormones have been used to reverse the effects
of ADH deficiency.
c. Pitressin tannate in oil 0.5 ml. may ameliorate symptoms for 24 to 48 hours.
d. Aqueous vasopressin tannate (Pitressin), 5 to 10 units,
can be given as frequently as necessary to prevent
polyuria.
e. 1-decamino, 8-D-arginine vasopressin (dDAVP), a synthetic analogue of vasopressin, can be administered
nasally as a spray (5 to 10 mg twice daily) and adjusted
as necessary.
4. Associated conditions
a. Patients with cerebral trauma are at increased risk,
and diabetes insipidus may be only one of many urgent problems facing the intensive care unit (ICU)
team.
b. Appropriate monitoring, including central venous
pressure and intracranial pressure, should be considered.

C. Precautions
1. Rapid correction of fluid deficits may result in cerebral edema and seizures result.
2. Glucose solutions may induce glucosuria and an osmotic diuresis that will confuse the picture.

DIABETIC KETOACIDOSIS (DKA)

Diabetic ketoacidosis is an urgent state of hyperglycemia, acidosis, dehydration, and, frequently, electrolyte abnormalities occurring in the patient with a relative insulin deficiency—usually a patient with diabetes mellitus. The mortality in treated cases is approximately 10%.

A. Recognition
1. Setting
   a. Patients with diabetes mellitus who are subjected to stress (i.e., surgery, sepsis, trauma)
2. Clinical findings
   a. Central nervous system
      (1) Confusion and somnolence progressing to stupor and coma
   b. Cardiovascular
      (1) Tachycardia
      (2) Normotensive or hypotensive secondary to dehydration
      (3) Dysrhythmias associated with hypokalemia
      (4) Deep, rapid breathing is characteristic (Kussmaul breathing) secondary to the acidosis
      (5) The breath odor may be "fruity"
   c. Gastrointestinal
      (1) Abdominal pain is a frequent (50%) finding.
      (2) Pain usually relents shortly after treatment is begun.
   d. Miscellaneous
      (1) Hypothermia
      (2) Gastric atony and ileus may accompany DKA
3. Laboratory studies
   a. Immediate (to establish diagnosis)
      (1) Serum glucose
      (2) Ketones

(3) Electrolytes (Na^+, K^+, HCO_3)

(4) Urine glucose (reducing substance) and ketones

(5) Arterial gases and pH

  b. Delayed

    (1) Creatinine

    (2) BUN

    (3) Serum and urine osmolality

    (4) Serial glucose and potassium determinations are critical to appropriate therapy

4. Roentgenograms and special studies

  a. Sepsis is a common precipitating event

  b. ECG to check for myocardial infarction and document dysrhythmias

B. Treatment

  1. Overall objective

    a. Reduce serum glucose

    b. Correct acidosis

    c. Increase intravascular and intracellular volume

    d. Reverse CNS

    e. Eliminate the inciting event

  2. Immediate therapy

    a. Intravenous hydration with a balanced salt solution

      (1) Use urine output with central monitoring

      (2) Increased urine volume may be secondary to osmotic diuresis and in itself is unreliable as a measure of hydration.

    b. Intravenous insulin

      (1) An initial bolus of 0.15 unit/kg of regular insulin followed by a constant infusion of approximately 0.15 unit/kg/hr

      (2) Serum glucose should decrease by approximately 100 mg/dl/hr to a level of approximately 250 mg/dl.

      (3) Urine insulin is not used as a measure of treatment.

      (4) Glucose (D5W) can (and should) be added to the maintenance intravenous fluids when serum glucose is approximately 200 to 300 mg/dl.

    c. In nonuremic patients with adequate urine output, potassium (20 to 40 mEq/L intravenous fluid) as potassium chloride should be added to the maintenance intravenous line.

      (1) Potassium deficits can be large and serum potassium must be monitored.

      (2) Serum measurements will dictate replacement.

      (3) All patients should have a cardiac monitor.

    d. Phosphate deficits may be large and should be replaced.

      (1) Serum phosphorus levels may be normal.

      (2) Phosphate can be administered intravenously as the potassium salt

    e. Bicarbonate is used with caution in patients with DKA.

      (1) If the acidosis is severe (pH <7.20), bicarbonate may be given slowly intravenously (never by bolus).

      (2) Hypokalemia and its associated dysrhythmias may result.

      (3) Hydration and insulin usually results in correction of the acidosis.

3. Sustained therapy

    a. Maintaining adequate hydration with a D5W-balanced salt solution

    b. Continuing constant-infusion insulin, adjusted using serum glucose as a guide (every 4 to 6 hours)

    c. Finding and treating the precipitating cause

4. Associated conditions during or after treatment of DKA

    a. The physician should be mindful of continued acidosis (hyperchloremic, lactic) and of the severe complication of cerebral edema (probably secondary to an osmotic difference in intracellular and extracellular fluid).

    b. Cerebral edema is best prevented by a relatively slow correction of the hyperglycemia and maintaining glucose greater than 200 mg/dl in the initial treatment period (48 to 72 hours).

NONKETOTIC HYPEROSMOLAR COMA

This is a comatose state associated with severe hyperglycemia and hyperosmolality. The absence of ketosis is a significant finding, not completely understood, which differentiates this entity from diabetic ketoacidosis.

A. Recognition
   1. Setting
      a. Nonketotic hyperosmolar coma frequently occurs or is cared for in an ICU setting.
      b. It tends to occur in elderly patients who may or may not be overtly diabetic.
      c. Latent diabetes mellitus or at least an abnormal glucose tolerance is usually manifest.
      d. Nonketotic hyperosmolar coma occurring as a result of intravenous or enteral hyperalimentation may not be associated with diabetes mellitus.
      e. Stress, trauma, surgery, or therapy with concentrated glucose intravenous solutions can be precipitating events.
      f. Of particular note is the occurrence of this syndrome in a previously stable ICU patient. Sepsis should be considered the overwhelmingly probable cause and should be actively sought.
   2. Clinical findings
      a. Central nervous system
         (1) Prominent and severe, ranging from lethargy and confusion to seizures and coma.
      b. Cardiopulmonary
         (1) Hypotension
         (2) Tachycardia and associated myocardial infarction
      c. Gastrointestinal
         (1) Nausea
         (2) Vomiting
         (3) Ileus
         (4) Diarrhea may or may not be present
   3. Laboratory studies
      a. Immediate
         (1) Serum electrolyte
         (2) Glucose

      (3) BUN

      (4) Arterial blood gases

      (5) Glucose levels may be massively elevated with associated hypokalemia and azotemia

      (6) Lactic acidosis is commonly present secondary to hypovolemia and decreased tissue perfusion

      (7) Urine glucose

      (8) Absence of serum-urine ketones

   b. Delayed

      (1) Serial determinations of electrolytes, especially potassium and glucose, will guide therapy.

      (2) These should initially be obtained at very frequent intervals.

 4. Roentgenograms and special studies

   a. Chest roentgenograms and blood cultures to rule out a septic event

   b. ECG to determine if an associated myocardial infarction has occurred

B. Treatment

 1. The overall objective

   a. Identical to that in diabetic ketoacidosis

      (1) Reduce serum glucose

      (2) Correct the acidosis

      (3) Increase the intravascular volume

   b. The precipitating event should be sought and treated

   c. A septic focus will be most common

 2. Immediate therapy

   a. Hydration with a balanced salt solution (normal saline is preferred) should be started. Large volumes will need to be infused, since a 20% total body fluid deficit is possible.

   b. Urine volume is a misleading measure of volume replacement because of the osmotic diuresis that will be present.

   c. Intravenous insulin

      An initial bolus of 0.15 unit/kg regular insulin followed by a constant infusion of 0.15 unit/kg/hr will usually be sufficient.

(1) Regular and frequent measurement of serum glucose is necessary.

(2) Serum glucose should decrease by approximately 100 mg/dl/hr and not drop below 200 to 250 mg/dl.

d. Intravenous fluids can be adjusted as necessary and should include glucose (D5W) and a balanced salt solution when serum glucose is in the 200 to 300 mg/dl range.

e. As with DKA, serum potassium deficits may be large and should be replaced as dictated by serial measurements of serum potassium.

3. Sustaining therapy
   a. Treatment of the inciting event
   b. Continued insulin therapy to maintain serum glucose greater than 150%

4. Associated conditions
   a. Continued acidosis and the possibility of cerebral edema
   b. Slow correction of serum glucose to minimize the development of cerebral edema

C. Precautions

1. Glucose intolerance in an ICU patient can quickly lead to nonketotic hyperosmolar coma. This should immediately lead the physician to suspect sepsis, and appropriate diagnostic tests should be ordered.

2. Immediate fluid therapy with a balanced salt solution is excellent for prevention of coma.

MYASTHENIC CRISIS

Myasthenic crisis is an acute exacerbation of the symptoms of myasthenia gravis resulting in life-threatening muscular weakness. Specifically, respiration is affected and rapid death results if supportive measures are not instituted. Patients with myasthenia gravis suffer a dysfunction at the myoneural junction. They are very sensitive to curare-like drugs and quaternary ammonium compounds.

A. Recognition
   1. Setting
      a. Myasthenic crisis occurs in patients with myasthenia gravis who are:
         (1) Stressed (trauma, sepsis, surgery)
         (2) React strongly to drugs blocking neuromuscular transmission
         (3) A common scenario occurs in the postoperative recovery room when a susceptible patient is extubated and suffers a rebound paralysis after administered neostigmine wears off. These patients may also not respond to usual doses of neostigmine.
      b. Patients operated on for thymoma may be susceptible.
   2. Clinical findings
      a. Central nervous system
         (1) Nonspecific; coma may lead to death
      b. Cardiopulmonary: Respiratory failure secondary to respiratory muscle weakness may be most urgent problem requiring immediate attention
      c. Musculoskeletal: Generalized progressive muscular weakness is the hallmark of disease
   3. Laboratory: none that acutely aid in diagnosis or treatment
   4. Roentgenograms, special studies: none specific
   5. Diagnosis: made with appropriate response to treatment
B. Treatment
   1. Overall objectives
      a. Reverse muscular weakness
      b. Restore patient's ability to respire
   2. Immediate therapy
      a. Ensure the patient's well-being and oxygenation
      b. Edrophonium (Tensilon), 10 mg IV (2 to 3 mg every 30 to 60 seconds) can help make diagnosis, but its short duration of action mitigates against its use
      c. Neostigmine (Prostigmin), 0.5 mg IM (or IV acutely) every 4 hours can reverse the acute syndrome

3. Sustaining therapy
   a. It is similar to that in myasthenia gravis.
   b. Most commonly therapy is pyridostigmine (Mestinon), 60 mg orally 3 times daily.
      (1) Dosage can be adjusted as necessary.
      (2) It should be the minimal dosage required to affect a beneficial result.
   c. Corticosteroid therapy is controversial and has not been shown to affect long-term outlook. Large acute doses may, in fact, exacerbate the crisis and probably should be avoided.
4. Associated conditions
   See "Setting," p. 617.
5. Follow-up
   Careful attention of a neurologist

C. Precautions
1. Immediate support of the patient is of paramount importance.
2. Drug therapy may or may not be immediately effective.

CHOLINERGIC CRISIS

This is a state resulting from excess anticholinesterase. Cholinergic crisis, which is quite rare, most commonly is iatrogenic and represents drug (neostigmine) overdose.

A. Recognition
1. Setting
   a. Generally patients requiring anticholinesteriase administration
   b. Patients may be particularly vulnerable in the postoperative period
2. Clinical findings
   a. Central nervous system
      (1) May vary from an exitatory state to coma
      (2) Pupillary miosis present
   b. Cardiopulmonary
      (1) Bradycardia
      (2) Increased bronchial secretion with coughing
      (3) Respiratory weakness may cause inadequate ventilation

  c. Gastrointestinal
     (1) Abdominal cramping
     (2) Diarrhea
     (3) Salivation
  d. Musculoskeletal
     (1) Muscular cramping and weakness may be pronounced.
     (2) Respiratory failure is a potentially lethal consequence.
3. Laboratory
   Not helpful in making the diagnosis.
4. Roentgenograms and special studies: none
5. Diagnosis
   a. Must rest on a clinical examination with a high index of suspicion
   b. Can be difficult and, in fact, may be confused with a myasthenic crisis
B. Treatment
   1. The overall objective
      a. Maintain the patient through the crisis until the symptoms abate
      b. Respiratory support is most crucial
   2. Immediate therapy
      a. General patient support
      b. Atropine, 0.4 to 1.0 mg intramuscularly or intravenously
      c. Ameliorate the symptoms of cholinergic stimulation
C. Precautions
   Distinguishing cholinergic excess may be very difficult. A high index of suspicion is necessary.

HYPOGLYCEMIA (INSULIN COMA)

Hypoglycemia is a state of mental confusion or coma resulting from decreased serum glucose levels. Decreased glucose production (liver dysfunction) or increased insulin activity (endogenous or *exogenous*) is responsible. Inadvertent excess exogenous insulin administration is the most common cause.

A. Recognition
  1. Setting
    a. Hypoglycemia most commonly occurs in patients with insulin-dependent diabetes mellitus who are stressed.
      (1) The postoperative period is a particularly vulnerable time.
      (2) The period shortly after weaning and discontinuing intravenous hyperalimentation is also a particularly dangerous period for the patient, since increased serum insulin levels may persist. This may be especially important in the ICU setting, where hyperalimentation lines may be used for other purposes during emergencies and other urgent situations.
    b. Hypoglycemia is common after major hepatic resections.
  2. Clinical findings
    a. Central nervous system
      (1) Confusion
      (2) Somnolence
      (3) Frank coma
    b. Cardiopulmonary
      (1) Hypotension   (2) Profuse diaphoresis
    c. Gastrointestinal
      (1) Nausea   (2) Vomiting
  3. Laboratory studies
    a. Serum glucose to confirm diagnosis
    b. Continued monitoring of serum glucose helpful
  4. Roentgenograms, special studies: none specific
  5. Diagnosis
    Established by a low serum glucose level with the appropriate clinical findings or reversal of signs and symptoms with glucose administration
B. Treatment
  1. Overall objectives
    a. Raise serum glucose levels
    b. Reverse the organ dysfunction
  2. Immediate therapy

a. Treatment should be presumptive and not await laboratory results.
b. After drawing serum glucose (but not awaiting the results), 25 ml of D50W should be administered by intravenous bolus.
   (1) If the problem is acute, the results are often dramatic with immediate clearing of confusion and reversal of coma.
   (2) If the hypoglycemia has existed for a period of time, the coma may be irreversible regardless of therapy.
c. Sustaining therapy: Adequate intravenous glucose (D5W usually sufficient); an adjustment of insulin dosage may be appropriate.
d. Associated conditions: Those mentioned under "Setting"
e. Follow-up: Adjustment of diabetic management

C. Precautions
1. Treatment with intravenous glucose should begin as soon as the diagnosis is suspected.
2. No harm results from administering 25 ml of D50W to any patient.

CARCINOID CRISIS (MALIGNANT CARCINOID SYNDROME)

The malignant carcinoid syndrome is manifest in patients with metastatic carcinoid tumor (primarily hepatic). The symptoms, as outlined below, result from the production and end-organ effects of serotonin, kallikrein, histamine, and possibly prostaglandins. 5-Hydroxyindoleacetic acid (5-HIAA), a metabolite of serotonin found in the urine, helps confirm the diagnosis.

A. Recognition
1. Setting
   Almost exclusively in patients with metastatic carcinoid tumor
2. Clinical findings
   a. Central nervous system
      (1) Vague findings; may be an excitatory state associated with the other symptoms

    b. Cardiopulmonary
      (1) Pulmonary wheezing may be prominent with tachycardia.
      (2) Blood pressure may be normal or elevated.
      (3) Heart failure may be superimposed in severe cases.
    c. Gastrointestinal
      (1) Crampy abdominal pain
      (2) Diarrhea
    d. Musculoskeletal
      (1) Cutaneous flushing of the face and trunk can be variable but spectacular findings.
      (2) Typically, the flushing is violaceous and precipitated by eating.
3. Laboratory
    a. Only useful in confirming the diagnosis of carcinoid tumor
    b. Urine 5-HIAA measurement (24-hour collection) is usually definitive
4. Roentgenograms and special studies
    Useful in the diagnosis and treatment of carcinoid tumors, but not particularly in carcinoid crisis
5. Diagnosis
    Made in the clinical setting as described
B. Treatment
  1. The objective (in the absence of resectable lesions): Abolish or ameliorate the systemic symptoms of the substances produced by the carcinoid tumor
  2. Immediate therapy
    a. Corticosteroids may significantly control symptoms.
    b. The dosage is extremely variable and should be tailored to the patient's needs.
  3. Sustaining therapy
    a. Chemotherapy against the tumor (generally unsatisfactory)
    b. Antiserotonin agents (e.g., cyproheptadise) which are of very limited benefit
    c. General patient support is the most one has to offer most patients

C. Additional consideration

Serious consideration should be given to removal of as much tumor as possible in young patients with liver involvement. This may significantly modify the severity of the syndrome.

PHEOCHROMOCYTOMA CRISIS (HYPERTENSIVE CRISIS)

Hypertensive crisis is the hypertension (and hypotension) that results from the catecholamine release of the adrenal or extraadrenal tumors known as pheochromocytomas.

A. Recognition

1. Setting

   a. Any patient with a diagnosed pheochromocytoma has the potential of a hypertensive crisis.

   b. Patients with medullary carcinoma of the thyroid who exhibit hypertension or labile blood pressure in the postoperative period (ICU setting) should be suspected of having a MEN II syndrome.

   c. Acute hypertensive crisis in a prior nonhypertensive patient (e.g., with anesthesia, with stress)

2. Clinical findings

   a. CNS: severe headache and seizures result from acute hypertension

   b. Cardiovascular-pulmonary

      (1) Vasomotor flushing of the skin

      (2) Tachycardia

      (3) Hypertension

      (4) Diaphoresis

      (5) Chest pain (may be angina)

   c. Gastrointestinal

      (1) Nausea

      (2) Vomiting

      (3) Abdominal pain and an urge to defecate

   d. Miscellaneous

      (1) All the symptoms and signs of malignant hypertension may be present.

      (2) Episodic and paraxysmal hypertension is characteristic of pheochromocytoma.

3. Laboratory

   a. Not helpful in the acute recognition or treatment

b. Serum catecholamine and their urinary metabolites are useful in confirming the diagnosis of pheochromocytoma

4. Roentgenograms, special studies: none specific.

5. Diagnosis

a. Diagnosis is presumptive unless a pheochromocytoma has been previously diagnosed.

b. This distinction is important since the treatment of catecholamine hypertension is difficult from that applied to hypertensive crisis of other etiology.

B. Treatment

1. Overall objective

a. Maintain a normal blood pressure.

b. Correct the volume deficit until definitive resection of the pheochromocytoma.

2. Immediate therapy.

a. Administration of a balanced salt solution

b. Pharmacologic control is as follows:

(1) Phentolamine (Regitine)

(a) Intravenous injection, 1 to 5 mg, can be immediately (within 30 seconds) effective.

(b) A constant infusion can be titrated (phentolamine, 30 mg/500 ml NS by minidrip).

(c) If the patient is or becomes refractory to phentolamine, sodium nitroprusside (Nipride) can be administered by constant infusion. (This does not counteract the catecholamine directly, but relaxes vascular smooth muscle.)

2. Oral phenoxybenzamine (Dibenzyline)

a. 20 to 40 mg/day in three divided doses should be started

b. Can be increased by 10 mg/day as necessary

3. Propranalol (Inderal)

a. 20 mg orally 3 times daily can be used to control tachycardia

b. Patients may be very sensitive to blockers and caution must be used

    c. Can also be given intravenously for cardiac rate arrhythmia

    d. Usually reserved until after α blockers are used, unless needed for arrhythmia control

  4. Definitive therapy

    a. Locate the tumor

    b. Surgical resection

    c. Malignant, metastatic pheochromocytoma may be quite difficult to control

C. Precautions

  1. The volume deficit in these patients may be significant.

  2. Hypotension secondary to vigorous pharmacologic control of the acute crisis is common.

SELECTED READINGS

Alberti K.G.M.M., and Thomas, D.J.V.: The management of diabetes during surgery, Br J Anaesth **51**:693, 1979.

Apgor, V., and Papper, F.M.: Pheochromocytoma—anesthetic management during surgical treatment, Arch. Surg. **62**:634, 1951.

Axelrod, L.: Glucocorticoid therapy, Medicine **55**:39, 1976.

Bradley, R.F.: Treatment of diabetic ketoacidosis in coma, Med. Clin. North Am. **49**:961, 1965.

Clowes, G.H.A., and Simeone, F.A.: Acute hypocalcemia in surgical patients, Ann. Surg. **146**:539, 1957.

Deftos, L.: Calcitonin as a drug, Ann. Intern. Med. **95**:192-197, 1981.

Edwards, C.R.W., and Besser, G.M.: Mitramycin treatment of malignant hypercalcemia, Br. Med. J. **3**:167, 1968.

Fernandes, M., and Bellini, G.: Management of the patient with pheochromocytoma, Drug Therapy, May, 1977, p. 43.

Henke, J.A., et al.: Immobilization hypercalcemic crisis, Arch. Surg. **110**:321, 1975.

Hoffenberg, R.: Thyroid emergencies, Clin. Endocrinol. Metab. **9**:503, 1980.

Ingbar, S.H., and Woeber, K.A.: The thyroid gland, *in* Williams, R.H. (editor): Textbook of endocrinology, ed. 6 Philadelphia, 1981, W.B. Saunders Co., p 209.

Leshin, M.: Acute adrenal insufficiency: recognition, management, and prevention., Urol. Clin. North Am. **9**:2, 1982.

Lewis, L., et al.: Fatal adrenal cortical insufficiency precipitated by surgery during prolonged continuous cortisone treatment, Ann. Intern. Med. **39**:116, 1953.

Mackin, J.F., Conary, J.J., and Pittman, C.S.: Thyroid storm and its management, N. Engl. J. Med. **291**:1396, 1974.

Massry, S.G.: Inorganic phosphate treatment of hypercalcemia, Arch. Intern. Med. **121**:307, 1968.

Morrison, G., and Murray, T.G.: Electrolyte, acid-base, and fluid homeostasis in chronic renal failure, Med. Clin. North Am. **65:**429, 1981.

Patten, B.E.: Myasthenia gravis: review of diagnosis and management, Muscle Nerve **1:**190, 1978.

Reddy, C.R., et al.: Studies on the mechanism of hypocalcemia of magnesium depletion, J. Clin. Invest. **52:**3000, 1973.

Sacks, H.S., et al.: Similar responsiveness of diabetic ketoacidosis to low-dose insulin by intramuscular injection and albumin-free infusion, Ann. Intern. Med. **90:**36, 1979.

Salassa, R., et al.: Postoperative adrenal cortical insufficiency: Occurrence in patients previously treated with cortisone, JAMA **152:**1509, 1953.

Slaney, G., and Brooke, B.: Postoperative collapse due to adrenal insufficiency following cortisone therapy, Lancet **1:**1167, 1957.

Walts, L.F., et al.: Perioperative management of diabetes mellitus, Anesthesiology **55:**104, 1981.

Weisenfeld, S., et al.: Absorption of insulin to infusion bottles and tubing, Diabetes **17:**766, 1968.

Wyngaarden, J.B., and Smith, L.H., Jr. (editors): Cecil's textbook of medicine, Philadelphia, 1982, W.B. Saunders Co.

25

Gastrointestinal problems in the critically ill

William Becker

Intraabdominal surgical problems are often the precipitating cause of a patient's entrance into the intensive care unit. The intent of this chapter is not to review intraabdominal surgical disease. However, a group of gastroenteric problems are more common in the critically ill. This section provides an overview of these conditions.

PAROTITIS

Responsible organisms for parotid bacterial infections are usually staphylococci and streptococci, though anaerobes may play a role.

A. Recognition
　　1. Setting
　　　　a. Dehydration
　　　　b. Malnutrition
　　　　c. Poor oral hygiene
　　　　d. Debilitating illness
　　　　e. Mucous plug in Stenson's duct causing occlusion with resultant pyogenic infection behind it
　　　　f. Presence of nasogastric (NG) tube
　　2. Clinical findings
　　　　a. Unilateral facial edema may be present, but in intubated patients this may not be as readily observed.
　　　　b. On oral examination with parotid manipulation, pus may be expressed from Stenson's duct.
B. Treatment
　　1. Hydration
　　2. Cephalosporins or beta-lactamase–resistant penicillin or vancomycin in atopic individuals

3. Daily manual compression of the parotid may keep a damaged or stenosed duct open
4. Extensive involvement may require drainage and debridement

THRUSH

Thrush is the oral overgrowth of *Candida albicans.*

A. Setting

Common in patients on broad-spectrum antibiotics

B. Treatment
1. Thrush can be readily avoided by nystatin (Mycostatin) irrigation of the oropharynx.
2. In patients on prolonged courses of broad-spectrum antibiotics, the addition of intravenous miconazole may be appropriate.

C. Precaution
1. Thrush is normally a self-limited and confined infection, although it may be painful and inhibit swallowing and coughing.
2. It provides, however, a chronic colonization of *Candida* that predisposes to involvement of the esophagus, stomach, duodenum, and lower gastrointestinal (GI) tract.
3. It may be the precondition for *Candida* pneumonia and even predispose to *Candida* line sepsis.

THE NASOGASTRIC TUBE

A. Pros
1. Decreases gastric air (especially in intubated patients and always in patients on continuous positive airway pressure (CPAP) therapy.
2. Decreases gastric secretion in ileus or fistulae
3. Excellent access for alkalinization and medication
4. Monitoring of gastric acidity

B. Cons

Impairs lower esophageal sphincter function, consequently:
1. Chronic peptic trauma to lower esophagus—esophagitis
2. May result in chronic aspiration or contamination of oral cavity and airway with enteric bacteria
3. Often results in chronic metabolic alkalosis, which may worsen ileus

    a. Goal of antacid therapy is pH 6 to 7

    b. pH of 9 to 10 unhelpful and may be harmful

TRACHEOESOPHAGEAL FISTULAE

A. Cause
1. Usually endotracheal or tracheal tube cuff trauma to the larynx
2. A long-term indwelling nasogastric (NG) tube provides a rigid structure that increases the abrasion insult

B. Prevention
1. When prolonged NG drainage is necessary in a patient with a tracheostomy, a gastrostomy may avoid this complication as well as the chronic aspiration of nasal-esophageal gastric drainage
2. Low-pressure cuffs on tracheostomy and endotracheal tubes
3. Removal of NG tubes as soon as possible
4. Enteric feeding tubes do not seem to have this problem.

C. Treatment
1. Direct repair or diversion procedure
2. Tracheal stenosis frequently accompanies fistula healing and may require resection

ESOPHAGITIS

A. Cause

Both NG intubation and *Candida* can cause esophageal mucositis, which may be so severe as to progress to stricture.

B. Prevention

NG intubation should be selectively used and esophagoscopy readily utilized in patients complaining of dysphagia or chest or back pain.

C. Treatment

Established invasive esophagitis requires miconazole or amphotericin therapy.

GASTRIC pH AND STRESS ULCERATION

Stress ulceration and upper gastrointestinal (UGI) bleeding is a serious complication that appears to be preventable. Vigorous control of gastric pH along with improved support care of intensive care unit (ICU) patients appear to have drastically decreased this complication.

A. Setting
   1. Critically ill patients are prone to develop gastroduodenal stress ulceration and upper gastrointestinal bleeding that may be massive. Such bleeding is associated with a mortality approaching 80%.
   2. Stress ulceration has been commonly associated with burn and neurosurgical patients.
B. Pathophysiology
   1. The pathophysiology of stress ulceration remains unclear.
   2. Altered blood flow, increased acid secretion, and breakdown of the gastroduodenal mucosal barrier may contribute to ulceration.
C. Protection and prevention
   1. Maintenance of the mucosal barrier affords protection.
      a. Improved maintenance of the mucosal barrier appears related to overall improvement of the management of critically ill patients with better support of cardiopulmonary and nutritional-metabolic function.
      b. To complement an aggressive general support of critically ill patients, a specific prophylactic approach to decrease acid production is warranted in most ICU patients.
      c. Although many agents have been used to reduce the incidence of gastroduodenal stress ulceration, the combination of H-2 blocker and an antacid appears to be the most useful in this setting.
      d. The use of H-2 receptor antagonists alone in the prophylaxis of stress ulceration is more controversial.
      e. A practical consideration in the selection of cimetidine versus hourly antacid should be the availability and reliability of nursing staff.
      f. The newer topical prostaglandins are in various stages of clinical testing.
      g. Enteral feeding appears to be the method of control.
   2. Prophylactic method
      a. An antacid is given every 2 hours.
      b. Gastric pH is recorded on an hourly basis initially.

    c. If this regimen will bring the pH above 5, a more frequent administration of antacid would seem unnecessary and will decrease the amount of nursing care involved.

    d. However, if gastric pH is not controlled, more frequent (hourly) and greater amounts of antacids (up to 120 ml/hr) may be required.

    e. H-2 receptor antagonists can be added at this point.

    f. When antacid frequency reaches every 30 minutes, H-2 receptor antagonists may be economical to add.

  3. Complications

    a. Complications associated with antacids and cimetidine include:

      (1) Mental confusion

      (2) Leukopenia

      (3) Diarrhea

      (4) Gastroesophageal regurgitation

    b. Rarely, however, is a complication severe enough to warrant discontinuation of either drug, except in the presence of multiple-systems organ failure, in which cimetidine has been associated with coma.

    c. In patients with renal failure, aluminum hydroxide gel can be used as the antacid.

ACALCULOUS CHOLECYSTITIS

A. Setting

Compromise of the gallbladder circulation resulting from burns, sepsis, trauma, or cardiovascular instability may result in a primary vascular insult leading to a tense nonviable gangrenous gallbladder. Perforation may be life threatening.

B. Clinical findings

  1. Fever

  2. Unexplained leukocytosis

  3. Right upper quadrant pain

  4. Elevated bilirubin and/or alkaline phosphatase (These findings should suggest acalculous cholecystitis regardless of the presence or absence of stones.)

C. Radiologic study

1. A PAPIDA or HIDA scan will rule out the presence of obstructive problems of the biliary tree.
2. ECHO test can detect stones, dilation, sledge, emphysema, and edema.

D. Treatment
   1. Surgery
   2. Percutaneous drainage—still somewhat experimental

PROLONGED ILEUS

A. Pathophysiology

Although postoperative ileus accompanies nearly every major abdominal operation, much remains to be learned about the pathophysiology of this entity.

1. The colon appears to be most sensitive to the operative insult.
2. Patients with ileostomy will often have return of bowel function on the second or third postoperative day.
3. The role of central, vagal, intramural, neurogenic, humoral, local, and intraluminal influences remains to be clearly defined (see box on opposite page).
4. The rapid appearance of ileus associated with sepsis may result in the syndrome of acute gastric dilation, with loss of several liters of fluid into the stomach and subsequent hypovolemic shock.

B. Setting

Although commonly seen in the absence of an NG tube (and readily treated by its insertion and fluid replacement), this syndrome may also occur when an NG tube has become occluded or is otherwise nonfunctional.

C. Obstruction versus ileus
   1. Classic clinical descriptions
      a. Obstruction
         (1) Distended, slightly tender abdomen
         (2) Hyperactive, high pitched, quiet bowel sounds as the duration of obstruction progresses
         (3) Absence of flatus and stool
         (4) Borborygmus should be the hallmark of partial obstruction with intermittent passage of stool and flatus

   b. Ileus
      (1) Quiet, nontender abdomen
      (2) Progressively distended abdomen if gastric secretions are not cleared
2. ICU presentation
   a. Bowel dysfunction in the critically ill and healing patient is an area requiring further research.
   b. The impact of anatomic, inflammatory, vasomotor, neurogenic, and humoral influences is poorly understood.
   c. Any abnormality of bowel function or delayed return of bowel function beyond the expected 2- to 5-day postoperative period should elicit:

**CAUSES OF PROLONGED ILEUS
IN CRITICALLY ILL PATIENTS**

A. Central
   Severe head injury or infection
B. Vagal
   Postvagotomy or therapy with anticholinergics
C. Intramural neural
   1. Diabetes mellitus
   2. Anorexia nervosa
   3. Cachexia
   4. Dysautonomias (Shy-Drager syndrome, etc.)
   5. Acquired Hirschsprung's disease
D. Humoral
   1. Burns
   2. Sepsis
   3. Pancreatitis
   4. Peritonitis
E. Local
   1. Dilation
   2. Obstruction
   3. Abdominal wall disruption
   4. Retroperitoneal hematoma, infection, pancreatitis
F. Intraluminal
   Change in flora

       (1) Thorough examination to rule out infection or obstruction

       (2) Electrolyte review to ensure metabolic stability

       (3) Careful reexamination of drug therapy to exclude unexpected toxicities and side effects

    d. Barium studies should be performed even in a quiet belly if prolonged ileus resists fluid, electrolyte, and nutritional therapy.

FISTULAE

A. Treatment

The fundamentals of the treatment of fistulae are simple on the surface, yet incredibly diffuse in their clinical ramifications.

   1. Establish adequate drainage (usually to the outside)

   2. Control sepsis

   3. Replace fluid-electrolyte losses

   4. Provide adequate nutrition

B. The combined impact of transhepatic biliary drainage, computed tomography (CT), or sonographic directed drainage, and endoscopy with enteral and parenteral nutrition has drastically reduced the need for emergent surgery in these often fragile, septic patients.

C. When the patient remains septic, rereviewing the adequacy and function of each of the drains in place is essential to ensure that loculation of infection has not occurred.

D. The purpose of surgery is either to explore and drain or to reestablish anatomic continuity.

   1. These two surgical goals must never be confused.

   2. Attempts to drain loculated pus and reestablish continuity at one setting are frequently doomed to failure.

ISCHEMIC BOWEL DISEASE

A. Causes (see box on opposite page)

   1. Cardiovascular instability of the critically ill

   2. Activation of procoagulants and other humoral factors

   3. Shifting splanchnic arterial and venous flow

   4. Concurrent anatomic insults of surgery and trauma

   5. Preexistent state of borderline atherosclerotic intestinal ischemia

B. Diagnosis

Although an extremely difficult diagnosis to make, it is critically important that the diagnosis be actively considered and aggressively sought before perforation and intractable sepsis supervenes.

1. Clinical findings
   a. Early postoperative bowel motility (24 to 48 hr)
   b. Bloody diarrhea
   c. Diffuse abdominal pain and distention
   d. Unexplained acidosis
   e. Hypovolemia
   f. Hypocalcemia
   g. Hyperphosphatemia
   h. Elevation of creatinine phosphokinase (CPK) BB fraction
   i. Mildly elevated lipase-amylase

CAUSES OF INTESTINAL ISCHEMIA

1. Low cardiac output
   a. Inadequate intravascular volume
   b. Impaired venous return
   c. Impaired left-side heart function
   d. Shock
2. Vascular
   a. Stenosis-occlusion
      (1) Aorta
      (2) Superior mesenteric artery
      (3) Inferior mesenteric artery
      (4) Colonic collaterals
         (a) Marginal artery of Drummond
         (b) Meandering mesenteric artery
         (c) Internal iliac—superior hemorrhoidal
   b. Portal venous thromboses
   c. Emboli
3. Hematologic
   a. Polycythemia vera
   b. Essential thrombocytosis
   c. DML
   d. Paroxysmal nocturnal hemoglobinuria
   e. Antithrombin III deficiency
   f. Protein C deficiency
   g. Paraproteinemia

---

2. Studies
   a. Sigmoidoscopy is not adequate to rule out.
   b. Colonoscopy is useful.
   c. Abdominal tap is useful.
C. Treatment
   1. Exploration with diversion-resection
   2. If bowel is ischemic but viable, embolectomy or revascularization of superior mesenteric artery (SMA) with second look at 48 hours
   3. The ready availability of home total parenteral nutrition (TPN) makes even total enterectomy a therapeutic consideration in an otherwise viable individual

CECITIS

A. Settings
   1. The cecum is most sensitive to the pressures generated by a large bowel obstruction, and even rectal obstruction will first manifest as cecal dilatation and perforation. Therefore, a cecal diameter of greater than 15 cm has often been deemed an indication for operation and transverse loop colostomy or end colostomy with mucous fistula.
   2. A number of severely ill transplant, immunocompromised, and debilitated patients have been described with full thickness inflammation of the right colon and inclusion bodies in the mucosa-submucosa on pathologic examination.
      a. Many of these patients have had simultaneous leukopenia and documented cytomegalovirus viremia.
      b. The local disease of the right colon may represent one aspect of a systemic viral illness involving lung, liver, and bone marrow.
B. Treatment
   1. Right colectomy with ileostomy and transverse mucous fistula for bleeding, perforation, or dilitation
   2. Whether antiviral therapy with acycloguanosine (Acyclovir) will have any impact on mortality is as yet unknown

PSEUDOMEMBRANOUS ENTEROCOLITIS

A. Setting and possible causes
   1. Patients who have been on long-term antibiotic therapy or bowel preparations before surgery may develop a form of diarrhea caused by the exotoxin of *Clostridium difficile*.
   2. The organism may be hospital acquired.
B. Clinical presentation
   1. High-output chronic diarrhea
   2. Acute diarrheal colitis with supervening sepsis
   3. The syndrome may be sufficiently severe to produce septic shock
C. Treatment
   1. Vancomycin when the diagnosis is suspected.
   2. Antidiarrheal agents are contraindicated.
   3. Culture of the offending organism is very difficult, and diagnosis depends on demonstration of the toxin.
   4. Mortality is 5% to 10%.

NEUTROPENIC COLITIS

A. Setting
   1. Leukemia
   2. Aplastic anemia
   3. Cancer chemotherapy
   4. Bone marrow transplantation
B. Clinical findings
   1. Diffuse or localized abdominal pain
   2. Ileus
   3. Obstipation or diarrhea
   4. Diffuse or localized rebound and a quiet, tense (though not rigid) abdomen with a relatively low-grade (<38.9° C, 102° F) temperature
C. Treatment
   1. Combination of nonabsorbable antibiotics (neomycin, 1 g every 4 to 6 hr with metronidazole and, possibly, oral mystatin (Mycostatin), ketaconazole, or miconazole
   2. Surgery probably contraindicated unless a frank perforation has occurred
   3. Recovery correlates with return of the peripheral neutrophil count

DIARRHEA IN THE ICU

A. Differential diagnosis of diarrhea in the critically ill patient
  1. Osmolar
     a. Excessive enteral feeding
     b. Occult partial-complete lactose deficiency
     c. Sorbitol or other nonabsorbable oral medications
     d. Antacid therapy
     e. Refeeding after cachexia
  2. Anatomic
     a. Dumping syndrome
     b. Blind loop syndrome with bacterial overgrowth
     c. Fistulae—gastrocolic, enteroenteric, enterocolic
     d. Partial bowel obstruction
     e. Impaction
  3. Secretory
     a. Endocrine
        (1) Hyperthyroidism
        (2) Zollinger-Ellison syndrome
        (3) Watery diarrhea, hypophosphotemia, acidosis syndrome
     b. Exocrine
        (1) Pancreatic insufficiency
        (2) Impaired bile reabsorption
  4. Infectious agents
     a. *Salmonella*
     b. *Shigella*
     c. *Escherichia coli*
     d. *Amoeba*
     e. *Clostridium difficile*
  5. Antibiotic induced
B. Diagnostic evaluation
  1. Rectal examination
  2. Inspection of the stool for fat, blood, guaiac, and mucus
  3. Stool culture for parasites and ova
  4. Reducing substance routine culture
  5. *C. difficile* culture and toxin
  6. Review of medication and nutritional therapy
  7. Upper and lower GI series to define anatomic abnormality

C. Treatment

Therapy with diphenyoxylate HCl (Lomotil) is usually contraindicated until a diagnosis is firmly established and appropriate treatment started.

JAUNDICE

Jaundice is a relatively frequent development in the surgical intensive care unit (SICU) patient. Based on the clinical situation and the judicious use of laboratory and radiologic evaluation, a cause for jaundice can be determined in most cases. Often an underlying cause requiring specific treatment will be discovered if one approaches jaundice in the SICU patient in a systemic and orderly fashion.

BILIRUBIN METABOLISM

A. Excretion
   1. Bilirubin, derived from the degradation of hemoglobin and bound to albumin, is carried in the plasma to the liver for exretion.
   2. Excretion from the liver via the biliary system to the intestine requires hepatic uptake, conjugation, and excretion into the biliary ductules.
   3. Bilirubin conjugated with glucuronide may be directly excreted in the stool or converted by gut bacteria to urobilinogen.
   4. The intestinal mucosa may reabsorb urobilinogen and excrete it in the urine.
B. Levels
   1. In the adult, normal bilirubin levels range from 0.5 to 1.0 mg/100 ml.
   2. Clinical jaundice is usually not detectable until the level of bilirubin rises to 2.5 to 3.0 mg/100 ml.
   3. Abnormalities at any stage of bilirubin metabolism give rise to jaundice.
C. Classification
   1. Dividing jaundice into three groups is clinically convenient. (See Table 25-1.)
      a. An increase in the production of pigment exceeds the liver's ability to excrete in a normal fashion.

Table 25-1. Clinical jaundice

Increased pigment	Hepatocellular damage or dysfunction	Biliary obstruction
Massive transfusions	Hepatitis	Common bile duct
Hematomas	Viral	Stones
Crush injury	Drug	Injury
Transfusion reactions	Anesthesia	Cholecystitis
Autotransfusion	Hypotension	Biliary and pancreatic
Cardiopulmonary bypass	Anoxia	tumors
Hemolytic anemias	Sepsis	Suppurative cholangitis
Sickle cell anemia	Cirrhosis	Bowel rest
Glucose-6-phosphate-dehydrogenase deficiency	Gilbert's disease	Sledge syndrome
	Dubin-Johnson syndrome	
	Injury to hepatic vasculature	
	Cholestatic drugs	
	Bowel rest	
	TPN	
	Excess glucose	
	? Cholestasis	

    b. Hepatocellular damage or dysfunction leads to abnormal bilirubin excretion.

    c. Obstruction of the biliary drainage system may lead to jaundice.

  2. The first two groups are often labeled "medical" jaundice and the third group "surgical" jaundice.

  3. In a critically ill patient, jaundice may result from a combination of any of the three groups. A patient with "medical" jaundice due to hepatocellular dysfunction from sepsis may well need a surgical procedure to correct the underlying cause.

DIAGNOSIS
Laboratory evaluation

A. A number of laboratory tests are useful in evaluating the jaundiced patient. These tests are interpreted in relation to one another and to the clinical setting.

B. Appropriate tests

  1. Direct and indirect bilirubin

2. Urinary examination for the presence or absence of bilirubin and urobilinogen
3. Serum enzyme assays for serum glutamic oxaloacetic transaminase (SGOT) and alkaline phosphatase
4. Serum glutamic pyruvic transaminase (SGPT) and 5'-nucleotidase to supplement the SGOT and alkaline phosphatase in the presence of bone disease and multiple organ damage
   a. They are more specific for hepatic and biliary disease.
   b. Alkaline phosphatase may also be fractionated by electrophoresis to distinguish its source.
5. Clotting time parameters
6. Prothrombin time
7. Partial thromboplastin time
   a. Tests 5 to 7 above provide information about clotting status.
   b. They also indicate the synthetic function of the liver, especially in response to Vitamin K.
8. Serum albumin to obtain information regarding the liver's synthetic function
9. Serum amylase to check for the possible presence of pancreatitis
10. Serologic tests for hepatitis
11. Other tests
    a. Serum ammonia
    b. Cholesterol and triglycerides
    c. Globulins by electrophoresis
    d. Immunoglobulins
    e. Specific amino acid levels

Radiologic evaluation

A. A number of diagnostic and therapeutic radiographic and radionuclide techniques may be advantageous
B. Plain chest and stomach roentgenograms
   1. May occasionally demonstrate abnormalities such as calcifications in the region of the gallbladder and biliary tree
   2. May be useful to localize underlying causes of jaundice (e.g., subphrenic abscess)

C. Ultrasound

Gray-scale ultrasound is one of the most useful tests in evaluating the jaundiced patient. The study requires a highly skilled technician to perform the examination.

1. Advantages
   a. Noninvasive
   b. Well tolerated
   c. Accurate
   d. Can often be done at bedside, eliminating the need to transfer a critically ill patient to the radiology department

2. Information provided
   a. Presence of absence of gallstones
   b. Size of the biliary ducts
   c. Thickness of the gallbladder wall
   d. Presence of liver metastases
   e. Presence of cirrhosis
   f. Presence of fatty infiltration
   g. Presence of severe hepatitis
   h. Presence of masses in the pancreas or intraabdominal abscesses

3. Accuracy
   a. Ninety percent to 97% accurate in differentiating between jaundice resulting from intrahepatic and extrahepatic causes
   b. In approximately 50% of patients, a specific diagnosis can be made on the basis of ultrasound examination alone
      (1) The upper limit of normal for the diameter of the common hepatic duct is approximately 7 mm
      (2) For the common bile duct, 10 mm
      (3) For the gallbladder wall, 3 mm
   c. Unsuccessful in about 5% of patients because of open wounds and interposed bowel gas

Computerized tomography (CT)

CT examination, with the use of newer generation scanners is also highly accurate in evaluating the biliary tract. When ultrasound is technically unsatisfactory, a CT scan may be a good alternative.

A. Advantages
   1. Can reliably detect dilated biliary ducts
   2. More accurate than ultrasound in the evaluation of the pancreas
   3. Useful in localizing in intraabdominal abscess and may be used in conjunction with percutaneous drainage of such an abscess
B. Disadvantages
   1. High cost
   2. Radiation exposure
   3. Need for oral and intravenous contrast

Radionuclide scanning

Several types of technetium-99–labeled radiopharmaceuticals are available for hepatobiliary scanning. These agents are rapidly concentrated in the biliary system and allow visualization of the liver, intrahepatic, and extrahepatic ducts and the duodenum in the normal patient.

A. Information provided
   1. Presence of acute cholecystitis
      a. Most useful function of scanning
      b. A normal scan with good visualization of the gallbladder effectively rules out acute cholecystitis
      c. False-positive examinations may occur in chronically starved patients or those on TPN.
   2. Biliary kinetics
   3. Distinction between intrahepatic and extrahepatic biliary obstruction
   4. Patency of the biliary system
   5. Presence of cystic duct
   6. Physiologic patency of the ducts even though visualization of the gallbladder and biliary ducts is variable at a bilirubin concentration of greater than 5 mg/100 ml.

Endoscopic retrograde cholangiography (ERCP)

A. ERCP is useful in the visualization of the pancreatic duct and the biliary tree.
   1. In experienced hands, a greater than 95% success rate occurs in visualizing the biliary system, with very low mortality.

2. In the evaluation of the jaundiced patient, ERCP is useful when extrahepatic biliary obstruction is strongly suspected but cannot be confirmed by less invasive procedures.
3. ERCP is also useful when a detailed picture of the anatomy is required before surgery.
B. ERCP can also be therapeutic in the treatment of biliary
obstruction secondary to choledocholithiasis or ampullary
stenosis or in the management of sledge that is refractory to
tube feeding.
1. Endoscopic spincterotomy is probably the initial treatment of choice for extrahepatic biliary obstruction resulting from choledocholithiasis or ampullary stenosis.
2. Stones can often be removed at the same procedure.
3. Success rates of 80% to 90% have been reported.

Percutaneous transhepatic cholangiography

A. Indications
1. They are generally similar to those for ERCP.
2. ERCP is probably a better choice when the ducts are not
dilated or when sphincterotomy is probably going to be
necessary.
B. Success rate
1. With a skinny needle, the procedure will be successful
in over 95% of patients with dilated bile ducts.
2. In patients with nondilated ducts, success rate is 70%.
C. Percutaneous transhepatic biliary drainage
1. This additional technique involves placement of a catheter into the biliary tree or even through the common bile
duct into the duodenum to allow internal drainage.
2. The procedure may be useful in critically ill patients with
biliary obstruction and jaundice who are poor risks for a
surgical procedure.

Oral and intravenous cholangiography

These procedures are of little or no use in the jaundiced
patient since they will usually fail to visualize the biliary system
if the bilirubin is greater than 3 mg/100 ml. The techniques
described above have supplanted these two.

Biliary sledge syndrome

A common association of extrahepatic biliary obstruction is with biliary tract dilation and sledge formation.

A. This commonly occurs in the presence of prolonged bowel rest, with or without the presence of TPN.

B. It seems to respond to the institution of the tube feeding and/or the administration of metronidazole (Flagyl).

1. With the institution of tube feeding, the bilirubin and alkaline phosphatase may rise before coming down.

SUGGESTED READINGS

Araki, T.: Cholecystitis: A comparison of real-time ultrasonography and technetium-99m hepatobiliary scintigraphy, Clin. Radiol. **31**:675, 1980.

Cerra, F.B., et al.: Mental status, the intensive care unit and cimetidine, Ann. Surg. **196**:565, 1982.

Deitch, E.A., and Engel J.M.: Acute acalculous cholecysitis, Am. J. Surg. **142**:290, 1981.

Dewbury, K.C., et al.: Ultrasound in the evaluation and diagnosis of jaundice, Br. J. Radiol. **52**:276, 1979.

Freitas, J.E., and Gulati, R.M.: Rapid evaluation of acute abdominal pain by hepatobiliary scanning, JAMA 244:1585, 1980.

Gregg, J.A., and McDonald, D.G.: Endoscopic retrograde cholangiopancreatography and gray-scale ultrasound in the diagnosis of jaundice, Am. J. Surg. **137**:611, 1979.

Hastings, P.R., et al.: Antacid titration in the prevention of acute gastrointestinal bleeding, N. Engl. J. Med. **298**:1041, 1978.

Khan, F., et al.: Results of gastric neutralization with hourly antacid and cimetidine in 320 intubated patients with respiratory failure, Chest **79**:409, 1981.

Kivilaakso, E., and Silen, W.: Pathogenesis of experimental gastric mucosal injury, N. Engl. J. Med. **301**:364, 1979.

Priebe, H.J., and Skillman, J.J.: Methods of prophylaxis in stress ulcer disease, World J. Surg. **5**:223, 1981.

Priebe, H.J., et al.: Antacid versus cimetadine in preventing acute gastrointestinal bleeding, N. Engl. J. Med. **302**:426, 1980.

Ranson, J.E.: Complications of small intestine surgery in complications in surgery and their management. J.D. Hardy, Philadelphia, 1981, W.B. Saunders Co., pp. 490-511.

Rubin, R.H., and Cosimi, A.B.: In Simmons, R.L., and Howard, R.J.: Surgical infectious disease, New York, 1982, Appleton Century Crofts, pp. 1118-1119.

Skillman, J.J., et al.: Respiratory failure, hypotension, sepsis and jaundice: A clinical syndrome associated with lethal hemorrhage from acute stress ulceration of the stomach, Am. J. Surg. **117**:523, 1969.

Wheeler, P.G., et al.: Noninvasive techniques in the diagnosis of jaundice-ultrasound and computer, Gut 20:196, 1979.

Zinner, M.T., et al.: The prevention of upper gastrointestinal tract bleeding in patients in an intensive care unit, Surg. Gynecol. Obstet. **153**:214, 1981.

26

Anaphylaxis

John Fath

A. Anaphylaxis is an acute, life-threatening, systemic response to chemical mediators released following activation of mast cell or mucosal-bound IgE.
   1. Variations on this mechanism, such as cold-induced anaphylaxis or exercise anaphylaxis, do not require presentation of an antigen.
   2. Some drugs, notably muscle relaxants and radiographic contrast agents, can mediate systemic release of chemical mediators without prior exposure to the drug in what is termed an "anaphylactoid response."
B. Mediators
   1. At the time of mast cell stimulation, they undergo degranulation and release granules that contain, among other things, preformed histamine and heparin.
      a. Other substances, such as the leukotrienes, which compose slow-reacting substance of anaphylaxis (SRSA), and prostaglandins are formed following stimulation.
   2. Release of these substances has a range of physiologic effects from mild urticarial rash to acute airway obstruction and cardiovascular collapse.
C. Physiology
   The mediation of this response is complex and not entirely understood.
   1. Histamine alone will cause tachycardia, flushing, headache, and increased blood pressure.
   2. In accompaniment with serotonin, fluid accumulation in the extracellular space is promoted through an increase in capillary permeability.

3. Pulmonary effects resulting from these mediator effects and secondary irritation of bronchial receptors include:
   a. Increased airway resistance
   b. Decreased compliance
   c. Hypoxia
4. Smooth muscle may constrict; contractions within the gastrointestinal and genitourinary system are common.
5. Other substances, notably the leukotrienes, may potentiate and extend the effects on any organ system.
6. Leukotrienes may also have primary effects of their own, such as negative inotropic cardiac depression.
7. Changes occur in the major shock organs: tracheobronchial endothelium, small airways, and the cardiovascular system.
   a. Cardiovascular
      (1) The peripheral vascular bed often dilates during an episode.
      (2) Decreased blood volume occurs as plasma leaks into the extracellular space.
      (3) Hemoconcentration can occur.
      (4) Cardiac output may fall secondary to decreased effective blood volume, hypoxia, or direct myocardial depression. This commonly leads to the otherwise rare cardiovascular response of decreased peripheral vascular resistance and decreased cardiac output.
   b. Pulmonary
      (1) Severe pulmonary compromise can evolve from upper airway obstruction resulting from laryngeal edema or from emphysematous air trapping due to lower airway bronchospasm.
      (2) Twenty-five percent of fatal cases involve laryngeal edema.
      (3) Twenty-five percent of fatal cases involve acute emphysema.
      (4) In the remainder of fatal cases, a mixed or cardiovascular lesion is felt to be the primary fatal event.

D. Diagnosis
   1. The diagnosis of anaphylaxis or anaphylactoid reactions may be difficult because many things can mimic the signs or symptoms.
   2. History
      a. A major differentiating factor is history of an allergy
      b. Use of muscle relaxants
      c. Administration of anesthesia-inducing agents
      d. Iodinated radiocontrast agents
   3. If only a single organ system is involved, other diagnoses should also be considered.
   4. Other problems that can lead to cardiovascular collapse include:
      a. Drug overdoses
      b. Hypoxia
      c. Hyperkalemia
      d. Myocardial infarction
      e. Arrhythmias
      f. Neurologic events
   5. Findings similar to allergic bronchospasm can be precipitated by:
      a. Plugged endotracheal tube
      b. Esophageal intubation
      c. Aspiration
      d. Pulmonary edema
      e. Asthma
      f. Chronic obstructive pulmonary disease (COPD)
E. Treatment (Table 26-1, box on p. 650)
   1. Goals
      a. Prevent further mediator release
      b. Block end-organ responses to the mediators
      c. Reverse what response have already occurred
   2. Primary treatment
      a. With rare exceptions, such as patients on beta-blockers or with idiopathic, hypertrophic, or subaortic stenosis, the primary treatment is with epinephrine.
         (1) Epinephrine mechanism
             (a) Increases cyclic adenosine monophosphate (CAMP) levels in most cells
             (b) Prevents further mediator release
             (c) Has balanced alpha and beta effects on end organs.

Table 26-1. Adult treatment

Drug	Form	Route	Dose
All symptoms			
Epinephrimine	1:1000	Subcutaneous, intramuscular, intralingual	0.1-0.5 ml every 5 to 15 min
Epinephrine	1:10,000	Intravenous	3 to 5 ml slowly intravenously over 5 min every 15 min
	1:10,000	Tracheobronchial	Inject via long catheter near carina, follow by 5 to 10 rapid breaths to disperse; repeat every 15 min
At injection site of subcutaneous antigen			
Epinephrine	1:1000		0.3 to 0.5 ml to delay absorption of antigen
Acute emphysema			
Nebulized bronchodilators			
Isoproterenol	1:200		0.5 ml in 1.5 ml normal saline every 4 hr
Intravenous			
Aminophylline			5 mg/kg body weight over 20 to 30 minutes, then 0.9 mg/kg/hr

(2) It can be given subcutaneously, intramuscularly, intralingually, intravenously, or intratracheally and repeated as necessary.

(3) If the reaction occurred secondary to a cutaneous injection, epinephrine can be injected locally to reduce absorption and a venous occlusive tourniquet placed proximal to the site.

b. Sometimes a single injection of epinephrine will abort the process. Other times, protracted resuscitation is necessary.

c. In cases of continued hypotension, volume expansion with crystalloid or preferably colloid is mandatory.

HYPOTENSION WITH APPROPRIATE FLUID RESUSCITATION

Dopamine Hcl (inotropic) — 200 mg/500 ml D5W (400 mEq/U) drip titrated to blood pressure (BP) response

Levarterenal bitartrate (Levophed) — 0.02% solution of bitartrate in 1 mg base/ml, 4 mg in 500 ml D5W (8 mEq/ml) titrated to BP response (1 to 4 mEq/min)

Cutaneous manifestations and as adjuvant in severe reactions

Diphenhydramine (Benadryl) — 25 to 50 mg intramuscularly or intravenously every 6 hours

Severe reactions, prolonged resuscitation or previously on β-blockade

Steroids

Dexamethasone (Decadron) — 4 to 8 mg intravenously every 6 hours for 24 hours longer as clinically indicated

Hydrocortisone succinate — 100 mg intramuscularly or intravenously every 3 to 6 hours for 24 to 48 hours

Special cases

Beta-blockade—These patients may be unresponsive to standard prescription, manifesting alpha-adrenergic effects only to epinephrine

(1) Sympathomimetics: Attempt to override beta-blockade
  Isoproterenol
  Dopamine

(2) Steroids: Possibly may improve adrenergic receptor availability

---

Documentation of this by central venous pressure (CVP) or pulmonary artery wedge pressure should be done before using pressor agents (other than epinephrine acutely).

(1) Currently, the pressor of choice is dopamine.

(2) Epinephrine drips have been associated with severe metabolic acidosis.

d. Steroids are commonly given in cases of severe anaphylaxis.

  (1) They may:
    (a) Reduce the severity of the later phases of the reaction
    (b) Prevent relapses after an initial successful resuscitation
    (c) Increase the responsiveness to exogenous pressor amines
  (2) They are relatively ineffective for the acute response.
  (3) If given too rapidly, they may cause hypotension and arrhythmias.
 e. Antihistamines, commonly diphenhydramine HCl (Benadryl), are given.
  (1) They relieve the cutaneous manifestations.
  (2) They do not avert or alter the cardiovascular response.

F. Prevention
 1. Pretreatment in patients at risk for reactions to iodinated contrast agents should include steroids.
  a. Prednisone: 50 mg orally every 6 hours for 3 doses, with last dose 1 hour before the study *or*
  b. Hydrocortisone succinate: 100 mg intramuscularly every 6 hours for 3 doses, with last dose 1 hour before study
 2. Antihistamines are often recommended.
  a. They have not been shown to avert the serious cardiovascular aspects of a reaction.
  b. Their use may block minor aspects of a reaction such as rash and subjective dyspnea and, consequently, delay the diagnosis of a major reaction.
  c. They are probably best reserved for use following epinephrine after a reaction has been diagnosed.

SECTION FOUR

THERAPEUTICS

27

Line access-drainage tubes

Arthur D. Santos

CENTRAL VENOUS LINES

A. Indications
 1. Volume status determination
 2. Hyperalimentation
 3. Chronic drug administration
 4. Cardiopulmonary functional assessment-resuscitation
 5. Central vein pressure and pulmonary artery pressure monitoring
 6. Flow monitoring
B. Anatomy (Fig. 27-1)
 1. Gross
  a. Pleura
   (1) Dome or cupola closer to left subclavian and jugular veins
   (2) Chronic obstructive pulmonary disease (COPD)—higher than usual pleural domes on both sides
   (3) Chest roentgenogram before proceeding with contralateral venous puncture
  b. Chest
   (1) Subclavian vein—between clavicle and first rib
   (2) Scalenus anticus—floor that phrenic nerve traverses
   (3) Subclavian artery—behind scalenus anticus and posterosuperior to vein
  c. Neck
   (1) Skin, subcutaneous tissue, fascia.
   (2) Sternocleidomastoid (SCM)
   (3) Carotid

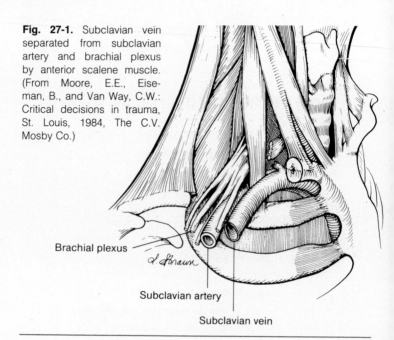

Fig. 27-1. Subclavian vein separated from subclavian artery and brachial plexus by anterior scalene muscle. (From Moore, E.E., Eiseman, B., and Van Way, C.W.: Critical decisions in trauma, St. Louis, 1984, The C.V. Mosby Co.)

Brachial plexus

Subclavian artery

Subclavian vein

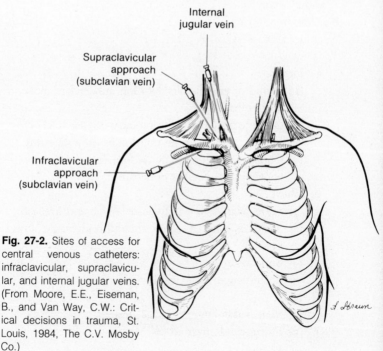

Internal jugular vein

Supraclavicular approach (subclavian vein)

Infraclavicular approach (subclavian vein)

Fig. 27-2. Sites of access for central venous catheters: infraclavicular, supraclavicular, and internal jugular veins. (From Moore, E.E., Eiseman, B., and Van Way, C.W.: Critical decisions in trauma, St. Louis, 1984, The C.V. Mosby Co.)

      (4) Nerves: eleventh, tenth, twelfth, sympathetic chain, recurrent laryngeal, cervical plexus

      (5) Thoracic duct—larger on left

  2. Ultrasound in location of jugular vein

    a. The level of the cricoid cartilage is location of largest diameter of jugular vein.

    b. Trendelenburg position of 15 degrees and Valsalva maneuver both cause similar venous distention.

    c. Carotid artery palpation decreases the size of jugular vein.

C. Approach and technique (Figs. 27-2 to 27-4)

  1. Sites

    a. Internal jugular

    b. Subclavian

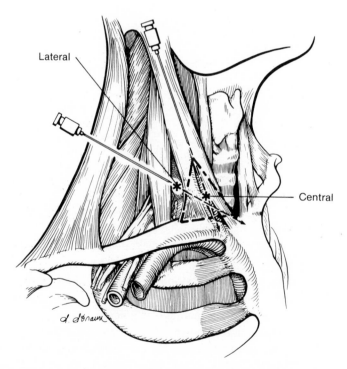

Fig. 27-3. Lateral and central approaches to internal jugular vein. (From Moore, E.E., Eiseman, B., and Van Way, C.W.: Critical disorders in trauma, St. Louis, 1984, The C.V. Mosby Co.)

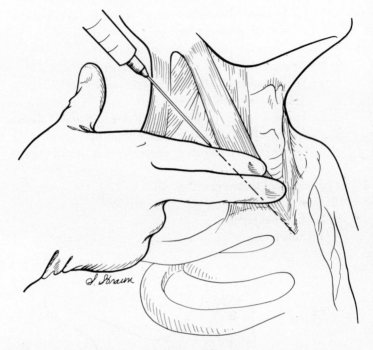

Fig. 27-4. Lateral approach with needle directed toward suprasternal notch. (From Moore, E.E., Eiseman, B., and Van Way, C.W.: Critical decision in trauma, St. Louis, 1984, The C.V. Mosby Co.)

    c. External jugular

    d. Long arm or peripherally inserted central catheter

  2. Internal jugular: right neck approach

    a. Patient's head turned left 90 degrees in supine position

    b. Trendelenburg position to prevent air emboli and cause venous distention

    c. Location of external jugular noted

    d. Prepare drape, gown, glove, mask; anesthetize just above external jugular vein as it crosses the SCM

    e. Vein located in coronal plane posterior to SCM above first rib insertion of scalenus anticus (scalene tubercle) parallel to axis of SCM

    f. Initial thrust is 30 degrees to sagittal plane parallel to coronal plane

    g. All initial attempts with 18-gauge needle

    h. One and one-half inches guidewire passed when located; guidewire is 0.021 inches in diameter and 80 cm in length; catheter placed over and secured with sutures.

    i. Wound dressed skillfully

    j. Chest roentgenogram for placement; adjust as necessary

3. Subclavian

    a. Patient in supine position with towel between shoulder blades

    b. Trendelenburg for above reason

    c. Location of clavicular notch (superior portions, deltopectoral groove, and approximately midportion of clavicle)

    d. Prepare drape, gown, glove, mask; anesthetize clavicle inferiorly along with skin and subcutaneous

    e. Using 18-gauge spinal needle, enter skin and step off clavicle; direct needle perpendicular to sagittal plane and parallel to coronal plane or the floor in the room

    f. Contact with underside of clavicle essential; maintenance of the above position is necessary for successful cannulation

    g. Vein is between clavicle and first rib

    h. Aspirate blood

    i. Place guidewire; guidewire is 0.021 inch in diameter, 80 cm in length

    j. Then cannulate with catheter secured and dress wound

    k. Chest roentgenogram taken

4. External jugular

    a. Risk of subclavian vein injury with stiff catheter

    b. Frequently used as peripheral line rather than for central catheter placement

5. Long arm

    a. High incidence of thrombophlebitis

    b. Good for short term (48 to 72 hours)

Table 27-1. Complications associated with central venous lines

Problem	Incidence	Cause	Prevention	Treatment
Pneumothorax	6%	Parenchymal lung perforation	Knowledge of anatomy subclavian vein (SC) stay close to clavicle Internal jugular vein (IJ) remain a needle distance from supraclavicular fossa	Observation Chest tube
Hemothorax	2%	Hemorrhagic pulmonary laceration	As above	Chest tube
Malposition	6%	Threading catheter when difficult	Smooth easy threading any obstruction Rethread	Chest roentgenogram
Arterial puncture	1%	Posterior thrust in SC Medial directed needle in IJ	Check for arterialized blood and pulsations	Compression
Intrapleural infusion	1%	Placement of catheter in pleura	Aspiration when catheter completely in place	Thoracentesis
Thrombosis		Infection Vessel wall injury	Silastic catheter Sterile dressings ? Heparin	Remove catheter ? Heparin
Myocardial perforation		Catheter in heart	Place catheter in superior vena cava (SVC)	Observe for tamponade remove and replace catheter

Arrhythmia	Catheter in heart	Place catheter in SVC	Pull back catheter
Subcutaneous emphysema	Puncture of trachea, esophagus, or lung	Knowledge of anatomy	Observation Chest roentgenogram, chest tube if necessary
Knotting of catheter	Catheter too long	Knowledge of distance to SVC to insertion	Chest roentgenogram
Thoracic duct perforation	Left-sided approach	Use right side Knowledge of anatomy	Observation
Catheter emboli	Failure to remove needle resulting in shearing of catheter	Remove both needle and catheter Measure length with known intact catheter	Angiography
Nerve injury	Too posterior in either SC or IJ approach	Knowledge of anatomy	Observation, check neurologic function
Catheter sepsis	Transcutaneous infection Result in positive blood culture Positive catheter tip culture If same organism will be diagnostic All lines colonize by skin Organism in 72 hours	Sterile dressing changes Rotate sites	Remove catheter culture

D. Internal jugular versus subclavian
   1. The right side is a straight course to right atrium; right internal jugular has lowest complication rate
   2. Carotid artery injury is more significant, but also more palpable than subclavian artery
   3. Thoracic duct larger on left
   4. Nerve damage potentially greater with internal jugular
   5. Patient comfort greater with subclavian
   6. Subclavian vein can be held open by surrounding structures
E. Complications (see Table 27-1)

SWAN-GANZ CATHETERS (PULMONARY ARTERY CATHETERS)

A. Anatomy and technique to gain access to central vein similar to central venous catheters
B. Technique to place catheter in wedge position
   1. All lines flushed; balloon tested and functional (Fig. 27-5)
   2. Catheter placed in introducer and advanced under pressure monitoring until in chest (Fig. 27-6); respiratory excursion seen and balloon inflated

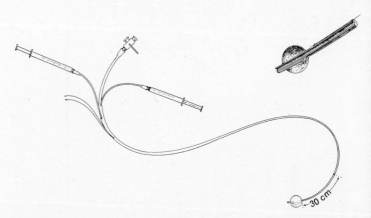

Fig. 27-5. The pulmonary artery balloon catheter. (From Van Way, C.W., and Buerk, C.A.: Surgical skills in patient care, 1978, The C.V. Mosby Co.)

3. Catheter advanced until right atrial tracing encountered
4. When catheter advances through right ventricle, potential for arrhythmia exists; systolic-diastolic pressure pattern seen
5. Pulmonary artery tracing is noted by increase in diastolic pressure and appearance of dicrotic notch
6. In wedge position drop balloon and there should be return of pulmonary artery tracing
7. Confirm position with chest roentgenogram; tip of catheter should be over vertebral column or in proximal right or left main pulmonary artery (PA)
8. See Fig. 27-7

C. Pressures
   1. Should be determined at end expiration
   2. Normal ranges

	Systolic (torr)	Diastolic (torr)	Mean (torr)
Right atrium (RA)	3 to 7	−2 to 2	−2 to 7
Right ventricle (RV)	15 to 30	0 to 7	
Pulmonary artery (PA)	15 to 30	5 to 15	10 to 20
Pulmonary artery wedge pressure (PAWP)			5 to 12
Left atrium (LA)			4 to 12

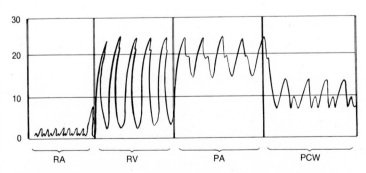

Fig. 27-6. Pressure monitoring in pulmonary artery catheterization. Pressures obtained as the pulmonary artery catheter is advanced into the right atrium *(RA),* the right ventricle *(RV),* pulmonary artery *(PA),* and the wedge position *(PCW).* (From Van Way, C.W., and Buerk, C.A.: Surgical skills in patient care, St. Louis, 1978, The C.V. Mosby Co.)

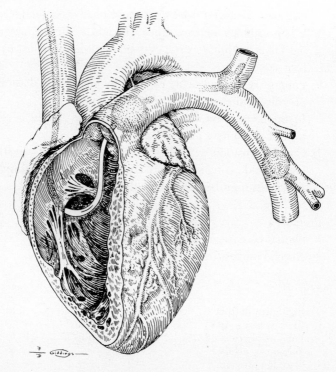

Fig. 27-7. The pulmonary artery catheter in place. (From Van Way, C.W., and Buerk, C.A.: Surgical skills in patient care, St. Louis, 1978, The C.V. Mosby Co.)

    3. Elevated RA pressure occurs with:
      a. RV failure
      b. Tricuspid stenosis and regurgitation
      c. Constrictive pericarditis
      d. Chronic left ventricular (LV) failure
      e. Volume overload
      f. Cardiac tamponade
    4. Elevation RV pressure occurs with:
      a. Pulmonary hypertension
      b. Pulmonic valvular stenosis
      c. RV failure
      d. Constrictive pericarditis
      e. Chronic congestive heart failure
      f. Ventricular septal defect (VSD)

5. Elevation of PA pressures occurs with
   a. Increased pulmonary blood flow—atrial septal defect (ASD), VSD
   b. Increased pulmonary vascular resistance
   c. Pulmonary parenchyme disease; increased pulmonary capillary pressure
   d. Increased pulmonary venous pressure
   e. Mitral stenosis and LV failure
6. Situations in which pulmonary artery diastolic pressure (PAD) may not equal PAWP or PAWP may not equal left ventricular end-diastolic pressure (LVEDP)
   a. Pulmonary disease—COPD and adult respiratory distress syndrome (ARDS)
   b. Increased pulmonary arteriolar resistance
   c. Heart rates greater than 125/min
   d. Zone IV placement of catheter
   e. Increased pulmonary interstitial pressure
   f. Constriction of pulmonary veins
7. Elevation of PAWP occurs with
   a. LV failure
   b. Mitral stenosis
   c. Mitral insufficiency
   d. Constrictive pericarditis
   e. Volume overload
   f. Pulmonary vein constriction
   g. Increased capillary-interstitial hydrostatic pressure—capillary leak syndromes

D. Miscellaneous
   1. Mixed venous gases can be drawn through PA catheter tip from RA port, if RA port is in lower RA.
   2. Respiratory and respirator variation is noted on pulmonary artery and wedge tracings.
      a. Readings should be obtained at end expiration.
      b. Significant change in pressure during respiratory cycle may suggest hypovolemia.
   3. Relative distances

15 cm from internal jugular (IJ) or subclavian (SC) vein	to RA
40 cm from right antecubital vein	to RA
50 cm from left antecubital vein	to RA
30 cm from femoral vein	to RA
add 15 cm to main pulmonary artery	

E. Complications (see Table 27-2)
   1. Fatal pulmonary rupture
      a. Incidence
         (1) 0.2% patients with one death in 1,500 catheterizations
      b. Clinical sign-settings
         (1) Patient with pulmonary artery catheter
         (2) Hemoptysis
         (3) Acute cardiopulmonary collapse
      c. Risk factors
         (1) Advanced age
         (2) Pulmonary artery hypertension–firm vessels
         (3) Clotting defects
         (4) Distal catheter placement
         (5) Balloon over inflation
         (6) Cardiopulmonary bypass manipulation and heparin
         (7) Tumor surrounding pulmonary artery
      d. Mechanisms for rupture of pulmonary artery
         (1) Balloon disrupts pulmonary artery
         (2) Balloon inflation propels tip through vessel wall (especially with eccentric balloon)
         (3) Catheter tip advanced too far peripherally
         (4) Inflation in small proximal pulmonary vessels
      e. Recommendations for minimizing its occurrence
         (1) Continuously monitor and evaluate RA, RV, PA and wedge pressures.
         (2) Confirm catheter location by chest roentgenogram at least daily.
         (3) Prevent overinflation of balloon and note volumes used to wedge previously.
         (4) Wedge only when needed.
         (5) Do not use fluid to inflate.
         (6) Attach empty syringe so accidental injections will not occur.
         (7) Prevent knotting and redundancy by "feel" and knowledge of distances. Use fluoroscopy if there

Table 27-2. Complications associated with pulmonary artery catheters

Problem	Cause	Prevention	Treatment
Vascular occlusion infarction	Balloon up too long	Remove all air and replace empty syringe	Withdraw catheter
Balloon rupture	Peripheral catheter	Pull back catheter, place centrally	Chest roentgenogram
	Placement of too much air in balloon	Use PAD pressures	Observation
		Limit air distention by fixed volume syringe	
Intracardiac knotting	Using more catheter than necessary to place in pulmonary artery	Knowledge of distance, chest roentgenogram	Withdraw catheter
Arrhythmias	Catheter contracts ventricular wall	Use as little catheter necessary to place—prevent redundancy	Lidocaine
Valvular injury	Perforation or failure to deflate balloon when withdrawing	Gently thread catheter, deflate on removal or withdrawal	Physical examination for murmur and angiography
Sepsis	Poor skin preparation	Prepare skin	Remove catheter
	Transcutaneous infection	Rotate catheter	Culture
	Wound dressing performed unsterilely	Sterile wound dressing	
		Usual transducer/line	
Subclavian thrombosis	Clot forms on catheter with vessel injury	Remove and rotate sites	Observation if only thrombosis
Pulmonary emboli	Clot breaks off and embolizes pulmonary artery	? Heparin	Heparin if pulmonary emboli and heparin not contraindicated

is a question of catheter positioning or difficulty in insertion.

(8) Do not leave catheter in wedge position.

f. Treatment

(1) Airway control

(2) Lobectomy-pneumonectomy, if needed

(3) Resusitation

(4) Usually not time for an angiogram

(5) Controversy exists over whether or not to pull catheter back or reinflate balloon

ARTERIAL LINES

A. Anatomy

1. Four major vessels

a. Radial

b. Brachial

c. Femoral

d. Dorsal pedals

B. Technique

1. Radial approach (Figs. 27-8 to 27-10)

a. Located on lateral anterior aspect of wrist

b. Most easily palpated and most superficial at wrist

c. Perform Allen test before draping

(1) Ulnar and radial artery is compressed with fist clenched or elevated to drain blood from the hand.

(2) The ulnar artery is released and the hand is observed for blushing.

(a) This indicates a patent palmar arch supplied by the ulnar artery.

(b) If radial occlusion occurs with the catheter, then the ulnar artery is usually capable of supplying the hand.

(3) Very few patients have inadequate palmar arch collateral. The risk is present when collateral flow is absent.

d. Sterile drape, glove, gown, mask, anesthetic given

e. Catheter needle system flushed and threaded

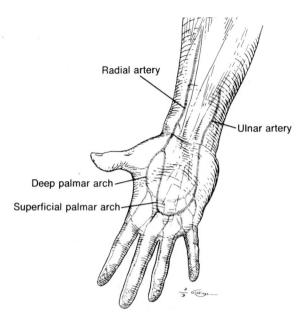

Fig. 27-8. Anatomy of the radial and ulnar arteries and the superficial and deep palmar arches. (From Van Way, C.W., and Buerk, C.A.: Surgical skills in patient care, St. Louis, 1978, The C.V. Mosby Co.)

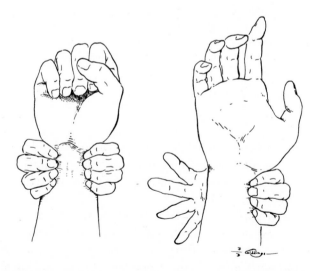

Fig. 27-9. Allen test for ulnar artery patency. (From Van Way, C.W., and Buerk, C.A.: Surgical skills in patient care, St. Louis, 1978, The C.V. Mosby Co.)

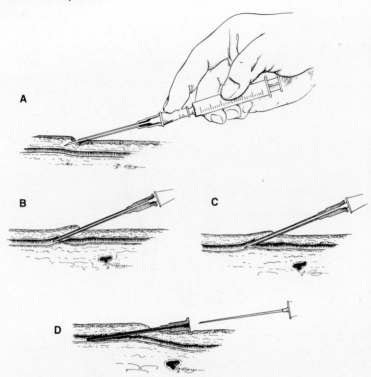

Fig. 27-10. Cannulation of an artery with an over-needle cannula. **A,** The needle and catheter have been inserted through the skin. **B,** The needle tip has been inserted into the artery. Blood can be aspirated, but the catheter is not yet in the artery. The needle tip should be raised and the needle advanced farther so that the catheter enters the artery, as in **C.** Then the catheter is threaded over the needle, into the artery, and the needle is removed, **D.** (From Van Way, C.W., and Buerk, C.A.: Surgical skills in patient care, St. Louis, 1978, The C.V. Mosby Co.)

  f. Pass catheter needle into arterial lumen by slowly advancing; blood return and arterial pressure tracing indicate intra-arterial position; thread catheter.

 2. Brachial approach

  In comparison with the radial artery, this vessel is larger and lies between the bicipital tendon and median nerve at the antecubital fossa. The technique is similar except that circulation to the hand and arm is compromised when thrombosis (<5%) occurs and nerve injury is more likely.

      a. Location of the artery is determined and the area cleaned.

      b. When blood is seen flowing retrograde and the pressure monitor shows the arterial tracing, the catheter is directed into the vessel lumen and threaded.

      c. Secure the line and apply sterile dressing.

  3. Femoral catheter

    The vessel is usually superficial and easy to palpate and puncture.

      a. Disadvantages

        (1) Difficult to control bleeding near the genital region

        (2) Catheter impairs mobility

        (3) Catheter can embolize peripherally or thrombose locally to cause vascular insufficiency

          (a) Peripheral pulses should be marked and checked frequently.

          (b) Thrombosis and emboli usually respond to arterotomy and Fogarty catheterization.

      b. Once the vessel is located in the inguinal region lateral to the pubic tubercle, the technique is similar to the previous approaches

  4. Dorsal pedal artery

    This artery can be dealt with as a radial arterial alternative. The technique is also the same.

C. Arterial pressure wave forms

  1. As the arterial catheter is monitored more peripherally from the aortic root:

      a. Peak systolic pressure increases as a result of an amplification effect in the arterial systems during systole.

      b. The dicrotic notch, which represents aortic valve closure, progressively moves down the downslope.

  2. A sharp upstroke, clear dicrotic notch, and end-diastolic phase should be present.

  3. Conversely, aortic stenosis creates a gradual upstroke and loss of dicrotic notch. The same phenomenon is demonstrated with overdamping of the system. Overdamping can occur from:

      a. Clot on the tip or in the catheter or transducer

    b. The contact of the catheter tip with vessel wall

    c. Overtightening of damping devices

       (1) These devices are necessary for accurate pressure readings.

       (2) A snap test accurately determines the correct degree of damping.

       (3) When too tight, the system can become overdamped.

  4. Respiratory variation of the arterial pressure tracing can occur in several situations. A pressure difference of greater than 10 torr is known as *pulsus paradoxus.*

    a. Cardiac tamponade

    b. Constrictive pericarditis

    c. Significant hypovolemia

    d. Positive-pressure ventilation

    e. Bronchospasm

    f. Thoracic tension (e.g., pneumothorax)

    g. Normal variant (diagnosis of exclusion)

D. Complications (see Table 27-3)

MILITARY ANTISHOCK TROUSER (MAST) SUIT OR PNEUMATIC ANTISHOCK GARMENT (PASG)

A MAST suit or PASG can facilitate shock management.

A. Mechanism

  1. Translocates vascular volume from the lower extremities to the upper half of the body

Table 27-3. Complications associated with arterial lines

Problem	Cause	Prevention	Treatment
Decreased or absent pulse distal to catheter	Arterial spasm Thrombosis	Atraumatic placement Immobilization Avoid low flow states	Remove catheter Vasodilator locally Thrombectomy
Local infection sepsis	Break in sterile technique, in placement, in maintenance, and in dressing change	Aseptic technique Rotate site after 72 to 96 hours	Remove catheter Blood cultures Catheter culture

      2. Increases local hydrostatic pressure
      3. Has an exoskeleton splinting action
B. Indications
      1. Splinting and control of hemorrhage from pelvic fractures
      2. Tamponading soft tissue hemorrhage
      3. Stabilizing multiple leg fractures
      4. Hypotension in trauma (controversial)
C. Contraindications
      1. Pulmonary edema
      2. Pregnancy and impaired pulmonary function are relative contraindications
D. Application of MAST suit (Figs. 27-11 to 27-16)

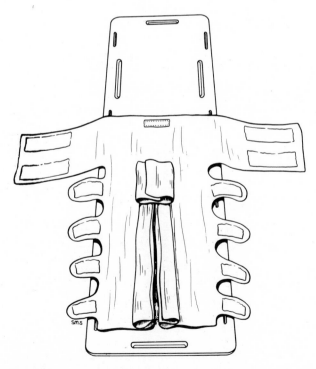

Fig. 27-11. MAST suit should be placed on stretcher before patient is positioned. (From Moore, E.E., Eiseman, B., and Van Way, C.W.: Critical decisions in trauma, St. Louis, 1984, The C.V. Mosby Co.)

1. Lay trousers flat and unfolded.
2. Slide underneath patient.
3. Fold straps about the legs first and fasten.
4. Fold about the abdomen.
5. Attach tubes to the pants' connections. Open all stopcocks.

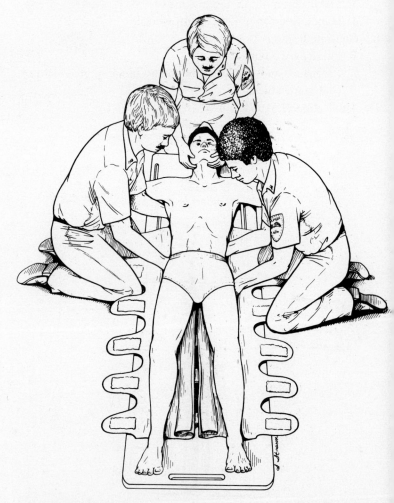

Fig. 27-12. Optimally, the patient's clothes should be removed to facilitate rapid perusal before MAST suit is fastened. (From Moore, E.E., Eiseman, B., and Van Way, C.W.: Critical decisions in trauma, St. Louis, 1984, The C.V. Mosby Co.)

6. Inflate legs first, then abdomen.
7. Inflate until the patient's blood pressure reaches 100 torr (systolic).
8. Turn stopcocks to maintain inflation.
9. Monitor patient's pressure and inflate to maintain that pressure.

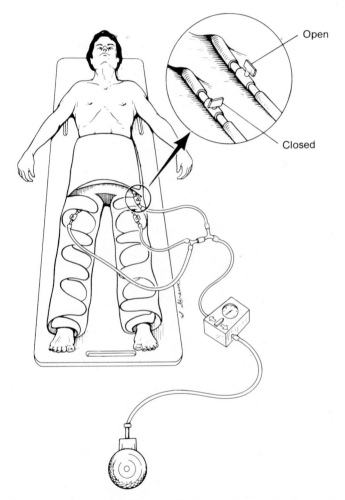

Open

Closed

Fig. 27-13. Tubing is connected to all three compartments. Insert illustrates closed and open positions for valves. (From Moore, E.E., Eiseman, B., and Van Way, C.W.: Critical decisions in trauma, St. Louis, 1984, The C.V. Mosby Co.)

E. Deflation
  1. Fluid resuscitation should occur before removal.
  2. The patient may be transported to surgery with trousers in place and inflated.
  3. Insert intravenous lines and administer blood volume.
  4. Monitor electrocardiogram (ECG).
  5. Open stopcock to abdominal section first.

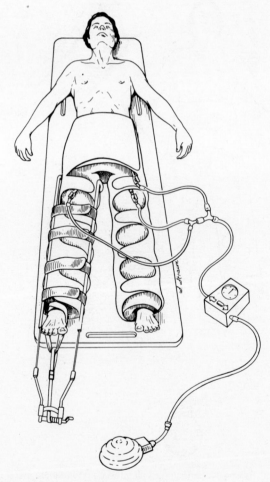

Fig. 27-14. If Hare traction splint is indicated, this should be placed before MAST suit is inflated. (From Moore, E.E., Eiseman, B., and Van Way, C.W.: Critical decisions in trauma, St. Louis, 1984, The C.V. Mosby Co.)

6. Stop deflation when blood pressure falls 10 torr and hold until additional fluids are given.
7. If blood pressure falls to a greater degree, reinflate trousers until more fluid and/or operation can be carried out to control hemorrhage.

F. Complications
   1. Reduction in local perfusion

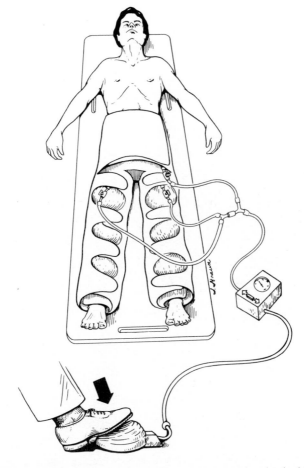

Fig. 27-15. Position of valves to each compartment must be checked before inflation. Leg sections should be inflated first. (From Moore, E.E., Eiseman, B., and Van Way, C.W.: Critical decisions in trauma, St. Louis, 1984, The C.V. Mosby Co.)

2. Potentiation of hypotension in settings of severe hypovolemia or incorrect application (abdomen first or with excessive pressure)

3. Skin necrosis, particularly in "thin" areas—over patella, malleolus

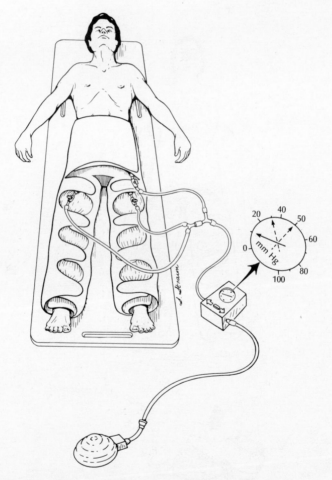

Fig. 27-16. Deflation of MAST suit must be done in careful, stepwise manner. Abdominal compartment should be released first in increments of 5 to 10 torr. (From Moore, E.E., Eiseman, B., and Van Way, C.W.: Critical decisions in trauma, St. Louis, 1984, The C.V. Mosby Co.)

CHEST TUBES

A. Indications
1. Chest tubes are helpful in removing excess air or blood from the intrapleural space.
a. If a major tracheobronchial injury is present, a persistent air leak occurs.
b. Blood filling a chest tube at a rate of 200 ml/hour over 2 to 3 hours may indicate the need to surgically control hemorrhage from injury of lung, heart, and great vessels.

B. Procedure for chest tube placement (Figs. 27-17 to 27-22)

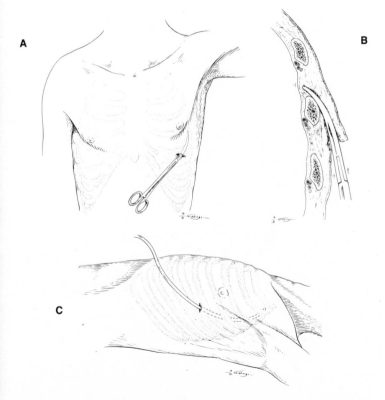

Fig. 27-17. Placing a chest tube. **A,** Site. **B,** Dissecting through chest wall. **C,** Final position. (From Van Way, C.W., and Buerk, C.A.: Surgical skills in patient care, St. Louis, 1978, The C.V. Mosby Co.)

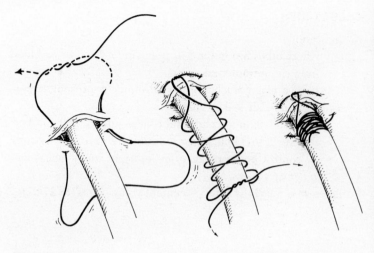

Fig. 27-18. Securing a chest tube. (From Van Way, C.W., and Buerk, C.A.: Surgical skills in patient care, St. Louis, 1978, The C.V. Mosby Co.)

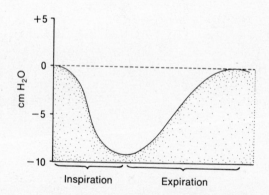

Fig. 27-19. Pressure in the pleural space. (From Van Way, C.W., and Buerk, C.A.: Surgical skills in patient care, St. Louis, 1978, The C.V. Mosby Co.)

Fig. 27-20. Heimlich valve. (From Van Way, C.W., and Buerk, C.A.: Surgical skills in patient care, St. Louis, 1978, The C.V. Mosby Co.)

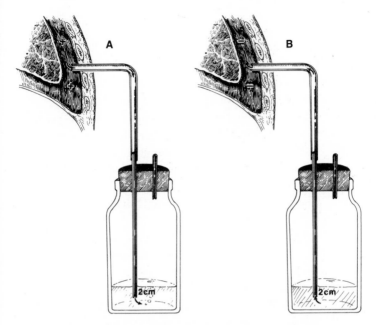

Fig. 27-21. Chest tube and chest bottle. **A,** Expiration—positive pleural pressure. **B,** Inspiration—negative pleural pressure. (From Van Way, C.W., and Buerk, C.A.: Surgical skills in patient care, St. Louis, 1978, The C.V. Mosby Co.)

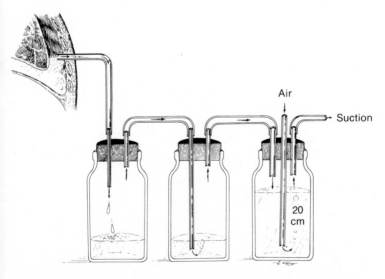

Fig. 27-22. Three-bottle system. (From Van Way, C.W., and Buerk, C.A.: Surgical skills in patient care, St. Louis, 1978, The C.V. Mosby Co.)

1. Start intravenous line.
2. Locate insertion site (usually ribs 5 to 8 in midaxillary line for trauma).
3. Prepare and drape site.
4. Anesthetize skin periosternum and pleura.
5. Make a 2 to 3 cm transverse incision at the predetermined site and bluntly dissect subcutaneous tissues, tunneling up and over the rib of choice.
6. Puncture pleura with tip of clamp and place gloved finger into incision to clear adhesions, clots, etc.
7. Clamp proximal end of chest tube. Advance desired length into pleural space.
8. Look for fogging of chest tube with expiration and listen for any movement. Palpate subcutaneous tissue superior to entrance into chest wall to determine if chest tube is in subcutaneous tissue.
9. Connect to water seal suction apparatus.
10. Suture in place and tape securely. Dress wound.
11. Obtain chest roentgenogram.

28

The use of blood and blood products in surgical and critically ill patients

Marvin A. McMillen

Surgical advances in cardiac, vascular, trauma, and preoperative surgery invariably require the support of an efficient blood banking service. The blood banks' resources are limited, however, and it is critical that they not be wasted. Reviewing the appropriate usages of blood component therapy and some of the key problems involved is the intent of this chapter.

A. Transfusion immunology
   1. ABO incompatibility
      a. Red cells are anuclear, amitochondrial, glycolysis-dependent packets of hemoglobin consisting primarily of a membrane rigidified by a cytoskeleton held in place by glycophorin protein molecules. Serinyl and threonyl residues on this glycophorin are linked to N-acetyl glucosamine-fucose (type O), N-acetyl glucosamine-galactose-fucose-M-acetyl galactosamine (type A), N-acetyl glucosamine-galactose-fucose galactose (type B). The terminal sugars alone determine the major antigenecity of the red cell. (The possibility exists that cleaving these terminal sugars could render all packed cells type O.)
      b. Nearly all individuals who lack the A and/or B antigens produce antibody against them.
         (1) The occurrence of significant hemolysis and its consequences is great in the individual administration of ABO mismatched blood.
         (2) The responsible antibody is usually a warm-reacting complement-fixing IgG, though some IgM is also produced.

2. Rh incompatibility
   a. The Rh system is far more complex than the ABO system and consists of multiple determinants, Cc, Dd, Ee, but antigenicity is primarily determined by the D structure.
   b. Among the 15% of the population who are Rh negative (i.e., lacking D), at least half will have anti-D IgG antibodies, capable of triggering a profound hemolysis.
      (1) If an Rh-negative person is inadvertently transfused with Rh-positive blood, the passive administration of anti-Rh antibody (Rhogam) within 3 to 7 days will prevent the development of anti-D antibody.
      (2) The dose is, however, substantial: 20 μg/ml of Rh + cells $\times$ 250 ml/unit = 5,000 μg/unit. The standard dose of Rhogam given to an Rh-negative mother delivered of an Rh-positive child is only 300 μg.
3. Other red cell antigens
   Kell, Duffy, Kidd, and Lutheran all refer to other red cell antigens capable of eliciting an IgM-mediated hemolytic response in the patient who has received multiple transfusions. Although other red cell antigens are known, they are seldom associated with clinical hemolysis.
4. White cell and platelet antigens
   a. The predominant cell structures by which the body's immune system recognized cells as "self" or "foreign" is the major histocompatibility complex.
      (1) These are cell surface glycoproteins present on most of the cells in the body, with the exception of neurons and erythrocytes.
      (2) In humans they are designated the HLA-A, B-, C-, and D-related (Dr) antigens.
      (3) Other non-MHC cell surface antigens ("minor antigens") are also capable of becoming the tar-

       gets of both immunoglobulins and cytolytic T-lymphocytes.

  b. White cell transfusions are usually not tissue typed before use, and repeated use of white cells may result in decreased life span and sensitization of recipients.

  c. Platelets have both histocompatability antigens and platelet-specific antigens (PIA 1, 2, 3) against which antibody can be directed in the multitransfused patient or in disease states (e.g., idiopathic thrombocytopenia [ITP]).

B. Transfusion therapy

  1. Fresh whole blood

    a. The ready availability of economical and efficient separation techniques has heralded the replacement of "fresh whole blood" by specific component therapy.

    b. "Fresh whole blood," in fact, is often neither fresh nor whole.

      (1) Platelets stored in the cold become irreversibly dysfunctional after only 1 or 2 hour's refrigeration.

      (2) Red cells stored at room temperature develop both membrane lesions and changes in O_2 affinity.

      (3) Factor V disappears from plasma.

      (4) Procoagulants appear that may promote disseminated intravascular coagulation (DIC).

      (5) Activation of vasoactive amines may trigger hypotension.

    c. If one hand-carries the unit of blood from donor to recipient, some advantages may accrue; otherwise, specific component therapy is preferable.

  2. Packed red cells

    a. Packed red cells are stored in a volume of 200 to 250 ml from a single donor at 4° C for up to 30 days at pH 5 in a glucose-citrate buffer.

    b. During storage changes occur (see Table 28-1).

Table 28-1. Effects of 4° C storage on one unit of whole blood preserved in CPD-AI

Component	Days	
	0	35
% Viable RBCs	100	79
Glucose (mg%)	44.0	22.9
K$^+$ (mEq)	1.3	8.2
Na$^+$ (mEq)	50.7	46.5
ATP (μmol/g Hgb)	4.18	2.4
2,3-DPG (μmol/g Hgb)	13.2	0.7
Lactate (mmol/L)	0	6.86
Ammonia (mg)	0	1157.7
pH	7.4	5.5-6.5
Factor I, V, VIII	100%	Near zero

(1) Red cell adenosine triphosphate (ATP) falls.
(2) 2,3-diphosphoglycerate (DPG) disappears over a 2-week period.
(3) Oxygen affinity changes:
  (a) Oxygen affinity and 2,3-DPG levels are adequate in 1- to 7-day-old blood.
  (b) Blood greater than one week old, however, has a markedly increased affinity for oxygen and consequent poorer delivery to the tissues. This lesion usually corrects within 24 hours in vivo and is of little consequence in the 1 or 2 unit transfusion.
  (c) Changes in red cell hemoglobin-oxygen affinity are a very real consideration in the massively transfused patient. In this setting, the freshest blood possible should be used.
3. Frozen red cells
  a. As blood freezes, extracellular ice formation renders the plasma intensely hypertonic. The red cell is subject to hypertonic lysis.
    (1) Addition of glycerol stabilizes red cells and protects them from the lesion.
    (2) Upon thawing, the cells must be washed to remove the glycerol.

(3) As such, the cells are free of white cell and platelet antigens, as well as plasma contaminants (such as IgA) to which some individuals may be sensitive.

b. The viability of frozen red cells is not as good as that of packed cells, but it is usually near 80%.

c. The O_2 affinity and 2,3-DPG levels are normal.

4. Granulocyte transfusions

a. Circulating polymorphonuclear leukocytes remain in the blood stream from 8 to 12 hours and, subsequently, migrate into the tissues.

b. Their functions are chemotatic, phagocytic, inflammatory, and bacteriostatic or bacteriocidal.

(1) Peripheral white cell counts below 1000 are associated with nearly 100% incidence of positive blood culture—usually secondary to gram-negative enteric organisms.

(2) White cell transfusions, however, are probably of little use with white counts over 500 to 1000.

(3) It has been questioned whether they should be used at all.

c. The cardinal signs of infection (erythema, induration, suppuration, and pain) require the presence of white cells; consequently, the neutropenic patient may develop a fulminant pneumonia, soft tissue infection, or abscess without an infiltrate or other signs.

d. Severely immunosuppressed neutropenic patients may develop a graft-versus-host–like syndrome from granulocyte transfusion contaminated by immunocompetent T-lymphocytes (fever, skin rash, hepatosplenomegaly with raised alkaline phosphatase and bilirubin). Irradiation (2,000 rad) prior to use may lessen this reaction.

C. Problems

1. Transfusion reactions

Transfusion reactions run the gamut from mild, otherwise asymptomatic, febrile reactions to profound anaphylactoid or hemolytic crises with vascular collapse. A pathophysiologic division of these reactions into febrile, allergic, anaphylactic, and hemolytic is clinically useful. Bacterially contaminated blood may present in an identical fashion as a hemolytic transfusion reaction and is included in the section.

a. Febrile reaction

    (1) Mild febrile reactions (38.3° C, 101° F) resulting from antibody against histocompatibility, white cell, or platelet antigens are commonly associated with packed cell, leukocyte, or platelet transfusions.

    (2) These patients usually will not have rigors, dyspnea, or urticaria.

    (3) If the clinical situation is urgent and the time constraints for new cross-match limited, transfusion can be continued once the blood is ascertained to be, in fact, the right unit for the right patient.

    (4) Acetaminophen (Tylenol), 10 g, or aspirin (ASA), 10 g orally or by suppository, will usually suffice to lower the temperature.

b. Allergic reaction

    (1) Atopic individuals and some patients with no history of allergy may experience symptoms ranging from pruritus and hives to acute anaphylaxis and shock.

    (2) Continuing transfusion in these patients involves a greater risk than in febrile reactions alone.

    (3) Generally, if this is a first allergic response, the unit should be taken down, retyped, and the patient treated with diphenhydramine HCl (Benadryl), 50 mg intramuscularly or intravenously.

    (4) In patients with a history of severe atopy (asthma, bee-sting anaphylaxis), antihistamine administration before transfusion is wise.

    (5) In patients with bronchospasm, transfusion should be discontinued immediately and the patient given diphenhydramine, 50 mg intramuscularly, epinephrine, 0.3 mg subcutaneously, and, if bronchospasm is severe, methylpredniso-

lone sodium succinate (Solu-Medrol), 2 g as an intravenous bolus. (Aminophylline or terbutaline may be ineffective in these individuals.)

c. Anaphylaxis
In full-blown anaphylaxis with laryngospasm, bronchospasm, and hypotension, epinephrine, diphenhydramine, steroids, fluids, and intubation are recommended.

d. Hemolytic reaction
(1) Patients with severe immunologically mediated hemolytic transfusion reactions are usually individuals with a history of prior transfusion or pregnancy.
   (a) They present with high fever (39° C, 102.5° F), rigors, headache, or loin or back pain, and they may develop oliguria and hypotension.
   (b) One third develop DIC.
   (c) The only clue to an intraoperative transfusion reaction may be the diffuse ooze of previously dry wound edges.
   (d) Therapy
      i.   Stop transfusion; check identification; culture and retype and cross.
      ii. Fluids—to a CVP of 10 or a wedge of 18 m to maintain an effective blood volume and adequate tissue oxygenation.
      iii. Diuretics (mannitol/furosemide [Lasix])—to maintain a urine volume of 50 to 100 ml/hr.
      iv. Steroids (Solu-Medrol, 30 mg/kg).

e. Anti-IgA reaction in IgA-deficient patients
(1) Between one in 600 and 800 patients have no demonstrable IgA.
(2) Extremely small amounts of IgA in transfused serum may cause a profound anaphylactic reaction with dyspnea, rigors, nausea, emesis, cramping, diarrhea, and circulatory collapse.
(3) Treatment is with epinephrine, steroids, and fluids.

    (4) The syndrome can be avoided with the use of washed red cells or frozen red cells.

  f. Bacterial contamination

    (1) *Pseudomonas aeruginosa* and some skin contaminants can grow at 4° C in citrated blood.

      (a) They may consume the citrate.

      (b) In vitro clotting may ensue.

    (2) Clinically, a rigor usually heralds circulatory collapse.

    (3) In addition to cultures, a Gram stain should be made of the transfused unit and organisms looked for.

    (4) The patient should be treated with fluids, steroids, and appropriate antibiotics for gram-negative infection.

  g. Delayed hemolysis

    (1) Sometimes hemolysis does not begin until 4 to 14 days after transfusion.

      (a) This response is the result of an anamnestic response in a prior transfused or parous patient rechallenged with the same antigen.

      (b) The disorder is usually mild.

      (c) The jaundice and anemia may, however, be confused with autoimmune hemolytic anemia.

2. Transfusion-borne infections

  a. Hepatitis

    The most common cause of posttransfusion hepatitis is probably hepatitis B (serum hepatitis or long-incubation type). Transfusions can, however, transmit hepatitis caused by non-A, non-B agent, hepatitis A agent, Epstein-Barr virus, cytomegalovirus, Q fever, coxsackie A and B virus, herpes simplex, adenovirus, and yellow fever.

    (1) Hepatitis B

      (a) The cause of hepatitis B is probably a 45 nm Dane particle that consists of a protein coat (the hepatitis B surface antigen, formerly the Australia antigen) and the hepatitis B core antigen.

(b) The existence of a large population of asymptomatic chronic carriers among addicts, male homosexuals, prisoners, and paid commercial donors makes the occurrence of posttransfusion hepatitis a recurrent problem (30,000 cases/year in the United States with probably another 150,000 asymptomatic).

   i. The incidence of subclinical or clinical hepatitis posttransfusion is probably 5%.

   ii. Some carriers (25% to 30%) chronically shed the surface antigen.

   iii. Many other chonic carriers, especially those repeatedly exposed to hepatitis B, carry antibody to hepatitis B in the sera.

(c) Posttransfusion hepatitis may be asymptomatic, severe, chronic, or fulminant with acute yellow atrophy.

(d) The treatment is expectant and supportive, identical to that of hepatitis of any other etiology.

(e) Hospital personnel inadvertently stuck or cut by contaminated needles or blades should receive a dose of 2 ml of gamma globulin or 0.2 ml of human hyperimmune serum globulin intramuscularly, especially when the patient has a history of hepatitis, dialysis, multiple transfusion, or homosexuality.

(f) Human IgG fractions separated by chemical methods have not been shown to transmit viral hepatitis.

(g) Studies with killed hepatitis B vaccine clearly demonstrate confirmed benefit, and vaccine should be recommended in high-risk hospital personnel.

(2) Cytomegalovirus

This causes an illness of fever, leukopenia, hepatosplenomegaly, and atypical lymphocytosis. It has been most commonly observed after open heart surgery. Diagnosis is made by a fourfold increase in anticytomegalovirus (CMV) antibody. Although CMV may cause severe icteric hepatitis, it is usually self-limited in the otherwise immunologically competent patient.

(3) Epstein-Barr virus (EBV)

The majority of adults, even in the absence of a history of infectious mononucleosis, have anti-EBV antibodies. When primary EBV infection occurs after transfusion, the syndrome is usually quite mild or asymptomatic, with fever, a mild jaundice, and atypical lymphocytes.

(4) Non-A, non-B hepatitis

Some authorities feel that the majority of post-transfusion hepatitides are a result of another as yet undefined agent. Recent work suggests a small ribonucleic acid (RNA) virus is responsible. Until a diagnostic test for this agent is readily available, this must remain a diagnosis of exclusion.

b. Syphilis

(1) Ninety-nine percent of patients with secondary or tertiary lues are seropositive. The Wasserman test performed on all blood donors will eliminate them.

(2) Approximately 35% of persons with primary syphillis are seronegative and may have spirochetemia.

(a) If the blood is used at under 5 days, transfusion induced syphilis may occur.

(b) Cold storage of blood beyond 5 days eradicates the treponeme.

(c) The use of commercial donor populations as platelet and white cell donors may, however, result in an increase of transfusion syphilis during the current veneral epidemic.

c. Brucellosis

Clinical illness caused by Brucella is primarily an occupational disease of farm workers and veterinarians. It should be a consideration, however, in patients who develop a febrile illness with jaundice and lymphoadenopathy 2 or 3 months after transfusion. Diagnosis is serologic.

d. Toxoplasmosis

Patients with toxoplasmosis may have asymptomatic parasitemia. The organism may remain viable in blood stored at 4° C. The only reported cases associated with transfusion have occurred in leukemia patients given white cell transfusions.

e. Malaria

The Vietnam war exposed a large number of donor-age Americans to the malaria-causing plasmodia. Although patients known to have malaria are excluded from voluntary donation, the same may not be true of (or may be concealed by) the financially motivated paid donor.

(1) The majority of reported cases have been *P. malariae*, with the remainder due to *P. vivax, P. falciparum,* and *P. ovale.*

(a) Any of these parasites will survive at least 14 days at 4° C (39.2° F).

(2) The indirect fluorescent antibody (IFA) is highly accurate in diagnosis.

f. Chagas' agent

In northern Argentina and southern Mexico, Chagas' disease infects over 7 million people, often causing a lethal cardiomyopathy. Blood transfusion is the second most common mode of transmission. Addition of crystal violet (125 mg) to a unit of blood will kill the parasite.

g. Babesiosis

Ticks endemic to Martha's Vineyard transmit babesiosis, a malaria-like illness. It may be mild or profoundly hemolytic. Intraerythrocyte diplococci, sometimes tetrad, are diagnostic. Although no therapy is currently known to be effective for killing the parasite, exchange transfusions have been reported effective in resolving the clinical disease.

h. Acquired immunodeficiency syndrome (AIDS)

(1) Caused by human T-lymphocytotropic virus (HTLV-III).

(2) Can be transmitted by transfusion.

(3) Elevated titers in donors imply viral exposure but are not diagnostic of AIDS.

(4) See Chapter 21.

C. The massively transfused patient (Table 28-2)

One of the greatest challenges in transfusion is the massively transfused patient. As a general rule, any emergency room patient requiring massive transfusion should receive warm, filtered, type-specific (typing requires 15 minutes) blood under 7 days old with one unit of fresh-frozen plasma/3 units packed cells.

1. Citrate toxicity

A warm adult with a normal liver appears to clear the citrate from one unit of blood every 5 minutes. Elevated citrate levels may cause metabolic acidosis and hypocalcemia.

Table 28-2. Pathophysiologic considerations in the massively transfused patient

Problem	Cause
1. Citrate toxicity	Hypocalcemia
2. Coagulation abnormalities	DIC
3. Altered hemoglobin function	Poor oxygen delivery to tissues
4. Acid-base alterations	Acidosis early, alkalosis later
5. Hypothermia	Platelets dysfunctional below 32.2° C (90° F), cardiac arrhythmias
6. Microembolization	↑ d A-a$_{DO_2}$
7. Plasticiser toxicity	
8. Denatured proteins	DIC
9. Vasoactive amines	Hypotension
10. Impaired reticuloendothelial system	
11. Potassium shifts	Hyperkalemia early, hypokalemia later
12. Impaired red cell deformability	Increased sequestration and clearance
13. PO$_4$ and NH$_4$ overload	Stresses liver
14. Interdonor incompatibility	May cause hemolysis
15. Graft-versus-host syndrome	Fever, pulmonary infiltration, skin lesions

   a. Citrate metabolism may be altered in hypotension and shock.

   b. In the event of impaired citrate clearance, calcium should be given over 5 minutes (1 amp calcium gluconate).

   c. Plasma levels of calcium should then be carefully monitored.

2. Coagulation abnormalities

   A large volume of blood has some procoagulant activity and very little factors V, VIII, and IX. In addition, impaired platelet function may occur with storage.

   a. One unit of fresh-frozen plasma should be given with every third unit of packed cells.

3. Altered hemoglobin function

   Stored blood loses 2,3-DPG and the oxygen affinity curve of hemoglobin shifts to the left, so that oxygen remains more tightly bound and is not as easily unloaded at the tissue level. Massive transfusion by itself exacerbates this condition even further.

   a. Massively transfused patients should receive blood less than 7 days old.

4. Acid-base alterations

   Three-week-old citrated blood contains 30 to 40 mEq of acid load.

   a. The liver's rapid metabolism of citrate makes routine alkalinization of massively transfused patients unnecessary.

   b. In settings of hepatic dysfunction with a reduced ability for citrate metabolism, alkalinization may be of value early on.

   c. In the presence of good hepatic function, alkalosis soon becomes a problem.

5. Hypothermia

   150 kcal of heat is required to warm 5 L of blood from 4° to 37° C (39.2° to 98.6° F). The massively transfused patient can ill afford this superimposed metabolic burden.

   a. The first sign of hypothermia in a cold patient may be unexplained atrial fibrillation, which may degenerate into a wide idioventricular rhythm and ventricular fibrillation as a function of decreasing temperature alone.

b. When this syndrome occurs, external warming blankets may be harmful.

    (1) They cause peripheral vasodilation and decrease the effective intravascular volume.

    (2) Consequently, cardiac work is increased in a patient with an already dysfunctional myocardium.

    (3) Skin burns occur easily.

    (4) Core warming may not be increased.

c. Keeping an unclothed patient covered with a regular blanket will decrease insensible heat loss.

d. Blood warmers should be used whenever possible. Rapid blood administration may be problematic with the current generation of warmers.

e. Peritoneal lavage or hemodialysis with a nonheparinizing system are faster ways of rewarming.

6. Microembolization

Stored blood develops microaggregates of fibrin, platelets, and white cells. The pathology caused by these aggregates is uncertain, but it is unlikely that they are good for the patient.

7. Plasticizer toxicity

Blood storage bags use di-2-ethyl-hexylphtalate (DEHP) as a plasticizer. This fat-soluble compound leaches into blood, and 3-week-old blood contains 250 mg/unit. The body metabolizes the material, and the biologic effects are currently unknown.

8. Denatured proteins

Denatured plasma proteins are probably worse for the hypotensive recipient than almost any other form of volume replacement.

a. A direct renal effect occurs with impaired glomular filtration despite normal renal plasma flow.

b. The microvascular pulmonary effects are still not defined but are, nevertheless, deleterious and associated with a widened $A\text{-}a_{D_{O_2}}$

9. Vasoactive amines

   Stored blood contains both serotonin from platelet breakdown and activated factor XII.

   a. Both of these substances activate the kininogen system.

   b. The metabolism of the kinin products occurs primarily in the lung.

   c. Pulmonary impairment may markedly alter kinin metabolism and prolong the effects.

10. Impaired host defenses

    Washed red cells result in less compromise of host defenses and leukocyte phagocytosis than packed cells.

11. Hyperkalemia

    After 3 weeks of storage, each unit of blood contains about 5 mEq $K+$/unit. Most of this excess $K+$ represents leakage from red cells whose $Na+ K+$ adenosine triphosphatase (ATP-ase) pump has been impaired by cold storage. Upon returning to the patient, stored red cells function as potassium "sponges." The massively transfused patient is more likely to become hypokalemic and metabolically alkalotic than hyperkalemic and acidotic.

    a. Impaired red cell deformability

       As red cells lose adenosine triphosphate (ATP), the membranes lose elasticity. Whether this impairs the function in the microcirculation is a theoretic, but unproved, consideration.

12. PO_4 and NH_{4+}

    Although phosphate increases in stored blood, it is not associated with clinical problems of hyperphosphatemia or hypocalcemia. NH_{4+}, on the other hand, may reach levels of 1 mg/dl of blood.

    a. This level may be a problem in patients with hepatic insufficiency.

    b. In patients with a history of hepatic coma, use of washed or frozen red cells plus fresh-frozen plasma (FFP) is recommended.

13. Interdonor incompatibility

In massively transfused patients receiving multiple units of red cells and FFP from different donor sources, the possibility of receiving antibody from one donor incompatible with blood from another is a real one. The likelihood of fulminant transfusion reaction is low, and these antibodies will usually merely produce a low-grade hemolysis. However, this may be a real problem in the trauma patient given O-negative blood in a crunch situation. If one switches to A, B or AB red cells, cross-matching must be performed as only a single unit of A, B, or AB may result in massive hemolysis from antibody in the transfused units of O. Type-specific uncross-matched blood is never appropriate after O-negative transfusion.

14. Graft-versus-host syndrome

Although the possibility of immunocompetent lymphocytes engrafting in the recipient exists, this is much more likely to occur with white cell or platelet transfusions.

15. Autotransfusion

a. Advantages

(1) Warm blood

(2) No cross-match problem

(3) Readily available

(4) Lack of 2,3-DPG problem

b. Disadvantages

(1) Hemolysis

(2) Presence of procoagulant

(3) Bacterial contamination

c. Potentially useful in settings of massive blood loss—trauma, vascular surgery

PRINCIPLES OF REPLACEMENT THERAPY FOR HEMOSTASIS

A. Platelet superpacks

1. Platelets are available as either platelet concentrates or platelet superpacks.

a. A superpack is a concentrate of 10 packs of regular platelets.

b. As such it contains approximately 7×10^{10} platelets in a volume of 200 ml.

    c. It can be expected to raise the platelet count of a 70 kg man to 100,000.

2. In the absence of antibody or sequestration, 10% of transfused platelets will remain in the peripheral circulation, except when splenectomy has been performed, when the yield will rise to 80% to 90%.
3. The half-life of transfused platelets is 12 to 18 hours.
    a. Consequently, the patient will usually require 1 to 2 superpacks daily or every other day.
    b. However, in febrile, septic individuals, the yield may drop to 30%, requiring 2 to 3 superpacks/day to achieve hemostasis.
4. Unlike many other blood components, platelets are not well preserved in cold storage at 4° C (39.2° F).
    a. They will lose their discoid shape, become spherical, and concomitantly lose their essential microtubular function.
    b. After several hours at 4° C (39.2° F), these changes are irreversible.
    c. Maximum viability is attained at 22° C (71.6° F).
    d. When maintained at room temperature, platelets can be used for 24 to 48 hours.
5. Fresh whole blood contains small numbers of platelets and most clotting factors.
    a. Since blood is usually stored cold, however, platelet function is rapidly lost.
    b. Platelet superpacks are vastly superior.
6. The indications for platelet transfusions are summarized in the box on p. 700. Counts need to be done and interpreted in the clinical setting. In general, with surgical bleeding, platelets need to be given to maintain a count ~100,000.

B. Problems of platelet transfusion
    1. Infection

    Because platelets are stored at room temperature, they are susceptible to bacterial contamination. However, a thrombocytopenic patient who becomes febrile and hypotensive during a platelet transfusion is probably experiencing an immunoglobulin-mediated transfusion reac-

---

INDICATIONS FOR PLATELET TRANSFUSIONS

COUNT	IMPACT/NEED
50,000 to 100,000	A. Probably adequate for minor surgery
	B. For major surgery—may need: One superpack before operation One superpack after operation One superpack first day after operation
25,000 to 50,000	A. For minor and major surgery needs: One unit preoperatively One unit postoperatively One unit first and second day postoperatively
	B. May also need therapy for epistaxis, menorrhagia, or hematurea on a similar schedule
5,000 to 25,000	A. Subject to recurrent or spontaneous bleeding
	B. May need steroids or splenectomy if underlying cause is chronic disorder (e.g., ITP)
<5000	A. Real and imminent danger of intracranial bleeding and immediate mortality 20% to 50%
	B. Need platelet superpacks immediately and then as needed; e.g., every 12 hr to keep platelet count >50,000 to 100,000

---

tion rather than receiving overtly contaminated superconcentrates.

2. Sensitization

Platelets bear HLA antigens on the surface and as such can sensitize the recipient to histocompatibility antigens.

a. This usually does not occur until repeated, multiple-donor (over 20) platelet transfusions have been given.

b. Sensitization has occurred, however, with only a single donor platelet transfusion.

c. Previous transfusion with whole blood or packed cells

        may also result in sensitization and decreased platelet half-life.

    d. Platelets should never be withheld from a bleeding patient when indicated because of theoretic sensitization to histocompatibility antigens.

  3. Graft-versus-host disease

    A small number of immunocompetent lymphocytes may contaminate platelet superpacks.

    a. Although unlikely, graft-versus-host–like syndromes should be considered in the immunosuppressed patient with a skin rash, fever, pulmonary infiltrates, and rising bilirubin.

    b. The number of other more likely possibilities in this clinical setting is legion, and graft-versus-host disease should be at the bottom of the list.

    c. In bone marrow transplantation and other immunodeficiency diseases, platelets should be irradiated (2000 R) before use.

C. Fresh-frozen plasma

  1. Storage

    a. Fresh-frozen plasma (FFP) from a single donor is stored in a volume of 250 ml frozen and has a long "shelf life."

    b. It is obtained either from banked blood or plasmapheresis and is anticoagulated with ACD or CPD.

    c. FFP for clinical use should not be thawed until just before its use:

      (1) Room temperature storage results in the production of fibrinogen degradation products that may have anticoagulant effects.

      (2) Factor V will quickly disappear from FFP at room temperature.

      (3) The vasoactive polypeptides that form may cause hypotension when transfused.

    d. Leukocyte and platelet antigens present in FFP may result in fever, urticaria, and erythema.

    e. Counts immediately after infusion and several hours later can document this phenomenon. When present and with a continued need for platelets, other options include:

    (1) Single donor plasma

    (2) HLA-matched plasma

2. Contents

  a. FFP contains basically all plasma proteins:

    (1) Clotting factors

    (2) Albumin

    (3) Immunoglobulins

    (4) Complement components

    (5) Fibrinolysin

    (6) The acute phase reactants (alpha-antitrypsin, $alpha_2$-macroglobulin, transferrin, ferritin, ceruloplasmin, heptoglobin, etc.)

  b. Current technology allows the separation and selective use of at least five different fractions.

    (1) Albumin

    (2) Gamma globulin

    (3) Fibrinogen

    (4) Prothrombin complex (factors II, VII, IX, and X)

    (5) Antihemophilic factor (factor VIII).

  c. All these products are made from pooled plasma.

  d. Use of the latter three products carries a significant risk of hepatitis.

  e. Albumin and plasma protein fraction (plasmanate) are heat stable and do not require refrigeration.

    (1) Hepatitis transmissability is prevented by 10-hour pasteurization at 60° C (140° F).

3. Uses

  a. FFP can be used for clotting factor replacement in a coumadinized patient or a patient with liver failure, hemophilia A or B, or other congenital factor deficiencies or DIC. However, a dose of 6 to 10 units per day (900 to 1500 ml of fluid), monitored by serial prothrombin time (PT) and partial thromboplastin time (PTT), may be necessary for factor replacement therapy.

  b. When used as a source of antithrombin III, only a single unit daily or every other day will probably be necessary.

    c. Some authors recommend the use of FFP or cryoprecipitate for correcting defective opsonization in septic patients.

D. Cryoprecipitate

    1. Cryoprecipitate is the undissolved precipitate that remains when FFP is thawed at 2° to 4° C (35.6° to 39.2° F).

    2. Cryoprecipitate is 10- to 30-fold enriched in factor VIII over FFP and is ⅓ fibrinogen (250 mg/unit).

    3. It has several advantages:

        a. Low cost

        b. Allows large amounts of factor to be given in a small volume

        c. Contains 80 to 100 units of factor VIII

        d. Contains fibronectin

    4. The minor disadvantages of cryoprecipitate can be overcome.

        a. Although it often contains small amounts of red and white cell antigens, inserting a Milipore filter in the system minimizes the febrile and allergic effects.

        b. The presence of these antigens, however, requires that cryoprecipitate be administered slowly over a period of 1 or 2 hours.

        c. A hepatitis risk is present.

    5. Uses

        a. Acute and chronic maintenance of patients with factor VIII deficiency (most common)

        b. Afibrinogenemia/hypofibrinogemia

        c. Von Willebrand's disease

        d. Factor XIII deficiency

        e. Component replacement in DIC

E. Factor VIII concentrate (antihemophilic factor [AHF], hemophil)

    1. Factor VIII may be purified by glycine or cold ethanolic precipitation to 10 to 40 × normal and further fractionated with polyethylene glycol.

    2. The advantages of factor VIII concentrate include:

        a. The lyophilized product is stable for long periods at 4° C (39.2° F).

    b. It is soluble in normal saline.

    c. It may be given as a bolus by syringe.

3. The increased incidence of hepatitis from this multiple-donor product offsets these advantages.

4. The dose of factor VIII concentrate is calculated by the formula:

    a. Acute:

$$\text{Dose} = (\text{desired factor VIII concentration*} \\ - \text{ patient's factor VIII}) \times \text{ plasma volume (40 ml/kg)}$$

    b. Maintenance:

$$\frac{1}{2} \text{ the dose every 12 hours}$$

    c. The activated PTT should be followed to ensure that a factor VIII inhibitor has not developed

F. Prothrombin complex (Konyne or Proplex)—factors II, VII, IX, and X

1. This complex of vitamin K–dependent factors can be absorbed out on tricalcium phosphate or diethylaminoethyl (DEAE) cellulose.

2. Its advantages include stability, convenience, and small volume.

3. Its disadvantages include:

    a. Expense

    b. The highest incidence of icteric hepatitis associated with its use of any blood product

4. The dose is calculated by the same formula as that of factor VIII.

    a. Because the half-life of factor IX is longer (24 hours), maintenance can be achieved with ½ the loading dose given daily.

5. Konyne is primarily used to treat hemophilia B (factor IX deficiency) and for acute bleeding and prophylaxis.

    a. Because of the high risk of icteric hepatitis, Konyne should not be used routinely to reverse the effects of Coumadin, except when time precludes reversal with phytonadione (Aquamephyton)—(1000 mg intravenously is effective in 80% within 8 hours—or volume considerations limit the use of FFP.

---

*Usually 30% to 50%.

b. Because Konyne contains no factor V, its use in patients with depressed coagulation secondary to hepatic insufficiency is not indicated.

c. Konyne has been used to initiate clotting in patients with hemophilia A and a factor VIII inhibitor. The risk of thrombosis is real, however, and this method should only be used in a carefully controlled and hemostatically monitored situation.

THE USE OF FFP, ALBUMIN, AND PLASMANATE IN THE HYPOVOLEMIC OR HYPOONCOTIC PATIENT

Two decades of controversy have not resolved whether crystalloid or colloid is superior as replacement fluid in the volume-depleted patient. One of the problems in resolving this issue has been a tendency to study a group of vastly different critically ill patients as if their single variable were a low central venous pressure (CVP), low wedge pressure, or low colloid oncotic pressure (COP). This is obviously not the case. Some general points:

1. The volume of crystalloid required to adequately resuscitate a patient is usually 1½ to 3 times that of a colloid-containing solution.

2. Total body salt and water, therefore, increases and much of this increase is sequestered in the interstitial space.

3. Pulmonary sequestration does not occur nearly as readily as interstitial sequestration because:

   a. Pulmonary lymphatics increase fluid clearance twentyfold.

   b. Pulmonary protein washes out as readily as serum protein. When the serum COP falls, so does the lung tissue oncotic pressure.

   c. The pulmonary vascularity is quite permeable to albumin (relative to the systemic vascularity) so the gradient across the pulmonary capillary bed remains small. The edema seen in peripheral tissues does not occur in the lung.

4. FFP, cryoprecipitate, plasmanate, and albumin are expensive.

5. Significant increases in COP do not occur until large doses are used.

6. Vasoactive amines in plasmanate and albumin may decrease A-a$_{D_{O_2}}$ and decrease glomerular filtration rate (GFR).

7. Hypotension occasionally occurs with plasmanate infusions.

8. Hypovolemia from bleeding is quickly remediable and should be an acute problem. Sepsis is more likely to be chronic.

9. When resuscitated to the same hemodynamic endpoint, crystalloid is associated with more lung edema, a greater A-a gradient, and a longer need for mechanical ventilation.

10. Crystalloid resuscitation can be associated with cerebral edema.

The peripheral edema in the hypooncotic critically ill patient may become profound, and the results of exogenous diuretics may be disappointing while the cost in terms of the metabolic alkalosis and hypokalemia is high. Edematous tissue sloughs and decubitises, so edema may trigger a cascade of iatrogenesis. In practice, FFP is often given to maintain an albumin of at least 2.5 to 3 g (albumin accounts for 20% of the COP) in the nutritionally comprised patient or to maintain a COP of 14 to 16 torr. The best source of colloid remains the patient's own adequately alimented liver.

SELECTED READINGS

Benson, R.E., and Isbister, J.P.: Massive blood transfusion, Anesth. Intensive Care **8**:152, 1980.

Civetta, J.M.: A new look at the Starling equation, Crit. Care Med. **7**:84, 1979.

Collins, J.A., Murawski, K., and Shafer, A.W.: Massive transfusion in surgery and trauma, New York, 1982, Alan R. Liss, Inc.

Colman, R.W., Robboy, S.J., and Minna, J.D.: Disseminated intravascular coagulation: a reappraisal, Ann. Rev. Med. **30**:359, 1979.

Hauer, J.M., Thiner, R.L., and Dawson, R.B.: Autotransfusion, New York, 1981, Elsevier–North Holland, p. 153.

Mant, M.J., and King, E.G.: Severe, acute disseminated intravascular coagulation. A reappraisal of its pathophysiology, clinical significance, and therapy based on 27 patients, Am. J. Med. **67**:557, 1979.

Owen, C.A., Bowie, E.J.W., and Thompson, J.H.: The diagnosis of bleeding disorders, Ed. 2, Boston, 1975, Little, Brown & Co.

Peta, L.D., and Swischer, S.N.: Clinical practice of blood transfusion, New York, 1981, Churchill Livingston.

Rackow, E.C., Fein, I.A., and Lepp, J.: Colloid osmotic pressure as a prognostic indicator of pulmonary edema and mortality in the critically ill, Chest **72**:709, 1977.

Rudowski, W.J.: Disorders of hemostasis in surgery, Hanover, New Hampshire, 1977, University Press of New England, p. 465.

29

Therapeutic guidelines for selected problems in the critically ill surgical patient

PART A GUIDELINES

HENRY J. MANN
DANIEL M. CANAFAX
JOHN H. RODMAN

The guidelines and general therapeutic principles in this chapter provide an appropriate starting point for drug therapy of commonly encountered problems in the critically ill surgical patient. However, the key to optimal therapy is a well-defined plan for periodic monitoring and subsequent individualizing of the patient's drug regimen to achieve well-defined end points. Rather than provide a comprehensive drug compendium, this chapter attempts to provide a concise overview of drugs commonly used in emergency situations. The dosage regimens suggested are consistent with the standard references listed at the conclusion of this chapter and reflect the current standard of practice in the Surgical Intensive Care Unit (SICU) at the University of Minnesota Hospitals.

WRITING AND GIVING ORDERS

The urgency of the situations in which many of the drugs discussed here are administered and the potency of these medications requires that utmost care be taken in formulating the order and that it be communicated clearly.

A. The components of a complete order are shown on p. 708.
B. It is preferable to write orders, but if that is not possible, verbal orders should be given in the same logical sequence and reduced to writing at the first opportunity.

C. If all of the components outlined below cannot be included in the order, consultation is needed. Only those orders carefully given can be carefully followed.

D. Several points deserve particular emphasis.

1. Trailing zeros after a decimal point should never be used (for example, 1.0 μg of dopamine hydrochloride). The easily overlooked decimal point can make an order of magnitude error.

2. Doses should not be expressed in micrograms per kilogram, but rather in absolute amounts. If the dose desired

---

WRITING ORDERS FOR PARENTERAL DRUGS

Preparation	Specify amount of drug and type of diluent.
Dosage	Include rate of drug administration (e.g., mg/min, rate of solution (e.g., ml/min), access site (e.g., right atrial line) and infusion apparatus.
Monitoring parameters	Indicate specific parameters and frequency.
Dosage adjustment	Define increments for dosage adjustment and frequency of dosage adjustment.
Alarms	Identify specific events that require notifying physician and/or stopping drug.

Example: lidocaine

1. 1 g of lidocaine in 500 ml of D5W.
2. Give 100 mg by slow IV push over 3 minutes, then begin constant infusion of 2 mg/min (1 ml/min) via peripheral IV site. Use volumetric infusion pump.
3. Blood pressure (BP) and heart rate (HR) every 15 minutes for 2 hours, then every hour. Observe for change in mental status.
4. If more than 10 premature ventricular contractions (PVCs) per minute or PVCs are coupled, give 75 mg of lidocaine over 3 minutes and increase infusion rate to 3 mg/min.
5. Notify physician if dosage is changed, BP is less than 90/60, or mental status changes.

is in micrograms per kilogram per minute, it should be multiplied out before it is ordered. The pharmacy and the nurses should double-check it.

3. Special care is needed to avoid confusion between abbreviations for milligrams (mg) and micrograms (μg).

4. The term *intravenous (IV) bolus* should never be used. Rather a specific rate of administration should be specified.

5. When the physician orders continuous infusions, he or she should specify both the rate of drug administration and the rate of solution delivery. These components provide a double-check against the total amount ordered in a given volume.

6. When drugs are given by continuous infusion, an infusion controller should always be used.

   a. The large number of infusion apparatuses now available preclude detailed recommendations.

   b. Every clinician should be familiar with at least a volumetric infusion device and a less expensive controller.

   c. Potent, rapid-acting drugs such as dopamine and sodium nitroprusside are most appropriately administered with a volumetric infusion pump.

7. Specific monitoring parameters and their frequency should be defined.

   a. Monitoring parameters must be interfaced with guidelines for upward or downward adjustment of dosage rates.

   b. Relying on standard protocols or leaving orders openended (such as "titrate to BP") does a disservice to both the patient and the nursing staff.

   c. Boundary values or alarm points should be outlined.

MEASURING DRUG CONCENTRATIONS AS THERAPEUTIC GUIDELINES

Advances in analytic methods now provide the clinician with another parameter to help guide therapy, ensure effective strategy for dosage requirements and reduce the risk of toxicity.

Measured drug concentrations should never be a sole end point for therapy, but they can be a valuable aid in optimizing therapy in patients with altered organ function and at increased risk for toxicity.

A. The key to maximizing the utility of measured drug concentrations is ordering the samples to be drawn at the appropriate time relative to the dose.

B. Correct interpretation requires knowing the exact times of drug administration and the exact time that the sample was obtained.

C. The timing and frequency of the samples will depend on the pharmacokinetics of the drug, the patient's ability to metabolize and eliminate the drug, and the objective of obtaining the measured drug concentrations.

   1. If the objective is to use the drug concentration to determine whether a higher dose would be appropriate, the patient should be at steady state.

   2. If drug concentrations are being monitored to detect accumulation, at least two samples, at an interval of one to two half-lives, are required.

D. Serially measured concentrations allow dosage regimen individualization for several drugs. This determination normally requires consultation with clinicians specifically trained in this area.

INOTROPES AND VASOPRESSORS

Refer to Table 29-1 for the sympathomimetic agents used for hemodynamic support.

Amrinone lactate (Inocor)

A. General considerations

   1. Amrinone is an inotropic agent that is not chemically related to catecholamines or digitalis.

   2. Vasodilation occurs with amrinone use, resulting in decreased systemic and peripheral vascular resistance.

   3. Major use is in congestive heart failure (CHF), where it increases cardiac output without increasing myocardial oxygen demand.

   4. It is a new agent with limited clinical experience.

Table 29-1. Sympathomimetic agents used for hemodynamic support

Drug	Initial dose	Time to effect	Duration of effect	Subsequent dosing
Epinephrine	0.5-1.0 mg IV infusion	Immediate	<10 min	0.5-1 mg IV q 5 min; IV infusion 1-4 µg/min p.r.n.
Levarterenol (norepinephrine)	0.3-0.5 mg subcutaneously	3-10 min	Several hours	IV infusion titrated to BP, usually 2-4 µg/min
	8-12 µg/min IV infusion	Immediate	<5 min after discontinuing infusion	
Dopamine Half-life = 2 min	1-5 µg/kg/min IV infusion	<5 min	<10 min	IV infusion titrated to BP, usually < 20 µg/kg/min
Dobutamine Half-life = 2 min	2.5 µg/kg/min IV infusion	<2 min	<10 min	IV infusion increasing by 2.5 µg/kg/min q.10 min to desired effect, usually less than 10 µg/kg/min
Isoproterenol	5 µg/min IV infusion	Immediate	<10 min p discontinuing infusion; may be prolonged with high dosages up to 50 min	IV infusion titrated by HR and BP, usually 1-4 µg/min
Phenylephrine for BP	100-180 µg/min	Immediate	<20 min p discontinuing infusion	40-60 µg/min after BP stabilized
Phenylephrine for paroxysmal supraventrical tachycardia (PSVT)	0.5-1 mg IV infusion over 30 sec	Immediate	<20 min	Increase by 0.1-0.2 mg each subsequent dose until PSVT controlled or systolic BP >160 torr May repeat q.1-2 min p.r.n.
Amrinone	0.75 mg/kg over 3 min	<5 min	<2 hr	5-10 µg/kg/min IV infusion may repeat loading dosage after 30 min

B. Initial dose
   1. Direct injection of 0.75 mg/kg IV push over 3 minutes
C. Maintenance dosage
   1. Continuous IV infusion of 5 to 10 μg/kg/min is required.
   2. Initial bolus dose may be repeated after 30 minutes if additional response is needed.
   3. Total daily dosage is usually less than 10 mg/kg.
D. Monitoring
   1. Monitor the following:
      a. HR
      b. BP
      c. Urine output
      d. Electrocardiogram (ECG)
      e. Platelet counts
   2. If possible, follow pulmonary capillary wedge pressure (PCWP) and cardiac index (CI).
   3. Reponse is related to concentration, and the therapeutic range is 0.5 to 7 μg/ml.
E. Adverse effects
   1. Asymptomatic thrombocytopenia (2.4%) is dose related and usually occurs within 3 days of initiating therapy
      a. Responds to decreasing dose or stopping amrinone
   2. Hypotension
   3. Arrhythmias
   4. Hepatotoxicity
   5. Gastrointestinal (GI) effects (nausea, vomiting, diarrhea)
F. Pharmacokinetics
   1. Onset of actions is less than 5 minutes.
   2. Peak effect occurs within 10 minutes.
   3. Duration of action ranges from 30 minutes to 2 hours
   4. Half-life is approximately 3.6 hours but may be prolonged to approximately 5.8 hours in CHF.
   5. Amrinone is 60% to 90% metabolized, and the metabolites and unchanged drug are excreted in the urine.
   6. Recommended doses result in concentrations of 2 to 3 μg/ml.
G. Interactions
   1. Digoxin and amrinone have additive inotropic effects.
   2. Disopyramide may potentiate the hypotensive effect.

    3. Dextrose solutions cause a slow inactivation of amrinone; approximately 13% over 24 hours.

H. Availability
    1. Amrinone injection of 5 mg/ml in 20 ml ampules

I. Preparation and administration
    1. Amrinone (100 mg in 50 ml of 0.45% or 0.9% sodium chloride) provides a concentration of 2 mg/ml.
    2. The drug may be administered peripherally.
    3. Administer the drug with a controller device.

Dobutamine HCl (Dobutrex)

A. General considerations
    1. Dobutamine stimulates $beta_1$-adrenergic receptors. Stimulation results in a positive inotropic effect on the heart.
    2. At high doses dobutamine will also stimulate $beta_2$-receptors. Peripheral vasodilation will result.
    3. Dobutamine will increase stroke volume and, to a lesser extent, HR.
    4. The drug is contraindicated in idiopathic hypertropic subaortic stenosis, as are inotropic agents in general.

B. Initial dose
    Begin with an IV infusion at 2.5 μg/kg/min.

C. Maintenance dosage
    1. Increase by 2.5 μg/kg/min every 10 minutes until the desired cardiac output is achieved.
    2. Dosages greater than 20 μg/kg/min are more likely to result in tachyarrhythmias.

D. Monitoring
    1. Monitor the following:
       a. HR   c. Urine output
       b. BP   d. ECG
    2. If possible, follow PCWP and CI.

E. Adverse effects
    1. Increases in HR, ventricular tachyarrhythmias, and increased systolic BP may occur as dosage increases.
    2. Arteriovenous (AV) conduction is facilitated by dobutamine. Patients with atrial fibrillation should be placed on digoxin to prevent rapid ventricular response.

F. Pharmacokinetics
  1. Onset of action is less than 2 minutes.
  2. Plasma half-life is less than 2 minutes.
  3. Duration of action is less than 10 minutes.
  4. Drug is metabolized to inactive substances which are excreted in the urine.
G. Interactions
  1. Beta-blockers will antagonize the effects of dobutamine.
  2. Sodium bicarbonate will inactivate dobutamine solutions.
  3. General anesthetics may cause ventricular arrhythmias when used with dobutamine.
H. Availability
  1. Available in a 20 ml vial containing 250 mg (12.5 mg/ml)
I. Preparation and administration
  Dobutamine (250 mg in 250 ml of IV solution) provides a concentration of 1000 μg/ml.

Dopamine

A. General considerations
  1. At doses of 1 to 10 μg/kg/min, dopamine predominantly stimulates:
    a. $Beta_1$-adrenergic receptors, providing an inotropic effect on the heart and peripheral vasodilation
    b. Dopaminergic receptors in the renal and mesenteric vascular beds resulting in vasodilation of these areas
  2. As the dose exceeds 10 μg/kg/min, alpha-adrenergic effects become prominent, and vasoconstriction in the periphery results. At higher doses, the dopaminergic effects are offset.
  3. Dopamine also causes a release of endogenous norepinephrine.
  4. Should extravasation occur, phentolamine, an alpha-adrenergic antagonist, 5 to 10 mg diluted with 10 to 15 ml of saline solution, should be infiltrated as soon as possible into the constricted area, using a syringe with a fine hypodermic needle. This is effective up to 12 hours after extravasation.

B. Initial dose
   1. Begin with an intravenous infusion at 4 µg/kg/min for serious hypotensive cases.
   2. Dose may start lower for less severe cases and for treating CHF.
   3. A large vein is preferred for dopamine administration.
   4. Increased renal perfusion effects occur at 0.5 to 2 µg/kg/min.
C. Maintenance dosage
   Dopamine infusion may be increased by 1 to 5 µg/kg/min every 10 minutes as required to maintain BP.
D. Monitoring
   1. Urine output should increase with dopamine use. If output begins to decrease, vasoconstriction may be too great.
   2. Usually titrate dosage by continuous BP monitoring.
   3. Optimize patient volume status.
   4. Monitor the ECG.
   5. Monitor the administration site for signs of extravasation.
   6. Vasoconstriction doses should be avoided; use a second or another agent if these doses are needed.
E. Adverse effects
   1. Low dose
      a. Hypotension
   2. Higher dose
      a. Premature beats
      b. Tachycardia
      c. Hypertension
      d. Vasoconstriction
   3. Extravasation may cause tissue necrosis and sloughing.
F. Pharmacokinetics
   1. Onset of action less than 5 minutes
   2. Plasma half-life is less than 2 minutes
   3. Duration of action is less than 10 minutes
   4. Metabolized to norepinephrine (25%), homovanillic acid, and 3,4-dihydroxyphenylactic acid (75%) which are excreted in the urine
G. Interactions
   1. Because monoamine oxidase (MAO) inhibitors will pro-

long the metabolism of dopamine significantly, start patients who have received these drugs within the previous 2 weeks at one tenth the usual dose.

2. Beta-blockers and alpha-adrenergic antagonist will reverse the cardiac and vasoconstriction actions of dopamine.

3. Alkaline solutions will inactivate dopamine.

4. Ergot alkaloids may potentiate the peripheral vasoconstriction seen with dopamine.

H. Availability
   1. Dopamine injection of 40, 80, and 160 mg/ml ampules, single dose vials, and syringes
   2. Prepared infusion solutions of 0.8, 1.6, and 3.2 mg/ml

I. Preparation and administration
   1. Dopamine (200 mg in 250 ml of intravenous solution) provides a concentration of 800 μg/ml.
      a. 400 mg in 250 = 1600 μg/ml
      b. 600 mg in 250 = 2400 μg/ml
      c. 800 mg in 250 = 3200 μg/ml
   2. Various concentrations may be needed, depending on the weight of the patient, dosage requirement, and fluid status.
   3. Administer the drug with a controller device.

Epinephrine HCl (Adrenalin chloride, Sus-Phrine)

A. General considerations
   1. Epinephrine acts on alpha- and beta-adrenergic receptors resulting in:
      a. Vasoconstriction
      b. Cardiac stimulation (chronotropic and inotropic)
      c. Bronchial smooth muscle relaxation
      d. Dilation of skeletal muscle vasculature
   2. Its major intravenous use is in cardiac arrest situations.
   3. Its major subcutaneous use is in treating status asthmaticus and severe anaphylaxis.

B. Initial dose
   1. Cardiac arrest
      a. By intravenous infusion
         (1) Epinephrine IV (0.5 to 1 mg slow push)

      (2) Dose should be diluted to 10 ml with normal saline if 1:1000 solution is used.
- b. Via endotracheal tube (ETT)
  - (1) If an intravenous line is not available, epinephrine (0.5 to 1 mg) may be instilled directly into the bronchial tree via an ET tube.
  - (2) Onset of action is within minutes with adequate cardiopulmonary resuscitation.
  - (3) Dilute the dose to 5 to 10 ml with sterile water.
- 2. Status asthmaticus and anaphylaxis
  - a. Repeat subcutaneous dose of 0.3 to 0.5 mg every 15 to 20 minutes for three doses.
  - b. Maximum single dose is 1 mg.
  - c. Total daily dose should not exceed 5 mg.

C. Maintenance dosage
  1. Epinephrine (0.5 mg IV slow push) may be repeated every 5 minutes as needed.
  2. If prolonged use is required, an epinephrine infusion can be administered at a rate of 1 to 4 µg/min.

D. Monitoring
  1. BP   3. Asthmatic or allergic symptoms
  2. HR

E. Adverse effects
  1. Hypertension and ventricular arrhythmias may occur. In the arrest situation in which epinephrine is indicated, however, these possible effects should not preclude using the drug.
  2. Repeated injections may cause local tissue necrosis.

F. Pharmacokinetics
  1. Onset of action is immediate for intravenous infusion and less than 10 minutes for subcutaneous dose.
  2. Duration of action is less than 10 minutes for intravenous infusion but may persist for several hours following subcutaneous dose.
  3. Effect is terminated by sympathetic nerve uptake and metabolism.

G. Interactions
  1. Beta-blockers *and* alpha-adrenergic antagonists can reverse the effects of epinephrine.

2. Sodium bicarbonate will inactivate epinephrine. Care must be taken to flush the IV tubing after sodium bicarbonate administration if epinephrine is to be injected through the same IV line.

3. Tricyclic antidepressants will increase the pressor response and the likelihood of cardiac dysrhythmia seen with epinephrine.

H. Availability
   1. Prefilled syringes: epinephrine (100 μg/ml) (1:10,000 solution) in 5 and 10 ml sizes
   2. Injection, United States Pharmacopeia (USP): epinephrine (1 mg/ml) (1:1000 solution) in 1 ml ampules, cartridges, syringes, and 30 ml vials (should be diluted before intravenous administration)
   3. 0.3 ml ampule and 5 ml vial of 1:200 solution

I. Preparation and administration
   1. Epinephrine (1 mg in 250 ml of intravenous solution) provides a concentration of 4 μg/ml.
   2. Administration rate should be 15 to 60 microdrops per minute with a controller device.

Isoproterenol HCl (Isuprel)

A. General considerations
   1. Isoproterenol is a beta-adrenergic agonist, which results in positive inotropic and chronotropic effects on the heart and bronchial relaxation in the lung.
   2. Isoproterenol increases cardiac output and venous return. It decreases peripheral vascular resistance.
   3. Isoproterenol has no vasopressor activity.
   4. Its use is contraindicated in tachycardia caused by digitalis intoxication.

B. Initial dose
   1. Begin with an infusion of isoproterenol (4 μg/min).
   2. Lower doses may be needed in patients with coronary insufficiency, diabetes, or hyperthyroidism.

C. Maintenance dosage
   1. Titrate dosage to desired BP and HR, usually less than 110 beats/min.

2. The usual dosage is 1 to 4 μg/min (0.05 to 0.3 μg/kg/min), but dosages up to 30 μg/min have been used in severe shock.

3. Significant inotropic effect can be achieved at dosages of 0.25 to 0.75 μg/min.

D. Monitoring

1. HR
2. BP
3. Central venous pressure (CVP)
4. ECG
5. PCWP
6. CI
7. Urine output

E. Adverse effects

1. Incidence of ventricular arrhythmias increases as the HR exceeds 130 beats/min.

2. Angina pain, restlessness, and nervousness may occur.

3. As the dosage increases in patients with poor response, hypotension may occur.

F. Pharmacokinetics

1. Onset of action immediate

2. Duration of action less than 10 minutes with normal doses but may be prolonged with larger doses

3. Approximately 50% metabolized and then excreted in urine

G. Interactions

1. Beta-blockers will antagonize the effects of isoproterenol.

2. Sodium bicarbonate can inactivate isoproterenol.

H. Availability

Isoproterenol injection USP (200 μg/ml) (1:5000 solution) in 5 ml and 10 ml syringes and 5 ml ampules and vials

I. Preparation and administration

1. Isoproterenol (1 mg) (5 ml of 200 μg/ml) added to 250 ml of D5W results in a concentration of 4 μg/ml.

2. Isoproterenol, (2 mg) (10 ml of 200 μg/ml), added to 250 ml of D5W results in a concentration of 8 μg/ml.

Norepinephrine bitartrate (Levophed)

A. General considerations

1. Norepinephrine acts primarily on alpha-adrenergic receptors. Vasoconstriction results.

2. Norepinephrine also has $beta_1$–stimulatory properties.

These are usually suppressed by a reflex bradycardia secondary to the alpha-adrenergic effect.

3. Should extravasation occur, phentolamine, an alpha-adrenergic antagonist (5 to 10 mg), diluted with 10 to 15 ml of saline solution, should be infiltrated as soon as possible into the constricted area, using a syringe with a fine hypodermic needle. This is effective for up to 12 hours after extravasation.

B. Initial dose

1. Begin with an intravenous infusion of norepinephrine base of 8 to 12 μg/min.

2. Larger veins are preferred for this infusion.

C. Maintenance dosage

1. Norepinephrine base (2 to 4 μg/min) is the usual adult maintenance requirement, but this must be titrated to the patient's BP response.

2. When the infusion is discontinued, a taper approach should be used.

D. Monitoring

1. Monitor BP and ECG continuously.

2. Monitor fluid status.

3. Monitor infusion site for signs of extravasation.

E. Adverse effects

1. Hypertension and reflex bradycardia are the most significant.

2. Extravasation of norepinephrine results in severe local vasoconstriction, which in turn leads to tissue necrosis and sloughing.

3. Headache may be a sign of hypertension.

4. Marked reduction in tissue perfusion can occur.

F. Pharmacokinetics

1. Onset of action is immediate.

2. Duration of action is less than 5 minutes.

3. Drug is metabolized to inactive substances that are excreted in the urine.

G. Interactions

1. Alpha-adrenergic antagonists can reverse the effects of norepinephrine.

2. Sodium bicarbonate inactivates norepinephrine.
3. Tricyclic antidepressants will increase the pressor response to norepinephrine. This interaction has also been seen with guanethidine and methyldopa.

H. Availability
1. Norepinephrine (2 mg) = norepinephrine base (1 mg).
2. Norepinephrine injection, USP, (2 mg/ml) (1 mg/ml norepinephrine base) in 4 ml ampules

I. Preparation and administration
1. Norepinephrine base (2 mg) in 250 ml of IV solution provides a concentration of 8 μg/ml.
2. Maintenance administration rate should be approximately 15 to 20 microdrops per minute regulated by a controller device.

Phenylephrine HCl (Neo-Synephrine)

A. General considerations
1. Phenylephrine is used only occasionally when alpha-adrenergic stimulation alone is needed.
2. Therapeutic doses stimulate alpha-receptors without affecting beta-receptors
3. Larger doses may activate $beta_1$-receptors in the heart.
4. Phenylephrine also causes a release of norepinephrine from storage sites.
5. Phenylephrine is not a substitute for adequate fluid replacement. For shock, dopamine has become the preferred agent.
6. Phenylephrine is occasionally useful for PSVT. However, other drugs are preferred.

B. Initial dose
1. For pressure support, initiate a continuous infusion beginning at 100 to 180 μg/min.
2. For treating PSVT, administer dosages of 0.5 to 1 mg over 30 seconds. This dosage may be increased by 0.1 to 0.2 mg with each successive dosage and repeated every 1 to 2 minutes until PSVT is controlled or the systolic BP exceeds 160 torr.

C. Maintenance dosage: As fluid volume is replaced, the maintenance dosage of phenylephrine infusion can be decreased to 40 to 60 μg/min.

D. Monitoring
1. Place patients on continuous telemetry with frequent monitoring of BP.
2. Closely monitor fluid status and HR.

E. Adverse effects
1. Headache which may be a sign of hypertension
2. Reflex bradycardia
3. Excitability
4. Restlessness
5. Rarely, arrhythmias

F. Pharmacokinetics
1. Onset of action is immediate following intravenous infusion and within 15 minutes following intramuscular (IM) or subcutaneous infusion.
2. Duration of action is approximately 20 minutes after intravenous administration and 1 hour after intramuscular or subcutaneous infusion.
3. Metabolized in the liver and intestine by MAO.

G. Interactions
1. MAO inhibitors will potentiate the pressor response of phenylephrine. This interaction has also been seen with tricyclic antidepressants and guanethidine.
2. Phentolamine can be used to control severe hypertensive responses.
3. Atropine sulfate blocks the reflex bradycardia seen with phenylephrine.

H. Availability
10 mg/ml (1%) ampules containing 1 ml

I. Preparation and administration
1. For IV infusion, addition of one ampule of 10 mg to a 500 ml bag of D5W results in a concentration of 20 μg/ml.
2. For direct intravenous injection in treating PSVT, the 1 ml ampule should be diluted with 9 ml of sterile water for injection, resulting in a solution of 1 mg/ml.
3. Dosage administration begins with 0.5 ml intravenous infusion over 30 seconds.

ANTIARRHYTHMICS
Bretylium tosylate (Bretylol)

A. General considerations
1. Bretylium is an adrenergic blocker.
2. Its mechanism is primarily via accumulation in sympathetic ganglia and postganglionic adrenergic neurons, where it inhibits norepinephrine release.
3. Hypotension is frequently observed but may be preceded by a transient rise in BP thought to be caused by bretylium-induced catecholamine release.
4. Bretylium is indicated for the treatment of ventricular fibrillation in conjunction with electrical cardioversion and ventricular tachycardia not responding to adequate doses of lidocaine HCl.

B. Initial dose
1. Ventricular fibrillation or immediately life-threatening ventricular tachycardia
   a. Never substitute bretylium for direct-current cardioversion.
   b. Give 5 mg/kg over 2 to 5 minutes.
   c. Repeat in 10 minutes if indicated.
2. Other serious ventricular arrhythmias
   a. 5 to 10 mg/kg at a rate no faster than 50 mg/min.
   b. Maximum initial doses should never exceed 40 mg/kg.

C. Maintenance dosages
1. Intermittent dosages at 6- to 8-hour intervals
2. Or a continuous infusion of 1 to 2 mg/min.

D. Monitoring
1. Continuous telemetry monitoring is mandatory.
2. Patients should be supine when bretylium is given.
3. Monitor vital signs at least every 10 minutes initially and then every 30 minutes.
4. Initial increases in BP will resolve without therapy.

E. Adverse effects
1. Most frequent
   a. Postural effects are seen in all patients.
   b. Significant hypotension occurs frequently.
2. Less frequent

    a. Bradycardia and initial increases in BP occur.

    b. Nausea and vomiting are common but can be minimized by slowing the rate of administration.

F. Pharmacokinetics

  1. The normal half-life of bretylium is 6 to 12 hours.

  2. Renal elimination is the predominant route of elimination. A half-life of more than 30 hours is likely when renal insufficiency is severe (creatinine clearance less than 5 ml/min).

G. Interactions

  1. The initial release of norephinephrine by bretylium may aggravate arrhythmias caused by digitalis toxicity.

H. Availability

  1. A 10 ml ampule containing 500 mg (50 mg/ml)

I. Preparation and administration

  1. Undiluted bretylium should ONLY be administered for immediately life-threatening ventricular arrhythmias.

  2. In all other instances, dilute bretylium to at least 10 mg/ml and give at a rate of 25 to 50 mg/min for initial doses.

  3. Maintenance dosages of 1 to 2 mg/min can be given if continued therapy is needed.

Lidocaine

A. General considerations

  1. Lidocaine is the drug of choice for parenteral therapy of ventricular arrhythmias and is not reliably effective for supraventricular arrhythmias. Lidocaine is less likely to impair cardiac output or conduction than other Class I antiarrhythmic drugs.

  2. In the presence of myocardial ischemia (MI), lidocaine is commonly indicated when one of the following exists:

    a. More than six ventricular ectopics per minute

    b. The ectopic beat encroaches on the T wave.

    c. Coupled ectopics or runs of ventricular tachycardia are experienced.

  3. Because of the extensive extravascular distribution (two-compartment behavior), dosage requirements in the first 1 to 3 hours of therapy are considerably greater than maintenance dosage requirements.

4. When lidocaine therapy is no longer required, the infusion can be discontinued without the common practice of weaning.

B. Initial dose
1. Loading dose: rapid infusion (not faster than 50 mg/min) of 1 to 2 ml/min.
2. May be repeated at 5-minute intervals to a total dose of 300 mg.

C. Maintenance dosage
1. *Continuous infusion:* 10 to 50 µg/kg/min (0.5 to 4 mg/min).
2. Reduce dosages for age over 70, Grade III New York Heart Association heart failure, or severe liver disease.
3. If major dose-related toxicity is observed, the drug should be stopped for at least 2 hours. If drug is restarted, the infusion rate should be cut in half.

D. Monitoring
1. Place patients on continuous telemetry.
2. Check vital signs and mental status at least every 2 hours.

E. Adverse effects
1. Most frequent: central nervous system (CNS) toxicity (decreased mentation, slurred speech, paresthesias, seizures)
2. Less frequent: cardiovascular toxicity, usually occurring with high drug concentrations or underlying severe heart disease

F. Pharmacokinetics
1. The liver primarily metabolizes lidocaine.
2. Normal half-life is about 2 hours.
   a. Decreased cardiac output significantly prolongs half-life.
   b. Half-lives of 4 to 6 hours are common in severe heart failure.
   c. Concurrent liver disease and heart failure may produce even slower elimination.
3. The kidneys eliminate less than 10% of lidocaine, but metabolites may accumulate in renal failure and contribute to toxicity.

4. Lidocaine serum concentrations of 1.5 to 5 µg/ml are considered therapeutic.
5. Levels of greater than 8 µg/ml are associated with increased incidence of toxicity.

G. Interactions
1. Propranolol HCl, metoprolol, and cimetidine, will decrease lidocaine elimination, and dosages should be adjusted downward. Ranitidine does not effect lidocaine clearance.
2. Increased concentrations of alpha$_1$–acid glycoprotein (associated with surgery, trauma, sepsis, and acute myocardial infarction) may increase protein binding and decrease lidocaine efficacy.

H. Availability
1. 50 and 100 mg prepacked syringes
2. 0.5, 1, 2 g vials
3. Prepared infusion 0.2%, 0.4%, 0.8% in 250 or 500 ml of D5W

I. Preparation and administration
1. Put 0.5 to 1 g in 250 to 1000 ml of D5W for a concentration of 1 to 4 mg/ml.
2. Avoid more than 1 g/U to minimize severity of inadvertent overdose.

Procainamide HCl (Pronestyl)

A. General considerations
1. Procainamide is effective for both ventricular and supraventricular arrhythmias.
2. Procainamide is more likely than lidocaine to decrease cardiac output or A-V nodal and ventricular conduction.
3. Fever, rash, or arthralgias in the initial 1 to 2 weeks of therapy may signal the procainamide-associated lupus syndrome.

B. Initial dose
1. Total loading dose will usually be 10 to 15 mg/kg.
2. Give 100 mg over 2 to 5 minutes at 10-minute intervals until arrhythmia responds or maximum dose is reached.
3. When administered intravenously, rate should never exceed 50 mg/min and preferably be no faster than 25 mg/min.

4. Reduced loading doses should be used in heart failure.

C. Maintenance dosage
1. If renal function is normal (creatinine clearance over 60 ml/min), maintenance dosage will be approximately one-half the loading dose given every 3 to 4 hours. It is usually administered by constant infusion.
2. Impaired renal function requires downward dose adjustment.
3. Maintenance infusion rates should not exceed 6 mg/min.
4. In renal failure, infusion rates should not exceed 3 mg/min unless monitored with serum concentrations.

D. Monitoring
1. Place patient on continuous telemetry.
2. Check BP and HR every 10 minutes during loading dosages.
3. Check BP and HR every 30 to 60 minutes during first 12 hours of therapy.
4. Adjust dosage in the following:
   a. Postural hypotension
   b. Prolonged QRS
   c. Prolonged Q-T interval
   d. Prolonged P-R interval
5. Measure serum concentrations 12 hours and 48 to 72 hours after starting therapy.

E. Adverse effects
1. Nausea, vomiting, and CNS effects may occur and are not necessarily dose related.
2. Hypotension and conduction disturbances are usually dose-related. They may resolve with temporary discontinuation for 3 to 6 hours, followed by resumption of dose at reduced rate.

F. Pharmacokinetics
1. The kidneys eliminate approximately 50% of procainamide unchanged.
2. Procainamide metabolism produces significant concentrations of the acetylated metabolite N-acetylprocainamide (NAPA). The kidneys eliminate 80% to 85% of NAPA.
3. Usual therapeutic concentrations of procainamide are 4 to 10 mg/L. Resistant arrhythmias may require higher concentrations.

4. NAPA concentrations should also be monitored. Values above 20 mg/L may contribute to toxicity.

G. Interactions
  1. Procainamide may antagonize the effects of cholinergic agents used in myasthenia and cause false edrophonium test results.
  2. Cimetidine reduces the renal excretion of procainamide and NAPA.

H. Availability
  1. 100 and 500 mg/ml for injection
  2. Capsules, tablets, and sustained released preparations for oral use

I. Preparation and administration
  1. Administer no more than 1000 mg in 250 to 500 ml of 5% dextrose (2 to 4 mg/ml).
  2. Always administer with a controlled infusion device.
  3. Risk of hypotension during loading doses can be minimized by NOT exceeding a rate of 25 mg/min.
  4. Always dilute to at least 10 mg/ml.

Propranolol (Inderal)

A. General considerations
  1. Parenteral administration of propranolol is usually confined to the treatment of SVTs or maintenance therapy when the oral route is not feasible.
  2. Small parenteral doses can rapidly and substantially alter adrenergic support of a patient's hemodynamics and must be used with great care.

B. Initial dose
  For control of the ventricular response in atrial flutter or fibrillation or conversion of PSVT, 1 mg over 1 minute can be given up to a total dosage of 10 mg.

C. Maintenance dosage
  1. For recurrence or loss of control of supraventricular tachyarrhythmias (SVTs), the initial dosages can be repeated every 2 to 6 hours.
  2. When continuous parenteral therapy is required, a continuous infusion of 1 to 4 mg/hr can be given.

D. Monitoring
   1. Initial therapy should only be performed under continuous electrocardiographic monitoring.
   2. Check vital signs every 5 to 10 minutes.
   3. Monitor patients closely for signs of bronchospasm and heart failure.
E. Adverse effects
   1. Most frequent: precipitation of heart failure, bronchospasm, and bradycardia.
      a. Patients with Wolff-Parkinson-White disease are at particular risk for severe bradycardia even with small doses.
      b. Isoproterenol (2 to 20 µg/min) will usually reverse persistent adverse effects.
F. Pharmacokinetics
   1. The half-life of propranolol varies between 2 and 6 hours.
   2. Elimination is almost exclusively hepatic. An active metabolite (4-hydroxypropranolol) is seen after oral but not parenteral doses.
   3. Serum concentrations increase disproportionately to dose.
G. Interactions
   1. Avoid concurrent administration with calcium–channel blockers because of additive effects on cardiac output and BP.
   2. Propranolol will slow elimination of drugs dependent on hepatic blood flow such as lidocaine.
   3. Use cautiously when other drugs are given that affect A-V node conduction, such as digitalis, quinidine, or procainamide.
   4. Glucose tolerance may be decreased in diabetic patients; this will require insulin adjustment.
   5. Cimetidine will decrease the clearance of propranolol; ranitidine does not.
   6. Propranolol may enhance rebound hypertension seen with clonidine HCl withdrawal.
   7. Epinephrine administration following beta-blockade can result in severe hypertension and reflex bradycardia.

H. Availability
   1. 1 ml ampules with 1 mg/ml.
   2. Tablets of 10, 20, 40, 60, and 80 mg.
I. Preparation and administration
   1. For intermittent dosage
      a. Dilute to 1 mg/10 ml of 5% dextrose or normal saline.
      b. Give at a rate no greater than 1 mg/min at 5-minute intervals for a total dosage of 10 mg.
   2. For continuous infusion
      a. Dilute to 10 mg/100 ml of D5W.
      b. Restrict total dosage prepared to 25 mg.

Verapamil (Isoptin)

A. General considerations
   1. Verapamil is most useful in terminating PSVTs and in controlling ventricular response in atrial fibrillation or flutter. Conversion of flutter on fibrillation occurs infrequently.
   2. Verapamil should not be used in the following situations:
      a. Severe heart failure or hypotension
      b. Sick sinus syndrome in the absence of a pacemaker
      c. Patients who have received parenteral beta-blockers within the previous 6 hours
B. Initial dose
   1. Verapamil should be given in a dose of 0.1 to 0.15 mg/kg up to a maximum of 10 mg as a 2- to 5-minute infusion.
   2. The same dosage can be repeated in 30 minutes if no response occurs.
C. Maintenance dosage
   1. Clinical experience with maintenance dosages of parenteral verapamil is limited.
   2. Recurrent PSVT could be treated with repeat doses scheduled p.r.n. but no more frequently than every 4 hours.
   3. Continuous infusions of 20 to 50 µg (0.02 to 0.05 mg)/min could be used if sustained effect is needed and intensive monitoring is available.

D. Monitoring
   1. Place patients on continuous telemetry.
   2. Check vital signs every 5 to 10 minutes for the first hour after verapamil administration.
   3. Monitor urine output and mental status closely.
E. Adverse effects
   1. Most common
      a. Hypotension
      b. Bradycardia
      c. Accelerated ventricular response
   2. Precipitation or exacerbation of heart failure is less common.
   3. Treatment
      a. Symptomatic bradycardia should be treated with isoproterenol (2 to 8 μg/min).
      b. Sustained hypotension may require treatment with IV fluids and isoproterenol, levarterenol, or dopamine.
F. Pharmacokinetics
   1. The half-life of verapamil varies between 2 and 7 hours.
   2. Hemodynamic effects are more transient than effects on rate after single parenteral doses.
   3. Elimination is primarily hepatic, but metabolites are renally excreted and may accumulate in renal failure.
   4. Extensive hepatic metabolism removes 70% to 90% of verapamil after oral dosages are given and results in much higher oral than parenteral dosages.
G. Interactions
   1. Concurrent therapy with parenteral beta-blockers or disopyramide can result in additive cardiodepressant effects.
   2. Concurrent digitalis, quinidine, or procainamide may result in pronounced effects on A-V nodal conduction.
   3. Verapamil can increase digoxin serum concentrations by inhibiting renal excretion of digoxin.
   4. Patients with severe cardiomyopathy or acute myocardial infarction may be at increased risk for hemodynamic effects.
   5. Calcium infusion will antagonize the effect of verapamil and can be used to treat an overdose.

H. Availability
  1. Ampules (2 ml each) with 5 mg/ml.
  2. Tablets of 80 and 120 mg.
I. Preparation and administration
  1. Verapamil should be diluted to a concentration of 1 mg/ml with normal saline (10 mg in 10 ml).
  2. The desired dosage should be given over 2 to 5 minutes.
  3. Continuous infusions must be given by a volumetric infusion pump.

ANTIHYPERTENSIVES
Diazoxide (Hyperstat)

A. General considerations
  1. Diazoxide is a potent, nondiuretic thiazide antihypertensive agent that reduces BP via direct relaxation of arterioles. Its antihypertensive effect is limited by reflex tachycardia and sodium and water retention; therefore, concurrent use of diuretics is recommended.
  2. Diazoxide induces mild hyperglycemia, and concomitant use of insulin may be required for diabetic patients.
  3. Diazoxide should not be used in the following situations:
    a. Compensatory hypertension (e.g., A-V shunt or coarctation of the aorta)
    b. Allergy to diazoxide, thiazides, or to sulfonamides.
    c. Recent acute myocardial infarction due to the increased myocardial oxygen demand secondary to reflex tachycardia caused by diazoxide.
    d. Oral diazoxide forms are not used to treat hypertension.
B. Initial dose
  1. Single dose
    a. 300 mg (or 5 mg/kg) administered IV over 30 seconds or less; may repeat in 30 minutes.
  2. Minibolus
    a. 1 to 3 mg/kg (max. 150 mg/dose) IV rapidly; may repeat every 5 to 15 minutes, until diastolic BP is less than 100 torr or a maximum dose of 600 mg is given.
  3. The minibolus is as effective as and safer than the single-dose method.

C. Maintenance dosage
   1. Repeat initial dosage every 4 to 24 hours, depending on clinical response.
   2. Oral antihypertensive therapy should be started as soon as possible.
   3. Therapy for more than 5 days is seldom necessary.
D. Monitoring
   1. BP and pulse
   2. Fluid status and renal function
   3. Uric acid and glucose
   4. Hematology
   5. ECG
   6. Total protein and albumin
   7. Injection site for extravasation
E. Adverse effects
   1. Most common are severe local pain or cellulitis from extravasation, water retention, tachycardia, or hyperglycemia.
   2. Less common are arrhythmias, myocardial or cerebral infarction, hyperuricemia, blood dyscrasias, and hypersensitivity.
F. Pharmacokinetics
   1. Onset of action is less than 2 minutes.
   2. Duration of action is 4 to 12 hours.
   3. Half-life: 28 hours (prolonged in renal failure).
   4. Protein binding = 94% (84% in renal failure).
   5. Drug is primarily metabolized in the liver with 20% excreted unchanged in the urine.
G. Interactions
   1. Concurrent administration with diuretics may result in additive hyperglycemic, hyperuricemic, and antihypertensive effects.
   2. Diazoxide may displace warfarin from protein-binding sites, resulting in higher blood levels of warfarin.
   3. Concurrent administration with methyldopa, reserpine, or direct vasodilators (such as hydralazine) may result in additive hypotension.

4. Diazoxide may increase the metabolism and/or decrease the protein binding of phenytoin, resulting in phenytoin toxicity or subtherapeutic effects.
5. Concurrent administration with hydrocortisone or phenothiazines results in additive hyperglycemia.

H. Availability
1. Diazoxide injection (15 mg/ml in 20 ml ampule)

I. Preparation and administration
1. Rapid diazoxide IV administration is used to immediately lower BP.
2. Inject only into a peripheral vein, avoid extravasation.
3. Should not be given by IM or subcutaneous routes because of its alkaline solution.

Hydralazine HCl (Apresoline)

A. General considerations
1. Hydralazine is used for the treatment of moderate to severe hypertension by means of direct relaxation of arterioles; however, its antihypertensive effect is limited by reflex tachycardia and sodium and water retention.
2. Hydralazine is used in combination with diuretics and beta-blockers to increase the antihypertensive effect and decrease the side effects.
3. Hydralazine is effective for treatment of severe CHF.
4. Hydralazine is contraindicated in coronary arterial disease, mitral valvular rheumatic disease, and allergy to the drug.

B. Initial doses
1. Oral: start with 10 mg q.i.d. for the first 2 to 4 days. Increase to 25 mg q.i.d. for the remainder of the week.
2. Parenteral: 10 to 20 mg intravenously or intramuscularly every 4 to 6 hours.

C. Maintenance dosage
1. May increase dosage to 50 mg orally q.i.d. in the second and subsequent weeks.
2. Twice daily dosage may be adequate.
3. Daily oral dosages greater than 200 mg are more likely to produce a lupus-like syndrome.

D. Monitoring
  1. BP and pulse
  2. Complete blood count and antinuclear antibody titer
  3. Fluid status
  4. Signs of lupus: fever and joint pain
E. Adverse effects
  1. Most common: headache, tachycardia, water retention.
  2. Less common: systemic lupus erythematosus, blood dyscrasia, and peripheral neuritis.
F. Pharmacokinetics
  1. Onset of action: oral 1 hour, IV administration 10 to 20 minutes, IM administration 20 to 40 minutes. Duration of action 3 to 8 hours.
  2. Half-life: 2 to 8 hours.
  3. Undergoes first-pass metabolism phenotype-dependent acetylation with bioavailability of 10% to 35%. Concomitant ingestion of food can increase bioavailability.
  4. Less than 10% of hydralazine is excreted unchanged in the urine.
G. Interactions
  1. Concurrent therapy with diuretics or other antihypertensive agents will result in additive hypotensive effect.
  2. Concurrent therapy with MAO inhibitors, will result in synergistic hypotensive effect.
  3. Concurrent therapy with beta-blockers may increase the bioavailability of the beta-blocker.
H. Availability
  1. Hydralazine tablets (10, 25, 50, 100 mg)
     Hydralazine injection (20 mg/ml in 1 ml ampules)
I. Preparation and administration
  1. Postoperatively, for essential hypertension, usually in combination with other drugs.
  2. Intravenously for severe essential hypertension.

Methyldopa (Aldomet)

A. General considerations
  1. Methyldopa acts through central stimulation of central inhibitory alpha-receptors and causes decreased peripheral vascular resistance.

2. Because of slow onset of methyldopa's action, IV nitroprusside or diazoxide is preferred in hypertensive crisis.

3. Methyldopa is generally most effective when used with a diuretic.

4. Methyldopa is contraindicated in active hepatic disease (e.g., active hepatitis or active cirrhosis), liver dysfunction associated with previous methyldopa therapy, and allergy to the drug.

B. Initial dose

1. 250 mg orally 2 or 3 times per day initially

2. 250 to 500 mg by IV infusion every 6 hours to maximum of 1 g every 6 hours

C. Maintenance dosage

1. The usual daily maintenance dosage is 500 mg to 2 g in 2 to 4 hours.

2. Adjust dosage according to patient's BP and tolerance at intervals of at least 2 days.

3. A single daily dose at bedtime is effective in some patients.

4. Give a larger dose at bedtime or start dosage increases in the evening to minimize the effect of drowsiness.

D. Monitoring

1. BP

2. CBC

3. Liver function tests

4. Direct Coombs' test

5. Hematology

E. Adverse effects

1. Drowsiness: most common—nasal congestion, depression, decreased mental acuity, hepatitis, hemolytic anemia (rare), positive result to Coombs' test (10% to 20%), and lupuslike syndrome.

F. Pharmacokinetics

1. Oral bioavailability varies from 25% to 50% caused by extensive first-pass metabolism. Intravenous bioavailability is similar to oral because of incomplete hydrolysis of the methyldopate ester.

2. Onset of action is approximately 2 to 6 hours following intravenous or oral administration.

3. Duration of action varies from 10 to 48 hours.
4. Plasma concentrations do not correlate with effect and the plasma half-time is approximately 2 hours.
5. Methyldopa is excreted in urine as both metabolite and unchanged drug.
6. Reduce dosage or increase dosage interval to 12 to 24 hours in renal failure patients.

G. Interactions
   1. Concurrent administration with diuretics, other antihypertensive agents, or anesthetics will result in additive antihypertensive effect.
   2. Sympathomimetic agents, phenothiazine, or tricyclic antidepressants may reduce the antihypertensive effect of methyldopa.
   3. Use with caution in patients receiving levodopa or lithium.
   4. Methyldopa may interfere with several lab tests, such as uric acid, serum creatinine, and serum glutamic oxaloacetic transaminase tests, and give a false-positive urinary catecholamine reaction.

H. Availability
   1. Methyldopa tablets 125, 250, 500 mg, suspension 250 mg/5 ml
      Methyldopate injection, 50 mg/ml intravenous infusions in 5 ml vials

I. Preparation and administration
   1. Intramuscular or subcutaneous administration is not recommended because absorption is unpredictable.
   2. Dilute intravenous dose in 5% dextrose injection to a maximum concentration of 10 mg/ml and infuse over 30 to 60 minutes.

Sodium nitroprusside (Nipride, Nitropress)

A. General considerations
   1. Nitroprusside is a direct-acting vasodilator used in treating hypertension and CHF.
   2. Decreases in afterload and preload will occur.
   3. A decrease in myocardial oxygen consumption may occur with nitroprusside use.

    4. Nitroprusside is contraindicated in compensatory hyper-
       tension (e.g., A-V shunt or coarctation of the aorta).

B. Initial dose
    1. Start a constant IV infusion at 0.5 μg/kg/min.
    2. In patients receiving other hypertensive agents and in
       elderly patients, smaller doses are required.

C. Maintenance dosage
    1. Increase dosage by 0.25-0.5 μg/kg/min every 5 minutes
       until the desired BP is achieved.
    2. The average dosage is 3 μg/kg/min with a range of 0.5-
       10 μg/kg/min. This dosage will cause approximately a
       30% to 40% decrease from the initial BP.
    3. Dosages greater than 10 μg/kg/min are more likely to
       cause cyanide and thiocyanate toxicity.
    4. Oral antihypertensive therapy should be started as soon
       as possible, while the nitroprusside infusion rate is being
       tapered and the BP response is being monitored.

D. Monitoring
    1. Frequently monitor BP until stable, then hourly, ideally
       with an arterial line. Avoid lowering the systolic BP be-
       low 60 torr.
    2. Check thiocyanate level daily if infusion exceeds 3 to 4
       days in patients with abnormal renal function.
    3. Thiocyanate concentration should not exceed 100 μg/ml.
    4. In patients with liver impairment, daily plasma cyanogen
       concentrations should be measured.
    5. Monitor hemodynamic parameters (e.g., PCWP, CO,
       PVR) blood pH, and serum bicarbonate when nitroprus-
       side is used to treat acute myocardial infarction or
       congestive heart failure.

E. Adverse effects
    1. Rapid infusion may produce nausea, vomiting, palpita-
       tions, muscle twitching, and abdominal pain. These are
       best relieved by slowing the infusion rate or temporarily
       discontinuing the drug.
    2. Thiocyanate toxicity
       a. Thiocyanate levels are greater than 100 μg/ml.
       b. Patients receiving prolonged infusion with impaired

  hepatic or renal function are more likely to develop thiocyanate toxicity.

  c. Condition is initially seen as neurotoxic symptoms (tinnitus, blurred vision, sedation, and delirium).

  d. Peritoneal dialysis or hemodialysis will remove thiocyanate.

 3. Cyanide toxicity

  a. Metabolic acidosis is the earliest sign of cyanide toxicity.

  b. Patients requiring higher doses because of blood pressure resistance to the drug are more likely to develop cyanide toxicity.

  c. Condition presents as dyspnea, tachycardia, ataxia, and loss of consciousness.

  d. Hydroxycobalamine may prevent cyanide toxicity. If toxicity develops, the infusion should be stopped and nitrite therapy for cyanide intoxication should be instituted.

 4. Hypothyroidism and methemoglobinemia may occur.

F. Pharmacokinetics

 1. Onset of action: 30 to 60 sec; duration: 3 to 5 min

 2. Half-life (thiocyanate) 1 week, prolonged in renal impairment

 3. Nitroprusside metabolized to cyanide in red blood cells, then converted to thiocyanate in the liver
  Metabolite (thiocyanate) renally excreted

G. Interactions

 1. Ganglionic blocking agents, anesthetics, and circulatory depressants can increase the hypotensive effect of nitroprusside.

 2. May aggravate vitamin B_{12} deficiency or hypothyroidism.

H. Availability

 Nitroprusside (50 mg of powder) for injection

I. Preparation and administration

 1. Powder is reconstituted with 3 ml of 5% dextrose for injection or sterile water for injection without preservatives.

 2. Dilute the concentrated solution (50 mg) in 250, 500, or 1000 ml of 5% dextrose to provide a concentration of 200, 100, or 50 μg/ml.

3. Solution must not be mixed with other drugs and is stable for 24 hours when protected from intense light. Discard solution if it becomes discolored.
4. Must be given by continuous infusion. Infuse into central line to avoid extravasation.
5. Administer intravenously by an infusion pump or similar rate-controlling device.

Trimethaphan camsylate (Arfonad)

A. General considerations
 1. Trimethaphan is a short-acting, nonselective ganglionic blocking drug. Toxicity from trimethaphan administration is common and related to parasympathetic inhibition.
 2. Trimethaphan is used for immediate reduction of BP in emergency hypertension and is the drug of choice in the patient with dissecting aortic aneurysm.
 3. It is often necessary to elevate the head of the bed to achieve an optimal effect.
 4. Trimethaphan is contraindicated in patients with glaucoma, in pregnancy, and when hypotension may subject the patient to undue risk, (e.g., anemia, hypovolemia, shock, respiratory insufficiency).
B. Initial dose
 1. Start IV infusion at 1 mg/min.
C. Maintenance dosage
 1. Increase dosage every 3 to 5 minutes until the desired BP is achieved.
 2. The range is usually from 0.3 to 6 mg/min.
 3. Oral antihypertensive therapy should be started as soon as possible.
D. Monitoring
 1. Monitor BP and HR.
 2. Monitor respiratory status.
E. Adverse effects
 1. Anticholinergic effects—urinary retension, dry mouth, tachycardia, cycloplegia
 2. Others—apnea and respiratory arrest

F. Pharmacokinetics
   1. Trimethaphan has an immediate onset of action.
   2. Duration of action is less than 10 minutes.
   3. Trimethaphan may be metabolized by pseudocholinesterase and excreted by the kidneys.
G. Interactions
   1. Concurrent administration with diuretics, other antihypertensive agents, or anesthetics, will result in an additive antihypertensive effect.
   2. Trimethaphan may prolong the effect of neuromuscular blocking agents.
   3. Use with caution in patients with arteriosclerosis; cardiac, hepatic, renal, or CNS disease; Addison's disease and diabetes; and in patients who are taking steroids.
H. Availability
   1. Trimethaphan camsylate injection 50 mg/ml in 10 ml ampules
I. Preparation and administration
   1. Dilute 500 mg (10 ml) of trimethaphan in 500 ml of 5% dextrose injection to provide a concentration of 1 mg/ml.
   2. Administer intravenously by an infusion pump or similar device.

MISCELLANEOUS DRUGS
Aminophylline

A. General considerations
   1. Aminophylline, a complex of theophylline and ethylenediamine, is equivalent to 80% theophylline on a weight basis.
   2. Theophylline directly relaxes respiratory smooth muscle, dilates pulmonary arterioles, reduces pulmonary hypertension and alveolar carbon dioxide tension, and increases pulmonary blood flow.
   3. At therapeutic levels, theophylline has a mild diuretic effect.
   4. In concentrations above the therapeutic range, theophylline causes a positive inotropic and chronotropic effect on the heart.

B. Initial dose
  1. In patients not previously receiving aminophylline (within 48 hours) administration of 7 mg/kg of lean body weight over a 20- to 60-minute perfusion should provide theophylline levels of about 12 μg/ml. Rapid IV injection may cause transitory hypotension.
  2. In patients taking the medication prior to admission, an estimate of their current theophylline level should be made, and a dose of 1 mg/kg for each 2 μg/ml increase desired should be given.
C. Maintenance dosage
  1. Begin a constant infusion following the initial dose on the basis of these factors:

	Aminophylline dose
Adults, healthy, smokers	0.9 mg/kg/hr
Adults, healthy, nonsmokers	0.6 mg/kg/hr
Adults with CHF, cor pulmonale, or liver dysfunction	0.25 mg/kg/hr

  2. Dosage adjustment should be based on patient response and serum theophylline levels. The effects of smoking can persist up to 2 years after stopping.
  3. When changing to oral aminophylline, a direct conversion of the total daily intravenous dose can be made. If a different theophylline salt is used, a conversion of theophylline administered over the daily dose (aminophylline dose × 0.8) must first be made.
  4. The first oral dose should be given when the IV infusion is stopped.
D. Monitoring
  1. Theophylline levels of 10 to 20 μg/ml are considered therapeutic in terms of bronchodilation and bronchospasm prevention.
    a. Some patients may respond at lower levels, and some may require higher serum theophylline levels.
    b. If a loading dose is administered, take the first measurement 30 minutes later.
    c. Measure theophylline levels a second time 8 hours after starting the maintenance infusion to determine clearance of the drug.

2. Measure theophylline levels daily for patients on intravenous theophylline.

E. Adverse effects
1. Levels over 20 μg/ml
   a. Nausea   d. Diarrhea
   b. Vomiting   e. Insomnia
   c. Headache
2. With increasing toxic concentrations
   a. Hyperglycemia   d. Seizures
   b. Hypotension   e. Brain damage
   c. Cardiac arrhythmias f. Death
3. Within the therapeutic range, tachyarrhythmias and premature beats are uncommon. If seen, other causes should be investigated.
4. If the theophylline level is greater than 60 μg/ml, charcoal hemoperfusion should be performed.
5. Less serious signs of theophylline toxicity occur in only 50% of patients with severe toxicity.

F. Pharmacokinetics

$$vd = 0.5 \text{ L/kg } (0.3 \text{ to } 0.7 \text{ L/kg})$$

Half-life: Adult nonsmoker, 7.9 hours
Adult smoker, 4 to 5 hours
CHF, 19 (3.1 to 82) hours
Cirrhosis, 32 (10 to 56) hours

1. A wide variety of dosage requirements may occur in patients with CHF, cor pulmonale, and liver disease. Dosages will require careful serum level monitoring.
2. Most healthy patients will exhibit linear dose-response curves; however, approximately 15% will show dose-dependent pharmacokinetics.

G. Interactions
1. Allopurinol in doses of 600 mg/day will decrease theophylline clearance by approximately 25%.
2. Cimetidine will double steady-state theophylline levels when added to a regimen. Ranitidine does not have this effect.
3. Isoproterenol infusions will increase theophylline clearance by approximately 19% (range 6% to 42%).

4. Phenytoin in therapeutic concentrations will increase theophylline clearance by approximately 75% after 10 days of concurrent administration. When given together orally, theophylline will inhibit phenytoin absorption.

H. Availability

1. Aminophylline is available as injection, oral solution, rectal solution, suppositories (erratic absorption), tablets, and extended-release tablets.

2. A large variety of other theophylline preparations are available.

3. Because all theophylline products are not bioequivalent, serum level monitoring should be done when changing brands or dosage forms.

I. Preparation and administration

1. Aminophylline injection is available in 250 mg/ml and 25 mg/ml concentrations.

2. For loading dosages aminophylline, 7 mg/kg, should be placed in sufficient intravenous solution to administer over 20 to 60 minutes and not to exceed a concentration of 40 mg/ml.

3. Maintenance infusions should be diluted in a volume not to exceed an 8-hour supply in order to minimize chances of toxicity from a runaway intravenous infusion.

Heparin sodium

A. General considerations

1. The dosage and monitoring of heparin differ, depending on whether the indication is prophylactic or therapeutic anticoagulation.

2. Guidelines provided here are for intravenous therapeutic coagulation in patients with deep vein thrombosis and/or associated pulmonary embolus.

3. Dosage should always be in units and never in milligrams.

4. Continuous-infusion heparin is more easily monitored with coagulation tests and is probably safer than giving intermittent dosages.

5. Prior to therapy, hematocrit, platelets, prothrombin

time, and activated partial thromboplastin time (APTT) should be obtained. Thrombin time may also be measured, and the activated coagulation time may be substituted for APTT.

    6. Heparin is also available as heparin calcium.

B. Initial dose

    1. Loading dose: 50 to 75 U/kg over 1 minute (may be omitted if risk of bleeding is high)

    2. Continuous infusion: 15 to 25 U/kg/hr (750 to 1500 U/hr) in 5% dextrose

C. Maintenance dosage

    1. Adjust daily to keep APTT between 1.5 and 2.5 times the control value.

    2. If APTT is between 100 and 120 sec, reduce rate by 10% to 20%.

    3. If APTT is greater than 130 sec, stop infusion for 2 hours and reduce rate by 20% to 35%.

D. Monitoring

    1. Obtain APTT, hematocrit, and platelets daily and observe for bleeding.

    2. High-risk patients may require more frequent (every 6 to 8 hours) coagulation monitoring at the outset of therapy.

    3. Heparin-induced thrombocytopenia occurs more frequently with beef lung than with porcine mucosal heparin.

    4. Obtain coagulation parameters *at least* 4 hours after a loading dose or a change in infusion rate.

    5. Evaluate platelet counts of less than 100,000 with aggregation studies; stop heparin if necessary and observe platelet count over the next 24 to 48 hours. If count is heparin induced, it will usually increase in that time.

E. Adverse effects

    1. Bleeding

    2. Thrombocytopenia

    3. Thrombosis resulting from increased platelet aggregation

F. Pharmacokinetics

    1. The half-life of heparin effect is usually 30 to 90 min, but it may be increased with high doses or prolonged therapy.

2. Dosage requirements are lower in older patients, females, and patients with uremia.

G. Interactions

1. Avoid IM injections and platelet-inhibiting drugs.

2. Heparin may prolong quick one-stage prothrombin time when used to adjust warfarin therapy. Therapeutic doses of warfarin may modestly prolong the APTT.

H. Availability

1000, 5000, 10,000, 20,000, and 40,000 U/ml from either porcine or bovine source

I. Preparation and administration

1. Use 5% dextrose.

2. Order no more than a 12-hour dose requirement per container of intravenous solution.

3. Use a controlled infusion device to ensure constant rate.

4. Instruct nursing staff *not* to attempt to "catch up" if infusion is behind schedule.

5. Avoid concomitant administration of other drugs in same line. Acidic drugs in high concentration will produce precipitate.

SELECTED READINGS

Billups, N.F.: American drug index, ed. 29, Philadelphia, 1985.

Evans, W.E., Schentay, J.J., and Jusko, W.J.: Applied pharmacokinetics. San Francisco, 1980, Applied Therapeutics, Inc.

Hansten, P.D.: Drug interactions, ed. 5, Philadelphia, 1985, Lea & Febiger.

Huff, B. (editor): Physician's desk reference, ed. 39, Oradell, N.J., 1985, Medical Economics Co. Inc.

Knobon, J.E., and Anderson, P.O.: Handbook of clinical drug data, ed. 5, Illinois, 1983, Hamilton.

McEvoy, G.K.: American Hospital Formulary Service drug information '85, Bethesda, Md., 1985, American Society of Hospital Pharmacists.

PART B ANESTHETICS
IAN GILMOUR

Although anesthetics do not play a central role in the surgical intensive care unit (SICU), it is unusual for a patient not to make at least one visit to the operating room. Because of the perioperative involvement of the SICU team, a section on anesthetics is included in this text. Since they are seldom indicated in SICU patients, however, preanesthetic medications will not be discussed; and because this section primarily explores the clinical pharmacology of anesthesia, mention of techniques, monitoring, and so on will be minimal.

IMPLICATIONS OF GENERAL ANESTHESIA FOR THE SICU PATIENT

General anesthesia occurs when a drug or a combination of drugs provides analgesia, amnesia, and obtundation of both somatic and autonomic responses to pain. When a general anesthetic is necessary for the intensive care patient, this must be provided in such a way that the very delicate physiologic balance of this patient is not disturbed.

A. In most cases, the maintenance of this balance requires the use of agents with minimal direct effect on cardiovascular equilibrium, but with sufficient efficacy to prevent reflex cardiovascular stimulation.

B. Although with one or two exceptions (ketamine, droperidol) anesthetic, are potent respiratory depressants, this is of less consequence in the typical intensive care patient because most are intubated and supported perioperatively by mechanical ventilation.

C. Anesthetic CNS effects are important because:

1. Continuous evaluation of the CNS is necessary to good intensive care.

2. In individuals with CNS dysfunction, anesthetic agents may have deleterious effects such as:

   a. Increases in cerebral blood flow causing increased intracranial pressure

  b. Prolonged obtundation

  c. Alteration of physical signs important in evaluation of these patients (e.g., pupil size, reflexes)

D. Additional possible effects include damage to:

 1. Kidneys

 2. GI tract

 3. Musculoskeletal system

 4. Integumentary system

E. The major guarantee of a patient's safety in the operating room is good anesthetic care; in unskilled or careless hands all anesthetic agents and methods are potentially lethal.

INDUCTION

Induction of anesthesia in the high-risk patient is always a crucial period.

A. During this time potent cardiopulmonary and autonomic nervous system depressants are introduced into patients who often have high levels of autonomic activity.

B. Control of the airway must be assured. Intubation is always a very dangerous period because of the potential for complications such as aspiration, loss of airway patency, inability to intubate, trauma to the upper airway, and the tremendous autonomic nervous system outflow associated with intubation.

C. Intubation (either oral or nasal) *without* any obtundation of reflexes may be indicated when:

 1. The patient has a full stomach (blood, food), upper gastrointestinal obstruction or ileus.

 2. A difficult intubation is contemplated.

 3. The patient is in extremis.

ANESTHETICS

Agents useful for induction provide rapid, smooth loss of consciousness, thus avoiding the excitation phase of anesthesia. This is particularly important in the SICU patient, because the increased CNS activity that occurs during this period increases the likelihood of such problems as regurgitation and aspiration, inability to physically restrain the patient, and maintenance of the airway.

A. In the United States, ultra-short-acting barbiturates (thiopental sodium, methohexital sodium, pentobarbitol) are most commonly used.

1. Advantages

   a. They provide rapid and smooth induction of anesthesia.

   b. They decrease intracranial pressure by decreasing cerebral blood flow.

   c. They decrease cerebral metabolic rate.

   d. They have excellent antiseizure activity (except methohexitol)

   e. Even in low doses, they can provide amnesia and sedation.

2. Disadvantages

   a. Their use is often associated with hypotension resulting from both autonomic blockade and direct depression of the myocardium.

   b. Since termination of action occurs by redistribution rather than excretion or metabolism, activity may be prolonged when large doses are used, (except with the use of methohexitol).

   c. Frequent administration leads to tachyphylaxis.

   d. They have a well-known ability to induce liver mitochondrial enzymes.

   e. They have antianalgesic effects, a distinct disadvantage in a surgical patient.

3. Usage

   Because of these disadvantages, barbiturates are seldom used for induction of anesthesia in seriously ill patients. They may be used in intermittent small doses to ensure amnesia.

B. Alternative induction agents include benzodiazepines, ketamine, steroid anesthetics (althesin, minoxalone), etomidate, and propanidid.

   Of these, only the benzodiazepines, etomidate, and ketamine are currently available in the United States.

MAINTENANCE

A. Inhalation agents—vapors

1. The older anesthetic agents, ether and cyclopropane, are no longer in common use primarily because they are flammable. They also present some disadvantages for the high-risk patient.

   a. At clinical concentrations they stimulated the autonomic nervous system.

   b. This stimulation is harmful in hypovolemic shock.

   c. Autonomic nervous system stimulation could be a problem with many types of cardiac dysfunction even though, in the intact healthy patient, the net effect was maintenance of stable cardiopulmonary function.

2. Inhalation agents currently in use in the United States are: halothane (a halogenated alkane), methoxyflurane, enflurane, and isoflurane (halogenated ethers).

   a. Advantages

      (1) Administration of these drugs is easily titrated to the patient's physiologic state.

      (2) The concentration of the agent may be changed rapidly via the respiratory tract when necessary.

      (3) They provide amnesia and analgesia at low doses, although at such doses they do not block potentially harmful autonomic reflexes.

      (4) They have minimal toxicity. Although the margin of safety between anesthetizing doses and potentially lethal side effects is relatively small, direct organ toxicity, even with halothane, is rare.

      (5) They work synergistically with muscle relaxants so that lower doses of the latter are needed to achieve a given degree of relaxation, thus minimizing interaction with aminoglycosides and other antibiotics.

      (6) All of the modern agents are bronchodilators, which can be valuable in patients with reactive airways.

      (7) A major advantage of all vapor and gaseous anesthetics is that their elimination is primarily a function of minute ventilation. In contrast, the metab-

olism and excretion of intravenous agents and their metabolites will be affected by hepatic and renal dysfunction.

b. Disadvantages

(1) Methoxyflurane produces a dose-related renal toxicity. Its use is limited to obstetric anesthesia.

(2) The drugs decrease myocardial contractility (halothane > enflurane > isoflurane).

(3) They sensitize the myocardium to catecholamines (halothane > isoflurane > enflurane).

(4) They cause arrhythmias (enflurane > isoflurane > halothane).

(5) They cause vasodilation (isoflurane > enflurane > halothane).

(6) They decrease pulmonary vascular resistance.

(a) Although this effect is generally of little clinical consequence, recent evidence suggests that specific vasodilation may occur in areas of the pulmonary vascular bed previously constricted because of hypoxia, thus increasing A-a DO_2.

(b) This effect can be crucial in an ICU patient, although most vasoactive drugs from dopamine to nitroprusside share this property.

(7) In clinical doses, both enflurane and halothane depress mucociliary activity. Data for isoflurane are not yet available. Depression of mucociliary activity may further compromise ICU patients with serious pulmonary dysfunction.

B. Anesthetic gases

Nitrous oxide (N_2O) is the only anesthetic gas in common use. Since it cannot provide anesthesia by itself, it is most often used with more potent agents to decrease the dosage of the more potent agent.

a. Formerly it was thought to be nontoxic and to have no side effects.

(1) Recently, however, toxic effects, especially with chronic exposure, have been reported.

(2) It has a direct negative inotropic effect.

(3) Its sympathomimetic properties can result in increased systemic vascular resistance and cardiac work.

b. Because N_2O is less depressant than other inhaled anesthetics, its combination with them usually causes less depression than the volatile agent alone would at comparable anesthetic levels.

c. On the other hand, combination with narcotics usually reveals the direct myocardial depressant effects of N_2O.

d. The effect of N_2O on hypoxic vasoconstriction is not clear.

C. Intravenous agents

Intravenous agents are used in anesthesia for a variety of reasons, and for this reason they come from across the pharmacologic spectrum. (Barbiturates are best used as induction agents and in repeated small doses may be used to ensure amnesia during surgery, but for reasons noted previously, use during surgery is not optimal.)

1. Benzodiazepines

a. Benzodiazepines provide excellent amnesia and sedation with significantly less respiratory and cardiovascular depression than barbiturates.

(1) When diazepam is used by itself even at high doses, changes in BP or cardiac output are less than 20% from baseline.

(2) Combined with narcotics, however, diazepam can cause profound cardiac depression.

b. Although the newer agents (midazolam, lorazepam) are water soluble, diazepam is not and is more likely to cause phlebitis.

c. A major difference from the ultra-short-acting barbiturates is a relatively prolonged duration of action which at least partially results from active metabolites. This makes the benzodiazepines less desirable when CNS assessment is necessary immediately postoperatively. Midazolam may be an exception to this rule.

2. Narcotic analgesics
   a. Advantages
      Narcotic analgesics have come into their own because they cause less cardiovascular depression than volatile anesthetics.
   b. Disadvantages
      (1) Histamine release causes arteriolar dilation and hypotension (morphine sulfate and demerol).
      (2) Cardiovascular side effects include negative inotropy and tachycardia (demerol), bradycardia secondary to vagal stimulation, hypertension, and, rarely, pulmonary hypertension (morphine sulfate, fentanyl citrate).
      (3) Very high dose requirements and postoperative nausea and constipation when used as the sole anesthetic agent are common. High doses mandate a relatively prolonged recovery period because even the so-called short-acting agents (fentanyl) are not so at high doses.
      (4) Except at very high doses (> 50 μg/kg fentanyl), they do not prevent untoward reflex responses to noxious stimuli and even at these doses, awareness during surgery has been reported.
   c. Short-acting synthetic narcotics
      (1) Short-acting synthetic narcotics (fentanyl, sufentanyl) have been developed that do not cause histamine release, have no direct myocardial depressant effects, and have some anesthetic activity.
      (2) These have made pure narcotic anesthesia (a high-dose narcotic + oxygen + muscle relaxant) very popular for use in high-risk patients in whom cardiovascular stability is of paramount importance.
3. Muscle-relaxant drugs
   The advent of muscle-relaxant drugs, the primary action of which is to prevent spontaneous or reflex contraction of striated muscle by blocking the myoneural junction, has allowed rapid advances in thoracoabdominal surgery.

a. Depolarizing agents
   (1) Depolarizing agents such as succinylcholine chloride (succinyldicholine) and hexamethonium act by:
      (a) Noncompetitively binding to receptor sites on the muscle side of the myoneural junction, thereby initiating a muscle contraction. They prevent postsynaptic acetylcholine stimulation by continuing to occupy the receptor.
   (2) Disadvantages
      (a) They are very short acting (succinyldicholine <5 minutes at usual doses in normal patients).
      (b) They cause generalized contractions of striated muscle resulting in increased gastric and ocular pressures.
      (c) They cause muscarinic effects, most notably bradycardia.
      (d) They have been associated with the development of malignant hyperthermia in susceptible individuals.
      (e) They cause muscle pain postoperatively.
   (3) Possible consequences
      (a) Hyperkalemia (especially in patients with neurologic dysfunction)
      (b) Regurgitation and aspiration of gastric contents
      (c) Extrusion of eyeball contents when the globe has been ruptured previously
      (d) Serious cardiac dysrhythmias, especially after two or three doses
b. Nondepolarizing agents
   Nondepolarizing relaxants (pancuronium bromide, gallamine triethiodide *d*-tubocurarine, vecuronium, and atracurium) interact competitively with the receptor.
   (1) Disadvantages
      (a) In general, duration of action is much longer than that of depolarizing agents (half-life greater than 20 minutes).
      (b) Their onset of action is much slower at normal doses.

(c) To varying degrees, most have both parasympatholytic and sympathomimetic activity that can cause serious cardiac dysrhythmias even in an otherwise normal patient. (The exceptions are vecuronium and atracurium).

(d) Some agents, notably *d*-tubocurarine, also cause histamine release. (The exceptions are vecuronium and gallamine).

(e) Renal and hepatic disease, both of which commonly occur in SICU patients, can affect significantly their duration of action. (The exception is atracevicus.)

(f) Their use mandates mechanical ventilatory support until the myoneural junction has recovered. This may be unwise in patients with conditions such as hypovolemic shock.

(g) These drugs interact with furosemide, nitroglycerin, local anesthetics, aminoglycosides, and other common SICU antibiotics.

(h) Their metabolites may have undesirable side effects (atracurium)

4. Ketamine

Ketamine, a derivative of phencyclidine HCl (Angel Dust) is a unique anesthetic agent that appears to cause dissociation between brainstem and cerebral cortex.

a. Advantages

(1) Although ketamine is a mild, direct myocardial depressant, its use is associated with increased sympathetic activity (typically increased cardiac output and BP), an effect of mixed benefit in the usual ICU patient.

(2) It is an excellent analgesic.

(3) Its relatively rapid onset of action makes it a reasonable induction agent.

b. Disadvantages

(1) Marked psychotropic dysfunction commonly results from its use, especially in high doses. This effect makes it less than the ideal agent for maintenance of anesthesia, especially in patients with

CNS dysfunction, since it also increases cerebral blood flow and oxygen consumption.

(2) However, recent data suggest that the psycho-tropic effects of ketamine are much less when it is administered by constant infusion rather than by intravenous or intramuscular bolus.

5. Droperidol

Droperidol, a butyrophenone, may be used on its own or in conjunction with a narcotic (fentanyl), the mixture known as Innovar.

a. Advantages

(1) Droperidol is a major tranquilizer.

(2) It has marked sedative and amnesic properties.

(3) It appears to potentiate the activity of narcotic an-algesics.

(4) It is a potent antimetic. For this reason, it is very useful for awake intubations.

b. Disadvantages

(1) Because of its prolonged duration of action, it is less than ideal in patients whose neurologic status is questionable.

(2) Like other butyrophenones and phenothiazines, its lack of significant cardiac depression is offset by a potent vasodilating action, both direct and indi-rect. Accordingly, droperidol is contraindicated in patients whose volume status is unknown.

(3) It tends to lower the seizure threshold.

(4) It may increase the frequency of dysrythmias.

GENERAL ANESTHETIC TECHNIQUES

By and large, ICU patients going to the operating room will receive either a local or general anesthetic rather than a re-gional conduction block.

A. Local or general anesthetic versus regional conduction block

1. The majority of intensive care patients coming to the op-erating room will already be intubated and receiving me-chanical ventilatory support with multiple sites of venous access. This makes the administration of a light general anesthetic enticingly simple and relatively safe.

2. Administration of a major regional block (subarachnoid block, epidural block) almost invariably involves disruption of autonomic homeostasis. Therefore, it may be less safe in this type of patient.

3. Conduction blocks (axillary, sciatic—femoral, intercostal with celiac plexus), largely avoid the cardiovascular side effects of subarachnoid or epidural blockade, but they are not without risk and require expertise sustained by frequent practice.

4. The CNS status of ICU patients is often such that they cannot be relied upon to lie quietly for any length of time.
   a. Therefore one is forced to use a significant amount of sedation or analgesia even in the presence of a satisfactory block.
   b. One might then reasonably question the advisability of performing two anesthetics.

5. Regional anesthesia is especially risky in patients with coagulopathies of any organ.

B. Balanced technique
   Frequently, the general anesthetic technique used in the seriously ill patient is a so-called balanced technique.
   1. The anesthesiologist is dividing the anesthetic into its component parts, selectively administering drugs to achieve each goal.
      a. Amnesia: N_2O, benzodiazepam
      b. Analgesia: narcotic, low-dose volatile agent
      c. Autonomic stability reflex blockade: narcotic, N_2O, low-dose volatile agent
      d. Blockade of somatic responses to noxious stimuli occurs via a muscle relaxant, usually in the nondepolarizing type.
   2. Because autonomic activity in these patients is often very high, agents causing sympathetic blockade or anesthesia so deep that it would block the stress response and destabilize the patient are avoided.
      a. Thus barbiturates, which have potent sympatholytic activity, are used infrequently and at low doses.
      b. In many cases, induction per se, does not occur: the

patient simply receives N_2O and increments of narcotic along with a muscle relaxant. In the highly stressed patient, even this might result in unacceptable lowering of autonomic nervous system tone with decreased cardiac output and BP.

c. Under certain circumstances, one might wait until surgery commences before providing analgesia, thus ensuring continued high sympathetic tone.

3. N_2O is avoided when:

a. Any depression of the cardiovascular system might tip the balance

b. High inspired oxygen concentrations are required

c. The patient has gas trapped within the body (bowel obstruction, pneumothorax)

d. Under these circumstances, other methods of amnesia must be sought.

(1) Ketamine or diazepam may be useful.

(2) In this type of patient, skill in conduction blockade is helpful.

4. When atherosclerotic heart disease is an underlying problem, much attention must be directed to lowering cardiac work, and maintaining myocardial O_2 delivery. Therefore any technique in these patients, regional or general, balanced or inhalation, must avoid extremes of blood pressure, tachycardia, increases in afterload, hypoxia, etc. In the less seriously ill patient or the patient with a different set of problems, other anesthetic agents may be useful.

a. When direct myocardial depression is of less consequence or when vasodilation may be beneficial, volatile anesthetics are useful.

(1) In all but the most seriously ill, halothane, enflurane, or isoflurane may be used with or instead of narcotics to provide analgesia and enhance amnesia.

(2) They have the added advantage of ease of administration, rapid excretion even with hepatic or renal failure, and synergism with muscle relaxants.

b. The addition of muscle relaxants will reduce anesthetic requirements, no matter which analgesic or amnesic drug is involved, even where muscle relaxation per se is not necessary to successful completion of the surgery. Care must be taken, however, to avoid the pitfall of inadequate anesthesia, because the increased cardiac work associated with sympathetic stimulation may be detrimental in a precariously balanced patient.

C. Pure techniques

"Pure" anesthetic techniques or cases in which only one anesthetic agent is used for maintenance of anesthesia are becoming increasingly rare even in healthy surgical patients.

1. Several reasons for this exist.

a. The balanced techniques have all the advantages noted above.

b. Pure techniques involving volatile anesthetics are more costly.

c. These volatile agents, at anesthetic levels, are potent cardiopulmonary depressants.

d. "Pure" techniques suitable for the high-risk patient such as fentanyl-oxygen or ketamine-oxygen are used, but they suffer from the drawbacks noted previously. However, administration by continuous infusion has been shown to lower doses and to decrease problems correspondingly.

LOCAL ANESTHETICS

Local anesthetics are tertiary amines separated from an aromatic ring by a carbon chain.

A. Although many local anesthetics are on the market, they can be divided by the chemistry of this chain into two basic types: amides and esters.

B. Although the mode of excretion is different, the local and toxic effects are similar.

1. The desired effect is blockade of nerve conduction, whether this be locally as in infiltration, or within larger areas of the body as during epidural anesthesia.

2. The effect of conduction block may be restricted to the distribution of the nerve or group of nerves (axillary block) being blocked.

3. In other cases (subarachnoid block), the whole body may be affected if the associated sympathetic blockade decreases venous return and cardiac output.

C. Choice of anesthetic

Obviously, the choice of anesthetic, whether it be general or regional, or one type of regional versus another, will be governed by the ability of the patient to tolerate the predictable side effects of any given method.

1. Recent data suggest that regional anesthesia is preferable in elderly patients undergoing hip surgery.

2. Regional anesthesia is thought to be preferable in patients with chronic obstructive pulmonary disease, especially with the advantages of continuous epidural analgesia in the postoperative period. However:

   a. Loss of sympathetic tone in the presence of the elevated mean intrathoracic pressure associated with forcible exhalation may augment cardiac side effects.

   b. The block can affect the accessory muscles of exhalation and precipitate acute respiratory failure.

   c. If the patient has chronic bronchitis and must lie supine for several hours, he almost certainly will develop atelectasis from sputum accumulation, the weight of abdominal contents, and surgical retraction.

3. Factors involved in choosing anesthetic agents

   a. Location of the block

   b. Expected duration and type of the surgical procedure

   c. Patient status

D. Toxicity

1. Local toxicity

   a. At concentrations greater than those achieved clinically, local anesthetics are neurotoxic.

   b. However, most local effects have to do with the accidental administration of a neurotoxic substance (preservative) or with trauma resulting from the technique itself.

2. Systemic toxicity
   a. Systemic toxicity is more likely to occur:
      (1) With blocks that require large volumes or concentrations of anesthetic such as epidurals
      (2) When the drug is accidentally administered intravenously
      (3) When the blockade is in a vascular area (intercostal), thus promoting vascular uptake
      (4) With amide drugs because they are not broken down by plasma cholinesterase
   b. Systemic toxicity is affected by such drug characteristics as fat solubility, protein binding, and potency.
   c. Systemic toxicity is manifested:
      (1) In the CNS by sedation and seizures
      (2) In the cardiovascular system with slowed conduction, myocardial depression, and arrythmias.
   d. Prilocaine HCl in large doses can cause methemoglobinemia.
E. Complications
   Complications of regional anesthesia can best be avoided by meticulous technique, asepsis, appropriate dosages, and continuous observation of the patient.

SELECTED READINGS
General

Bonica, J.J.: Principles and practice of obstetric analgesia and anesthesia, New York, 1967, F.A. Davis Co.

Bromage, P.R.: Epidural analgesia, Philadelphia, 1978, W.B. Saunders Co.

DeJong, R.H.: Local anesthetics, Springfield, 1977, Charles C Thomas.

Miller, R.D. (editor): Anesthesia, New York, 1981, Churchill Livingston, Inc.

Wood-Smith, F.G., Vickers, M.S., and Steward, H.C.: Drugs in anesthetic practice, London, 1973, Butterworths.

General anesthesia

Booji, L.H.D.J., et al.: Cardiovascular and neuromuscular effects of Org NC45, pancuronium, metocurine and d-tubocurarine in dogs, Anesth. Analg. 59:26, 1980.

Linde, H.W., et al.: Cardiovascular effects of isoflurane and halothane during controlled ventilation in older patients, Anesth. Analg. 54:701, 1976.

Mainzer, J., Jr.: Awareness, muscle relaxants, and balanced anesthesia, Can. Anaesth. Soc. J. 20:386, 1979.

Mathias, J.A., Evans-Prosser, C.D.G., and Churchill Davidson, H.C.: The role of nondepolarizing drugs in the prevention of suxamethonium bradycardia, Br. J. Anaesth. **42**:609, 1970.

Philbin, D.M., (editor): Anesthetic management of the patient with cardiovascular disease, Int. Anesthiol. Clin. **17**:1, 1979.

Shapiro, H.M.: Intracranial hypertension: therapeutics and anesthetic considerations, Anesthesiology **43**:45, 1975.

Regional anesthesia

Cusick, J.F., Mylkebust, J.B., and Abram, S.E.: Differential neural effects of epidural anesthetics, Anesthesiology **53**:299, 1980.

DeJong, R.H.: Toxic effects of local anesthetics, JAMA **239**:1166, 1978.

Moore, D.C.: Regional Anesthesia, Philadelphia, 1969, F.A. Davis Co.

White, W.D., Pearce, D., and Norman, J.: Postoperative analgesia: a comparison of intravenous on demand fentanyl with epidural bupivicaine, Br. Med. J. **2**:166–167, 1979.

30

The high-risk surgical patient

Arthur D. Santos

With current improvement in anesthetic and surgical technique, reductions in operative mortality have been significant. With an older population, more complex medical problems, and improved surgical techniques, a rather large group of operative candidates exists with an increased surgical risk. The high-risk patient has compromised single or multiple organ systems that can alter the response to surgery or increase morbidity or mortality. Appropriate preoperative preparation can reduce morbidity and mortality to acceptable levels in many cases.

A. Assessing risk
 1. Organ reserve
  a. To assess risk, one must consider the reserve present in each specific organ system.
   (1) Reserve is the organ's ability to respond to stress physiologically. This response usually requires placing an additional burden on that organ system.
   (2) The stress of surgery requires some element of reserve for the patient to survive the postoperative state.
   (3) Although many patients are not stressed to maximal reserve, others have borderline reserve and should be studied to evaluate the potential outcome of an operation. Stratification of these patients into groups based on mortality or functional deficit can be beneficial.
   (4) Questions to ask when dealing with high-risk patients
    (a) Does the patient have organ system reserve?
    (b) By what criteria can the reserve be evaluated?

(c) Is this reserve adequate for the patient to tolerate an operation?

(d) If it is not adequate, can the physician(s) manipulate the reserve to optimize the organ's function?

(e) Does optimization then improve mortality and morbidity?

2. Actual mortality

a. With the technology of single-system support, mortality becomes subdivided into its components.

(1) Myocardial infarction (a significant cause of cardiac deaths) or failure

(2) Ventilatory failure

(3) Systemic sepsis and wound infections in nutrition

(4) Renal failure

(5) Hepatic failure

(6) Malnutrition

b. When a significant complication has been sustained, single-system organ failure can proceed to multiple-system organ failure with its resultant high mortality (see Chapter 20).

c. Key tasks then become:

(1) Maintaining oxygen transport to support peripheral and central tissue metabolism

(2) Removing or controlling sepsis sites

(3) Maintaining hepatic protein synthesis via individualized nutritional support

(4) Excising all possible dead/injured tissue

3. Risk categories

a. General areas of limited reserve in an organ system

(1) Coronary artery disease

(2) Smoking and chronic obstructive pulmonary disease

(3) Renal failure

(4) Cirrhosis

b. Pulmonary, liver, and renal risk and assessment are discussed in those respective chapters. Cardiovascular factors and risk assessment will be discussed here.

    c. Any risk must be viewed in the clinical context and the decision to operate on the risk/benefit assessment.

CARDIOVASCULAR

In dealing with the high-risk patient with a cardiovascular condition, coronary artery obstruction is the primary disease and myocardial infarction or failure are the events.

A. Myocardial infarction
   1. Patients with atherosclerotic heart disease but with no history of a myocardial infarction have a 6.6% operative mortality.
   2. Patients with no atherosclerotic heart disease have an operative mortality of 2.9%.
   3. The reinfarction rate correlates with the interval between the myocardial infarction and the anticipated date of operation:
      a. 6-week- to 3-month-interval = 37% reinfarction rate
      b. 3-month- to 6-month-interval = 16%
      c. Greater than 6 months = 5%
         (1) The curve flattens here, and additional improvement is not noted over a period of 1 to 2 years.
         (2) Thus perhaps one can look at this as the safe interval.
         (3) One should wait following a myocardial infarction to perform elective surgery.
         (4) The mortality of the postoperative myocardial infarction in one series was 54%.
         (5) The most common day for a myocardial infarction to occur in the postoperative period is the third day. This is followed by the first and the fourth days in terms of incidence.
         (6) More recent data suggest that interventional monitoring can lower the risk in the 6 to 18 weeks after an infarction.
B. Predicting likelihood of a cardiac event
   1. Cardiac event
      a. Myocardial infarction (most common)
      b. Ventricular tachycardia
      c. Pulmonary edema

2. Goldman's nine variables
   a. The nine variables are divided into history, physical examination, electrocardiogram (ECG) findings, laboratory data, and the anticipated operation and its urgency.
   b. Each of the nine variables is assigned a point value.
      (1) The variables with the highest point value are those of congestive heart failure, an S3 gallop, or jugular venous distention.
      (2) Myocardial infarction less than 6 months before surgery is the second highest.
   c. With the use of the history, physical examination, and ECG findings, the variables with the highest point value are identified.
   d. Once one has evaluated a patient completely according to the nine variables and has totaled the number of points per patient, one can then apply the classification system to the point value and predict minor or no complications or life-threatening complications and cardiac death.
      (1) Sum total < 5 points = class 1. The number of life-threatening complications and the risk of cardiac death is minimal.
      (2) Class 2 = 6 to 12 points
      (3) Class 3 = 3 to 25 points
      (4) > 26 points = an incidence of life-threatening complications at 22% and a cardiac death at 56%.
   e. Classes define
      (1) Static cardiac risk
      (2) Its relationship with a cardiac event
      (3) Its potential mortality and morbidity
   f. Classes do not define
      (1) Myocardial reserve
      (2) Criteria to evaluate myocardial reserve
      (3) Correlation between presence or absence of reserve with mortality and morbidity
3. American Society of Anesthesiologist classification (ASA) of physical status with postoperative cardiac events

      a. Does not predict cardiac death as accurately as Goldman's variables

      b. Does predict overall mortality very well

  4. New York Heart Association (NYHA) functional classification

      a. Does not correlate strongly with postoperative cardiac events

      b. Therefore does not predict cardiac events in the postoperative period better than the Goldman criteria

      c. However, it does predict overall mortality as did the ASA classification.

C. Preoperative study

  1. In subendocardial infarctions, obtaining CPK-MB isoenzymes is important.

      a. An ECG may not give the information needed on the basis of the usual transmural criteria for infarction.

  2. Until now, treadmill ECGs have been very important in diagnosing significant coronary artery disease. Unfortunately, the accuracy is only 65%.

  3. The advent of the nuclear medicine scans has become important in diagnosing significant coronary artery disease.

      a. With computer assistance, one can evaluate ventricular wall function with a multigated blood pool study (MUGA scan). With the use of this scan, one can obtain a 95% accuracy.

      b. Two other scans, the stress thallium-201 scanning and the dynamic myocardial scintigraphy scan, seem to be most helpful in detecting myocardial ischemia at rest or during stress and may be useful in determining myocardial reserve.

      c. The technetium-99 stannous pyrophosphate scan is most helpful in diagnosing myocardial infarctions after the 36-hour period.

      d. The thalium 201-scan is excellent in diagnosing an acute myocardial infarction within the initial 12 hours.

    e. The coronary angiogram is very useful for diagnosing significant coronary artery disease.

      (1) Defines the anatomy and the obstructive lesions

      (2) Shows spasm, bypassable lesions, and lesions that are a minimal to ballon angioplasty

      (3) Shows left ventricular function

      (4) Shows areas of akinesia, hypokinesia, and good wall motion

      (5) Shows valvular dysfunction

      (6) Can measure end diastolic pressures

D. Improving mortality rates in coronary artery disease

  1. The operative mortality in patients with significant coronary artery disease can be improved by operatively bypassing the coronary arteries and then performing elective surgery.

    a. Particularly applicable to patients who have

      (1) Unstable angina

      (2) Left main disease

      (3) Triple vessel disease with muscle dysfunction

    b. Some of the high-risk procedures include those which require major transfusions and have anticipated periods of hypotension, including abdominal aortic aneurysms.

  2. Accumulating data indicate that appropriate preoperative preparation may reduce operative mortality.

    a. Principles

      (1) Adjust blood volume and cardiac function to reduce the risk of hypoperfusion during anesthetic induction and during the operative procedure.

      (2) Assess cardiac reserve for "fluid distribution" that may be necessary, particularly in settings of potentially high blood loss.

      (3) Assess the presence and severity of pulmonary artery hypertension and its response to dilating therapy.

      (4) Correct hemoglobin and electrolyte imbalance.

        (a) Potassium loading to correct serum and total body deficits, particularly in the presence of chronic or acute aggressive diuresis

      (5) Vasodilate with nitrates.

3. The functional defects in myocardial function can be defined and optimized preoperatively by performing a preoperative "tune-up."
   a. Pulmonary artery catheter is placed and baseline function data obtained.
   b. The response to volume loading is determined.
      (1) The patient is challenged with 200 ml of colloid, and baseline parameters are again measured.
   c. One-half inch of nitropaste is applied or low-dose intravenous nitroglycerine given, and baseline parameters are again taken.
   d. Volume loading is again performed, and a Starling curve plotted.
      (1) The optimum filling pressure and stroke volume are determined.
      (2) Fluid distribution ability is determined.
      (3) A determination is made as to whether inotropes and afterload reduction are necessary.
   e. The use of these parameters simplifies
      (1) Determining myocardial reserve
      (2) Determining the criteria that define reserve
      (3) Optimizing myocardial function
E. Other cardiovascular risk settings
   1. Congestive heart failure
      a. Preoperative heart failure can predict a recurrence postoperatively.
         (1) Increasing the functional class of the NYHA increases the incidence of failure.
         (2) The mortality varies from 15% to 20%. With coronary heart disease, the mortality is higher (25% to 70%).
         (3) Predictors
            (a) New gallop
            (b) Developing signs of left- or right-sided failure
            (c) The clinical setting
   2. Hypertension
      The risk of diastolic hypertension per se is minimal in patients without significant renal disease or heart failure.

The absence of central lesions in the coronary, cerebral, renal, and carotid circulation also lessens the risk.

a. Risk entails:
   (1) Cerebral hemorrhage
   (2) Thrombosis
   (3) Myocardial infarct ischemia

b. The most hazardous period is during induction of anesthesia.
   (1) Hypotension or hypertension can occur.
   (2) The patient's electrolytes and volume status must be optimal (especially if on diuretics).
   (3) Antihypertensives are continued up until the day of operation; abrupt withdrawal may precipitate acute hypertension.
      (a) Clonidine
      (b) Propranolol
   (4) Use of anesthetics that have less myocardial depressant activity is appropriate.
   (5) However, maintaining normal blood pressure in a severely hypertensive patient may:
      (a) Induce a low-flow state
      (b) Inadequately perfuse the cerebral circulation which leads to strokes
      (c) Jeopardize myocardial blood flow leading to myocardial ischemia

3. Carotid disease and operative risk
The data relating to postoperative stroke in the general surgery patient are sparse.

a. Physicians disagree regarding prophylactic surgery for significant stenosis in the absence of symptoms.
   (1) Most authors agree that in symptomatic patients and selected asymptomatic patients that an endarterectomy is protective against a stroke when performed as an elective procedure.
      (a) In one study by oculoplethysmography, patients with a 60% or less stenosis had a 2% risk of stroke, whereas patients with a significant stenosis greater than 60% had a 16.2% risk of stroke which fell to a 1.9% risk after carotid endarterectomy.

(b) Digital subtraction angiography or Doppler analysis are useful screening agents.

(2) Carotid endarterectomy would not affect one half of strokes because they would be caused by hemorrhage, intracerebral thrombosis, lacunar infarct, intracerebral aneurysms or embolisms from the heart.

Prophylactic antibiotics

A. Recommended in presence of:
  1. Prosthetic valves or devices
  2. Prior endocarditis
  3. Valvular or congenital heart disease
  4. Mitral valve prolapse
  5. Idiopathic hypertrophic subaortic stenosis
B. Recommended for:
  1. Dental surgery
  2. Oral or upper respiratory tract surgery
  3. Gastrointestinal and/or genitourinary tract surgery
  4. Surgery through or in the presence of active infection
C. Endocarditis prophylaxis
  1. Dental procedures and surgery of the upper respiratory tract
    a. Regimen A
      (1) Combined oral parenteral penicillin—aqueous crystalline penicillin G (1,000,000 U intramuscularly) *mixed with* procaine penicillin G (600,000 U M). Give 30 minutes to 1 hour prior to procedure and follow with penicillin V 500 mg postoperatively q. 6h for 8 dosages.
      (2) Oral penicillin—penicillin V, 2.0 grams postoperatively 30 minutes to 1 hour prior to procedure followed by 500 mg postoperatively q. 6h for 8 dosages.
      (3) For patients allergic to penicillin—erythromycin 1 G 1½ to 2 hours prior to procedure followed by 500 mg postoperatively q. 6h for 8 dosages *or* vancomycin (see Regimen B).

   b. Regimen B (prosthetic heart valves)
      (1) Penicillin plus streptomycin—aqueous crystalline penicillin G (1,000,000 U intramuscularly) *mixed with* procaine penicillin G (600,000 U intramuscularly) *plus* streptomycin (1 g intramuscularly). Give 30 minutes to 1 hour prior to procedure and follow with penicillin V 500 mg postoperatively q. 6h for 8 doses.
      (2) For patients allergic to penicillin—vancomycin (1 g IV over 30 minutes to 1 hour) started 30 minutes to 1 hour prior to procedure and followed by erythromycin 500 mg postoperatively q. 6h for 8 dosages.
 2. Gastrointestinal/genitourinary surgery and instrumentation
    a. Aqueous penicillin G, 2,000,000 U intramuscularly or intravenously or ampicillin, 1 g intramuscularly or intravenously with gentamycin intramuscularly or intravenously 1.5 mg/kg (80 mg maximum)
    b. For patients allergic to penicillin:
       (1) Vancomycin, 1 g intravenously, over 30 to 60 minutes and streptomycin, 1 g intramuscularly
    c. Dose to be administered 30 minutes prior to procedure; may repeat in 12 hours

Prosthetic heart valves and anticoagulation

A. Aortic valve
   1. Stop anticoagulation 2 to 3 days preoperatively.
   2. Restart within 48 hours postoperatively.
B. Mitral valve (alone or in combination)
   1. Stop anticoagulation 1 to 2 days preoperatively.
   2. Start heparin 12 to 24 hours postoperatively.
   3. Restart sodium warfarin.

SELECTED READINGS

Bellocci, F., et al.: The risk of cardiac complications in surgical patients with bifascicular block: a clinical and electrophysiologic study in 98 patients, Chest **77**:343, 1980.

Crawford, E.S., et al.: Operative risk in patients with previous coronary artery bypass, Ann. Thorac. Surg. **26**:215, 1978.

Goldman, L.: Guidelines for evaluating and preparing the cardiac patient for general surgery, J. Cardiovasc. Med. **5**:637, 1980.

Goldman, L.: Non-cardiac surgery in patients receiving propranolol, Arch. Intern. Med. **141**:193, 1981.

Goldman, L., and Caldera, D.L.: Risk of general anesthesia and elective operations in the hypertensive patient, Anesthesiology **50**:285, 1979.

Goldman, L., et al.: Multifactorial index of cardiac risk in non-cardiac surgical procedures, N. Engl. J. Med. **297**:845, 1977.

Goldman, L., et al.: Cardiac risk factors and complications in noncardiac surgery, Medicine **57**:357, 1978.

Katholi, R.E., Nolan, S.P., and McGuire, L.B.: Living with prosthetic heart valves—subsequent noncardiac operations and the risk of thromboembolism or hemorrhage, Am. Heart J. **92**:162, 1976.

Knapp, R.B., Topkins, M.J., and Artusio, J.F.: The cerebrovascular accident and coronary occlusion in anesthesia, JAMA, **182**:106, 1962.

Mauney, F.M., Ebert, P.D., and Sabiston, D.C. Jr.: Post-operative myocardial infarction: a study of predisposing factors, diagnosis and mortality in a high risk group of surgical patients, Ann. Surg. **172**:497, 1970.

Medical evaluation of the preoperative patient, Med. Clin. North Am. **63**(5): 1979.

Moran, J.M., et al.: Coronary revascularization in patients receiving propranolol, Circulation **50** supp. 2:116, 1974.

Prys-Roberts, C., Meloche, R., and Foëx, P.: Studies of anesthesia in relation to hypertension: I. Cardiovascular responses of treated and untreated patients, Br. J. Anaesth. **43**:112, 1971.

Reves, J.G., et al.: Calcium channel blockers: uses and implications for anesthesiologists, Anesthesiology **57**:504, 1982.

Smilyan, H., Weinberg, S.E., and Howanitz, P.J.: Continuous propranolol infusion following abdominal surgery, JAMA **247**:2539, 1982.

Tarhan, S., et al.: Myocardial infarction after general anesthesia, JAMA **220**:1451, 1972.

Tinker, J.H., and Tarhan, S.: Discontinuing anticoagulant therapy in surgical patients with cardiac valve prostheses, JAMA **239**:738, 1978.

Whiting, R.B.: Ventricular premature contractions. Which should be treated? Arch. Intern. Med. **140**:1423, 1980.

Index